Craig Swan

# Study Guide for

# Principles and Policy
## Sixth Edition

William J. Baumol
Alan S. Blinder

The Dryden Press
**Harcourt Brace College Publishers**
Fort Worth   Philadelphia   San Diego   New York   Orlando   Austin   San Antonio
Toronto   Montreal   London   Sydney   Tokyo

**Cover Image:** Tommy Lynn

*Address for Editorial Correspondence*
The Dryden Press, 301 Commerce Street, Suite 3700, Fort Worth, TX 76102

*Address for Orders*
The Dryden Press, 6277 Sea Harbor Drive, Orlando, FL 32887
1-800-782-4479, or 1-800-433-0001 (in Florida)

ISBN: 0-03-098445-9

Printed in the United States of America

4 5 6 7 8 9 0 1 2 3   021   9 8 7 6 5 4 3 2 1

The Dryden Press
Harcourt Brace College Publishers

# Table of Contents

# Introduction

This study guide is designed to be used with *Microeconomics: Principles and Policy*, Sixth Edition, by William J. Baumol and Alan S. Blinder. This guide is not a substitute for the basic textbook; rather, experience has shown that conscientious use of a supplement such as this guide can lead to greater learning and understanding of the course material. It might also improve your grade.

The chapters in this book parallel those in *Microeconomics: Principles and Policy*, Sixth Edition. Each chapter here is a review of the material covered in the textbook chapters. You should first read and study each chapter in the textbook and then use the corresponding chapter in this book. "Use" is the correct verb, as chapters in this book are designed for your *active* participation.

The material with which you will be working is organized into the following elements.

## LEARNING OBJECTIVES

Each chapter starts with a set of behavioral learning objectives. These indicate the things you should be able to do upon completing each chapter.

## IMPORTANT TERMS AND CONCEPTS

As one of the learning objectives for each chapter states, you should be able to define, understand, and use correctly the terms and concepts that are listed in this section. They parallel the important terms and concepts listed at the end of the text chapter. Being able to *define* these terms is likely to be important for your grade. But to really *understand* what they mean, rather than to temporarily memorize their definition, is even better. The ultimate test of your understanding will be your ability to *use correctly* the terms and concepts in real-life situations.

## CHAPTER REVIEW

Each review section has a summary discussion of the major points of each chapter. The reviews are designed to be used actively. Frequently, you will need to supply the appropriate missing term or to choose between pairs of alternative words. Some of the missing words are quite specific and can be found in the list of important terms and concepts. At other times, the answers are less clear-cut, as the following hypothetical example illustrates: "If people expect inflation at higher rates than before, nominal interest rates are likely to _____." Any of the following would be correct answers: increase, rise, go up. In cases like this, do not get concerned if the answer you choose is different from the one in the back of the book.

## IMPORTANT TERMS AND CONCEPTS QUIZ

Each chapter contains an important terms and concepts quiz to help you review important terms and concepts. Match each term with the most appropriate definition.

## BASIC EXERCISE

Most chapters have one or more exercises that are designed for you to use as a check on your understanding of a basic principle discussed in the chapter. Many of the exercises use simple arithmetic or geometry. While getting the correct answers is one measure of understanding, do not mistake the arithmetic manipulations for the economic content of the problems. A hand calculator may make the arithmetic less burdensome.

## SELF-TEST FOR UNDERSTANDING

Each chapter has a set of multiple choice and true-false questions for you to use as a further check on your understanding. It is important to know not only the correct answers but also why other answers are wrong. When considering the true-false questions especially, be sure you understand why the false statements are false. Answers for the Self-Tests are in the back of this guide and include page references to the textbook to help you understand correct choices.

## APPENDIX

Many chapters in the text contain an appendix, which generally is designed to supplement the chapter content with material that is either a bit more difficult or offers further exposition of a particular economic concept. In some cases, the review material for the appendix parallels that for the chapter, including learning objectives, important terms and concepts, and so forth. In other cases, the appendix material is reviewed here in the form of an additional exercise designed to illustrate the principals discussed in the appendix.

## SUPPLEMENTARY EXERCISE

Many chapters end with a supplementary exercise, which may be either an additional mathematical exercise or some suggestions that allow you to use what you have learned in real-world situations. Some exercises use more advanced mathematics. Since many of these exercises review Basic Exercise material, they illustrate how economists use mathematics and are included for students with appropriate training. Most importantly, understand the economic principles that underlie the Basic Exercise, something that does not depend upon advanced mathematics.

## ECONOMICS IN ACTION

Most chapters include a brief example, mostly from recent newspapers or magazines. Each example has been chosen to show how economic concepts and ideas can help one understand real world problems and issues.

## STUDY QUESTIONS

Each chapter ends with a short list of study questions. Working with friends on these questions is a useful way to review chapter material and should help on examinations.

Being introduced to economics for the first time should be exciting and fun. For many, it is likely to be hard work, but hard work does not have to be dull and uninteresting. Do not look for a pat set of answers with universal applicability. Economics does not offer answers but rather a way of looking at the world and thinking systematically about issues. As the English economist John Maynard Keynes said:

> The theory of economics does not furnish a body of settled conclusions immediately applicable to policy. It is a method rather than a doctrine, an apparatus of the mind, a technique of thinking, which helps its possessor to draw correct conclusions.

Bertrand Russell, the distinguished British philosopher and mathematician, had considered studying economics but decided it was too easy. The Nobel prize-winning physicist, Max Planck, also considered studying economics but decided it was too hard. Whether, like Russell, you find economics easy or, like Planck, you find it hard, I trust that with the use of this guide you will find it relevant and exciting!

The preparation of this guide would not have been possible without the help and contributions of others. I especially want to acknowledge the contributions of Dr. Marianne Felton of Indiana University, Southeast, Jack Stecher, and my wife, Janet.

Craig Swan

# What Is Economics?

## LEARNING OBJECTIVES

After completing this chapter, you should be able to:

♦ explain the role of abstraction, or simplification, in economic theory.

♦ explain the role of theory as a guide to understanding real-world phenomena.

♦ explain why correlation need not imply causation.

♦ explain why imperfect information and value judgments will always mean that economics cannot provide definitive answers to all social problems.

## IMPORTANT TERMS AND CONCEPTS

Voluntary exchange
Comparative advantage
Productivity
Externalities
Marginal analysis
Marginal costs
Abstraction and generalization
Theory
Correlation versus causation
Economic model
Opportunity Cost

## CHAPTER REVIEW

Chapter 1 has two objectives: It introduces the types of problems that concern economists, offering 12 important ideas for Beyond the Final Exam, and it discusses the methods of economic analysis, in particular the role of theory in economics.

Problems discussed in the first part of the chapter have been chosen to illustrate 12 basic economic issues to be remembered beyond the final exam. You should not only read this material now, but re-examine the list at the end of the course. Understanding the economic principles that underlie these 12 basic issues is the real final examination in economics.

The methods of economic inquiry are best described as "eclectic," meaning they are drawn from many sources according to their usefulness to the subject matter. Economists borrow from the social sciences to theorize about human behavior. They borrow from mathematics to express theories concisely. And they borrow from statistics to make inferences from real-world data about hypotheses suggested by economic theory.

Economists are interested in understanding human behavior not only for its own sake, but for the policy implications of this knowledge. How can we know what to expect from changes resulting from public policy or business decisions unless we understand why people behave the way they do? Consider the 12 ideas discussed in the first part of this chapter. Each derives from economic theory. As you will learn, each idea also offers insight into actual experience and is an important guide to evaluating future changes.

As in other scientific disciplines, theory in economics is an abstraction, or simplification, of innumerable complex relationships in the real world. When thinking about some aspects of behavior, say a family's spending decisions or why the price of wheat fluctuates so much, economists will develop a model that attempts to explain the behavior under examination. Elements of the model derive from economic theory. Economists study the model to see what hypotheses, or predictions, it suggests. These can then be checked against real-world data. An economist's model will typically be built not with hammer and nails, but with pencil, paper, and computers. The appropriate degree of abstraction for an economic model is determined, to a large extent, by the problem at hand and is not something that can be specified in advance for all problems.

Economists believe they can make a significant contribution to resolving many important social issues. It is hoped that by the time you finish this course, you will agree with this belief. At the same time, you should realize that economics offers a way of looking at questions rather than a comprehensive set of answers to all questions. Economists will always have differences of opinion on final policy recommendations because of

**(1)** incomplete_____ and different _____ judgments.

## IMPORTANT TERMS AND CONCEPTS

Choose the best definition for the following terms.

1. ____f____ Voluntary exchange
2. ____b____ Comparative advantage
3. ____e____ Productivity
4. ____g____ Externalities
5. ____l____ Marginal analysis
6. ____a____ Marginal costs
7. ____c____ Abstraction
8. ____i____ Theory
9. ____d____ Correlation
10. ____k____ Model
11. ____j____ Opportunity cost

a. Additional cost incurred by a one–unit increase in output.
b. Ability to produce a good less inefficiently than other goods.
c. Ignoring many details to focus on essential parts of a problem.
d. Situation in which the movements of two variables are linked, whether or not a causal relation exists.
e. Output produced by a unit of input.
f. Trade in which both parties are willing participants.
g. Effects on third parties that are not part of an economic transaction.
h. Cost per unit produced.
i. Deliberate simplification of relationships to explain how those relationships work.
j. Value of the next best alternative.
k. Simplified version of some aspect of the economy.
l. Evaluation of the impact of changes.

## SELF-TESTS FOR UNDERSTANDING

### Test A

Circle the most appropriate answer.

1. Most economists believe that policies to reduce inflation will
   a. permanently increase unemployment.
   b. never be adopted in democracies.
   c. increase unemployment for a time.
   d. have immediate and lasting impact.

2. In addition to interest rates, information about _____ is necessary to investigate the real cost of borrowing and lending.
   a. the inflation rate
   b. exchange rates
   c. the unemployment rate
   d. marginal cost

3. Economic analysis shows that federal budget deficits
   a. are a significant burden on future generations.
   b. are really of no concern.
   c. produce an impact that will depend on particular circumstances.
   d. are, in reality, usually beneficial.

4. Small differences in the productivity growth rate
   a. make little difference, even over periods as long as a century.
   b. can compound into significant differences.
   c. can be safely ignored by citizens and politicians.
   d. will lead only to small differences in the standard of living between countries.

5. Most economists believe that exchange
   a. is likely to be considered mutually advantageous to both parties when it is voluntary.
   b. only takes place when one side can extract a profit from the other.
   c. usually makes both parties worse off.
   d. is best when strictly regulated by the government.

6. With respect to international trade,
   a. a country can gain only if its neighbors lose.
   b. countries should try to be self-sufficient of all goods.
   c. only those countries with the highest productivity levels will gain.
   d. a country can gain by producing those goods in which it has a comparative advantage.

7. Most economists believe that attempts to set prices by decree
   a. will work best in the long run.
   b. are likely to create significant new problems.
   c. are the only way to establish fair prices.
   d. have a history of practical effectiveness.

8. When the actions of some economic agents impose cost on others, for example the polluting smoke of a factory or power plant,
   a. market mechanisms may exist that can help remedy the situation.
   b. the only answer is government regulation.
   c. there is very little one can do; such is the price of progress.
   d. it is always best to close down the offending action.

9. Economists define opportunity cost as
   a. the money price of goods and services.
   b. the lowest price you can bargain for.
   (c.) the value of the next best alternative.
   d. the time you must spend when shopping.

10. Marginal analysis is concerned with the study of
    a. buying stocks and bonds on credit.
    b. those groups that operate on the margins of the market economy.
    (c.) changes, such as the increase in cost when output increases.
    d. an engineer's fudge factor for possible errors.

11. The cost disease of personal services
    a. could be eliminated if only the government would regulate prices.
    b. would be eliminated if everyone practiced safe sex.
    c. is only an excuse for the government's inability to control its own spending.
    (d.) refers to the impact of differential rates of growth of productivity between the manufacturing and service sectors of the economy.

12. Economic analysis suggests that
    a. policies that promote the highest rate of economic growth unambiguously improve the distribution of income.
    b. policies to increase equality may reduce output.
    c. incentives for work and savings have almost no impact on people's behavior.
    (d.) there is no tradeoff between the size of the economic pie and how the pie is divided.

## Test B

Circle T or F for true or false.

T (F) 1. Economic models are no good unless they include all of the detail that characterizes the real world.

T (F) 2. Material in this text will reveal the answer to many important social problems.

(T) F 3. Opportunity cost is measured by considering the best alternative foregone.

(T) F 4. Economists' policy prescriptions will always differ because of incomplete information and different value judgments.

T (F) 5. Theory and practical policy have nothing to do with each other.

(T) F 6. If two variables are correlated, we can be certain that one causes the other.

T (F) 7. The best economic models all use the same degree of abstraction.

(T) F 8. An economist tests a hypothesis when she deliberately simplifies the nature of relationships in order to explain cause and effect.

T (F) 9. No business should ever sell its output at a price that does not cover full cost.

T (F) 10. There is no tradeoff between policies that increase output and those that equalize income.

## SUPPLEMENTARY EXERCISE

The following suggested readings offer an excellent introduction to the ideas and lives of economists past and present:

1. *The Worldly Philosophers: The Lives, Times & Ideas of the Great Economic Thinkers*, 6th ed., by Robert L. Heilbroner (Touchstone Books, 1987).

2. In recent years, *The Quarterly Review* of the Banca Nazionale del Lavoro and *The American Economist*, published by Omicron Delta Epsilon, the undergraduate economics honors society, have published recollections and reflections by distinguished economists. Read what these authors have to say about their lives as economists. The December 1983 issue of *The Quarterly Review* contains reflections by William Baumol.

3. *Lives of the Laureates: Ten Nobel Economists*, edited by William Breit and Roger W. Spencer (MIT Press, 1990). This is a collection of recollections by ten winners of the Nobel Prize in Economics.

## STUDY QUESTIONS

1. Explain the relationships between theories, models, and hypotheses.

2. Why are theories necessary for understanding the causal links between economic variables? Why can't the facts speak for themselves?

3. Many trace the establishment of economics as a field of study to the publication of Adam Smith's *Wealth of Nations* in 1776. Why, after more than 200 years, do so many questions remain?

## ECONOMICS IN ACTION

### Play Ball

Are baseball players overpaid? Contracts worth $3 million to $5 million a year seemed common in the early 1990s. Even after adjusting for inflation, Babe Ruth's highest salary is estimated to have been less than $700,000. What accounts for the difference, and does it make economic sense?

Writing in *Scientific American*, Paul Wallich and Elizabeth Corcoran explain the difference through the concepts of opportunity cost and marginal analysis, ideas introduced in this chapter. Under the reserve clause, in effect from 1903 until the mid-1970s, a baseball player who did not like his contract had little choice other than retiring from baseball. Players were not free to bargain with other teams. After the introduction of free agency, baseball players could sell their services to the team with the best offer.

Gerald Scully, in his book *The Business of Major League Baseball*, uses statistical techniques to see how hitting and pitching help determine a team's winning percentage and how a team's revenue relates to its record and the size of the market in which it plays. He then estimates how adding a particular player might add to a team's performance and hence its revenue.

Using data from the late 1980s, Scully finds that the performance of selected superstars increased team revenues by $2 million to $3 million, numbers consistent with the highest salaries at the time. Using data from the late 1960s, he estimates that superstars increased team revenues by $600,000 to $1 million and notes that the highest salaries were only $100,000 to $125,000.

1. How does the concept of opportunity cost help explain baseball salaries while the reserve clause was in effect? What was the opportunity cost of a baseball player's time? How did free agency change the opportunity cost for a player deciding whether to stay with a team?

2. How would marginal analysis help a team determine how much it should offer a free agent?

SOURCES: Paul Wallich and Elizabeth Corcoran, "The MBAs of Summer," *Scientific American*, (June 1992): p. 120.
Gerald W. Scully, *The Business of Major League Baseball*, (Chicago: University of Chicago Press, 1989).

# Appendix: The Graphs Used in Economic Analysis

## LEARNING OBJECTIVES

After completing the material in this appendix, you should be able to:

♦ interpret various graphs:
  - use a two-variable graph to determine what combinations of variables go together.
  - use a three-variable graph to determine what combinations of the $X$ and $Y$ variables are consistent with the same value for the $Z$ variable.
♦ construct two-variable and three-variable graphs.
♦ compute the slope of a straight line and explain what it measures.
♦ explain how to compute the slope of a curved line.
♦ explain how a 45–degree line can divide a graph into two regions, one in which the $Y$ variable exceeds the $X$ variable, and another in which the $X$ variable exceeds the $Y$ variable.

## IMPORTANT TERMS AND CONCEPTS

Variable
Two-variable diagram
Horizontal and vertical axes
Origin (of a graph)
Slope of a straight (or curved) line
Negative, positive, zero, and infinite slope
Tangent to a curve
$Y$-intercept
Ray through the origin, or ray 45–degree line
Contour map

## APPENDIX REVIEW

Economists like to draw pictures, primarily *graphs*. Your textbook and this study guide also make extensive use of graphs. There is nothing very difficult about graphs, but understanding them from the beginning will help you avoid mistakes later on.

(1)    All the graphs we will use start with two straight lines, one on the bottom and one on the left side. These edges of the graph will usually have labels to indicate what is being measured in both the vertical and horizontal directions. The line on the bottom is called the (horizontal/vertical) axis, and the line running up the side is called the _____ axis. The point at which the two lines meet is called the _____. The variable measured along the horizontal axis is often called the $X$ variable, while the term $Y$ variable is often used to refer to the variable measured along the vertical axis.

Figure 1-1 is a two-variable diagram plotting expenditures on alcoholic beverages and ministers' salaries. Does this graph imply that wealthier clergymen drink more, or does it suggest that more drinking in general is increasing the demand for, and hence the salaries of, clergymen? Most likely neither interpretation is correct; just because you can plot two variables does not mean that one caused the other.

Many two-variable diagrams encountered in introductory economics use *straight lines*, primarily for simplicity. An important characteristic of a straight line is its *slope*, measured by comparing differences

(2) between two points. To calculate the slope of a straight line, divide the (<u>horizontal/vertical</u>) change by the corresponding _____ change as you move to the right along the line. The change between any two points can be used to compute the slope because the slope of a straight line is _____. If the straight line shows that both the horizontal and vertical variables increase together, then the line is said to have a (<u>positive/negative</u>) slope; that is, as we move to the right, the line slopes (<u>up/down</u>). If one variable decreases as the other variable increases, the line is said to have a _____ slope. A line with a zero slope shows _____ change in the *Y* variable as the *X* variable changes.

A special type of straight line passes through the origin of a graph. This is called a _____

(3) through the origin. Its slope is measured the same as the slope of any other straight line. A special type of ray is one that connects all points where the vertical and horizontal variables are equal. If the vertical and horizontal variables are measured in the same units, then this line has a slope of +1 and is called the _____ line.

Like straight lines, curved lines also have slopes, but the slope of a curved line is not constant. We measure the slope of a curved line at any point by the slope of the one straight line that just touches,

(4) or is _____ to, the line at that point.

A third type of graph is used by economists as well as cartographers. Such a graph can represent

(5) three dimensions on a diagram with only two axes by the use of _____ lines. A traditional application of such a graph in economics is a diagram that measures inputs along the horizontal and vertical axes and then uses contour lines to show what different combinations of inputs can be used to produced the same amount of output.

**FIGURE 1-1**
**MINISTERS' SALARIES AND**
**EXPENDITURES ON ALCOHOL**
Source: U.S. Labor Department; U.S. Commerce Department

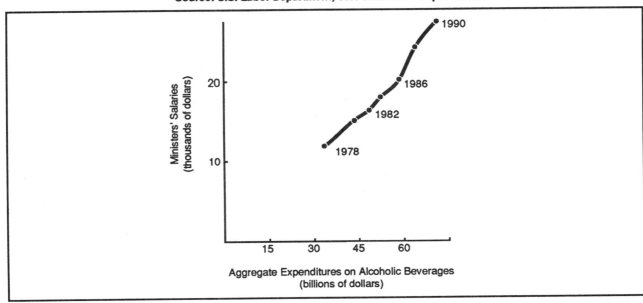

## IMPORTANT TERMS AND CONCEPTS QUIZ

Choose the best definition for the following terms.

1. _____ Variable
2. _____ Two-variable diagram
3. _____ Horizontal axis
4. _____ Vertical axis
5. _____ Origin
6. _____ Slope
7. _____ Negative slope
8. _____ Positive slope
9. _____ Zero slope
10. _____ Infinite slope
11. _____ Tangent to a curve
12. _____ Y-intercept
13. _____ Ray
14. _____ 45-degree line
15. _____ Contour map

a. Graph of how a variable changes over time.
b. Vertical line segment.
c. Straight line, touching a curve at a point without cutting the curve.
d. The bottom line of a graph.
e. Straight line emanating from the origin.
f. Object whose magnitude is measured by a number.
g. Simultaneous representation of the magnitudes of two variables.
h. Point where both axes meet and where both variables are zero.
i. Straight line through the origin with a slope of +1.
j. Point at which a straight line cuts the vertical axis.
k. Line that goes down, moving from left to right.
l. Line that neither rises nor falls, moving from left to right.
m. The side of a graph.
n. Two-dimensional representation of three variables.
o. Ratio of vertical change to corresponding horizontal change.
p. Line that rises, moving from left to right.

## BASIC EXERCISES
### Reading Graphs

These exercises are designed to give practice working with two-variable diagrams.

1. **Understanding a Demand Curve**
   The demand curve in Figure 1-2 represents the demand for new Ph.D. economists.
   a. What quantity would colleges and universities demand if they have to pay a salary of $45,000?
   _____
   b. What does the graph indicate would happen to the quantity demanded if salaries fall to $35,000? The quantity demanded would (<u>increase/decrease</u>) to _____
   c. What would happen to the quantity demanded if salaries were $50,000? It would (<u>increase/decrease</u>) to _____
   d. What is the slope of the demand curve? _____
   e. Explain how the slope of the demand curve provides information about the change in the number of new Ph.D. economists demanded as salary changes.

2. **Understanding a 45–degree Line**

   Figure 1-3 shows data on grade point averages for Valerie and her friends. Overall averages are measured along the horizontal axis while GPAs for courses in economics are measured along the vertical axis. Figure 1-3 also includes a 45–degree line.

   a. How many individuals have higher overall GPAs than economics GPAs?
   _____

   b. How many individuals do better in economics courses than in their other courses?
   _____

   c. If all of Valerie's friends had their best grades in economics courses, all of the points in Figure 1-3 would lie (<u>above/below</u>) the 45–degree line.

   d. If all of the points in Figure 1-3 were below the 45–degree line, we could conclude that Valerie and her friends did better in (<u>economics/non-economics</u>) courses.

**FIGURE 1-2**
**THE DEMAND FOR NEW Ph.D. ECONOMISTS**

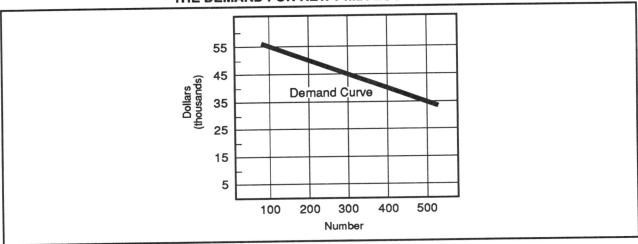

**FIGURE 1-3**
**GRADE POINT AVERAGES**

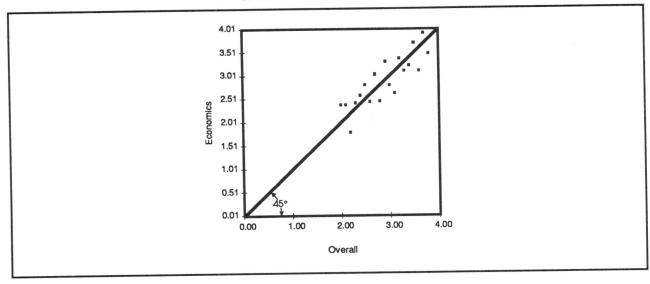

### 3. Understanding Slopes

Table 1-1 contains data on the cost of producing widgets.

a. Plot this data in Figure 1-4. The points appear to lie along a (curved/straight) line.

b. Draw the appropriate line through these points and extend it to the vertical axis. What is the mathematical value for the slope of the line? _____. Can you provide an economic meaning for this number?

c. What is the mathematical value for the Y–intercept of your line? _____. Can you provide an economic meaning for this number?

d. Now consider Figure 1-5, which shows how the cost of producing gadgets varies with output. Describe how the slope of the curved line varies as output increases. Can you provide an economic interpretation for your answer?

### TABLE 1-1

| Output | Cost |
|--------|--------|
| 0 | $1,000 |
| 200 | $2,000 |
| 400 | $3,000 |
| 600 | $4,000 |
| 800 | $5,000 |
| 1,000 | $6,000 |

### FIGURE 1-4
### TOTAL COST AND OUTPUT: WIDGETS

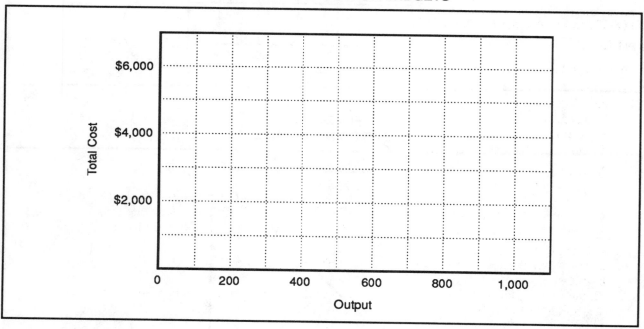

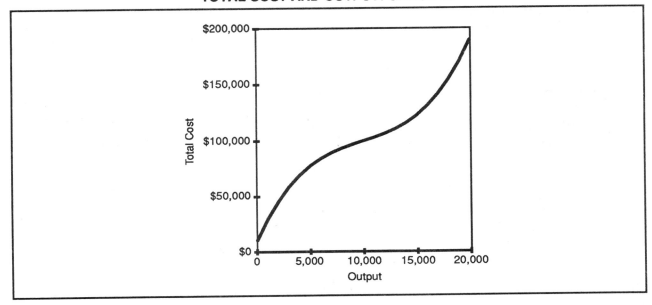

**FIGURE 1-5**
**TOTAL COST AND OUTPUT: GADGETS**

---

## SELF-TESTS FOR UNDERSTANDING

### Test A

Circle the most appropriate answer.

1. The vertical line on the left side of a two-variable diagram is called the
   a. ray through the origin.
   b. vertical axis.
   c. X axis.
   d. slope of the graph.

2. A two-variable diagram
   a. can only be drawn when one variable causes another.
   b. is a useful way to show how two variables change simultaneously.
   c. is a useful way of summarizing the influence of all factors that affect the Y variable.
   d. can only be used when relationships between variables can be represented by straight lines.

3. The origin of a two–variable graph is
   a. found in the lower right corner of a graph.
   b. the same as the Y–intercept.
   c. the intersection of the vertical and horizontal axes where both variables are equal to zero.
   d. found by following the slope to the point where it equals zero.

4. The slope of a straight line is found by dividing the
   a. Y variable by the X variable.
   b. vertical axis by the horizontal axis.
   c. largest value of the Y variable by the smallest value of the X variable.
   d. vertical change by the corresponding horizontal change.

5. The slope of a straight line
   a. is the same at all points.
   b. increases moving to the right.
   c. will be zero when the X variable equals to zero.
   d. is always positive.

6. If a straight line has a positive slope, then we know that
   a. it runs uphill, moving to the right.
   b. the slope of the line will be greater than that of a 45–degree line.
   c. it must also have a positive Y–intercept.
   d. it will reach its maximum value when its slope is zero.

7. Referring to parts (1), (2), (3), and (4) of Figure 1-6, determine which line has a(n)
   a. positive slope _____3_____.
   b. negative slope _____1_____.
   c. zero slope _____2_____.
   d. infinite slope _____4_____.

**FIGURE 1-6**

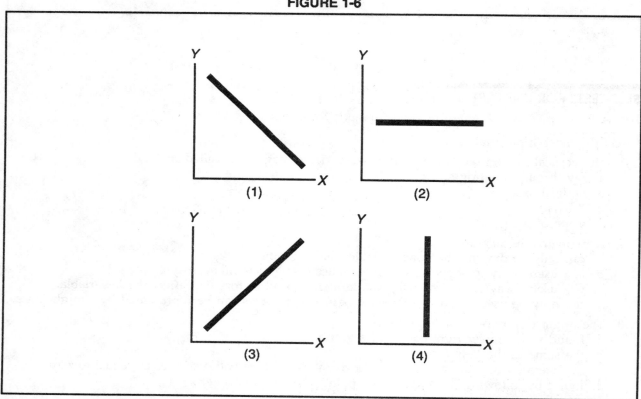

**FIGURE 1-7**

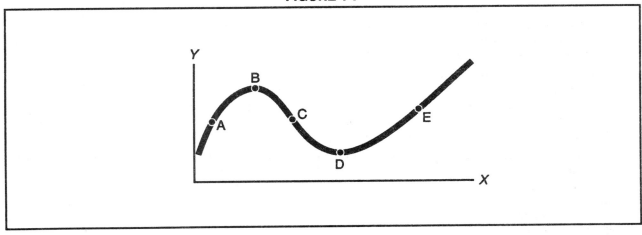

8. Referring to Figure 1-7, determine at which points the curved line has a(n)
    a. positive slope ____A____ ____E____ _____.
    b. negative slope ____C____ _____ _____.
    c. zero slope ____B____ ____D____ _____.
    d. infinite slope _____ _____ _____.

9. If when X = 5, Y = 16 and when X = 8, Y = 10, then the
    a. line connecting X and Y has a positive slope.
    b. line connecting X and Y is a ray through the origin.
    c. slope of the line connecting X and Y is +6.
    d. slope of the line connecting X and Y is –2.

10. The slope of a curved line is
    a. the same at all points on the line.
    b. found by dividing the Y variable by the X variable.
    c. found by determining the slope of a straight line tangent to the curved line at the point of interest.
    d. always positive.

11. If a curved line is in the shape of a hill, then the point of zero slope will occur at the
    a. origin of the line.
    b. highest point of the line.
    c. Y–intercept of the line.
    d. point where a ray from the origin intercepts the line.

12. The Y–intercept is
    a. the same as the origin of a graph.
    b. the point where a straight line cuts the Y axis.
    c. usually equal to the X–intercept.
    d. equal to the reciprocal of the slope of a straight line.

13. If the Y–intercept of a straight line is equal to zero, then this line is called
    a. the opportunity cost of a graph.
    b. a ray through the origin.
    c. the 45–degree line.
    d. the X axis.

14. A ray is
    a. any straight line with a slope of +1.
    b. any line, straight or curved, that passes through the origin of a graph.
    c. a straight line with a positive Y–intercept.
    d. a straight line that passes through the origin.

15. If the X and Y variables are measured in the same units, a 45–degree line will
    a. have a positive Y–intercept.
    b. have a negative slope.
    c. show all points where X and Y are equal.
    d. be steeper than the Y axis.

16. If $X$ and $Y$ are measured in the same units, and we consider a point that lies below a 45–degree line, then we know that for the $X$ and $Y$ combination associated with this point,
    a. the $X$ variable is greater than the $Y$ variable.
    b. a line from the origin through this point will be a ray and will have a slope greater than +1.
    c. the $Y$ variable is greater than the $X$ variable.
    d. the slope of the point is less than 1.

17. Referring to parts (1), (2), (3), and (4) of Figure 1-8, determine which part(s) show a ray through the origin.
    a. (2)
    b. (1) and (3)
    c. (1) and (4)
    d. (3) and (4)

## FIGURE 1-8

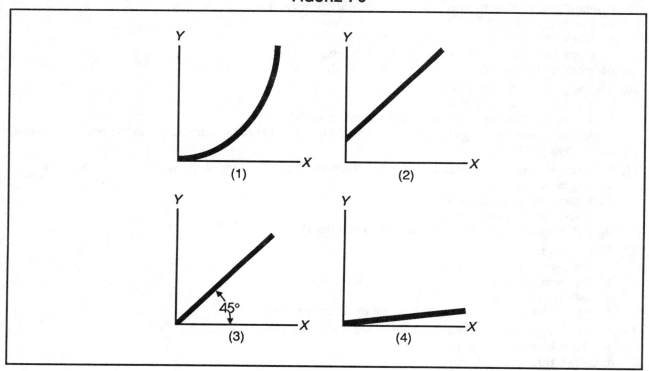

18. If in part (4) of Figure 1-8, the Y variable changes by 2 units when the X variable changes by 5 units, then the slope of the line is
    a. .4 (2/5).
    b. 2.5 (5/2).
    c. 10 (2 × 5).
    d. insufficient information to compute.

19. If two straight line have the same slope, then they
    a. must also have the same Y–intercept.
    b. will show the same change in Y for similar changes in X.
    c. will both pass through the origin.
    d. are said to be complements.

20. A contour map
    a. is always better than a two-variable diagram.
    b. is a way of collapsing three variables into a two-variable diagram.
    c. shows how the Y variable changes when the X variable is held constant.
    d. is only of relevance to geographers.

## Test B

Circle T or F for true or false.

T (F)  1. The line along the bottom of a two–variable graph is called the vertical axis.

T (F)  2. The slope of a line measures the value of the Y variable when the X variable is equal to zero.

(T) F  3. The slope of a straight line is the same at all points on the line.

(T) F  4. A negative slope means that the Y variable decreases when the X variable increases.

T (F)  5. The slope of a curved line cannot be measured.

(T) F  6. A straight line that has a Y–intercept of zero is also called a ray through the origin.

T (F)  7. All rays through the origin have the same slope.

(T) F  8. If X and Y are measured in the same units, then a 45–degree line is a ray through the origin with a slope of +1.

(T) F  9. If X and Y are measured in the same units, then any point above a 45–degree line is a point at which the Y variable is greater than the X variable.

T (F) 10. A contour map is a way to show the relationship between two variables in three dimensions.

*Chapter* **2**

# A Profile of the U.S. Economy

## LEARNING OBJECTIVES

After completing this chapter, you should be able to:

- ◆ explain the difference between inputs and outputs.
- ◆ explain why total output of the American economy is larger than that of other nations.
- ◆ explain why real GDP per capita is a better measure of living standards than GDP.
- ◆ explain the difference between a closed and open economy.
- ◆ describe in general terms the growth experience of the American economy.
- ◆ describe the broad changes in American work experience: Who goes to work outside the home? What sorts of jobs do they hold? What sorts of goods and services do they produce?
- ◆ describe who gets what proportion of national income.
- ◆ describe the common forms of business organization.
- ◆ describe the role of government in the American economy.
- ◆ explain the implications of the pitfalls of time series graphs:
  - • failure to adjust for changes in prices and/or population.
  - • the use of short time periods with unique features.
  - • omitting the origin.
  - • the use of different units to measure the same variable.

## IMPORTANT TERMS AND CONCEPTS

Economy
Inputs (factors of production)
Outputs
Gross domestic product (GDP)
Real GDP
Open economy
Closed economy
Inflation
Recession
Sole proprietorship
Partnership
Corporation
Transfer payments
Mixed economy

## CHAPTER REVIEW

This chapter offers an introduction to and overview of the American economy. The money value of total
**(1)** output of the American economy is usually measured by something called gross_____
_____or _____for short. American GDP is so large because of the size of the
work force and the productivity of American workers. Other countries, for example China and India, have
larger populations, but the productivity of workers there does not compare with that of American workers.

Why is the American economy so productive? It is useful to view an economic system as a social
**(2)** mechanism that organizes (<u>inputs/outputs</u>) to produce _____. Many believe that the
productivity of the American economy is a reflection of business competition fostered by the extensive
use of_____ markets and _____ enterprise.

No economy is self–sufficient. All economies trade with each other, although their reliance on trade
varies. The average of exports and imports as a percentage of GDP is often used as a measure of the degree
**(3)** to which an economy can be called _____ or _____. Compared to other
industrialized countries, the United State would look like a(n) (<u>closed/open</u>) economy. While exports and
imports have both increased since World War II, they are currently just a bit more than 10 percent of
American GDP.

Because it uses money values to add up different types of outputs, i.e, food, clothes, cars, medical
services, and new houses, GDP will increase when prices increase even if there is no change in production.
**(4)** A sustained increase in prices on average is referred to as _____. A time series graph
of American GDP since World War II shows significant growth. As with all time series graphs, one needs
to be careful about exactly how the variable of interest is measured. If one is interested in consumption
possibilities, it is best to correct for inflation by looking at GDP measured in dollars of constant purchasing
power or _____ GDP. It may also be useful to adjust real GDP by the growth in
population for a measure of GDP _____ _____. Adjusting for inflation and population
growth still shows a doubling of per capita real GDP over the past 40 years.

While the time series graph of real GDP for the United States shows significant growth since World
War II, it has not been continual growth. There have been periods when total output declined. These
**(5)** periods are called _____. How the government should respond during or in
anticipation of a period of recession continues to spark controversy.

(6)      Organizing inputs, also called factors of _____, is a central issue that any economy must address. For the most part, output in the United States is produced by private firms that compete in free markets. Most economists believe that having to meet the competition is an important reason why the American economy is so productive. Inputs include labor, machinery, buildings, and natural resources. It is the revenue from selling output that creates income for these factors of production.

In the United States the largest share of income accrues to which factor of production?
(7)  _____. The income earned by those who put up the money to buy buildings and machinery comes in the form of interest and profits. Together, these two forms of income receive about _____ of each sales dollar. Most Americans work in (manufacturing/service) industries.

A business may be owned and operated by a single individual, in which case it is called a
(8) sole_____. If a business is run by a fixed number of individuals, it is called a _____. However, most output is produced by _____, fictitious legal entities that have the status of individuals. Most large corporations are owned by stockholders and run by managers. While almost 90 percent of output in the United States is produced by privately owned businesses, most observers would say that the American economy is best described as a (laissez faire/mixed/socialistic) economy. That is, there is important public influence over the private market along with a mixture of public and private ownership.

The discussion in the text lists five roles for government:

1) To provide certain goods and services.
2) To raise taxes to finance its operations.
3) To redistribute income.
4) To regulate business.
5) To enforce the rules of business and society, including property rights.

This or any other list does not say whether particular actions are best done by the government or by the private economy. Are there legitimate unmet needs that should be addressed by government, or is government already too big? Much of the material in subsequent chapters is designed to help you understand what markets do well and what they do poorly. It is hoped that a better understanding of the insights from economic analysis will help you decide where you would draw the line between markets and government.

## Appendix

As illustrated in the text, economists make extensive use of time series graphs. These are two variable
(9) graphs with time measured along the (horizontal/vertical) axis and one or more variables of interest measured along the _____ axis. Time series graphs are an effective way to convey a lot of information, but they also can be misleading if misused either inadvertently or deliberately.

When making or interpreting time series graphs you should be aware of the following pitfalls:
- Failing to adjust for inflation or population growth can give a misleading impression of growth.
- Showing only a brief period of time and/or one with an atypical beginning or ending can give a distorted impression of actual experience.
- Omitting the origin can give an exaggerated impression of changes.
- Changing the units of measurement, say from pounds to ounces or dollars to pennies, can make a graph arbitrarily steeper or flatter.

## IMPORTANT TERMS AND CONCEPTS QUIZ

Choose the most appropriate definition for the following terms.

1. _____ Economy
2. _____ Inputs (factors of production)
3. _____ Outputs
4. _____ Gross domestic product (GDP)
5. _____ Real GDP
6. _____ Open economy
7. _____ Closed economy
8. _____ Inflation
9. _____ Recession
10. _____ Sole proprietorship
11. _____ Partnership
12. _____ Corporation
13. _____ Transfer payments
14. _____ Mixed economy

a. Money value of all goods and services produced in a year.
b. A business owned by a fixed number of individuals.
c. A sustained increase in the average level of prices.

d. A collection of markets in a specified geographic area.
e. Economy in which exports and imports are small relative to GDP.
f. A measure of how prices today compare to prices during a specified base period.
g. Value of goods and services produced in a year measured by dollars of constant purchasing power.
h. A period when real GDP declines.
i. Labor, machinery, buildings, and natural resource used to produce goods and services.
j. A business owned by a single individual or family.
k. International trade is a large promotion of GDP.
l. Economy with public influence over the workings of free markets and a mix of public and private ownership.
m. Goods and services desired by consumers.
n. A business that has the legal status of a fictitious individual.
o. Money that individuals receive from the government as grants.

## BASIC EXERCISES

These exercises are designed to introduce facts about the American economy and to offer practice working with graphs and economic data.

1. **Growth Trends**
   a. Look at Table 2-1, which has data on personal income after taxes. The data show that between 1960 and 1990 aggregate personal income after taxes increased more than eleven fold (4,042.9 ÷ 360.5 = 11.2). Do you agree that individuals in 1990 were eleven times richer than individuals in 1960? Could they buy eleven times as many goods and services as they could in 1960?
   b. For each year in Table 2-1 divide aggregate income by the corresponding population to compute income per capita rather than aggregate income. Rather than a twenty-five fold increase, per capita income in 1990 was only _____ times its 1960 level.
   c. For each year divide income per capita by the corresponding price level and multiply by 100 to compute income per capita in constant prices. The figures in the last column of Table 2-1 will tell us how per capita purchasing power, or real income, has changed since 1960. (The appendix to Chapter 6 contains more information about how a price index is constructed and what can be done with it.) In 1990, per capita purchasing power was _____ times its 1960 level.

## TABLE 2-1
## PERSONAL INCOME AFTER TAXES

| Year | Aggregate Personal Income After Taxes (billions) | Population (millions) | Income per Capita | Price Index 1987 = 100 | Real Income per Capita (1987 prices) |
|------|------|------|------|------|------|
| 1960 | $360.5 | 180,671 | $_____ | 27.5 | $_____ |
| 1970 | $722.0 | 205,052 | $_____ | 46.4 | $_____ |
| 1980 | $1,952.9 | 227,726 | $_____ | 80.9 | $_____ |
| 1990 | $4,042.9 | 249,924 | $_____ | 105.7 | $_____ |

SOURCE: 1993 Economic Report of the President, Tables B-3, B-24, B-29

### 2. Rock Concerts: Adjusting for Inflation

Who paid more to attend their favorite rock concert, you or your parents? Table 2-2 has data on ticket prices of stadium rock concerts. Use the data on consumer prices to express ticket prices for earlier years in 1993 dollars. (Divide each ticket price by the value of the price index and multiply by 100.)

### TABLE 2-2

| Year | Concert | Ticket Price | Consumer Price Index (1993 = 100) | Ticket Price in 1993 Dollars |
|------|---------|------|------|------|
| 1965 | Beatles | $3.50 | 21.9 | $_____ |
| 1971 | The Band, Muddy Waters, John Sebastian, Paul Butterfield Blues Band | $8.00 | 28.1 | $_____ |
| 1976 | Fleetwood Mac, Jeff Beck | $9.00 | 39.5 | $_____ |
| 1978 | Eagles, Steve Miller | $10.00 | 45.3 | $_____ |
| 1982 | The Who | $16.00 | 60.1 | $_____ |
| 1983 | Simon and Garfunkel | $20.00 | 69.2 | $_____ |
| 1985 | Bruce Springsteen | $17.50 | 74.7 | $_____ |
| 1986 | Bob Dylan, Grateful Dead | $20.00 | 76.1 | $_____ |
| 1988 | Pink Floyd | $22.50 | 82.2 | $_____ |
| 1989 | Rolling Stones | $28.50 | 86.1 | $_____ |
| 1993 | Paul McCartney | $32.50 | 100.0 | $_____ |

SOURCE: Minneapolis StarTribune, May 21, 1993. 1993 Economic Report of the President

**FIGURE 2-1A**
**Housing Starts: January-June, 1993**

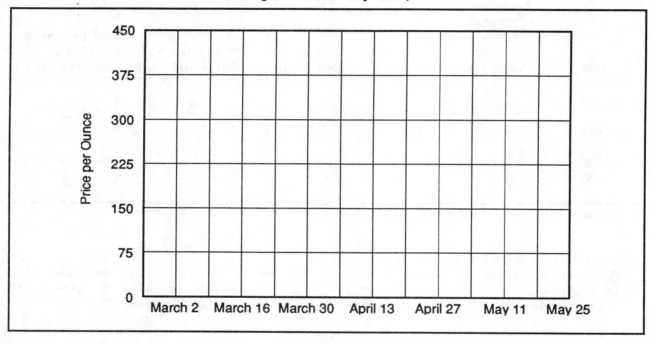

### 3. Dangers of Omitting the Origin

Table 2-3 contains data on gold prices during the late winter and early spring of 1993. Plot this data in Figures 2-1a and 2-1b. Which figure gives the more accurate representation of the increase in gold prices and why?

**TABLE 2-3**
**The Price of Gold**
**March 2, 1993—May 25, 1993**

| Date | Dollars per Ounce |
| --- | --- |
| March 2 | $328.95 |
| March 9 | $326.45 |
| March 16 | $328.75 |
| March 23 | $331.75 |
| March 30 | $336.15 |
| April 6 | $338.15 |
| April 13 | $337.15 |
| April 20 | $340.25 |
| April 27 | $350.55 |
| May 4 | $354.70 |
| May 11 | $356.45 |
| May 18 | $366.75 |
| May 25 | $374.45 |

SOURCE: *The Economist*, various issues

**FIGURE 2-1B**
**Housing Starts: January-June, 1993**

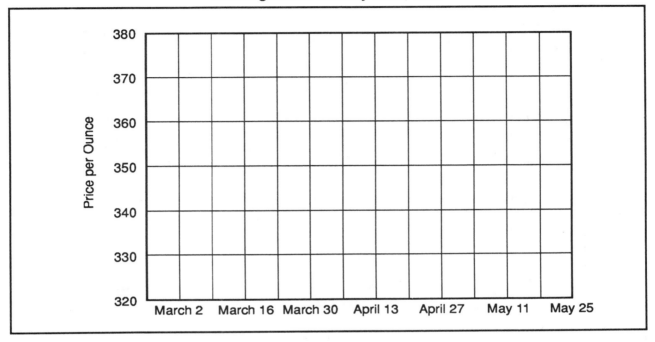

**FIGURE 2-2**

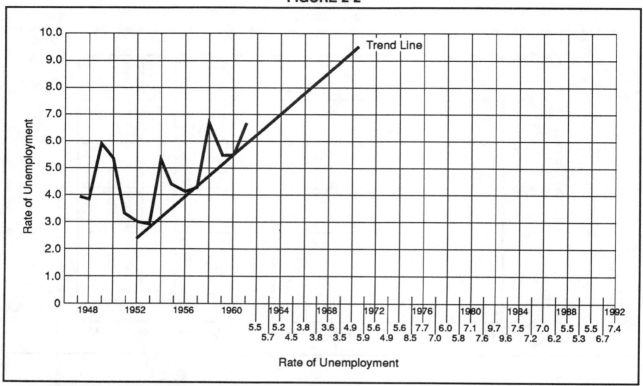

SOURCE: 1993 Economic Report of the President, Table B-30.

## 4. Choice of Time Periods

In 1960, John F. Kennedy campaigned on a promise to get the country moving, including more rapid economic expansion. When Kennedy was elected president the unemployment rate was rising and the economy was slipping into a recession. Many observers were claiming that for a variety of "structural" reasons the United States was entering an era of permanently higher unemployment. A major piece of evidence used to support this line of thinking was the rising succession of lowest unemployment rates in each postwar business expansion up to the early 1960s. The data are presented here, in Figure 2-2, together with a trend line connecting the succession of lowest unemployment rates. Use the data in Figure 2-2 to extend the time series graph and to check the accuracy of this argument. If the graph were restricted to data from 1968 to 1983, what would a similar trend line over this period show? What could one conclude from such a trend line?

## SELF-TESTS FOR UNDERSTANDING

### Test A

Circle the most appropriate answer.

1. Which of the following help to explain why output of the American economy is as high as it is? (There may be more than one correct answer to this question.)
   a. The size of the labor force.
   b. The amount of money provided by the government.
   c. Business regulation.
   d. The productivity of American workers.

2. Total output of the United States economy
   a. is slightly less than that of Japan.
   b. is comparable to that of other industrialized countries.
   c. exceeds that of all other national economies.
   d. is among the lowest for industrialized countries.

3. Gross domestic product measures
   a. consumer spending.
   b. the vulgarness of many consumer goods.
   c. unpaid economic activity that takes place inside households.
   d. the money value of all the goods and services produced in an economy in a year.

4. Gross domestic product per capita refers to
   a. GDP per person (GDP/population).
   b. GDP times population (GDP × population).
   c. GDP per worker (GDP/employment).
   d. GDP measured in dollars of constant purchasing power.

5. The average standard of living over time is best measured by
   a. GDP.
   b. GDP per capita.
   c. real GDP.
   d. real GDP per capita.

6. If the price of everything increases, but the production of specific goods and services is unchanged,
   a. real GDP will actually decline.
   b. real GDP will remain unchanged.
   c. real GDP will increase as prices increase.

7. Inflation refers to
   a. an increase in the stock of money.
   b. an increase in the price of any single commodity.
   c. a sustained increase in the average level of prices.
   d. an increase in GDP.

8. The term *recession* refers to
   a. a period of inflation.
   b. a period of above–average economic growth.
   c. automatic reductions in government spending designed to reduce the deficit.
   d. a period when real GDP declines.

9. When referring to inputs, the term *capital* refers to
    a. money business firms need to borrow.
    b. the importance of a firm's head office.
    c. machines and buildings used to produce output.
    d. all of a firm's factors of production.

10. Which of the following would not be classified as an input?
    a. A farmer's time to grow wheat.
    b. The farmer's tractor.
    c. The farmer's land.
    d. The bread that is made from the wheat.

11. The majority of American workers work for
    a. manufacturing companies.
    b. the federal government.
    c. state and local governments.
    d. firms that produce a variety of services, including retail and wholesale trade.

12. Most business firms are
    a. corporations.
    b. partnerships.
    c. proprietorships.

13. Which business firms account for the greatest share of output?
    a. Corporations.
    b. Partnerships.
    c. Proprietorships.

14. The term *concentration ratio* refers to the
    a. purity of products produced by large consumer firms.
    b. proportion of output produced by the largest four firms in an industry.
    c. production process for reconstituted fruit juices.
    d. increasing power of the federal government.

15. When Americans buy goods produced abroad, _____ increase.
    a. exports
    b. taxes
    c. transfer payments
    d. imports

16. When Americans are able to sell goods to foreigners, this adds to
    a. exports.
    b. taxes.
    c. transfer payments.
    d. imports.

17. Consumer spending accounts for _____ of American GDP.
    a. less than a fifth
    b. about a third
    c. about half
    d. about two–thirds
    e. about three–quarters

18. National defense accounts for _____ of federal government spending.
    a. less than a fifth
    b. about a third
    c. about half
    d. about two–thirds

19. For the most part, the United States has chosen to let markets determine pre–tax income and then uses taxes and _____ to reduce income inequalities.
   a. tariffs
   b. inflation
   c. transfer payments
   d. government production

20. Compared to other industrialized countries, taxes as a percent of GDP in the United States are
   a. among the lowest.
   b. about the same as most other industrialized countries.
   c. among the highest.

## Test B

Circle T or F for true or false.

T  F  1. An economic system is a social mechanism that organizes inputs to produce outputs.

T  F  2. Since World War II American real GDP has increased every year without interruption.

T  F  3. The American economy is a more open economy than other industrialized economies.

T  F  4. The American economy relies on free markets and private enterprise to a greater extent than most other industrialized economies.

T  F  5. During a recession, unemployment usually increases.

T  F  6. Government production accounts for more than half of American GDP.

T  F  7. Women hold more than half of the jobs outside the home.

T  F  8. Most American workers still produce goods rather than services.

T  F  9. Labor gets most of the income generated in the United States.

T  F  10. Most businesses in the United States are sole proprietorships.


## SUPPLEMENTARY EXERCISE

Table 2-4 reports data on tuition and required fees for four–year universities. How do increases in tuition and fees compare to the increase in prices in general and increases in income? You can adjust the data on nominal tuition and fees by dividing it by the price index from Table 2-1. An increase in real tuition and fees would indicate that this element of the cost of college has increased faster than prices in general. Once you have computed tuition and fees in terms of 1987 purchasing power, divide these figures by real per capita income calculated in Table 2-1 to see how tuition and fees have changed relative to real income per capita.

What has happened to tuition and fees at the college or university you attend? The appropriate office at your institution should be able to provide current and historical data on tuition and fees.

Information on prices and income can be found in the most recent *Economic Report of the President*.

### TABLE 2-4
### TUITION AND REQUIRED FEES
#### 4-Year Universities

| Year | Public | Private |
|------|--------|---------|
| 1970-71 | $478 | $1,980 |
| 1980-81 | $915 | $4,275 |
| 1990-91 | $2,159 | $11,379 |

SOURCE: *Digest of Education Statistics*, 1992, National Center for Education Statistics, U.S. Department of Education, Table 301.

## STUDY QUESTIONS

1. What is the difference between inputs and outputs? How would you categorize the steel used in new cars or home appliances?

2. How can output of the American economy be greater than that of countries like China and India with larger populations?

3. What measure(s) of economic activity would you use to compare living standards, either over time for a single country or between countries at a point in time? Why?

4. What does the historical record show regarding the growth in real GDP and real GDP per capita in the United States?

5. What is meant by a closed or open economy? How would you characterize the United States?

6. In the United States, who works outside the home for wages and salary and what types of jobs do they hold?

7. How is income in the United States distributed among factors of production?

8. What are the common forms of business organization? Which tend to be larger? Which smaller? Why?

9. How does the role of government in the American economy compare with that of other industrialized countries?

10. What are some of the common pitfalls of time series graphs and how can you avoid them?

## ECONOMICS IN ACTION

### The Proper Role for Government

How far should the government go when regulating business? If the government is to provide some goods and services, what principles determine which goods and services? How far should the government go in redistributing income?

Noted economist Milton Friedman has consistently argued for a limited role for government. In a widely publicized PBS series, Friedman and his wife, Rose, advocated four principles as tests of the appropriate business of government. National defense, domestic police and justice, the provision of goods and services in the limited cases where markets do not work well, and protection for citizens who cannot protect themselves, (e.g., children) define the Friedmans' four principles. These principles, especially the third, could be seen as justifying a range of government action. The Friedmans are as concerned with government failures as with market failures. They note that once started, government initiatives are rarely stopped. In their view the burden of proof should be on the proponents of government action.

The Friedmans see government as created by the citizenry. They argue that government should be organized to maximize individual "freedom to choose as individuals, as families, as members of voluntary groups." They endorse the view of Adam Smith that as long as individuals do not violate the laws of justice, they should be free to pursue their own interests and that competitive markets rather than government regulation are usually the most effective forms of social organization. "We can shape our institutions. Physical and human characteristics limit the alternatives available to us. But none prevents us, if we will, from building a society that relies primarily on voluntary cooperation to organize both economic and other activity, a society that preserves and expands human freedom, that keeps government in its place, keeping it our servant and not letting it become our master."[1]

The equally renowned John Kenneth Galbraith, on the other hand, argues that increasing affluence has led to an imbalance between private and public goods. Goods and services that are marketable to individuals allow private producers to accumulate the financial resources that give them control of labor,

[1]Milton and Rose Friedman, *Free to Choose: A Personal Statement*, Harcourt Brace Jovanovich, 1980.

capital, and raw materials. Sophisticated advertising creates and sustains demand for private goods, generating more income and profits. This affluence of the private sector is in marked contrast to the poverty of the public sector. Galbraith argues that society needs a balance between private and public goods but that the pernicious effects of advertising that creates the demand that sustains the production of private goods gives rise to a serious imbalance. One result is an increasing demand for private goods and services to protect individuals from the poverty of public goods and services, such as elaborate alarm systems and private guards to counteract the lack of police.

How much increase in public spending is necessary to redress the balance? Galbraith will only say that the distance is considerable. "When we arrive, the opulence of our private consumption will no longer be in contrast with the poverty of our schools, the unloveliness and congestion of our cities, our inability to get to work without a struggle, and the social disorder that is associated with imbalance. . . the precise point of balance will never be defined. This will be of comfort only to those who believe that any failure of definition can be made to score decisively against the larger idea."[2]

1. How would you define the proper role of government? Where would you draw the line between those activities best left to individual initiative and markets and those that are the appropriate business of government?

---

[2] John Kenneth Galbraith, *The Affluent Society*, Houghton Mifflin, 1958.

*Chapter* **3**

# Scarcity and Choice:
# The Economic Problem

## LEARNING OBJECTIVES

After completing this chapter, you should be able to:

♦ explain why the true cost of any decision is its opportunity cost.

♦ explain the link between market prices and opportunity costs.

♦ explain why the scarcity of goods and services (outputs) must be attributed to a scarcity of resources, or inputs, used in production processes.

♦ draw a production possibilities frontier for a firm or for the economy.

♦ explain how the production possibility frontier contains information about the opportunity cost of changing output combinations.

♦ explain why specialized resources mean that a firm's or economy's production possibilities frontier is likely to bow outward.

♦ explain how an economy can shift its production possibilities frontier.

♦ explain why production efficiency requires that an economy produce on, rather than inside, its production possibilities frontier.

♦ describe the three coordination tasks that every economy must confront.

♦ explain why specialization and division of labor are likely to require the use of markets.

♦ describe how a market economy solves the three coordination tasks.

## IMPORTANT TERMS AND CONCEPTS

| | |
|---|---|
| Resources | Economic growth |
| Scarcity | Consumption goods |
| Choice | Capital goods |
| Rational decision | Efficiency |
| Opportunity cost | Specialization |
| Outputs | Division of labor |
| Inputs (means of production) | Exchange |
| Production possibilities frontier | Market system |
| Allocation of resources | Three coordination tasks |
| Principle of increasing costs | |

## CHAPTER REVIEW

### "You can't always get what you want" Mike Jaeger

Scarcity and the resulting necessity to make choices are fundamental concerns of economics. This chapter is an introduction to these issues, although they have already been implicitly introduced in many of the 12 ideas for Beyond the Final Exam, and will reappear throughout the text.

(1)  The importance of *choice* starts with the fact that virtually all resources are _____. Most people's desires exceed their incomes, and, thus, everyone makes buying choices all the time. Similarly, firms, educational institutions, and government agencies make choices between what kinds of outputs to produce and what combination of inputs to use. An economist studying the use of inputs for the overall economy is studying the allocation of resources.

  What is a good way to make choices? The obvious answer is to consider the alternatives. Economists
(2) call these forgone alternatives the _____ _____ of a decision. Imagine it is the night before the first midterm in Introductory Economics, which will cover Chapters 1-6, and here you are only on Chapter 3. A friend suggests a night at the movies and even offers to buy your ticket so "it won't cost you anything." Do you agree that the evening out won't cost anything? What will you be giving up?

  At first the idea of choices for the economy may sound strange. It may be easiest to imagine such choices being made by bureaucrats in a centrally planned economy. Even though there is no central planning bureau for the U.S. economy, it is useful to think of opportunities available to the American economy. The opportunities selected result from the combined spending and production decisions of all citizens, firms, and governmental units, decisions coordinated by our reliance on markets.

  The *production possibilities frontier* is a useful diagram for representing the choices available to a firm or
(3) an economy. The frontier will tend to slope downward to the right because resources are (scarce/specialized). The frontier will tend to bow out because most resources are _____. For any one year the resources available to an economy—the number of workers, factories, and machines, and the state of technology—are essentially fixed. Over time, an economy can increase its resources if it produces (more/fewer) consumption goods and _____ capital goods. Similarly, technological advancements are more likely if an economy devotes (more/fewer) resources to research and development. In terms of a frontier showing possible combinations of consumption and capital goods, the true cost of faster economic growth is given by the foregone output of _____ goods.

  Opportunity cost is the best measure of the true cost of any decision. For a single firm or an economy as a whole, with choices represented by a production possibilities frontier, the opportunity cost of changing
(4) the composition of output can be measured by the_____ of the production possibilities frontier.

(5) As an economy produces more and more of one good, say automobiles, the opportunity cost of further increases is likely to (increase/decrease). This change in opportunity cost illustrates the principle of_____ cost and is a result of the fact that most resources are (scarce/specialized).

For given amounts of all but one good, the production possibilities frontier for an economy measures the maximum amount of the remaining good that can be produced. Thus the production possibilities frontier defines maximum outputs or efficient production. There is, of course, no guarantee that the economy will operate on its frontier. If there is unemployment, then the economy is operating (on/inside) the frontier. If a firm or economy operates inside its production possibilities frontier, it is said to be _____ that is, with the same resources the firm or the economy could have produced more of some commodities.

(6)

All economies must answer three questions:
1. How can we use resources efficiently to operate on the production possibilities frontier?
2. What combinations of output shall we produce: that is, where on the frontier shall we produce?
3. To whom shall we distribute what is produced?

(7) The American economy answers these questions through the use of markets and prices. If markets are functioning well, then money prices (will/will not) be a reliable guide to opportunity costs. Problems arise when markets do not function well and when items do not have explicit price tags.

## IMPORTANT TERMS AND CONCEPTS QUIZ

Choose the best definition for the following terms.

1. _____ Resources
2. _____ Scarcity
3. _____ Choice
4. _____ Rational decision
5. _____ Opportunity cost
6. _____ Outputs
7. _____ Inputs
8. _____ Production possibilities frontier
9. _____ Allocation of resources
10. _____ Principle of increasing costs
11. _____ Consumption goods
12. _____ Capital goods
13. _____ Economic growth
14. _____ Efficiency
15. _____ Specialization
16. _____ Division of labor
17. _____ Exchange
18. _____ Market system
19. _____ Three coordination tasks

a. Resources used in production process.
b. Produced goods used to produce other goods in the future.
c. System in which allocation decisions are made in accordance with centralized direction.
d. Breaking tasks into smaller jobs.
e. Outward shift of the production possibilities frontier.
f. Decision on how to divide scarce resources among different uses.
g. Instruments used to create the goods and services people desire.
h. Process whereby a worker becomes more adept at a particular job.
i. Situation in which the amount of an item available is less than people want.
j. Goods and services that firms produce.
k. System in which decisions on resource allocation come from independent decisions of consumers and producers.
l. Absence of waste.
m. Foregone value of the next best alternative.
n. Decision made from a set of alternatives.
o. System in which people can trade with others.
p. Item available for immediate use by households.
q. Tendency for the opportunity cost of an additional unit of output to rise as production increases.
r. A decision that best serves the decision maker's objectives.
s. Graph of combinations of goods that can be produced with available inputs and technology.
t. Decisions on what goods to produce, how to produce them, and how to distribute them.

## BASIC EXERCISES

These exercises are designed to explore more fully some of the implications of the production possibilities frontier for an economy.

1. Figure 3-1 shows the production possibilities frontier (PPF) for the economy of Adirondack, which produces consumption and capital goods, here called bread and computers.
    a. If all resources are devoted to the production of bread, Adirondack can produce _____ loaves of bread. In order to produce 1000 computers, the opportunity cost in terms of bread is _____ loaves. To produce another 1000 computers, the opportunity cost (<u>rises/falls</u>) to _____ loaves. As long as the PPF continues to curve downward, the opportunity costs of increased computer output will (<u>continue to rise/start to fall</u>). These changes are the result, not of scarce resources per se, but of _____ resources. (You might try drawing a PPF on the assumption that all resources are equally productive in the production of both outputs. Can you convince yourself that it should be a straight line?)
    b. Find the output combination of 2500 computers and 320,000 loaves on Figure 3-1. Label this point *A*. Is it an attainable combination for Adirondack? Label the output combination 1500 computers and 400,000 loaves *B*. Is this combination attainable? Finally, label the output combination 1000 computers and 520,000 loaves *C*. Is this combination attainable? We can conclude that the attainable output combinations for Adirondack are (<u>on/inside/outside</u>) the production possibilities frontier.
    c. An output combination is inefficient if it is possible to produce more of one or both goods. Which, if any, of the output combinations identified in question b is an inefficient combination? _____. Show that this point is inefficient by shading in all attainable points indicating more of one or both goods.

### FIGURE 3-1

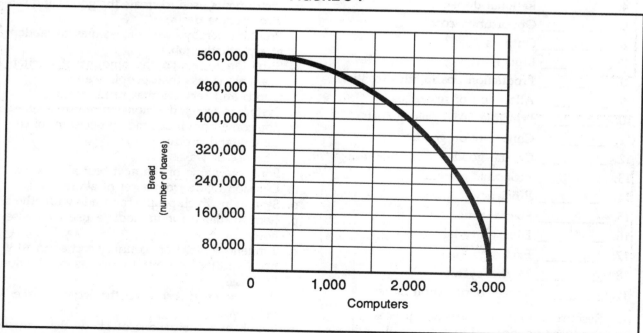

2. Figure 3-2 shows a PPF is applicable for two identical economies Catskill and Adirondack. The only difference is that Catskill produces 2,500 computers and 280,000 loaves of bread, point D, and Adirondack produces 2,000 computers and 400,000 loaves of bread, point E. Remember that computers stand for all capital goods and that the production of capital goods adds to the productive resources of an economy.

   a. The production of capital goods this year should cause the PPF for both economies to shift out next year. Figure 3-3 shows the new and initial PPFs for Adirondack following the production of 2,000 computers. Note that the new PPF lies outside the initial PPF. Draw the new PPF for Catskill. Has the PPF for Catskill shifted by more or less than that of Adirondack? Why?

   b. Describe how you would measure the cost of growth for the economy with the higher rate of economic growth?

FIGURE 3-2

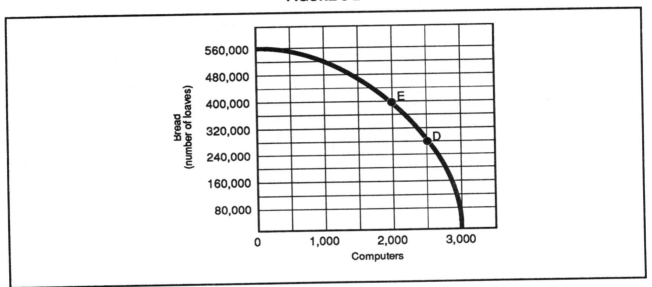

FIGURE 3-3

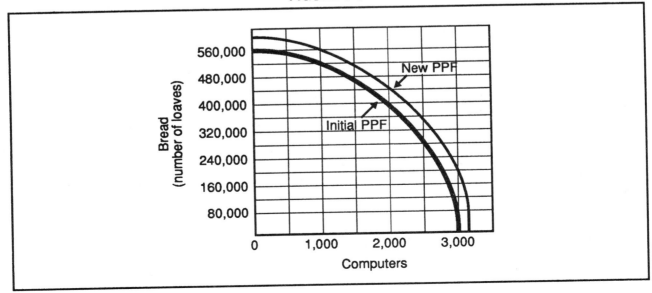

## SELF-TESTS FOR UNDERSTANDING
### Test A

Circle the most appropriate answer.

1. Economists define opportunity cost as
   a. the dollar price of goods and services.
   b. the hidden cost imposed by inflation.
   c. the value of the next best alternative use that is not chosen.
   d. the time spent shopping.

2. The position of an economy's production possibilities frontier is determined by all but which one of the following?
   a. The size of the labor force.
   b. Labor skills and training.
   c. The amount of consumption goods the economy can produce.
   d. Current technology.

3. A firm's production possibilities frontier shows
   a. the best combination of output for a firm to produce.
   b. its plans for increasing production over time.
   c. the architectural drawings of its most productive plant.
   d. different combinations of goods it can produce with a designated quantity of resources and available technology.

4. An efficient economy utilizes all available resources and produces the _____ output its technology permits.
   a. minimum amount of
   b. best combination of
   c. one combination of
   d. maximum amount of

5. The fact that resources are scarce implies that the production possibility frontier will
   a. have a negative slope.
   b. be a straight line.
   c. shift out over time.
   d. bow out from the origin.

6. Which of the following statements imply that production possibilities frontiers are likely to be curved, rather than straightlines?
   a. Ultimately all resources are scarce.
   b. Most resources are more productive in certain uses than in others.
   c. Unemployment is a more serious problem for some social groups than for others.
   d. Economists are notoriously poor at drawing straight lines.

7. The set of attainable points for a firm that produces two goods is given by
   a. all points on the production possibilities frontier.
   b. all points inside the production possibilities frontier.
   c. all points on or inside the production possibilities frontier.
   d. none of the above.

8. If an economy is operating efficiently, it will be producing
   a. inside its production possibilities frontier.
   b. on its production possibilities frontier.
   c. outside its production possibilities frontier.
   d. the maximum amount of necessities and the minimum amount of luxuries.

9. The principle of increasing cost is consistent with a _____ production possibilities frontier.
   a. straight–line
   b. bowed–in
   c. shifting
   d. bowed–out

10. The inability of the economy to produce as much as everyone would like is ultimately a reflection of
    a. a lack of money in the economy.
    b. congressional gridlock.
    c. the inability of a market economy to perform the necessary coordination tasks.
    d. a limited amount of productive resources.

11. The process of economic growth will be accompanied by
    a. a steeper production possibilities frontier.
    b. a production possibilities frontier that has shifted out.
    c. a smaller share of output devoted to government spending.
    d. an increase in the birth rate.

12. When, in Figure 3-1, the production of bread is increased from 280,000 loaves to 400,000 loaves, the opportunity cost in terms of reduced output of computers is
    a. 0
    b. 500
    c. 2,000
    d. 2,500

13. Which of the following implies a shift in the production possibilities frontier for a shoe firm?
    a. Raising all prices by 10 percent.
    b. Borrowing money to hire more workers and buying more machines.
    c. Changing the composition output toward more women's shoes and fewer men's shoes.
    d. Expanding the advertising budget.

14. Consider a production possibility frontier showing alternative combinations of corn and computers that can be produced in Cimonoce, a small island in the South Pacific. The opportunity cost of more computers can be measured by
    a. the slope of the production possibility frontier.
    b. the X-intercept of the production possibility frontier.
    c. the Y-intercept of the production possibility frontier
    d. the area under the production possibility frontier.

15. Which one of the following situations reflects a shift of the economy's production possibilities frontier?
    a. The proportion of labor devoted to the production of agricultural products has declined from 21 percent in 1929 to less than 3 percent in 1990.
    b. Total real output for the U.S. economy in 1990 was about six times greater than in 1929.
    c. Between 1990 and 1991 total real output of the U.S. economy declined by $35 billion as the unemployment rate rose from 5.5 to 6.7 percent.
    d. From 1979 to 1980 the inflation rate was about 13.5 percent.

16. Which of the following would not shift an economy's production possibilities frontier?
    a. A doubling of the labor force.
    b. A doubling of the number of machines.
    c. A doubling of the money supply.
    d. More advanced technology.

17. A rational decision is one that
    a. will win a majority if put to a vote.
    b. is supported unanimously.
    c. best serves the objectives of the decision maker.
    d. is supported by *The New York Times*.

18. If exchange is voluntary,
    a. there can be mutual gain even if no new goods are produced.
    b. one party will always get the better of the other.
    c. there can be mutual gain only if new goods are produced as a result of the trade.
    d. there can be mutual gain only if government oversees the trade.

19. All but which one of the following are examples of waste and inefficiency?
    a. Employment discrimination against women and people of color.
    b. Operating on an economy's production possibilities frontier.
    c. High levels of unemployment.
    d. Quotas that limit the educational opportunities of particular ethnic groups.

20. The three coordination tasks that all economies must perform
    a. can only be done by a central planning bureau.
    b. can only be done by markets.
    c. can only be done inefficiently.
    d. can be done by planning bureaus or markets.

## Test B

Circle T or F for true or false.

T  F  1. There can never be any real scarcity of manufactured goods, as we can always produce more.

T  F  2. Market prices are always a good measure of opportunity cost.

T  F  3. The principle of increasing costs is a reflection of the fact that most productive resources tend to be best at producing a limited number of things.

T  F  4. An economy can shift its production possibilities frontier outward by the process of economic growth.

T  F  5. Because they have the power to tax, governments do not need to make choices.

T  F  6. The existence of specialized resources means that a firm's production possibilities frontier will be a straight line.

T  F  7. The existence of widespread unemployment means that an economy is operating inside its production possibilities frontier.

T  F  8. An economy using its resources efficiently is operating on its production possibilities frontier.

T  F  9. Because they are nonprofit organizations, colleges and universities do not have to make choices.

T  F  10. A sudden increase in the number of dollar bills will shift the economy's production possibilities frontier.

## SUPPLEMENTARY EXERCISES

### 1. The Cost of College

Those of you paying your way through college may not need to be reminded that the opportunity cost of lost wages is an important part of the cost of education. You can estimate the cost of your education as follows: Estimate what you could earn if instead of attending classes and studying you used those hours to work. Add in the direct outlays on tuition, books, and any differential living expenses incurred because you go to school. (Why only differential living expenses?)

2. **The Cost of Children**

   Bob and Jane both took Sociology 1 last year. As part of the course they were asked to compute the cost of raising a child. Bob estimated the cost at $184,000, an average of $5,000 a year in increased family expenditures for the first 12 years, then $6,000 a year for the next six years, and finally four years of college at $22,000 per year. Jane also was enrolled in Economics 1. She estimated the cost at $300,000. She started with all the same outlays that Bob did but also included $29,000 a year for four years as the opportunity cost of the parent who stayed at home to care for the child. Which calculation better reflects the cost of raising a child? What would be the cost of a second child?

3. Consider an economy with a production possibilities frontier between cars (C) and tanks (T) given by

$$C = 6L^5K^5 - 0.3T^2$$

   where $L$ is the size of the labor force (50,000 people) and $K$ is the number of machines, also 50,000.
   a. What is the maximum number of cars that can be produced? Call this number of cars $C^*$. The maximum number of tanks? Call this number of tanks $T^*$.
   b. Draw a PPF graph.
   c. Is this frontier consistent with the principle of increasing costs?
   d. Is the output combination $(1/2 C^*, 1/2 T^*)$ attainable? Is the output combination $(1/2 C^*, 1/2 T^*)$ efficient? Why or why not?
   e. What is the opportunity cost of more tanks when 10 tanks are produced? 50 tanks? 200 tanks?
   f. Find a mathematical expression for the opportunity cost of tanks in terms of cars. Is this mathematical expression consistent with the principle of increasing cost?
   g. Draw the new PPF if the labor force and the number of machines both increase by 10 percent. Where does this frontier lie relative to the original frontier?

4. **The Cost of Economic Growth**

   If you have access to a microcomputer, you might try programming this small recursive model to investigate the cost of economic growth. You could either try writing your own program in BASIC or some other programming language, or you could use a spreadsheet program. Some programming hints are given at the end of the problem.

   Imagine an economy that produces bundles of consumption goods $C$, and investment goods, $I$, with the help of labor, $L$, and machines, $M$, that exist at the beginning of the year. The production of consumption and investment goods is described by equation (1)

   (1)  $$C + I = (L)^{.75} \bullet (M)^{.25}$$

   Some machines wear out each year. The number of machines at the beginning of the next year is equal to 92 percent of the machines at the beginning of the year plus investment during the year, or $.92 \bullet M + I$. The number of machines will be constant when investment is sufficient to replace the 8 percent that wear out. If investment is greater, then the number of machines will increase, and the economy's production possibilities frontier will shift out.

   This economy has 10,000 laborers, $L = 10,000$, and originally there are 20,000 machines, $M = 20,000$.
   a. Verify that if $I = 1,600$, output and consumption will be constant.
   b. What happens to output and consumption over time if $I$ increases by 25 percent to 2,000?
   c. In question b you should find that consumption initially declines as some output is diverted from consumption to investment. However, over time, the output of consumption goods should increase and surpass its earlier value found in a. If an increase in investment from 1,600 to 2,000 is a good thing, what about an increase from 2,000 to 2,400? How does the eventual increase in consumption following this increase compare with what you found in b?
   d. Can there ever be too much investment? Try additional increases in investment and watch what happens to the eventual level of consumption. Can you explain what is going on?

**Programming Hints**   Columns in a spreadsheet would correspond to the following equations where subscripts refer to time periods. Note that equations for $I$ and $C$ are the same for all periods. Following the initial period you will need to be sure that your expression for the number of machines incorporates the subtraction of machines that have worn out and the addition of new machines from the production of investment goods. You will probably want to set your program or spreadsheet to run for about 100 periods.

$$M_t = 20,000 \qquad\qquad t = 1$$
$$I_t = 1,600 \qquad\qquad t = 1, 2, \ldots$$
$$C_t = (10,000)^{.75} \cdot (M_t)^{.25} - I_t \qquad t = 1, 2, \ldots$$
$$M_t = .92 \cdot M_{t-1} + I_t \qquad\qquad t = 2, 3, \ldots$$

## ECONOMICS IN ACTION

In 1971 the Brookings Institution published the first of a sequence of studies of the President's budget proposal called <u>Setting National Priorities</u>. The following is from the introduction to the first study.

> The United States budget is not the document of an executive whose decisions are law, nor of a prime minister whose party must support him or bring down the government. It is, rather, a set of proposals to the Congress for action on appropriations and tax measures. Precisely because it must advocate the course recommended by the President, the budget cannot emphasize the difficulty of the choices made. It records the President's decisions, but it does not identify the close ones. Alternatives that were serious contenders for adoption but were finally rejected are seldom if ever mentioned. In some cases, programs generally recognized as ineffective or of low priority are debated but finally left unchanged because all participants in the debate realize how few are the lances a President can afford to break against politically impregnable targets. Thus, the budget is a document designed to persuade an independent Congress rather than to analyze policy alternatives.

> The following pages seek to illuminate some of the President's budgetary choices for 1971. The study will (1) identify the major choices in fiscal policy and in specific expenditure programs; (2) consider some of the available alternatives and the reasoning behind the choices actually proposed; (3) discuss, by way of example, several federal programs that continue to be supported despite attempts by several administrations to alter or eliminate them; and (4) project to fiscal 1975 the revenue yield of existing tax laws and the expenditure consequences of current and proposed programs in order to estimate the likely size of the "fiscal dividends" over the next four years. The 1971 budget is the first in history to present longer-term projections. The projections offered in this study are spelled out in somewhat greater detail than those presented in the budget and include a range of alternatives that would depend on budgetary policies adopted in coming years.

> The purpose of the study is to contribute to informed discussion of the budget, not to propose a different budget. It *examines* alternatives; it does not *recommend* alternatives. Its aim is to show the difficulty of making choices in a complex and uncertain world, not to criticize those who had to make them.

1. What sort of information would you need if you had to make decisions about defense spending or the structure of a national health insurance plan?

2. Are you likely to find the information for these and other decisions in the President's budget?

3. If not, what is the role of the President's budget?

---

SOURCE: From *Setting National Priorities. The 1971 Budget*, Charles L. Schultze, et. al., The Brookings Institution et. al. (Washington, D.C. 1970): p. 4.

## STUDY QUESTIONS

1. How do markets help an economy address the three coordination tasks of deciding "how," "what," and "to whom"?

2. Explain when market prices are likely to be a good measure of opportunity cost and when they are not.

3. How do specialization and the division of labor enhance economic efficiency? Why do they require a system of exchange?

4. How can an economy choose to grow faster, and how can you use a production possibilities frontier to measure the cost of faster growth?

5. What is the difference between attainable points of production and efficient points of production? (It may be easiest to illustrate your answer using a diagram of a production possibilities frontier. Be sure that you can define and identify those points that are attainable and those points that are efficient.)

6. What is the difference between resources being scarce and resources being specialized? What are the implications of scarcity and specialization for the production possibilities frontier?

# Chapter 4

# Supply and Demand:
# An Initial Look

## LEARNING OBJECTIVES

After completing this chapter, you should be able to:

- draw a demand curve, given appropriate information from a demand schedule of possible prices and the associated quantity demanded.

- draw a supply curve, given appropriate information from a supply schedule of possible prices and the associated quantity supplied.

- explain why demand curves usually slope downward and supply curves usually slope upward.

- determine the equilibrium price and quantity, given a demand and supply curve.

- explain what forces tend to move market prices and quantities toward their equilibrium values.

- analyze the impact on prices and quantities of shifts in the demand curve, supply curve, or both.

- distinguish between a shift in and a movement along either the demand or supply curve.

- distinguish between price ceilings and price floors.

- explain the likely consequences of government interference with market-determined prices.

## IMPORTANT TERMS AND CONCEPTS

Quantity demanded
Demand schedule
Demand curve
Quantity supplied
Supply schedule
Supply curve
Supply-demand diagram
Shortage

Surplus
Equilibrium
Equilibrium price and quantity
Law of supply and demand
Shifts in (versus) movements along supply and demand curves
Price ceiling
Price floor

# CHAPTER REVIEW

Along with scarcity and the need for choice, *demand* and *supply analysis* is a fundamental idea that pervades all of economics. After studying this chapter, look back at the 12 ideas for Beyond the Final Exam in Chapter 1 and see how many concern the "law" of supply and demand.

Economists use a *demand curve* as a summary of the factors influencing people's demand for different commodities. A demand curve shows how, during a specified period, the quantity demanded of some

(1) good changes as the _____ of that good changes, holding all other determinants of demand constant. A demand curve usually has a (negative/positive) slope, indicating that as the price of a good declines, people will demand (more/less) of it. A particular quantity demanded is represented by a point on the demand curve. The change in the quantity demanded as price changes is a (shift in/movement along) the demand curve. Quantity demanded is also influenced by other factors, such as consumer incomes and tastes, population and the prices of related goods. Changes in any of these factors will result in a (shift in/movement along) the demand curve. Remember, a demand curve is defined for a particular period—a week, a month, or a year.

Economists use a *supply curve* to summarize the factors influencing producers' decisions. Like the demand curve, the supply curve is a relationship between quantity and _____. Supply curves

(2) usually have a (negative/positive) slope, indicating that at higher prices producers will be willing to supply (more/less) of the good in question. Like quantity demanded, quantity supplied is also influenced by factors other than price. The size of the industry, the state of technology, the prices of inputs, and the price of related outputs are important determinants. Changes in any of these factors will change the quantity supplied and can be represented by a (shift in/movement along) the supply curve.

Demand and supply curves are hypothetical constructs that answer what-if questions. For example, the supply curve answers the question, "What quantity of milk would be supplied if its price were $10 a gallon?" At this point it is not fair to ask whether anyone would buy milk at that price. Information

(3) about the quantity demanded is given by the _____ curve, which answers the question, "What quantity would be demanded if its price were $10 a gallon?" The viability of a price of $10 will be determined when we consider both curves simultaneously.

Figure 4-1 shows a demand and supply curve for stereo sets. The market outcome will be a price

(4) of $_____ and a quantity of_____. If the price is $400, then the quantity demanded will be (less/more) than the quantity supplied. In particular, from Figure 4-1 we can see that at a price of $400, producers will supply _____ sets _____ while consumers will demand _____ sets. This imbalance is a (shortage/surplus) and will lead to a(n) (increase/reduction) in price as inventories start piling up and suppliers compete for sales. If, instead, the price of stereo sets is only $200, there will be a (shortage/surplus) as the quantity (demanded/supplied) exceeds the quantity _____. Price is apt to (decrease/increase) as consumers scramble for a limited number of stereos at what appear to be bargain prices.

These forces working to raise or lower prices will continue until price and quantity settle down at

(5) values given by the_____ of the demand and supply curves. At this point, barring outside changes that would shift either curve, there will be no further tendency for change. Market-determined price and quantity are then said to be in _____. This price and quantity combination is the only one in which consumers demand exactly what suppliers produce. There are no frustrated consumers or producers. However, equilibrium price and quantity will change if anything happens to shift either the demand or supply curves. The Basic Exercise in this chapter asks you to examine a number of shifts in demand and supply curves.

Often factors affect demand but not supply, and vice versa. For example, changes in consumer

(6) incomes and tastes will shift the (demand/supply) curve but not the _____ curve. Following a shift in the demand curve, price must change to re-establish equilibrium. The change in price will lead to a (shift in/movement along) the supply curve until equilibrium is re-established at the intersection of the new demand curve and the original supply curve. Similarly a change in technology or the price of inputs will shift the _____ curve but not the _____

curve. Equilibrium will be re–established as the price change induced by the shift in the supply curve leads to a movement along the _____ curve to the new intersection.

In many cases the government intervenes in the market mechanism in an attempt to control prices. Some price controls dictate a particular price; other controls set maximum or minimum prices. A *price*
(7) *ceiling* is a (maximum/minimum) legal price, typically below the market-determined equilibrium price. Examples of price ceilings include rent controls and usury laws. A *price floor* sets a _____ legal price. To be effective, the price floor would have to be above the equilibrium price. Price floors are often used in agricultural programs.

In general, economists argue that interferences with the market mechanism are likely to have a number of undesirable features. Price controls will almost surely lead to a misallocation of resources, as it is unlikely legislated prices will equal opportunity cost. If there are a large number of suppliers, price
(8) controls will be (hard/easy) to monitor and evasion will be hard to police. In order to prevent the breakdown of price controls, governments quite likely find it necessary to introduce a large number of _____ _____. The enforcement of price controls can provide opportunities for favoritism and corruption. If all of this is not enough, price controls are almost certain to produce groups with a monetary stake in preserving controls.
(9) Price ceilings have a history of persistent (shortages/surpluses) and the development of black markets. Prices in the illegal market are likely to be greater than those that would have prevailed in a free market, with substantial income going to those whose only business is circumventing the controls. Over a longer period of time new investment is likely to (decrease/increase) as controlled prices reduce the profitability of investment in the industry.

Firms try to get around effective price floors by offering nonprice inducements for consumers to buy from them rather than from someone else. (Remember that effective price floors result in excess supply.) These nonprice inducements are apt to be less preferred by consumers than would a general reduction in prices. Price floors will also result in inefficiencies as high-cost firms are protected from failing by
(10) artificially (high/low) prices. Another form of inefficiency involves the use of time and resources to evade effective controls.

**FIGURE 4-1**

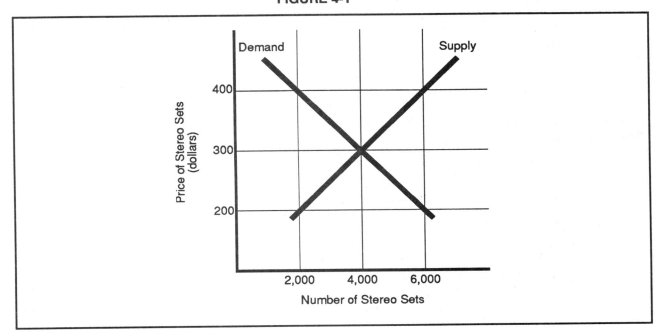

## IMPORTANT TERMS AND CONCEPTS QUIZ

Choose the best definition for the following terms.

1. _____ Quantity supplied
2. _____ Quantity demanded
3. _____ Demand schedule
4. _____ Demand curve
5. _____ Supply schedule
6. _____ Supply curve
7. _____ Supply-demand diagram
8. _____ Shortage
9. _____ Surplus
10. _____ Equilibrium
11. _____ Equilibrium price and quantity
12. _____ Shifts in supply or demand curves
13. _____ Movement along a supply or demand curve
14. _____ Price ceiling
15. _____ Price floor
16. _____ Law of supply and demand

a. Observation that in a free market, price tends to level where quantity supplied equals quantity demanded.
b. Legal minimum price that may be charged.
c. Graph depicting how quantity demanded changes as price changes.
d. Change in price causing a change in quantity supplied or demanded.
e. Number of units consumers want to buy at a given price.
f. Price/quantity pair at which quantity demanded equals quantity supplied.
g. Table depicting how the quantity demanded changes as price changes.
h. Situation in which there are no inherent forces producing change.
i. Table depicting how quantity supplied changes as price changes.
j. Legal maximum price that may be charged.
k. Number of units producers want to sell at a given price.
l. Table depicting the changes in both quantity demanded and quantity supplied as price changes.
m. Change in a variable other than price that affects quantity supplied or demanded.
n. Excess of quantity supplied over quantity demanded.
o. Graph depicting the changes in both quantity supplied and quantity demanded as price changes.
p. Excess of quantity demanded over quantity supplied.
q. Graph depicting how quantity supplied changes as price changes.

## BASIC EXERCISES

These exercises ask you to analyze the impact of changes in factors that affect demand and supply.
1.  a.  Table 4-1 has data on the quantity of candy bars that would be demanded and supplied at various prices. Use the data to draw the demand curve and the supply curve for candy bars in Figure 4-2.
    b.  From the information given in Table 4-1 and represented in Figure 4-2, the equilibrium price is _____ cents and the equilibrium quantity is _____.
    c.  Now assume that increases in income and population mean the demand curve has shifted. Assume the shift is such that, at each price, the quantity demanded has increased by 300 candy bars. Draw the new demand curve. At the new equilibrium, price has (increased/decreased) to _____ cents, and quantity has (increased/decreased) to _____ million candy bars.

d. Next assume that an increase in the price of sugar has shifted the supply curve. Specifically, assume that, at each price, the quantity supplied has been reduced by 150 candy bars. Draw the new supply curve. The shift in the supply curve following the increase in the price of sugar will (increase/decrease) equilibrium price and _____ the equilibrium quantity. Using the demand curve you drew in part c, above, the new equilibrium price following the increase in the price of sugar will be _____ cents and the equilibrium quantity will be _____ million candy bars.

### TABLE 4-1
### DEMAND AND SUPPLY SCHEDULES
### FOR CANDY BARS

| Quantity Demanded (millions) | Price per Bar (cents) | Quantity Supplied (millions) |
|---|---|---|
| 1200 | 35 | 1050 |
| 1100 | 40 | 1100 |
| 900 | 50 | 1200 |
| 800 | 55 | 1250 |
| 700 | 60 | 1300 |

### FIGURE 4-2

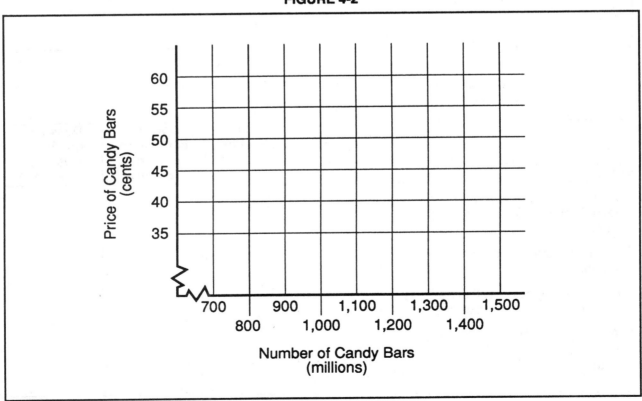

2. Figure 4-3 shows the demand and supply of chicken. Fill in Table 4-2 to trace the effects of various events on the equilibrium price and quantity.

**FIGURE 4-3**
**THE DEMAND AND SUPPLY OF CHICKEN**

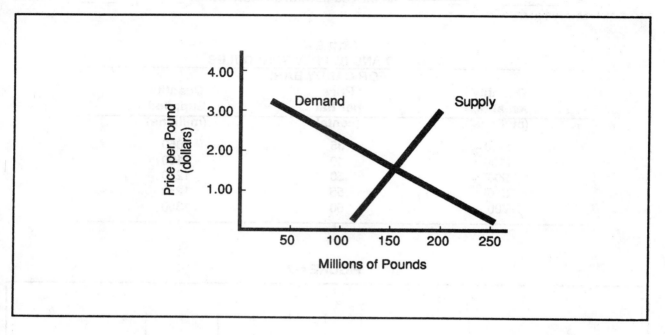

**TABLE 4-2**

| Event | Which curve shifts? | Is the direction left or right? | Does the equilibrium price rise or fall? | Does the equilibrium quantity rise or fall? |
|---|---|---|---|---|
| a. A sharp increase in the price of beef leads many consumers to switch from beef to chicken. | | | | |
| b. A bumper grain crop cuts the cost of chicken feed in half. | | | | |
| c. Extraordinarily cold weather destroys a significant number of chickens. | | | | |
| d. A sudden interest in eastern religions converts many chicken eaters to vegetarians. | | | | |

3. Figure 4-4 shows the demand and supply of compact discs. Complete Table 4-3 to examine the impact of price ceilings and price floors. What conclusion can you draw about when ceilings and floors will affect market outcomes?

**FIGURE 4-4**
**THE DEMAND AND SUPPLY OF DISCS**

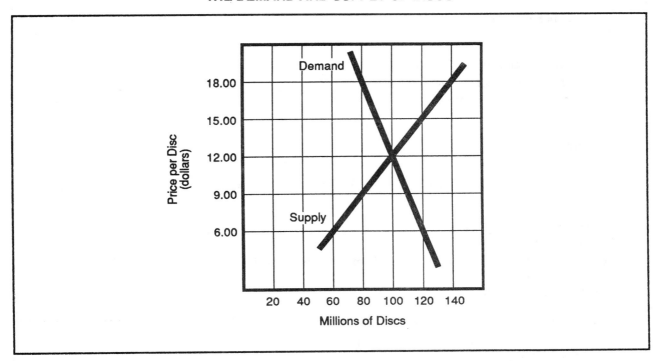

**TABLE 4-3**

| | Quantity Demanded | Quantity Supplied | Shortage or Surplus |
|---|---|---|---|
| a. Price ceiling = $18 | | | |
| b. Price ceiling = $9 | | | |
| c. Price floor = $15 | | | |
| d. Price floor = $6 | | | |

## SELF-TESTS FOR UNDERSTANDING
### Test A

Circle the most appropriate answer.

1. A demand curve is a graph showing how the quantity demanded changes when _____ changes.
   a. consumer income
   b. population
   c. price
   d. the price of closely related goods

2. The slope of a demand curve is usually _____, indicating that as price declines the quantity demanded increases.
   a. negative
   b. positive
   c. infinite
   d. zero

3. If price decreases, the quantity supplied usually
   a. increases.
   b. is unchanged.
   c. decreases.
   d. goes to zero.

4. Quantity demanded is likely to depend upon all but which one of the following?
   a. Consumer tastes.
   b. Consumer income.
   c. Price.
   d. The size of the industry producing the good in question.

5. A supply curve is a graphical representation of information in a(n)
   a. demand schedule.
   b. equilibrium.
   c. supply schedule.
   d. balance sheet.

6. The entire supply curve is likely to shift when all but which one of the following change?
   a. The size of the industry.
   b. Price.
   c. The price of important inputs.
   d. Technology that reduces the production cost.

7. There will likely be a movement along a fixed supply curve if which one of the following changes?
   a. Price.
   b. Technology that reduces the production cost.
   c. The price of important inputs.
   d. The size of the industry.

8. There will be a movement along the demand curve when which one of the following changes?
   a. The size of the industry producing the good.
   b. Population.
   c. Consumer incomes.
   d. The price of related goods.

9. Graphically, the equilibrium price and quantity in a free market will be given by
   a. the Y axis–intercept of the demand curve.
   b. the X axis–intercept of the supply curve.
   c. the point of maximum vertical difference between the demand and supply curves.
   d. the intersection of the demand and supply curves.

10. When the demand curve shifts to the right, which of the following is likely to occur?
    a. Equilibrium price rises and equilibrium quantity declines.
    b. Equilibrium price rises and equilibrium quantity rises.
    c. Equilibrium price declines and equilibrium quantity rises.
    d. Equilibrium price declines and equilibrium quantity declines.

11. If equilibrium price and quantity both decrease, it is likely that
    a. the supply curve has shifted to the right.
    b. the demand curve has shifted to the right.
    c. the demand curve has shifted to the left.
    d. the supply curve has shifted to the left.

12. A shift in the demand curve for sailboats resulting from a general increase in incomes will lead to
    a. higher prices.
    b. lower prices.
    c. a shift in the supply curve.
    d. lower output.

13. A shift in the supply curve of bicycles resulting from higher steel prices will lead to
    a. higher prices.
    b. lower prices.
    c. a shift in the demand curve.
    d. larger output.

14. Which of the following is likely to result in a shift in the supply curve for dresses? (There may be more than one correct answer.)
    a. An increase in consumer incomes.
    b. An increase in tariffs that forces manufacturers to import cotton cloth at higher prices.
    c. An increase in dress prices.
    d. Higher prices for skirts, pants, and blouses.

15. From an initial equilibrium, which of the following changes will lead to a shift in the supply curve for Chevrolets?
    a. Import restrictions on Japanese cars.
    b. New environmental protection measures that raise the cost of producing steel.
    c. A decrease in the price of Fords.
    d. Increases in the cost of gasoline.

16. If the price of oil, a close substitute for coal, increases, then
    a. the supply curve for coal will shift to the right.
    b. the demand curve for coal will shift to the right.
    c. the equilibrium price and quantity of coal will not change.
    d. the quantity of coal demanded will decline.

17. If the price of shoes is initially above the equilibrium value, which of the following is likely to occur?
    a. Stores inventories will decrease as consumers buy more shoes than shoe companies produce.
    b. The demand curve for shoes will shift in response to higher prices.
    c. Shoe stores and companies likely will reduce prices in order to increase sales, leading to a lower equilibrium price.
    d. Equilibrium will be re–established at the original price as the supply curve shifts to the left.

18. Price floors are likely to
    a. lead to a reduction in the volume of transactions, as we move along the demand curve, above the equilibrium price to the higher price floor.
    b. result in increased sales as suppliers react to higher prices.
    c. lead to shortages.
    d. be effective only if they are set at levels below the market equilibrium level.

19. Effective price ceilings are likely to
    a. result in surpluses.
    b. increase the volume of transactions as we move along the demand curve.
    c. increase production as producers respond to higher consumer demand at the low ceiling price.
    d. result in the development of black markets.

20. A surplus results when
    a. the quantity demanded exceeds the quantity supplied.
    b. the quantity supplied exceeds the quantity demanded.
    c. the demand curve shifts to the right.
    d. effective price ceilings are imposed.

## Test B

Circle T or F for true or false.

T  F   1.   The Law of Supply and Demand was passed by Congress in 1776.

T  F   2.   The demand curve for hamburgers is a graph showing the quantity of hamburgers that would be demanded during a specified period at each possible price.

T  F   3.   The slope of the supply curve indicates the increase in price necessary to get producers to increase output.

T  F   4.   An increase in consumer income will shift both the supply and demand curves.

T  F   5.   Both demand and supply curves usually have positive slopes.

T  F   6.   If at a particular price the quantity supplied exceeds the quantity demanded, then price is likely to fall as suppliers compete.

T  F   7.   Equilibrium price and quantity are determined by the intersection of the demand and supply curves.

T  F   8.   Since equilibrium is defined as a situation with no inherent forces producing change, the equilibrium price and quantity will not change following an increase in consumer income.

T  F   9.   A change in the price of important inputs will change the quantity supplied but will not shift the supply curve.

T  F  10.   Price ceilings likely will result in the development of black markets.

T  F  11.   Price controls, whether floors or ceilings, likely will increase the volume of transactions from what it would be without controls.

T  F  12.   An effective price ceiling is normally accompanied by shortages.

T  F  13.   An effective price floor is normally accompanied by shortages.

T  F  14.   An increase in both the market price and quantity of beef following an increase in consumer incomes proves that demand curves do not always have a negative slope.

## STUDY QUESTIONS

1. Why do economists argue that neither quantity demanded nor quantity supplied is likely to be a fixed number?

2. What adjustment mechanisms are likely to ensure that free–market prices move toward their equilibrium values given by the intersection of the demand and supply curves?

3. Why are changes in all of the supply determinants, except price, said to shift the entire supply curve while changes in price are said to give rise to a movement along a fixed supply curve?

4. How do factors that shift the entire supply curve usually give rise to a movement along a given demand curve?

5. If price cannot adjust, say due to an effective price ceiling, what factors will likely allocate the quantity supplied among consumers?

6. Consider the demand for a necessity (for example, food), and the demand for a luxury (for example, home hot tubs). For which good would you expect the quantity demanded to show a greater response to changes in price? Why? For which good would you expect the demand curve to be steeper? Why? For which good would you expect the demand curve to show a greater shift in response to changes in consumer income? Why?

## ECONOMICS IN ACTION

1. **Energy Policy—The Mix of Politics and Economics**

   The following quotation, written in the spring of 1977, is by Robert E. Hall and Robert S. Pindyck. As you read it, try to understand Hall's and Pindyck's argument in terms of simple demand and supply analysis.

   National energy policy faces a deep conflict in objectives, which has been a major reason for the failure to adopt rational measures: Consumers want cheap energy, but producers need high prices to justify expanded production. So far the goal of low prices has dominated. Through a combination of measures, some longstanding and some thrown together quickly during the energy crisis of 1974, the price of energy to consumers in the United States has been held far below the world level. Domestic producers have been prohibited from taking advantage of the higher world price, and in the case of oil, a heavy tax has been imposed on domestic production to finance the subsidization of imports. These steps have caused demand to increase more rapidly than production, and energy imports have risen to fill the gap. If recent policies are continued, imports will continue to grow. Some painful choices regarding the objectives of energy policy will force themselves upon the United States in the next few years.

   The economics of the nation's energy problem involves little more than the principle that higher prices result in less demand and more supply. The exact size and timing of the effects of price on demand and supply are still open to debate, but a summary of recent evidence indicates that demand falls by about one per cent for each four-percent increase in price, and supply rises by about one percent for each five-percent increase in price. Of course several years must pass before demand and supply fully respond to changes in price, and there is some uncertainty over the magnitude and speed of the supply response, but these numbers provide a reasonable basis for an initial description of the energy market in the United States. Policies in effect today have depressed the domestic price of energy, on the average, by about 30 percent below the world price. Consumption, then, is about eight-percent higher than it would be otherwise, and supply is about six-percent lower. Stated in oil-equivalents, the total consumption of energy in the United States is about 38 million barrels per day: 31 million barrels are filled by domestically produced oil, natural gas, and coal, and the rest is imported. Eight percent of consumption is just over three million barrels per day, and six percent of domestic production is just under two million barrels, so the policy of depressing prices has the net effect of increasing imports by about five million barrels. But current imports are around seven million barrels per day, so a striking conclusion emerges from these simple calculations *The problem of rising imports is largely of our own making.* Imports might well be much lower had our energy policy not been based on maintaining low prices.[1]

Table 4-3 presents data on U.S. demand for energy in oil equivalents and domestic U.S. supply, consistent with Hall's and Pindyck's argument.

a. From the data in Table 4-3, plot the demand and domestic supply curves. In 1977 the controlled U.S. price was $8.75 a barrel. What was the domestic demand for energy and what was the domestic supply? What was the demand for imports (the difference between demand and domestic supply)?

b. Hall and Pindyck indicate that the world price of energy in 1977 was $12.50 a barrel. What would have happened to demand, domestic supply, and imports if the price of energy in the United States had been permitted to rise to the world price?

c. What would have happened to energy prices and consumption if we had banned all imports and allowed domestic supply and demand to determine the equilibrium price and quantity?

d. Some people have argued that the demand and supply curves are actually much steeper. They contend that higher prices will not reduce demand by as much as Hall and Pindyck estimate and neither will higher prices increase supply by as much. Draw new, steeper demand and supply curves and examine the impacts of a market solution to the energy problem. (The new curves should intersect the original curves at a price of $8.75)

### TABLE 4-3

| Demand Quantity of Energy (millions of oil barrel equivalents | Price per Barrel (dollars) | Domestic Supply Quantity of Energy (millions of oil barrel equivalents) |
|---|---|---|
| 33.2 | 15 | 34.5 |
| 35.1 | 12 | 33.0 |
| 37.7 | 9 | 31.2 |
| 41.8 | 6 | 28.7 |

## 2. Hey, Buddy...

Scalping tickets—selling tickets at whatever the market will bear rather than at face value—is illegal in a number of states, including New York, where the high demand for tickets to a retrospective exhibition of Henri Matisse at the Museum of Modern Art in late 1992 prompted renewed interest in the economic effects of scalping. Admission was by special ticket. By the time the exhibit opened, all advance sale tickets had been sold. A limited number of tickets were available each day. Art lovers typically had to wait in line for up to two hours early in the morning to purchase these tickets at $12.50 each. Tickets also were available without the wait at $20 to $50 from scalpers who evaded the police.

Some economists view scalpers as providing a service to those who have not planned ahead or do not wish to stand in line. They point out that other businesses, such as airlines, charge a hefty price for last–minute purchases.

Scalpers also do a lively business at the Super Bowl and the Final Four of the NCAA basketball playoffs. Why doesn't the National Football League and the NCAA simply raise the price of tickets?

[1] E. Hall and Robert S. Pindyck, "The Conflicting Goals of National Energy Policy." Reprinted with the permission of the authors from: *The Public Interest*, No. 47 (Spring 1977), page 3–4, 977 by National Affairs, Inc.

Some would argue that they, along with other businesses, are concerned with "goodwill." Even if higher profits could be earned from higher ticket prices, it might come by sacrificing profits over the long run as goodwill is replaced by ill will and a growing lack of consumer interest.

Some argue that scalping should be illegal, as it makes events unaffordable for the average person. Others wonder whether the average person ever gets tickets to such events and, if he does, whether he might not prefer the option of selling his tickets at a handsome profit.

Some economists have proposed a two-tier system. First a limited number of tickets would be sold at lower prices to those willing to stand in line or enter a lottery. Then the remaining tickets would be sold at whatever price the market will bear.

1. Who is harmed when scalping is illegal?
2. Would you expect legalizing scalping to affect the price of tickets from scalpers? Why?
3. Evaluate the pros and cons of a two-tier system.

SOURCE: "Tickets: Supply Meets Demand on Sidewalk," *New York Times*, December 26, 1992.

## SUPPLEMENTARY EXERCISE

Imagine that the demand curve for tomatoes can be represented as

$$Q = 1000 - 250\ P.$$

The supply curve is a bit trickier. Farmers must make planting decisions on what they anticipate prices to be. Once they have made these decisions, there is little room for increases or decreases in the quantity supplied. Except for disastrously low prices, it will almost certainly pay a farmer to harvest and market his tomatoes. Assuming that farmers forecast price on the basis of the price last period, we can represent the supply curve for tomatoes as

$$Q = 200 + 150\ P_{-1,}$$

where $P_{-1}$ refers to price in the previous period. Initial equilibrium price and quantity of tomatoes are $2 and 500, respectively. Verify that at this price the quantity supplied is equal to the quantity demanded. (Equilibrium implies the same price in each period.)

Now assume that an increase in income has shifted the demand curve to

$$Q = 1,400 - 250\ P.$$

Starting with the initial equilibrium price, trace the evolution of price and quantity over time. Do prices and quantities seem to be approaching some sort of equilibrium? If so, what? You might try programming this example on a microcomputer or simulating it with a spreadsheet program. What happens if the slope of the demand and/or supply curve changes?

Ask your instructor about cobweb models. Do you think looking at last period's price is a good way to forecast prices?

*C h a p t e r* **5**

# Deciding on Output and Price: The Importance of Marginal Analysis

## LEARNING OBJECTIVES

After completing this chapter you should be able to:

- explain why a firm can make a decision about output or price, but not usually about both.
- calculate total and marginal revenue from data on the demand curve.
- explain why the demand curve is the curve of average revenue.
- calculate average and marginal cost from data on total cost.
- use data on costs and revenues to compute the level of output that maximizes profits.
- explain why the point of maximum profit cannot be associated with a positive or negative marginal profit.
- explain why comparing marginal revenue and marginal cost is equivalent to looking at marginal profit.
- explain why profit can be maximized only when marginal revenue is (approximately) equal to marginal cost.
- explain how and why an economist's definition of profit differs from that of an accountant.
- explain how selling at a price above marginal cost can increase profits even if the price is below average cost.

## IMPORTANT TERMS AND CONCEPTS

Profit maximization
Satisficing
Total profit
Economic profit
Total revenue and cost
Average revenue and cost
Marginal revenue and cost
Marginal analysis

## CHAPTER REVIEW

This is the first of four chapters exploring what lies behind the demand and supply curves introduced in Chapter 4. This chapter also introduces the concept of marginal analysis, one of the most important tools an economist has. In this chapter marginal analysis is used to help decide how much output a firm should produce to maximize its profits.

While marginal analysis is a powerful tool for business decision making, it is applicable in many nonbusiness situations as well. For example. how much should the government spend to clean up the environment? Or a related question: To clean up our lakes and rivers, should the government require all industries and towns to reduce their discharges by an equal percentage, or is there a more efficient alternative? As discussed in Chapter 21, marginal analysis can help answer these questions.

You may already have had more experience with marginal analysis than you realize. Have you ever had to pay federal income taxes? If so, you might dig out your records and make two calculations. Your
(1) total taxes divided by your total income would be your (average/marginal) tax rate. Now assume that you had $100 more income. Figure out how much more taxes you would have owed. This increase in taxes divided by the $100 additional income would be your (average/marginal) tax rate.

Your grade point average is another example of the distinction between marginal and average. If you want to raise your overall GPA, what sorts of grades do you need? The grades you earn this semester are the marginal contribution to your overall grade average. Similarly, a baseball player's daily batting record is a marginal measure when compared with his season's batting average.

In whatever context, marginal analysis focuses on the effect of changes. For business output decisions, marginal analysis looks at the effect on costs, revenues, and profits as output changes. The change in total
(2) cost from changing output by one unit is called _____ cost. The change in total revenue from producing and selling one more unit is _____ revenue. Marginal profit is the change in total _____ as output expands by one unit. Because profits equal revenue minus costs, marginal profit equals marginal _____ minus marginal _____.

(3) Economists usually assume that business firms are interested in maximizing (average/marginal/total) profit. This assumption need not be true for all firms, but economists have found that models based on this assumption provide useful insights into actual events. (Refer back to the discussion in Chapter 1 about the role of abstraction in theory.) Economists are interested in marginal profit, not as an end in itself, but because marginal profit is an extremely useful guide to maximizing total profit.

It should be common sense that any firm interested in maximizing profit will want to expand output as long as the increase in total revenue exceeds the increase in total costs. Rather than looking at total revenue and total cost, we could just as easily look at the changes in revenue and cost as output changes. An increase in output will add to profits if the increase in revenue is greater than the increase in costs. An economist might make the same point by saying that an increase in output will add to profits if
(4) (marginal/average) revenue exceeds (marginal/average) cost. We could also say that an increase in output will add to total profits as long as marginal profits are (positive/zero/negative). Total profits will stop rising when marginal profits fail to _____, that is, when marginal revenue _____ marginal costs.

## IMPORTANT TERMS AND CONCEPTS QUIZ

Choose the best definition for the following terms.

1. _____ Profit maximization
2. _____ Satisficing
3. _____ Total profit
4. _____ Economic profit
5. _____ Total revenue
6. _____ Total cost
7. _____ Average revenue
8. _____ Average cost
9. _____ Marginal revenue
10. _____ Marginal cost
11. _____ Marginal analysis

a. Net earnings minus a firm's opportunity cost of capital.
b. Total revenue divided by quantity of output.

c. Decision rules that look at the impact of changes.
d. Amount firm must spend to produce a given quantity of output.
e. Difference between total revenue and total costs.
f. Addition to total cost when producing one more unit of output.
g. Decision-making rule that seeks no more than satisfactory solutions.
h. Addition to profit from producing an additional unit of output.
i. Level of output where revenue minus cost is greatest.
j. Total cost divided by quantity of output.
k. Price of output times quantity sold.
l. Addition to total revenue when producing one more unit of output.

## BASIC EXERCISES

1. This exercise is designed to review the use of marginal revenue and marginal cost as a guide to the maximization of profits.
   a. Table 5-1 has data on demand for widgets from Wanda's Widget Company as well as data on production costs. Total revenue and total cost are plotted in the top panel of Figure 5-1. Fill in the column on total profits by subtracting total cost from total revenue. Plot the data on total profit in the second panel of Figure 5-1. Looking just at your graph of total profit, what output level maximizes total profits?

### TABLE 5-1
### WANDA'S WIDGET COMPANY

| Marginal Revenue | Total Revenue | Demand Price (dollars) | Output | Total Cost (dollars) | Marginal Cost | Total Profits |
|---|---|---|---|---|---|---|
| | 3,500 | 3,500 | 1 | 2,000 | | _____ |
| _____ | 6,600 | 3,300 | 2 | 3,000 | _____ | _____ |
| _____ | 9,300 | 3,100 | 3 | 4,100 | _____ | _____ |
| _____ | 11,600 | 2,900 | 4 | 5,300 | _____ | _____ |
| _____ | 13,500 | 2,700 | 5 | 6,900 | _____ | _____ |
| _____ | 15,000 | 2,500 | 6 | 8,900 | _____ | _____ |
| _____ | 16,100 | 2,300 | 7 | 11,100 | _____ | _____ |
| _____ | 16,800 | 2,100 | 8 | 13,400 | _____ | _____ |
| _____ | 17,100 | 1,900 | 9 | 15,800 | _____ | _____ |
| _____ | 17,000 | 1,700 | 10 | 18,300 | _____ | _____ |

b. Complete Table 5-1 by computing marginal cost and marginal revenue. Plot these series in the bottom panel of Figure 5-1. Marginal revenue exceeds marginal cost up to what level of output? _____ Looking just at your graph of marginal cost and marginal revenue, what output level maximizes total profits? Is this the same answer as above?

**FIGURE 5-1**

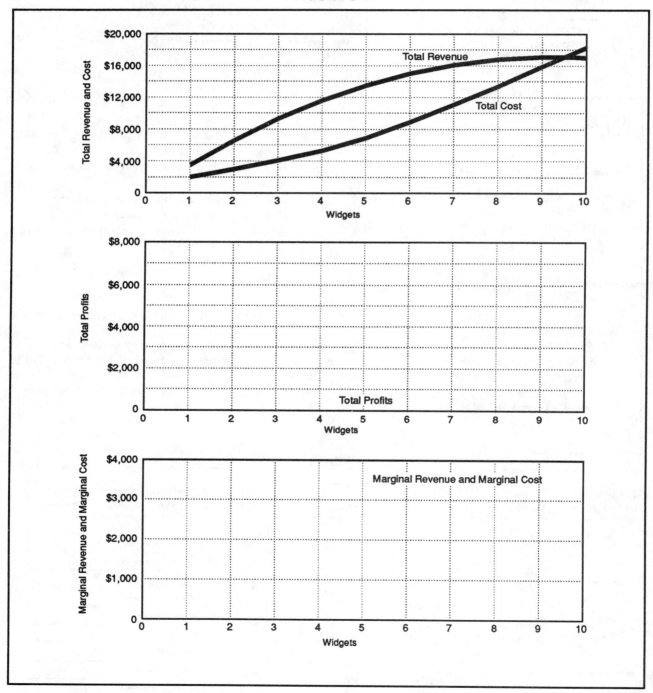

c. Figure 5-2 plots the average cost of producing widgets. Plot the data on the demand curve from Table 5-1. Using the profit–maximizing level of output determined above, find the profit–maximizing price on the demand curve. Draw the rectangle for total revenue and shade it lightly with positively sloped lines. Using the average cost curve, draw the rectangle for total cost and shade it lightly with negatively sloped lines. This rectangle should overlap a part of the rectangle for total revenue. The non-overlapped part of the total revenue rectangle is also a measure of total _____. Maximizing total profit maximizes the size of this rectangle. It (<u>does/does not</u>) maximize the difference between average revenue and average cost. It (<u>does/does not</u>) imply that output should increase whenever average revenue exceeds average cost.

**FIGURE 5-2**

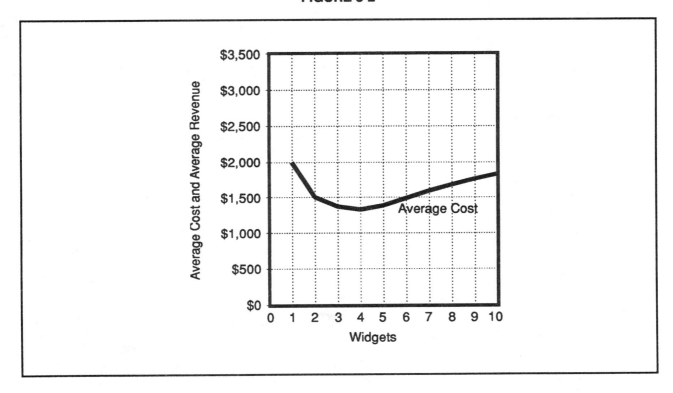

**FIGURE 5-3**
**THE DEMAND FOR MEDALIST BICYCLES**

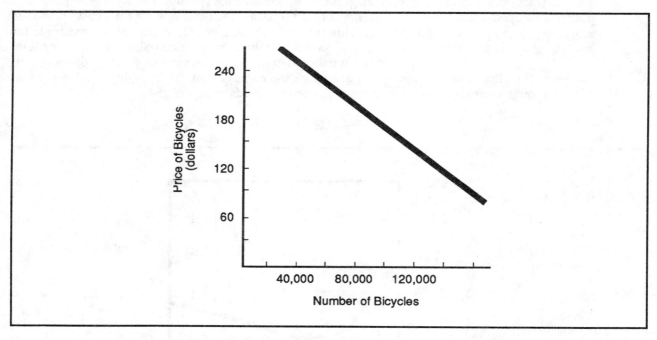

2. The geometry of marginal revenue
   a. Figure 5-3 shows the demand curve for Medalist bicycles. Draw a rectangle for total revenue on the assumption that 100,000 bicycles are sold. Lightly shade this rectangle with horizontal lines.
   b. Assume now that 120,000 bicycles are sold rather than 100,000. Draw a rectangle for total revenue at this higher level of sales. Lightly shade this rectangle with vertical lines.

If you have drawn and shaded the rectangles correctly, you should have a large, cross-hatched rectangle and two smaller rectangles: one long, horizontal rectangle on the top of the cross-hatched rectangle and one thin, vertical rectangle on the right side. The thin, vertical rectangle represents revenue from additional sales at the new lower price. This rectangle (is/is not) a complete measure of marginal revenue. It measures the receipts of additional sales but neglects the drop in revenue from the reduction in price that is necessary to expand sales in the first place. This reduction in revenue on previous units is represented by the _____ rectangle. The geometric representation of marginal revenue is the (vertical/horizontal) rectangle minus the _____ rectangle.

---

## SELF-TESTS FOR UNDERSTANDING

### Test A

Circle the most appropriate answer.

1. The logic of the demand curve says that business firms can choose
   a. the profit–maximizing level of output and the profit–maximizing level of prices.
   b. the profit–maximizing level of output or the profit–maximizing level of prices but not both.
   c. to sell whatever quantity they want at whatever price.
   d. only those levels of output where marginal cost equals marginal revenue.

---

2. The assumption of profit maximization is
   a. likely to be true for all firms.
   b. the same as the assumption of satisficing.
   c. a useful abstraction that gives sharp insights.
   d. the best description of what firms actually do.

3. Total profit is equal to
   a. average revenue minus average cost.
   b. marginal revenue minus marginal cost.
   c. total revenue minus total cost.
   d. zero when marginal cost equals marginal revenue.

4. Marginal profit is
   a. the difference between total revenue and total cost.
   b. only positive at the profit–maximizing output level.
   c. another term for the return on an owner's own time and resources.
   d. the addition to profit when output increases by one unit.

5. If total costs are increasing then
   a. marginal cost must also be increasing.
   b. marginal cost must be positive.
   c. average cost must be greater than marginal costs.
   d. average cost must be increasing.

6. Average cost is found by
   a. dividing total cost by output.
   b. multiplying marginal cost by output.
   c. looking at how total cost changes when output changes.
   d. considering how price changes with quantity along the demand curve.

7. Marginal cost equals
   a. total cost divided by total output.
   b. the change in total cost associated with an additional unit of output.
   c. the change in average cost.
   d. the slope of the average cost curve.

8. The demand curve is the curve of
   a. total revenue.
   b. marginal revenue.
   c. variable revenue.
   d. average revenue.

9. Marginal revenue to a firm is
   a. the same as the demand curve for the firm's output.
   b. found by dividing price by output.
   c. found by dividing output by price.
   d. the change in revenue associated with an additional unit of output.

10. When output increases by one unit, marginal revenue will typically be
    a. less than the new lower price.
    b. equal to the new lower price.
    c. greater than the new lower price.

11. Marginal profit equals the difference between
    a. total revenue and total cost.
    b. average revenue and average cost.
    c. marginal revenue and marginal cost.
    d. the demand curve and the marginal cost curve.

12. If a firm has chosen an output level that maximizes profits, then at this level
    a. marginal profits are also maximized.
    b. average cost is minimized.
    c. further increases in output will involve negative marginal profits.
    d. the difference between average revenue and average cost is maximized.

13. Which of the following is consistent with profit maximization?
    a. Produce where marginal cost is minimized.
    b. Produce where average cost is minimized.
    c. Produce where marginal revenue equals marginal cost.
    d. Produce where marginal revenue is maximized

14. If marginal revenue is greater than marginal cost, then a firm interested in maximizing profits should probably
    a. reduce output.
    b. increase output.
    c. leave output unchanged.

15. As long as total revenue is greater than total cost,
    a. marginal profit must be positive.
    b. total profit must be increasing.
    c. total profit will be positive.
    d. marginal profit will be positive.

16. Once a firm has determined the output level that maximizes profits, it can determine the profit–maximizing price from
    a. the demand curve.
    b. setting its usual markup on average cost.
    c. adding marginal cost to marginal revenue.
    d. adding marginal cost and average cost.

17. Producing where marginal revenue equals marginal cost is the same as producing where
    a. average cost is minimized.
    b. total profit is maximized.
    c. average cost equals average revenue.
    d. marginal profit is maximized.

18. An economist's definition of profit differs from that of an accountant because
    a. the economist is only interested in marginal cost and marginal revenue.
    b. the economist includes the opportunity cost of owner-supplied inputs in total cost.
    c. accountants cannot maximize.
    d. economists cannot add or subtract correctly.

19. If accounting profits are zero, it is likely that economic profits are
    a. negative.
    b. also zero.
    c. positive.

20. If marginal revenue is less than average cost, a firm
    a. should reduce output; it loses the additional revenue but saves more in cost.
    b. must be losing money.
    c. should consider a temporary shutdown.
    d. can still increase profits if marginal revenue exceeds marginal cost.

## Test B

Circle T or F for true or false.

T F  1.  Business firms can decide both the price and quantity of their output.

T  F   2.  Firms always make optimal decisions.

T  F   3.  The demand curve for a firm's product is also the firm's marginal revenue curve.

T  F   4.  Marginal cost is computed by dividing total cost by the quantity of output.

T  F   5.  Marginal revenue is simply the price of the last unit sold.

T  F   6.  An output decision will generally not be optimal unless it corresponds to a zero marginal profit.

T  F   7.  Marginal profit will be zero when marginal revenue equals marginal cost.

T  F   8.  An economist's measure of profit would typically be smaller than an accountant's.

T  F   9.  As long as average revenue exceeds average cost, a firm is making profits and should increase output.

T  F  10.  It never pays to sell below average cost.

# Appendix: The Relationships Among Total, Average, and Marginal Data

## BASIC EXERCISES

These questions are designed to help review the relationships between total, average, and marginal measures described in the appendix to Chapter 5.

1.  Table 5-2 contains information on Kristen's first ten games with the college softball team. The table includes her batting performance for each game, a marginal measure, as well as her season average updated to include the results of each game. Answer the following questions to see if the marginal data, Kristen's daily batting record, is consistent with the average data, her season batting average. It may be useful to first plot both the marginal and average data in Figure 5-4.

    a.  According to Rule 3, the marginal and average records should be equal on the first day of the season. Is this the case?

    b.  According to Rule 4, if the marginal data is equal to the average, the average should be unchanged. Check to see if this is always the case.

    c.  According to Rule 4, if the marginal data is less than the average, the average should decline. Check to see if this is always the case.

    d.  According to Rule 4, if the marginal data is greater than the average, the average should increase. Check to see if this is always the case.

**TABLE 5-2**

| Game | At–bats | Hits | Daily Batting Average | Season Batting Average |
|------|---------|------|-----------------------|------------------------|
| 1 | 4 | 2 | .500 | .500 |
| 2 | 4 | 2 | .500 | .500 |
| 3 | 4 | 1 | .250 | .417 |
| 4 | 3 | 1 | .333 | .400 |
| 5 | 4 | 3 | .750 | .474 |
| 6 | 3 | 1 | .333 | .455 |
| 7 | 6 | 2 | .333 | .429 |
| 8 | 3 | 0 | .000 | .387 |
| 9 | 4 | 2 | .500 | .400 |
| 10 | 5 | 2 | .400 | .400 |

**FIGURE 5-4**
**KRISTEN'S BATTING**

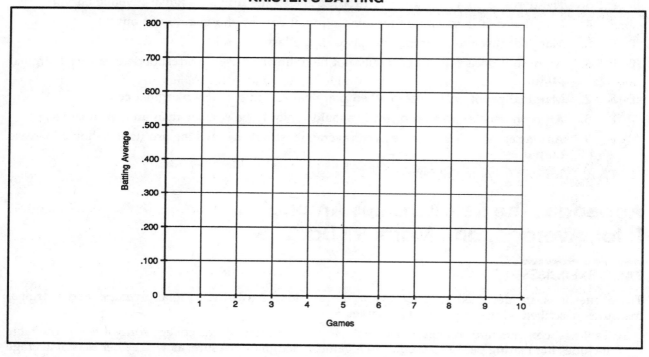

**FIGURE 5-5**

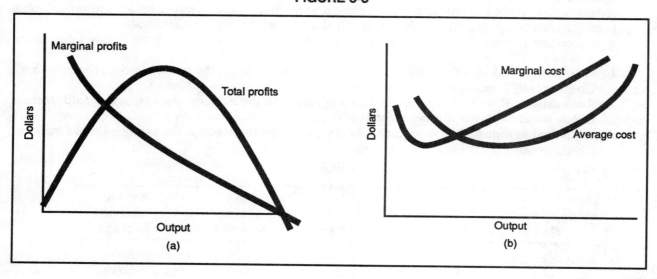

2. a. Explain what is wrong with both of the illustrations below.
   b. For part (a) of Figure 5-5, assume that the total profit curve is correct and draw an appropriate marginal profit curve.
   c. For part (b) of Figure 5-5, assume that the average cost curve is correct and draw an appropriate marginal cost curve.

## SUPPLEMENTARY EXERCISES

### A Mathematical Example of Profit Maximization

The demand for Acme stereos is

$$Q = 1,200 - 4 P,$$

where $Q$ represents output measured in thousands of sets and $P$ represents price. The total cost of producing stereos is given by

$$TC = 16,000 + 120 Q - .4 Q^2 + .002 Q^3.$$

 a. What are Acme's fixed costs?
 b. What mathematical expression describes average costs? Marginal costs?
 c. Plot average cost and marginal cost. Does your marginal cost curve go through the minimum point of your average cost curve?
 d. Use the information from the demand curve to derive a mathematical expression for marginal revenue.
 e. On the same graph as in c draw the demand curve (the average revenue curve) and the marginal revenue curve.
 f. What does your graph suggest about the profit–maximizing level of output?
 g. Does your answer in f coincide with a direct mathematical solution for $Q$ where MR = MC? It should. (To answer this question you will need to use the expressions you derived for marginal revenue and marginal cost).
 h. What is Acme's maximum profit?
 i. Shade in the portion of your graph that represents maximum profit.
 j. What if fixed cost were $20,000? How, if at all, do your answers to b, c, d, g, and h change?

## ECONOMICS IN ACTION

### Fair Trade, Free Trade, and Marginal Cost

American trade laws, like those of many other countries, include anti-dumping provisions. Foreign producers are not supposed to have access to American markets if they sell their output at unfairly low prices. The concern is that a foreign producer might drive American competitors out of business and then be in a position to act as a monopolist, raising prices and restricting output. Such actions are sometimes called ruinous competition.

Complaints about dumping are typically initiated by American producers, not consumers. If a complaint is found to have cause by the Commerce Department, the government can impose anti-dumping tariffs on specific foreign manufacturers that are intended to establish prices that reflect "fair value," that is, raise prices to a level sufficient to cover fully allocated costs plus a normal profit. Two of the most notable recent examples involve Korean computer chip manufacturers and steel manufacturers from 19 countries.

Assume that fully allocated cost is another term for the average cost of purchased inputs, including labor, and that normal profit refers to the opportunity cost of the investment by a firm's owners. (As we have seen, economists include both measures when they talk of average cost.)

The material in this chapter has suggested that, in the long run, price must be sufficient to cover average costs and that the entry and exit of firms will move prices to this level. But characteristics of long–run equilibrium are not a forecast of prices tomorrow or next week.

 1. Are there conditions under which domestic producers would willingly sell output for less than "fair value," that is, less than average cost? From an initial position of equilibrium, how would a domestic producer respond to a temporary shift of the demand curve to the left during a recession?

2. How does one distinguish possible ruinous competition from normal market fluctuations and the natural tendency of all producers to exploit opportunities to limit competition? Should foreign producers be prohibited from behavior that domestic producers are likely to engage in on a regular basis?

---

SOURCE: "Cement Shoes for Venezuela," Peter Passell, *New York Times*, September 25, 1991.

## STUDY QUESTIONS

1. Why can't firms sell as much output as they want at whatever price they want?

2. The condition for profit maximization is stated in terms of marginal revenue and marginal cost. What would happen to total profits if instead a firm produced where average revenue equaled average cost?

3. Why isn't marginal revenue equal to the price of the last unit sold?

4. Why does profit maximization require that marginal profit be equal to zero rather than positive?

5. What are the differences between profits as measured by an economist and profits as measured by an accountant? Which is likely to be larger? Why?

# Chapter 6

# Input Decisions and Production Costs

## LEARNING OBJECTIVES

After completing this chapter, you should be able to:

- ◆ compute the average and marginal physical product for a single input given total output at different input levels.
- ◆ explain the "law" of diminishing marginal returns.
- ◆ compute the marginal revenue product for additional units of some input given information on the marginal physical product and on the price of the output.
- ◆ explain why a profit–maximizing firm will expand the use of each input until the marginal revenue product equals the price of the input.
- ◆ explain why the law of diminishing returns implies that a profit–maximizing firm will use less of an input following a price increase.
- ◆ explain the importance of opportunity cost when distinguishing between total cost and total expenditure.
- ◆ explain the difference between fixed and variable costs.
- ◆ explain why fixed costs, administrative problems of large organizations, and the law of diminishing returns imply that the short-run average cost curve is usually U–shaped.
- ◆ describe the difference between the short run and long run.
- ◆ explain how to determine the long-run average cost curve from a set of short-run average cost curves.
- ◆ show how information on a firm's production function allows you to investigate the substitutability of inputs.
- ◆ explain how and why the ratio of input prices and the ratio of marginal physical products is relevant to the choice of input combinations.
- ◆ explain how total costs—and hence average costs—can be computed given information on the production function and input prices.
- ◆ determine whether a particular production function shows increasing, decreasing, or constant returns to scale, given data on output and on various input combinations.
- ◆ explain the relationship between returns to scale and the long-run average cost curve.
- ◆ distinguish between diminishing returns to increases of a single productive input and economies of scale when all inputs change.
- ◆ explain the difference between analytical and historical cost curves.

## IMPORTANT TERMS AND CONCEPTS

Total physical product (TPP)
Average physical product (APP)
Marginal physical product (MPP)
Marginal revenue product (MRP)
"Law" of diminishing marginal returns
Fixed cost
Variable cost
Sunk cost
Increasing (decreasing) average cost
Short and long runs
Substitutability of inputs
Cost minimization
Rule for optimal input use
Production function
Economies of scale (increasing returns to scale)
Constant returns to scale
Decreasing returns to scale
Historical versus analytical cost relationships

## CHAPTER REVIEW

In this chapter we will make extensive use of the concept of *marginal analysis* as a guide to optimal decision making. We will see how marginal analysis can help a firm make optimal decisions about the use of production inputs and how these decisions can be used to derive cost curves.

This chapter introduces a potentially bewildering array of curves and concepts—marginal physical product, marginal revenue product, fixed costs, variable costs, long run, short run. All of these curves and concepts relate to each other and underlie optimal firm decisions. Spending time now to get these relationships clear will save you time in later chapters and the night before the exam.

(1) In deciding whether to use an additional unit of some input, say, hiring more workers, a firm should look at the contribution of the additional workers to both total revenue and total cost. If the increase in revenue exceeds the increase in cost, then profits will (increase/decrease). The increase in revenue comes from producing and selling additional units of output. Economists call the amount of additional output from the use of one more unit of input the marginal (physical/revenue) product of the input. For a firm selling its output at a constant price, the increase in revenue comes from multiplying the additional output by the price at which it can be sold. Economists call this the marginal _____ product.

(2) Common sense tells us that a profit-maximizing firm should use additional units of any input if the addition to total revenue exceeds the addition to total cost. Another way of saying the same thing is that the firm should consider using more of an input as long as the marginal (physical/revenue) product exceeds the _____ of the input. A firm has clearly gone too far if additions to revenue are less than additions to cost. Thus a profit-maximizing firm should expand the use of any factor until the marginal revenue product equals the price of the input.

If the price of an input is constant, firms will use more and more units of this input until the marginal revenue product falls to a point where it equals the input price. As a result, firms will usually expand the use of any input past any region of increasing marginal returns and into the region of decreasing returns to the one input.

We have talked about the optimal use of one input. Our rule holds true for more than one input. The idea is to adjust the use of all inputs until the marginal physical product divided by the input price is equal for all inputs. In symbols, assuming the use of two inputs A and B, we have

$$\frac{MPP_A}{P_A} = \frac{MPP_B}{P_B}$$

as the condition for an optimal input combination. Either fraction shows you how output will change per dollar spent on that input. When the fraction is high, one gets a lot of output per dollar spent. A low fraction means less output per dollar spent. If this ratio were initially high for input B and low for input

(3) A, a firm would want to use (less/more) of input B and _____ of input A. Making these adjustments should (increase/reduce) the MPP of input B and _____ the MPP of input A, moving the fractions toward the equality necessary for the optimal input combination.

What about our original result that we should adjust the use of a single input until marginal revenue product equals the price of the input? Is it still valid when there is more than one input? Yes. Remember that for input A, $MRP_A = MPP_A \cdot P_{OUTPUT}$. Following our earlier rule, we would adjust the use of input A until $P_A = MRP_A$ or until $P_A = MPP_A \cdot P_{OUTPUT}$. The use of input B should be adjusted until $P_B = MPP_B \cdot P_{OUTPUT}$. A little multiplication and division should show that when the prices of inputs and output are constant, making these adjustments individually also results in the optimal input combination.[1]

If the price of an input changes, it is natural to expect the firm's optimal input combination to change.
(4) Specifically, it is natural to expect that a profit-maximizing firm will (reduce/increase) the use of any factor whose price has risen. Changing the quantity of one input will typically affect the marginal physical product of other inputs. As a result, a firm will want to rethink its use of all inputs following a change in price of any one input. It is quite likely that following an increase in the price of one input, a profit-maximizing firm will decide to use relatively (less/more) of the more expensive input and relatively _____ of the inputs with unchanged prices.

The relationship between inputs and outputs has been formalized by economists into something that measures the maximum amount of output that can be produced from any specified combination of inputs
(5) given current technology, or, for short, the _____ function. Information about the marginal physical product for a single factor comes from the production function. (The appendix to this chapter discusses one geometrical representation of such a function through the use of a contour-line diagram.) The concept of a production function is also useful in separating what happens if we increase the use of all factors or of just one factor. If all inputs are increased by the same percentage amount, then the percentage increase in output is used to indicate the degree of *economies of scale*. If output increases by more than the common percentage increase in all inputs, the production function exhibits _____ returns to scale. If output increases by less, there are _____ returns to scale, and if output increases by the same percentage, we would say that returns to scale are _____.

Information from the production function can be used to construct *cost curves* for a firm. Over a very short time horizon, previous commitments may limit a firm's ability to adjust all inputs. These commitments often imply that at least one input is predetermined and cannot be adjusted immediately. Imagine a farmer with a five-year lease on a parcel of land and unable to rent additional land. The interval of
(6) time over which none of a firm's fixed commitments can be adjusted is called the (long/short) run.

---

[1] When the $MRP_A$ is equal to the price of input A, we can write the same thing in symbols as $MPP_A \cdot P_{OUTPUT} = P_A$. Dividing both sides of this equality by $MPP_A$ we see that $P_{OUTPUT} = P_A/MPP_A$. Similar results hold for input B. That is, setting $MRP_B$ equal to the price of input B also sets $P_{OUTPUT} = P_B/MPP_B$. Since both fractions are equal to the price of output, they are equal to each other and their reciprocals are also equal, that is, if $P_A/MPP_A = P_B/MPP_B$ then $MPP_A/P_A = MPP_B/P_B$, our condition for the optimal input combination.

The total cost of producing any given output in the short run can be computed with the help of the production function, input prices and any relevant opportunity costs. We will be interested only in minimum total costs for any level of output. We can use what we know about optimal factor use to help figure the most efficient combination of variable inputs. We can then compute minimum total cost. As an example, assume that production requires two inputs, one of which is fixed in the short run. To compute total cost, the firm must first use the production function to see what amount of the variable input is necessary to produce different levels of output. Then it can compute total cost for each level of output by multiplying the quantity of the fixed input and the optimal quantity of the variable input by their prices, remembering relevant opportunity costs, and adding the results. After computing total cost, the firm can

(7) compute average cost by dividing total cost by the associated level of _____.
The firm can also compute marginal cost by examining the way (<u>average/total</u>) cost changes when output changes.

The period of time over which a firm can adjust all its fixed commitments is called the

(8) _____. Long-run cost curves can be derived by either of two equivalent methods. One procedure would first derive short-run cost curves for each possible amount of the fixed input. We would then determine the long-run cost curve by joining the _____ segments of the short-run cost curves. An alternative and equivalent method would treat both factors as variable. One would first use the production function and input prices to determine the optimal level of both inputs to produce any given level of output. Total cost for each output level is computed from input prices and from optimal input levels by multiplication and addition. Average and marginal cost are then easily computed.

(9) Since in the long run all factors can be changed, the shape of the long-run average cost curve is related to economies of scale. Constant returns to scale imply that a doubling of output requires twice as much of all inputs. In this case, total costs also double and average cost (<u>falls/is unchanged/rises</u>). Increasing returns to scale mean that twice the output can be produced with (<u>more/less</u>) than twice the inputs and average cost will (<u>fall/rise</u>). With decreasing returns to scale, twice the output requires _____ than twice the inputs and average cost _____.

(10) Fixed costs refer to the costs of (<u>indivisible/variable</u>) inputs, that is, inputs that are necessary for any production but do not vary with the level of output. If car insurance for a traveling salesman does not vary with the number of miles he drives, this would be an example of fixed costs. Sunk costs refer to costs incurred because of previous purchases or commitments. Even if no output is produced, a firm will be obligated to cover its sunk costs.

We've covered a lot of ground and a lot of curves. You may want to take a deep breath before a quick review. The production function contains the basic technical information about inputs and output. From this information we can derive total physical product and marginal physical product for a single input. Knowing the price of output will let us compute marginal revenue product. Comparing marginal revenue product with input prices will determine the optimal input quantities. Optimal input quantities in turn, determine (minimum) total cost for alternative levels of output. Once we know total cost, we can easily compute average and marginal cost. In the short run, there may be fixed costs. In the long run, all inputs, and hence all costs, are variable. In either run, the same optimizing principles apply.

## IMPORTANT TERMS AND CONCEPTS QUIZ

Choose the best definition for the following terms.

1. _____ Total physical product
2. _____ Average physical product
3. _____ Marginal physical product
4. _____ Marginal revenue product
5. _____ "Law" of diminishing marginal returns
6. _____ Fixed costs
7. _____ Variable costs
8. _____ Sunk cost
9. _____ Short run
10. _____ Long run
11. _____ Production function
12. _____ Economies of scale
13. _____ Returns to scale
14. _____ Analytic cost curves
15. _____ Historic cost curves

a. Curve showing how average cost at a single point in time varies with output.

b. Observation that marginal physical product eventually declines.

c. Cost of indivisible inputs necessary for any production.

d. Savings acquired through increases in quantities produced.

e. Period of time long enough for all of a firm's commitments to end.

f. Dollar value of output produced by an extra unit of input.

g. Graph of output generated by various quantities of one input, holding other inputs fixed.

h. Total output divided by total quantity of input.

i. Cost to which a firm is precommitted.

j. Maximum amount of product obtainable from any specified combination of inputs, given the current state of knowledge.

k. Increase in output that results from an additional unit of a given input, holding all other inputs constant.

l. A graph showing how average cost has changed over time.

m. Change in profits resulting from a change in price.

n. Period of time during which some, but not all, of a firm's commitments will have ended.

o. Costs that change as the level of production changes.

p. Relation of percentage change in output to proportionate change in all inputs.

## BASIC EXERCISES

These questions review the concept of a production function and optimal input decisions

Megan and Jamie have invested in Greenacre Farms to grow cornbeans. Since they both work in the city, they will need to hire workers for the farm. Table 6-1 has data on various input combinations and the resulting output of cornbeans.

1. Using the data in Table 6-1, draw on Figure 6-1 the relationship between total output and labor input for 100 acres of land.

   What is the region of increasing marginal returns _____

   What is the region of decreasing marginal returns? _____

   What is the region of negative marginal returns? _____

2. Use Figure 6-1 to draw the relationship between total output and labor input, assuming the use of 200 acres of land. Identify the regions of increasing, decreasing, and negative returns.

   Do the same assuming 300 acres of land. How does the output-labor curve i.e., the curve of total physical product, shift when more land is used?

3. Fill in the middle part of Table 6-1 by computing the marginal physical product of each worker. Check to see that the regions of increasing, diminishing, and negative returns that you identified above correspond to information about the marginal physical product of labor. (You might also check to see that your entries in the middle of Table 6-1 equal the slopes of the total product curves you drew in Figure 6-1.)

4. Your answers to questions 1, 2, and 3 should confirm that the production function for cornbeans eventually shows decreasing returns to labor for all three potential farm sizes. (What about returns to the increased use of land for a fixed amount of labor?)

5. Now consider the following pairs of inputs (acres, workers) and indicate for each whether economies of scale are increasing, decreasing, or constant.

**ECONOMIES OF SCALE**

|  |  |
|---|---|
| (100, 1) to (200, 2) | _____ |
| (100, 2) to (200, 4) | _____ |
| (100, 3) to (200, 6) | _____ |
| (200, 2) to (300, 3) | _____ |
| (200, 4) to (300, 6) | _____ |

## TABLE 6-1
### TOTAL OUTPUT OF CORNBEANS
#### (thousands of tons)
#### Number of Workers

|  |  | 1 | 2 | 3 | 4 | 5 | 6 |
|---|---|---|---|---|---|---|---|
| Acres | 100 | 1 | 4 | 6 | 7 | 6 | 4 |
| of | 200 | 2 | 6 | 9.5 | 12 | 13 | 12 |
| Land | 300 | 3 | 7.5 | 11 | 14 | 16 | 17 |

#### Marginal Physical Product of Labor

|  |  | 1 | 2 | 3 | 4 | 5 | 6 |
|---|---|---|---|---|---|---|---|
| Acres | 100 | ___ | ___ | ___ | ___ | ___ | ___ |
| of | 200 | ___ | ___ | ___ | ___ | ___ | ___ |
| Land | 300 | ___ | ___ | ___ | ___ | ___ | ___ |

#### Marginal Revenue Product of Labor

|  |  | 1 | 2 | 3 | 4 | 5 | 6 |
|---|---|---|---|---|---|---|---|
| Acres of Land | 200 | ___ | ___ | ___ | ___ | ___ | ___ |

### FIGURE 6-1
### TOTAL OUTPUT OF CORNBEANS

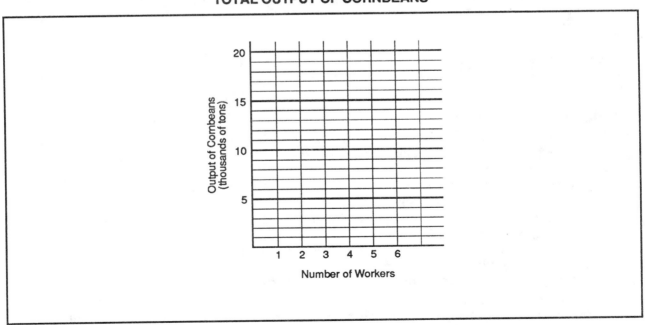

**FIGURE 6-2**
**MARGINAL REVENUE PRODUCT**

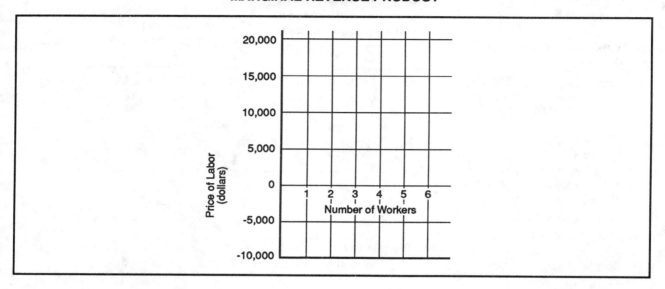

6. Assume that cornbeans can be sold for $5 a ton. Greenacre Farms has 200 acres of land. Calculate the marginal revenue product of labor for 200 acres of land in the bottom part of Table 6-1. Plot the marginal revenue product in Figure 6-2. Hired help costs $8,000. Draw a horizontal line in Figure 6-2 at $8,000 to indicate the price of labor. How many workers should Megan and Jamie hire? _____. At the level of labor input you just determined, what is the difference between the proceeds from selling cornbeans (output) and labor costs? _____. (Check to see that your labor input choice maximizes this difference by considering the use of one more or one fewer worker.)

## SELF-TESTS FOR UNDERSTANDING

### Test A

Circle the most appropriate answer.

1. A graph of total physical product shows how output changes as
   a. all inputs are increased simultaneously.
   b. the firm adopts new technologies.
   c. the scale of production varies.
   d. one input is increased, holding all others constant.

2. For a production process that uses just one input, average physical product is found by
   a. graphing total output against the number of units of input.
   b. computing the change in output for a unit change in input.
   c. dividing total output by the number of units of input.
   d. multiplying the number of units of input by their cost.

3. The "law" of diminishing marginal returns
   a. says that eventually the marginal physical product of any input must become negative.
   b. applies to only a simultaneous increase in all inputs.
   c. can only be true for a production function with decreasing returns to scale.
   d. refers to what happens to output as only one factor is increased, all other inputs being held constant.

4. When looking at the curve for total physical product, the region of diminishing marginal returns is given by the region where marginal physical product is
   a. negative.
   b. positive.
   c. positive and increasing.
   d. positive and decreasing.

5. Consider the following data on workers and output.

| Workers | 1 | 2 | 3 | 4 | 5 |
|---------|----|----|----|----|----|
| Output | 10 | 25 | 35 | 42 | 40 |

   Where do diminishing marginal returns to workers begin to set in?
   a. After the first worker.
   b. After the second worker.
   c. After the third worker.
   d. After the fourth worker.

6. Marginal physical product refers to
   a. the increased revenue from employing an additional worker.
   b. the change in total output from a one-unit increase in a variable input.
   c. total output divided by total input.
   d. total output divided by total cost.

7. For a production process that uses just one input, a firm should expand output as long as
   a. marginal revenue product is greater than the price of the input.
   b. marginal physical product is positive.
   c. average cost is declining.
   d. marginal physical product is greater than average physical product.

8. The rule for optimal input use implies that a firm should use additional units of an input until
   a. average cost equals the price of the input.
   b. marginal physical product is maximized.
   c. marginal revenue product equals the price of the input
   d. increasing returns to scale are exhausted.

9. A change in fixed costs affect
   a. marginal physical product of the variable input.
   b. average physical product of the variable input.
   c. marginal cost associated with changes in the variable input.
   d. average cost associated with changes in total output.

10. In the short run, decisions to vary the amount of output will affect all but which one of the following?
    a. sunk costs.
    b. variable costs.
    c. marginal physical product.
    d. average costs.

11. As output increases, average fixed costs
    a. first decline and then increase.
    b. decrease continuously.
    c. are constant.
    d. increase more or less continuously.

12. As output increases, average total costs typically
    a. first decline and then increase.
    b. decrease continuously.
    c. are constant.
    d. increase more or less continuously.

13. A change in which of the following will *not* shift the short-run average cost curve?
    a. The price of output.
    b. The price of inputs.
    c. The quantity of fixed factors.
    d. The marginal physical product of variable inputs.

14. The term *economies of scale* refers to
    a. the change over time in average cost as firms grow larger.
    b. the percentage change in the marginal revenue product divided by the percentage change of the associated input.
    c. the increase in output when only one input is increased.
    d. what happens to total output following a simultaneous and equal percentage increase in all inputs.

15. If all inputs are doubled and output more than doubles, one would say that the production relationship
    a. shows decreasing returns to scale.
    b. shows constant returns to scale.
    c. shows increasing returns to scale.
    d. violates the "law" of diminishing returns.

16. In the long run,
    a. inputs are likely to be less substitutable than in the short run.
    b. all production functions will exhibit constant returns to scale.
    c. a firm is assumed to be able to make adjustments in all its fixed commitments
    d. average cost must decline.

17. The optimal choice of input combinations
    a. is a purely technological decision, unaffected by input prices, and better left to engineers than economists.
    b. can be determined by looking at information on the marginal revenue product and the prices of various inputs.
    c. will always be the same in both the short and long run.
    d. is likely to include more of an input if its price rises and if other input prices are unchanged .

18. Assume that on a small farm with 10 workers, the hiring of an 11th worker actually lowers total output. Which of the following statements is not necessarily true?
    a. The marginal physical product of the last worker is negative.
    b. The marginal revenue product of the last worker is negative.
    c. A profit-maximizing firm would never hire the 11th worker.
    d. The production function shows decreasing returns to scale.

19. Marginal revenue product (MRP) is equal to
    a. $MPP \bullet P_{OUTPUT}$ .
    b. $MPP / P_{OUTPUT}$ .
    c. $P_{OUTPUT} / MPP$.
    d. the marginal cost of increasing output.

20. The ratio of a productive input's marginal physical product (MPP) to its price is a measure of the
    a. marginal cost of expanding output.
    b. average cost of expanding output.
    c. efficiency of production.
    d. increase in output from spending an extra dollar on this input.

21. To maximize profits, firms should increase the use of inputs with _____ ratios of MPP to price and reduce the use of inputs with _____ ratios of MPP to price.
    a. high; low
    b. low; high

**Test B**

Circle T or F for true or false.

T  F  1.  The "law" of diminishing returns says that economies of scale can never be increasing.

T  F  2.  The marginal physical product of an input refers to the increase in output associated with an additional unit of that input when all other inputs are held constant.

T  F  3.  The marginal revenue product measures the total revenue that a firm will have at different use levels of a particular input.

T  F  4.  If a production function shows increasing returns to scale from the additional use of all inputs, it violates the "law" of diminishing returns.

T  F  5.  If a production function shows decreasing returns to scale, it is likely that long-run average costs will be increasing.

T  F  6.  The short run is defined as any time less than six months.

T  F  7.  The curve of average fixed cost is usually U-shaped.

T  F  8.  Long-run cost curves will always lie above short-run cost curves.

T  F  9.  Inputs are likely to be more substitutable in the long run than in the short run.

T  F  10. Historical data on costs and output is a good guide to the relevant cost curves for a firm's current decisions.

# Appendix: Production Indifference Curves

## LEARNING OBJECTIVES

After completing this appendix, you should be able to:

♦ describe how diminishing returns to a single factor help determine the shape of a typical production indifference curve.

♦ determine what input combination will minimize costs for a given level of output, given information about production indifference curves and input prices.

♦ explain how a firm's expansion path helps determine (minimum) total cost for every possible output level.

♦ use a production indifference curve to explain how a change in the price of one productive factor can affect the least cost combination of inputs.

## IMPORTANT TERMS AND CONCEPTS

Production indifference curve
Budget line
Expansion path
Point of tangency between the budget line and the corresponding production indifference curve

## APPENDIX REVIEW

A set of *production indifference curves,* or isoquants, is a geometrical device that can be used to represent a production function involving two inputs and one output. The horizontal and vertical axes are used to measure quantities of each input. A line connecting all input combinations capable of producing the

(1) same amount of output is called the _____ _____ curve. Each separate curve represents a particular output level. Higher curves will mean (more/less) output.

(2)      Production indifference curves will usually have a (negative/positive) slope and (will/will not) bow in toward the origin. This last property follows from the "law" of _____ returns. Production indifference curves (do/do not) cross.

     Production indifference curves tell a firm what alternative combinations of inputs will produce the same amount of output. An optimizing firm should not be indifferent to these alternatives. To make an optimal decision, the firm will need to know the price of each input. From this information the firm can construct a budget line showing combinations of inputs that can be purchased for the same total cost. The budget line is a (curved/straight) line. The slope of the budget line is given by the ratio of input prices.

(3) The price of the input measured on the (horizontal/vertical) axis goes on the top of the ratio. The intercept on each axis comes from dividing the total budget by the price of input measured on that axis.

     To minimize cost for a given level of output, the firm chooses that combination of inputs lying on

(4) the (highest/lowest) budget line consistent with the given level of output. For smooth and convex production indifference curves, we choose an input combination such that a budget line is just tangent to the relevant production indifference curve. A change in the price of either input will shift the budget line and result in a new optimal input combination.

     This procedure will determine the optimal input combination to minimize cost for a given output target. Using the same procedure to find the lowest cost input combination for different levels of output

(5) defines the firm's _____ path. It also allows us to compute total cost for any level of output. At this point, division and subtraction will allow us to compute average and marginal cost. Which level of output maximizes profits was addressed in Chapter 5 and comes from an analysis of marginal revenue and marginal cost.

     Is the solution to the question of optimal input in this appendix consistent with the earlier discussion about the ratio of input prices and marginal physical products? Yes. Although it may not be immediately obvious, the slope of the production indifference curve equals the ratio of marginal physical products. When we choose the optimal input combination from the point of tangency where the slope of the production indifference curve equals the slope of the budget line, we set the ratio of marginal products equal to the ratio of input prices. In symbols, assuming that our two inputs are A and B, choosing the point of tangency between the production indifference curve and the budget line means that

$$\frac{MPP_A}{MPP_B} = \frac{P_A}{P_B}$$

Some multiplication and division[2] allows us to rewrite this expression as

$$\frac{MPP_A}{P_A} = \frac{MPP_B}{P_B},$$

our earlier condition for the optimal use of inputs.

---

[2]Multiply both sides of the expression by $MPP_B$ and divide both sides by $P_A$.

# IMPORTANT TERMS AND CONCEPTS QUIZ

Choose the best definition for the following terms.

1. _____ Production indifference curve
2. _____ Budget line
3. _____ Expansion path

a. Locus of firm's cost-minimizing input levels for different output levels.
b. Graph showing how total output varies as one input is increased.
c. Graph depicting all combinations of input quantities that yield a given level of output.
d. Representation of equally costly input combinations.

# BASIC EXERCISES

Figure 6-3 shows a production indifference curve for producing 6,000 tons of cornbeans. This curve is derived from data given in Table 6-1.

1. (Read all of this question before answering.) If land can be rented at $65 an acre a year and if labor costs work out to $8,000 a worker, what is the least cost combination for producing 6,000 tons of cornbeans? Restrict your answer to the dots in Figure 6-3 that correspond to data from Table 6-1.
   _____ acres and _____ workers.
   If land rents for $125 a year and labor costs $8,000 a worker, what is the least cost input combination for producing 6,000 tons of cornbeans? _____ acres and _____ workers.
   Remember that the ratio of input prices determines the slope of the budget line. For a given set of input prices draw the budget lines that pass through each of the three input combinations. Remember that these lines should be parallel. For a given set of input prices, the least cost combination is given by the lowest budget line. Can you explain why?

## FIGURE 6-3
## PRODUCTION INDIFFERENCE CURVE

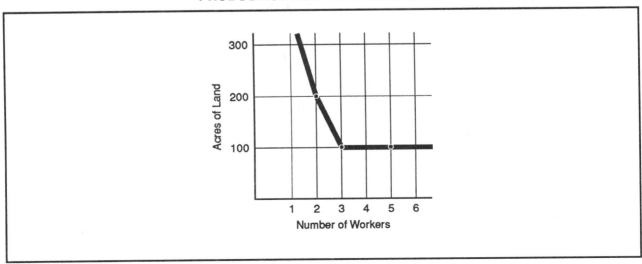

2. From your answer to the previous question, you know that if the cost of using land is relatively low, the least cost input combination will use more land with a smaller number of workers. You also know that if the cost of using land rises enough, an optimizing farmer would be induced to use less land and more workers. What is the rental price of land that just tips the balance away from the input combination of 200 acres and two workers to the combination of 100 acres and three workers? $_____.

   You should be able to answer this question by "rotating" a budget line around the outside of the production indifference curve. For given input prices, find the one budget line that just touches, or is tangent to, the production indifference curve. This point will show the lowest cost-input combination. As one input price changes, the slope of the budget line will change and the tangency point will move as the lowest cost-budget line rotates around the outside of the production indifference curve. If the price of land is low, the input combination of 200 acres and two workers will be on the lowest budget line. As the price of land rises, the slope of the budget line becomes flatter, and there will come a point where suddenly the input combination of 100 acres and three workers is on the lowest budget line.

## SELF-TESTS FOR UNDERSTANDING

### Test A

Circle the most appropriate answer.

1. A production indifference curve shows
   a. different levels of output that can be produced with a given amount of inputs.
   b. levels of output about which producers should be indifferent.
   c. what changes in one input are necessary to keep the marginal physical product of a second input constant.
   d. what input combinations can be used to produce a given output.

2. Which of the following properties is *not* true of production indifference curves?
   a. They have a negative slope.
   b. Their slope is always equal to the ratio of input prices.
   c. They bow in toward the origin because of the "law" of diminishing returns.
   d. The amount of output is the same for all points on the production indifference curve.

3. A single budget line shows
   a. how total cost varies when the level of output changes.
   b. how production costs vary when the price of inputs changes.
   c. what different combinations of inputs can be purchased with a fixed budget.
   d. how production costs have changed over time.

4. The budget line relevant for choosing the optimal amount of two inputs
   a. has a positive slope.
   b. will shift in a parallel fashion in response to an increase in the price of one input.
   c. is a straight line with a negative slope reflecting relative input prices.
   d. will have a different slope following an equal percentage change in the price of all inputs.

5. When the price of one input increases,
   a. the budget line will shift out in parallel fashion.
   b. the budget line will shift in a parallel fashion.
   c. the slope of the budget line will change.
   d. the production indifference curves will shift.

6. If production requires two inputs, labor and capital, and the price of both doubles,
   a. the slope of the budget line will double.
   b. production indifference curves will become steeper.
   c. the marginal physical product of the more expensive input will decline.
   d. the slope of the budget line and the least costly input combination do not change.

7. Which one of the following will not occur after a reduction in the price of one input?
   a. The budget line will shift in such a way that a fixed production budget can now buy more of the cheaper input.
   b. The optimal input combination for a given level of output is likely to involve the use of more of the cheaper input.
   c. The minimum total cost for producing a given level of output will fall.
   d. Each production indifference curve will show a parallel shift.

## Test B

Circle T or F for true or false.

T   F   1.   Production indifference curves have a positive slope because higher output usually requires more of both inputs.

T   F   2.   Typically, a production indifference curve will bow in at the middle because of the "law" of diminishing returns.

T   F   3.   A firm minimizes cost for any level of output by choosing the input combination given by the tangency of the budget line to the production indifference curve.

T   F   4.   An increase in the price of either input will make the budget line steeper.

T   F   5.   If production requires the use of two inputs, $x_1$ and $x_2$, a change in the price of $x_1$ will never affect the optimal use of $x_2$.

T   F   6.   A change in the price of output will change the cost-minimizing input combination for a given level of output.

T   F   7.   For given input prices, the tangencies of production indifference curves with alternative budget lines trace out a firm's expansion path.

## SUPPLEMENTARY EXERCISE

Assume that the production of widgets ($W$) requires labor ($L$) and machines ($M$) and can be represented by the production function*

$$W = L^{1/2} M^{1/2}.$$

1. Draw a production indifference curve for the production of 500,000 widgets.

2. $L$ measures labor hours and $M$ measures machine hours. In the long run, both machine and labor hours are variable. If machine hours cost $48 and labor hours cost $12, what is the cost-minimizing number of labor and machine hours to produce 500,000 widgets? (Whether it is profitable to produce 500,000 widgets depends on the price of widgets.)

*This particular mathematical representation of a production function is called the Cobb-Douglas production function. Cobb was a mathematician. Douglas was president of the American Economic Association and United States senator from Illinois from 1948 to 1966. You might enjoy reading the comments by Albert Rees and Paul Samuelson about Douglas and his work in the *Journal of Political Economy*, October 1979, Part 1.

3. Assume that the firm has 125 machines capable of supplying 250,000 machine hours.
   a. Draw a picture of total output as a function of the number of labor hours.
   b. Use the production function to derive an expression for the marginal physical product of labor conditional on the 250,000 machine hours. Draw a picture of this function. What, if any, is the connection between your picture of total output and the marginal physical product?
   c. Divide your picture of the marginal physical product into regions of increasing, decreasing, and negative marginal returns to labor. (Note: Not all areas of need exist.)
   d. If the price of widgets is $50 and the price of labor is $12 per hour, what is the optimal number of labor hours that the firm should use? How many widgets will the firm produce?

4. Graph the expansion path for this production function on the assumption that labor hours cost $12 and machine hours cost $48.

5. Are returns to scale in the production of widgets constant, increasing, or decreasing?

6. Assume the demand for widgets is given by

$$W = 2,500,000 - 25,000\ P_w$$

where $P_w$ = price of widgets.

   a. If a firm can purchase labor services at $12 per hour and machines can be rented at $48 per hour, what is the marginal cost? What is the profit maximizing level of output? What is the market price of widgets?
   b. Assume now that the firm owns 100 machines that supply 200,000 machine hours and that the firm can purchase labor at a cost of $12 per hour. Derive an expression for marginal cost and determine the profit maximizing level of output. What is the market price of widgets?

## STUDY QUESTIONS

1. What is the difference between diminishing marginal returns and negative marginal returns?
2. Which do fixed costs affect and why—average cost or marginal cost?
3. Which do variable costs affect and why—average or marginal cost?
4. What is the difference between fixed costs and sunk costs?
5. Why do economists typically use a U-shaped curve to represent an average cost curve?
6. If a firm's production function shows increasing returns to scale, what will its long-run average cost curve look like and why?
7. Why isn't a firm's long-run average cost curve found by connecting the minimum points of its short-run average cost curves?
8. Consider a production function that involves the input of two factors. For each factor individually, increases in inputs lead to diminishing returns. However, when both inputs are increased simultaneously, there are increasing returns to scale. Can this be possible? Explain why.
9. If output can be produced with varying quantities of different inputs, how can a firm figure out the cost-minimizing input combination?
10. Why should a firm interested in profit maximization make no changes in output or prices following an increase in fixed costs?

*Chapter* **7**
# Demand and Elasticity

## LEARNING OBJECTIVES

After completing this chapter you should be able to:

- compute the elasticity of demand, given data from a demand curve.
- describe how various factors affect the elasticity of demand.
- explain why the price elasticity of demand is a better measure of the price sensitivity of demand than the slope of the demand curve.
- explain how the impact of a change in price on total revenue and consumer expenditures depends on the price elasticity of demand.
- explain how the concept of cross elasticity of demand relates to the concepts of substitutes and complements.
- explain how factors other than price can affect the quantity demanded.

## IMPORTANT TERMS AND CONCEPTS

(Price) elasticity of demand
Elastic, inelastic, and unit-elastic demand curves
Complements
Substitutes
Cross elasticity of demand
Shift in a demand curve

## CHAPTER REVIEW

The material in this chapter offers an intensive look at demand curves. Demand curves provide important information for analyzing business decisions, market structures, and public policies.

An important property of demand curves is the responsiveness of demand to a change in price. If a firm raises its price, how big a sales drop is likely? If a firm lowers its price, how large an increase in sales will there be?

To avoid problems with changing units, economists measure these changes as percentages. If, for a given change in price, we divide the percentage change in the quantity demanded by the percentage change in the price producing the change in quantity and ignore the negative sign, we have just computed
(1) the price _____ of _____. Remember, this calculation ignores minus signs and uses the average price and quantity to compute percentage changes.

It is useful to know the elasticity properties of certain, special types of demand curves. If the demand curve is truly a vertical line, then there is no change in the quantity demanded following any change in
(2) price, and the elasticity of demand is _____. (No demand curve is likely to be vertical for all prices, but it may be for some.) The other extreme is a perfectly horizontal demand curve where a small change in price produces a very large change in the quantity demanded. Such a demand curve implies that if price declines, even just a little, the quantity demanded will be infinite, while if the price rises, even a little, the quantity demanded will fall to zero. In this case a very small percentage change in price produces a very large percentage change in the quantity demanded, and the price elasticity of demand is, in the limit, _____. The price elasticity of demand along a negatively sloped straight-line demand curve (is constant/changes). One of the basic exercises illustrates just this point.

A demand curve with a price elasticity of demand greater than 1.0 is commonly called
(3) _____ while demand curves with a price elasticity of demand less than 1.0 are called _____. If the price elasticity of demand is exactly 1.0 the demand curve is said to be a _____ demand curve.

Some simple arithmetic, not economics, can show the connection between the price elasticity of demand and the change in total consumer expenditure (or, equivalently, the change in sales revenue) following a change in price. We know that total expenditures or revenues are simply price times quantity, or

$$\begin{array}{ccccc} \text{Consumer} & & \text{Sales} & & \\ \text{expenditures} & = & \text{revenues} & = & p \times q. \end{array}$$

A decrease in price will increase quantity as we move along a given demand curve. Whether total revenue increases clearly depends on whether the increase in quantity is big enough to outweigh the decline in price. (Remember the old saying: "We lose a little on each sale but make it up on volume.")

Again, it is mathematics, not economics, that tells us the percentage change in total expenditures or revenue is equal to the sum of the percentage change in price and the percentage change in quantity.[1]

$$\left[\begin{array}{c} \text{Percentage} \\ \text{change in} \\ \text{sales revenues} \end{array}\right] = \left[\begin{array}{c} \text{Percentage} \\ \text{change in} \\ \text{price} \end{array}\right] + \left[\begin{array}{c} \text{Percentage} \\ \text{change in} \\ \text{quantity} \end{array}\right]$$

Remember that as we move along a given demand curve, a positive change in price will lead to a negative change in quantity, and vice versa.

If the absolute value of the percentage change in quantity is equal to the absolute value of the
(4) percentage change in price, then total revenue (will/will not) change following a change in price. In this case, the price elasticity of demand is equal to _____.

When the elasticity of demand is greater than 1, the absolute value of the percentage change in quantity will be (greater/less) than the percentage change in price. An increase in price that reduces the quantity demanded will (decrease/increase) total revenue, and a reduction in price that increases the quantity demanded will (decrease/increase) total revenue. Opposite conclusions apply when the price elasticity of demand is
(5) less than 1.0. In this case the percentage change in quantity (will/will not) offset the percentage change in price. An increase in price that reduces the quantity demanded will (decrease/increase) total revenue, and a reduction in price that increases the quantity demanded will (decrease/increase) total revenue.

---

[1] This result is strictly true only for very small changes in $p$ and $q$. Total revenue always equals $p \times q$, but this simple way of calculating the percentage change in total revenue is only true for small changes

The price elasticity of demand refers to the impact on the quantity demanded of a change in a commodity's price. A related elasticity concept compares the change in the quantity demanded of one

**(6)** good with a change in the price of another good. This quotient is called the _____ elasticity of demand. In this case we must keep track of any negative signs.

Some goods, such as knives and forks, film and cameras, are usually demanded together. Such pairs

**(7)** are called _____ and are likely to have a (<u>positive</u>/negative) cross elasticity of demand. For example a decline in the price of cameras is likely to (decrease/<u>increase</u>) the demand for film. That is, following a decline in the price of cameras, the demand curve for film will likely shift to the (left/<u>right</u>).

**(8)** Other goods, such as different brands of toothpaste, are probably close _____ and are likely to have a _____ cross elasticity of demand. What is the likely impact on the demand for Colgate toothpaste of a change in the price of Crest? A decrease in the price of Crest toothpaste would likely (<u>decrease</u>/increase) the demand for Colgate toothpaste. Alternatively, one could say that a decrease in the price of Crest will likely shift the Colgate demand curve to the (<u>left</u>/right).

The price of a commodity is not the only variable influencing demand. Changes in other factors, say, advertising, consumers' income, tastes, or the price of a close substitute or complement, will mean

**(9)** a (<u>shift in</u>/movement along) a demand curve drawn against price. Finally, remember that a demand curve refers to a particular period of time.

## IMPORTANT TERMS AND CONCEPTS QUIZ

Choose the best definition for the following terms.

1. _____ Price elasticity of demand
2. _____ Elastic demand curve
3. _____ Inelastic demand curve
4. _____ Unit-elastic demand curve
5. _____ Complements
6. _____ Substitutes
7. _____ Cross elasticity of demand
8. _____ Shift in demand curve

a. Ratio of percent change in quantity demanded of one product to the percent change in the price of another.

b. A change in price leads to a less than proportionate change in quantity demanded.

c. Good for which an increase in price leads to higher demand.

d. An increase in price of one good decreases the demand for the other.

e. A change in price leads to a more than proportionate change in quantity demanded.

f. Ratio of percent change in quantity demanded to percent change in price.

g. A change in price accompanied by an equal proportionate change in quantity demanded.

h. An increase in the price of one good increases the demand for the other.

i. Change in the quantity demanded due to a change in any determinant of demand except price.

## BASIC EXERCISES

These exercises offer practice in calculating and interpreting price elasticities of demand.

1. Table 7-1 contains data on possible prices and the associated quantity of demand for jeans in Collegetown. Plot this demand curve in Figure 7-1. It is a _____ line.
   a. Using the data in Table 7-1, compute the elasticity of demand for each change in price.[2] What general conclusion can you draw about the elasticity of demand along a straight-line demand curve? The elasticity of demand (<u>increases/decreases</u>) as one moves down and to the right along a straight-line demand curve.
   b. Use the same data to compute total revenue for each price-quantity pair in Table 7-1. Compare the change in total revenue to the elasticity of demand. What conclusion can you draw about this relationship?

### TABLE 7-1
### THE DEMAND FOR JEANS

| Price (dollars) | Quantity Demanded | Percentage Change Price | Percentage Change Quantity | Elasticity of Demand | Total Revenue |
|---|---|---|---|---|---|
| 24 | 24,000 | | | | _____ |
| 20 | 32,000 | _____ | _____ | _____ | _____ |
| 16 | 40,000 | _____ | _____ | _____ | _____ |
| 12 | 48,000 | _____ | _____ | _____ | _____ |
| 8 | 56,000 | _____ | _____ | _____ | _____ |

### FIGURE 7-1

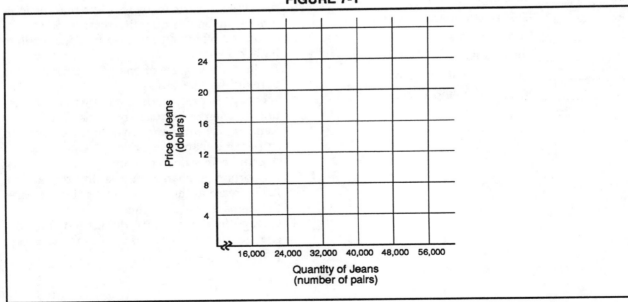

---

[2]Remember to use the average of the two prices and quantities. For a change in price from $24 to $20 compute the elasticity of demand as

$$\frac{8,000}{28,000} \div \frac{4}{22}.$$

2. The Price Elasticity of Demand
   a. Table 7-2 has data on possible prices and the associated demand for schmoos and gizmos. Use these data to plot the demand curves in Figures 7-2 and 7-3. Looking at these demand curves, which curve looks more elastic? More inelastic?
   b. Now use the data in Table 7-2 to calculate the elasticity of demand for schmoos for a change in price from $60 to $50.[3] It is

   _____.

### TABLE 7-2

| The Demand for Schmoos | | The Demand for Gizmos | |
|---|---|---|---|
| Price (dollars) | Quantity | Price (dollars) | Quantity |
| 60 | 200 | 2.00 | 2,000 |
| 50 | 240 | 1.25 | 3,200 |
| 48 | 250 | 1.00 | 4,000 |
| 40 | 300 | 0.50 | 8,000 |

### FIGURE 7-2

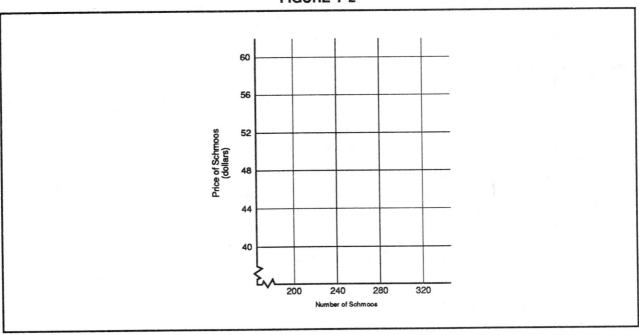

[3]Remember to use the average of the two prices or quantities when computing each percentage change. For example, compute the elasticity of demand when the price changes from $60 to $50 as

$$\left[\frac{40}{220}\right] \div \left[\frac{10}{55}\right].$$

**FIGURE 7-3**

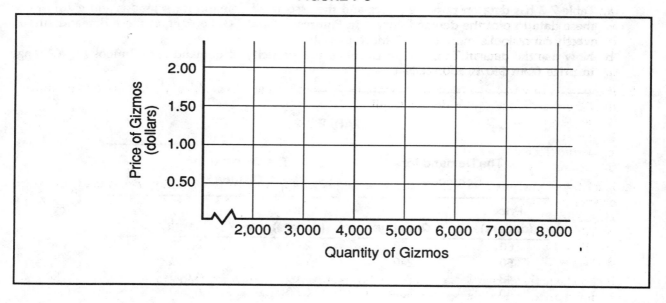

c. Use the same data to calculate the elasticity of demand for gizmos for a change in price from $1 to 50 cents. It is _____.

d. For these changes, which demand curve is more elastic? In fact, if you look closely at the underlying data for both curves—for example, by computing the total revenue—you will see that for both curves the elasticity of demand is _____.

## SELF-TESTS FOR UNDERSTANDING

### Test A

Circle the most appropriate answer.

1. Looking just at the demand curve, the price responsiveness of demand is given by
   a. the Y-intercept.
   b. the slope of the demand curve.
   c. the slope of a ray from the origin to a point on the demand curve.
   d. the product of price times quantity.

2. If when price increases the quantity demanded declines, we know that
   a. the demand curve has a negative slope.
   b. the price elasticity of demand is less than 1.0.
   c. total sales revenue will increase.
   d. total sales revenue will decrease.

3. The price elasticity of demand is defined as the _____ change in the quantity demanded divided by the _____ change in price.
   a. percentage; absolute
   b. absolute; absolute
   c. percentage; percentage
   d. absolute; percentage

4. If the price elasticity of demand is less than 1.0, then for a 10 percent change in price the quantity demanded will change by
   a. less than 10 percent.
   b. exactly 10 percent.
   c. more than 10 percent.
   d. There is not enough information.

5. If the units in which the quantity demanded is measured are changed, say from pounds to ounces, then the price elasticity of demand will
   a. decrease.
   b. increase.
   c. be unaffected.
   d. increase by a factor of 16.

6. If a 10 percent price increase leads to a 12 percent decline in the quantity demanded, the price elasticity of demand is
   a. $(10 + 12) = .83$.
   b. $(12 + 10) = 1.2$.
   c. $(12 - 10) = 2$.
   d. $(12 + 10) = 22$.

7. If the elasticity of demand is equal to 1.0, then a change in price leads to
   a. no change in the quantity demanded.
   b. a reduction in total revenue.
   c. a shift in the demand curve.
   d. an equal (ignoring any negative signs), proportionate change in the quantity demanded.

8. If the elasticity of demand is greater than 1.0, a reduction in price will
   a. decrease total sales revenue.
   b. increase total sales revenue.
   c. leave total sales revenue unchanged.
   d. lead to a reduction in the quantity demanded.

9. Sales revenue will not change following an increase in price if
   a. the price elasticity of demand is equal to 1.0.
   b. the demand curve is a straight line.
   c. the cross elasticity of demand is positive.
   d. the quantity demanded doesn't change.

10. If the demand for apples is inelastic, apple producers could increase total revenue by
    a. decreasing price.
    b. increasing price.
    c. changing price will not affect total revenue.

11. If a 20 percent decrease in the price of long-distance phone calls leads to a 35 percent increase in the quantity of calls demanded, we can conclude that the demand for phone calls is
    a. elastic.
    b. inelastic.
    c. unit elastic.

12. From the data given above, what would happen to total revenue following a 20 percent decrease in the price of long- distance phone calls? It would
    a. decrease.
    b. increase.
    c. remain the same.

13. Angelita manufactures artificial valves used in open-heart surgery. She is contemplating increasing prices. Total revenue will decrease unless the demand for valves is
    a. elastic.
    b. inelastic.
    c. unit elastic.

14. Goods that are usually used together are said to be
    a. complements.
    b. inelastic.
    c. spin-offs.
    d. substitutes.

15. If goods are substitutes, then the cross elasticity of demand is likely to be
    a. equal to 1.0.
    b. negative.
    c. positive.
    d. zero.

16. The cross elasticity of demand between frozen pizza and home-delivered pizza would be computed as the percentage change in the quantity of frozen pizza demanded divided by
    a. the percentage change in the price of frozen pizza.
    b. the percentage change in the quantity of home-delivery pizza demanded.
    c. the percentage change in the price of home-delivery pizza.
    d. the change in the price of mozzarella cheese.

17. If, following an increase in the price of schmoos, the quantity demanded of gizmos declined, we would conclude that
    a. the demand for gizmos is inelastic.
    b. gizmos and schmoos are substitutes.
    c. gizmos and schmoos are complements.
    d. schmoos are likely to be a luxury good.

18. If the cross elasticity of demand between two goods is positive, we would conclude that the two goods are
    a. substitutes.
    b. complements.
    c. necessities.
    d. both likely to have inelastic demand curves.

19. If the price of Sony 90-minute audio tapes increases, the demand curve for JVC audio tapes is likely to
    a. shift to the right.
    b. shift to the left.
    c. be unchanged.
    d. become vertical.

20. If skis and boots are complements, then which one of the following statements is false?
    a. A reduction in the price of skis is likely to increase the sales of boots.
    b. Revenue from ski sales will increase following a reduction in the price of ski boots.
    c. An increase in the price of boots will likely reduce the sales of skis.
    d. The cross elasticity of demand between skis and boots will likely be positive.

21. The income elasticity of demand is measured as the percentage change in
    a. price divided by the percentage change in income.
    b. the quantity demanded divided by the percentage change in income that changes demand.
    c. income divided by the change in demand.
    d. income divided by the percentage change in price.

## Test B

Circle T or F for true or false.

T  F  1. The price elasticity of demand is defined as the change in quantity divided by the change in price.

T  F  2. The elasticity of demand will be the same at all points along a straight-line demand curve.

T  F  3. A vertical demand curve would have a price elasticity of zero.

T  F  4. A demand curve is elastic if, following a decrease in price, the quantity demanded increases.

T  F  5. If demand is inelastic, an increase in price will actually increase the quantity demanded.

T  F  6. If the demand for airplane travel is elastic, then a reduction in the price of airline tickets will increase total expenditures on airplane trips.

T  F  7. If two goods are substitutes, then an increase in the price of one good is likely to reduce the demand for the other good.

T  F  8. The cross elasticity of demand between complements is normally negative.

T  F  9. If sales of Whoppers at Burger King increase following an increase in the price of Big Macs at McDonald's we can conclude that Whoppers and Big Macs are complements.

T  F  10. The price elasticity of demand for Pontiacs is likely to be greater than that for cars as a whole.

T  F  11. A demand curve will shift to the left following an increase in price of a close complement.

T  F  12. An increase in consumer income will shift the demand curve for most goods to the left.

T  F  13. The income elasticity of demand is defined as the percentage change in income divided by the percentage change in price.

T  F  14. Plotting price and quantity for a period of months or years is a good way to estimate a demand curve.

# Appendix: Statistical Analysis of Demand Relationships

## BASIC EXERCISES

Completing these exercises should help underscore the necessity and difficulty of distinguishing between a demand curve and observations on price and quantity that are determined by the intersection of demand and supply curves.

1. Consider the data on cheese consumption and prices for the period 1970 to 1980 in Table 7-3. Plot these data. What does this say about the demand for cheese? Why?

**TABLE 7-3**

| Year | Quantity (millions of pounds) | Price (dollars per pound) |
| --- | --- | --- |
| 1970 | 2,356 | 0.65 |
| 1971 | 2,490 | 0.67 |
| 1972 | 2,757 | 0.71 |
| 1973 | 2,891 | 0.84 |
| 1974 | 3,077 | 0.97 |
| 1975 | 3,017 | 1.04 |
| 1976 | 3,423 | 1.16 |
| 1977 | 3,577 | 1.19 |
| 1978 | 3,794 | 1.30 |
| 1979 | 3,888 | 1.41 |
| 1980 | 4,149 | 1.56 |

SOURCE: Computed from *Survey of Current Business*, various issues.

2. Assume that the demand for hand-held calculators depends on consumer income and price as follows:

$$Q^D = -100 + 0.2Y - 5P$$

where

$$
\begin{aligned}
Q^D &= \text{quantity demanded (thousands)} \\
Y &= \text{consumer income, and} \\
P &= \text{price (dollars).}
\end{aligned}
$$

Supply is assumed to be determined as follows:

$$Q^S = 50 + 15P$$

where $Q^S$ = quantity supplied (millions of pounds).

a. Compute the equilibrium price and quantity for 1990, 1991, and 1992, given that consumer income was as follows:

| Year | Consumer Income |
|------|-----------------|
| 1990 | $3,000 |
| 1991 | 3,100 |
| 1992 | 3,200 |

Plot these price-quantity pairs for each year on a two-variable diagram. Are these points a good estimate of the demand curve? Why? Why not?

b. Assume now that the supply curve for calculators shifts each year in response to technical advances in the production process. To capture these technical advances, we need a new supply curve for each year as follows:

| | | | | | | |
|------|------|---|-----|---|-----|
| 1990 | $Q^s$ | = | 50 | + | $15P$ |
| 1991 | $Q^s$ | = | 100 | + | $15P$ |
| 1992 | $Q^s$ | = | 300 | + | $15P$ |

Compute and plot equilibrium price and quantity for each year. (Remember to include the effect of the change in consumer income in the demand curve.) Are these points a good estimate of the demand curve? Why? Why not?

## SUPPLEMENTARY EXERCISE

1. **Profit Maximization and the Elasticity of Demand**

   A profit-maximizing firm will not try to produce so much output that it is operating in the inelastic portion of its demand curve. Why not? If demand is inelastic, total revenue will increase following a reduction in output (The higher price more than compensates for the reduction in output.) Total costs will decline if output is reduced. Thus, profits—revenue minus costs—must increase following a decline in output if a firm is originally operating in the inelastic portion of its demand curve. What are the elastic and inelastic portions of the demand for Acme stereos described in Supplementary Exercise 1, Chapter 5? Was your profit-maximizing level of output in the elastic or inelastic region?

## ECONOMICS IN ACTION

1. Howard Grant operates a movie theater in New Jersey, just across the Hudson River from New York. He used to show the most recently released movies at a ticket price of $6.50. He was especially discouraged when attendance dropped to 212 people over a full weekend. He then changed the format to show still current but previously released movies, and he reduced his ticket price to $1. Weekend attendance jumped to 3,782 people. (*The New York Times*, March 20, 1992)
   a. Using the numbers above, what is the elasticity of demand for movies at Mr. Grant's theater?
   b. What would happen to Mr. Grant's attendance if other theaters adopted his format and lowered their prices?

2. In the late spring of 1992 Northwest Airlines offered a promotional fare advertised as parents fly free with children. The program cut airline fares in half for family travel. American Airlines, which had unsuccessfully tried earlier to reduce the number of special promotional airfares, responded by halving all fares purchased seven days in advance. To avoid the anger of passengers who had bought tickets earlier, the airlines agreed that these passengers could reticket at the new, lower fares. Not

surprisingly, airlines and travel agents were swamped with calls. At one point, new bookings were so heavy that some airline executives were reported saying that total sales revenue might not drop "because of the extraordinary high response." (*The New York Times*, June 2, 1992)

a. What would the price elasticity of demand for air travel have to be if these airlines executives were correct?

b. How would we know whether the reduction in ticket prices did double the demand for air travel? Consider the following. In the summer of 1991, June through September, travel on domestic airlines totaled 120 billion passenger miles. In 1992, summer travel totaled 134.5 billion passenger miles. Discuss the relevance of this information for an evaluation of the impact of the reduction in airfares.

## STUDY QUESTIONS

1. Why is elasticity measured as the ratio of percentage changes and not just as the ratio of the change in quantity demanded to the change in price?

2. What is the logic behind the statement in the text that the demand for narrowly defined commodities, for example a particular brand of clothing, is more elastic than the demand for broadly defined commodities, that is, all clothing?

3. Which is likely to be larger and why, the price elasticity of demand for luxuries or the price elasticity of demand for necessities?

4. What is meant by the terms "perfectly elastic" and "perfectly inelastic"? What do these demand curves look like and why?

5. How does the elasticity of demand help determine whether a change in price will raise or lower total sales revenue?

6. If a government is interested in increasing revenue, will it want to impose tariffs or sales taxes on goods with a high or low price elasticity of demand? Why?

7. What is the cross elasticity of demand and how does its numerical value help to determine whether goods are complements or substitutes?

8. Consider the demand for pretzels. Why does the change in the price of a complement, say, beer, or the change in the price of a close substitute, say, potato chips, lead to shift in the demand curve for pretzels rather than a movement along the curve? What exactly is the nature of the shifts?

*Chapter* **8**

# Consumer Choice and the Individual's Demand Curve

## LEARNING OBJECTIVES

After completing this chapter, you should be able to:

- distinguish between total and marginal utility.
- explain the role of marginal utility as a guide to maximizing consumer surplus.
- explain how the law of diminishing marginal utility can be used to derive an optimal purchase rule.
- explain how the optimal purchase rule can be used to derive a demand curve.
- explain how the concept of consumer surplus helps explain why mutual gain arises from voluntary exchange.
- explain what economists mean by inferior goods and why inferior goods may have demand curves that slope upward.
- distinguish between the income and substitution effects of a price change.
- derive a market demand curve given information on individual demand curves.
- explain why a market demand curve can have a negative slope even if individual demand curves do not.

## IMPORTANT TERMS AND CONCEPTS

Marginal analysis
Total utility
Marginal utility
The "law" of diminishing marginal utility
Optimal purchase rule ($P=MU$)
Scarcity and marginal utility
Consumer's surplus
Inferior goods
Income effect
Substitution effect
Individual and market demand

## CHAPTER REVIEW

This chapter discusses economic models of consumer choice. These models are what lie behind negatively sloped demand curves. The appendix to the chapter discusses indifference curve analysis, which is a more sophisticated treatment of the same material.

Economists derive implications for individual demand curves by starting with assumptions about individual behavior. One relatively innocent assumption should be sufficient. It concerns consumer preferences and is called the "law" of diminishing marginal utility. Perhaps we should first start with utility.

The term *utility* refers to the benefits people derive from consuming goods and services. The actual utility is unique to each one of us and thus is incapable of being measured. To get around the measurement problem, we will use the term *total utility* to refer to the maximum amount a consumer will pay for a given quantity of the commodity. (It should be obvious that this amount will be influenced by a person's income and preferences.) Rather than focusing on total utility, however, economists have found it useful to pay attention to the additional amount of money that a consumer would pay for one more unit of the

(1) commodity, or _____ utility, measured in money terms. (Marginal utility (will/will not) also be influenced by a person's income and preferences.) The law of diminishing marginal utility is a hypothesis about consumer preferences. It says that normally additional units of any commodity provide less and less satisfaction. As a result, the additional amount a consumer will pay for an additional unit of some commodity will (increase/decrease) the more units she is already consuming.

The law of diminishing marginal utility can be used as a guide to optimal commodity purchases. Optimal purchases are ones that maximize the difference between total utility and total expenditures on a commodity.

(2) This difference is called _____ surplus[1]. That is, optimal purchases yield maximum total utility for a given level of income and maximum _____. Our optimal purchase rule says that an individual consumer should buy additional units of a commodity as long as the marginal utility of the additional units exceeds the _____ of the commodity. If marginal utility exceeds price, the addition to total utility from consuming one more unit will be (greater/less) than the addition to total spending, and consumer's surplus will (increase/decrease).

This notion of optimal purchases and purchasing more until marginal utility falls below price is all well and good for a single commodity, but couldn't a consumer run out of income before she has considered optimal purchases of all goods and services? When one looks at demand curves commodity by commodity, this seems a real possibility. But remember that demand is influenced by income and preferences. Total utility measures what people are willing to pay, given their preferences, their income, and the prices of other goods, not what they desire. As Mick Jagger and the Rolling Stones said, "You can't always get what you want." The appendix to this chapter shows geometrically how total income constrains the demand for individual commodities.

With our optimal purchase rule it is easy to derive an individual *demand curve*. A demand curve shows the quantity demanded at different prices, holding all other things constant. (Look back at Chapter 4 if necessary.) To derive an individual demand curve we confront our consumer with different prices and see how the quantity demanded changes. Our optimal purchase rule tells us that she will purchase

(3) more units as long as the marginal utility is (greater/less) than the price of the unit. She will stop when

---

[1]There is a geometric interpretation of consumer surplus. As the demand curve is the curve of marginal utility, the area under the demand curve equals total utility. If a consumer can buy as much as he wants at market prices, total expenditures are price times the quantity purchased. The result is that consumer surplus can be represented as the area under the demand curve and above the horizontal line drawn at the market price. For a straightline demand curve consumer surplus is a triangle, e.g. triangle DAA in Figure 88-2(a) on page 203 of the text.

the two are equal. If we now lower the price, we know that she will again try to equate price and (marginal/total) utility, which she does by considering buying (more/less). Thus, as price goes down the quantity demanded goes (down/up), and this individual demand curve has a (positive/negative) slope.

Income also affects an individual's demand for various commodities. We saw in Chapter 4 that a
(4) change in income will mean a (shift in/movement along) the demand curve. In terms of the concepts of this chapter, a change in income will influence how much a person would spend to buy various commodities; that is, a change in income will influence total and marginal _____.
Following a change in income, we could again conduct our demand curve experiment, and it would not be surprising if the resulting demand curve had shifted. An increase in income will typically mean an increase in the demand for most commodities, but occasionally the demand for some commodity decreases following an increase in income. Commodities whose consumption increases as a consumer's income increases are called _____ goods, and commodities whose consumption decreases are called _____ goods.

We can now use the possibility of inferior goods to see why the quantity demanded might decrease following a reduction in price. We start by noting that the impact of a price change can be divided into an *income effect* and a *substitution effect*. Consider a price reduction on some good, say potatoes. The fact that potatoes are now cheaper relative to other goods implies an increase in demand for potatoes. This
(5) relative price effect is also called the _____ effect. But that is not the whole story. Following the price decline, a consumer could buy the same amount of all commodities, including potatoes, as she did before and still have money leftover. This leftover money comes from the decline in the price of potatoes, and it is similar to an increase in income, which will, as noted above, affect her demand for all goods. This leftover money effect is also called the _____ effect of a price change. If potatoes were an inferior good, then increased income would lead our consumer to demand (fewer/more) potatoes. The final change in demand for potatoes, or any other commodity following a price change, will be determined by the net effect of the _____ and _____ effects of a price change. Demand curves for normal goods will always have a (positive/negative) slope, as the substitution and income effects of a price change work in the same direction. Demand curves for inferior goods will also have a negative slope as long as the _____ effect is stronger than the _____ effect.

Individual demand curves are a critical building block to market demand curves. If people determine their own demands without regard to the purchases of others, then we can derive the market demand
(6) curve by the (horizontal/vertical) summation of individual demand curves. For each price we simply add up the individual quantities demanded. If individual demand curves each have a negative slope, the market demand curve must also have a _____ slope. Even if individual demand curves are vertical, that is, individuals purchase only a fixed quantity, the market demand curve is still likely to have a negative slope as lower prices attract new consumers and higher prices drive some consumers away.

## IMPORTANT TERMS AND CONCEPTS QUIZ

Choose the best definition for the following terms.

1. _____ Marginal analysis
2. _____ Total utility
3. _____ Marginal utility
4. _____ "Law" of diminishing marginal utility
5. _____ Consumer's surplus
6. _____ Inferior goods
7. _____ Income effect
8. _____ Substitution effect

a. Impact on demand from change in purchasing power when the price of a good changes.
b. Difference between total utility and total expenditures for a given quantity of some commodity.
c. Change in quantity demanded of a good resulting from change in its relative price, holding real income constant.
d. Evaluation of the effects of small changes.
e. Maximum amount of money a consumer will pay for an additional unit of some commodity.
f. Quantity demanded increases when consumer real income rises.
g. Quantity demanded declines when consumer real income rises.
h. Maximum amount of money a consumer will give in exchange for a quantity of some commodity.
i. Observation that additional units of a given commodity generally have decreasing value for a consumer.

## BASIC EXERCISES

These exercises review how we use the law of diminishing marginal utility to derive a negatively sloped demand curve.

1. Table 8-1 presents data on Dolores' evaluation of different quantities of dresses.
   a. Use these data to compute the marginal utility of each dress.
   b. The optimal purchase rule says to buy more dresses as long as the marginal utility of the next dress exceeds the price of the dress. According to this rule, how many dresses should Dolores buy if they cost
   $90 each? _____
   $60 each? _____
   $40 each? _____

### TABLE 8-1

| Dresses | Total Utility | Marginal Utility |
|---------|---------------|------------------|
| 1 | $110 | $ _____ |
| 2 | $210 | $ _____ |
| 3 | $290 | $ _____ |
| 4 | $360 | $ _____ |
| 5 | $410 | $ _____ |
| 6 | $440 | $ _____ |
| 7 | $460 | $ _____ |

c. Now, fill in columns 3, 5, and 7 of Table 8-2 to compute the difference between total utility and total expenditures for each price. What quantity maximizes the difference between total utility and total expenditures when price equals

$90 _____

$60 _____

$40 _____

d. The text defines total utility as the maximum amount Dolores would pay for various quantities of dresses. The difference between what she would be willing to pay and what she has to pay is called _____ surplus. How do the quantities determined using the optimal purchase rule in question 2 compare with those determined by maximizing consumer surplus in question 3?

e. Use the information in Table 8-1 to plot Dolores' demand curve for dresses in Figure 8-1. Is your demand curve consistent with your answers to questions 2 and 3? (It should be.)

**TABLE 8-2**

| Dresses | Price = $90 Total Expenditure | Difference* | Price = $60 Total Expenditure | Difference* | Price = $40 Total Expenditure | Difference* |
|---------|---------------------------|-------------|---------------------------|-------------|---------------------------|-------------|
| 1 | $ 90 | _____ | $ 60 | _____ | $ 40 | _____ |
| 2 | 180 | _____ | 120 | _____ | 80 | _____ |
| 3 | 270 | _____ | 180 | _____ | 120 | _____ |
| 4 | 360 | _____ | 240 | _____ | 160 | _____ |
| 5 | 450 | _____ | 300 | _____ | 200 | _____ |
| 6 | 540 | _____ | 360 | _____ | 240 | _____ |
| 7 | 630 | _____ | 420 | _____ | 280 | _____ |

*Differences between total utility and total expenditures

**FIGURE 8-1**

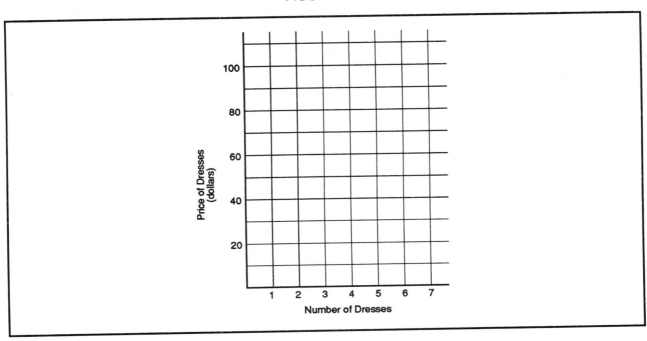

2. Consider the following information on Joel's total utility for CDs purchases:

| Number of CDs | Total Utility |
|:---:|:---:|
| 1 | $25 |
| 2 | $45 |
| 3 | $63 |
| 4 | $78 |
| 5 | $90 |
| 6 | $100 |
| 7 | $106 |
| 8 | $110 |

a. What marginal utility is associated with the purchase of the third CD?
   1. $18
   2. $21
   3. $45
   4. $63

b. What is Joel's consumer surplus if he purchases 3 CDs at $11 apiece?
   1. $30
   2. $33
   3. $63
   4. $96

c. What would happen to Joel's consumer surplus if he purchased an additional CD at $11?
   1. Consumer surplus declines by $11.
   2. Consumer surplus increases by $11.
   3. Consumer surplus increases by $15.
   4. Consumer surplus increases by $4.

d. How many CDs should Joel buy when they cost $11 apiece?
   1. 0
   2. 3
   3. 5
   4. 7

e. What is Joel's consumer surplus at the optimal number of record purchases?
   1. $ 35
   2. $ 55
   3. $ 79
   4. $100

f. If the CDs go on sale and their price drops to $8, how many CDs do you expect Joel to buy?
   1. 5
   2. 6
   3. 7
   4. 8

## SELF-TESTS FOR UNDERSTANDING

### Test A

Circle the most appropriate answer.

1. The total utility of any commodity bundle
   a. should be the same for all individuals.
   b. is defined as the maximum amount a consumer will spend for the bundle.
   c. will equal expenditures on the commodity in question.
   d. is not likely to change even if a consumer's income changes.

2. The law of diminishing marginal utility
   a. implies that total utility declines as a consumer buys more of any good.
   b. is an important psychological premise that helps explain why all demand curves have a negative slope.
   c. must hold for every commodity and every individual.
   d. says that increments to total utility will decrease as an individual consumes more of a commodity.

3. Rick is willing to spend up to $200 for one ski trip this winter and up to $300 for two trips. The marginal utility of the second trip to Rick is
   a. $100.
   b. $200.
   c. $300.
   d. $500.

4. Consumer's surplus refers to the
   a. money a consumer has left over at the end of the month.
   b. accumulation of garbage that could be but is not recycled.
   c. difference between total expenditures and what a consumer would have been willing to pay for the same purchases.
   d. the pleasure a consumer takes when she finds an especially good deal.

5. Consumer's surplus will increase as long as the marginal utility of each additional purchase is
   a. positive.
   b. increasing.
   c. greater than total utility.
   d. greater than the price of the commodity.

6. The optimal purchase rule says that to maximize the difference between total utility, measured in money terms, and total expenditures a consumer should purchase additional units
   a. as long as total utility is increasing.
   b. until marginal utility equals zero.
   c. as long as marginal utility exceeds price.
   d. until marginal utility equals total utility.

7. If consumers act to maximize consumer's surplus, price will be closely related to
   a. total utility.
   b. average utility.
   c. marginal utility.
   d. consumer's surplus.

8. The law of diminishing marginal utility implies that individual demand curves will typically
   a. have a negative slope.
   b. show no response to a change in price.
   c. slope up and to the right.
   d. have a positive slope.

9. Scarcity raises _____ utility but lowers _____.
   a. total; price
   b. marginal; price
   c. marginal; total utility
   d. total; marginal utility

10. The caviar-bread paradox indicates that
    a. contrary to economists' assumptions, consumers are really irrational.
    b. price is more closely related to marginal utility than to total utility.
    c. bread is an inferior good.
    d. the demand for caviar is very elastic.

11. The effect of an increase in income on quantity demanded
    a. is always positive.
    b. may be positive or negative.
    c. is positive for necessities and negative for luxuries.
    d. depends on the price elasticity of demand.

12. When economists say that some commodity is an inferior or a normal good, they are referring to the impact of
    a. a change in price on the quantity demanded.
    b. an increase in the quantity consumed on total utility.
    c. an increase in the quantity consumed on marginal utility.
    d. a change in income on the quantity demanded.

13. For an inferior good, the demand curve
    a. must have a negative slope.
    b. is likely to be horizontal.
    c. must have a positive slope.
    d. may have a positive slope.

14. Whenever it is possible to switch between goods or services, the substitution effect of a reduction in price
    a. should lead to a decrease in the quantity demanded.
    b. should lead to no change in the quantity demanded.
    c. should lead to an increase in the quantity demanded.
    d. may be positive or negative.

15. The term inferior good refers to goods
    a. made with substandard materials.
    b. that economists dislike.
    c. for which the quantity demanded declines when real income increases.
    d. advertised in the *National Enquirer.*

16. If, following a decrease in price, the quantity demanded also decreases, we can be reasonably certain that
    a. the good in question is an inferior good.
    b. the substitution effect is greater than the income effect.
    c. the good in question is not an inferior good.
    d. the income effect would show an increase in the quantity demanded as real income increases.

17. The impact of a change in the price of cheese on the demand for cheese can be divided into
    a. micro and macro effects.
    b. inflation and price-level effects.
    c. income and substitution effects.
    d. general and partial effects.

18. If cheap hamburger meat with a high fat content is an inferior good, then we know that
    a. the demand curve for this good must slope upward.
    b. consumer demand may increase following a price increase.
    c. the income effect of a price reduction works in the same direction as the substitution effect.
    d. the income effect of a price increase works in the same direction as the substitution effect.

19. If restaurant meals are not inferior goods, then the income effect of a price change
    a. will work in the same direction as the substitution effect.
    b. will work in the opposite direction from the substitution effect.
    c. implies, on balance, that people will demand fewer restaurant meals following a price reduction.
    d. means that at higher prices people may demand more, not fewer, restaurant meals.

20. Market demand curves can be constructed by
    a. the vertical summation of individual demand curves.
    b. varying the number of people in the market.
    c. charging different people different prices and observing their behavior.
    d. the horizontal summation of individual demand curves.

## Test B

Circle T or F for true or false.

T F 1. The term *marginal utility* refers to the amount of dollars that consumers will pay for a particular commodity bundle.

T F 2. The term *inferior good* refers to those commodities that economists do not like.

T F 3. If the law of diminishing marginal utility holds for pizza, and if pizzas are not an inferior good, then the demand curve for pizza will have a negative slope.

T F 4. If, following a reduction in price, the quantity of potatoes demanded declines, we can conclude that potatoes are an inferior good.

T F 5. If a consumer is interested in maximizing the difference between total utility and expenditures, it is optimal to consume more of a commodity as long as the marginal utility of additional units exceeds the market price.

T F 6. The income and substitution effects of a change in price always work in the same direction, implying that a reduction in price must increase the quantity demanded.

T F 7. Part of the impact of a price increase for any good can be analyzed as a reduction in income.

T F 8. If a consumer is rational, he will never buy an inferior good.

T F 9. Consumer's surplus is defined as the difference between price and marginal utility.

T F 10. A market demand curve can have a negative slope only if all individual demand curves have a negative slope.

## ECONOMICS IN ACTION

Judging from the past two decades, drought appears to be a regular visitor to California. A year or two of below-average rain and snowfall can seriously deplete the state's reservoirs. As the effects of a water shortage become progressively more severe, there is discussion of various schemes for water rationing, but typically none of these schemes involve using prices to ration water. Most water districts set price to cover cost and do not think very much about price as a variable that might limit demand when drought limits supply.

A typical sequence of events will start with a campaign to encourage voluntary reduction in water usage. As drought persists, many areas establish quotas for water usage, usually based on family size, with stiff increases in price for water consumption in excess of the quota. (The dashed line in Figure 8-4 illustrates such a quota-high price scheme. The dashed line indicates the total water bill. The price per gallon is given by the slope of the line.)

The quota-high-price scheme offers a strong incentive to limit water consumption to the basic quota, but there is little monetary incentive to reduce water consumption below the quota. Economist Milton Friedman suggested that rather than impose quotas with high prices for excess consumption, water districts should charge a very high price for *all* water consumption, with a rebate to consumers with especially low water consumption. (See *Newsweek*, March 21, 1977.)

The solid line in Figure 8-4 illustrates a possible high-price-rebate scheme. To ensure that a water district has enough money to cover its fixed costs, the position and/or slope of the solid line could be adjusted. Parallel shifts of the solid line would affect the maximum rebate and the no-charge point, but not the price of a gallon of water. Shifts in the slope would change the price. For example, pivoting the solid line on point A would change both the price and the maximum rebate, while leaving the cost of the basic quota unchanged.

Ross and Judy live in San Francisco. During 1976, in response to the growing concern about water conservation, they voluntarily cut their water consumption significantly below the quotas established by other water districts. The San Francisco rationing scheme, adopted in early 1977, mandated that all San Francisco residents reduce their consumption below 1976 levels by the same percentage. When drought returned to California in the mid 80's, Ross and Judy were heard telling their friends that they were using all the water they could to increase their base use.

1. What advice would you give to a water district dealing with a drought? How much reliance should be placed on campaigns for voluntary reductions? How much reliance should be placed on prices? If prices, what short of scheme would you recommend and why—a quota with high price scheme or a high price with rebate scheme or something else? Do you think price affects people's demand for water? What about businesses, government, and farmers?

## FIGURE 8-4

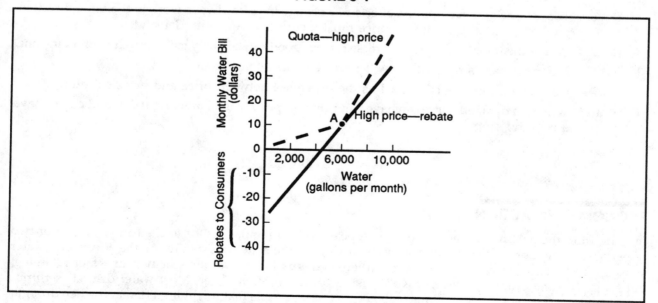

# Appendix: Indifference Curve Analysis

## LEARNING OBJECTIVES

After completing this appendix, you should be able to:

◆ draw a budget line, given data on prices and money income.

◆ explain why economists usually assume that indifference curves (1) never intersect, (2) have a negative slope, and (3) are bowed in toward the origin.

◆ explain why higher indifference curves are preferred to lower indifference curves.

◆ determine optimal commodity bundle(s) for a consumer, given a budget line and a set of indifference curves.

◆ explain why, if indifference curves are smooth and bowed in to the origin, the optimal commodity bundle is the one for which the marginal rate of substitution equals the ratio of commodity prices.

◆ use indifference curve analysis to derive a demand curve, that is, show the change in the quantity demanded of a good as its price changes.

◆ use indifference curve analysis to analyze the impact on commodity demands of a change in income.

## IMPORTANT TERMS AND CONCEPTS

Budget line
Indifference curves
Marginal rate of substitution
Slope of an indifference curve
Slope of a budget line

## APPENDIX REVIEW

Indifference curve analysis is a more rigorous treatment of the material covered in Chapter 8. As the appendix shows, we can study consumer choices by confronting a consumer's desires or preferences, indicated by indifference curves, with a consumer's opportunities, indicated by a budget line. This approach shows how total purchases are constrained by income.

(1)   The *budget line* represents all possible combinations of commodities that a consumer can buy, given her income. The arithmetic of a budget line for two commodities shows that it is a (straight/curved) line with a (positive/negative) slope. An increase in money income will produce a change in the (intercept/slope) of the budget line. A change in the price of either commodity will mean a change in the _____ of the budget line. The slope of the budget line is equal to the ratio of the prices of the two commodities. (The price of the commodity measured along the horizontal axis goes on top.)

(2)   The budget line indicates only all the different ways a consumer could spend her income. In order to figure out what consumption bundle is best for her, we must examine her own personal preferences. Economists use the concept of _____ curves to summarize an individual's preferences. These curves are derived from a person's ranking of alternative commodity bundles. For two commodities, a single indifference curve is a line connecting all possible combinations (bundles) of the two commodities between which our consumer is _____. From the assumption

that more is better, we can deduce (1) that higher indifference curves (are/are not) preferred to lower indifference curves, (2) that indifference curves (never/often) intersect, and (3) that indifference curves will have a (positive/negative) slope.

(3)    Indifference curves are usually assumed to be curved lines that are bowed (in/out). The slope of an indifference curve indicates the terms of trade between commodities that our consumer is indifferent about. For a given reduction in one commodity the slope tells us how much (more/less) of the other commodity is necessary to keep our consumer as well off as before. The slope of the indifference curve is also known as the marginal rate of _____. If indifference curves are bowed in, or convex to the origin, the marginal rate of substitution (increases/decreases) as we move from left to right along a given indifference curve. This change in the marginal rate of substitution is a psychological premise similar to our earlier assumption about declining marginal utility, and it is what makes the indifference curves convex to the origin.

We can now determine optimal consumer choices. The optimal choice is the commodity bundle that makes our consumer as satisfied as possible, given her opportunities. In this case, opportunities are (4) represented by the _____ line, and the evaluation of alternative commodity bundles is given by the _____ curves. The best choice is a commodity bundle that puts our consumer on her (highest/lowest) possible indifference curve. This consumption bundle is indicated by the indifference curve that is just tangent to the _____.

From the definition of the slope of a curved line (Chapter 1) we know that at the point of tangency the slope of the associated indifference curve will equal the slope of the budget line. Since the slope of the budget line is given by the ratio of the prices of the two goods, we know that at the optimal decision the slope of the indifference curve, or the marginal rate of substitution, will equal the ratio of prices.

The marginal rate of substitution tells how our consumer is willing to trade goods, and the price ratio tells us how she can trade goods in the market by buying more of one good and less of the other. If these two trading ratios are different, our consumer can make herself better off by changing her purchases. It is only when the two trading ratios are equal that her opportunities for gain have been eliminated.

Once you master the logic and mechanics of indifference curve analysis, you can use it to investigate the impact on demand of changes in price or incomes. A change in either income or prices will shift the (5) _____ _____. It is the resulting change in the optimal commodity bundle that helps trace out a movement along the demand curve in the case of a change in prices, and the shift in the demand curve, in the case of a change in income. (It is possible to show the income and substitution effects on the indifference curve diagram. If interested, ask your instructor.)

## IMPORTANT TERMS AND CONCEPTS QUIZ

Choose the best definition for the following terms.

1. _____ Budget line
2. _____ Indifference curves
3. _____ Marginal rate of substitution
4. _____ Slope of budget line

a. Maximum amount of one commodity a consumer will give up for an extra unit of another commodity.

b. Lines connecting all combinations of commodities on a consumer's utility function.

c. Line showing all possible combinations of two commodities a consumer can purchase given prices and the consumer's income.

d. Lines connecting all combinations of commodities that a consumer finds equally desirable.

e. Ratio of commodity prices.

## BASIC EXERCISES

These problems are designed to review the logic of the rule for optimal consumer choice using indifference curve analysis, which says that a consumer should choose the commodity bundle associated with the point of tangency between the budget line and the highest indifference curve.

1. Figure 8-2 shows a set of indifference curves for Gloria between books and hamburgers.
    a. Gloria has an income of $80 that she will spend on books and hamburgers. Hamburgers cost $2 each and paperback books $4 each. Draw the budget line in Figure 8-2 that constrains Gloria's choices. (You might first compute the maximum number of hamburgers Gloria can buy; then determine the maximum number of books; then connect these points with a straight line.)
    b. How many hamburgers will Gloria buy?

    _____

    How many books will she buy?

    _____

    In Figure 8-2, label this combination $B$ for best choice. (If you drew the budget line correctly, this point should lie on indifference curve $I_3$.)
    c. The combination of 30 hamburgers and five books, point Z, is obviously not a better choice, as it lies on a lower indifference curve. Assume that Gloria tentatively chooses point Z and is considering whether this choice is best. If you put a ruler along indifference curve $I_2$, you should be able to verify that at point Z the marginal rate of substitution of hamburgers for books is 3. This means that Gloria would be willing to give up _____ hamburgers in order to be able to buy one more book. (You can check this by noting that the combination of 27 hamburgers and six books is on the same indifference curve.[1] However, since books cost only $4 while hamburgers cost $2 Gloria has only to give up _____ hamburgers in order to buy one book. This is clearly a good deal for Gloria, and she will reduce her consumption of hamburgers in order to buy more books; that is, she will move down the budget line away from point Z.

### FIGURE 8-2 GLORIA'S INDIFFERENCE CURVES

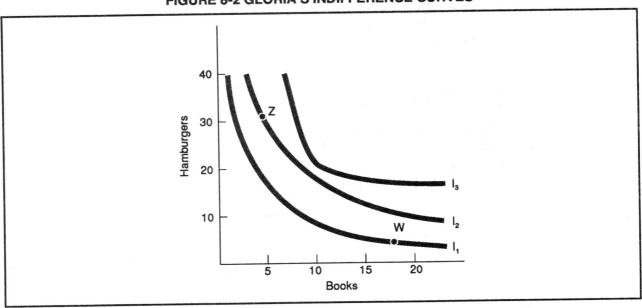

---

[1]Most indifference curves do not have straight-line segments. The straight-line segment is used for convenience; the general argument is still correct.

d. Consider point $W$, on indifference curve $I_1$. Think about the trade off Gloria would accept as given by the slope of her indifference curve and the trade off available in the market as given by the slope of the budget line. Explain why Gloria will be better off moving to the left along the budget line away from point $W$.

e. Arguments similar to those in c and d indicate that for smooth indifference curves as in Figure 8-2, the optimal consumer choice cannot involve a commodity bundle for which the marginal rate of substitution differs from the ratio of market prices. The conclusion is that the optimal decision must be the commodity bundle for which the marginal rate of substitution _____.

2. Figure 8-3 assumes that Sharon spends all of her income on pizza and baseball tickets. The budget line $P_1B_1$ reflects Sharon's initial income and market prices for pizza and baseball tickets. Her preferences are shown by the curved indifference curves. Initially, Sharon chooses to consume at point $X$.

a. Change in income. Where will Sharon consume following a change in income that shifts the budget line to $P_2B_2$? _____ Is either good an inferior good? How do you know?

b. Change in price. Where will Sharon consume following a reduction in the price of pizzas that shifts the budget line to $P_3B_1$?

## FIGURE 8-3

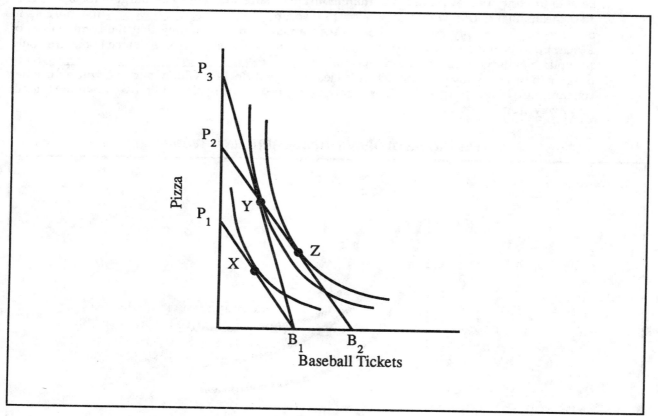

## SELF-TESTS FOR UNDERSTANDING

### Test A

Circle the most appropriate answer.

1. The budget line
   a. determines an individual's optimal consumption bundle.
   b. will not shift at all if prices of both commodities increase and income is unchanged.
   c. determines an individual's possible consumption bundles.
   d. is a straight line whose slope is given by the rate of inflation.

2. The slope of the budget line
   a. is equal to the marginal rate of substitution.
   b. depends upon a consumer's income.
   c. is determined by commodity prices.
   d. should be positive.

3. If a consumer chooses to allocate his income between two goods, a decrease in the price of either good will
   a. make the budget line flatter.
   b. make the budget line steeper.
   c. shift the budget line out in a parallel fashion.
   d. change the slope of the budget line.

4. Following an increase in income,
   a. a consumer's indifference curves will shift.
   b. the slope of the budget line will increase.
   c. individual commodity demand curves will not shift.
   d. the budget line will shift in a parallel fashion.

5. A set of indifference curves is
   a. usually assumed to have a positive slope.
   b. used by economists to represent a person's preferences among different commodity bundles.
   c. the same for everyone.

6. The marginal rate of substitution refers to the slope of
   a. an individual's demand curve.
   b. the budget line.
   c. the market demand curve.
   d. indifference curves.

7. The slope of an indifference curve
   a. is constant if the indifference curve is convex to the origin.
   b. always equals the slope of the budget line.
   c. indicates what commodity trades an individual would be indifferent about.

8. Indifference curve analysis shows that an increase in the price of one commodity will
   a. cause the resulting budget line to lie inside the original budget line.
   b. lead a consumer to choose a new commodity bundle, but one that is on the same indifference curve.
   c. shift consumer preferences.
   d. necessarily lead to a reduction in the demand for both commodities.

9. The assumption that more is preferred to less is sufficient to prove all but which one of the following?
   a. Indifference curves never intersect.
   b. Indifference curves bow in toward origin.
   c. Higher indifference curves are preferred to lower ones.
   d. Indifference curves have a negative slope.

10. If when choosing between beer and pretzels, a consumer is always willing to trade one beer for one bag of pretzels, the resulting indifference curve will
    a. still bow in toward the origin.
    b. be a straight line.
    c. bow out away from the origin.

## Test B

Circle T or F for true or false.

T  F  1.  The budget line is a curved line, convex to the origin.

T  F  2.  A change in the price of one commodity will change the slope of the budget line.

T  F  3.  A change in income will also change the slope of the budget line.

T  F  4.  The assumption that consumers prefer more to less is sufficient to establish that indifference curves will be convex to the origin.

T  F  5.  The slope of indifference curves at any point is given by the ratio of prices.

T  F  6.  The slope of an indifference curve is also called the marginal rate of substitution.

T  F  7.  Optimal decision making implies that a consumer should never choose a commodity bundle for which the marginal rate of substitution equals the ratio of market prices.

T  F  8.  Indifference curve analysis shows that consumers should be indifferent about all the commodity bundles along the budget line, e.g., consumers should be indifferent as between points Y and Z in Figure 8-3.

T  F  9.  Indifference curve analysis shows us that the demand for all goods is interrelated in the sense that changes in the price of one good can affect the demand for other goods.

T  F  10.  Indifference curve analysis suggests that a doubling of all prices and of income will not change optimal consumption bundles.

## SUPPLEMENTARY EXERCISE

Consider a consumer whose total utility can be represented as

$$U = (F + 12)(C + 20)$$

where $F$ = quantity of food, $C$ = quantity of clothing, and $U$ = the arbitrary level of utility associated with a particular indifference curve. (A different value for $U$ will imply a different indifference curve.)

1. Draw a typical indifference curve. (Try $U = 7840$.)

2. Can you derive an expression for the demand for food? For clothing? (Can you use the equation for the indifference curves and what you know about optimal consumer choice to derive an equation that expresses $F$ or $C$ as a function of prices and income? The particular form of these demand curves comes from the mathematical specification of the indifference curves. A different specification of the indifference curves would lead to a different demand function.)

3. If food costs $1.50, clothing $3, and income is $300, what combination of food and clothing will maximize utility?

4. Assume the price of food rises to $2. Now what combination of food and clothing maximizes utility?

5. Assume income increases to $330. What happens to the demand for food and clothing? Is either good an inferior good?

## STUDY QUESTIONS

1. How is it that total utility can increase while marginal utility decreases?

2. Why do economists expect a close relation between price and marginal utility rather than total utility?

3. Why does water, which is essential for life, cost so much less than diamonds? *Hint:* For which is total utility likely to be larger? For which is marginal utility likely to be larger?

4. How can there be mutual gain from voluntary trade when no new goods are produced?

5. Economists have a particular definition of inferior goods that does not refer to the quality of product but may be correlated with quality. What is the economist's definition of an inferior good?

6. Explain how the substitution effect of a price change implies that demand curves will have a negative slope while the income effect allows for the possibility that the demand curves for some goods might have a positive slope.

*C h a p t e r* **9**

# The Firm and the Industry Under Perfect Competition

## LEARNING OBJECTIVES

After completing this chapter, you should be able to:

- describe the conditions that distinguish perfect competition from other market structures.
- explain why the study of perfect competition can be profitable even if few industries satisfy the conditions of perfect competition exactly.
- explain why under perfect competition the firm faces a horizontal demand curve while the industry faces a downward-sloping demand curve.
- explain the relation of price, average revenue, and marginal revenue as seen by individual firms under perfect competition.
- find the profit-maximizing output level for a perfectly competitive firm given information on the firm's marginal cost curve and the market price for its output.
- explain why a perfectly competitive firm's short-run supply curve is the portion of its marginal cost curve that is above average variable costs.
- derive an industry's short-run supply curve given information on the supply curves for individual firms.
- use the concept of opportunity cost to reconcile economic and accounting profits.
- explain how freedom of entry and exit imply that in the long run firms operating under perfect competition will earn zero economic profit.
- explain why the long-run supply curve for a competitive industry is given by the industry's long-run average cost curve.
- explain how perfect competition implies the efficient production of goods and services.

## IMPORTANT TERMS AND CONCEPTS

Market
Perfect competition
Pure monopoly
Monopolistic competition
Oligopoly
Price taker
Horizontal demand curve
Short-run equilibrium
Sunk cost
Variable cost
Supply curve of the firm
Supply curve of the industry
Long-run equilibrium
Opportunity cost
Economic profit

## CHAPTER REVIEW

This chapter uses the concepts developed in earlier chapters to study in more detail the supply decisions of firms. The discussion also adds important material about *market structures*. The decisions of individual firms depend not only upon their production functions and cost curves, but also upon the type of market structure the firm faces. Among other things, different market structures have important implications for demand conditions that firms face. This chapter focuses on the abstraction of the market structure of perfect competition. Later chapters will investigate other market structures—monopolistic competition, oligopoly, and pure monopoly.

Perfect competition is distinguished from other market structures by four conditions:

(1)    1. (Few/Many) buyers and sellers.

2. (Differentiated/Identical) product

3. (Easy/Difficult) entry and exit.

4. (Perfect/Imperfect) information.

Conditions 1, 2, and 4 imply that the actions of individual buyers and sellers (do/do not) affect the market price for the identical product. Condition 3 implies that the number of firms can easily expand or contract and leads to the condition that long-run equilibrium will be characterized by (positive/zero/negative) economic profits.

An important first step to analyzing the firm's decisions in a particular market structure is to be careful about what the market structure implies for the firm's demand curve and its marginal revenue. Let us first consider the short-run supply decision of an individual firm under perfect competition. Since the actions of this firm will not affect the market price, the firm can sell as much or as little as it wants
(2)    at the prevailing market price. Alternatively, we may say that the firm faces a (horizontal/vertical) demand curve. In Chapter 6 we saw that the demand curve is also the curve of average revenue. If the demand curve is horizontal, then besides being the curve of average revenue it is also the curve of _____ revenue. (Remember the picture of marginal revenue in the Basic Exercise to Chapter 5 of this study guide. If the demand curve is horizontal, there is no horizontal rectangle to subtract.) As we saw in Chapter 5, the firm maximizes profits by producing where MC = MR. Under perfect competition, MR = $P$, thus under perfect competition the firm should produce where MC = MR = $P$.

We can now derive the short-run supply curve for the firm by imagining that the firm faces a variety of possible prices and considering what output the firm would supply at each price. These price-output

pairs will define the firm's short-run supply curve. For many possible prices, short-run supply will be
(3) given by the intersection of price and the (average/marginal) cost curve. If price drops below the minimum of the average total cost curve, the MC = P rule maximizes profits by minimizing _____.
Even if price is less than average total cost, the firm should continue to produce as long as price exceeds average _____ cost. If the firm decides to produce nothing it still must cover its (variable/sunk) costs. As long as price exceeds average variable cost, there will be something left over to help cover sunk costs. Putting all of this together, we can conclude that under perfect competition a firm's short-run supply curve is given by the portion of the _____
_____ curve above average _____ cost.

(4) The industry short-run supply curve is given by the (horizontal/vertical) summation of individual firms' supply curves. Market price, the variable so crucial to individual firms' decisions, will be given by the intersection of the market _____ and _____ curves.
In the short run, the number of firms in the industry is fixed; and the short-run industry supply curve will come from the supply decisions of existing firms.
In the long run, there will be more (fewer) firms if the short-run equilibrium involves economic profits (losses). For example, if general market returns are around 8 percent and investments in the firm show
(5) a return of 6 percent, an economist would conclude that the firm has an economic (loss/profit) of _____ percent. In this case, by investing elsewhere and earning 8 percent, the firm's owners would be (better/worse) off. The 8 percent is the _____ cost of capital to the firm and it is an important part of costs as counted by the economist. Thus, economists focus on economic profits as the indicator of entry or exit rather than on accounting profits. The condition of long-run equilibrium that (accounting/economic) profits be zero is consistent with _____ profits equal to general market rates of return.
As firms enter or leave, the industry short-run supply curve will shift appropriately, price will adjust as we move along the industry demand curve, and industry long-run equilibrium will be achieved when there are no further incentives for entry or exit. Figure 9-1(a) illustrates a firm in a perfectly competitive industry. Figure 9-1(b) shows the industry demand and supply. The illustrated firm will be making economic (profits/losses). Shade in the appropriate rectangle showing economic profits or losses. There will be an incentive for some firms to (enter/leave) the industry. As the number of firms in the industry
(6) changes, the supply curve in Figure 9-1(b) will shift to the (right/left) and price will (rise/fall). If the cost curves in Figure 9-1(a) are representative of long-run costs for all current and potential firms in the industry, long-run equilibrium will involve a price of $_____. Note that at all times our representative firm is producing where MC = P. But in the long-run equilibrium, MC = P = minimum _____ _____ _____ cost. It is this last condition that explains the efficiency of perfectly competitive markets.

**FIGURE 9-1**

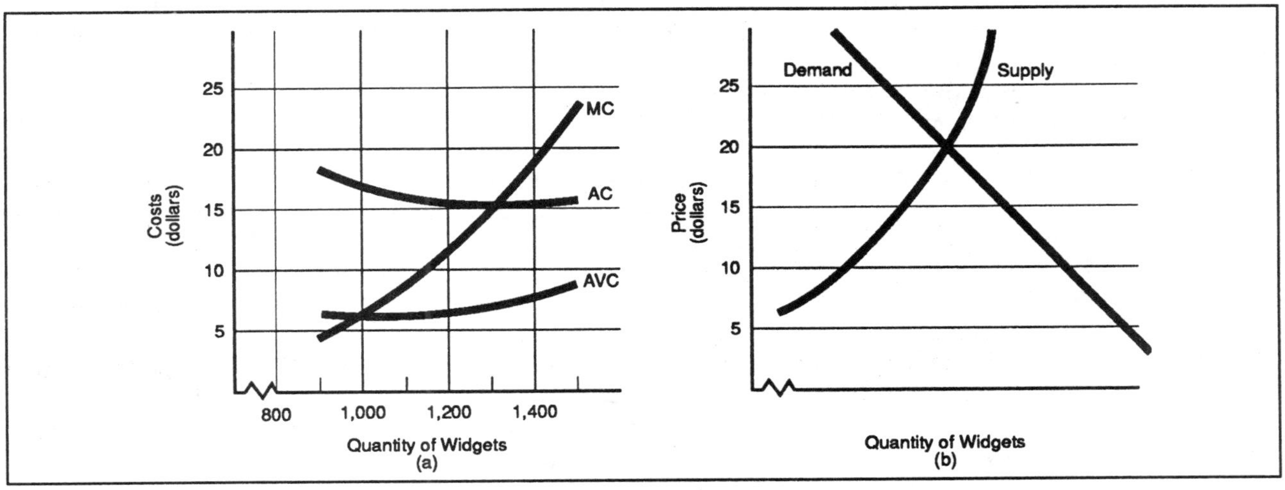

## IMPORTANT TERMS AND CONCEPTS QUIZ

Choose the best definition for the following terms.

1. _____ Market
2. _____ Perfect competition
3. _____ Pure monopoly
4. _____ Monopolistic competition
5. _____ Oligopoly
6. _____ Price taker
7. _____ Horizontal demand curve
8. _____ Sunk cost
9. _____ Variable cost
10. _____ Supply curve of the firm
11. _____ Supply curve of the industry
12. _____ Short-run equilibrium
13. _____ Long-run equilibrium
14. _____ Economic profit

a. Industry composed of a few large rival firms.
b. The part of the marginal cost curve that exceeds average variable cost.
c. Industry with only one supplier.

d. Return to an owner's investment in her firm in excess of the return on alternative investments.
e. Single buyer in a market.
f. Costs related to previous decisions and independent of this period's output.
g. Set of buyers and sellers whose actions affect the price of some commodity.
h. Market price that provides no incentive for firms to enter or leave the industry.
i. Horizontal sum of supply curves for each firm in the industry.
j. Costs that depend upon the production level.
k. Agent or firm too small to affect the market price.
l. Market price that differs from minimum long-run average cost.
m. Many small firms selling an identical product.
n. Many small firms selling slightly differentiated products.
o. Demand curve as seen by firms in a perfectly competitive industry.

## BASIC EXERCISE

This exercise is designed to explore the short-run supply curve for a firm under perfect competition.

Assume that widgets are produced by perfectly competitive firms. The data in Table 9-1 are consistent with Figure 9-1 and are for a representative widget firm. Although not listed separately in Table 9-1, producing widgets involves fixed costs of $10,140.

1. If the price of widgets is $19.10, what is the profit-maximizing level of output? _____. What are economic profits at this level of output? $_____. Check that this level of output maximizes profits by calculating profits for output levels 100 units higher and lower.
   Economic profits at higher output = $_____
   Economic profits at lower output  = $_____

2. What is the profit-maximizing level of output if the price of widgets falls to $11.50, below all values for average cost? _____. What are economic profits at this level of output? $_____. Again check that this level of output maximizes profits or minimizes losses by considering output levels 100 units higher, 100 units lower, and no production.
   Economic losses at higher output  = $_____
   Economic losses at lower output   = $_____
   Economic losses at zero output    = $_____

### TABLE 9-1
### COSTS OF PRODUCING WIDGETS

| Quantity | Average Cost (dollars) | Average Variable Cost (dollars) | Marginal Cost (dollars) |
|---|---|---|---|
| 900 | 17.67 | 6.40 | 4.60 |
| 1000 | 16.44 | 6.30 | 6.30 |
| 1100 | 15.62 | 6.40 | 8.60 |
| 1200 | 15.15 | 6.70 | 11.50 |
| 1300 | 15.00 | 7.20 | 15.00 |
| 1400 | 15.14 | 7.90 | 19.10 |
| 1500 | 15.56 | 8.80 | 23.80 |

3. If the price of widgets is $6.00, what is the profit maximizing level of output? Why?

_____.

4. What general conclusion can you draw about the short-run supply curve for a firm operating under conditions of perfect competition? _____

_____

5. Note that in question 1, when the market price was assumed to be $19.10, the profit-maximizing level of output was at a point where price exceeded both average cost and average variable cost. Remembering that under perfect competition a firm can sell as much output as it wants at the given market price, why isn't it profitable for the firm to produce even more when price exceeds average costs? _____

_____

6. If many firms can produce widgets with the same cost functions, what is the long-run equilibrium price of widgets? $_____. What is the associated level of production for the representative firm? _____.

## SELF-TESTS FOR UNDERSTANDING

### Test A

Circle the most appropriate answer.

1. Which of the following is not a condition for perfect competition?
   a. Perfect information about products.
   b. One firm producing many products.
   c. Freedom of entry.
   d. Freedom of exit.

2. If production is limited to a few large firms, the resulting market structure is called
   a. perfect competition.
   b. monopolistic competition.
   c. oligopoly.
   d. pure monopoly.

3. If a firm can sell any amount of output without affecting price, we say that the demand curve for this firm is
   a. horizontal.
   b. inelastic.
   c. equal to the marginal cost curve.
   d. indeterminate.

4. Which one of the following is not true under perfect competition?
   a. The firm's demand curve is horizontal.
   b. The firm's demand curve is also the curve of average revenue.
   c. The firm's demand curve is also the curve of marginal revenue.
   d. The firm's demand curve is inelastic.

5. If a firm's demand curve is horizontal, marginal revenue equals
   a. average cost.
   b. marginal cost.
   c. average revenue.
   d. minimum long-run average cost.

6. If a firm's demand curve is horizontal, it should produce
   a. as much output as it can.
   b. more output as long as price exceeds average variable cost.
   c. at the point where marginal cost equals price.
   d. at the minimum of its long-run average cost curve.

7. Under perfect competition, a profit-maximizing firm should shut down when price falls below
   a. average cost.
   b. average variable cost.
   c. marginal cost.
   d. sunk costs.

8. The short-run supply curve for a firm under perfect competition is the portion of the firm's marginal cost curve that is above the
   a. average total cost curve.
   b. average fixed cost curve.
   c. average variable cost curve.
   d. minimum of the marginal cost curve.

9. Under perfect competition, industry supply in the short run is given by
   a. the intersection of market demand and average cost.
   b. the horizontal sum of firms' short-run supply curves.
   c. the horizontal sum of firms' average cost curves.
   d. a fixed markup over average variable cost.

10. Which of the following is not a characteristic of long-run equilibrium under perfect competition?
    a. Production where $P$ = MC.
    b. Zero accounting profits.
    c. Zero economic profits.
    d. Production where $P$ = minimum average cost.

11. Which of the following explains why in the long run economic profits in a perfectly competitive industry will equal zero?
    a. The assumption of perfect information.
    b. The elasticity of market demand.
    c. The ease of entry and exit by new and existing firms.
    d. The existence of fixed costs that must be covered in the long run.

12. When economic profits equal zero, we know that accounting profits will
    a. also be zero.
    b. likely understate economic profits.
    c. be at their minimum.
    d. equal the opportunity cost of an owner's investment in her firm.

13. In long-run equilibrium under perfect competition, all but which one of the following are equal?
    a. Average cost.
    b. Average revenue.
    c. Marginal revenue.
    d. Sunk cost.

14. Under perfect competition, price will equal average cost
    a. in the short run.
    b. in the long run.
    c. always.
    d. never.

15. Under perfect competition, firms will produce where MC = $P$
    a. in the short run.
    b. in the long run.
    c. in both the short and long run.
    d. never.

16. Under perfect competition, price is determined by the intersection of the industry supply and demand curves
    a. in the short run.
    b. in the long run.
    c. in both the short and long run.
    d. never.

17. Firms will pay a larger share of any tax increase when
    a. consumer demand is responsive to price.
    b. marginal cost lies below average cost.
    c. demand curves are steep.
    d. an industry is in long-run equilibrium.

18. The analysis of market equilibrium shows that following the imposition a tax per unit output,
    a. price will typically rise, but by less than the tax.
    b. firms can easily pass on all of the tax in the form of higher prices.
    c. firms usually use the imposition of the tax to increase their own profits.
    d. price will not change if marginal cost exceeds average cost.

19. Imagine that pencils are produced by firms with U-shaped average costs under conditions of perfect competition. A large expansion of federal government aid to education has disturbed the original long-run equilibrium by shifting the demand curve for pencils to the right. Which one of the following is not a likely response?
    a. Pencil prices rise initially in response to the increase in demand.
    b. Existing firms are likely to earn positive economic profits in the short run.
    c. Existing firms in the industry initially expand output to the point where average cost equals the new, higher price.
    d. New firms are likely to enter the industry in response to earnings above the opportunity cost of capital.

20. Widgets are produced by perfectly competitive firms. The demand curve for widgets has a negative slope. A technological innovation dramatically reduces average and marginal costs for current and potential widget manufacturers. All but which one of the following will occur?
    a. The quantity supplied increases in the short run.
    b. The price of widgets declines in the short run.
    c. Economic profits increase in the short run.
    d. Economic profits will be positive in the long run.

## Test B

Circle T or F for true or false.

T  F  1.  Perfect competition is characterized by many firms producing similar but not identical products.

T  F  2.  Under perfect competition, firms will maximize profits by always producing at the minimum of their average cost.

T  F  3.  Freedom of entry and exit are really unnecessary for the existence of perfect competition.

T  F  4.  Under perfect competition a firm is always guaranteed to earn positive economic profits if it produces where MC = $P$.

T  F  5.  Under perfect competition, the demand curve facing the industry is horizontal.

T  F  6.  A competitive firm should always expand output as long as price exceeds average cost.

T  F  7.  The firm's short-run supply curve is given by the portion of its marginal cost curve with a positive slope.

T  F  8.  In long-run equilibrium, perfectly competitive firms will show positive accounting profits but zero economic profits.

T  F  9.  If price is less than average cost, a firm is always better off shutting down.

T  F  10.  Perfect competition is studied because a very large number of markets satisfy the conditions for perfect competition.

## SUPPLEMENTARY EXERCISE

Consider a firm with the following total cost curve:

$$TC = 10{,}140 + .00001\, Q^3 - .02\, Q^2 + 16.3\, Q$$

where $Q$ is output. (This cost curve is consistent with the Basic Exercise.)

1. Derive equations for the firm's
   a. average cost.
   b. average variable cost.
   c. marginal cost.

2. Draw a picture showing these various measures of cost as a function of output.

3. Verify that the marginal cost curve goes through the bottom of the average cost curve and the average variable cost curve.

4. Assume this firm operates in a perfectly competitive market. Derive a mathematical expression for the firm's supply curve.

# ECONOMICS IN ACTION

## Three R's and One C?

The quality of education in public schools and what to do about it has become a major issue in election campaigns for everything from local school boards to President of the United States. Declining test scores, mathematical abilities that rank among the lowest in the world, drugs and drinking at school are all common stories in newspapers. A recent report about education in America viewed the situation with such alarm that it was entitled "A Nation at Risk." Everything from smaller classes and higher pay for teachers to more computers and mandatory standardized tests have been proposed. Some, like English Professor E. D. Hirsch, have developed elaborate curricular proposals they would like to see adopted.

Some argue that spending more money or requiring extensive testing within the present structure of public schools will make little difference. They see schools as too bureaucratic and too involved in politics to be responsive to the concerns of individual parents or children. A solution favored by some would introduce market competition into primary and secondary schooling. In its most radical form these proposals would abolish public schools, take the current money spent on schooling, divide it by the number of students, and give every parent of school-age children a voucher for this amount to be spent at the school of their choice. A school's revenue would depend upon its ability to attract and enroll students. Advocates of these plans argue that as schools compete for students the quality of education will increase, and likely without increased spending. Money currently spent on bloated bureaucracies would be channeled to direct instruction. Bad schools would fail to attract students while innovations that increase learning would spread as they were copied by competing schools.

Opponents of voucher systems argue that the market is an inappropriate solution to the problems of public schools. They argue that goods are allocated in markets according to the ability of customers to pay while schooling should not be. Private schools look like a panacea because they can be selective about whom they admit. Taking the best students, they leave public schools, especially large urban schools, with a disproportionate number of students with serious emotional and learning disabilities. Over time a voucher system might also lead to a widening gap between socioeconomic groups as continuing concerns about the level of public spending brings budgetary pressures to reduce the size of vouchers. Wealthy families would have the resources to supplement the voucher; poor households would not. The result would be a two-track schooling system that belies the traditional American commitment to equal opportunity for all.

1. Is the market an appropriate institution for the delivery of primary and secondary education? What are the conditions for the efficiency of competitive markets? Are they likely to apply in this case? Do equity considerations argue for public schools or market competition?

# STUDY QUESTIONS

1. What are the conditions necessary for perfect competition?
2. Which of these conditions helps to ensure that in the long run economic profits are driven to zero? Explain.
3. How can firms in a perfectly competitive industry face a horizontal demand curve when the demand curve for the industry is sloping downward?
4. Explain the difference between average and marginal cost. Which is relevant for the short-run supply decisions of firms in a perfectly competitive industry? Why?
5. How can it be profitable for a firm to stay in business if price is less than average cost?
6. Often firms think that if they lower their price just a bit they may attract enough customers from their competitors to increase profits. Why wouldn't a firm in a perfectly competitive industry do the same thing?

7. What is meant by the efficient production of commodities and how is it fostered by market forces under perfect competition?

8. The discussion of equilibrium makes a distinction between the short run and the long run. What is it that is different between the short run and the long run for firms and for an industry of perfectly competitive firms?

*Chapter* **10**

# The Price System and the Case for Laissez Faire

## LEARNING OBJECTIVES

After completing this chapter, you should be able to:

♦ list the three coordination tasks that must be solved by any system of resource allocation.

♦ explain the difference between an efficient and inefficient allocation of resources.

♦ explain how competitive markets, in which all producers and consumers respond to common market prices, can efficiently allocate resources.

♦ describe situations in which price increases may be in society's best interest.

♦ describe the conditions under which an inefficient allocation of resources might be preferred to an efficient allocation.

## IMPORTANT TERMS AND CONCEPTS

Efficient allocation of resources
Coordination tasks: output selection, production planning, distribution of goods
Laissez faire
Input-output analysis
MC = P requirement of perfect competition
MC = MU efficiency requirement

## CHAPTER REVIEW

This chapter discusses how prices work to allocate resources and how they affect the efficiency of the economy. In particular, it is shown that in a competitive economy, the self-serving actions of utility-maximizing individuals and profit-maximizing firms can lead to an efficient allocation of the economy's resources. The complete, rigorous proof of this proposition is usually discussed only in graduate courses in economic theory and involves the use of some fairly advanced mathematics. This chapter offers a simpler introduction to this material.

CHAPTER 10 / THE PRICE SYSTEM AND THE CASE FOR LAISSEZ FAIRE

The efficiency implications of a laissez-faire, competitive economy are important reasons why economists have great respect for the workings of the price system. But the proof of this abstract proposition is not a proof that we should dismantle the federal government and that all markets should be unregulated. The proposition refers to the efficiency of a perfectly competitive economy. Many aspects (1) of the American economy (are/are not) consistent with the requirements for a competitive economy. The implications of these real-world imperfections are the subject of Chapters 11–18. Also, efficiency is not the only way to judge the workings of an economy. Notions of fairness, or equity, are also important and may at times lead to a preference for less efficient, but fairer, nonmarket procedures.

Sometimes proposals to change prices for efficiency reasons are opposed because of their potentially adverse impact on a particular group. For example, higher taxes on energy to foster conservation and the development of alternative energy sources to reduce our dependence on foreign energy are often opposed because they will increase the cost of living for poor households. These equity considerations are an important part of any final decision. However, many economists argue that it is preferable to address the issue of income distribution through general taxes or transfers rather than by limiting changes in prices that promote efficiency. For example, changes in the earned income credit, personal exemptions or the standard deduction could be used to provide protection to lower income households while letting higher energy prices provide an incentive for all households to reduce their use of energy.

(2)     All economies must answer three questions. First there is the question of output _____: How much of each type of good and service should be produced? Next, there is the question of production _____: How should various productive inputs be allocated among the millions of firms and plants in order to meet the original output decisions? Finally, there is the question of the _____ of products: How are the available goods and services to be divided among consumers? How do we evaluate the job that an economy does in answering these questions? Economists typically use two yardsticks: efficiency and equity. This chapter concentrates on efficiency.

*Economic efficiency* is an important but relatively abstract concept. If by redistributing the commodities that are produced we can make everyone better off in his or her own estimation, we would say that the (3) initial allocation of commodities (was/was not) efficient. It is only when there are no more opportunities to make some individuals better off while not worsening the situation of others that economists would characterize the economy as _____.

There are usually many efficient allocations of resources. Each point on an economy's production (4) possibilities frontier is (efficient/inefficient) in terms of the production of output. If an economy is operating on this frontier, it is impossible to increase the output of one good without _____ the output of one or more other goods. Whether the economy is efficient or fair in terms of distributing this output is another question.

Let us consider in more detail how a competitive economy achieves efficiency in the selection of output. (The appendix to this chapter discusses efficiency in production planning and output distribution.) Efficiency in the selection of output requires that, for the quantity produced, the marginal (5) _____ of the last unit to consumers must equal the marginal _____ of producers.

Why is this condition necessary for an efficient output selection? Remember that the definition of efficiency refers to consumers' evaluations of their own well-being, an evaluation that economists assume consumers are making when they maximize the difference between total utility and spending. If the marginal utility of some good exceeds the marginal cost of producing more units, then the production (6) of at least one more unit of output will result in a net (increase/decrease) in consumer well-being. Consumers benefit by the increase in their utility while the cost to society of additional production is given by the marginal _____. If marginal utility exceeds marginal cost, the benefit to consumers from increased production will be (greater/less) than the cost to society, and the initial output selection (is/is not) efficient. It is only when marginal utility (exceeds/equals/is less than) marginal cost that there are no more opportunities for net gains.

It is one of the beauties of a competitive economy that utility-maximizing individuals and profit-maximizing firms will, while pursuing their own self-interests, make decisions that result in marginal utility being equal to marginal cost. Our optimal purchase rule of Chapter 8 showed that utility-maximizing consumers will purchase additional units until the marginal utility of the last unit consumed equals the (7) _____ of the commodity. The discussion in Chapter 5 showed that profit-maximizing firms will equate marginal revenue and _____ _____. The discussion in Chapter 9 showed that for a firm under perfect competition, marginal revenue is equal to _____. Thus a profit-maximizing firm under perfect competition, producing where marginal cost equals marginal revenue, will be producing where the marginal cost of the last unit produced equals the _____ of the commodity.

(8) To summarize, utility-maximizing consumers set marginal _____ equal to price, and profit-maximizing competitive firms set marginal _____ equal to price. The result is that marginal utility (exceeds/equals/is less than) marginal cost, our condition for efficiency in the selection of output.

A centrally planned economy would attempt to answer the three basic questions of output selection, production planning, and product distribution by direct decree, without the use of prices. Often in these economies decisions about output selection were made with little attention to individual consumer preferences. More weight was typically given to the planners' preferences for such things as increased production of steel and electricity, although periodic newspaper accounts of a readjustment of production goals in response to consumer unrest and the final collapse of central planning in Eastern Europe and the Soviet Union showed that even planners cannot forget entirely about consumers.

Once decisions about output levels have been made, a central planner must be sure that productive inputs are allocated to ensure that the production goals can in fact be achieved. One type of analysis that takes account of the interindustry flows of inputs necessary for the production of goods for final use is (9) _____ — _____ analysis. A major limitation of this analysis is the enormity and complexity of the sets of equations. It is a major conceptual advantage that the price system in a competitive economy does not require that this information be centralized.

## IMPORTANT TERMS AND CONCEPTS QUIZ

Choose the best definition for the following terms.

1. _____ Efficient allocation of resources
2. _____ Output selection
3. _____ Production planning
4. _____ Distribution of output
5. _____ Laissez faire
6. _____ Input-output analysis

a. Decisions on what quantities of each input to use to produce each good.
b. Technique of simultaneously solving equations that link necessary inputs to output for all industries.
c. Situation that takes advantage of every opportunity to make some individuals feel better off without harming others.
d. Situation in which an agent's welfare can be improved without injury to anyone else.
e. Decisions on the division of output among consumers.
f. Decisions on how much of each commodity to produce.
g. Program of minimal interference with the workings of the free market.

## BASIC EXERCISE

This problem is designed to illustrate the logic of the rule for efficiency in output selection. Discussion in the chapter indicated that efficiency in the selection of output requires that marginal utility equals marginal cost for all commodities. If not, it is possible, by changing the selection of output, to improve consumers' well-being.

Consider an economy's production of shirts. Assume that at the current level of shirt output, the marginal utility of shirts is $22 and the marginal cost is $12.

1. The production of one more shirt will increase total utility by $_____. The production of one more shirt will cost society $_____.

2. In Chapter 8 we saw that utility-maximizing consumers will maximize the difference between total utility and total spending. This difference equals the money value of their well-being. Looking at the change in both utility and cost, we can see that the production of one more shirt will increase consumer well-being by $_____. Efficiency in the production of shirts requires (more/fewer) shirts.

3. What if the marginal utility of an additional shirt is $15 and the marginal cost is $18? Then the production of an additional shirt will (increase/decrease) consumer well-being by $_____ and efficiency in the production of shirts will call for (more/fewer) shirts.

4. If the marginal cost of additional shirts is constant at $18, then in order that there be no opportunity for a change in the production of shirts to increase consumer well-being, enough shirts should be produced so that the marginal utility of an additional shirt is $_____.

## SELF-TESTS FOR UNDERSTANDING

### Test A

Circle the most appropriate answer.

1. For any economy that uses the price system, which of the following is not necessarily true?
   a. Prices play an important role in shaping the allocation of resources.
   b. Prices play an important role in shaping the distribution of income and wealth.
   c. Prices will reflect consumer preference and income.
   d. Prices of necessities will be low, and prices of luxuries will be high.

2. The price system distributes goods and services on the basis of income and
   a. scarcity.
   b. consumer preferences.
   c. education.
   d. planner preferences.

3. The three basic coordination tasks for resource allocation that economies may solve by markets or planning include all but which one of the following?
   a. The distribution of output among consumers.
   b. How much of different goods to produce.
   c. The allocation of available resources to the production of different goods.
   d. The amount of money that the government will print.

4. The use of prices to allocate goods among consumers means that
   a. all consumers will be able to buy an equal share of all outputs.
   b. the resulting allocation must necessarily be inefficient.
   c. wealthy consumers will be able to command a greater amount of output.
   d. there must be persistent inflation in order to choke off consumer demand.

5. Prices in competitive markets affect all but which one of the following?
   a. The allocation of inputs among competing producers.
   b. The allocation of output among consumers.
   c. The distribution of income.
   d. The slope of the production possibilities frontier.

6. Consider the production possibilities frontier shown in Figure 10-1. Efficiency in production is given by
   a. all of the points inside the frontier.
   b. all of the points on or inside the frontier.
   c. all of the points on the frontier.
   d. the point of equal output of all goods.

7. Consider production at point P in Figure 10-1. If the economy produces at point P, one would say that output selection is
   a. efficient
   b. inefficient
   c. efficient or inefficient depending upon consumers' preferences.

8. Under conditions of perfect competition, firms will choose to produce the quantity of output such that
   a. MC = MU.
   b. MU= P.
   c. MC = P.
   d. MRP=P.

9. In competitive markets consumers will demand particular commodities up to the point where
   a. MU = MC
   b. MU = P.
   c. MC = P.
   d. MU = O.

**FIGURE 10-1**

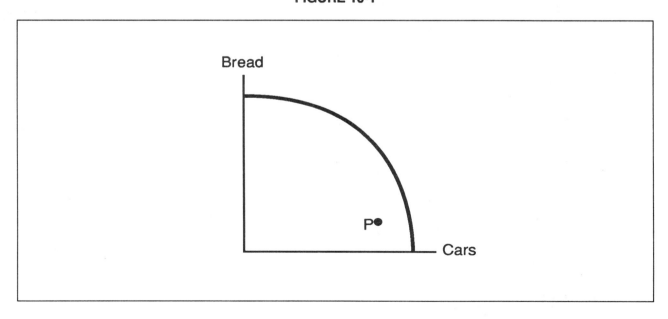

10. The condition for optimal output selection is
    a. MC = P.
    b. MC = MU.
    c. MRP = P.
    d. MU = P.

11. Competitive markets can meet the criterion for efficiency in production planning
    a. through the use of input-output tables.
    b. only after the Congress approves the President's budget proposal.
    c. automatically.
    d. less efficiently than centrally planned economies.

12. If the marginal utility of color television sets is $400 and the marginal cost is $300, then efficiency in output selection requires that the production of color television sets should
    a. increase.
    b. decrease.
    c. neither increase nor decrease.

13. The change in the production of color television sets from question 4 will likely
    a. increase marginal cost and marginal utility.
    b. increase marginal cost and decrease marginal utility.
    c. decrease marginal cost and marginal utility.
    d. decrease marginal cost and increase marginal utility.

14. An efficient allocation of resources
    a. will always be fair.
    b. is the best allocation possible.
    c. means the economy is operating somewhere on its production opportunity frontier.
    d. is always better than an inefficient allocation.

15. Leon does not now own a motorcycle. He would pay up to $2,000 for one. Motorcycles produced by competitive firms in long-run equilibrium, earning zero economic profit, cost $4,000 to produce. Which of the following is false?
    a. Leon is not likely to buy a motorcycle.
    b. Since Leon's marginal utility is less than the marginal cost of production, there would be a social gain if direct government controls reduced the production of motorcycles.
    c. The marginal utility of a motorcycle to someone must be at least $2,000.

16. If resources have been allocated in a way that meets the requirements of economic efficiency, then we know that
    a. output is being produced in accordance with the preferences of the Council of Economic Advisers.
    b. production occurs at a point inside the economy's production possibilities frontier.
    c. there is no reallocation of resources that can make some individuals better off without making others worse off.
    d. the marginal cost of producing every commodity has been minimized.

17. Efficiency in the distribution of output among consumers requires that
    a. all consumers must face the same price for any single commodity.
    b. the price of all goods must be the same.
    c. marginal cost equal marginal revenue.
    d. income be equally distributed among all consumers.

18. Efficiency in the distribution of output requires that
    a. the price of all goods be the same.
    b. all firms are able to sell a given product at the same price.
    c. firms set marginal utility equal to marginal revenue product.
    d. marginal cost be minimized.

**Test B**

Circle T or F for true or false.

T F 1. The term *laissez faire* refers to an economy with minimal economic regulation by government.

T F 2. If resources are being allocated efficiently, we know that there is no better allocation possible.

T F 3. Efficient resource allocation always requires the intervention of a central planner to set prices correctly.

T F 4. Efficiency in the selection of output requires that the marginal utility of every commodity be equal to its marginal cost.

T F 5. An unregulated competitive economy is incapable of seeing that appropriate efficiency conditions are achieved for all commodities.

T F 6. Input-output analysis is a mathematical tool to aid in the distribution of output among consumers without using the price system.

T F 7. Charging higher prices on public transportation during rush hours is an example of using the price system to increase efficiency.

T F 8. Considerations of fairness may sometimes lead a society to prefer an inefficient allocation to an efficient one.

T F 9. Efficiency in the distribution of goods implies that everyone will get an equal share of all goods.

T F 10. Competitive markets promote efficiency in output selection because both firms and consumers respond to the same price.

# Appendix: The Invisible Hand in the Distribution of Goods and in Production Planning

## BASIC EXERCISES

These exercises illustrate the implications of the rules for efficiency in the allocation of productive inputs and in the allocation of output between consumers, as discussed in the appendix to Chapter 10.

1. **Efficiency in the Distribution of Output Among Consumers**

The rule for efficiency in the distribution of output among consumers is that _____
_____
_____ .

Imagine that Todd and Nicole both consume steaks and pizzas. The initial allocation of steak and pizza has resulted in the following marginal utilities:

MARGINAL UTILITY

|        | Todd | Nicole |
|--------|------|--------|
| Steaks | $9   | $6     |
| Pizzas | 4    | 4      |

a. Is the condition for efficiency in the distribution of output satisfied? _____ . If not, there should be some, possibly many, reallocations of output that will increase either Todd's or Nicole's total utility (or both) without reducing total utility for the other.

b. Imagine that Nicole gives Todd one steak in exchange for two pizzas. On net, considering the full effects of the trade, what is the change in Todd's utility? (<u>increase/decrease</u>) $_____ Nicole's utility? (<u>increase/decrease</u>) $_____ An implication of the utility changes of the reallocation is that the initial allocation was (<u>efficient/inefficient</u>).

c. How do competitive markets work to ensure that uncoordinated individual demands will satisfy the condition for efficiency in the distribution of output among consumers?

2. **Efficiency in the Allocation of Productive Inputs**

Our rule for efficiency says that if two inputs, labor and land, are both used to produce corn and tomatoes, then inputs should be assigned to each output until the_____

_____.

a. We know from Chapter 6 that this condition will be automatically satisfied under perfect competition for profit-maximizing firms that can buy inputs at given prices. Perhaps less clear is that if this condition is not satisfied, then it would be possible to reallocate inputs among firms and produce more total output—with the same amount of inputs. Consider the following table showing the initial marginal physical products of land and labor in the production of corn and tomatoes.

### MARGINAL PHYSICAL PRODUCT OF LABOR AND LAND IN THE PRODUCTION OF CORN AND TOMATOES

|  | Corn (bushels) | Tomatoes (pounds) |
| --- | --- | --- |
| Labor (person) | 120 | 1,200 |
| Land (acre) | 40 | 200 |

Consider the reallocation of one worker from corn production to tomato production. As a result of this reallocation of labor, the production of corn will fall by _____ bushels and the production of tomatoes will rise by _____ pounds. Now consider moving four acres of land from tomato production to corn production. As a result of the reallocation of land, the production of corn will rise by _____ bushels and the production of tomatoes will fall by _____ pounds. Counting the reallocation of both land and labor, the production of corn changes by _____ bushels and the production of tomatoes changes by _____ pounds.

b. Efficiency in the selection of inputs helps to achieve efficiency in the choice of outputs. We have seen that efficiency in the selection of outputs requires that MU = MC. In competitive markets, MU = MC because utility-maximizing individuals see to it that MU = P. Efficiency in the selection of input sets MC = P.

We saw in Chapter 6 that our rule for optimal use of inputs could also be expressed in terms of marginal revenue product. Using symbols, our optimal input rule says

$$P_Q\text{MPP}_X = P_{X'}$$

where $P_Q$ is the product price, $P_X$ is the input price, and $\text{MPP}_X$ is the marginal physical product of input X in the production of Q. If we divide both sides of the equation by $\text{MPP}_X$ we get

$$P_Q = \frac{P_X}{\text{MPP}_X}$$

Note that $P_x/\text{MPP}_x$ is the marginal cost of producing more output by using more of input X. If we buy one more unit of input X, we spend $P_x$ and get $\text{MPP}_x$ more units of output at a cost of $P_x/\text{MPP}_x$ per unit of additional output. A profit-maximizing firm will use the optimal input rule for all its inputs. Thus, the marginal cost of an output expansion by the use of any single input, of the many that a firm may use, will be equal to the marginal cost from the additional use of any other input.

c. How do competitive markets work to ensure that the uncoordinated decisions of firms satisfy the condition for efficiency in the allocation of productive inputs?

## SUPPLEMENTARY EXERCISE

Go to the library and look up information about the most recent input-output table for the U.S. economy. (Information about input-output tables can be found about once a year in the *Survey of Current Business*, a monthly publication of the U.S. Commerce Department.)

There are several input-output tables. One table indicates which industries use which commodities. Another table indicates which industries produce which commodities. The table of direct requirements shows what direct inputs are necessary per unit of output of each industry. The table of direct and indirect requirements solves all the input-output relationships and shows how the output of every industry must adjust in order to increase the output of any one industry. It is this table that takes account of such indirect requirements as increased electricity to make more steel in order to increase the output of cars. Input-output tables are constructed each year after allocating the output of the economy across 85 sectors. Every five years more detailed tables are constructed for 541 industries and commodities.

1. How many separate pieces of information do these input-output tables contain? How long do you think it would take to construct such a table? How long do you think it would take you to solve all the interrelationships and produce a table of direct and indirect requirements?

2. Which industries produce mainly for final uses and which produce mainly intermediate outputs, that is, inputs for other industries?

3. The November 1969 *Survey of Current Business* contains data for the 1963 input-output table. Compare these data to the most recent table you can find. Pick one or two favorite industries and see how total and direct requirements have changed over time. If you are a planner concerned with the year 2000, how should you determine what input-output requirements are relevant?

## ECONOMICS IN ACTION

### Hi-Ho, Hi-Ho, It's Off to Work We Go

It's not only bridges that get congested. On Sunday morning, additional cars do not seem to interfere with the traffic flow on most urban highway systems, but on Monday morning each additional driver adds to congestion, makes every other driver's commute take longer, and seems to turn many highways into linear parking lots.

The highway and road systems of most large cities seem to be a clear case of too many vehicles and too few roads. Yet building more roads seems only to increase the traffic without solving the problem. Economist Kenneth A. Small, writing in *The Brookings Review*, Spring 1993, talks of a reservoir of potential drivers, deterred from driving by existing congestion, who quickly fill up new roads as they are completed. Small is skeptical that policies such as campaigns to promote ride-sharing, mass transit, staggered work hours, or high-occupancy-vehicle lanes will have more than a temporary impact on urban congestion. Are there market mechanisms that would improve the situation? Small believes there are, specifically congestion pricing—"charging motorists a very high premium for using the most popular roads during peak hours."

Small argues that congestion pricing provides an incentive for drivers to consider alternative routes, alternative times, and/or alternative means of transportation. The policies listed above focus on only a subset of travelers while providing no incentive for the vast majority of drivers to change their behavior. While no one likes paying tolls, not many of us like being stuck in traffic, either.

To be successful, Small argues that congestion pricing must impose tolls that vary widely by time of day and are sufficiently high at peak demand to have a measurable impact. Although not its primary purpose, Small believes congestion pricing also would improve air quality by reducing both the volume of traffic and the higher emissions associated with congestion.

Small is concerned that congestion prices might be a burden for lower income families. He argues that a portion of the revenues collected should be used in ways that benefit low-income households. Using the Los Angeles region as an example, Small suggests a congestion price of 15¢ a mile or $66 a month for a commuter who has a 20-mile round trip commute each day. He estimates net revenues of around $3 billion a year and proposes using one-third for reimbursements to travelers through an employee commuting allowance and fuel tax reduction; another third for reductions of the portion of sales and property taxes that subsidize highways and transportation; and the remaining third for improvements to transportation services, including mass transit and critical highway projects.

1. What is your evaluation of Small's proposal?

## STUDY QUESTIONS

1. What are the three coordination tasks that must be solved by any system of resource allocation?

2. Why is the determination of efficient allocations a largely technical exercise with many potential solutions rather than a method for determining the best allocation for the economy?

3. Why isn't point P in Figure 10-1 an example of efficiency in output selection? Starting at point P, show what other possible points of production dominate point P in terms of efficiency considerations. Is there only one such point or a set of points? If a set, how can there be more than one?

4. Is it ever possible that society would be better off with higher rather than lower prices? Explain.

5. Should an economy always prefer an efficient allocation to an inefficient allocation? Explain.

6. How can a price system (market mechanism) hope to solve the large number of coordination decisions that are included in the mathematics of an input-output table for the entire economy?

## Chapter **11**

# Monopoly

## LEARNING OBJECTIVES

After completing this chapter, you should be able to:

- calculate a monopolist's profit-maximizing price and output, given information on costs and demand.
- explain why for a monopolist marginal revenue is less than price.
- describe what factors allow a particular monopoly to persist.
- explain why, unlike with a competitive firm, there is no supply curve for a monopolist.
- explain why a monopolist will receive positive economic profits in both the short and long runs.
- describe why a monopolist's demand and cost curves may differ from those of a comparable competitive industry.
- explain how a monopoly can give rise to an inefficient allocation of resources.
- explain why a monopolist cannot pass on all of any pollution charge or other increase in cost.

## IMPORTANT TERMS AND CONCEPTS

Pure monopoly
Barriers to entry
Patents
Natural monopoly
Monopoly profits
Inefficiency of monopoly
Shifting of pollution charges

## CHAPTER REVIEW

In Chapter 9 we studied the decisions of firms operating in markets characterized as perfect competition, that is, markets with lots of firms competing to produce and sell one good. Chapter 6 considered optimal firm decisions and Chapter 10 considered the implications of these decisions for the efficiency of resource (1) allocation. This chapter will consider a *pure monopoly*, a market with (<u>one/many</u>) firm(s) producing a single good with (<u>no/lots of</u>) close substitutes. The essence of a pure monopoly is one producer without effective competition.

A pure monopoly may arise for one of two reasons. If the technology of large-scale production enables one firm to produce enough to satisfy the whole market at lower average costs than a number

(2) of smaller firms can, the result is a _____ monopoly. Legal restrictions such as exclusive licensing or patents; advantages the monopolist acquires for himself, such as control of a vital input or technical superiority; or special risks faced by potential entrants who must spend large amounts on factories or advertising before realizing any revenue can also create a pure monopoly. All of these factors would deter potential competitors and are called _____ to _____ .

The study of a pure monopoly often starts by assuming that some enterprising entrepreneur is able to monopolize a previously competitive industry. It is also traditional to assume that the monopolist initially faces the previous industry demand curve and operates with the same cost curves.

Under pure competition, individual firms face demand curves that are horizontal; that is, the firm can sell as much as it wants at the market price. A monopolist will face the industry demand curve with

(3) a (<u>positive/negative/zero</u>) slope. The monopolist who wants to sell more must (<u>raise/lower</u>) her price.

The monopolist maximizes profit just like any other profit-maximizing firm; that is, the monopolist

(4) chooses the output level at which (<u>marginal/average</u>) cost equals (<u>marginal/average</u>) _____ revenue. Now the only trick is to figure out what the relevant cost and revenue curves look like. Marginal cost comes from the monopolist's total costs in exactly the same way that it does for anyone else. The tricky part is marginal revenue. Marginal revenue is the addition to total revenue from producing and selling one more unit. Under pure competition, the actions of an individual firm have no effect on the market price and marginal revenue equals _____ . But with a monopolist, quantity decisions do affect price and marginal revenue (<u>is/is not</u>) equal to price.

(5) Remember from Chapter 5 that the demand curve is the curve of (<u>average/total</u>) revenue. From Rule 4 in the Appendix to Chapter 5 we know that when average revenue is declining, marginal revenue will be (<u>less/more</u>) than average revenue. In other words, for the monopolist with a downward-sloping demand curve, the curve of marginal revenue will lie (<u>above/below</u>) the curve of average revenue. (Remember the geometry of marginal revenue in the exercise to Chapter 5 in the Study Guide or in Figure 11-3 in the text.) A similar use of Rule 4 indicates that when average cost is rising, the marginal cost curve will lie _____ the average cost curve.

Once we have used the marginal cost and marginal revenue curves to compute the monopolist's

(6) profit-maximizing output level, we can use the (<u>demand/supply</u>) curve to figure out what price she should charge. We know that since the curve of marginal revenue lies below the demand curve, the monopolist's market price will be (<u>greater/less</u>) than both marginal revenue and marginal cost. We also know that if average cost is rising, average cost will be (<u>greater/less</u>) than marginal cost and hence also (<u>greater/less</u>) than the market price given by the demand curve. Thus, for a profit-maximizing monopolist, operating at a level where average cost is rising, price will be greater than average cost and the monopolist will receive positive economic profits. Since, by definition, the monopolist is the only supplier, new firms (<u>will/will not</u>) arise to compete away these profits. Compared with results under pure competition, the monopolist's profit-maximizing behavior will result in a (<u>higher/lower</u>) price and a (<u>higher/lower</u>) level of output in both the short and long run. (If average costs are not rising, the long-run viability of the monopolist requires that price exceed average cost.)

In Chapter 10 we saw that pure competition leads to an efficient allocation of resources. Efficient resource allocation requires that the marginal utility (MU) of each commodity equal its marginal cost (MC).

(7) Optimal consumer decisions lead to the result that MU equals _____ . Under perfect competition, optimal firm decisions imply that MC equals _____ . The upshot is clearly that under pure competition MU equals MC. With a pure monopoly as outlined above— that is, with the same demand and cost curves—we know that while consumers will continue to equate

MU and $P$, the monopolist will equate MC to _____, which is (greater/less) than $P$. The result is that with a pure monopoly, MU is (greater/less) than MC. Increased quantity of the monopolized commodity would yield marginal benefits, measured by MU, that are (greater/less) than marginal costs. In this sense the monopoly leads to an inefficient allocation of resources.

(8)     It's important to note that the monopolist faces demand and cost curves that are the same as those of the previously competitive industry. However, several factors could shift these curves following a change in market structure. Advertising might shift demand and cost curves. Savings from centralizing various operations and avoiding duplication might shift the cost curves (up/down). Greater inefficiencies from greater size would have the opposite effect. Particular results will depend upon particular circumstances.

(9)     Why do we say there is no supply curve for a monopolist? Remember that the supply curve shows the relationship between each possible market price and the quantity supplied. Under pure competition a firm takes price as given and then decides how much to produce, knowing that its individual quantity decision (will/will not) affect the market price. The firm's supply curve comes from considering its reaction to possible prices. But the monopolist (does/does not) take price as given. The monopolist is interested in trading off the revenue implications of different price-quantity combinations, as shown by the demand curve, against the cost implications of producing those different amounts. The monopolist chooses the one quantity that maximizes profits and receives the price given by the point on the demand curve consistent with the quantity. The monopolist is a price (maker/taker).

## IMPORTANT TERMS AND CONCEPTS QUIZ

Choose the best definition for the following terms.

1. _____ Pure monopoly
2. _____ Barriers to entry
3. _____ Patents
4. _____ Natural monopoly
5. _____ Monopoly profits

a. Impediments preventing potential rivals from entering an industry.
b. Industry in which advantages of large-scale production enable a single firm to supply the market demand at a lower average cost than a number of smaller firms could.
c. Industry with a single buyer for the entire market.
d. Temporary government grants of exclusive production rights to products' inventors.
e. Industry with single supplier of a product for which there are no close substitutes.
f. Economic profits that persist in the long run.
g. Accounting profits that do not disappear in the long run.

138

CHAPTER 11 / MONOPOLY

## BASIC EXERCISES

These exercises are designed to offer practice in computing the profit-maximizing quantity and price for a monopolist. Mario has a monopoly in the production of widgets.

1. Table 11-1 contains data on the demand for widgets and the cost of producing them. Use this data to compute Mario's profit-maximizing quantity and the associated price.
   a. One way is to fill in columns 2 and 5 of Table 11-3 by computing total revenue and total cost. Next, choose the output level that maximizes the difference. That level of output is _____ widgets.
   b. The second way is to fill in columns 3 and 4 of Table 11-3 by computing marginal revenue and marginal cost. Mario could maximize profits by increasing production as long as marginal _____ exceeds marginal _____. In this case, Mario maximizes profits by producing _____ widgets.
   c. To maximize profits Mario should charge a price of $_____.

2. Unfortunately, the production of widgets involves significant pollution, and the government has imposed a pollution charge that costs Mario $1,000 a widget. Table 11-2 contains the original data on demand along with the new average cost data that reflect the $1,000 a widget pollution charge.

### TABLE 11-1

| Quantity | Average Revenue (Price) | Average Cost |
|---|---|---|
| 12 | $9,500 | $7,068.00 |
| 13 | 9,300 | 6,957.00 |
| 14 | 9,100 | 6,894.00 |
| 15 | 8,900 | 6,869.40 |
| 16 | 8,700 | 6,876.00 |

### TABLE 11-2

| Quantity | Average Revenue (Price) | Average Cost |
|---|---|---|
| 12 | $9,500 | $8,068.00 |
| 13 | 9.300 | 7,957.00 |
| 14 | 9,100 | 7,894.00 |
| 15 | 8,900 | 7,869.40 |
| 16 | 8,700 | 7,876.00 |

### TABLE 11-3

| (1) Quantity | (2) Total Revenue | (3) Marginal Revenue | (4) Marginal Cost | (5) Total Cost |
|---|---|---|---|---|
| 12 | | | | |
| 13 | | | | |
| 14 | | | | |
| 15 | | | | |
| 16 | | | | |

**TABLE 11-4**

| (1)<br>Quantity | (2)<br>Total<br>Revenue | (3)<br>Marginal<br>Revenue | (4)<br>Marginal<br>Cost | (5)<br>Total<br>Cost |
|---|---|---|---|---|
| 12 | | | | |
| 13 | | | | |
| 14 | | | | |
| 15 | | | | |
| 16 | | | | |

    a. Use Table 11-4 to compute the new profit-maximizing output level. Mario's new profit-maximizing output level is _____ and the associated price is $_____. How much pollution tax does Mario pay? $_____. Note that while the pollution charge is $1,000 a widget, Mario's profit-maximizing price increases by only $_____. Why doesn't Mario simply raise his price by the full $1,000?

    b. What is the new level of profits? $_____.

3. (Optional) Your answer to question 2 should indicate that the pollution tax has reduced both the output of widgets and the associated volume of pollution. What would have happened if, instead of a per-unit tax, the government had simply fined Mario $13,000 for polluting and imposed no further charges? Compared with the initial situation in question 1, what happens to Mario's profit-maximizing level of output, the associated level of pollution output, and actual profits with this lump-sum pollution charge? (When answering this question be sure you are working with the correct cost curves. Adjust Table 11-3, remembering that at each output level, total costs will now be $13,000 higher than the entries in column 5.)

## SELF-TESTS FOR UNDERSTANDING

### Test A

Circle the most appropriate answer.

    1. Pure monopoly is characterized by
        a. many firms producing slightly different products.
        b. many firms producing slightly different products that are close substitutes.
        c. such a small number of firms that each must figure out how the others will respond to its own actions.
        d. one firm, with no competitors, producing a product with no close substitutes.

    2. Which one of the following is not likely to lead to a monopoly?
        a. Patents.
        b. Control of the sole source of an important commodity.
        c. A commodity with many close substitutes.
        d. Significant increasing returns to scale.

3. A natural monopoly arises when
    a. natural resources are an important input.
    b. there are significant cost advantages to large scale production.
    c. the government prohibits entry.
    d. patents protect a firm's technology.

4. Which of the following is not an example of a barrier to entry?
    a. Patents that give exclusive rights to production.
    b. The existence of large sunk costs before one can begin production.
    c. A legal charter that grants its holder the right to be the sole supplier.
    d. None of the above.

5. Which of the following is likely to represent a monopoly?
    a. The largest department store in town.
    b. The University of Iowa, which is the largest employer in Iowa City.
    c. The local TV cable company, which operates under an exclusive contract from the city.
    d. Amtrak.

6. If in order to sell more, a firm must reduce the price on all units sold, we can conclude that the firm's demand curve
    a. has a positive slope.
    b. is horizontal.
    c. slopes down and to the right.

7. Under the conditions of question 6, we know that marginal revenue will
    a. exceed average revenue.
    b. equal average revenue.
    c. be less than average revenue.

8. If average costs are increasing, marginal cost will be
    a. greater than average cost.
    b. less than average cost.
    c. equal to average cost.
    d. there's insufficient information to determine whether marginal cost will be above or below average cost.

9. A monopolist maximizes profit by producing where
    a. marginal cost equals marginal revenue.
    b. marginal cost equals marginal utility.
    c. average cost equals average revenue.
    d. the difference between average cost and average revenue is greatest.

10. Once a monopolist has determined the profit maximizing level of output, the price she should charge is given by
    a. the curve of marginal revenue.
    b. the curve of marginal cost.
    c. the curve of average cost.
    d. the curve of average revenue.

11. A monopolist's profits are found by multiplying the quantity produced by the difference between
    a. marginal cost and marginal revenue.
    b. marginal cost and average revenue.
    c. average cost and average revenue.
    d. average cost and marginal revenue.

12. A monopolist's economic profits will
    a. be competed away in the long run.
    b. be driven to the opportunity cost of capital.
    c. persist in the long run.
    d. be limited by usury laws.

13. Because a monopolist is a price maker, it is typically said that he has
    a. an inelastic demand curve.
    b. no demand curve.
    c. no supply curve.
    d. an upward sloping demand curve.

14. An entrepreneur who monopolizes a previously competitive industry and now faces the same demand curve and produces with the same cost function will typically maximize profits by
    a. forcing consumers to buy more at a higher price.
    b. producing less but charging a higher price.
    c. increasing volume.
    d. lowering both output and price.

15. Pollution charges or other taxes that are levied on each unit of output will lead to a shift in all but which one of the following?
    a. marginal cost.
    b. marginal revenue.
    c. average cost.
    d. none of the above.

16. An increase in a monopolist's average cost will lead to a(n)
    a. increase in price by the same amount, as the monopolist passes on the price increase.
    b. increase in price only if marginal cost also increases.
    c. decrease in price as the monopolist needs to sell more in order to cover increased costs.
    d. increase in price only if the elasticity of demand is less than 1.0.

17. A monopolist cannot simply pass on any increase in costs such as a pollution tax because
    a. marginal cost exceeds average cost.
    b. the average cost curve often has a positive slope.
    c. the demand curve for the output is typically downward sloping.
    d. of concerns about excessive profiteering.

18. Some argue that because they control the whole market and can thus garner all of the benefits, monopolies are more likely to foster innovations. Statistical evidence
    a. confirms this argument.
    b. suggests exactly the reverse.
    c. lacks a firm conclusion.

19. An increase in a monopolist's fixed cost will
    a. reduce the profit-maximizing level of output.
    b. not affect the profit-maximizing level of output.
    c. increase the profit-maximizing level of output as the monopolist needs to sell more to cover costs.

20. If marginal cost is greater than zero, we know that a monopolist will produce where the elasticity of demand is
    a. greater than unity.
    b. equal to unity.
    c. less than unity.

## Test B

Circle T or F for true or false.

T F 1. A pure monopoly results when only a few firms supply a particular commodity for which there are no close substitutes.

T F 2. Significant increasing returns to scale, which reduce average costs as output expands, may result in a natural monopoly.

T F 3. A pure monopolist can earn positive economic profits only in the long run.

T F 4. An entrepreneur who successfully monopolizes a competitive industry will face a horizontal demand curve just like each of the previous competitive firms.

T F 5. A monopolist maximizes profits by producing at the point at which marginal cost equals marginal revenue.

T F 6. If in a monopolistic industry, demand and cost curves are identical to a comparable competitive industry, and the demand curve slopes downward while the average cost curve slopes upward, then the monopolist's price will always exceed the competitive industry's price, but the monopolist's output will be larger.

T F 7. A monopolist has a greater incentive to advertise than does an individual firm under pure competition.

T F 8. When market price is greater than average cost, a monopolist can always increase profits by producing more.

T F 9. A monopolist will be able to increase price by the full amount of any per-unit tax, such as a per-unit pollution charge.

T F 10. A firm operating under conditions of pure competition will not be able to pass on any of a per-unit pollution tax and must therefore pay the whole tax out of reduced profits.

## SUPPLEMENTARY EXERCISES

1. The demand curve for the problem in the Basic Exercise is

$$Q = 59.5 - .005P.$$

In question 1 of the Basic Exercise, the total cost curve is

$$TC = 52,416 + 225Q^2.$$

a. Derive mathematical expressions for total revenue, marginal revenue, average cost, and marginal cost.

b. Plot the demand, marginal revenue, and marginal cost curves.

c. Use your expressions for marginal revenue and marginal cost to solve for the profit-maximizing level of output. Is your answer consistent with your graph in part b and your answer to the Basic Exercise?

d. What is the impact of the per-unit pollution tax and the fixed-charge pollution tax on your expressions for total, average, and marginal cost? Do differences here help explain the impact of these taxes on the profit-maximizing level of output?

2. Why is (a) the correct answer to question 10 in Test A? (You might want to refer back to Chapter 5.)

## ECONOMICS IN ACTION

### The High Cost of New Drugs

President Clinton's promise for health-care reform focused attention on the pricing policies of drug companies in early 1993. On March 28, 1993, *The New York Times* reported that Tacrine, the first drug to treat Alzheimer's disease, had recently been recommended by an advisory panel of the Food and Drug Administration. Industry observers were expecting Tacrine would cost more than $1,000 a year even though it was not effective for most patients. What explains such high prices for this and other new drugs?

Some point to the high cost of drug research and the fact that most new ideas are not successful as justification for the high cost of drugs. Pharmaceutical manufacturers argue that drugs save money, as even expensive drugs are often cheaper than hospitalization or surgery.

Regulating drug prices to allow manufacturers a reasonable rate of return while recognizing the significant research and development costs a company incurs—that is, setting prices on the basis of cost-plus pricing—has been advocated by some. Others are concerned that this approach may subsidize and encourage wasteful and mediocre research. Sam Peltzman, a professor of economics at the University of Chicago, argues that one should not be surprised by high prices. Patents mean that drug companies enjoy a ten-year monopoly. As Peltzman puts it, "These companies are not charities—they are charging what the market will allow."

Are there other solutions? Peltzman has advocated limiting patent monopolies to five years. Others argue that the concept of managed competition, under which patients are organized into large groups to bargain with drug companies and other health providers, is necessary for patients to get the best price. Some are less optimistic that patients, even if organized into large groups, will be successful in bargaining with drug companies who hold a monopoly position unless patients are willing to refuse drug treatments that cost too much.

1. How would you determine a fair price for new drugs?
2. Do prices determined in competitive markets meet your criteria for fairness?
3. What would it take to enforce your concept of fair prices and what side effects are likely to be associated with enforcement?
4. What do you think explains the high price of new drugs?

## STUDY QUESTIONS

1. Who has the greater incentive to advertise and why, a firm in a purely competitive industry or a monopolist?

2. Why are barriers to entry important for the preservation of a monopolist's monopoly?

3. What is the difference between a price taker and a price maker? Which description is relevant for a monopolist?

4. Why do economists argue that monopoly leads to an inefficient allocation of resources?

5. Are there conditions under which society might benefit from a monopoly? Explain.

6. Why doesn't a monopolist simply raise her price by the full cost of things like pollution charges?

7. If both monopolists and competitive firms produce where marginal revenue equals marginal cost, why are the results of a competitive industry and a monopolized industry different?

*Chapter* **12**

# Between Competition and Monopoly

## LEARNING OBJECTIVES

After completing this chapter, you should be able to:

- compare the four conditions that define monopolistic competition with those of perfect competition.
- explain why and how the long-run equilibrium of a firm under monopolistic competition differs from that of a firm under pure competition.
- explain why monopolistic competitors are said to have excess capacity.
- explain why it is so difficult to make a formal analysis of an oligopolistic market structure.
- describe briefly the alternative approaches to modeling oligopolistic behavior.
- explain why most economists believe it is difficult to maintain the discipline necessary to sustain a cartel.
- use marginal cost and marginal revenue curves to derive the implications for price and quantity of sales maximization as opposed to profit maximization.
- use the maximin criterion to determine the final outcome in a game-theory setting.
- use marginal cost and marginal revenue curves to explain how a kinked demand curve can imply sticky prices.
- explain how the concept of contestable markets means that even in an industry with few firms, no firm will earn long-run profits in excess of the opportunity cost of capital, and inefficient firms will not survive if entry and exit is costless.

# IMPORTANT TERMS AND CONCEPTS

Monopolistic competition
Excess capacity theorem
Oligopoly
Oligopolistic interdependence
Cartel
Price leadership
Sales maximization
Game theory
Maximin criterion
Kinked demand curve
Sticky price
Perfectly contestable markets

# CHAPTER REVIEW

Pure competition and pure monopoly are the polar examples of market structure most easily analyzed in textbooks. Actual markets tend more toward *monopolistic competition* and *oligopoly*, which are the subjects of this chapter. It is harder to model firm behavior in these market structures, especially in the case of oligopoly. However, profit maximization remains a dominant characteristic of most firms and marginal cost and marginal revenue curves still are important tools when analyzing the decisions firms make.

(1) A market structure in which there are numerous participants, freedom of entry and exit, perfect information, and product heterogeneity is referred to as _____ competition. Because each seller is able to partially differentiate his product, individual firms will face a demand curve with a (negative/positive/zero) slope. At each point in time, profit-maximizing firms will try to produce at the output level where _____ _____ equals _____. The assumption of freedom of entry and exit implies that in the long run under monopolistic competition firms will earn (negative/positive/zero) economic profit. If an individual firm is earning positive economic profits, the (entry/exit) of new firms will shift the demand curve down (and may raise costs) until the demand curve is just tangent to the (average/marginal) cost curve.

(2) A market structure with only a few firms producing a similar or identical product, and in which some firms are very large, is called a(n) _____. Formal analysis of such market structures is difficult when considering the decisions of one firm, one must also take into account the possible reactions of competitors. No single model describes all the possible outcomes under oligopoly, and economists have found it useful to consider a number of possible models and outcomes. If firms in an oligopolistic market band together and act like a single profit-maximizing monopolist, the resulting group is called a _____. If most firms look to pricing decisions made by a dominant firm, economists refer to the outcome as one of _____

_____.

Oligopolistic firms tend to be large corporations with professional managers. Some argue that managers are likely to be more interested in maximizing total revenue than in maximizing profits. This outcome is more likely if the compensation of managers depends more upon the size of the firm than upon its profitability. A firm interested in maximizing sales revenue will increase output until marginal

(3) revenue equals _____. Compared with profit maximization, sales maximization will mean a (<u>higher/lower</u>) price and a _____ quantity.

      Game theory has been fruitfully used in the study of oligopolistic behavior by a number of economists. Game theory involves listing the possible outcomes of your moves and your opponents' countermoves in

(4) a(n)_____ matrix and then choosing an appropriate _____.

      Another traditional element of the analysis of oligopoly is the concept of a kinked demand curve.

(5) Such a demand curve comes from assuming that your competitors (<u>will/will not</u>) match any decrease in your price but (<u>will/will not</u>) match any increase in your price. As a result, there is a gap in the (<u>marginal/average</u>) revenue curve, and profit-maximizing prices may not change unless there is a significant shift in the marginal_____ curve.

      The concept of perfectly contestable markets suggests that even oligopolists may be limited in their

(6) ability to earn monopolistic profits. The crucial condition for perfect contestability is that _____ and _____ are costless and unimpeded. In such a case, competitors would get into and out of the market whenever profits exceeded the _____ _____ of_____. While no market may be perfectly contestable, the extent to which markets are contestable will limit the ability of firms to charge monopolistic prices.

## IMPORTANT TERMS AND CONCEPTS QUIZ

Choose the best definition for the following terms.

1. _____ Monopolistic competition
2. _____ Excess capacity theorem
3. _____ Oligopoly
4. _____ Cartel
5. _____ Price leadership
6. _____ Sales maximization
7. _____ Game theory
8. _____ Maximin criterion
9. _____ Kinked demand curve
10. _____ Perfectly contestable markets

a. Group of sellers who join together to control production, sales, and price.
b. Industry with a single purchaser.
c. Notion that under monopolistic competition firms will tend to produce at less than capacity, i.e., minimum average cost.

d. Market in which entry and exit are costless and unimpeded.
e. Mathematical analysis of the behavior of competing firms.
f. Industry composed of a few large rival firms.
g. Many firms selling slightly different products.
h. Selecting the strategy that yields the maximum profit, assuming an opponent tries to damage you as much as possible.
i. Situation where one firm sets the price and other firms follow.
j. Expanding output to the point where marginal revenue equals zero.
k. Situation where price declines are matched by competitors while price increases are not.

148

## BASIC EXERCISES

These problems explore several important issues in the analysis of monopolistic competition and oligopoly.

1. Our discussion of monopolistic competition argued that long-run equilibrium implies the firm's demand curve will be tangent to its average cost curve. We have also argued that profit maximization requires that marginal revenue equal marginal cost (or, alternatively, that firms should expand output as long as marginal revenue exceeds marginal cost). How do we know that marginal revenue equals marginal cost at the quantity given by the tangency between the demand curve and the average cost curve?

   a. Table 12-1 contains data on weekly costs and revenue for Gretchen's restaurant. Average revenue and average cost are plotted in Figure 12-1. Note that the demand curve is tangent to the average cost curve. Plot total profits in the left half of Figure 12-1. What output level maximizes profits?

   b. Use the data in Table 12-1 to compute marginal revenue and marginal cost in Table 12-2. According to Table 12-2, what level of output maximizes profits? Why?

### TABLE 12-1

| Quantity | Average Revenue | Average Cost | Total Revenue | Total Cost | Total Profit |
| --- | --- | --- | --- | --- | --- |
| 600 | $19 | $21.67 | $11,400 | $13,002 | $–1,602 |
| 800 | 17 | 17.50 | 13,600 | 14,000 | –400 |
| 1,000 | 15 | 15.00 | 15,000 | 15,000 | 0 |
| 1,200 | 13 | 13.33 | 15,600 | 15,996 | –396 |
| 1,400 | 11 | 12.14 | 15,400 | 16,996 | –1,596 |

### FIGURE 12-1

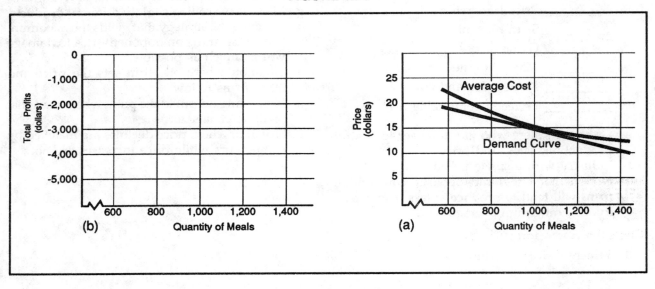

**TABLE 12-2**

| Quántity | Marginal Revenue | Marginal Cost |
|---|---|---|
| 600 | | |
| 800 | | |
| 1,000 | | |
| 1,200 | | |
| 1,400 | | |

**FIGURE 12-2**

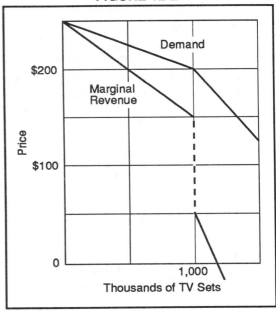

2. Figure 12-2 shows the kinked demand curve for a profit-maximizing firm that produces TV sets in an oligopolistic situation.
   a. What is the profit-maximizing level of output and the corresponding price if TVs can be produced at a marginal cost of $100?

   Quantity _____

   Price _____

   b. Assume that marginal cost increases by 40 percent to $140 per TV. Describe what happens to the profit-maximizing levels of price and quantity following this increase in marginal cost.
   _____
   c. What increase in marginal cost is necessary to induce a change in behavior on the part of this oligopolist and why? _____
   d. What decrease in marginal cost is necessary to induce a change in behavior on the part of this oligopolist and why? _____

## SELF-TESTS FOR UNDERSTANDING

### Test A

Circle the most appropriate answer.

1. Which of the following is the important difference between perfect and monopolistic competition?
   a. Few sellers rather than many.
   b. Heterogeneous rather than homogeneous product.
   c. Barriers to entry rather than freedom of entry.
   d. Long-run positive economic profits rather than zero economic profits.

2. Monopolistic competition would be most appropriate when describing which of the following?
   a. Collusion between contractors when bidding for government contracts.
   b. The production of automobiles in the United States.
   c. Much retail trade in the United States.
   d. Most production for export.

3. Under monopolistic competition the heterogeneity of output implies that
   a. individual firms face downward-sloping demand curves.
   b. both marginal cost and marginal revenue will increase with additional units of output.
   c. individual firms can make positive economic profits even in the long run.
   d. in the long run, individual firms will produce at minimum average cost.

4. Free entry and exit under monopolistic competition means that in the long run
   a. firms will earn economic profits.
   b. a firm's demand curve will be tangent to its average cost curve.
   c. a firm will operate where marginal cost exceeds marginal revenue.
   d. only one firm can survive.

5. Under monopolistic competition firms are likely to produce
   a. to the left of the point of minimum average cost.
   b. to the right of the point of minimum average cost.
   c. at the point of minimum average cost.

6. Which of the following is most likely an example of monopolistic competition?
   a. The airline industry.
   b. Restaurants in Denver.
   c. Competition between television networks.
   d. Cable television in Atlanta.

7. Which of the following characterizes a firm's short-run equilibrium under monopolistic competition?
   a. Production where average cost equals price.
   b. Production at minimum average cost.
   c. Production where marginal revenue equals marginal cost.
   d. Zero economic profits.

8. Which of the following does not characterize a firm's long-run equilibrium under monopolistic competition?
   a. Production where average cost equals price.
   b. Production at minimum average cost.
   c. Production where marginal revenue equals marginal cost.
   d. Zero economic profits.

9. If long-run economic profits are zero, we know that firms are producing where
   a. marginal cost equals marginal revenue.
   b. marginal revenue equals average cost.
   c. marginal cost equals price.
   d. average cost equals price.

10. The situation where a few large firms produce similar products is referred to as
    a. monopolistic competition.
    b. an oligopoly.
    c. contestable markets.
    d. price leadership.

11. Oligopoly may be associated with all but which one of the following?
    a. Price leadership.
    b. Collusive behavior.
    c. Advertising.
    d. Lots of firms.

12. If oligopolistic firms get together to carve up the market and act like a monopolist, the result is called a
    a. cabal.
    b. contestable market.
    c. cartel.
    d. natural monopoly.

13. A firm interested in maximizing sales revenue will produce at a point where
    a. marginal revenue equals marginal cost.
    b. average cost is minimized.
    c. marginal revenue equals zero.
    d. average revenue equals average cost.

14. A firm that maximizes sales revenues instead of profits will charge
    a. a higher price.
    b. a lower price.
    c. the same price but will advertise more.

15. Game theory may be especially useful in analyzing a firm's behavior under conditions of
    a. pure competition.
    b. monopolistic competition.
    c. oligopoly.
    d. pure monopoly.

16. The term *payoff matrix* refers to
    a. bribes paid by cartels.
    b. the structure of winnings in an office pool on the NCAA basketball championship.
    c. the set of possible outcomes in a game theory situation.
    d. players' shares in the NFL playoffs.

17. The term *kinked demand curve* refers to
    a. economists' inability to draw straight lines.
    b. the demand for X-rated movies.
    c. industries with substantial economies of scale.
    d. a situation where competitors match price decreases but not price increases.

18. If a firm faces a kinked demand curve, the demand curve for price increases will likely
    a. be steeper than for price decreases.
    b. have a positive slope.
    c. be more elastic than for price decreases.
    d. be less elastic than for price decreases.

19. Markets can be perfectly contestable if
    a. products are identical.
    b. entry and exit is free and easy.
    c. only two firms are bidding against each other.
    d. long-run economic profits are zero.

20. All but which one of the following market structures are likely to result in a misallocation of resources?
    a. Perfect competition.
    b. Monopolistic competition.
    c. Oligopoly.
    d. Monopoly.

## Test B

Circle T or F for true or false.

T  F   1.  Firms that operate under conditions of oligopoly are likely to engage in lots of advertising.

T  F   2.  Heterogeneity of output is an important feature of monopolistic competition.

T  F   3.  Under monopolistic competition, freedom of entry and exit will guarantee that a firm always earns a zero economic profit, in both the short run and the long run.

T  F   4.  Under monopolistic competition, marginal revenue equals marginal cost in the short run but not in the long run.

T  F   5.  There would be an unambiguous social gain if some firms in a market with monopolistic competition were forced by regulation to stop producing.

T  F   6.  Oligopoly is characterized by a small number of firms, some very large, producing an identical or similar product.

T  F   7.  Arrangements such as price leadership and tacit collusion can be important in oligopolistic markets.

T  F   8.  A firm that maximizes sales revenue will typically charge a higher price than a firm that maximizes profits.

T  F   9.  An oligopolist facing a kinked demand curve will see a more elastic demand curve for price increases than for price decreases.

T  F  10.  Perfectly contestable markets are only possible when there are a large number of competing firms.

## SUPPLEMENTARY EXERCISE

The equations below for demand and total cost underlie the first problem in the Basic Exercises. Use these equations to derive explicit expressions for marginal cost, marginal revenue, and average cost. Now solve for the level of output that maximizes profits. Compare your answer with the results you obtained in the Basic Exercises.

$$Q = 2500 - 100\ P$$
(demand curve)
$$TC = 10,000 + 5\ Q$$
(total cost curve)

where $Q$ = total quantity, $P$ = price, and TC = total cost.

## ECONOMICS IN ACTION

New planes and the 1990 recession left airlines in the United States with more seats than passengers. Fierce price competition to fill seats resulted in large reported losses for the next three years. In the spring of 1992, Robert Crandall, president of American Airlines, introduced a fare structure that was intended to limit the number of low–priced tickets that airlines had been offering. *The New York Times* described Crandall's announcement as an attempt "to discipline the industry and the business traveler by curbing the use of discount fares and other loopholes." (May 29, 1992). Seven weeks later when Northwest Airlines tried offering half–priced tickets to families, American responded with a general two–for–one offer that was matched by other airlines. The result was a bargain for travelers and continued red ink for airlines. The *Times* described these actions by American as another warning by Crandall of his determination.

In the winter of 1993, Northwest Airlines tried again, offering discounts of 20 to 40 percent to groups of two to four travelers when they purchased 14-day advance tickets. When these discounts were matched by Delta and American, Northwest withdrew its fare reductions and also rescinded a fare increase that was to have been implemented following the availability of the discount fares. Michael Levine, Northwest's executive vice president for marketing, said, "Unfortunately, competitive response eliminated the possibility of realizing the revenue enhancement that we and the industry need. Our competitors choose to broaden our offer and risk industry pricing havoc." (Minneapolis *StarTribune.*)

1. How do the concepts of price leadership and a kinked demand curve help to explain:
   a) The fare structure that American Airlines tried to introduce in 1992.
   b) The response by other airlines to meet or exceed the price reductions offered by Northwest in 1992 and 1993.
   c) Northwest's decision to abandon its previously announced fare increase in 1993.

## STUDY QUESTIONS

1. How does monopolistic competition differ from perfect competition?

2. What is meant by the notion that monopolistic competition leads to excess capacity?

3. "As monopolistic competition leads to excess capacity, there will be an unambiguous social gain if government regulation reduces the number of firms and eliminates the excess capacity." Do you agree or disagree? Why?

4. What difference would it make if a firm acts to maximize profits or to maximize sales?

5. As a cartel is assumed to act to maximize profits, why do economists believe that cartels are difficult to establish and tend to self-destruct?

6. How can a kinked demand curve help explain price stickiness in an oligopolistic setting?

7. What is the maximin criterion for choosing among strategies in a game theory setting?

8. Even if there are few firms in a market, the power of these firms to charge high prices will be limited if markets are contestable. Why is free and easy exit as important to contestable markets as free and easy entry?

*C h a p t e r* **13**

# The Market Mechanism: Shortcomings and Remedies

## LEARNING OBJECTIVES

After completing this chapter, you should be able to:

- list the major shortcomings of free markets.
- explain why detrimental externalities mean that marginal private costs will understate marginal social costs.
- explain why the existence of externalities, whether beneficial or detrimental, will result in an inefficient allocation of resources.
- describe the important characteristics of public goods.
- explain why these characteristics mean that private profit-maximizing firms will not supply public goods.
- explain why some people believe that free markets are unlikely to result in an appropriate allocation of resources between the present and the future.
- explain how uneven productivity growth results in the cost disease of personal services.

## IMPORTANT TERMS AND CONCEPTS

Opportunity cost
Resource misallocation
Production possibilities frontier
Price above and below marginal cost
Externalities (detrimental and beneficial)
Marginal social cost and marginal private cost
Public goods
Private goods
Excludability

Depletability
Irreversible decisions
Asymmetric information
Principals
Agents
Rent seeking
Moral hazard
Cost disease of personal services

# CHAPTER REVIEW

This chapter lists seven issues often seen as shortcomings of unregulated markets. Some have been discussed in previous chapters, and several others will receive a more complete treatment later. The discussion here focuses on four of the seven: externalities, public goods, the trade-off between present and future consumption, and the cost disease of personal services.

(1) The material in Chapter 3 introduced the concept of an economy's *production possibilities frontier*. We saw that the slope of the frontier measured how much the output of one commodity must decrease in order to increase the production of another commodity. In other words, the slope of the production possibilities frontier measures the _____ cost of increasing the output of any one commodity.

(2) Chapter 10 explained how a market economy can lead to an *efficient allocation of resources*; that is, one where marginal utilities and marginal costs are equal. If the marginal utility of the last unit of some good is not equal to the marginal cost of producing that last unit, the result is a *misallocation of resources*. The virtue of competitive markets is that firms maximize profits by producing where price equals _____, and individuals maximize by consuming where price equals _____. Thus, our condition for an efficient allocation is automatically satisfied. An economy that satisfies all of the assumptions necessary for perfect competition will automatically result in an efficient allocation of resources. The economy will operate (on/inside) the production possibilities frontier.

(3) Many of the reasons mentioned at the beginning of the chapter may imply that an economy does not satisfy the conditions for perfect competition. In this case the wrong prices may get established, leading to an inefficient allocation of resources. If price is greater than marginal cost, the economy will tend to produce too (much/little) of a good to maximize consumer benefits. There may be a case for government intervention to allocate resources directly or, preferably, to help establish prices that will lead to an efficient allocation.

## Externalities

(4) Many economic activities impose incidental burdens or benefits on other individuals for which there is no compensation. These sorts of activities are said to involve _____. If an activity, such as pollution, harms others and there is no compensation, we say that there are _____ externalities. If an activity benefits others who do not pay for the benefits they receive, we say that there are _____ _____.

(5) Externalities imply that many activities are likely to have private benefits and costs that are different from social benefits and costs. In the case of detrimental externalities, social costs will be (higher/lower) than private costs, while in the case of beneficial externalities, social benefits will be _____ than private benefits.

(6) Private profit-maximizing firms will base their production decisions on (private/social) costs. If there are detrimental externalities, the result will be an (efficient/inefficient) use of resources. From a social viewpoint, too (much/little) of the commodity in question will be produced. In the case of beneficial externalities, unregulated markets are likely to produce (less/more) output than is socially desirable. Schemes for taxes and subsidies are, in principle, capable of adjusting private costs and benefits to more adequately reflect social costs and benefits.

## Public Goods

(7) Most goods provided by private profit-maximizing firms have two primary characteristics. The first is that the more of a good you use, the less there is for someone else. This characteristic is called _____. The second is that you must pay for goods in order to use them. This characteristic is called _____. Goods that have neither of these characteristics are called _____ goods. Things like national defense, police protection, beautiful parks, and clean streets are examples of such goods.

(8) Once public goods are provided to one individual, their benefits cannot easily be restricted to just a few people. It is (difficult/easy) to exclude nonpayers. As a result, it is difficult to get individuals to pay for the goods they can enjoy for free when someone else is paying for them. This is sometimes referred to as the free-_____ problem.

(9) Besides the problem of lack of excludability, one person's use of public goods, such as enjoying a park, does not usually deplete the supply for others. In technical language, the marginal cost of serving additional users is _____. This contrasts with private goods, where providing additional units of output does require additional resources and does entail a positive marginal cost. An efficient allocation of resources requires that price equal marginal social cost. The clear implication is that from an efficiency standpoint, public goods should be priced at _____ and one should not be surprised if profit-maximizing firms fail to provide public goods.

## Present and Future Consumption

The productive use of resources is time-specific. Loafing today will not make tomorrow twice as long. A machine that is idle one day does not mean that twice as many machine hours will be available the next day. While the use of resources is time-specific, the consumption of output is not. Output can be saved, either directly by adding to inventories in warehouses or indirectly by building plants and machines. Thus, an economy does have the ability to transfer consumption through time by acts of saving and investment.

The rate of interest is an important determinant of how much investment will actually take place. A number of observers have questioned whether the private economy will result in interest rates and investment spending that are socially optimal. In the real world, monetary and fiscal policies can be used to manipulate interest rates and hence to influence investment. Some observers, such as the English economist A. G. Pigou, have argued that people are simply shortsighted when it comes to saving for the future.

(10) Individual investment projects often entail great risk for the individual investors but little risk for society. Bankruptcy may wipe out an investor's financial investment, but it (does/does not) destroy buildings and machines. These capital goods will still be around for others to use. It has been argued that the high individual risk will result in a level of investment that is (less/more) than socially optimal.

(11) Many decisions, such as damming a canyon, are essentially _____, and some people are concerned that unregulated market decisions in these cases do not adequately represent the interests of future generations. These arguments suggest that even competitive markets are likely to result in inappropriate decisions about saving and investments.

## Cost Disease of Personal Services

(12) Many services—doctor visits, education, police protection—require mainly labor input and offer (limited/substantial) opportunities for increases in labor productivity. By contrast, increasing mechanization and technological innovations have resulted in substantial increases in labor productivity in the production of many commodities. Increased labor productivity has led to higher wages for workers in these industries. Since workers can move among occupations, the wages of teachers and police, for example, have had to increase to remain competitive with opportunities in other jobs. In manufacturing industries, increased labor productivity helps offset the cost pressures from higher wages. In service industries there are little or no increases in labor productivity to help contain cost pressures. The result is that many personal services have become more expensive over time because of the uneven pattern of increases in labor productivity. Increases in productivity always make an economy better off in the sense that it can now produce more of all goods, including personal services. But at the same time, society will find that lagging productivity in service industries means that the cost of these services has increased. Concerns about controlling costs may be misdirected if the major problem is the natural market response to differential productivity growth.

## IMPORTANT TERMS AND CONCEPTS QUIZ

Choose the best definition for the following terms.

1. _____ Opportunity cost
2. _____ Resource misallocation
3. _____ Production possibilities frontier
4. _____ Externalities
5. _____ Marginal private cost
6. _____ Marginal social cost
7. _____ Excludability
8. _____ Depletability
9. _____ Public good
10. _____ Private good
11. _____ Asymmetric information
12. _____ Principals
13. _____ Agents
14. _____ Rent seeking
15. _____ Moral hazard
16. _____ Cost disease of personal services

a. Tendency of clients who have the lowest risks to be the most likely insurance customers.
b. Results of activities that provide incidental harm or benefit to others.
c. Tendency of the real cost of services to increase because of difficulty of increasing productivity.
d. Decision makers who delegate their power to others.

e. Graph depicting the combinations of various goods that can be produced with available resources and existing technology.
f. Commodity or service whose benefits are not depleted by an additional user and for which it is difficult to exclude people from enjoying its benefits.
g. Unproductive activity in pursuit of profit.
h. Utility of an increase in output differs from its opportunity cost.
i. Parties to a transaction know different things about the item to be exchanged.
j. Marginal private cost plus costs imposed on others.
k. Commodity or service whose benefits are depleted by an additional user and for which people are excluded from its benefits unless they pay.
l. The ability to keep someone who does not pay from enjoying a commodity.
m. Tendency of insurance to encourage risk taking.
n. Share of marginal cost for an activity that those who engage in the activity pay.
o. Those to whom decision-making authority is delegated.
p. Commodity is used up when consumed.
q. Foregone value of next best alternative that is not chosen.

## BASIC EXERCISE

This exercise is designed to illustrate the cost disease of personal services.

Table 13-1 has spaces to compute the costs of producing both widgets and police services; both are assumed to be produced with only labor input. (Wages for police officers and for workers in the widget factory are assumed to be equal, as individuals can choose between these occupations.)

1. Fill in the missing spaces in the first column to determine the cost per widget of producing 240,000 widgets and the cost per hour of 200,000 hours of police services.
2. The first entry in the second column assumes that labor productivity in the production of widgets has risen by 4.17 percent. The earnings of widget workers and police officers are assumed to increase by the same percentage as productivity. Now fill in the rest of the second column. What has happened to the average cost of producing one widget? What about the cost of producing one hour of police services?
3. The first entry in column 3 assumes that the growth in average labor productivity continues for another 10 years. Again, the growth in earnings is assumed to match the growth in productivity. Fill in the rest of column 3. What is the increase in the cost of producing one widget?

_____ What about the cost of one hour of police services? _____.

4. One way to hold the line on police costs is to refuse to increase salaries for police officers. Another way is to reduce the number of police officers. What are the long-run implications of both these policies?

### TABLE 13-1
### COSTS OF PRODUCING 240,000 WIDGETS

|  | (1) | (2) | (3) |
| --- | --- | --- | --- |
| Widgets per worker | 1,920 | 2,000 | 3,000 |
| Number of workers[a] | 125 | _____ | _____ |
| Annual earnings per worker | $21,120 | $22,000 | $33,000 |
| Total labor costs (total cost) | _____ | _____ | _____ |
| Cost per widget | _____ | _____ | _____ |

### COSTS OF PRODUCING 200,000 HOURS OF POLICE SERVICES

|  | (1) | (2) | (3) |
| --- | --- | --- | --- |
| Hours per police officer | 2,000 | 2,000 | 2,000 |
| Number of police officers[b] | 100 | _____ | _____ |
| Annual earnings per police officer | $21,120 | $22,000 | $33,000 |
| Total labor cost (total cost) | _____ | _____ | _____ |
| Cost per hour of police services | _____ | _____ | _____ |

[a]240,000 + widgets per worker
[b]200,000 + hours per police officer

## SELF-TESTS FOR UNDERSTANDING

### Test A

Circle the most appropriate answer.

1. The condition for efficient resource allocation is
   a. MC = MR.
   b. P = Average Revenue.
   c. MU = MC.
   d. MU = Price.

2. Which of the following is a clear indicator of a misallocation of resources?
   a. Barney and Michelle, who subscribe to *Gourmet* magazine, despair over the increasing number of fast-food outlets.
   b. In the long run, farmer Fran makes zero economic profit.
   c. After careful study, economists have concluded that the economy of Arcadia is operating at a point inside its production possibilities frontier.
   d. The latest census survey indicates that the top 10 percent of the income distribution has an average income that is more than 12 times that of the bottom 10 percent.

3. The term *externalities* is used by economists to describe
   a. economic decisions by foreign governments.
   b. occupants of extraterrestrial space ships.
   c. all economic activity that takes place outside the classroom.
   d. activities that impose costs or benefits on third parties.

4. Economists expect profit–maximizing competitive firms to expand production as long as price exceeds
    a. marginal social cost.
    b. marginal utility.
    c. marginal private cost.
    d. average cost.

5. Which of the following is an externality?
    a. Imperfect information.
    b. Your pride in the new stereo system you just purchased at a bargain price.
    c. Natural monopolies, such as the local electric utility.
    d. The new road built for the NASA tracking station that has substantially reduced transportation costs for local farmers.

6. A detrimental externality arises when
    a. the actions of a firm provide unintended benefits for third parties.
    b. having bought insurance, Jason figures he doesn't need to buy as sturdy a bike lock.
    c. a firm's managers cannot be closely monitored by stockholders.
    d. the actions of a firm impose costs on families living near the firm's plants.

7. In the presence of detrimental externalities, marginal private cost is usually
    a. less than marginal social cost.
    b. equal to marginal social cost.
    c. greater than marginal social cost.

8. Economists argue that if the production of paper is associated with detrimental externalities, a free market will likely
    a. produce more paper than is socially desirable.
    b. produce less paper than is socially desirable.
    c. produce the socially optimal quantity of paper in spite of the detrimental externality.

9. If the production of gizmos involves beneficial externalities, then it is likely that
    a. marginal private benefits are less than marginal social benefits.
    b. a free market will produce too many gizmos.
    c. a tax on the production of gizmos will lead to a more efficient allocation.
    d. the use of gizmos does not involve depletion.

10. Economists define public goods as
    a. all things the government spends money on.
    b. economic activities that impose costs or benefits on third parties.
    c. goods and services that many people can enjoy at the same time and from which it is difficult to exclude potential customers who do want to pay.
    d. goods and services that should receive public subsidy such as improved health care and better housing for poor families.

11. Economists expect that profit–maximizing firms in competitive markets will produce _____ public goods.
    a. too few
    b. too many
    c. about the right quantity
    d. no

12. For a pure public good, the marginal cost of serving an additional user is equal to
    a. marginal social cost.
    b. marginal private cost.
    c. zero.
    d. marginal utility.

13. Which of the following does not have the characteristics of a public good?
    a. Clean rivers.
    b. Visits to the doctor.
    c. Police and fire protection.
    d. Unscrambled radio and television signals.

14. The "free-rider" problem refers to
    a. the difficulty of stopping kids from sneaking onto the local merry-go-round.
    b. the difficulty of getting people to voluntarily contribute to pay for public goods.
    c. using subsidies to encourage the production of goods with beneficial externalities.
    d. increasing problems with hitchhikers on the interstate highways.

15. Which of the following is an example of rent seeking?
    a. The efforts of lobbyists to get Congress to restrict the import of foreign steel.
    b. The hours Juan and Ramona spend working in their own restaurant.
    c. The time and effort Julie spends studying to be a doctor.
    d. Cleon's efforts to find an inexpensive apartment before school starts.

16. As used by economists, the term *moral hazard* refers to the
    a. temptations of large cities on impressionable teen–agers.
    b. state of much television programming
    c. tendency of insurance to make people less concerned about risky behavior.
    d. widespread incidence of sexually transmitted diseases among single men and women.

17. Decisions by company managers that make their own lives more comfortable at the cost of reducing stockholder profits are examples of
    a. moral hazards.
    b. principal-agent problems.
    c. deterimental externalities.
    d. public goods.

18. Which of the following explains the cost disease of personal services?
    a. The supply effects of price controls, such as rent control.
    b. The existence of monopoly elements in the economy.
    c. Detrimental externalities.
    d. The uneven prospects for improved labor productivity in different sectors of the economy.

19. Which of the following is *not* likely to suffer from the cost disease of personal services?
    a. Individual piano lessons.
    b. The production of television sets.
    c. Small liberal arts colleges that maintain an unchanged student-faculty ratio.
    d. Orchestras and symphonies.

20. Which of the following is *not* an argument that free markets will result in an inappropriate amount of saving and investment?
    a. Investment projects are often riskier to individuals than to the community.
    b. During periods of inflation, nominal interest rates will rise to incorporate expectations of continuing inflations.
    c. Due to "defective telescopic faculties," people do not give enough consideration to the future.
    d. Many decisions concerning natural resources are made without enough consideration given to their irreversible consequences.

## Test B

Circle T or F for true or false.

T  F  1.  An unregulated market economy would never have business cycles.

T  F  2.  Externalities, whether beneficial or detrimental, imply that marginal social cost is always less than marginal private cost.

T  F  3.  An activity that causes damage to someone else and for which there is no compensation is said to involve a detrimental externality.

T  F  4.  A beneficial externality is likely to result in marginal private benefits exceeding marginal social benefits.

T  F  5.  Economists define public goods as anything for which the government spends money.

T  F  6.  The fact that it is difficult to restrict the use of public goods to those who are willing to pay is the problem of depletability.

T  F  7.  The provision of public goods is complicated by the "free-rider" problem.

T  F  8.  The fact that public goods are not depleted by use implies that the marginal cost of providing the goods to one more consumer is zero.

T  F  9.  The interest rate plays an important role in the allocation of resources between the present and the future, because it affects the profitability of investment projects.

T  F  10.  Many investment projects will entail less risk for the individual investor than for the community as a whole.

## SUPPLEMENTARY EXERCISES

1.  Consider the economy of Beethovia, which produces two goods: widgets and music recitals. Widgets are manufactured with capital and labor according to the following production function:

$$W = 60 \ L^{1/2} \ K^{1/2},$$

where $L$ = number of workers producing widgets and $K$ = number of machines. Music recitals are labor intensive and produced according to the following production function:

$$M = 50 \times L.$$

Initially there are 40,000 workers in Beethovia, meaning that the sum of labor allocated to the production of widgets or recitals cannot exceed 40,000. Initially, there are 22,500 machines, or $K$ = 22,500.

a.  Draw the production possibilities frontier for Beethovia showing the trade-off between the production of widgets and recitals. (It is probably easiest to arbitrarily fix the number of recitals and then calculate the maximum production of widgets with the remaining labor and all the machines.)

b.  Competitive markets have resulted in 39,601 widget workers and 399 musicians. At this allocation, what is the marginal product and average product of labor in the production of widgets? In the production of recitals?

c. Saving and investment by the people of Beethovia have increased the number of machines to 28,900. At the initial allocation of labor, but with the new number of machines, what is the marginal and average product of labor in the production of widgets? What has happened to the productivity of workers in the production of recitals?

d. What has happened to the opportunity cost of music recitals; that is, what is the new slope of the production possibilities frontier at the allocation specified in question b? To answer this question, either draw a new production possibilities frontier or derive a mathematical expression for the slope of the frontier.

e. If you have answered question d correctly, you should have determined that the cost of recitals has increased. Recitals suffer from the cost disease of personal services. At the same time, how can you show that the increase in productivity has made Beethovia unambiguously richer?

2. Go to the library or bookstore and get a copy of *Encounters with the Archdruid* (New York: Farrar, Stoav's and Giroux, 1971) by John McPhee. The book reports on three encounters between David Brower, who was president of the Sierra Club, and other individuals who want to dam the Colorado River, build a copper mine in the Cascades, and develop Hilton Head Island. Many think that McPhee's description of the raft trip down the Colorado River with Brower and Floyd Dominy, who was head of the Bureau of Reclamation, is especially good.

Whose position do you favor?

Is Brower always right? Is he ever right?

## ECONOMICS IN ACTION

### Standards or Taxes

In 1975, after the first increase in oil prices, the Energy Policy and Conservation Act mandated minimum corporate average fuel economy (CAFE) standards for new passenger cars sold in the United States. Originally established at 18.5 miles per gallon (mpg) for 1978, the CAFE standard is now close to 30 mpg. An increase to 40 mpg by the beginning of the next century has been proposed. The CAFE standards were adopted in an effort to reduce American dependency on foreign oil. Increases are now proposed to help reduce carbon dioxide emissions.

Writing in *The Journal of Economic Perspectives*, Spring 1992, economist Robert Crandall compares the efficiency of CAFE standards with that of a fuel tax. Crandall notes that cars consume 55 percent of motor vehicle fuel and account for about 13 percent of carbon emissions. New cars make up about 7 percent of all cars on the road and account for 9 percent of passenger car miles driven. As petroleum is used for things other than motor vehicle fuels, Crandall estimates that new cars account for about 2 percent of annual petroleum consumption.

He argues that while CAFE standards will eventually improve the fuel efficiency of cars, they have some perverse effects in the short run. By increasing the cost of new cars, higher CAFE standards induce some drivers to hold on to their less efficient older cars. By lowering the marginal cost of driving, higher CAFE standards might increase the number of miles driven by new car owners. In contrast, a fuel tax has opposite effects. It provides an incentive to get rid of older, less efficient cars for newer cars while increasing the marginal cost of driving for all drivers. Crandall argues that a fuel tax also has the edge on safety considerations as it leads to a greater reduction in total miles driven and induces less vehicle downsizing than higher CAFE standards. While some worry about the impact of higher gasoline taxes on the poor, Crandall cites research that suggests automatic adjustment of transfer payments to increases in the consumer price index may offset higher gasoline taxes for poor households.

CAFE standards may be preferred by legislators because their cost is hidden in the price of new cars. An increased gasoline tax would be quite visible. Crandall cites a study by Charles River Associates that estimates it would take a tax of 25¢ a gallon to match the fuel savings of a 40 mpg CAFE standard. If the tax were to be levied on all petroleum consumption, the study by Charles River Associates estimates that it need only be about 10¢ to induce an equivalent reduction in petroleum use. Crandall estimates that CAFE standards would end up costing 7 to 10 times as much as a broad–based petroleum tax.

    1. Which do you favor, higher CAFE standards or higher gasoline taxes? Which do you think would be more effective in reducing oil consumption? Which do you think is fairer? Why?

## STUDY QUESTIONS

1. Why do economists argue that externalities, whether beneficial or detrimental, are likely to lead to a misallocation of resources?

2. Why does a free market tend to overproduce goods with detrimental externalities?

3. How can the price system help correct the problems of externalities?

4. What is the difference between private and public goods?

5. What are the distinguishing characteristics of a public good as compared with a private good?

6. Why can't we leave the provision of public goods to profit–maximizing firms?

7. Do you believe that unregulated private markets will save too little or too much? Why?

8. Colleges and universities have been urged to hold tuition increases under the inflation rate. What does the concept of the cost disease of personal services suggest would happen if such a policy were followed for the next 10 years?

*C h a p t e r* **14**

# Real Firms and Their Financing: Stocks and Bonds

## LEARNING OBJECTIVES

After completing this chapter, you should be able to:

- explain the major advantages and disadvantages of alternative forms of business organization.
- explain why investors in common stock are not penalized in the form of lower rates of return from the double taxation of corporate dividends.
- explain how double taxation can affect the business investment decisions of corporations and may lead to inefficient resource allocation.
- explain the advantages of plowback as a source of funds to a corporation.
- explain why bond prices fall when interest rates go up and vice versa.
- explain how the use of stocks or bonds shifts risk between a corporation and financial investors.
- describe how portfolio diversification can reduce the risk faced by a financial investor.
- explain why the stock market is of critical importance to the financing of corporations even though new stock issues account for only a small proportion of new funds raised by corporations.
- discuss the advantages and disadvantages of corporate takeovers.
- discuss the role of speculation both in the economy and in the securities markets.

## IMPORTANT TERMS AND CONCEPTS

Proprietorship
Unlimited liability
Partnership
Corporation
Limited liability
Double taxation
Plowback or retained earnings

Common stock
Bond
Portfolio diversification
Stock exchanges
Takeovers
Speculation
Random walk

## CHAPTER REVIEW

This chapter explores the advantages and disadvantages of alternative legal forms of business organization. Special attention is given to the different ways in which corporations raise funds and to the markets on which corporate securities are traded.

(1)　　　A business owned and operated by an individual is called a _____. This is by far the most common form of business organization in the United States. When a firm's ownership and decision making are shared by a fixed number of individuals, the business is called a _____. Another form of business organization is one in which the firm has the legal status of a fictional individual and is owned by a large number of stockholders and run by an elected board of directors and officers. This form of organization is called a _____. A major advantage here is that stockholders, the legal owners of the business, are not liable for the firm's debts. Having _____ liability makes it possible for corporations to raise very large sums of money in the pursuit of profits.

　　　A corporation that raises funds by selling shares of ownership and offering a stake in profits is issuing

(2) (stock/bonds). If a corporation issues securities that promise to pay fixed sums as interest and principal, it is issuing _____. Corporations can also borrow directly from large financial institutions, such as banks or insurance companies. The most common way of raising funds is to directly reinvest part of a corporation's profits. This method of raising funds is called _____. Corporations typically prefer to use plowback to finance corporate investments as it avoids the cost and scrutiny that accompany new issues of stocks and bonds.

　　　Assuming a firm does not become bankrupt, a bond that is held to maturity offers the bondholder a

(3) fixed stream of payments. Investing in stock promises dividend payments and stock prices that (are/are not) known at the time of purchase. The greater uncertainty of dividends and stock prices as compared to bond payments leads many investors to conclude that stocks are (more/less) risky than bonds. From the viewpoint of a firm, (bonds/stocks) are more risky, because a failure to (meet bond payments/pay dividends) can force bankruptcy.

　　　This comparison understates the riskiness to individual investors of investing in bonds. If a bond must be sold before maturity and interest rates have changed, the market price of the bond will also change. If interest rates have risen, existing bonds with low coupon payments will look less attractive

(4) unless their price (rises/falls). Holders of these bonds will suffer a (gain/loss). Conversely, if interest rates have fallen, competition for existing bonds with high coupon payments will (increase/decrease) the price of existing bonds.

　　　Shares of stock offer investors returns in the form of dividend payments and/or changes in the stock price. Investors have the option of buying shares of only one company or shares of several companies.

(5) Buying shares of several companies is an example of _____. Institutional investors who use computers to make automatic trading decisions are engaging in _____ trading. One assumes control of an existing corporation by buying a sufficient number of current shares of stock. When such an action is contested, it is called a _____ battle and can be an effective way to remove incompetent management. There is concern that these struggles lead to wasteful and costly actions on both sides.

　　　Stocks and bonds are traded in markets that sometimes have a specific location, such as the New York Stock Exchange, but they are also traded by dealers and brokers who keep track, by telephone or

(6) computer, of the latest price changes. New stock issues (are/are not) usually sold through established exchanges. Two important functions served by established exchanges include (1) reducing the _____ of stock ownership by providing a secondary market in existing shares and (2) determining the current price of a company's stock. In the latter role, established exchanges help allocate the economy's resources to those firms that, in the market's judgment, are expected to make the most profitable use of those resources.

　　　Speculators are not much different from most investors who hope to profit from increases in stock prices. From a general perspective, speculation serves two important functions. First, it can help decrease price fluctuations. Buying at low prices in anticipation of being able to sell next year at high prices will,

(7) in fact, make prices today (<u>higher/lower</u>) than they otherwise would be and will also make prices next year _____ than they otherwise would be. The second function of speculation is that it can provide _____ for those who want to avoid taking risks. Commodity speculators will agree now on a price to be paid or buying crops next year, thus insuring a farmer against the adverse effects of a decrease in price. Other speculators may agree now on a price at which to sell crops next year to a milling company, thus insuring the miller against the adverse effects of an increase in price.

    The behavior of individual stock prices has long fascinated investors. Much time and effort is spent trying to forecast price movements. Some investors look at things like a firm's earnings and its current stock price; others plot recent stock prices and try to discover laws of motion in their graphs. Economists have also studied the changes in individual stock prices. Much of this research supports the conclusion

(8) that changes in stock prices are essentially unpredictable; that is, they look like a _____ _____. Such a result could arise because of essentially random waves of buying and selling as investors try to outguess each other. It could also arise from investors' careful study and analysis of individual companies, study that is so complete that all anticipated events are fully reflected in current stock prices. The expectation today of higher profits tomorrow raises stock prices (<u>today/tomorrow</u>). In this view, changes in stock prices can only reflect currently unanticipated events, events that will likely look like random events. This viewpoint has been formalized in the hypothesis of "efficient markets." Much advanced research in financial economics is concerned with testing this hypothesis.

## IMPORTANT TERMS AND CONCEPTS QUIZ

Choose the best definition for the following terms.

1. _____ Proprietorship
2. _____ Unlimited liability
3. _____ Partnership
4. _____ Corporation
5. _____ Limited liability
6. _____ Double taxation
7. _____ Retained earnings (plowback)
8. _____ Common stock
9. _____ Bond
10. _____ Portfolio diversification
11. _____ Takeovers
12. _____ Speculation
13. _____ Random walk
14. _____ Stock exchange

a. Change in variable is completely unpredictable.

b. Legal obligation to repay company debts only with money owners have already invested in the firm.

c. Purchase of risky assets in anticipation of favorable price changes.

d. Corporation's promise to pay a fixed sum at maturity plus annual interest.

e. Firm owned by an individual.

f. Portion of a corporation's profits that management returns to shareholders.

g. Holding a number and variety of stocks, bonds, and other assets in an attempt to find offsetting risks.

h. A group of individuals not currently in control of a firm buys enough stock to gain control.

i. Legal obligation to repay company's debts with whatever resources owners may have.

j. Piece of paper that gives holder a share of ownership in a company.

k. Firm owned by a fixed number of individuals.

l. Portion of a corporation's profits that management decides to keep and reinvest.

m. Firm owned by stockholders, with the legal status of a fictitious individual.

n. Taxes on corporate profits before distribution to shareholders and taxes on dividends received by shareholders.

o. Organized market for trading corporate shares.

## BASIC EXERCISES

### 1. Double Taxation

This exercise is designed to illustrate how market forces adjust stock prices to reflect alternative yields available to investors and to ensure that the returns to shareholders are not reduced by the double taxation of corporate profits.

The XYZ Corporation earns $80 million in profits and pays $28 million in profits tax to the government, leaving $52 million that is paid out as a $4 dividend on each of 13 million shares of stock. (XYZ does not plowback any of its after-tax profits.) Investors in XYZ stock have the option of investing in corporate bonds and earning a return of 10 percent on which they will have to pay income taxes, just as they must pay taxes on dividend income.

| Stock Price | Dividend Before Taxes | Dividend Yield (col. 2 + col. 1) |
|---|---|---|
| $ 25 | $4 | _____ |
| 40 | 4 | _____ |
| 64 | 4 | _____ |
| 100 | 4 | _____ |

a. Fill in the blank column to compute the dividend yield on a share of XYZ stock at various prices.
b. Assume that the XYZ dividend has always been $4 and is expected to remain $4. Further, since XYZ does not plowback any of its after-tax profits, the price of XYZ stock is not expected to change. If investors require the same return on shares of XYZ stock as they do on corporate bonds, what will be the price of XYZ stock? _____ Do investors in XYZ stock receive a lower rate of return because of the double taxation of corporate income—once as corporate profits and then again as dividends? Why or why not?
c. What is likely to happen to the price of XYZ stock if the interest rate of government bonds rises to 16 percent? Falls to 6.25 percent?
d. Suddenly and unexpectedly, the president of XYZ announces that oil has been discovered on company property. The revenues from this discovery will double profits for the foreseeable future. Furthermore, XYZ announces that starting next year and continuing into the future, the dividend per share will also double to $8. Why will the price of XYZ stock rise immediately rather than waiting until next year when higher dividend payments start?
e. If everyone believes that dividends on XYZ stock will double beginning next year, and if alternative investments continue to yield 10 percent, what is the likely new stock price? Why?

### 2. Portfolio Diversification

This exercise is meant to illustrate the principle of diversification. Assume you invested $10,000 on December 31, 1991, and sold your holdings on December 31, 1992. Table 14-1 shows the results of dividing your investment among each of 10 stocks. The entries in Table 14-2 assume that your $10,000 was invested in just one company. Column (1) shows the number of shares purchased on December 31, 1991. Column (2) reports stock prices on December 31, 1991.

a. Column (3) has spaces for the value of your stock holdings on December 31, 1992. Complete this column in both tables by multiplying stock prices on December 31, 1992, by the number of shares; that is, multiply each entry in column (2) by the corresponding entry in column (1).
b. Complete column (5) by adding the dividends you received in 1992, column (4), to the value of your stock holdings in column (3). Column (5) shows the total return, dividends plus the change in stock prices. Be sure to sum all of the entries in column (5) for Table 14-1.
c. Each entry in column (5), Table 14-2, shows how you would have done had you invested all your money in the stock of one company. The sum for column (5), Table 14-1, shows the results of a ten-stock portfolio. How do your results illustrate the link between portfolio diversification and risk?

**TABLE 14-1**

| Company | (1)<br>Number of<br>Shares if<br>Investing<br>$1,000<br>12/31/91 | (2)<br>Price per<br>Share on<br>12/31/92 | (3)<br>Value of<br>Shares on<br>12/31/92<br><br>(1) × (2) | (4)<br>Dividends<br>Received<br>during 1992 | (5)<br>Total<br>Returns for<br>1992<br><br>(3) + (4) |
|---|---|---|---|---|---|
| AT&T | 25.56 | $51.00 | | $ 33.74 | |
| Boeing | 20.94 | $40.13 | | $ 20.94 | |
| Chrysler | 85.11 | $32.00 | | $ 51.06 | |
| Citicorp | 96.39 | $22.25 | | $578.31 | |
| Du Pont | 21.45 | $47.13 | | $ 37.32 | |
| Exxon | 16.43 | $61.13 | | $ 46.49 | |
| IBM | 11.24 | $50.38 | | $ 54.38 | |
| Maytag | 65.04 | $14.88 | | $ 32.52 | |
| Reebok | 30.19 | $34.00 | | $ 9.06 | |
| Xerox | 14.60 | $79.25 | | $ 43.80 | |

Total Portfolio  _____

**TABLE 14-2**

| Company | (1)<br>Number of<br>Shares if<br>Investing<br>$10,000<br>12/31/91 | (2)<br>Price per<br>Share on<br>12/31/92 | (3)<br>Value of<br>Shares on<br>12/31/92<br><br>(1) × (2) | (4)<br>Dividends<br>Received<br>during 1992 | (5)<br>Total<br>Returns for<br>1992<br><br>(3) + (4) |
|---|---|---|---|---|---|
| AT&T | 255.60 | $51.00 | | $ 33.74 | |
| Boeing | 209.40 | $40.13 | | $ 20.94 | |
| Chrysler | 851.10 | $32.00 | | $ 51.06 | |
| Citicorp | 963.90 | $22.25 | | $578.31 | |
| Du Pont | 214.50 | $47.13 | | $ 37.32 | |
| Exxon | 164.30 | $61.13 | | $ 46.49 | |
| IBM | 112.40 | $50.38 | | $ 54.38 | |
| Maytag | 650.40 | $14.88 | | $ 32.52 | |
| Reebok | 301.90 | $34.00 | | $ 9.06 | |
| Xerox | 146.00 | $79.25 | | $ 43.80 | |

## SELF-TESTS FOR UNDERSTANDING
### Test A

Circle the most appropriate answer.

1. Most business firms are
   a. corporations.
   b. proprietorships.
   c. partnerships.
   d. financed by issuing stock.

2. What form of business accounts for the largest share of output?
   a. Corporations.
   b. Limited partnerships.
   c. Partnerships.
   d. Proprietorships.

3. Which one of the following is *not* true of proprietorships?
   a. The proprietor has complete and full personal control of the business.
   b. Limited liability on the part of the proprietor for the debts of the business.
   c. Income is only taxed once.
   d. Few legal complications.

4. Disadvantages of partnerships include all but which one of the following?
   a. Unlimited liability of partners for the debts of the partnership.
   b. Pooling of the resources and expertise of partners.
   c. The difficulty of getting partners to agree on important issues.
   d. Legal difficulties associated with changes in partners.

5. What form of business offers owners limited liability for the debts of the business?
   a. Corporations.
   b. Partnerships.
   c. Proprietorships.

6. In which form of business is income subject to double taxation?
   a. Proprietorship.
   b. Partnership.
   c. Corporation.

7. Ways in which corporations can raise money include all but which one of the following?
   a. Issuing shares of stock.
   b. Borrowing money in the form of bonds.
   c. The reinvestment, or plowback, of profits.
   d. Paying dividends.

8. Which of the following is the most important source of new funds for corporations?
   a. New stock issues.
   b. Corporate bonds.
   c. Retained earnings.
   d. Bank loans.

9. Why do economists expect that corporations will ignore business opportunities offering profitable but limited returns?
   a. The difficulty of getting agreement from millions of owners.
   b. The double taxation of corporate income.
   c. Limited liability for stockholders.
   d. Corporate managers will be more concerned with their welfare than that of the stockholders.

10. If held to maturity and there is no risk of bankruptcy, bonds offer investors
    a. greater returns because interest payments as opposed to dividend payments are not subject to double taxation.
    b. unknown interest payments that will fluctuate with profits.
    c. returns that are usually greater than those available from stocks.
    d. known interest payments.

11. A decrease in interest rates will tend to
    a. increase bond prices.
    b. lower bond prices.
    c. have no effect on bond prices.

12. Emerson purchased a newly issued General Electric bond several years ago with coupon payments offering an interest rate of 10 percent. Since then, market interest rates on similar bonds have fallen to 8 percent. Which of the following is true?
    a. The market value of the bonds that Emerson bought will have increased from the price he paid.
    b. If held to maturity and General Electric does not default, Emerson will earn 8 percent on his investment.
    c. Anyone purchasing such bonds today at their current market price and holding them to maturity can expect to earn 10 percent on the investment.
    d. If Emerson sold his bonds today at their current market price, he would have to sell them for less than he paid.

13. Five million shares of stock are outstanding in XYZ Corporation. If the price of XYZ stock rises by $1, then
    a. XYZ Corporation will have $5 million more to invest or use to pay higher dividends.
    b. existing shareholders will benefit by $1 a share.
    c. investors who hold XYZ bonds will have suffered a capital loss.
    d. XYZ Corporation will owe federal tax on the increased stock price.

14. A limit order specifies
    a. the number of shares you will buy at the prevailing market price.
    b. trading between bonds and stocks.
    c. the price at which you are willing to buy or sell shares of stock.
    d. the time at which you are willing to buy or sell shares of stock.

15. Program trading refers to
    a. a systematic plan for building an investment portfolio.
    b. individuals who purchase stocks recommended by individuals appearing on the television program *Wall Street Week*.
    c. the use of computers to design and execute buying and selling of stocks.
    d. the activities of market specialists.

16. Which of the following $100,000 investments offers the most diversification?
    a. $100,000 of Boeing stock.
    b. $100,000 of New York City bonds.
    c. $100,000 of gold.
    d. $25,000 invested in each of the following: Kodak, Sears, Du Pont, and Shell Oil.

17. The important economic functions of organized stock exchanges include all but which one of the following?
    a. Offering investors insurance against the risk of changes in stock prices.
    b. Reducing the risk of purchasing stock by offering investors a place to sell their shares should they need the funds for some other purpose.
    c. Helping allocate the economy's resources, since companies with high current stock prices will find it easier to raise additional funds to pursue investment opportunities.

18. If Maxine is to be a successful speculator she must
   a. buy during a period of excess supply and sell during a period of excess supply.
   b. buy during a period of excess supply and sell during a period of excess demand.
   c. buy during a period of excess demand and sell during a period of excess demand.
   d. buy during a period of excess demand and sell during a period of excess supply.

19. Advantages to existing stockholders from takeovers can include all but which one of the following?
   a. The elimination of incompetent management.
   b. Increasing the price of an undervalued company.
   c. A greater chance that low earnings will grow to match their potential.
   d. The time and effort of top management in responding to the takeover bid.

20. To say that stock prices follow a random walk is to say that
   a. stock prices are easily predicted given information about past prices.
   b. the predictions of stock analysts are uniformly better than those of individual investors.
   c. day–to–day changes in stock prices are essentially unpredictable.
   d. over the long run, individual investors will only lose money by buying stocks.

## Test B

Circle T or F for true or false.

T F 1. Corporations, while constituting a minority of the *number* of business organizations, are the most important form of organization when measured by total sales.

T F 2. When measured by the number of firms, proprietorships are the most common form of business organization in the United States.

T F 3. The double taxation of corporate income—once as corporate profits and again as dividends—means that investors in the stock market must settle for a lower rate of return on stocks.

T F 4. Assuming no bankruptcy, a corporate bond is a riskless investment even if the bond must be sold before maturity.

T F 5. Any individual who wants to buy or sell shares of stock can do so by walking onto the floor of the New York Stock Exchange and announcing her intentions.

T F 6. Whenever a share of Xerox stock is sold on the New York Stock Exchange, Xerox gets the proceeds.

T F 7. A corporation that decides to issue stock will typically offer the shares initially through one of the regional stock exchanges.

T F 8. Established stock exchanges, such as the New York Stock Exchange, are really just a form of legalized gambling and serve no social function.

T F 9. The finding that stock prices follow a random walk implies that investing in stock is essentially a gamble.

T F 10. Profitable speculation involves buying high and selling low.

## SUPPLEMENTARY EXERCISES

### 1. Stocks and Bonds

Consult the financial page of any newspaper that lists bonds. Find the listing for several regular bonds of corporations with a similar maturity date sometime past 2005. Write down their coupon rate, current yield, and market price. Also note stock prices for the same companies. After three months, again check the stock prices and the current yield and price of the bonds. Note if any increase (or decrease) in the current yield is matched by an opposite movement in the bond price. Had you actually bought these bonds, would you now have a gain or loss? What if you had bought shares of stock? Have all or most of the bond prices moved together? Have all the stock prices moved together? (It would not be surprising if the prices of bonds of different corporations rose or fell together. Stock prices are less likely to change together. Can you explain why?)

2. **Bond Prices and Interest Rates**

   The market price of a $1,000 bond paying interest once a year can be calculated by computing the present value of future payments:

   $$\text{Price} = \sum_{t=1}^{N} \frac{\text{INT}}{(1+i)^t} + \frac{1,000}{(1+i)^N}$$

   where Price = market price, $i$ = market interest rate, $N$ = number of years to maturity, and INT = interest payment. See the appendix to chapter 15 for a discussion of this equation.

   It may be easiest to complete the following exercises if you have access to a microcomputer or sophisticated hand calculator.

   a. Show that if INT = $80 and $i$ = .08, the market price of this bond will be $1,000 for all values of $N$.

   b. Now vary $i$, holding INT constant at $80 and $N$ constant at 25 years. Note how the price of a bond issued with a coupon payment of $80 changes as market interest rates change. You should find that price is less than $1,000 when $i$ is greater than .08 and price is greater than $1,000 when $i$ is less than .08.

   c. Choose a particular value for $i$, say .07, and see how the difference in price from the original $1,000 varies as $N$ varies from one year to 25 years. You should find that the difference in price is greater as $N$ gets larger; that is, longer term bonds show a greater change in price for a given change in interest rates.

## ECONOMICS IN ACTION

### If You're So Smart, Why Aren't You Rich?

Can you or your stock broker consistently beat the market? Many economists would answer no unless you have inside information, on which it is illegal to trade. Presumptions about the inability of individuals to beat the market are closely linked to notions of efficient markets and random walks. The notion of efficient markets implies that stock prices reflect all available information about future profitability. Should the profit prospects from investing in stock X improve, the price of stock X should rise as investors and stock managers seek to take advantage of this information. In this way all available information is incorporated into current stock prices. On this view, stock prices change only as new information becomes available. New information that is easily foreseen would already be incorporated into stock prices. The conclusion is that new information must be unpredictable and changes in the price of individual stocks will follow a random walk. Some stocks are riskier than others and need to offer a higher expected return to compensate for the possibility that they may turn out to be a bust. Riskier stocks with above average returns are not a violation of the efficient markets hypothesis, as the risk of such investments is part of currently available information.

Does all this mean that one cannot make money in the stock market? No, one can make money, but once you have decided how much risk you are willing to accept, do not expect that you or your stockbroker can consistently do better than other investors. In any given year some investors and investment professionals will do better than others. The efficient markets hypothesis suggests that over a period of years no one will consistently beat the market. Some have likened beating the market to guessing whether a fair coin toss will come up heads or tails. Imagine you asked this question of everyone attending a Michigan-Notre Dame football game in Ann Arbor. If half the crowd said heads and half said tails, more than 50,000 people would have predicted the coin toss correctly. After 12 flips about 24 people would have a perfect record of prediction. Do they know something we don't know? Would you want to bet on their continued ability to predict?

The discussion of efficient markets has a certain surface plausibility, but how does one test whether markets are in fact efficient? Economists have defined three notions of efficiency—weak, semi-strong, and strong. Weak efficiency requires that information on past prices of stock X is of no use in forecasting. Semi-strong efficiency requires that no publicly available information is helpful, while strong efficiency says that no relevant information, published or not, helps to forecast stock prices. Tests for various forms of efficiency involve elaborate computer estimation and/or simulation of trading rules based on past prices and other information. Remember that any profit from a particular trading rule has to be sufficient to offset the trading costs of implementing the rule.

As computers have become more powerful it has been possible to test for a wider range of trading rules. In a recent survey[1], *The Economist* noted a number of apparent anomalies, cases where there appear to be small but predictable returns in excess of the market average. One of the best known of these is the so-called "January effect" where portfolios of the shares of small companies have consistently done better in January than the stock market as a whole. What explains such inefficiencies? No one is sure. If the decisions of a sufficient number of investors are determined by mood and feeling rather than hard-headed analysis, it might be possible that inefficiencies could persist with smart traders winning at the expense of others. It may also be that the identification of trading rules that beat the market will work to eliminate their profit potential as they are adopted on a wide scale basis.

What is an individual investor to do?

---

[1] "Beating the Market", *The Economist*, December 5, 1992. You might also want to look at the symposium of papers on the stock market and speculative bubbles in the Spring 1990 issue of *The Journal of Economic Perspectives*.

## STUDY QUESTIONS

1. The text points out that although a small percentage of business firms, corporations account for a much larger percentage of business sales and output. This difference arises because the biggest firms are corporations. Why are the biggest firms corporations?

2. How can it be that investors in stock are not penalized by the double taxation of income to corporations?

3. Why is most business investment financed by plowback or retained earnings rather than by new stock issues or bonds?

4. What explains the inverse relationship between market interest rates and bond prices?

5. Why is it often said that bonds are riskier than stock to a corporation but stocks are riskier than bonds for investors?

6. Why do economists argue that portfolio diversification reduces the risk of investing in stocks?

7. What is the economic role of the stock market if new stock issues are seldom used to finance business investment?

8. Many people would like to regulate speculators on the belief that they are greedy predators who profit only on the misfortune of others. Why do economists often disagree with this assessment?

## Chapter 15

# Pricing the Factors of Production

## LEARNING OBJECTIVES

After completing this chapter, you should be able to:

- explain why the demand curve for a factor of production is the downward sloping portion of its marginal revenue product curve.
- explain why the demand for inputs is a derived demand.
- distinguish between investment and capital.
- explain how changes in interest rates may affect the profitability of specific investment decisions and hence the demand for funds.
- explain who gains, who loses, and why, under an effective usury ceiling.
- distinguish between land rents and economic rents.
- identify input units that receive economic rent, given supply curves of various slopes.
- explain why the fact that apartment buildings need to be maintained and that they can be reproduced at close to constant cost implies that, in the long run, rent control measures will be self-defeating.
- explain why, in the real world, profits are likely to offer returns in excess of the interest rate.
- explain how the concept of economic rent is relevant to issues concerning the taxation of profits.

## IMPORTANT TERMS AND CONCEPTS

Factors of production
Entrepreneurship
Marginal productivity principle
Marginal physical product
Marginal revenue product
Derived demand
Usury laws
Investment
Capital
Interest
Discounting
Marginal land
Economic rent
Entrepreneurs
Risk bearing
Invention versus innovation

## CHAPTER REVIEW

This chapter initiates the discussion of input prices by considering what determines the rental price of money, the rental price of land, and the income of entrepreneurs. If this material is combined with the material in Chapter 16 on wages—the rental price for labor services—and material in Chapter 21 on the price of natural resources, we have a complete theory of income distribution based on marginal

(1) _____. This chapter and Chapter 16 build upon our earlier discussion of optimal input use by firms. In Chapter 6 we saw that the demand for factors of production can be derived from profit-maximizing considerations. A firm is willing to pay for labor, land, natural resources, and so forth because it can use these factors to produce and sell output. In Chapter 6 we also learned that the demand curve for a particular factor of production is simply the downward-sloping portion of the marginal _____ product curve.

*Interest rates* adjust to balance the demand for funds by borrowers and the supply of funds from
(2) lenders. The demand curve for funds has a (<u>negative/positive</u>) slope, indicating that at lower interest people will want to borrow (<u>less/more</u>). The supply curve of funds will have a (<u>negative/positive</u>) slope, indicating that a (<u>higher/lower</u>) interest rate is necessary to induce lenders to increase the supply of loans. An effective usury ceiling would impose an interest rate (<u>above/below</u>) the market clearing rate as determined by the _____ of the demand and supply curves.

The demand for funds for business borrowing derives from a consideration of the profitability of investment projects. In earlier chapters we talked about capital and labor as factors of production. Investment projects add to the stock of capital. The profitability of investment projects is another way of referring to the marginal revenue product of more capital. The profitability of investment projects is complicated because most projects require dollar outlays immediately while offering returns in the future. To evaluate the profitability of an investment we need some way of comparing current and future dollars. Economists and business people compare future and present dollars through a process called
(3) _____. As explained in the appendix to this chapter, this process relies on interest rate calculations. Higher interest rates will mean that (<u>fewer/more</u>) investment projects will be profitable. Thus higher interest rates will be associated with a (<u>higher/lower</u>) quantity of funds demanded and imply a (<u>negatively/positively</u>) sloped demand curve for business borrowing.

When considering the notion of *rent*, remember that economists use the term in a special way different
(4) from everyday usage. Most of the rent that you may pay for an apartment (<u>is/is not</u>) economic rent.

Economic rent refers to the earnings of a factor of production that exceed the minimum amount necessary to keep that factor in its current employment.

(5) If the supply curve of some factor, such as land, is really vertical, it means that the factor would be willing to work for as little as nothing. It also means that it is impossible to duplicate this factor at any cost; otherwise, a high enough price would induce an increase in supply, and the supply curve would not be vertical. In the case of a vertical supply curve, (some/all) of any market price would be economic rent. If the supply curve of some factor is a horizontal line, the market price will reflect exactly what is necessary to induce any supply. In this case an economist would say that the factor receives _____ economic rent.

(6) An upward-sloping supply curve means that higher prices will induce an increase in supply, but there will be some units of supply that would have been present at lower prices. In this case (most/all) units of the factor will receive economic rent. In fact, it is only the marginal unit, the unit on the supply curve at the market equilibrium price, that earns no economic rent. The market price is as high as it is to induce this last unit to supply itself. All other units would have been available at a lower price, and thus (part/all) of their earnings are economic rent. Land is a traditional input to use when talking about rent, but remember that land is not the only factor to earn economic rent. Anyone who would stay in a particular job for less pay, because he or she likes the work or the location, or for any other reason, (is/is not) earning some economic rent.

(7) When considering land rentals it is clear that not all land is the same: Some parcels are more productive or better located than others. Economists would expect that land rentals, the price for using a piece of land for a period of time, will adjust to reflect these differences. More productive land that produces the same output at lower cost will receive a (higher/lower) land rent. In equilibrium, rents should adjust so that the cost of producing the same quantity of output, including land rents, will be _____ on all parcels of land. If not, there is a clear incentive to use the land with lower total cost. This incentive to switch parcels increases the rent on the originally (low/high)-cost piece of land and decreases rent on the other pieces of land. The process stops only when land rentals have adjusted to again equate total cost.

(8) As with any other productive factor, an increase in the demand for goods produced with land will (decrease/increase) the demand for land. Poor quality land, whose use was unprofitable at lower output prices, will now become profitable to use. Thus, more land will be used, and land rents will again adjust to equalize the costs of production on all parcels. As a result, the rent on previously used, higher quality land will (increase/decrease). An additional part of the response to increased land demand is likely to be (more/less) intensive use of existing land.

*Profits* are a residual item after revenues have been used to pay other costs—labor, material inputs, interest on borrowed funds, and taxes. Profits also represent the return on equity investments in a firm.[1] In a world of perfect certainty, capitalists should expect the profits on their investments to offer a return just equal to the interest rate. The rate of interest would be the opportunity cost of their equity investment in the firm. Any higher return would be competed away. Any lower return would lead some funds to be invested elsewhere in the pursuit of returns at least equal to the interest rate. (Remember that in competitive markets, economic profits equal zero in long-run equilibrium.)

(9) In the real world, investments are not certain. Many business investments look like uncertain gambles. If entrepreneurs dislike taking risks, then profits will have to offer them the expectation of returns that are (greater/less) than the rate of interest. Profits that are the result of monopoly power would be (greater/less) than the interest rate. Finally, successful (innovation/invention) will often give an entrepreneur temporary monopoly profits and lead to a rate of profit that is (greater/less) than the interest rate. The effects of taxing profits will depend upon whether profits are mostly economic rents or mostly a necessary return to attract entrepreneurial talent.

---

[1]Equity refers here to the amount of their own money the owners have tied up in the firm. Specifically, if they sold the firm and paid off their creditors, the amount left over is their equity.

## IMPORTANT TERMS AND CONCEPTS QUIZ

Choose the best definition for the following terms.

1. _____ Factors of production
2. _____ Entrepreneurship
3. _____ Marginal productivity principle
4. _____ Marginal physical product
5. _____ Marginal revenue product
6. _____ Usury law
7. _____ Investment
8. _____ Capital
9. _____ Interest
10. _____ Discounting
11. _____ Marginal land
12. _____ Economic rent
13. _____ Invention
14. _____ Innovation

a. Payment to a factor of production in excess of the minimum amount necessary to keep the factor in its present employment.
b. Additional units of a given input add diminishing amounts to total output.

c. Starting firms, introducing innovations, and taking the necessary risks in seeking business opportunities.
d. The change in sales revenue from selling the marginal physical product of an additional unit of input.
e. Flow of resources into the production of new capital.
f. Act of generating a new idea.
g. Inputs used in the production process.
h. Payment for the use of funds.
i. Land on the borderline of being used.
j. Profit-maximizing firm should hire that quantity of an input at which marginal revenue product equals the price of the input.
k. Using interest rates to determine the present worth of a sum of money receivable or payable at a future date.
l. Act of putting a new idea into practical use.
m. Increase in output resulting from a one-unit increase in a given input.
n. Stock of plant, equipment, and other productive resources.
o. Maximum legally permissible interest rate.

## BASIC EXERCISE

This exercise is designed to illustrate how differences in land rents reflect differences in productivity.

Darlene can work as a checker at the local grocery store for as many hours as she wants, earning $8 an hour. She also is considering raising flowers for sale on one of two plots of land. The sunny plot has good soil, and Darlene estimates that if she worked 40 hours a week she could earn $400 a week raising flowers on this land. The second plot is marginal land available for free. It would require the use of fertilizer and special mulches to raise the same quantity of flowers. Darlene estimates these extra costs would total $30 a week.

1. Calculate Darlene's profit from using the marginal plot of land on the assumption that it is available at zero rent. Do not forget to include the opportunity cost of Darlene's own work as an element of cost.
2. If Darlene's estimate of the increased cost of using the marginal land is typical of other uses, what market rent would you expect will be charged for the use of the sunny plot and why?
3. Explain why the profit that Darlene could earn from using the marginal plot of land limits the rent the owner of the sunny plot will be able to charge.

## SELF-TESTS FOR UNDERSTANDING

### Test A

Circle the most appropriate answer.

1. Economists argue that the demand for factors of production is
   a. an applied demand.
   b. insensitive to changes in the price of factors.
   c. best represented as an upward–sloping curve.
   d. a derived demand.

2. Profit-maximizing firms will use more of a productive factor as long as the price of the factor is less than its
   a. marginal revenue product.
   b. marginal cost.
   c. marginal physical product.
   d. average product.

3. The demand curve for productive factors is the downward-sloping portion of the relevant
   a. marginal physical product curve.
   b. marginal cost curve.
   c. marginal revenue product curve.
   d. average cost curve.

4. If the price of widgets increases,
   a. we should see a movement along the demand curves for factors producing widgets.
   b. there should be a shift in the demand curves for factors producing widgets.
   c. the best guess is that there will be little change in the demand for factors producing widgets.
   d. the demand curves for factors producing widgets should shift to the left.

5. The concept of discounting suggests that when compared with a dollar next year, a dollar today is worth
   a. less.
   b. more.
   c. the same.

6. If interest rates increase, the difference in the value of $100 today compared with $100 next year will
   a. decrease.
   b. be unchanged.
   c. increase.
   d. be impossible to determine.

7. Firms produce output using land, labor, exhaustible resources, entrepreneurship, and
   a. capital.
   b. investment.
   c. interest.
   d. economic rent.

8. Firms undertake _____ to add to the stock of _____.
   a. innovation; invention
   b. discounting; investment
   c. investment; capital
   d. capital; investment

9. Which of the following is an example of investment as opposed to capital?
   a. The fleet of 747s owned by American Airlines.
   b. Julia's purchase of 100 shares of Xerox stock.
   c. The five apartment buildings owned by Ralph.
   d. The expanded warehouse facilities that Norma will have built this year.

10. Economists expect that land rents will
    a. adjust to equalize total costs of production across different parcels of land.
    b. mean that more productive parcels of land receive higher rents.
    c. result in more intensive use of more productive parcels of land.
    d. all of the above.

11. Parcel of land B can be used to raise corn at a cost of $50,000. The same amount of corn can be raised on parcel P for $75,000. An economist would expect the rent on parcel B to exceed that on parcel P by
    a. $25,000.
    b. $50,000.
    c. $75,000.
    d. $125,000.

12. Marginal land refers to land that
    a. is most productive for growing any given crop.
    b. is on the borderline of being used in productive activity.
    c. earns economic rent.
    d. borders interstate highways in rural areas.

13. The term *economic rent* refers to
    a. any rent paid by someone as part of an economic transaction.
    b. rent paid by economists for their apartments.
    c. earnings by factors of production greater than they would settle for.
    d. land rents.

14. If the supply curve for some factor of production can be represented as a horizontal line, an economist would say that _____ of the income earned by this factor is economic rent.
    a. none
    b. some
    c. all

15. An input will earn pure economic rent if the supply curve for the input is
    a. horizontal.
    b. upward sloping.
    c. vertical.

16. Which of the following individuals are earning economic rent?
    a. Ruth, who says, "If this job paid any less I'd quit; it wouldn't be worth the hassle."
    b. Sergio, who says, "This job is so interesting I'd work here even for a lot less."
    c. Nick, whose purchase of an apartment building should bring him a return equal to the interest rate.
    d. Sophia, who is expecting a substantial profit from her investment in the manufacture of solar energy panels to compensate her for the risks she is taking.

17. Rent seeking refers to
    a. efforts of college students to find apartments each fall.
    b. the use of productive resources in the pursuit of economic profits.
    c. attempts to get departments within a company to pay for space they occupy.
    d. a landlord's efforts to collect from deadbeat tenants.

18. In a world of competitive firms with no uncertainty or risk, economists expect that the profit rate will be
    a. less than the rate of interest.
    b. equal to the rate of interest.
    c. higher than the rate of interest.

19. Monopoly power, whether permanent or temporary, means that profits are
    a. less than the rate of interest.
    b. equal to the rate of interest.
    c. higher than the rate of interest.

20. Higher taxes on profits will have little impact if
    a. profits are mostly economic rent.
    b. profits are equal to nominal interest rates.
    c. profits are growing.
    d. the supply curve for entrepreneurial talent is horizontal.

## Test B

Circle T or F for true or false.

T   F   1. The demand curve for a factor of production is identical to its curve of marginal physical productivity.

T   F   2. Interest rates represent the market price for the use of funds.

T   F   3. Discounting means using the rate of interest to compare future and present dollars.

T   F   4. The factories that the Ford Motor Company uses to produce cars are an example of investment rather than capital.

T   F   5. According to economists, only land earns economic rent.

T   F   6. Inputs available in perfectly elastic supply will earn no economic rent.

T   F   7. The rent on any piece of land will equal the difference between production costs on that piece of land and production costs on the next-best available piece of land.

T   F   8. The law of diminishing returns implies that an increase in the demand for land will actually reduce the rent paid on most parcels of land.

T   F   9. The reason that most rent-control laws have adverse effects in the long run is that the long-run supply of structures, as opposed to land, is likely to be quite elastic.

T   F   10. Economic theory proves that the rate of profits must equal the rate of interest.

# Appendix: Discounting and Present Value

## LEARNING OBJECTIVE

After completing the exercises below, you should be able to appreciate how discounting, or present value, calculations can help when considering investment decisions.

## IMPORTANT TERMS AND CONCEPTS

Discounting
Present value

## IMPORTANT TERM AND CONCEPT QUIZ

Choose the best definition for the following term.

1. _____ Present value

    a. Using interest rates to determine the current value of dollars to be received or paid at various dates in the future.

    b. Future worth of a sum of money receivable or payable at the present date.

## BASIC EXERCISES

1. **Discounting and Investment Decision**

Eric has an opportunity to purchase a machine to make gyros. The machine cost $4,000 and is expected to last two years. After other expenses, Eric expects to net $2,000 next year and $2,500 in two years. Assume that Eric has the $4,000 to buy the machine now. Is it a good investment?

a. Fill in the column of Table 15-1 to compute the present value of costs and returns on the assumption that the interest rate is 10 percent.

b. Add up the present value of the returns and compare this sum with the present value of the cost. Which is greater? _____. If the interest rate is 10%, should Eric purchase the machine?

c. Assume now that the interest rate is 5 percent. Fill in the relevant column of the table to compute the present value of the returns at an interest rate of 5 percent.

d. Sum the present value of the returns and compare this sum with the present value of the cost. Which is greater? _____ If the interest rate is 5%, should Eric purchase the machine? _____.

e. The decision rule discussed in the text, and the one you should have used when answering questions b and d, compares the present value of future returns to the present value of costs. If the present value of the returns exceeds the present value of the cost, it means that Eric can do better by undertaking the investment than by investing in financial assets that yield the rate of interest we used to compute the present values. If the present value of the returns is less than the present value of the cost, it means that Eric would do better with a financial investment. You can verify that this is the case by filling in the missing parts of Table 15-2 for interest rates of 5 and 10 percent.

### TABLE 15-1
### ERIC'S GYRO MACHINE

| Time | Item | Amount | Present Value* $i = 5$ percent | Present Value* $i = 10$ percent |
|------|------|--------|------------------|-------------------|
| Now | Cost | $4,000 | _____ | _____ |
| One year | Return | 2,000 | _____ | _____ |
| Two years | Return | 2,500 | _____ | _____ |
| | Present value of all returns | | _____ | _____ |
| | Net present value of project | | _____ | _____ |

*Present value = $\dfrac{\text{dollars in n years}}{(1 + i)^n}$

    = (dollars in the $n^{th}$ year) divided by (1 plus the rate of interest multiplied by itself $n$ times)

**TABLE 15-2**
**CAN ERIC DO AS WELL BY INVESTING $4,000 AT THE RATE OF INTEREST?**

| | Interest Rate | |
| --- | --- | --- |
| | 5 percent | 10 percent |
| 1. Initial deposit | $4,000 | $4,000 |
| 2. Interest after one year (5 percent and 10 percent of line 1) | _____ | _____ |
| 3. Balance after one year (line 1 plus line 2) | _____ | _____ |
| 4. Withdrawal after one year* | $2,000 | $2,000 |
| 5. New balance (line 3 minus line 4) | _____ | _____ |
| 6. Interest during second year (5 percent and 10 percent of line 5) | _____ | _____ |
| 7. Balance after second year (line 5 plus line 6) | _____ | _____ |

Compare line 7 with the $2,500 Eric would have received in the second year if he had bought the gyro machine. Line 7 should be greater (less) if the net present value of the project in Table 15-1 is negative (positive). That is, if the net present value of the project is negative (positive), Eric will do better (worse) by making a financial investment at the given rate of interest.

*This $2,000 matches the return after one year from the gyro investment.

**TABLE 15-3**
**WHAT IF ERIC HAD TO BORROW THE $4,000?**

| | Interest Rate | |
| --- | --- | --- |
| | 5 percent | 10 percent |
| 1. Amount borrowed | $4,000 | $4,000 |
| 2. Interest due at end of first year | $ 200 | $ 400 |
| 3. Cash flow from investment | $2,000 | $2,000 |
| 4. Net cash flow after interest payment (line 3 minus line 2) | _____ | _____ |
| 5. Interest earned during second year by investing net cash flow (5 percent and 10 percent of line 4) | _____ | _____ |
| 6. Cash flow from investment | $2,500 | $2,500 |
| 7. Total at end of second year (line 4 plus line 5 plus line 6) | _____ | _____ |
| 8. Interest due at end of second year | $ 200 | $ 400 |
| 9. Loan repayment | $4,000 | $4,000 |
| 10. Net (line 7 minus line 8 and line 9) | _____ | _____ |

The crucial question is whether the gyro investment offers any return after paying back the loan with interest. Any dollars left over are pure profit for Eric since he did not invest any of his own money. It should be true that Eric will have a positive (negative) net if the present value of returns is greater (less) than the present value of costs. Is it?

(The entries on line 10 are dollars in the second year. What is the present value of these dollars? How do these present values compare with the net present values calculated in Table 15-1 above?)

f. What if Eric had to borrow the money? Would the same sorts of calculations be sufficient to help you decide whether he should borrow the money? The answer is yes. The reason is that while figuring the present value of the returns, you are accounting for interest payments whether Eric has the money or not. If he does not have the money, he will need to pay a lender. Even if he does have the money he will need to "pay" himself as much as he might have earned in some other investment. That is, he will need to meet the opportunity cost of his own money. Fill in the missing parts of Table 15-3, which has been constructed to illustrate just this point.

To summarize

a. Present value calculations use interest rates to transform dollars in the future into their equivalent today.

b. Comparing the present value of returns and cost is a good way to evaluate investment opportunities.

c. Comparing present value of returns and cost is a good procedure whether you have to borrow the money or not, assuming that you can borrow or lend at the same rate of interest you are using in your present value calculations.

d. If the present value of returns equals the present value of cost, an investment opportunity offers the same return as investing at the rate of interest.

e. If the present value of returns exceeds the present value of costs, an investment opportunity offers a greater return than investing at the rate of interest.

f. If the present value of returns is less than the present value of costs, an investment opportunity offers a worse return than investing at the rate of interest.

2. **When is $1,000,000 not $1,000,000?**

On Wednesday, April 14, 1993, Don Calhoun earned $1,000,000 for about 5 seconds of work. Or did he? After reluctantly accompanying a friend to a basketball game between the Chicago Bulls and Miami Heat, Mr. Calhoun was chosen at random from the audience. Standing at one free–throw line, he was given one shot at the basket at the other end of the court. His baseball-like hurl was all net.

The million dollars that Mr. Calhoun will receive is actually $50,000 a year for 20 years, not $1,000,000 immediately. What is the cost of Mr. Calhoun's $1,000,000 to the restaurant and soft–drink sponsors of the long free–throw contest? Why is it less than $1,000,000?

## SUPPLEMENTARY EXERCISE

### Can You Share in Monopoly Profits?

Assume that the major oil companies are able to exercise considerable monopoly power and, as a result, earn substantial monopoly profits on their investments, far in excess of the interest rate. Can you share these profits and earn the same high rate of return by buying oil company stocks?

What determines the price of oil company stocks? An economist would expect the market price to be close to the present value of the future returns from owning the stock, that is, close to the present value of expected future dividends and capital gains. Thus if dividends are high because of huge monopoly profits, the price of the stock will be _____. If huge monopoly profits and the resulting future dividends were known for sure, what rate of return do you think you could earn by buying oil company stocks? Just who does earn those monopoly profits?

## ECONOMICS IN ACTION

### Nice Work if You Can Get It

A number of observers have charged that compensation for executives of American corporations is excessive. Certainly the compensation received by some individuals has been eye-catching, notably the $550 million that Michael Milken received in 1987. Too often it seems that newspapers report increases in executive compensation while companies report negative profits and declining stock values. Critics charge that since executives sit on each other's boards of directors they are hardly the ones to be trusted when it comes to setting each other's compensation. U.S. representative Martin Sabo (D-Minnesota) recently introduced a bill in Congress to limit the ability of corporations to deduct executive compensation from taxable income to the first $1,000,000.

Economists Michael Jensen and Kevin Murphy take a contrary view as they argue that the problem with CEO compensation is not the level of pay but the manner of payment.[2] Specifically, Jensen and Murphy argue that compensation should be more closely linked to performance. "On average, corporate America pays its most important leaders like bureaucrats," they write. "Is it any wonder then that so many CEOs act like bureaucrats rather than the value-maximizing entrepreneurs companies need to enhance their standing in world markets?"

Jensen and Murphy looked at salaries and bonuses for more than 2,500 CEOs in 1,400 publicly held companies from 1974 to 1988. While increases in CEO compensation through the 1980s sparked much of the recent criticism, Jensen and Murphy find that after correcting for inflation, average salaries and bonuses from 1982 to 1988 were a bit less than during the 1930s. More importantly, they argue that there should be a tighter link between company performance and CEO compensation. Good years and bad years make little difference in CEO compensation. The authors argue that executives are agents of the stockholders and should act to maximize value for stockholders. The best way to insure that executives act in the interests of stockholders is to link executive compensation to stock market values. Jensen and Murphy argue that their approach would result in "big rewards for outstanding performance and meaningful penalties for poor performance." If on average this means even higher executive compensation, Jensen and Murphy argue that such an increase is justified if it is a reward for superior performance. They see their approach as offering a much stronger incentive than is typical at most companies for superior performance that benefits all stockholders.

1. Is executive compensation excessive?
2. What sorts of incentives and rewards for executive performance are in the best interests of stockholders? of the economy?
3. Should there be limits on executive compensation? If so, what and why? What would be the effect on incentives of different limits?

---

[2]Michael C. Jensen and Kevin J. Murphy, "CEO Incentives—It's Not How Much You Pay, But How," *Harvard Business Review*, May-June 1990, pp. 138-153.

## STUDY QUESTIONS

1. What does it mean to say that the demand for a factor of production is a derived demand?
2. Why is the demand curve for a factor of production the downward–sloping portion of the factor's curve of marginal revenue product?
3. What is the difference between investment and capital?
4. How does discounting help a firm determine the profitability of investment projects?
5. How is the profitability of investment projects affected when interest rates change?
6. Why isn't the rent you pay for an apartment economic rent?
7. What is meant by the statement in the text that almost all employees earn some economic rent?
8. What explains differences in rent for different parcels of land?
9. Why doesn't competition work to limit profits to the rate of interest?

*C h a p t e r* **16**

# Labor: The Human Input

## LEARNING OBJECTIVES

After completing this chapter, you should be able to:

- explain how income and substitution effects influence the slope of the supply curve of labor.
- explain how the demand for labor is derived from a firm's profit-maximizing decisions about the use of factors of production.
- use demand and supply curves to determine the equilibrium wage and employment in a competitive labor market.
- explain why wages for some individuals contain substantial economic rent.
- discuss the factors that help explain why wages differ among individuals.
- discuss how human capital theory explains the observed correlation between more education and higher wages.
- discuss some of the alternative views of the role of education.
- use demand and supply curves to analyze the impact of minimum wage legislation.
- describe the history of unions and major labor legislation in the United States.
- use demand and supply curves to describe labor union's possible alternative goals.
- describe the strategies a union might follow to increase wages.
- distinguish between a monopsonist and a monopolist.
- describe the differences between arbitration and mediation.

## IMPORTANT TERMS AND CONCEPTS

Minimum wage law
Income and substitution effects
Backward-bending supply curve
Economic rent
Investments in human capital
Human capital theory
Dual labor markets
Union
Industrial and craft unions

Taft-Hartley Act (1947)
Closed shop
Union shop
Seniority rules
Monopsony
Bilateral monopoly
Collective bargaining
Mediation
Arbitration

## CHAPTER REVIEW

In a competitive market without minimum wages or unions, wages and employment—the price and quantity of labor services—will be determined by the interaction of the demand for and the supply of labor services and can be analyzed with tools that should now be familiar—demand and supply curves.

The supply of labor comes from individual decisions to work. Individual decisions to supply work are simultaneously decisions to forgo leisure. Thus, a decision to supply less labor is simultaneously a
**(1)** decision to demand _____. At higher wages, the same number of working hours will mean a larger income. If leisure is not an inferior good, people are apt to demand (<u>more/less</u>) leisure as their income increases. This suggests that the supply of labor might (<u>increase/decrease</u>) as wages increase. This is called the (<u>income/substitution</u>) effect of higher wages, but it is only part of the story.

Higher wages also increase the opportunity cost of an hour of leisure. As a result we expect that
**(2)** as wages increase the substitution effect will lead people to work (<u>more/less</u>). The ultimate effect of increased wages comes from the sum of the income and substitution effects. Statistical evidence suggests that at low wages the _____ effect predominates and labor supply (<u>increases/decreases</u>) with an increase in wages, while at high wages the two effects tend to (<u>enhance/offset</u>) each other. The response of individuals to a change in wages, the income and substitution effects, helps determine the (<u>slope/position</u>) of the labor supply curve. Other factors, such as the size of the available working population and nonmonetary aspects of many jobs, help determine the _____ of the labor supply curve. The strength of the (<u>income/substitution</u>) effect is important for an understanding of the historical evidence on real wages and average weekly hours in the United States.

The demand for labor comes from the decisions of firms to use labor as one of many factors of production. Labor services are valuable because they add to output and, it is hoped, to profits. Thus the demand for labor is a derived demand. The discussion in Chapters 5 and 15 of how a profit-maximizing firm makes optimal decisions about the use of factors of production showed us that a firm should use more of any factor as long as the addition to revenue exceeds the addition to cost or, in technical terms, as long as the marginal revenue product of the factor is greater than the marginal cost of the factor. The demand curve for labor is determined by the marginal revenue product curve. The curve has a negative slope because of the law of diminishing marginal returns.

In competitive markets, equilibrium wages and employment are determined by the intersection of the market demand and supply curves, which come from the horizontal summation of firms' demand curves and individuals' supply curves. Any factor that shifts either curve will change equilibrium wages and employment. For example, an increase in the demand for a firm's output or a technological innovation
**(3)** that increases the productivity of labor will shift the (<u>demand/supply</u>) curve and lead to (<u>higher/lower</u>) wages, employment, or both.

Wages will differ for a number of reasons. Differences in abilities and work effort will affect individual wages. Differing amounts of other factors of production would also be expected to affect the marginal physical product of labor and hence wages. If individual skills are not easily duplicated, as may be the case for star athletes or performers, wages will be high as they contain significant economic rents. If skills are easily duplicated, one would expect that competition in the form of entry would work to keep wages in line with the costs of acquiring skills.

Education and wages are positively correlated—people with more education typically earn higher wages. Human capital theory views these higher wages as the return from investments in human capital— that is, the time, money, and effort spent on schooling and training. Other theories hold that rather than enhancing skills, schooling only sorts workers by their innate abilities, helping employers identify those who will be most productive. Radical critics charge that schooling only sustains existing class differences by teaching discipline and obedience. Theories of dual labor markets combine alternative approaches, arguing that schooling sorts workers into good and bad jobs. In the primary labor market with good jobs,

(4) education (does/does not) enhance the skills and wages of workers. In the secondary labor market, workers (do/do not) have an incentive to invest in their own skills.

In some cases the market determination of wages and employment is affected by a legal floor on

(5) wages rates, or a(n) _____ wage. Chapter 4 discussed the effects of price floors. One should expect similar results from minimum wages. To be effective, the minimum wage must be (higher/lower) than the market wage. Imposing a minimum wage will (increase/decrease) the volume of employment as firms move backward and to the left along their demand curves for labor. At the same time the promise of higher wages is apt to increase the (demand/supply) of labor. The net result will be higher wages and income for those lucky enough to have jobs, but only frustration for others seeking work. While these effects are clear in theory, statistical evidence of the impact of minimum wage laws on the level of employment is controversial.

(6) Minimum wage laws affect primarily (skilled/unskilled) labor markets. A major noncompetitive feature in many skilled labor markets is the existence of labor _____. Currently, about one-sixth of American workers belong to a union. The development of unions in America can be traced back about 100 years. Significant union gains were made during the 1930s with the passage of the Wagner, or _____ _____ _____ Act, which guaranteed workers the right to form unions and established the National Labor Relations Board to ensure that these rights were not violated. Some union practices were declared illegal by the _____—_____ Act, passed in 1947.

In some labor markets, unions are the only supplier of labor services; that is, they are

(7) a (monopolist/monopsonist). As such, they face a trade-off between wages and employment just as a monopoly supplier of widgets faces a trade-off between price and output. Geometrically, a union, as a monopolist, can choose any point on the relevant _____ curve for labor. The trade-off between wages and employment comes because the demand curve for labor has a negative slope. A union might be able to raise both wages and employment if it can shift the demand curve for labor to the (right/left). Increasing the demand for union-made products or featherbedding and other restrictive work practices will have the desired impact on the demand for union labor. (In terms of efforts to increase wages and income, do not limit your conception of unions to the AFL-CIO or to the Teamsters. Many professional organizations, such as the American Medical Association attempt to enhance the income of their members, often by limiting supply.) Efforts to increase productivity are an alternative way to increase the demand for labor.

Sometimes a union, as a monopolistic supplier of labor, faces a single buyer of labor services. When

(8) one buyer constitutes the entire market demand, the buyer is called a _____. Both monopolists and monopsonists realize that their decisions about quantity of labor must at the same time affect _____. Monopolists who want to sell more must accept a (higher/lower) price, and monopsonists who want to buy more must pay a _____ price. If a monopsonist faces a monopolist, then the whole market has only _____ participants. The technical term for this situation is _____ monopoly. Each will consider the actions of the other, and, as for oligopoly, the outcome is difficult to predict.

(9) When union and management sit down to decide the terms and conditions of employment, they are engaging in _____ _____. This process establishes not only wages but also fringe benefits, overtime premiums, grievance procedures, and a host

of other details. If both sides cannot come to an agreement and wish to avoid a strike, they may agree to _____ or _____. If this person only helps labor and management to reach an agreement but has no power to enforce a settlement, she is called a(n) _____. If she listens to the arguments of both sides and then also makes the final decisions, she is called a(n) _____.

## IMPORTANT TERMS AND CONCEPTS QUIZ

Choose the most appropriate definition for the following terms.

1. _____ Minimum wage law
2. _____ Income effect (of higher wages)
3. _____ Substitution effect (of higher wages)
4. _____ Backward-bending supply curve of labor
5. _____ Human capital theory
6. _____ Dual labor markets
7. _____ Industrial union
8. _____ Craft union
9. _____ Closed shop
10. _____ Union shop
11. _____ Seniority rules
12. _____ Monopsony
13. _____ Bilateral monopoly
14. _____ Collective bargaining
15. _____ Mediation
16. _____ Arbitration

a. All workers must join the union.
b. Reduction in supply of labor as wages increase.
c. Legal floor on wages for all workers.
d. Viewing education as an investment in a person's earning potential.
e. Market composed of a single seller and a single buyer.

f. Group representing similar-skilled workers in all industries.
g. Market situation in which there is only one producer.
h. Impact on demand for increased leisure from higher income when wages increase.
i. Intervention of an impartial individual who is empowered to impose binding decisions on unresolved issues.
j. Market situation in which there is only one buyer.
k. Group representing all types of workers in a single industry.
l. Increased opportunity cost of leisure as wages increase.
m. Hiring only union members.
n. Discussions between labor and management to determine wages and conditions of employment.
o. Intervention of an impartial observer who attempts to hasten the bargaining process.
p. Substitution effect of higher wages outweighs income effect.
q. Notion that there are mainly two types of jobs: those offering opportunities for acquisition of skills and promotions, and "dead-end jobs."
r. Job-related advantages to workers who have held their jobs longest.

## BASIC EXERCISE

This problem illustrates the determination of wages and employment in both a competitive market and a market monopolized by a labor union.

Tony runs a small company, Bearpaw Boots, that manufactures hiking boots. Table 16-1 shows output per month for different quantities of labor.

1. Fill in the third column by using the data in the second column to compute the marginal physical product of each additional worker.

2. Tony can sell boots for $60 a pair. Each boot contains $20 worth of leather, leaving $40 for wages or profits. As Tony has a small firm, the prices of boots is unaffected by the quantity that he sells. Fill in the fourth column by computing the marginal revenue products of each worker. Be sure to use the $40 net figure rather than the $60 gross.

3. Tony wants to maximize profits. How many workers should he employ if monthly wages are $1,100? _____

4. Show that your answer to question 3 maximizes profits by computing total profits for one more and for one less worker.

### TABLE 16-1
### OUTPUT FIGURES FOR BEARPAW BOOTS

| Number of Bootmakers | Total Number of Pairs of Boots per Month | Marginal Physical Product (boots) | Marginal Revenue Product (dollars) |
|---|---|---|---|
| 1 | 60 | _____ | _____ |
| 2 | 115 | _____ | _____ |
| 3 | 165 | _____ | _____ |
| 4 | 210 | _____ | _____ |
| 5 | 250 | _____ | _____ |
| 6 | 285 | _____ | _____ |
| 7 | 315 | _____ | _____ |
| 8 | 340 | _____ | _____ |
| 9 | 360 | _____ | _____ |
| 10 | 375 | _____ | _____ |

5. Figure 16-1 shows the supply of bootmakers for the entire industry. Assume there are 100 competitive firms just like Tony's. Using your data on the marginal revenue product for a typical firm, plot the market demand for bootmakers. What is the equilibrium market wage and employment? $_____ and _____. At the equilibrium market wage, how many workers should Tony employ? _____ What are Tony's profits? _____.

### FIGURE 16-1

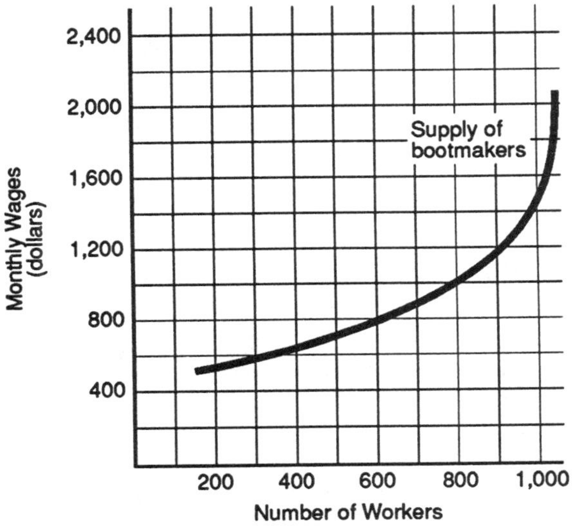

6. Assume now that the International Association of Bootmakers has been successful in unionizing bootmakers. In order to evaluate possible alternative goals, the union has asked you to use your knowledge of the industry demand curve to answer the following questions:
    a. If union membership is limited to 400 persons, what is the maximum monthly wage the union can get from employers? _____
    b. If the union wage is set at $700 a month, what is the maximum amount of employment? _____
    c. What wage and employment combination will maximize total wage payments? _____.

# SELF-TESTS FOR UNDERSTANDING

## Test A

Circle the most appropriate answer.

1. A change in which of the following will affect the slope of the labor supply curve?
    a. An increase in the working age population.
    b. A technological innovation that increases labor productivity.
    c. An increase in the price of a competitive firm's output.
    d. An increase in the willingness of people to trade higher money incomes for more leisure.

2. A change in which of the following will affect the position of the labor supply curve?
    a. An increase in the working age population.
    b. A technological innovation that increases labor productivity.
    c. An increase in the price of a competitive firm's output.
    d. An increase in the willingness of people to work longer hours in return for higher wages.

3. The income and substitution effects mean that the supply of labor _____ when wages increase.
    a. will always increase
    b. may rise or fall
    c. will always decline

4. Empirical evidence about labor supply suggests that
    a. the substitution effect is usually stronger than the income effect.
    b. the income effect outweighs the substitution effect for most workers.
    c. except at low wages, the income and substitution effects tend to offset each other.
    d. higher wages will lead to a shift in the supply of labor schedule.

5. The demand for labor is the downward-sloping portion of the _____ curve for labor.
    a. marginal physical product
    b. marginal revenue product
    c. marginal cost
    d. average revenue

6. A change in which of the following will affect the demand for labor by affecting the marginal physical product of labor?
    a. The demand for a firm's output.
    b. The amount of other factors of production per worker.
    c. The supply of labor.
    d. The minimum wage.

7. A change in which of the following will affect the demand for labor by affecting the marginal revenue product of labor?
   a. The demand for a firm's output.
   b. Union militancy.
   c. The supply of labor.
   d. The minimum wage.

8. Historical data that show a declining work week along with rising real wages are probably reflecting
   a. minimum wage laws.
   b. the income effect of higher wages.
   c. the substitution effect of higher wages.
   d. the Taft-Hartley Act.

9. The text refers to a study at Princeton that showed a 10 percent increase in wages results in a 3 percent increase in the supply of labor. According to this data, the price elasticity of the supply of labor is
   a. .3 ($^3/_{10}$).
   b. 3.3 ($^{10}/_3$).
   c. 13 percent (10 + 3).
   d. Insufficient information to determine.

10. If the supply of labor is backward bending, then
    a. we're probably talking about manual labor.
    b. even higher wages are needed to increase supply
    c. the income effect is greater than the substitution effect.
    d. the incentive to work more hours when wages are higher is outweighing the income effect of higher wages.

11. Wages are likely to contain a large component of economic rent when
    a. significant training is involved in learning valuable skills.
    b. schooling works only to sort individuals into good or bad jobs.
    c. minimum wage laws are effective.
    d. valuable skills are virtually impossible to duplicate.

12. The supply curve for schmoos is upward sloping. An increase in the demand for schmoos (the demand curve shifts to the right) will lead to all but which one of the following?
    a. The price of schmoos increases.
    b. The marginal physical product of labor schedule shifts upward.
    c. The marginal revenue product of labor schedule shifts upward.
    d. The demand curve for labor to produce schmoos shifts upward.
    e. More employment and/or higher wages in the schmoo industry.

13. The theory of human capital says that
    a. individuals can repair their own bodies with artificial parts, just like machines.
    b. soon all work will be done by robots.
    c. individual decisions to seek training and new skills can be modeled in the same way as ordinary investment decisions, involving present costs in the expectation of future returns.
    d. slavery in the United States was doomed because it was uneconomical.

14. Human capital theory explains the correlation between education and wages as the result of
    a. learning in school that enhances productivity.
    b. sorting by social class.
    c. the dual labor market.
    d. the growing influence of white collar unions.

15. What percent of American workers belong to unions?
    a. 100 percent.
    b. 50 percent.
    c. 33 percent.
    d. less than 20 percent.

16. In contrast with unions in Europe and Japan, unions in America
    a. are much more political.
    b. have resulted in almost twice the level of strike activity found in any other country.
    c. involve a smaller percentage of the labor force than in most countries.
    d. have been less adversarial than unions in Japan.

17. The Taft-Hartley Act
    a. permitted states to ban union shops.
    b. legalized closed shops.
    c. created the National Labor Relations Board.
    d. increased the minimum wage.

18. A single union that controls the supply of labor to many small firms is a
    a. socialist.
    b. monopsonist.
    c. oligopolist.
    d. monopolist.

19. Unless a union can shift the demand curve for labor, it can increase wages only if it is willing to
    a. strike.
    b. accept lower employment.
    c. submit to binding arbitration
    d. engage in a secondary boycott.

20. Which of the following are examples of

    mediation _____

    arbitration _____

    strike _____

    featherbedding _____

    work slowdown _____

    union shop _____

    closed shop _____

    a. Public school teachers and the local school board, unable to reach agreement, consent to accept the determination of a three-person board.
    b. Plane schedules are delayed as air traffic controllers "do it by the book" in their handling of planes.
    c. Anyone may seek work at the local meat-packing plant, but once employed she must join the union.
    d. In an attempt to avert a steel strike, the secretary of labor helps the United Steelworkers and the steel companies to resolve their differences.
    e. The United Mine Workers start picketing after contract negotiations fail.
    f. none.

**Test B**

Circle T or F for true or false.

T F 1. Information on the marginal revenue product of labor can be used to derive a firm's demand for labor.

T F 2. The law of diminishing returns implies that the demand curve for labor will have a negative slope.

T F 3. The income effect of higher wages suggests that the supply of labor schedule may have a positively sloped portion.

T F 4. An increase in wages that increases the quantity of labor supplied is represented as a shift in the supply curve.

T F 5. Raising the minimum wage will raise the income of all people earning less than the minimum wage.

T F 6. If a labor union has complete control over the supply of a particular type of labor, it is a monopsonist.

T F 7. A market with a single buyer and a single seller is called an oligopoly.

T F 8. In general there is no conflict between union attempts to maximize wages for current union members and attempts to provide employment for the largest possible number of workers.

T F 9. Statistical evidence suggests that unions have been successful in raising wages by 50 to 100 percent above their competitive level.

T F 10. If a union and employer, unable to reach agreement on a new contract, agree to accept the decision of an impartial third party, they have agreed to settle their differences by arbitration.

# Appendix: The Effects of Union and Minimum Wages Under Monopsony

## LEARNING OBJECTIVE

The exercise below is designed to increase your understanding of the material in the appendix to Chapter 16.

## IMPORTANT TERMS AND CONCEPTS

Marginal labor costs

## IMPORTANT TERMS AND CONCEPTS QUIZ

Choose the most appropriate definition for the following term.

1. _____ Marginal labor cost

a. Wage rate.
b. Change in total wages paid as employment increases.
c. Change in total wages as percent of change in total cost.

## BASIC EXERCISE

This problem illustrates what can happen when unorganized workers face a monopsonistic employer.

Assume that Bearpaw Boots (the subject of the Basic Exercise for the chapter) is located in a small, isolated town in northern Maine and is the sole employer of bootmakers. Tony still sells his boots in a competitive market for a net price of $40. Table 16-2 contains data on what wages Tony must pay to get various numbers of employees.

1. Use the data in the first two columns of Table 16-2 to plot the supply curve of labor in Figure 16-2. Use the data on the marginal revenue product computed in Table 16-1 to plot the demand curve for labor in Figure 16-2. These curves intersect where wages are $_____ and the number of employees is _____. Will Tony pay this wage and employ this many workers? (yes/no) Why?

### TABLE 16-2
### SUPPLY OF BOOTMAKERS IN A SMALL, ISOLATED TOWN

| Number of Bootmakers | Monthly Wage (dollars) | Total Labor Cost (dollars) | Marginal Labor Costs (dollars) |
|---|---|---|---|
| 1 | 300 | _____ | _____ |
| 2 | 400 | _____ | _____ |
| 3 | 500 | _____ | _____ |
| 4 | 600 | _____ | _____ |
| 5 | 700 | _____ | _____ |
| 6 | 800 | _____ | _____ |
| 7 | 900 | _____ | _____ |
| 8 | 1,000 | _____ | _____ |
| 9 | 1,100 | _____ | _____ |
| 10 | 1,200 | _____ | _____ |

### FIGURE 16-2
### DEMAND FOR AND SUPPLY OF BOOTMAKERS

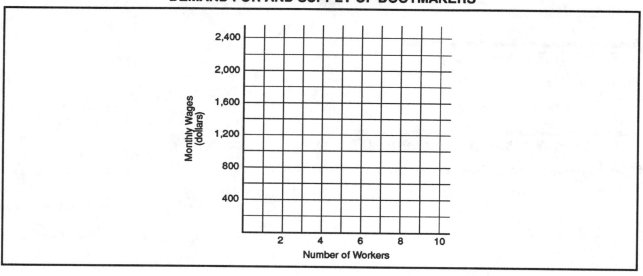

2. Remember, Tony is the only employer of bootmakers in town. As he employs additional workers, he must pay a higher wage not only to each new employee but also to all existing employees. Thus the marginal labor cost of an additional worker is (greater/less) than the wage. Fill in the remaining columns of Table 16-2 to compute Tony's marginal labor costs.

3. Plot the figures on marginal labor costs in Figure 16-2.

4. Tony's profit-maximizing level of employment is _____ workers.

5. What is the lowest wage that Tony must offer in order to attract the profit-maximizing number of workers? $_____

6. What are Tony's profits (net revenue minus total wages)? $_____

7. If Tony were forced to pay a minimum wage of $1,100 a month, what would happen to wages and employment as compared with your answers to questions 4 and 5? _____

8. Would a union necessarily force the minimum wage solution to question 7 on Tony? Why or why not?

## SUPPLEMENTARY EXERCISE

### Does College Pay?

Data on income distribution for 1990 report an average income of $28,744 for heads of households completing four years of high school and an income of $50,549 for those who have completed four or more years of college. If we assume that average college graduates will earn the $21,805 difference every year they work, is college a good financial investment?

To answer this question you will need to compare the present value of the cost of college to the present value of the earnings differential. Remember from the Supplementary Exercise to Chapter 3 that the cost of college includes the opportunity cost of lost wages from not working, spending on tuition, fees, and books, and any differential living expenses. Basic room and board should not be included, as a person would incur those expenses whether going to school or not. Table 16-3 contains an illustrative calculation on the assumption that one spends four years in college from ages 19 to 22 and then works for 43 years until age 65. An interest rate of 8 percent has been used to calculate present values. What would such a calculation show for you? How would a change in the rate of interest affect the net present value? Why might someone value a college education even if it did not promise a financial return?

**TABLE 16-3**

|  | Public | Private |
|---|---|---|
| **Cost of College for each of four years** |  |  |
| Lost wages | $28,744 | $28,744 |
| Tuition and fees | $2,159 | $11,379 |
| Books and incidentals | $2,000 | $2,000 |
| **Present value at age 19 of the cost of college[1]** | $117,697 | $150,678 |
| **Present value at age 19 of income differential[2]** | $179,361 | $179,361 |
| **Net present value** | $61,664 | $28,683 |

1. $PV = \sum_{t=0}^{3} \dfrac{\text{Total cost}}{(1.1)^t}$

    All costs are assumed to be paid at the beginning of the year.

2. $PV = \sum_{t=23}^{65} \dfrac{\text{Income Differential}}{(1.1)^{t-19}} \quad \sum_{t=23}^{65} \dfrac{\$21{,}805}{(1.1)^{t-19}}$

    All income is assumed to be earned at the end of the year.

The calculations in Table 16-3 are meant to be illustrative not definitive. The $28,744 income figure is an average for all high school graduates. We would expect that recent graduates would earn less, lowering the cost of college. Similarly, the income differential between college and high school graduates is likely to be small at first and grow over time. Finally, while financial return is an important part of many decisions to attend college, it is only one factor that should be considered.

## ECONOMICS IN ACTION
### 9 to 5 or 9 to 9?

*The New York Times* noted that in April 1993 average overtime for factory workers rose to 4.3 hours per week. ("Fewer Jobs Filled as Factories Rely on Overtime Pay," *The New York Times*, May 16, 1993.) While some increase in average overtime is to be expected during a business recovery, the 4.3-hour figure was an all-time high since data on overtime hours were first collected in 1948. It was estimated that if firms hired new workers instead of paying overtime the unemployment rate would drop by a full percentage point, from 7 to 6 percent. Why has there been such an increase in overtime work when overtime pay is 50 percent more expensive than straight wages?

Many workers welcome the opportunity to work overtime, and many companies find it the most profitable way to expand production, especially when they are not sure whether demand for their products will remain high. The rising cost of fringe benefits—health insurance, unemployment compensation, retirement, social security—is also cited as an important factor that leads companies to prefer expanding overtime to hiring new workers. By 1993 these extra costs amounted to 28 percent of a worker's wages. James Waters of Towers Perrin, a personnel consulting firm, put the matter somewhat differently when he said, "Benefit costs, including health costs, are a major factor, but there is more concern about all the costs of recruiting people, training them, carrying them until they become fully productive, and then the cost of firing them if production slacks off. A weak economy has made employers very cautious."

Overtime is quite common in manufacturing where workers are generally highly skilled and the hiring of new workers takes time and effort for recruitment and training. In contrast, the work force for retail sales and food industries is less skilled with more extensive use of part-time workers and contract workers without benefits. The result has been less overtime and more new hires in service sectors than in manufacturing.

Some blame large health insurance costs, typically paid for each full-time worker regardless of the number of hours worked, as a major factor in explaining the increased overtime. Paying overtime may cost more in terms of salary but does not add to a company's health insurance costs the way hiring new workers would. Those concerned about the impact of health insurance costs on employment and overtime see a payroll tax for health care or some other form of government-financed health insurance as helping reduce the cost of new hires to private firms.

1. Firms can increase employment by hiring new workers or increasing hours for their current workers. Analyze the factors affecting a firm's decision to increase overtime or hire new workers when, in addition to hourly wages and fringe benefits, there is a significant fixed cost to hiring new workers.

2. Consider each of the following elements of labor compensation: Wages, social security taxes, retirement contributions, health insurance benefits, training costs, costs of hiring and firing. Which vary directly with the number of hours worked and which operate like fixed costs, that is, which vary with the number of workers and which with the number of hours worked?

3. Extra pay for overtime work was instituted during the 1930s to discourage overtime and to encourage employers to hire more workers. Is there a need for additional steps today? If yes, what steps would you recommend and why? If no, why not?

## STUDY QUESTIONS

1. Why does the income effect of an increase in wages tend to reduce the supply of labor when wages increase?

2. Why does the substitution effect of an increase in wages tend to increase the supply of labor when wages increase?

3. How can distinguishing between the income and substitution effects of an increase in wages help one understand the historical record of increasing real wages and a declining work week?

4. What explains the demand for labor?

5. When will wages contain significant economic rent?

6. Demand and supply analysis seems to suggest that there should be a single wage, yet there is significant variation in the wages individuals receive. What other factors explain the significant difference in wages among individuals? Which of these factors can be seen as factors affecting the demand and supply curves and which cannot?

7. What is human capital theory and how might it explain differences in wages?

8. What would you expect to happen if the minimum wage is increased? Why?

9. Economists often argue that a union can only raise wages by accepting a reduction in employment. When does a union face this sort of trade-off and what might it do to try and increase both employment and wages?

10. What is the difference between mediation and arbitration? Is one better than the other? Why?

## Chapter 17

# Poverty, Inequality, and Discrimination

## LEARNING OBJECTIVES

After completing this chapter, you should be able to:

- discuss some of the facts of poverty and income distribution.
- describe the implications of the use of absolute or relative concepts of poverty.
- explain what a Lorenz curve is.
- draw a Lorenz curve, given data on population and income.
- describe what factors account for differences in incomes, how some of these factors reflect voluntary choices, and why these factors make identifying economic discrimination so difficult.
- explain how competition can minimize some forms of discrimination but not others.
- explain why the trade-off between equality and efficiency implies that the optimal distribution of income will involve some inequality.
- explain the concept of a negative income tax and how it affects work incentives.
- describe the controversy surrounding programs for affirmative action and comparable worth.

## IMPORTANT TERMS AND CONCEPTS

Poverty line
Absolute and relative concepts of poverty
Lorenz curve
Economic discrimination
Statistical discrimination
Optimal amount of inequality
Trade-off between equality and efficiency
Aid to Families with Dependent Children (AFDC)

Food stamps
Negative income tax (NIT)
Civil Rights Act
Equal Employment Opportunities Commission (EEOC)
Affirmative action
Comparable worth

## CHAPTER REVIEW

Discussions of poverty in America usually focus on the number of families below the *poverty line*. In 1992
(1) this dividing line was about $_____ a year for a family of four. It is
adjusted every year for changes in prices. Since the yearly adjustment reflects only prices and not general
increases in real income, the poverty line is a(n) (absolute/relative) concept of poverty rather than a(n)
_____ concept.

The facts about the distribution of income can be presented in a number of different ways. Economists
(2) often use a form of graphical representation called a(n)_____ curve. To construct such
a curve, one first orders families or individuals by income, lowest to highest. Then the cumulative percentage
of total income is plotted against the cumulative percentage of families (or individuals). The Lorenz curve
starts at the origin, where zero percent of families have _____ percent of
income. Perfect equality in the distribution of income would result in a Lorenz curve that coincided with
the _____ line. In real economies, with inequality in the distribution of income,
the Lorenz curve has a _____ slope and lies (above/below) the 45-degree
line. (Can you convince yourself that the Lorenz curve never has a negative slope and that it never crosses
the 45-degree line?) In fact, some researchers measure the degree of inequality by the area between the
Lorenz curve and the 45-degree line as a proportion of the total area under the 45-degree line. Over the
last 30 years this measure shows (no/very little/significant) change in inequality of the distribution of
income in the United States.

U.S. income data show that in 1991, families with incomes above $63,000 were in the top 20 percent
of the income distribution, while families with incomes below approximately $14,350 were in the bottom
(3) 20 percent. The top 20 percent of families received _____ percent of income while
the bottom 20 percent received _____ percent.

Why do incomes differ? The list of reasons is long and includes differences in abilities, intensity of
work, risk taking, wage differentials for unpleasant or hazardous tasks, schooling and training, work
experience, inherited wealth, luck, and discrimination. Some of the reasons for differences in incomes
represent voluntary choices by individuals to work harder, take more risks, or accept unpleasant work
in order to earn higher incomes. Measures to equalize incomes may adversely affect the work effort of
these individuals. In more technical terms, efforts for greater equality may mean reduced
(4) _____. This important trade-off does not mean that all efforts to increase
equality should be abandoned. It does mean that efforts to increase equality have a price and should not
be pushed beyond the point where the marginal gains from further equality are worth less than the
marginal loss from reduced efficiency. Exactly where this point is reached is the subject of continuing
political debate.

The trade-off between equality and efficiency also suggests that in the fight for greater equality one
should choose policies with small rather than large effects on efficiency. Economists argue that many
welfare programs are inefficient. One important reason is the relatively large reduction in benefits for each
(5) additional dollar of earned income. These high implicit (marginal/average) tax rates (increase/decrease)
the incentive for increased work effort on the part of welfare recipients who are able to work.

Many economists favor replacing the current welfare system with a negative income tax, that is, a
system of direct cash grants tied to income levels and linked to the tax system. These schemes usually
(6) start with a minimum guaranteed level of income and a tax rate that specifies the (increase/decrease) in
the cash grant for every dollar increase in income. A low tax rate will retain significant work incentives;
however, a low tax rate also means that grants continue until income is quite high. The point where
payments from the government stop and payments to the government start is called the
_____ level of income. A negative income tax with a low marginal tax rate
can offer significantly better work incentives to those currently receiving welfare, but there will be
(positive/negative) work incentives for those not now on welfare. Recent negative income tax experiments
have investigated the size of these negative work incentives and found them to be (large/small).

(7) Economic discrimination is defined as a situation in which equal factors of production receive _____ payments for equal contributions to output. Average differences in income between large social groups, such as men and women or blacks and whites, (are/are not) sufficient proof of economic discrimination. These average differences tend to (overstate/understate) the amount of economic discrimination. To accurately measure the impact of possible discrimination, we must first correct for the factors listed above that could create differences in income without implying economic discrimination. Some factors, such as schooling, are tricky. For instance, differences in wages associated with differences in schooling would not imply any discrimination if everyone has had an equal opportunity for the same amount of schooling. But it is unclear whether observed differences in schooling represent voluntary choices or another form of discrimination. Public policy makes it illegal to discriminate, but the evidence concerning what constitutes discrimination is subject to dispute. Competitive markets can work to decrease some forms of discrimination, especially discrimination by (employers/employees). Dissatisfaction with apparent continuing discrimination has led to the adoption of policies for affirmative action and comparable worth adjustments in wages.

## IMPORTANT TERMS AND CONCEPTS QUIZ

Choose the most appropriate definition for the following terms.

1. _____ Poverty line
2. _____ Lorenz curve
3. _____ Economic discrimination
4. _____ Statistical discrimination
5. _____ Affirmative action
6. _____ Comparable worth
7. _____ AFDC
8. _____ Negative income tax
9. _____ Food stamps

a. Amount of income below which a family is considered "poor."
b. Active efforts to recruit and hire members of underrepresented groups.

c. Graph depicting the distribution of income.
d. Income share of poorest quartile of income distribution.
e. Public assistance to families with children but no working parent.
f. Pay standards that assign equal wages to jobs deemed "comparable."
g. Estimating a worker's productivity as low solely because that worker belongs to some group.
h. Stamps that allow families to buy food at subsidized prices.
i. Paying different amounts to equivalent factors of production for equal contributions to output.
j. Income-conditioned cash grants available to all families as an entitlement.

## BASIC EXERCISE

This problem illustrates the high marginal tax rates that often result from combining welfare programs. The numbers in this problem do not come from any specific welfare program but illustrate many.

Imagine a welfare system that offers a family of four the following forms of public support.

- *General assistance* in the form of a basic grant of $300 a month. The first $50 of earned income every month is assumed to be for work-related expenses and does not reduce benefits. After that, benefits are reduced by 50 cents for every dollar of earned income.
- *Food stamps* that offer the family $2,500 a year but require payments equal to 25 percent of gross wage earnings.
- *Medicaid benefits* of $1,500 a year. The family is assumed to receive these benefits as long as it is eligible for general assistance.
- *Housing subsidy* that gives the family an apartment worth $4,400 a year in rent. The family must pay rent equal to 25 percent of its net income, which is determined as gross wage earnings plus general assistance minus $500 for each dependent.

1. Fill in column 7 of Table 17-1 by computing net income after taxes and after welfare payments for the different levels of earned income.
2. Use the data in columns 1 and 7 to plot net income against earned income in Figure 17-1. Plot each pair of points and then connect successive pairs with a straight line. What does the graph suggest about work incentives under these programs?
3. Use the data in Table 17-1 to complete Table 17-2, computing the implicit marginal tax rates that this family faces as it earns income. What is the relationship between the implicit marginal tax rates you computed in Table 17-2 and the slope of the graph in Figure 17-1? (How do these marginal rates compare with marginal rates under the positive portion of federal income taxes of 15, 28, and 33 percent?)
4. One could reduce the implicit marginal tax rate by lowering the rate at which benefits are reduced under any of the programs. To investigate the impact of such reductions, construct a new version of Table 17-1 in which general assistance payments are reduced by only 25 cents for every dollar reduction in income, and the food stamp subsidy is reduced by only 10 cents. What happens to the magnitude of the subsidy payments at each level of income? What happens to the break-even levels of income for each program, that is, to the level of income when a family is no longer eligible? What would happen to total public outlays for these programs?

## TABLE 17-1
### (dollars)

| (1) Earned Income | (2) Social Security and Income Taxes* | (3) General Assistance | (4) Food Stamps | (5) Medicaid Subsidy | (6) Housing Subsidy | (7) Net Income (1) + (2) + (3) + (4) + (5) + (6) |
|---|---|---|---|---|---|---|
| 0 | 0 | 3,600 | 2,500 | 1,500 | 4,400 | _____ |
| 600** | 65 | 3,600 | 2,350 | 1,500 | 4,250 | _____ |
| 6,500 | 702 | 650 | 875 | 1,500 | 3,513 | _____ |
| 7,799 | 787 | 1 | 550 | 1,500 | 3,350 | _____ |
| 7,800 | 787 | 0 | 550 | 0 | 3,350 | _____ |
| 10,000 | 619 | 0 | 0 | 0 | 2,800 | _____ |
| 10,250 | 600 | 0 | 0 | 0 | 2,738 | _____ |
| 13,200 | 199 | 0 | 0 | 0 | 2,000 | _____ |
| 19 350 | −1,694 | 0 | 0 | 0 | 463 | _____ |
| 21,200 | −2,353 | 0 | 0 | 0 | 0 | _____ |

*Income taxes include earned income credit at low levels of income and are based on 1992 tax rates.
**Assume $50 a month.

**FIGURE 17-1**

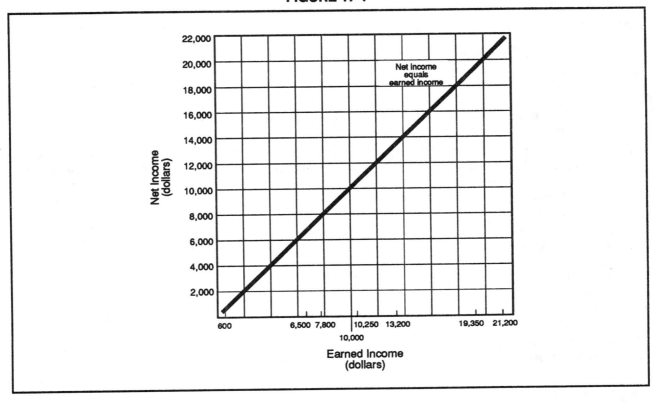

Earned Income
(dollars)

**TABLE 17-2**

| (1)<br>Earned<br>Income<br>(dollars) | (2)<br>Change in<br>Earned<br>Income<br>(dollars) | (3)<br>Net Income<br>(Table 17-1,<br>column 7)<br>(dollars) | (4)<br>Change in<br>Net Income<br>(dollars) | (5)<br>"Implicit Taxes"<br>(2) - (4)<br>(dollars) | (6)<br>Implicit Marginal<br>Tax Rate<br>(5) ÷ (2)<br>(percent) |
|---|---|---|---|---|---|
| 0 | | | | | |
| | 600 | | | | |
| 600 | | | | | |
| | 5,900 | | | | |
| 6,500 | | | | | |
| | 1,299 | | | | |
| 7,799 | | | | | |
| | 1 | | | | |
| 7,800 | | | | | |
| | 2,200 | | | | |
| 10,000 | | | | | |
| | 250 | | | | |
| 10,250 | | | | | |
| | 2,950 | | | | |
| 13,200 | | | | | |
| | 6,150 | | | | |
| 19,350 | | | | | |
| | 1,850 | | | | |
| 21,200 | | | | | |

## SELF-TESTS FOR UNDERSTANDING

### Test A

Circle the most appropriate answer.

1. The facts on income distribution in the United States show
   a. a substantial move toward equality over the last 30 years.
   b. that the richest 20 percent of families receive about 80 percent of the total income.
   c. that the poorest 20 percent of families receive less than 2 percent of income.
   d. a Lorenz curve that sags below the 45–degree line.

2. The poverty line computed by the government, estimated to be $14,350 in 1992, is an example of
   a. statistical discrimination.
   b. a relative concept of poverty.
   c. an absolute concept of poverty.
   d. economic discrimination.

3. Defining poor people as those who fall in the bottom 20 percent of the income distribution
   a. is an absolute concept of poverty.
   b. is a relative concept of poverty.
   c. means that continued economic growth will eliminate poverty.
   d. implies that the Lorenz curve is a straight line.

4. Between 1983 and 1992, the proportion of families with incomes below the official poverty line
   a. decreased but remained above previous low values.
   b. stayed about the same.
   c. rose substantially.
   d. declined to its lowest point ever.

5. The Lorenz curve
   a. is the same for all countries.
   b. is a graph of the cumulative percentage of families (or persons) and the associated cumulative percentage of income they receive.
   c. is a measure of economic discrimination.
   d. shows the growth in income one might expect as she accumulates work experience.

6. If income were equally divided among all families, the Lorenz curve would
   a. lie above the 45-degree line.
   b. follow the horizontal axis.
   c. be the 45-degree straight line.
   d. lie below the 45-degree line.

7. If there were no economic discrimination, the Lorenz curve would
   a. lie above the 45-degree line.
   b. follow the horizontal axis.
   c. be the 45-degree straight line.
   d. lie below the 45-degree line.

8. Compared with other industrial countries, data on the distribution of income in the United States show
   a. more inequality than most other countries.
   b. about the same degree of inequality.
   c. much more equality.

9. In 1992, the richest 20 percent of families received about _____ percent of total income.
   a. 20 percent
   b. 32 percent
   c. 40 percent
   d. 44 percent

10. In 1992, the poorest 20 percent of families received about _____ percent of total income.
    a. 2 percent
    b. 5 percent
    c. 10 percent
    d. 20 percent

11. In 1992, families with an income above _____ were in the top 20 percent of the income distribution.
    a. $36,000
    b. $63,000
    c. $100,000
    d. $200,000

12. Consider a negative income tax scheme with a guaranteed minimum income of $6,000 for a family of four and a tax rate of 50 percent. The break-even level of income will be
    a. $3,000
    b. $6,000
    c. $9,000
    d. $12,000

13. If the Vincents earn $8,000 in wages, their total income will be
    a. $6,000.
    b. $8,000.
    c. $10,000.
    d. $14,000.

14. Reducing the tax rate while retaining the same minimum guarantee will
    a. reduce the break-even level of income.
    b. leave the break-even level of income unchanged.
    c. increase the break-even level of income.
    d. there's too little information to know.

15. If a negative income tax system is to be financed within a given budget, then a reduction in the negative tax rate to increase work incentives
    a. must be offset by a reduction in the minimum guaranteed level of income.
    b. needs no change in the minimum guaranteed level of income.
    c. must be offset by an increase in the minimum guaranteed level of income.

16. Choose all of the actions that would reduce the break-even level of income.
    a. Lower the minimum guarantee level.
    b. Lower the tax rate on earned income.
    c. Increase the minimum guarantee level.
    d. Increase the tax rate on earned income.

17. If two individuals with similar productivity receive different pay for the same work, one would call this evidence of
    a. economic discrimination.
    b. prejudice.
    c. statistical discrimination.
    d. luck.

18. All but which one of the following could give rise to differences in income without implying discrimination?
    a. Schooling.
    b. Ability.
    c. Compensating wage differential for night work.
    d. Intensity of work effort.

19. Which of the following would be an example of economic discrimination?
    a. Census data showing that, on average, women earn less than men.
    b. Nurses earn less than doctors.
    c. Over the period 1980 to 1990, plumbers and electricians received larger percentage wage increases than did college professors.
    d. A careful study showing that among blacks and whites with identical education, work experience, productivity, and motivation, blacks earn less than whites.

20. Competitive markets work to erode what type of discrimination?
    a. Discrimination by employees.
    b. Discrimination by employers.
    c. Statistical discrimination.

## Test B

Circle T or F for true or false.

T  F   1. Continued economic growth is capable of eliminating poverty as measured by an absolute standard, but not as measured by a relative standard.

T  F   2. U.S. data show no change in poverty as measured by the number of families below the poverty line since 1960.

T  F   3. In the United States, the 20 percent of families that are poorest receive about 20 percent of total income.

T  F   4. Perfect equality in the distribution of income would result in a Lorenz curve that lies on the 45-degree line.

T  F   5. Data for the last 40 years show little change in the Lorenz curve for the United States.

T  F   6. The fact that women, white or black, have lower average incomes than men, is sufficient proof of economic discrimination.

T  F   7. Competitive markets can help reduce discrimination by employers.

T  F   8. In the absence of monopolies, unregulated markets would result in an equal distribution of income.

T  F   9. Some differences in income reflect voluntary choices, such as decisions to work more hours or to take early retirement.

T  F  10. The federal personal income tax system has substantially reduced the degree of income inequality in the United States.

## SUPPLEMENTARY EXERCISES

1. Table 17-3 shows data on the distribution of income for 12 Organization for Economic Cooperation and Development (OECD) countries. Which countries have the greatest equality in the distribution of income? You might try drawing a Lorenz curve for several countries to help you decide. For example, consider Japan and Sweden. Use one large piece of graph paper to draw a Lorenz curve for both countries. In which country is income distributed more equally?

If you have access to a microcomputer, try writing a small program to compute the area between the line of equality and the Lorenz curve for each of the countries in Table 17-3.

Compare these data on income distribution for industrialized countries with similar data for lower-income developing countries. *World Development Report*, published annually by the World Bank, reports data on income distribution for a large number of countries.

2. Following is a suggested list of additional readings on three important topics covered in this chapter.

On the general issue of trade-offs between increased equality and reduced efficiency, read Arthur Okun's *Equality and Efficiency: The Big Trade-off*, published by the Brookings Institution, 1975. This important book is the source of the "leaky bucket" analogy used in the text.

For an excellent discussion of how existing welfare schemes confront poor people with "economic choices no rational person would want to make," read *Why Is Welfare So Hard to Reform?* by Henry J. Aaron, published by the Brookings Institution, 1973. The book was written following the Nixon administration's attempt to implement a negative income tax.

Martin Anderson's book, *Welfare: The Political Economy of Welfare Reform in the United States*, Hoover Institution Press, 1978, argues that existing welfare programs have essentially eliminated poverty as a critical social issue. Anderson served for a while as one of President Reagan's White House aides for domestic policy. More recent data on the impact of noncash benefits can be found in *The Statistical Abstract of the United States*.

3. Women now account for more than 45 percent of the American labor force. Economic issues concerning the role of women in the labor force are examined by Claudia Goldin in *Understanding the Gender Gap: An Economic History of American Women*, Oxford University Press, 1990.

4. Investigate the details of welfare programs in the city or county in which you live. Use this information to construct your version of Table 17-1.

**TABLE 17-3**
**PERCENTAGE OF POST-TAX INCOME RECEIVED BY POPULATION DECILES**

| | | Population Deciles | | | | | | | | | |
|---|---|---|---|---|---|---|---|---|---|---|---|
| | Year | 1 | 2 | 3 | 4 | 5 | 6 | 7 | 8 | 9 | 10 |
| Australia | 1966-67 | 2.1 | 4.5 | 6.2 | 7.3 | 8.3 | 9.5 | 10.9 | 12.5 | 15.1 | 23.7 |
| Canada | 1969 | 1.5 | 3.5 | 5.1 | 6.7 | 8.2 | 9.7 | 11.2 | 13.1 | 15.9 | 25.1 |
| France | 1970 | 1.4 | 2.9 | 4.2 | 5.6 | 7.4 | 8.9 | 9.7 | 13.0 | 16.5 | 30.4 |
| Germany | 1973 | 2.8 | 3.7 | 4.6 | 5.7 | 6.8 | 8.2 | 9.8 | 12.1 | 15.8 | 30.3 |
| Italy | 1969 | 1.7 | 3.4 | 4.7 | 5.8 | 7.0 | 9.2 | 9.8 | 11.9 | 15.6 | 30.9 |
| Japan | 1969 | 3.0 | 4.9 | 6.1 | 7.0 | 7.9 | 8.9 | 9.9 | 11.3 | 13.8 | 27.2 |
| Netherlands | 1967 | 2.6 | 3.9 | 5.2 | 6.4 | 7.6 | 8.8 | 10.3 | 12.4 | 15.2 | 27.7 |
| Norway | 1970 | 2.3 | 4.0 | 5.6 | 7.3 | 8.6 | 10.2 | 11.7 | 13.0 | 15.1 | 22.2 |
| Spain | 1973-74 | 2.1 | 3.9 | 5.3 | 6.5 | 7.8 | 9.1 | 10.6 | 12.5 | 15.6 | 26.7 |
| Sweden | 1972 | 2.2 | 4.4 | 5.9 | 7.2 | 8.5 | 10.0 | 11.5 | 13.3 | 15.7 | 21.3 |
| United Kingdom | 1973 | 2.5 | 3.8 | 5.5 | 7.1 | 8.5 | 9.9 | 11.1 | 12.8 | 15.2 | 23.5 |
| United States | 1972 | 1.5 | 3.0 | 4.5 | 6.2 | 7.8 | 9.5 | 11.3 | 13.4 | 16.3 | 26.5 |

SOURCE: Malcolm Sawyer, "Income Distribution in OECD Countries." *OECD Occasional Studies*. July 1978, Table 4, page 14. Reprinted by permission.

## STUDY QUESTIONS

1. What do you believe happened to the degree of inequality in the distribution of income in the United States over the past decade? Why?

2. Which is the most meaningful measure of poverty, an absolute standard or a relative standard? Why?

3. What is a Lorenz curve and how does it provide information about the distribution of income?

4. Differences in income may be related to a number of factors. What factors reflect voluntary choices and what factors might reflect economic discrimination?

5. What is the difference between statistical discrimination and economic discrimination? Does statistical discrimination always lead to economic discrimination? Is economic discrimination always the result of statistical discrimination?

6. Competitive market forces can be counted on to help reduce some forms of discrimination but not others. When will market forces work to eliminate discrimination and when might additional measures be needed?

7. What is meant by the optimal degree of inequality? Why isn't it zero?

8. How does a negative income tax improve work incentives as compared with a system of overlapping poverty programs?

## ECONOMICS IN ACTION
### Employment, Wages, and Poverty

The economic expansion from 1982 to 1990 was the second longest in U.S. history. Poverty rates declined but not by as much as one would have expected from experience during the 1960s. Why was economic expansion less effective in reducing poverty in the 1980s than in the 1960s?

Economist Rebecca Blank has considered a number of explanations.[1] For example, Census data on the incidence of poverty focuses on cash income. There was a substantial expansion of in-kind transfer programs between the 1960s and the 1980s, food stamps, housing subsidies, and medicaid being the primary examples. Might these changes explain differences in the 1980s as compared with the 1960s? Blank is skeptical. While the level of in-kind transfers were higher in the 1980s and measures of poverty that include in-kind transfer were thus lower, she can find little evidence of any substantial increase in these programs over the 1980s. Including in-kind transfers makes little difference in the decline in the poverty rate during the 1980s. Other possibilities that Blank investigated include changes in the regional location of the poor, changes in public assistance programs, and changes in the types of families that are poor. In all cases, she concludes that these factors were either unimportant or too small to explain why the reduction in the poverty rate over the 1980s lagged experience of the 1960s.

What does explain the difference? Blank finds evidence that over the 1980s there was a decline in the real wages of low-wage workers and this explains why economic growth was less effective in reducing poverty. According to Blank, "The primary reason why the poor 'catch up' in economic booms is expanded employment opportunities. The incidence of unemployment, non-employment, and part-time employment is heavily skewed toward the bottom of the income distribution; when employment grows it is the unemployed, the non-employed, and part-time employed who are most able to take advantage of that growth." Blank found that economic growth in the 1980s did lead to increased employment opportunities for low-income families. If anything, employment and weeks of work for low-income families expanded more rapidly in the 1980s than in the 1960s. However, the increased hours of work were largely offset by declines in real wages. Blank's findings are consistent with information from the 1990 Census that shows a widening differential in the earnings of college graduates compared with high school graduates and dropouts.

---

[1] Rebecca M. Blank, "Why Were Poverty Rates So High in the 1980s?," NBER Working Paper No. 3878, October 1991.

---

What explains the decline in the real wages of low-wage workers? Blank does not offer a particular reason but speculates on a combination of factors, "changes in unionization, changes in technology, changes in international markets . . . and changes in the relative supply of more and less skilled workers relative to a rapidly growing demand for labor market skills by employers."

1. What do you think explains why the economic expansion of the 1980s did not result in a larger decline in the poverty rate?
2. What are the implications for public policy?

*Chapter* **18**

# Limiting Market Power: Regulation of Industry

## LEARNING OBJECTIVES

After completing this chapter, you should be able to:

- describe the two major purposes of regulation.
- identify the major regulatory agencies and the industries they regulate.
- critically evaluate the arguments supporting regulation.
- explain why regulators often raise prices.
- discuss the implications of "fully distributed costs" as a basis for price floors.
- explain why marginal cost pricing may be infeasible in an industry with significant economies of scale.
- explain why allowing a firm to earn profits equal to the opportunity cost of its capital provides little incentive for increased efficiency.
- evaluate the alternatives suggested for present regulatory practices.
- summarize recent experience under deregulation of several industries.
- discuss the experience of nationalized and regulated industries.

## IMPORTANT TERMS AND CONCEPTS

Regulation
Nationalization
Privatization
Price floor
Price ceiling
Natural monopoly
Economies of scale
Economies of scope

Cross-subsidization
Self-destructive competition
Fully distributed cost
Marginal cost pricing
Ramsey Pricing Rule
Stand-alone cost
Regulatory lag
Price caps

## CHAPTER REVIEW

(1) Generally, the United States has chosen to (<u>regulate/nationalize</u>) rather than to _____ industries where there is concern about the exploitation of excessive market power. This chapter discusses the controversies about regulatory practices and the roles played by the regulatory agencies.

Regulatory procedures have been adopted basically for four reasons:

1. To regulate the actions of natural monopolies in industries where economies of
(2) _____ and economies of_____ mean that free competition between a large number of suppliers (<u>is/is not</u>) sustainable.

2. To ensure service at reasonable prices to isolated areas. It is argued that regulation is necessary so that suppliers can offset (<u>above/below</u>)-cost prices in isolated areas with (<u>above/below</u>)-cost prices elsewhere and thus be protected from competitors who concentrate only on the profitable markets.

3. To avoid self-destructive competition among firms in industries with high (<u>fixed/marginal</u>) costs and low short-run _____ costs.

4. To protect consumers, employees, and the environment from unscrupulous business practices.

The first three justifications often lead to direct regulation of prices and/or earnings. The last reason, concerning consumer, employee, and environmental protection, usually does not involve the direct regulation of prices, although compliance can impose substantial costs on firms.

Regulation of prices has to be a very complicated undertaking. Established to prevent abuses of monopoly such as charging prices that are "too high," the regulatory agencies have, in many cases, actually
(3) raised prices. In these cases, regulation preserves the shadow of competition only by protecting (<u>high/low</u>)-cost, inefficient firms.

Several criteria have been proposed to evaluate whether prices are "fair." One method looks at all costs related to a given line of business as well as some portion of shared overhead. This method leads
(4) to what is called _____ _____ costs. Economists typically argue for the use of _____ cost as a more appropriate basis for price floors. One can conceive of cases, often in connection with regulated earnings, where any price above long-run marginal cost yet below fully distributed costs will allow (<u>higher/lower</u>) prices for all of a firm's customers.

The application of marginal cost pricing is difficult in an industry with significant economies of scale. In this case, average cost will decline as output increases. When average cost declines, marginal
(5) cost is (<u>greater/less</u>) than average cost. Economists and some regulators have urged use of the Ramsey Pricing Rule, under which the excess of price over marginal cost depends upon the elasticity of _____. Difficulties with implementing the Ramsey Pricing Rule have led to interest in the concept of stand-alone cost. Under this approach, regulators would not set price but rather floors and ceilings within which prices could vary. Price floors would reflect minimal competitive prices, or (<u>marginal/average</u>) cost. Price ceilings would reflect the competitive costs of providing the service or good in question, or_____ _____ cost.

A number of alternatives to the present system of regulation have been considered. In some markets it
(6) appears that viable competition is now possible. In these cases, many observers have argued for (<u>more/less</u>) regulation. Recently there has been significant deregulation of airlines, trucking, railroads, telecommunications, and banking. In other cases, the problem of efficiency incentives might be addressed by the use of explicit _____ criteria, which would reward firms for measurable increased efficiency.

Sometimes regulation limits overall profitability rather than prices. For example, a firm's rate of return might be limited to 10 percent. While such regulation might seem to limit the ability of firms to exercise
(7) monopoly power, it also (<u>enhances/reduces</u>) the incentive for firms to be efficient. In the absence of profit regulation, successful efforts to reduce costs will be rewarded with higher profits. If profits are regulated, there is less incentive to seek out the most efficient means of production. The term *regulatory lag* has been coined to describe the drawn out regulatory process. Some suggest that this process itself offers one of the few incentives for efficiency and innovation, since it actually builds in some penalty for (<u>efficiency/inefficiency</u>) and some reward for _____. A variant of this notion would predetermine price ceilings and leave firms free to earn higher profits through even greater efficiency.

Experience with deregulation, especially in airline, transportation, and telephone service, is now more than a decade old, and a number of trends have emerged.

1. Prices have generally declined.
2. Local airline service has not suffered, as was feared, due to the establishment of specialized commuter airlines.
3. New firms have entered previously regulated industries, although not all have survived.
4. Unions in previously regulated industries have been under significant pressure to reduce wages and adjust work rules.
5. Mergers have increased the average size of the largest firms.

Items 4 and 5 need careful interpretation. To the extent that regulation allowed firms to easily pass on increased labor costs, unions will find the bargaining position of firms now subject to competitive market pressures much tougher. Mergers are understandable if regulation was originally concentrated on industries with economies of scale. We now need to balance the potential cost savings from larger firms against the potential of monopoly abuses.

While the United States has chosen, with some exceptions, to regulate industries, a number of other countries have chosen to nationalize industries. No clear–cut evidence exists on which approach is superior. One can find cases where nationalized industries are a model of efficiency and others where they are not. An important limitation of nationalization as a general solution is the absence of a systematic incentive for efficiency like that provided by the profit motive for private enterprises. Much seems to depend upon particular circumstances, especially the rules adopted by government agencies.

## IMPORTANT TERMS AND CONCEPTS QUIZ

Choose the most appropriate definition for the following terms.

1. _____ Regulation
2. _____ Nationalization
3. _____ Privatization
4. _____ Price floor
5. _____ Price ceiling
6. _____ Natural monopoly
7. _____ Economies of scale
8. _____ Economies of scope
9. _____ Cross-subsidization
10. _____ Ramsey Pricing Rule
11. _____ Fully distributed cost
12. _____ Stand-alone cost
13. _____ Regulatory lag
14. _____ Price caps

a. Losses on one product balanced by profits on another.
b. Principle that, in a multiproduct, regulated firm where price must exceed marginal cost for the firm to break even, the ratio of price to marginal cost should be highest for the products with the lowest demand elasticities.
c. Legal restrictions or controls or business decisions of firms.
d. Fair share of a firm's total cost as determined by accounting conventions.
e. Industry in which a single firm is able to supply the market output at lower average cost than a number of smaller firms could.
f. Savings acquired through simultaneous production of different products.
g. Government ownership and operation of a business firm.
h. Hypothetical cost for an efficient firm to supply a particular service.
i. Prices based on incremental costs.
j. Delays in considering requests for price changes.
k. Legal minimum price.
l. Savings acquired through increases in quantities produced.
m. Pre assigned price ceilings that decline in future years in anticipation of future productivity growth.
n. Selling previously nationalized or public firms to private owners.
o. Legal maximum price.

## BASIC EXERCISE

This exercise illustrates the difficulty of marginal cost pricing when average cost declines.

Imagine that the efficient provision of telephone calls in a medium-sized city involves an initial investment of $100 million financed by borrowing at 6.75 percent and variable cost of 15 cents a phone call. The phone company's annual fixed cost would be $6.75 million (6.75 percent of $100 million).

1. Use this information about costs to plot marginal cost and average total cost in Figure 18-1. (Use the $6.75 million figure for annual fixed cost.)
2. Assume that regulators set price at 15 cents, the level of marginal cost. What is the firm's profit position if 60 million calls a year are demanded at that price? 90 million? 150 million?
3. Is setting price equal to marginal cost a viable option in this case? Why or why not?

**FIGURE 18-1**

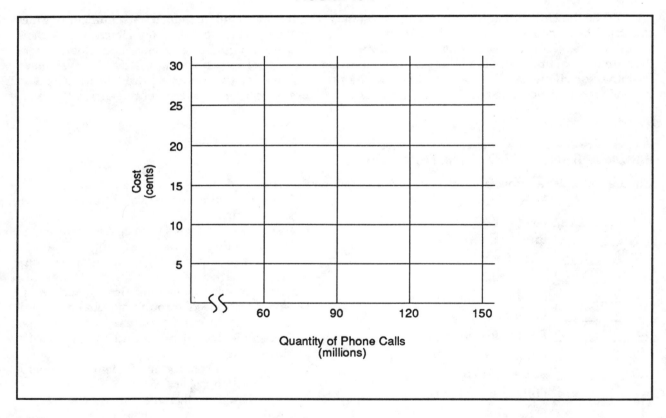

## SELF-TESTS FOR UNDERSTANDING

### Test A

Circle the most appropriate answer.

1. Match each of these regulatory agencies with the appropriate industries from the list below.

   Interstate Commerce Commission (ICC)

   _____

   Federal Communications Commission (FCC)

   _____

   Federal Energy Regulatory Commission (FERC)

   _____

   Federal Reserve

   _____

   Securities and Exchange Commission (SEC)

   _____

   a. Banking
   b. Automobile manufacturers
   c. Broadcasting and telecommunications
   d. Railroads, barges, pipelines, and some trucking
   e. Telephone
   f. Securities (stocks and bonds)
   g. Interstate transmission of electric power and sales of natural gas
   h. Pharmaceuticals

2. Regulation proponents would disagree with which one of the following?
   a. The public needs to be protected from the potential abuses of natural monopolies.
   b. Destructive competition may benefit consumers in the short run but will leave them open to monopoly abuses in the long run.
   c. "Caveat emptor" is an appropriate principle for the marketplace.
   d. In the absence of regulation, many isolated communities might find themselves without vital services.

3. Economies of scale and economies of scope are examples of a
   a. nationalized industry.
   b. natural monopoly.
   c. regulated industry.
   d. competitive industry.

4. Which of the following is an example of economies of scale?
   a. Anna finds her costs increasing as she tries to increase the production of her custom designed clothes.
   b. Jim discovers that a 15 percent reduction in price leads to a 30 percent increase in sales.
   c. Sarah realizes that her firm's expertise and experience in producing specialized medical equipment will be useful in the production of testing equipment for physicists.
   d. IBM is able to reduce unit costs when it doubles production of the IBM PC.

5. Which of the following is an example of economies of scope?
   a. An increase in circulation for the *Daily Planet* would involve only printing costs and require no increase in the editorial staff.
   b. Ramona and Ricardo have invested their wealth in a portfolio of stocks, bonds, and real estate.
   c. In an effort to keep production lines busy all year, Arctic Enterprises produces a variety of small-engine home and garden tools in addition to its successful line of snowblowers.
   d. Ma Bell formerly used profits from long-distance calls to reduce monthly charges for local phone service.

6. The term *cross subsidy* refers to
   a. an angry firm that does not receive a subsidy.
   b. higher prices on some products that help to cover costs on other products.
   c. Congressional subsidies for agriculture.
   d. the financing of Christian churches.

7. Regulation has promoted cross-subsidization as a way of
   a. dealing with universal service to isolated, high-cost locations.
   b. accounting for fully distributed costs.
   c. promoting efficiencies from synergetic business combinations.
   d. addressing the effects of self-destructive competition.

8. The term *fully distributed costs* refers to
   a. marginal cost.
   b. average variable cost.
   c. average variable cost plus some allocation of shared or overhead costs.
   d. average fixed cost.

9. Prices based on fully distributed costs
   a. would be identical to those based on long-run marginal costs.
   b. would be identical to Ramsey prices.
   c. have been proposed as a way of ensuring that prices on all lines of business are fair to customers and competitors alike.
   d. provide strong incentives for increased efficiency.

10. Marginal cost pricing is not feasible in industries characterized by
    a. low fixed costs and rising marginal cost.
    b. constant returns to scale.
    c. rising average costs.
    d. high fixed costs and falling average costs.

11. The Ramsey Pricing Rule is an attempt to solve the problem of appropriate pricing in
    a. nationalized industries.
    b. single-product, regulated firms.
    c. the telephone and telecommunications industry.
    d. multiproduct, regulated firms where prices must exceed marginal cost for the firm to break even.

12. According to the Ramsey rule, the ratio of price to marginal cost should be largest for those products with the
    a. largest fully distributed costs.
    b. largest income elasticity of demand.
    c. largest stand-alone costs.
    d. smallest price elasticity of demand.

13. Which of the following pricing rules is likely to result in the lowest prices to consumers?
    a. Stand-alone cost pricing.
    b. Fully distributed cost pricing.
    c. Marginal cost pricing.
    d. Average cost pricing.

14. The term *regulatory lag* refers to
    a. the time it takes people to respond to a change in prices.
    b. the long time it may take for a change in regulated prices to be approved.
    c. the slowness of moves to deregulation.
    d. the delay that occurs on many long-distance phone calls.

15. The term *price caps* refers to
    a. price floors.
    b. price ceilings that are adjusted in anticipation of future efficiencies.
    c. limits on a firm's overall profits.
    d. attempts to control inflationary increases in prices.

16. The use of *price caps* is an example of
    a. using regulatory lags to provide some incentive for increased efficiency.
    b. successful nationalization.
    c. rate-of-return regulation.
    d. cross-subsidization.

17. Which of the following *does not* provide a strong incentive for increased efficiency on the part of regulated firms?
    a. Regulating profits so they equal the opportunity cost of capital.
    b. Deregulation.
    c. Performance criteria.
    d. Regulatory lag.

18. Which one of the following is not among the alternatives proposed to the present system of regulation?
    a. Deregulation of industries where there appears to be sufficient competition.
    b. The use of explicit performance criteria where feasible.
    c. An institutionalized regulatory lag in an effort to promote efficiency.
    d. More extensive use of fully distributed costs.

19. Deregulation of the airline industry has produced all but which one of the following?
    a. Lower prices on average.
    b. Reduced frills and other forms of nonprice competition.
    c. Pressures on unions for wage concessions as firms attempt to lower costs.
    d. A reduction in merger activity compared with the preceding period of regulation.

20. In the United States natural monopolies tend to be regulated while in Europe they have tended to be
    a. nationalized.
    b. privatized.
    c. revitalized.
    d. capitalized.

## Test B

Circle T or F for true or false.

T  F  1. Regulators are exclusively concerned with getting regulated industries to lower prices.

T  F  2. The term *economies of scope* refers to the reduction in average costs that come from large-scale production.

T  F  3. Fair-rate-of-return regulations—that is, price controls that allow firms in an industry to earn profits sufficient to cover the opportunity cost of their capital—offer strong incentives for efficiency and innovation.

T  F  4. The term *regulatory lag* refers to the lag between actual regulatory practice and the conventional wisdom as to the best practice.

T  F  5. In the absence of regulation, firms required to provide service to isolated communities at high cost might find their more profitable low-cost markets taken over by competitors through a process called cream-skimming.

T  F  6. Self-destructive competition is often used as an argument for regulation.

T  F  7. Stand-alone cost, based on the idea of contestable markets, has been proposed as an alternative to direct regulation of prices.

T  F  8. Non economists who talk about fully distributed costs and economists who talk about long-run marginal costs are using different language to describe the same thing.

T  F  9. A limitation of nationalization as a solution to the problem of natural monopolies is that there are few systematic mechanisms to promote efficiency in nationalized industries.

T  F 10. Nationalized industries in all countries are terribly inefficient.

## SUPPLEMENTARY EXERCISE

Pick your favorite regulatory agency, then go to the library and look up the appropriate annual reports to find out who has served on the regulatory commission recently. Use biographical information, such as is found in *Who's Who in America*, to trace the careers of these individuals. Did these commissioners come from the industry they regulated? After leaving the government did they take a job with the industry they regulated? Who is regulating whom?

## STUDY QUESTIONS

1. What is the difference between economies of scale and economies of scope?

2. Do you believe regulation is necessary to prevent self-destructive competition? Why? Why not?

3. Why do regulators often work to increase rather than limit prices?

4. What is the difference between prices based on fully distributed costs and prices based on marginal cost?

5. Why aren't prices based on marginal cost, a feasible alternative in case of natural monopolies arising from economies of scale?

6. What pricing principle should be followed if it is necessary to establish price floors in a particular industry? Why?

7. How can regulatory lags provide incentives for efficiency?

8. What is your evaluation of the American experience with deregulation?

9. What are the advantages and disadvantages of regulation as opposed to nationalization for dealing with a natural monopoly?

## ECONOMICS IN ACTION

### Fear of Flying

Airline deregulation appears to have raised more questions than it answered. By the spring of 1993 as this edition of the Study Guide was being written, air fares for Americans were among the least expensive in the world. A careful traveler was able to take advantage of low-priced, advance-purchase fares. On balance, the hub-and-spoke system had made it easier for travelers from mid-sized cities—one flight to a major hub opened up the rest of the country. But were these advantages just a temporary illusion? The airlines had cumulative losses totaling almost $10 billion. This appeared to be a classic case of an industry with high fixed costs and low marginal costs. Had competitive pressures forced airlines into a no-win price war with prices close to marginal costs but insufficient to cover total costs? While travelers benefited in the short run, wouldn't they pay in the long run?

Concerns about the viability of American airlines gave rise to a number of remedies. Tax rebates, direct government subsidies, and a return to regulated airfares to enforce prices high enough to cover costs were among the proposed solutions. President Clinton was moved to establish a presidential commission on the future of the American air industry.

Others were not so sure that massive government intervention was needed. They argued that many problems were of the industry's own making and would solve themselves as the economy recovered. Excess capacity reflected both the slow economic recovery and overly optimistic purchases of new planes. The debt load of some airlines that added to their fixed costs was in part the result of earlier leveraged buyouts. Labor costs reflected earlier voluntary settlements with powerful unions. Some airlines were able to protect themselves through Chapter 11 bankruptcy proceedings.

Those who counseled against special actions argued that bankruptcy would not destroy planes but would allow new ownership to start over without the large debt service or high labor costs that encumbered previous owners. They expected that as economic growth recovered, the demand for air travel and the profits of airlines would follow suit. Moves by the government to provide subsidies or to increase prices would only sustain the management that was responsible for current problems. While one could make a case for government action that would eliminate remaining barriers to competition, in particular long-term leases that allowed particular airlines to dominate boarding gates along with take-off and landing slots at congested airports, these actions were quite different from direct subsidies or indirect subsidies through regulated prices.

1. What has happened to American airlines since the spring of 1993? Do you agree with the recommendations of the presidential commission? If you were in charge, what would you have done in the spring of 1993?

# Chapter 19
# Limiting Market Power: Antitrust Policy

## LEARNING OBJECTIVES

After completing this chapter, you should be able to:

- explain the major features of each of the five basic antitrust laws.
- describe the shift in judicial emphasis from conduct to structure as grounds for identifying illegal monopolies.
- describe the evidence of changes in concentration in the United States.
- explain the differences in vertical, horizontal, and conglomerate mergers.
- discuss the major arguments for and against bigness per se.
- describe how concentration may or may not be related to market power.
- evaluate arguments supporting price discrimination.

## IMPORTANT TERMS AND CONCEPTS

Antitrust policy
Sherman Act
Clayton Act
Price discrimination
Celler-Kefauver Antimerger Act
Federal Trade Commission Act
Robinson-Patman Act
Rule of reason
Structure versus conduct
Horizontal merger
Vertical merger
Conglomerate merger
Concentration of industry
Concentration ratio
Patent
Market power

## CHAPTER REVIEW

This chapter discusses antitrust policy, which is designed to control the growth of monopolies and prevent undesirable behavior from powerful firms. The history of antitrust legislation in the United States starts

**(1)** with the _____ Act, enacted in 1890. This act declared illegal any actions in restraint of trade and any attempts to monopolize trade. Vigorous antitrust legal action (<u>was/was not</u>) immediately adopted.

The next important pieces of legislation were both enacted in 1914. The Federal Trade Commission Act

**(2)** established the Federal Trade Commission, and the _____ Act prohibited a number of practices, including preferential prices to some buyers that were not based on cost differences, known as _____ _____; requirements that buyers purchase not only what they want but also other goods exclusively from the same seller, called _____ contracts; having the same individuals serve as directors of two or more competing firms, or _____ _____; and the purchasing of a competitor's stock if that acquisition tended to reduce competition.

**(3)** At this time, court decisions in antitrust cases were based on the rule of _____ which said that size per se (<u>is/is not</u>) illegal; rather, the focus was on firm _____. In the Alcoa case, decided in 1945, the Supreme Court ruled that in addition to illegal conduct, size per se (<u>was/was not</u>) sufficient grounds for antitrust actions.

A firm can grow bigger by expanding its own factories or building new ones. A firm can also become

**(4)** bigger by buying up other firms. Combining two firms into one is a _____. When two companies, one of which sells inputs to the other, merge it is called a (<u>vertical/horizontal</u>) merger. Mergers between competitors are called _____ mergers. The merger of two unrelated firms is called a _____ merger.

Economists and others have long argued whether bigness per se is good or bad. Opponents contend that the flow of wealth to firms with significant market power is socially undesirable and should be

**(5)** restrained; profit-maximizing monopolists are likely to produce (<u>more/less</u>) output than is socially desirable; and large firms with significant market power have little inducement for _____.

Proponents counter that large firms are necessary for successful innovation. They maintain that many

**(6)** big firms, because of (<u>increasing/decreasing</u>) returns to scale, can yield benefits to the public as a result of the associated (<u>reduction/increase</u>) in unit cost that accompanies large-scale production. To break up these firms into smaller units would (<u>increase/decrease</u>) costs.

There is no perfect measure of how concentrated an industry is. One widely used gauge looks at the percent of industry output accounted for by the four largest firms. This measure is called a four-firm

**(7)** _____ ratio. In this century, concentration ratios in the United States have shown (<u>much/little</u>) change.

## IMPORTANT TERMS AND CONCEPTS QUIZ

Choose the most appropriate definition for the following terms.

1. _____ Antitrust policy
2. _____ Price discrimination
3. _____ Horizontal merger
4. _____ Vertical merger
5. _____ Conglomerate merger
6. _____ Concentration ratio
7. _____ Patent
8. _____ Market power

a. Temporary grant of monopoly rights over an invention.
b. Joining firms that produce similar products into a single firm.

c. Ability of a firm to affect the price of its output for its own benefit.
d. Programs designed to control growth of monopoly and to prevent powerful firms from engaging in "undesirable" practices.
e. Temporary grant of monopoly rights over a publication.
f. Charging different buyers different prices for the same product.
g. Combining two unrelated firms into a single firm.
h. Percentage of an industry's output produced by its four largest firms.
i. Joining firms, one of which supplies input(s) to the other, into a single firm.

## BASIC EXERCISE

This exercise illustrates how a monopolist may be able to increase her profits by engaging in price discrimination. Table 19-1 contains data on the demand for snow tires in Centerville and Middletown. Centerville does not get much snow, and the demand for snow tires is quite elastic. Middletown is smaller, and gets more snow; it should not be surprising that the demand for snow tires in Middletown is less elastic than in Centerville. Snow tires are supplied to both cities by a monopolist who can produce tires with a fixed cost of $2,500,000 and a constant marginal cost of $10 a tire.

1. Assume that the monopolist charges the same price in both towns. Use the data on total demand to compute the monopolist's profit-maximizing level of output and price. First compute total revenue in order to compute marginal revenue per tire by dividing the change in total revenue by the change in output. Then compare marginal revenue to the monopolist's marginal cost of $10 to determine the profit-maximizing level of output.

### TABLE 19-1

| Price | Quantity Demanded Centerville | Middletown | Total Demand | Total Revenue | Marginal Revenue |
|-------|-------------|------------|--------------|---------------|------------------|
| $48 | 10,000 | 40,000 | 50,000 | _____ | _____ |
| 45 | 25,000 | 43,750 | 68,750 | _____ | _____ |
| 42 | 40,000 | 47,500 | 87,500 | _____ | _____ |
| 39 | 55,000 | 51,250 | 106,250 | _____ | _____ |
| 36 | 70,000 | 55,000 | 125,000 | _____ | _____ |
| 33 | 85,000 | 58,750 | 143,750 | _____ | _____ |
| 30 | 100,000 | 62,500 | 162,500 | _____ | _____ |
| 27 | 115,000 | 66,250 | 181,250 | _____ | _____ |

**TABLE 19-2**

| | Centerville | | | Middletown | | |
|---|---|---|---|---|---|---|
| Price | Total Revenue | Marginal Revenue | | Total Revenue | Marginal Revenue | |
| $48 | _____ | _____ | | _____ | _____ | |
| 45 | _____ | _____ | | _____ | _____ | |
| 42 | _____ | _____ | | _____ | _____ | |
| 39 | _____ | _____ | | _____ | _____ | |
| 36 | _____ | _____ | | _____ | _____ | |
| 33 | _____ | _____ | | _____ | _____ | |
| 30 | _____ | _____ | | _____ | _____ | |
| 27 | _____ | _____ | | _____ | _____ | |

Price? $_____

Output?_____

Profits? $_____

2. Assume that the monopolist can charge different prices in the towns; that is, she is a price discriminator. Can the monopolist increase her profits by charging different prices? Complete Table 19-2 to answer this question.

Profit-maximizing price in Centerville: $_____

Profit-maximizing price in Middletown: $_____

Quantity of snow tires in Centerville: _____

Quantity of snow tires in Middletown: _____

Total Profits: $_____

3. In which town did the monopolist raise the price? In which town did she lower the price? The monopolist should charge a higher price in the town with the lower elasticity of demand. Can you explain why? Is that the case here?

## SELF-TESTS FOR UNDERSTANDING

### Test A

Circle the most appropriate answer.

1. Regarding the Sherman Act, which of the following is *not true*?
   a. It prohibited contracts, combinations, and conspiracies in restraint of trade.
   b. It prohibited acts that attempt monopolization of trade.
   c. It declared any firm with 50 percent of an industry's output to be an illegal monopoly.
   d. It contained no mechanism for enforcement.

2. The Clayton Act prohibits all but which one of the following?
   a. The direct purchase of a competitor's assets.
   b. Tying contracts.
   c. Price discrimination.
   d. Interlocking directorates.

3. Price fixing is illegal under the
   a. Sherman Act.
   b. Clayton Act.
   c. Federal Trade Commission Act.
   d. Celler-Kefauver Act.

4. The rule of reason said that
    a. reasonable people could determine what levels of concentration ratios imply excessive market power.
    b. reasonable prices, even if fixed by competing firms, were not illegal.
    c. size is illegal only if acquired or maintained through objectionable overt acts that tend to monopolize trade.
    d. it is reasonable to prosecute a firm under the Sherman Act when it controls an excessive proportion of industry output.

5. Tying contracts
    a. require purchasing firms to sign long-term exclusive purchase agreements.
    b. are often used by companies that sell rope and string.
    c. require retailers to tie their sales price to a manufacturer's suggested price.
    d. require buyers to one good to also buy other goods from the same seller.

6. Price discounts that tend to reduce competition were declared illegal under the
    a. Sherman Act.
    b. Federal Trade Commission Act.
    c. Robinson-Patman Act.
    d. Celler-Kefauver Act.

7. The actions described in question 6 were designed to
    a. lower prices to consumers.
    b. protect small retail outlets from the competition of large discount stores.
    c. insure that all manufacturers receive a fair rate of return.
    d. enhance competition among retailers.

8. An interlocking directorate refers to
    a. the special locks many corporations now use on their office doors.
    b. overly complicated directions often issued by large companies.
    c. situations when the same individual serves as a member of the boards of directors of competing firms.
    d. the organization chart of the Pentagon.

9. Which of the following cases illustrates interlocking directorate?
    a. Abby Aldrich serves as a director of Alcoa and of Shell Oil.
    b. Franklin Fish serves as a director of Pillsbury and of United Airlines.
    c. Carlos Calvo serves as a director of Bank of America and of General Motors.
    d. Brenda Buchanan serves as a director of IBM and Apple Computer.

10. Which of the following indicates that structure per se, rather than conduct, may be used as evidence of an illegal monopoly?
    a. The Clayton Act.
    b. The Celler-Kefauver Act.
    c. The Alcoa case.
    d. The General Electric-Westinghouse price-fixing case.

11. A horizontal merger occurs when
    a. one firm buys another.
    b. a supplier buys one of its customers.
    c. a firm buys one of its competitors.
    d. a successful antitrust case forces a large firm to spin off competing divisions.

12. Which of the following would constitute a vertical merger?
    a. A grocery chain merges with the bakery that supplies it with bread.
    b. Two television manufacturers merge.
    c. Mobil Oil buys Montgomery Ward.
    d. U.S. Steel buys Marathon Oil.

13. Which of the following would be a horizontal merger?
    a. DuPont buys Texaco.
    b. General Electric merges with *The New York Times.*
    c. Ford Motor Company merges with Goodyear Tire.
    d. TWA merges with United Airlines.

14. Which of the following would be a conglomerate merger?
    a. Ford merges with Goodyear.
    b. General Electric merges with *The New York Times.*
    c. TWA merges with United.
    d. Apple buys IBM.

15. Following guidelines issued by the Justice Department in the early 1980s there was
    a. a decrease in merger activity.
    b. little change in merger activity.
    c. an increase in merger activity.
    d. a significant increase in court cases prosecuted by the Justice Department.

16. If an industry is composed of 10 firms, each the same size, then the four–firm concentration ratio would be
    a. 4
    b. 10
    c. 40
    d. 100

17. Data for the United States suggest that industrial concentration
    a. has declined significantly since passage of the Clayton Act.
    b. has shown little trend during the past 90 years.
    c. has increased dramatically since World War ll.

18. Studies of concentration and market power conclude that
    a. any increase in concentration ratios tends to increase prices.
    b. contestable markets are the most susceptible to the exercise of market power.
    c. whether increases in concentration will allow firms to exercise more market power depends upon whether other factors favor collusion.
    d. no correlation exists between concentration and the use of market power.

19. Proponents of vigorous antitrust policy argue that bigness per se is bad for all but which one of the following reasons?
    a. Bigness may lead to undesirable concentrations of political and economic power.
    b. Monopolies may not feel competitive pressures to be innovative.
    c. Monopolies, in the pursuit of maximum profits, will usually restrict output below socially desirable levels.
    d. Large-scale firms may imply significant economies of scale.

20. An inefficient firm that attempts to limit the competitive practices of more efficient competitors by using anti-trust laws would be said to engage in
    a. a tying contract.
    b. rent seeking.
    c. price discrimination.
    d. economic discrimination.

## Test B

Circle T or F for true or false.

T  F  1.  A government antitrust case always imposes a large financial burden on a company whether it has engaged in illegal actions or not.

T  F  2.  The Sherman Act outlawed actions in restraint of trade and monopolization of trade.

T F 3. The Clayton Act established the Federal Trade Commission.

T F 4. A manufacturing firm that merges with its supplier is engaging in a horizontal merger.

T F 5. A four-firm concentration ratio is the percentage of industry output produced by the four largest firms.

T F 6. Experience clearly shows that any increase in concentration leads to an increase in market power.

T F 7. Actual evidence on four-firm concentration ratios indicates a significant increase in concentration of American business over the last 80 years.

T F 8. A technological innovation that favors large-scale production will always increase concentration in an industry.

T F 9. Research by economists suggests that only the largest firms can afford to engage in research and development.

T F 10. Price discrimination is always unfair.


## SUPPLEMENTARY EXERCISE

The two lists in Table 19-3 identify the 25 largest industrial firms in the United States in 1929 and 1955, ranked by assets. The list for 1955 comes from the first *Fortune*[1] list of the 500 largest industrial companies. The list for 1929 comes from work by two economists, Norman Collins and Lee Preston.[2]

**TABLE 19-3**

| 1929 | Rank | 1955 |
|---|---|---|
| U.S. Steel | 1 | Standard Oil (N.J.) |
| Standard Oil (N.J.) | 2 | General Motors |
| General Motors | 3 | U.S. Steel |
| Bethlehem Steel | 4 | Du Pont |
| Anaconda | 5 | Mobil Oil |
| Ford Motor Company | 6 | Standard Oil (Ind.) |
| Mobil Oil | 7 | Gulf Oil |
| Standard Oil (Ind.) | 8 | Texaco |
| Gulf Oil | 9 | General Electric |
| Shell Oil | 10 | Standard Oil (Cal.) |
| Texaco | 11 | Bethlehem Steel |
| Standard Oil (Cal.) | 12 | Westinghouse |
| Du Pont | 13 | Union Carbide |
| General Electric | 14 | Sinclair Oil |
| Armour | 15 | Phillips Petroleum |
| Sinclair Oil | 16 | Western Electric |
| Allied Chemical | 17 | Cities Service |
| International Harvester | 18 | Shell Oil |
| Western Electric | 19 | Chrysler |
| Union Oil | 20 | International Harvester |
| Union Carbide | 21 | Alcoa |
| Swift | 22 | Anaconda |
| Kennecott Copper | 23 | American Tobacco |
| International Paper | 24 | Republic Steel |
| Republic Steel | 25 | Kennecott Copper |

[1]*Fortune*, July 1956, Supplement, page 2. Reprinted with permission.
[2]Norman R. Collins and Lee E. Preston, "The Size Structure of the Largest Industrial Firms, 1901–1958", *American Economic Review*, vol. 51, Number 5, December 1961, pages 986-1011.

See if you can list the largest industrial firms today. Then go to the library and look up the most recent list of the *Fortune* 500. It is usually in the May issue. How many of these corporations are still in the top 25? How many corporations have slipped in ranking? How many have gained?

In 1955 these companies had sales that totaled $46.8 billion. Their sales equaled 12 percent of GNP. What are comparable figures today?

*Fortune* ranks firms by sales and assets. How do these rankings compare?

*Fortune* also publishes a list of the 500 largest industrial firms in the world. How big are the biggest American firms when compared to their international competition?

## STUDY QUESTIONS

1. Can price discrimination ever benefit consumers?
2. What is the difference between conglomerate, horizontal, and vertical mergers?
3. Should antitrust policy be based on conduct or structure? Explain.
4. How are concentration ratios measured?
5. Has American business become more or less concentrated over the last 50 years?
6. What does the evidence suggest about increasing concentration and the use of market power?
7. Consider antitrust policy that divided the largest firms whenever the four–firm concentration ratio in any industry exceeded 50 percent. Would such a policy be good for the country? Why? Why not?
8. Should American antitrust laws include an explicit exclusion for cooperative research and development activities? Why?
9. How effective do you believe American antitrust laws have been?

## ECONOMICS IN ACTION

### Trustbusting 101

Even though they are not organized to make a profit, colleges and universities are often seen as big business. Should they be subject to the same restraints on price collusion as other businesses? "Under the Sherman act, a combination formed for the purpose and with the effect of raising, depressing, fixing, pegging or stabilizing the price of a commodity in interstate commerce is illegal per se." (*U.S. v. Socony-Vacuum Oil Co.*)

As explained in the box in Chapter 19, a number of eastern colleges, the Overlap Group, would meet annually to review financial aid decisions. They argued that these meetings allowed prospective students to decide what school to attend on purely educational grounds. By agreeing on common definitions for measuring financial need and awarding financial aid, the out–of–pocket cost to students would be the same at each school even if tuition were different. William R. Cotter, president of Colby College, argued that without such agreements, students and their families "would find the already difficult task of choosing a college distorted by the varied grant offers." With the agreements, students are able to make choices "on the basis of the most appropriate academic program, not the cost to the family." (*Chronicle of Higher Education*, October 4, 1989)

Writing in the <u>Journal of Economic Perspectives,</u> Summer 1991, economists Stephen Salop and Lawrence White were skeptical that this argument would be acceptable to the courts. They left little doubt how they and the courts would evaluate an argument from executives of Ford, Chrysler, and General Motors that an agreement on common prices for mid-size cars was designed to let consumers decide among competing models on the basis of comfort and style, not price.

Writing in <u>The Brookings Review</u>, Winter 1993, after the Justice Department prevailed in its court case against MIT, William Bowen and David Breneman, both economists and both former university presidents, argued that student aid at a school like MIT is most appropriately seen as an educational investment and not a price discount. A school that has trouble meeting its enrollment and income targets will offer financial aid as long as net tuition income is greater than variable costs. Bowen and Breneman argue that in this case financial aid is a price discount designed to increase net revenues. On the other hand, they assert, a school like MIT could meet its enrollment target without offering any financial aid as its applicant pool contains a sufficient number of qualified applicants willing to pay full tuition. In this case Bowen and Breneman argue that financial aid does not affect the size of the entering class, but can have important impacts on its composition. "For MIT and similarly situated institutions, student aid enables the college to attract qualified students who could not afford to come otherwise, including students who will contribute to the diversity of the student population and, ultimately, to the needs of the nation for more well-educated students from racial minorities and disadvantaged backgrounds." In their view this a critical difference that makes action under the Sherman Act inappropriate. Rather than raising prices and reducing output, MIT and others are using scarce resources efficiently. Bowen and Breneman argue that "Options for 'consumers' (students) are increased, since awarding a budgeted amount of aid strictly on the basis of need gives more students a chance to attend an expensive institution."

Assume you were an economist working for the Department of Justice in 1991. Would you have recommended legal action against the Overlap Group? Why? Why not?

*C h a p t e r* **20**

# Taxation, Government Spending, and Resource Allocation

## LEARNING OBJECTIVES

After completing this chapter, you should be able to:

- distinguish between progressive, proportional, and regressive tax systems.
- describe the major taxes levied by the federal, state, and local governments and identify which are direct taxes and which are indirect taxes.
- explain why the payroll tax is regressive.
- explain what issues make the social security system controversial.
- explain the concept of fiscal federalism.
- contrast various concepts of fair or equitable taxation.
- explain the difference between the burden and the excess burden of a tax.
- explain how changes in economic behavior can enable individuals to shift the burden of a tax, that is, explain what is wrong with the flypaper theory of tax incidence.
- explain what factors influence how the burden of a tax will be shared by consumers and suppliers.
- explain how some taxes can lead to efficiency gains, not losses.

## IMPORTANT TERMS AND CONCEPTS

Progressive, proportional, and regressive taxes
Average and marginal tax rates
Direct and indirect taxes
Personal income tax
Payroll tax
Corporate income tax
Excise tax
Tax loopholes
Tax Reform Act of 1986
Social security system
Property tax

Fiscal federalism
Horizontal and vertical equity
Ability-to-pay principle
Benefits principle of taxation
Economic efficiency
Burden of a tax
Excess burden
Incidence of a tax
Flypaper theory of incidence
Tax shifting

## CHAPTER REVIEW

This chapter concentrates on taxes: What taxes are collected in America and what economic effects they have. Few people like paying taxes. In fact, many people make adjustments in their behavior to reduce the taxes they must pay. It is these adjustments that measure the economic effects of taxes, an aspect often overlooked in popular discussions.

(1) Taxes are levied by federal, state, and local governments. For the most part, federal taxes tend to be (direct/indirect) taxes, while state and local governments rely more on _____ taxes. The largest revenue raiser for the federal government is the _____ _____ tax. Next in line in terms of revenue raised is the _____ tax. Other important federal taxes include the _____ income tax and excise taxes.

(2) When talking about income tax systems it is important to distinguish between *average* and *marginal* tax rates. The fraction of total income paid as income taxes is the (average/marginal) tax rate, while the fraction of each additional dollar of income paid as taxes is the _____ tax rate. If the average tax rate increases with income, the tax system is called _____. If the average tax rate stays constant for all levels of income, the tax system is said to be _____, while if the average tax rate falls as income increases, the result is a _____ tax system. Changes under the Tax Reform Act of 1986 reduced marginal income tax rates and enhanced the efficiency of the U.S. federal personal income tax by closing a number of loopholes.

(3) The social security system is financed by (income/payroll) taxes. These taxes are considered (regressive/progressive) because they (do/do not) apply to all sources of income and because after a certain level of income the marginal tax rate becomes _____. Social security benefits do not work like private pension funds, because benefits are not limited by individual contributions.

The social security system has been able to offer retired people good benefits for two reasons: (1) Real wages and incomes of those currently employed have shown substantial growth; and (2) the number of working people has been large relative to the number of retired individuals. The continued operation of both these factors has recently been called into question by the slowdown in the growth of real wages and population. Recent adjustments in both taxes and benefits have attempted to solve the problem by accumulating a surplus in the social security trust fund to pay future benefits.

(4) The major state and local taxes, _____ taxes, and _____ taxes, are indirect taxes. In the aggregate, state income taxes raise a smaller percentage of state revenues, but their importance is growing. Property taxes are usually levied as a percent of (assessed/market) value rather than _____ value. Numerous inequities arise as market values change almost continuously, while assessments for tax purposes are usually made infrequently. There (is/is not) general agreement about the progressivity or regressivity of the property tax. In addition to the taxes raised by state governments, there is a system of transfers from the federal to state governments called fiscal _____.

(5) Economists use their dual criteria of equity and efficiency to judge taxes. When talking about the fairness of a tax, we talk about _____. Various criteria have been advanced to judge the fairness of a particular tax. The principle that equally situated individuals should pay equal taxes is referred to as _____. The principle that differentially situated individuals should be taxed in ways that society deems fair is referred to as _____ _____. The ability-to-pay principle is an example of _____ equity. Rather than looking at the income and wealth of families, there is an alternative approach to taxation that says people should pay in proportion to what they get from public services. This principle for taxation is called the _____ principle. User fees for a variety of public services, such as garbage collection, the use of parks, and street cleaning, are an example of the _____ principle.

(6) Efficiency is the other criterion that economists use to judge taxes. Almost all taxes cause some inefficiency. The amount of money that would make an individual as well off with a tax as she was without the tax is called the _____ of the tax. Sometimes it just equals the tax payment an individual makes, but more generally it is (greater/less) than an individual's tax payment. The difference between the total burden and tax payments is called the _____ _____.

The reason that tax payments typically understate the total burden of a tax is that the existence of the tax will often induce a change in behavior. Measuring only the taxes paid (does/does not) take account of the loss of satisfaction resulting from the induced change in behavior. The excess burden is the measure of the inefficiency of a particular tax. Thus the principle of efficiency in taxation calls for using taxes that raise the same revenue but with the (largest/smallest) excess burden. That is, the principle of efficiency calls for using taxes that induce the smallest changes in behavior.

Often taxes will affect even those people who do not pay them. Imagine that the government imposes a $50 excise tax on bicycles, paid by consumers at the time of purchase. Even though paid by consumers, it may be easiest to examine the impact of this tax by viewing it as a shift in the supply curve, as illustrated in Figure 20-1. Consumers do not care why the price of bicycles has increased; there is no reason for their demand curve to shift. Suppliers collect the tax for the government and are concerned with what is left over after taxes in order to pay their suppliers and cover their labor cost and the opportunity cost of their capital. How suppliers will respond to the after-tax price is given by the original supply curve. The before-tax supply curve comes from adding the excise tax onto the original supply curve and is given by the dashed line in Figure 20-1.

(7) Looking at Figure 20-1 we see that compared with the original equilibrium, the new equilibrium involves a (higher/lower) price to consumers, a (higher/lower) price to suppliers, and a (larger/smaller) quantity of bicycles produced. It would not be surprising if the change in supply resulted in unemployed bicycle workers, lower wages for employed bicycle workers, and fewer bicycle firms. None of these workers or firms paid the tax, yet all were affected by it.

In the bicycle example, as consumers adjusted to the new tax, they shifted part of the burden onto others. The question of how the burden of taxes is divided among different groups is the question of tax

(8) _____. At first glance it might appear that the burden of the tax is borne entirely by consumers who pay it at the time of sale. The notion that the burden of the tax rests with those who pay the tax is called the _____ theory of tax incidence. As the bicycle example makes clear, if consumers change their behavior as a result of the tax, they may succeed in _____ part of the burden of the tax.

(9) The study of tax incidence suggests that the incidence of excise or sales taxes depends on the slopes of both the _____ and _____ curves. Payroll taxes, such as social security taxes, are like an excise tax on labor services. Statistical work suggests that for most workers the supply of labor services is relatively (elastic/inelastic) with respect to wage rates, which in turn suggests that (workers/firms) rather than _____ bear most of the burden of the payroll tax.

**FIGURE 20-1**
**DEMAND FOR AND SUPPLY OF BICYCLES**

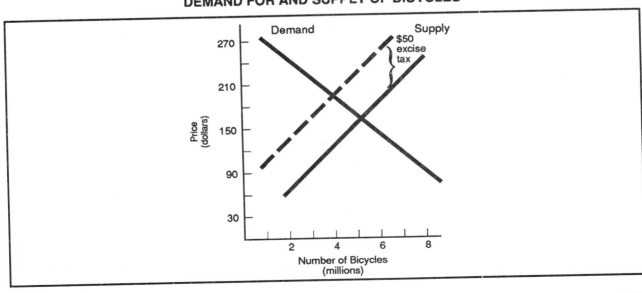

## IMPORTANT TERMS AND CONCEPTS QUIZ

Choose the most appropriate definition for the following terms.

1. _____ Progressive tax
2. _____ Proportional tax
3. _____ Regressive tax
4. _____ Average tax rate
5. _____ Marginal tax rate
6. _____ Direct taxes
7. _____ Indirect taxes
8. _____ Excise tax
9. _____ Tax loophole
10. _____ Fiscal federalism
11. _____ Horizontal equity
12. _____ Vertical equity
13. _____ Ability to pay principle
14. _____ Benefits principle of taxation
15. _____ Burden of a tax
16. _____ Excess burden
17. _____ Incidence of a tax
18. _____ Flypaper theory of incidence
19. _____ Tax shifting

a. Provision in the tax code that reduces taxes below statutory rates if certain conditions are met.
b. Average tax rate increases with income.
c. People who derive benefits from a government-provided service should pay the taxes to support it.

d. Amount an individual would have to receive to make her as well off with the tax as she was without it.
e. Allocation of the burden of a tax to specific groups.
f. Notion that the burden of a tax is borne by those who pay it.
g. Taxes levied on people.
h. Equally situated individuals should be taxed equally.
i. Average tax rate falls as income rises.
j. Frequency with which a tax is levied.
k. Sales tax on a specific commodity.
l. Situation where economic reactions to a tax mean others bear part of the burden of the tax.
m. System of grants from one level of government to the next.
n. Ratio of taxes to income.
o. Wealthier people should pay higher taxes.
p. Average tax rate is the same at all income levels.
q. Amount by which the burden of a tax exceeds the tax paid.
r. Fraction of each additional dollar of income that is paid in taxes.
s. Taxes levied on specific economic activities.
t. Differently situated individuals should be taxed differently in accordance with social norms.

## BASIC EXERCISE

This exercise is designed to illustrate how the incidence of an excise tax depends on the elasticity (slope) of the demand and supply curves.

1. Table 20-1 has data on the demand and supply of running shoes. Plot the demand curve from column 1 and the supply curve from column 3 in Figure 20-2.

2. Determine the initial equilibrium price and quantity of running shoes.

   Price $_____

   Quantity _____

3. Now assume that in a fit of pique, non-running legislators impose a fitness tax of $10 on each pair of shoes. Draw the new supply curve by shifting the original supply curve by the magnitude of the excise tax. The new equilibrium price is $_____ and the new equilibrium quantity is _____.

**TABLE 20-1**
**DEMAND FOR AND SUPPLY OF**
**RUNNING SHOES**

| (1) Demand (millions of pairs) | (2) | Price (dollars) | (3) Supply (millions of pairs) | (4) |
|---|---|---|---|---|
| 68 | 53.0 | 30 | 38 | 48.00 |
| 65 | 52.5 | 32 | 40 | 48.33 |
| 62 | 52.0 | 34 | 42 | 48.67 |
| 59 | 51.5 | 36 | 44 | 49.00 |
| 56 | 51.0 | 38 | 46 | 49.33 |
| 53 | 50.5 | 40 | 48 | 49.67 |
| 50 | 50.0 | 42 | 50 | 50.00 |
| 47 | 49.5 | 44 | 52 | 50.33 |
| 44 | 49.0 | 46 | 54 | 50.67 |
| 41 | 48.5 | 48 | 56 | 51.00 |
| 38 | 48.0 | 50 | 58 | 51.33 |
| 35 | 47.5 | 52 | 60 | 51.60 |
| 32 | 47.0 | 54 | 62 | 52.00 |

**FIGURE 20-2**
**DEMAND FOR AND SUPPLY OF RUNNING SHOES**

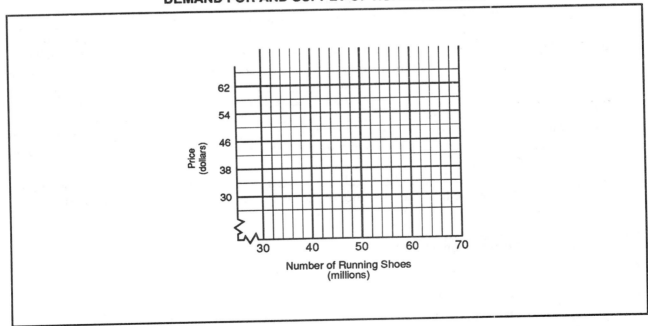

**FIGURE 20-3**
**DEMAND FOR AND SUPPLY OF RUNNING SHOES**

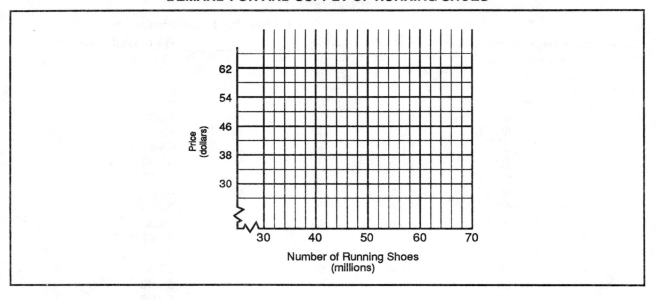

4. How much more do consumers, who continue to buy running shoes, pay? $_____.
   How does this increase in price compare with the excise tax of $10?

5. What is likely to happen to employment, wages, and profits in the running-shoe industry?

6. On Figure 20-3, plot the demand curve from column 2 and supply curve from column 3 of Table
   20-1. Comparing Figures 20-2 and 20-3, we have the same supply curve but different demand curves.
   Both figures should show the same initial equilibrium price and quantity.

7. At the initial equilibrium price and quantity, which demand curve is more elastic? _____.
   (Review the appropriate material in Chapter 7 if you do not remember how to compute the price
   elasticity of a demand curve. Remember this distinction when it comes to comparing results.)

8. Now analyze the impact of the imposition of the same excise tax of $10 per pair of running shoes
   using Figure 20-3. The new equilibrium price is $_____ and the new equilibrium
   quantity _____. In which case, Figure 20-2 or Figure 20-3, does the equilibrium price
   of running shoes rise the most? _____. In which case are the volume of employment and the level of wages likely to fall the least? _____. From this comparison we can conclude that the more inelastic the demand curve, the more the burden of an excise
   tax will be borne by _____.

9. Use information on demand from either column 1 or 2 and the two supply curves in columns 3 and
   4 in Table 20-1 to analyze how the incidence of the tax is affected as the elasticity of supply changes

## SELF-TESTS FOR UNDERSTANDING

### Test A

Circle the most appropriate answer.

1. In the United States since 1950, federal taxes as a proportion of GDP have
   a. declined.
   b. fluctuated but shown little trend.
   c. increased dramatically.

2. In the United States, state and local taxes as a percentage of GDP have
   a. declined since 1960.
   b. shown virtually no change over the last 60 years.
   c. increased from 1945 to the early 1970s and shown little trend since then.

3. For the most part the federal government relies on _____ taxes while state and local governments rely on _____ taxes.
   a. excise; property
   b. sales; income
   c. property; sales
   d. direct; indirect

4. Direct taxes are levied on
   a. specific economic activities.
   b. reproducible property.
   c. people.
   d. the value added at each stage of production.

5. Which of the following is an indirect tax?
   a. Income taxes.
   b. Inheritance taxes.
   c. Head taxes.
   d. Sales taxes.

6. Fiscal federalism refers to
   a. Alexander Hamilton's plan for assuming the debts of the individual states.
   b. federal government control of state and local spending.
   c. grants from one level of government to another.
   d. the balance between taxes paid to the federal government and the value of federal contracts received, measured on a state-by-state basis.

7. If income taxes are progressive, then the average tax rate
   a. decreases as income increases.
   b. is unchanged as income increases.
   c. increases as income increases.
   d. Insufficient information to determine.

8. If income taxes are progressive, then the marginal tax rate
   a. decreases as income increases.
   b. is unchanged as income increases.
   c. increases as income increases.
   d. Insufficient information to determine.

9. Christopher earned $20,000 last year and paid 10 percent or $2,000 in taxes. His marginal income tax rate is 15 percent. If his income rises this year, say to $25,000, his average tax rate will
   a. decrease.
   b. remain unchanged.
   c. increase.

10. The Abbotts have an income of $20,000 a year and pay $2,000 a year in income taxes. The Beards have an income of $40,000 a year and pay $5,000 a year in income taxes. From this information we can conclude that this tax system
    a. is regressive.
    b. is proportional.
    c. is progressive.
    d. satisfies the benefits principle of taxation.

11. The ability-to-pay principle of taxation is an example of
    a. horizontal equity.
    b. vertical equity.
    c. the benefits principle.
    d. fiscal federalism.

12. If two families are identical in all respects, the principle of horizontal equity says that
    a. both families should pay more income taxes than other families with less income.
    b. both families should pay the same income tax.
    c. both families should have a lower average tax rate than a richer family.
    d. income taxes are, from a social viewpoint, a more appropriate form of taxation than are payroll taxes.

13. Which of the following is an example of the benefits principle of taxation?
    a. Excise taxes on cigarettes.
    b. Higher property taxes as a percent of market value for more expensive homes.
    c. Special assessments on homeowners in proportion to their street frontage to help pay for repairs to curbs and gutters.
    d. Social security taxes.

14. The burden of a tax is defined as
    a. revenue raised minus the cost of collection.
    b. the proportion of taxes paid by individuals rather than corporations.
    c. the amount of money that would make a taxpayer as well off as he was before the tax was introduced.
    d. revenue raised plus the cost of collection.

15. The burden of most taxes is _____ the revenue raised.
    a. less than
    b. equal to
    c. greater than

16. The excess burden of a tax is
    a. the cost of collecting the tax.
    b. a measure of the inefficiency of the tax.
    c. best measured by the amount of complaining done by taxpayers.
    d. highest when the tax induces the least change in behavior.

17. A sales tax on which of the following will involve a small excess burden?
    a. A tax on a commodity with a zero price elasticity of demand.
    b. A tax on a commodity with a very high elasticity of demand.
    c. A tax on a commodity consumed primarily by poor families.
    d. A tax on a commodity consumed primarily by rich families.

18. The flypaper theory of tax incidence
    a. is a shorthand reference to such sticky issues as the appropriate degree of progressivity in the personal income tax.
    b. implies that if a tax induces changes in economic behavior, part of the burden of the tax may be shifted to other economic agents.
    c. is usually right regarding who bears the burden of a tax.
    d. says that the burden of a tax is borne by those who pay the tax.

19. Tax loopholes typically introduce new inefficiencies and _____ the progressivity of the income tax.
    a. reduce
    b. have little effect on
    c. increase

20. The Tax Reform Act of 1986
   a. reduced marginal tax rates.
   b. introduced significant loopholes.
   c. increased personal income taxes in order to reduce corporate taxes.
   d. is generally conceded to have worsened the efficiency of the American tax system.

## Test B

Circle T or F for true or false.

T  F  1.  Over the past 35 years federal government taxes have taken an ever-increasing share of the GNP.

T  F  2.  Federal payroll taxes are a less important source of revenue than either the federal personal income tax or the federal corporate income tax.

T  F  3.  State personal income taxes are an example of a direct, as opposed to indirect, tax.

T  F  4.  State taxes are primarily indirect taxes.

T  F  5.  The principle of horizontal equity says that equally situated individuals should be taxed equally.

T  F  6.  The ability-to-pay principle says that people who derive benefits from a particular public service should pay the taxes to finance it.

T  F  7.  The burden of a tax is normally less than the revenue raised by the tax.

T  F  8.  If a tax does not induce a change in economic behavior, then there is no excess burden.

T  F  9.  The flypaper theory of incidence is correct in regards to social security taxes.

T  F  10.  The concept of excess burden proves that taxes can never improve efficiency.

## SUPPLEMENTARY EXERCISE

In the spring of 1993 there was considerable discussion of a possible increase in the federal tax on cigarettes. Some saw an increase as a cash cow to finance medical care reform or to help reduce the federal deficit. If interested in maximizing the amount of revenue, one would need to be careful not to raise the tax so high that demand fell too much and tax revenues actually declined.

Writing separately in *The New York Times* in June of 1993, economists Jeffrey Harris and Michael Grossman offered dramatically different estimates of the demand elasticity. Drawing on Canadian experience, Harris suggested that the price elasticity of demand for cigarettes was around 0.25. He estimated that a $2 increase in cigarette taxes would raise an additional $28 billion in revenue each year. Grossman argued that because of the addictive properties of smoking, the response to a change in price would be small in the short run but much larger in the long run.

The following straight line demand curves are approximations of the Harris estimate and Grossman's long run demand curve. Both of these demand curves have been constructed to mimic actual price and quantity data for 1992 when 24.9 billion packs of cigarettes were sold in the United States at an average price of $2 a pack that included a tax of $.24.

$$\text{Harris:} \quad Q = 30.80 - 2.95\,(P + T)$$
$$\text{Grossman:} \quad Q = 46.72 - 10.91\,(P + T)$$

1. Verify that when P+T = 2 each demand curve is consistent with the 1992 quantity and price combination.
2. On the assumption that the supply curve for cigarettes is horizontal at a net-of-tax price of $1.76 a pack, i.e; P = 1.76, what tax maximizes tax revenues? (If you have access to a spreadsheet program on a microcomputer you might set up a small example that calculates the quantity demanded and then tax revenue at different taxes. Alternatively, after writing down the expression for total tax revenues, you could differentiate the expression to find the value of T that maximizes revenue.)

3. What is the price elasticity of demand for each equation? Consider a $.50 increase in cigarette taxes. What do the two equations estimate would happen to demand? Use these answers to estimate the price elasticity of demand in 1992. You might also try plotting both demand curves on the same demand-supply diagram.

4. Actual tax revenues will depend upon the price elasticity of supply as well as the price elasticity of demand. Question 2 assumed that the price elasticity of supply was infinite. What would happen if it were zero or somewhere in between?

## STUDY QUESTIONS

1. Should income taxes be progressive or proportional? Explain your reasoning.

2. Without changing the level of spending, should your state increase income taxes in order to reduce sales taxes or increase sales taxes to reduce income taxes? Why?

3. Why do economists consider the social security tax to be regressive?

4. In the final analysis, who pays the social security tax, workers or firms?

5. What is fiscal federalism?

6. What is the difference between horizontal and vertical equity?

7. If a progressive income tax meets social concerns about vertical equity, can it also satisfy concerns about horizontal equity? Explain.

8. What is the difference between the benefits principle of taxation and the concept of ability to pay?

9. Why do economists say that the burden of a tax is usually greater than the revenue raised by the tax?

10. Is it true that the more elastic the demand curve, the smaller the amount of any sales tax that consumers will pay? Explain.

## ECONOMICS IN ACTION

### The Flat Tax

Writing in 1985, economists Robert E. Hall and Alvin Rabushka advocated what they call the flat tax. (*The Flat Tax*, Hoover Institution Press, Stanford, California, 1985) Jerry Brown, a perennial candidate for the Democratic Party presidential nomination, advocated a version of the Hall-Rabushka tax during the presidential primaries of 1992. What is the Hall-Rabushka flat tax?

Hall and Rabushka propose a single tax rate of 19 percent for everyone. After allowing for personal deductions, wage, salary, and pension, income would be taxed at the flat rate of 19 percent. Personal exemptions of $12,600 for a family of four adjusted for inflation would be $16,200 in 1992. Thus a family of four with wage, salary, and pension income of $46,200 in 1992 would owe 19 percent of $30,000 or $5,700 in individual income taxes. Note that the Hall-Rabushka proposal makes no allowance for deductions for medical expenses, charitable contributions, mortgage interest, or state income taxes.

What about interest, dividends, and other forms of business and investment income? Would these escape taxation? The Hall-Rabushka proposal includes a 19 percent business tax that they view as an efficient withholding tax on these forms of income. The business portion of the Hall-Rabushka flat tax is calculated as follows: A business first lists all income from the sale of products and services it produces. It then subtracts wage, salary, and pension payments. It also deducts the cost of material inputs, i.e. purchases from other firms, and it deducts expenditures on new plant, equipment, and land. Whatever is left is taxed at 19 percent. Note that interest and dividend payments are not deductible by businesses and individuals do not pay any additional tax on them. Note also that fringe benefits, e.g. health insurance and retirement contributions, are not deductible from the business tax. Hall and Rabushka argue that these are forms of income often as valuable to workers as take-home pay and should be taxed accordingly.

Hall and Rabushka believe their flat tax forms need only be the size of a postcard and would minimize the demand for high cost tax lawyers and accountants. Under the Hall-Rabushka proposal there is no taxation of capital gains on stocks or houses. With regard to stocks, Hall and Rabushka argue that stock values should reflect future business income that is best taxed as it is earned. With respect to houses, they note that most capital gains on houses escape taxes at present.

1. Economists evaluate tax proposals on grounds of equity and efficiency. How does the Hall-Rabushka proposal rank on these criteria as compared with the existing system of individual and business taxes?

Chapter **21**

# Environmental Protection and Resource Conservation

## LEARNING OBJECTIVES

After completing this chapter, you should be able to:

♦ explain why, in most cases, it is undesirable to reduce pollution to zero.

♦ explain why unrestricted competitive markets are likely to result in a socially unacceptable level of pollution.

♦ explain why it is unlikely that profit-maximizing private firms can be expected to clean up the environment.

♦ describe the major approaches to limiting pollution.

♦ compare the advantages and disadvantages of using taxes and permits to control pollution.

♦ explain why, under perfect competition and negligible extraction costs, the price of depletable resources would be expected to rise at the rate of interest.

♦ explain how and why actual prices of depletable resources have behaved differently over most of the twentieth century.

♦ describe the three virtues of rising prices for scarce resources.

♦ explain why known reserves for many resources have not tended to fall over time.

## IMPORTANT TERMS AND CONCEPTS

Externality
Direct controls
Pollution charges (taxes on emissions)
Subsidies for reduced emissions
Emissions permits
Known reserves
Organization of Petroleum Exporting Countries (OPEC)
Rationing
Paradox of growing reserves of finite resources

## CHAPTER REVIEW

This chapter explores the economics of environmental protection and resource conservation, with emphasis on the strengths and weaknesses of a market economy in dealing with both issues.

### Environmental Protection

Pollution is one example of instances in which unregulated markets will fail to achieve an efficient allocation of resources. Typically, pollution imposes little or no cost on the polluter, yet it imposes costs

(1) on others. In the language of economists, pollution is an example of a detrimental _____.
Pollution happens because individuals, firms, and government agencies use the air, land, and waterways as free dumping grounds for their waste. Economists believe that if there is a high cost to using these public resources, then the volume of pollution will (increase/decrease) because people will be more careful about producing wastes and/or they will choose less costly alternatives for waste disposal. One way to make the use of public resources costly is to impose (taxes/subsidies) in direct proportion to the volume of pollution emitted. This is an example of using the price system to clean up the environment.

(2)      Many government policies have relied on voluntarism and direct _____. Both policies have their place in a coordinated attempt to clean up the environment. Economists, though, are skeptical of relying on voluntary cooperation as a long-range solution. Cleaning up the environment is costly, and firms that voluntarily incur these costs are likely to be undersold by less public-spirited competitors.

     A government ruling that mandates an equal percentage reduction in pollution activity by all polluters is an example of a direct control. Economists argue that since the costs of reducing pollution are apt to vary

(3) among polluters, an equal percentage reduction by all polluters is likely to be (efficient/inefficient) compared with other alternatives, such as emissions taxes. From a social viewpoint, unequal reductions in pollution will be more _____, as it is likely to cost less for some firms to reduce pollution. Faced with an emissions tax, firms will reduce pollution until the (marginal/average) cost of further reductions exceeds the tax. Firms that continue to pollute will pay the tax; other firms will pay for pollution-control devices. All firms will choose the least costly alternative.

### Resource Conservation

Some resources, such as trees and fish, are called renewable resources. As long as breeding stocks are not destroyed, these resources will replenish themselves. The rest of this chapter concentrates on non-renewable or depletable resources such as minerals and oil. In this case there is no reproduction, although in some cases there may be recycling.

     Many observers have voiced concern that the world is running out of natural resources. They allege that soon the quantity of resources supplied will not be able to keep up with the quantity of resources demanded and that the result will be massive shortages and chaos. Yet, in a free market we know that

(4) the quantity demanded (can/can never) exceed the quantity supplied, because demand and supply will always be brought into equilibrium by adjustments in _____. This fundamental mechanism of free markets, first discussed in Chapter 4, is as applicable to the supply and demand of scarce resources as it is to any other commodity.

     Harold Hotelling first described the special behavior of the prices of depletable resources in free markets. He discovered that if the costs of extraction are negligible, the price of depletable resources must

(5) rise at a rate equal to the rate of _____. This result follows from relatively simple considerations. Assets held in the form of bank deposits or bonds earn interest for their owners. Owners of natural resource reserves expect their asset—the reserves—to earn a similar risk-adjusted return.

If increases in the price of future resources offer a less attractive return than do interest rates, resource owners will sell their resources and put the money in the bank. This action decreases the current price of resources. There will be a continuing incentive to sell, with downward pressure on current resource prices, until the return from holding resources again provides a return competitive with interest rates. Similarly, if the future return from holding resources is expected to be extremely high, more investors will want to buy resource inventories, (increasing/decreasing) current prices. These pressures will continue until holding resource inventories again offers a risk-adjusted return comparable to that of investments in the bank.

**(6)** This theory suggests that the prices of depletable resources should show a rising trend at a rate equal to the rate of _____. The unexpected discovery of resource reserves, technological progress that reduces the cost of extraction, and government attempts at price controls can all make prices behave differently. Data on known reserves, rather than declining as implied in the literal interpretation of a nonrenewable resource, have typically shown slight increases. These increases in reserves reflect the workings of the price system as the pressure for higher prices has induced new exploration and made the use of high cost deposits profitable. It is important to remember that pressure for higher prices is what equates demand and supply, avoids chaos, and facilitates the adjustment to alternative technologies.

Many economists see increasing prices for depletable resources as an important virtue of free markets. Increasing prices help to deal with the problem of declining reserves in three important ways:

**(7)**
1. Increasing prices (encourage/discourage) consumption and waste and provide a(n) (disincentive/incentive) for conservation on the part of consumers.
2. Increasing prices (encourage/discourage) more efficient use of scarce resources in the production of commodities.
3. Increasing prices provide a(n) (disincentive/incentive) for technological innovation and the use of substitutes as well as (encouraging/discouraging) additional exploration and the exploitation of high-cost sources of supply.

## IMPORTANT TERMS AND CONCEPTS QUIZ

Choose the most appropriate definition for the following terms.

1. _____ Externality
2. _____ Direct controls
3. _____ Pollution charges
4. _____ Emissions permit
5. _____ Known reserves
6. _____ Organization of Petroleum Exporting Countries
7. _____ Rationing

a. Cartel of oil-rich nations that has attempted to control oil markets.
b. Monetary incentives and penalties used to make polluting financially unattractive.
c. Fees paid to polluting firms in exchange for reductions in pollution.
d. Result of activities that affect other people, without corresponding compensation.
e. Authorization to pollute up to a specified level.
f. Legal limits on pollution emissions or performance specifications for polluting activities.
g. Nonprice methods of distributing scarce supplies.
h. Amount of a resource available if one relies solely on existing technology and already discovered sources.

## BASIC EXERCISES

1. This exercise examines the implications of alternative pollution taxes.

    Assume that plastic trash bags are produced in a market that is best characterized as one of perfect competition. Manufacturers have long used local rivers as convenient dumping grounds for their industrial wastes. Figure 21-1 plots the average cost of producing trash bags. These data are applicable for each firm.

    a. In the absence of pollution-control measures, what is the long-run equilibrium price of plastic bags? $_____. What is the long-run equilibrium level of output for each firm? _____. (To answer this question you may want to review the material in Chapter 9 about long-run equilibrium under perfect competition.)

    b. The amount of pollution discharge is directly proportional to the number of bags produced. Assume that the government imposes a pollution charge of 5 cents per bag. Draw in the new average cost curve on Figure 21-1. Will there be an increase, a decrease, or no change in each of the following as a result of the pollution charge? (Assume for now that there is no pollution-control technology, that each firm must pay the tax, and that the demand for plastic bags declines as price rises.)

| | |
|---|---|
| Industry output | _____ |
| Price | _____ |
| Number of firms in the industry | _____ |
| Average cost curve for each firm | _____ |
| Output level of each firm | _____ |
| Total pollution | _____ |

    c. Assume that pollution-control equipment becomes available. This equipment will eliminate 75 percent of pollution at an average cost of 4 cents per bag. Explain why no firm will adopt the pollution-control equipment if the pollution charge is unchanged at 5 cents a bag. (Assume that the cost of the control equipment is all variable cost at 4 cents per bag and that there is no fixed-cost component.)

### FIGURE 21-1

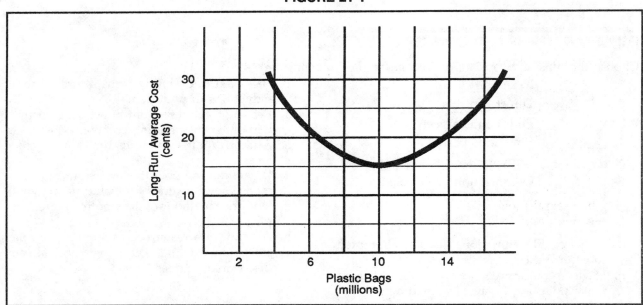

d. Assume now that the tax is shifted to the volume of emissions, not to the number of bags produced, and that it is equivalent to 5 cents a bag if no pollution-control equipment is installed. Will any firm purchase the pollution-control equipment?

e. With the emissions tax at a rate of 5 cents per bag, to what rate must the cost of pollution control decline before firms will use it? If the cost of pollution control is constant at 4 cents, to what rate must the tax increase to induce firms to install the pollution-control equipment?

f. Assume now that the costs of reducing pollution are not identical for all firms. For simplicity, assume that there are two types of firms, low-cost pollution-control firms and high-cost pollution-control firms. The low-cost firms can eliminate pollution at costs lower than the emissions tax but the high-cost firms cannot. What is the result of imposing an emissions tax? What will happen to total industry output? Will any firms leave the industry? If so, which ones, the high-cost or the low-cost firms? Why?

2. a. Table 21-1 contains data on real output and energy consumption for the U.S. economy. Use these data to compute the use of energy per thousand dollars of GDP.

**TABLE 21-1**

| Year | Real GDP (billions of 1987 $) | Energy Consumption (quadrillion BTUs) | Energy Consumption per $1,000 GDP (thousands of BTUs) |
|------|------|------|------|
| 1970 | 2,873.9 | 66.4 | _____ |
| 1971 | 2,955.9 | 67.9 | _____ |
| 1972 | 3,107.1 | 71.3 | _____ |
| 1973 | 3,268.6 | 74.3 | _____ |
| 1974 | 3,248.1 | 72.5 | _____ |
| 1975 | 3,221.7 | 70.5 | _____ |
| 1976 | 3,380.8 | 74.4 | _____ |
| 1977 | 3,533.3 | 76.3 | _____ |
| 1978 | 3,703.5 | 78.1 | _____ |
| 1979 | 3,796.8 | 78.9 | _____ |
| 1980 | 3,776.3 | 76.0 | _____ |
| 1981 | 3,843.1 | 74.0 | _____ |
| 1982 | 3,760.3 | 70.8 | _____ |
| 1983 | 3,906.6 | 70.5 | _____ |
| 1984 | 4,148.5 | 74.1 | _____ |
| 1985 | 4,279.8 | 74.0 | _____ |
| 1986 | 4,404.5 | 74.2 | _____ |
| 1987 | 4,539.9 | 76.8 | _____ |
| 1988 | 4,718.6 | 80.2 | _____ |
| 1989 | 4,838.0 | 81.3 | _____ |
| 1990 | 4,877.5 | 81.3 | _____ |
| 1991 | 4,821.0 | 81.1 | _____ |
| 1992 | 4,922.6 | 81.9 | _____ |

SOURCES: GDP: *Economic Report of the President*, 1989, Table B-2; Energy: *Statistical Abstract of the United States*, 1990, Table 940; and *Monthly Energy Review*, January 1993, Table 1.2.

**FIGURE 21-2**
**ENERGY PRICES AND CONSUMPTION**

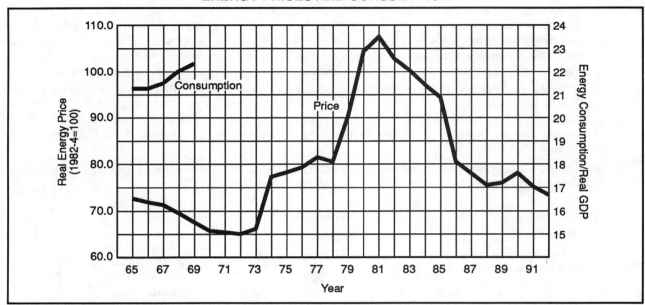

b. Figure 21-2 shows real energy prices, i.e., energy prices divided by the consumer price index. Complete Figure 21-2 by plotting the data on energy consumption per thousand dollars of GDP. Use this graph to discuss the pattern of energy consumption over the last 25 years.

## SELF-TESTS FOR UNDERSTANDING

### Test A

Circle the most appropriate answer.

1. Which of the following suggests that, except for recycling, all economic activity results in a disposal problem?
   a. The edifice complex.
   b. The law of conservation of energy and matter.
   c. Emissions permits.
   d. Externalities.

2. Which of the following countries has avoided significant pollution problems?
   a. China.
   b. Russia.
   c. The United States.
   d. Poland.
   e. None of the above.

3. Economists view pollution as a textbook example of
   a. public goods.
   b. externalities.
   c. increasing returns to scale.
   d. the evils of monopoly.

4. Significant pollution is caused by the actions of
   a. business.
   b. government.
   c. consumers.
   d. All of the above.

5. The fact that pollution is often a detrimental externality suggests that
   a. cleaning up the environment must be done by direct government expenditures.
   b. without government intervention, profit-maximizing private firms cannot be expected to clean up the environment.
   c. public agencies have been responsible for most pollution.
   d. direct controls are superior to other forms of government intervention.

6. Which of the following is not an example of using financial incentives to clean up the environment?
   a. Mandated pollution-control equipment in an attempt to reduce automobile emissions.
   b. A graduated tax that increases with the polluting characteristics of each automobile engine.
   c. The sale of a limited number of permits to control emissions into Lake Erie.
   d. Allowing firms to buy and sell emission rights originally assigned under a program of direct controls.

7. The use of pollution charges as a means of cleaning up the environment
   a. is the predominant form of pollution control in the United States.
   b. is likely to be more efficient than a system of direct controls.
   c. would be most appropriate in situations calling for sudden action, such as a serious smog condition.
   d. would have exactly the same effects on the volume of pollution as do subsidies for pollution-control equipment.

8. As a strategy to control pollution, voluntarism
   a. is the best long-run strategy.
   b. may be the only practical alternative in cases were surveillance is impractical.
   c. should be the most effective alternative.
   d. has significant efficiency advantages as compared with pollution taxes.

9. Economists typically argue that _____ are likely to be most effective in reducing pollution over the long run.
   a. direct controls
   b. taxes on emissions
   c. voluntary programs
   d. specifications as to allowable equipment and/or procedures

10. Pollution charges are likely to be more efficient than direct controls because
    a. most of the reduction in pollution will be done by those who can implement reductions at low cost.
    b. everyone will be forced to show the same percentage reduction in pollution.
    c. no one likes paying taxes.
    d. pollution is a detrimental externality.

11. Compared with a system of direct controls, pollution charges
    a. are basically a "carrot" approach, relying on everyone's voluntary cooperation.
    b. are likely to lead to an equal percentage reduction in emissions from all pollution sources.
    c. will not reduce pollution, as firms will simply pass on these costs to their consumers with no impact on output levels.
    d. offer an incentive for continually reducing emissions, rather than reducing them just to some mandated level.

12. Harold Hotelling argued that, in competitive markets, even if extraction costs are negligible, the price of depletable resources will rise at a rate equal to the rate of
    a. inflation.
    b. unemployment.
    c. interest.
    d. growth of real income.

13. Which one of the following would be expected to reduce the price of a natural resource?
    a. The establishment of an effective producer cartel.
    b. The discovery of previously unknown reserves.
    c. An increase in the rate of inflation.
    d. An increase in GDP.

14. The quantity demanded of a scarce resource can exceed the quantity supplied
    a. if there is a sudden surge in demand.
    b. as economic growth increase demand.
    c. if monopolistic suppliers withhold supply.
    d. only if something prevents prices from adjusting.

15. Which of the following reflects a movement along the demand curve for energy?
    a. Reductions in the use of energy induced by higher prices.
    b. The development of new lower cost-extraction procedures.
    c. Increased demand from increases in GDP.
    d. The building of manufacturing capacity to extract oil from shale.

16. The record of resource prices in the twentieth century shows
    a. most have increased in line with the Hotelling principle.
    b. most have shown even greater increases in price.
    c. little trend in the real price of many resources.
    d. a steady trend toward lower real prices for almost all resources.

17. Rising resource prices can be a virtue as they lead to all but which one of the following?
    a. Increased waste.
    b. Increased use of substitutes.
    c. Increased conservation.
    d. Increased innovation.

18. Data for 1950-1980 suggest that the known reserves of some natural resources
    a. declined.
    b. remained roughly constant.
    c. increased.

19. Measured relative to total output, i.e., GDP, the use of energy in the United States is now
    a. about as high as it has ever been.
    b. about the same as it has been for the last 20 years.
    c. significantly lower than it was 20 years ago.

20. Effective price ceilings for natural resources are likely to
    a. provide an increased incentive for further exploration.
    b. shift the demand curve to the left.
    c. induce consumers to conserve.
    d. lead to resource shortages.

## Test B

Circle T or F for true or false.

T  F  1. Pollution has become a serious problem only since World War II.

T  F  2. Only capitalist economies suffer from extensive pollution.

T  F  3. When considering public policies to limit discharges of wastes into a river basin, an equal percentage reduction by all polluters is likely to be the most economically efficient policy.

T  F  4. Pollution charges imposed on monopolist firms will have no effect on the volume of their polluting activity, because they will simply pass on the higher costs in the form of higher prices.

T  F  5. Efficiency considerations strongly suggest that society should spend enough to reduce all pollution to zero.

T  F  6. If left unchecked, the free-market mechanism will cause the demand for natural resources to exceed supply.

T  F  7. For much of the twentieth century the relative prices of most natural resources have shown dramatic increases.

T  F  8. Hotelling argued that, in free markets and with constant extraction costs, the price of natural resources will rise at the rate of inflation.

T  F  9. The unexpected discovery of resource deposits would reduce prices and delay the onset of the Hotelling pricing principle.

T  F  10. Rising prices can help control resource depletion as they induce firms and households to conserve.

## SUPPLEMENTARY EXERCISES

1. **Pollution and Prices**

   Can a producer simply pass on to her customers any pollution charge imposed on her? This numerical example expands upon the problem in the Basic Exercise.

   Consider the production of plastic bags, which cause pollution in direct proportion to the volume of production. The demand for bags is given by

   $$Q = 2{,}600 - 40P$$

   where Q is measured in millions of bags.

   a. Assume that plastic bags are produced by a monopolist at a cost of 15¢ a bag; that is,

      $$TC = 15 \times Q.$$

      Plot the demand, marginal revenue, average cost, and marginal cost curves on a piece of graph paper. What is the monopolist's profit–maximizing level of output, the associated price, and her profits?

   b. The government now imposes a pollution tax of 5¢ a bag, that is, TC = 20 x Q. What happens to output, prices, and profits if the monopolist simply raises her price by 5¢? Can she do better by charging a different price? If so, what is that price, the associated quantity, and the new level of profits?

   c. Assume now that bags are produced by identical small firms under conditions of perfect competition. Each firm produces bags with average cost given by

      $$AC = .4(Q - 10)^2 + 15.$$

      What is the long-run market equilibrium price and quantity? How many firms are in the industry? How many bags does each firm produce?

    d. Again the government imposes a pollution tax of 5¢ a bag on each producer. What happens in the short run when there are still the same number of bag producers? What about the long run? How many firms will produce how many bags at what price?

2. You might enjoy reading Robert M. Solow, "The Economics of Resources or the Resources of Economics," *American Economic Review,* May 1974, pages 1–14, for a nontechnical discussion of the implications of the Hotelling pricing principle.

    You might enjoy the following exchange about limits to growth:

    Council on Environmental Quality and the Department of State (Gerald O. Barney, study director), *Global 2000 Report to the President of the U.S., Entering the 21st Century* (U.S. GPO, 1980–1981); also (Pergamon Press, 1980–1981).

    Herman Kahn and Julian L. Simon, editors, *The Resourceful Earth: A Response to 'Global 2000,'* (Basil Blackwell, 1984).

## STUDY QUESTIONS

1. What do economists mean when they say pollution is an externality?

2. Why do unregulated competitive markets tend to produce more pollution than is socially desirable?

3. Would it be a good idea to reduce all pollution to zero?

4. Why do you think business firms prefer government regulation to voluntary compliance with pollution standards?

5. Why do economists argue that emission taxes are a more efficient means of reducing pollution than direct controls?

6. What is the Hotelling principle of resource pricing?

7. Is the history of resource prices over the twentieth century consistent with the Hotelling principle?

8. Under what circumstances can the quantity demanded of a depletable resource exceed the quantity supplied?

9. What are the three virtues of rising prices for natural resources?

10. Why haven't reserves for many resources been falling over time as use of these resources continues every year?

## ECONOMICS IN ACTION
### Heavy Metal

It seems like we cannot pick up a newspaper without reading about some impending ecological disaster or some resource that is about to disappear. Economist Julian Simon is an outspoken critic of such doomsday forecasts. He points out that our ancestors faced similar apparent disasters and, with some effort, overcame them. In many cases this involved learning how to use new metals or new sources of energy. According to Simon, the ultimate resource is human ingenuity. He is fond of quoting Henry George: "Both the jayhawk and the man eat chickens, but the more jayhawks, the fewer the chickens, while the more men, the more chickens."

In 1980 Simon issued a challenge to those predicting disaster. He argued that if resources were becoming increasingly scarce, their real price should increase. Simon offered the following $1,000 bet: Pick any resource(s) and any future date. On that date, we will look to see if resource prices have risen by more or less than inflation. If prices were to rise by more than inflation, Simon would pay. If prices had not risen as fast as inflation Simon, would collect.

Simon's challenge was accepted in October 1980 by Paul Ehrlich, author of *Population Bomb,* along with John Harte and John Holdren. They chose five metals: chrome, copper, nickel, tin, and tungsten. On paper, they spent $200 on each metal, buying 51.28 pounds of chrome, 196.56 pounds of copper, 65.32 pounds of nickel, 229.16 pounds of tin, and 13.64 pounds of tungsten. The bet was to look at the inflation-adjusted price of this market basket of metal in October 1990. If, after adjusting for inflation, the market basket of metal cost more than $1,000, Simon would pay Ehrlich, Harte and Holdren the difference from $1,000. On the other hand, if the total cost were less than $1,000, Ehrlich, Harte and Holdren owed Simon the difference.

1. If you could choose either side of a similar bet today, which would you take and why? Who do you think won? What was the payoff?

# The Realm of Macroeconomics

## LEARNING OBJECTIVES

After completing this chapter you should be able to:

♦ explain the difference between microeconomics and macroeconomics.

♦ determine whether particular problems are within the realm of microeconomics or macroeconomics.

♦ describe the role of economic aggregates in macroeconomics.

♦ explain how supply-demand analysis can be used to study inflation, recessions, and stabilization policy.

♦ distinguish between real and nominal GDP.

♦ explain how GDP is a measure of economic production, not economic well-being.

♦ characterize, in general terms, the movement in prices and output over the last 100 years.

♦ use aggregate demand and supply curves to explain how stabilization policy addresses problems of unemployment and inflation.

## IMPORTANT TERMS AND CONCEPTS

Microeconomics
Macroeconomics
Domestic product
Aggregation
Aggregate demand and aggregate supply curves
Inflation
Deflation
Recession
Gross domestic product (GDP)
Nominal versus real GDP
Final goods and services
Intermediate goods
Stagflation
Stabilization policy

# CHAPTER REVIEW

Economic theory is traditionally split into two parts, microeconomics and macroeconomics. If one studies
(1) the behavior of individual decision-making units, one is studying _____. If one studies the behavior of entire economies, one is studying _____. This chapter is an introduction to macroeconomics.

The American economy is made up of tens of millions of firms, hundreds of millions of individuals, and innumerable different goods and services. Since it would be impossible to list each of these firms, individuals, and commodities, economists have found it useful to use certain overall averages or aggregates. The concept of *domestic product* is an example. If we concentrate on macroeconomic aggregates, we ignore much of the micro detail; whereas by concentrating on the micro detail, we may ignore much of the overall picture. The two forms of analysis are not substitutes; rather, they can be usefully employed together. (Remember the map example in Chapter 1 of the text.) It has been argued that only successful macro-economic policy leads to a situation in which the study of microeconomics is important, and vice versa.

Supply and demand analysis is a fundamental tool of both micro and macro theory. In microeconomics one looks at the supply and demand for individual commodities, while in macroeconomics one studies aggregate supply and aggregate demand. The intersection of the demand and supply curves in
(2) microeconomics determines equilibrium _____ and _____. In macroeconomics the intersection of the aggregate demand and supply curves determines the cost of living, or the price level, and aggregate output, or the gross _____ _____.

(3) A sustained increase in the price level would be called _____, whereas a sustained decrease would be called _____. Domestic product in the U.S. economy usually increases every year for reasons that will be discussed in Chapters 34 and 38. Periods when domestic product declines are referred to as _____. With an unchanged aggregate supply curve, an outward (rightward) shift of the aggregate demand curve would lead to (higher/lower) prices and (higher/lower) output. Higher prices would also result if the aggregate supply curve shifted to the (left/right), but, this time, higher prices would be associated with a(n) (increase/decrease) in output. Such a combination of rising prices and declining output is called _____. If both curves shift to the right at the same rate, then it is possible to have increased output with constant prices.

(4) Gross domestic product is defined as the sum of the _____ values of all _____ goods and services produced in the domestic economy during a year. Economists and national income statisticians use prices to add up the different kinds of output. If one uses today's prices, the result is (nominal/real) GDP. If one values output by prices from some base period, one gets _____ GDP. Which is the better measure of changes in output? (Nominal/Real) GDP. If all prices rise and all outputs are unchanged, (nominal/real) GDP will increase while _____ GDP will not. It is important to remember that GDP is a measure of production; it (is/is not) a measure of economic well-being.

If you look at a long period of American history, you will see that there have been periods when
(5) both output and prices have risen and fallen. The long-term trend for output is (up/down). The overall trend for prices (depends/does not depend) upon the period you are reviewing. Up until World War II, prices rose and fell whereas since 1945, prices seem only to have _____.

The government would like to keep output growing, thus avoiding recession; at the same time,
(6) it would like to keep prices from rising, thus avoiding (inflation/deflation). Attempts to do just this
are called _____ policy. The American government has been
formally committed to such policies only since the end of World War II. A look at Figures 22-3 and
22-4 in the text suggests that since 1950 stabilization policy has done a good job avoiding
_____ but not of avoiding _____. Chapter 33
discusses why this result is not surprising; that is, why, if one concentrates on maintaining high levels
of employment and output, the result is likely to be higher prices.

## IMPORTANT TERMS AND CONCEPTS QUIZ

Choose the best definition for the following terms.

1. _____ Microeconomics
2. _____ Macroeconomics
3. _____ Domestic product
4. _____ Aggregation
5. _____ Aggregate demand curve
6. _____ Aggregate supply curve
7. _____ Inflation
8. _____ Deflation
9. _____ Recession
10. _____ Gross domestic product
11. _____ Nominal GDP
12. _____ Real GDP
13. _____ Final goods and services
14. _____ Intermediate goods
15. _____ Stagflation
16. _____ Stabilization policy

a. Period of expansion in an economy's total output.
b. Period of decline in an economy's total output.
c. Inflation occurring while the economy is growing slowly or in a recession.

d. Gross domestic product calculated at current price levels.
e. Total production of a nation's economy.
f. Government programs designed to prevent or shorten recessions and to counteract inflation.
g. Products purchased by their ultimate users.
h. Study of behavior of an entire economy.
i. Combining individual markets into a single, overall market.
j. Gross domestic product calculated using prices from some agreed-upon year.
k. Products purchased for resale or for their use in producing other products.
l. Sustained decrease in general price level.
m. Graph of quantity of domestic product demanded at each possible price level.
n. Sum of money values of all final goods and services produced in the domestic economy within the year.
o. Graph of quantity of domestic product produced at each possible price level.
p. Study of behavior of individual decision-making units.
q. Sustained increase in general price level.

## FIGURE 22-1

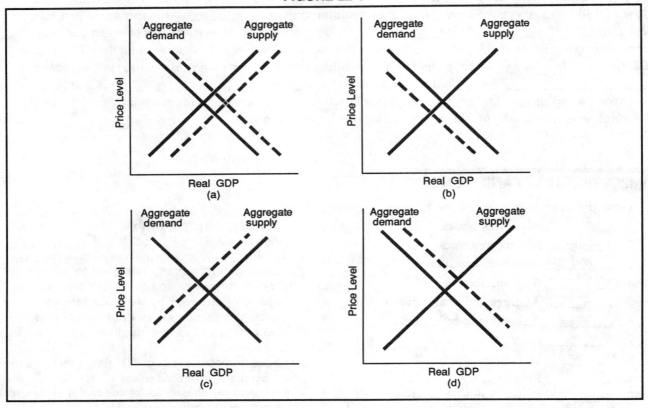

## BASIC EXERCISES

These exercises use the aggregate demand–aggregate supply diagram to review a few basic concepts.

1. Figure 22-1 has four panels. The solid lines indicate the initial situation, and the dashed lines indicate a shift in one or both curves.
   a. Which diagram(s) suggests a period, or periods, of inflation? ___C, d___
   b. Which diagram(s) suggests a period, or periods, of deflation? ___b___
      (Have prices in the U.S. economy ever declined in the twentieth century? ___Yes___
      If so, when? ___After WWII___ )
   c. Which diagram(s) illustrates growth in real output with stable prices? ___a___
   d. Which diagram(s) illustrates stagflation? ___c___

2. Stabilization policy involves changes in government policies designed to shorten recessions and stabilize prices. For reasons explored in Chapters 28 through 33, stabilization policies have their primary effect on the aggregate demand curve. For the cases listed below explain how stabilization policy can reestablish the initial levels of output and prices. Do this by indicating the appropriate shift in the aggregate demand curve. (The exact policies that will achieve these shifts will be described in detail in Chapters 28 through 33.)
   a. Inflation [diagram (d)]
   b. Recession [diagram (b)]
   c. Consider diagram (c), the case of stagflation. If the government is restricted to policies that shift the aggregate demand curve, what will happen to output if the government adopts policies to combat inflation and restore the original price level? What happens to prices if the government is committed to maintaining the original level of output?

## TABLE 22-1

| | Price (1) | 1992 Quantity (2) | Money Value (3) | Price (4) | 1993 Quantity (5) | Money Value (6) |
|---|---|---|---|---|---|---|
| Hamburgers | $2.00 | 300 | _____ | $2.80 | 310 | _____ |
| Shakes | 1.00 | 300 | _____ | 1.30 | 320 | _____ |
| Fries | 0.75 | 300 | _____ | 0.90 | 330 | _____ |
| | | Nominal GDP | _____ | | Nominal GDP | _____ |

3. Table 22-1 contains data on output and prices in a hypothetical economy that produces only fast food.
   a. Calculate the money value of the production of hamburgers, shakes, and fries by multiplying price and quantity. Sum these results to calculate nominal gross domestic product (GDP) for each year.
   b. What is the percentage increase in nominal GDP from 1992 to 1993?

   _____
   c. Use 1992 prices to compute real GDP for 1993 based on 1992 prices.
      Value of 1993 hamburger production using 1992 prices        _____
      Value of 1993 shake production using 1992 prices            _____
      Value of 1993 fries production using 1992 prices            _____
      Real GDP for 1993 (expressed in terms of 1992 prices)       _____
   d. Calculate the percentage increase in real GDP from 1992 to 1993. _____
   e. How does this figure compare to the increase in nominal GDP calculated in question b? Which is the better measure of the increase in production?_____

   _____

## SELF-TESTS FOR UNDERSTANDING

### Test A

Circle the most appropriate answer.

1. Microeconomics is concerned with
   a. economic aggregates.
   b. the actions of individual economic decision-making units.
   c. small people.
   d. small countries.

2. The study of macroeconomics focuses on
   a. the economic actions of large people.
   b. decisions by the largest 500 industrial companies.
   c. the prices and output of all firms in an industry.
   d. the behavior of entire economies.

3. Which of the following is an example of a macroeconomic aggregate?
   a. The national output of Haiti.
   b. The total output of General Motors.
   c. Employment at Sears.
   d. The price Exxon charges for unleaded gas.

4. The aggregate demand curve shows
   a. the history of real GDP over the recent past.
   b. alternative levels of domestic output that policy makers might choose.
   c. how the quantity of domestic product demanded changes with changes in the price level.
   d. the demand for goods and services by the federal government.

5. The graph showing how the quantity of output produced by all firms depends upon the price level is called the
   a. aggregate supply curve.
   b. Phillips curve.
   c. production possibilities frontier.
   d. economy's aggregate indifference curve.

6. GDP measures the sum of money values of
   a. all goods sold in the domestic economy during the past year.
   b. all final goods and services produced in the domestic economy during the past year.
   c. attendance at all the worst movies during the past year.
   d. all payments to household domestic help during the past year.

7. GDP is designed to be a measure of
   a. economic activity conducted through organized markets.
   b. national well-being.
   c. all economic activity during the preceding year.
   d. all economic transactions involving checks or cash during the preceding year.

8. Using today's prices to aggregate all final output in the economy will yield
   a. nominal GDP.
   b. real GDP.
   c. the cost of living.
   d. GDP in constant dollars.

9. Real GDP is computed by valuing output by
   a. manufacturers' costs.
   b. current prices.
   c. some fixed set of prices.
   d. last year's rate of inflation.

10. Which of the following would not be included in GDP for 1994?
    a. The production of refrigerators in 1994.
    b. The government's purchase of paper clips in 1994.
    c. Consumer expenditures on haircuts in 1994.
    d. General Motors' expenditures on steel for producing Cadillacs in 1994.

11. Which of the following would not be part of GDP for 1994?
    a. Stacey's purchase of a 1994 Pontiac.
    b. Tanya's purchase of the latest microcomputer produced by Apple.
    c. Ramon's expenditures on new furniture for his apartment.
    d. Jamal's purchase of a guitar originally used by John Lennon in 1965.

12. Which of the following is measured by the GDP statisticians?
    a. Jerita's purchase of Boeing stock from Walter.
    b. Your spending on tuition and fees for this year.
    c. Durwood's winnings from his bookie.
    d. The value of Yvonne's volunteer time at her daughter's school.

13. Which of the following will be measured as an increase in GDP but need not reflect an increase in economic well-being?
    a. Expenditures to clean up a major oil spill in Prince William Sound.
    b. The value of the time Roland spends painting his own house.
    c. The cost of new medical care that reduces infant mortality.
    d. Earnings of numbers runners in Chicago.

14. In 1974 nominal GDP was $1.459 trillion. In 1975 nominal GDP increased to $1.768 trillion. On the basis of just this information, which of the following statements is true?
    a. Total output of the American economy was greater in 1975 than in 1974.
    b. The whole increase in nominal GDP was the result of inflation.
    c. Actual output increased by 8.50 percent.
        $[(1.598 - 1.473) + (1.473)] \times 100$.
    d. It is impossible to determine what happened to prices and output from data on nominal GDP alone.

15. A recession is likely to occur if
    a. unemployment is falling.
    b. the aggregate supply curve shifts to the right.
    c. the increase in nominal GDP exceeds the increase in real GDP.
    d. the aggregate demand curve shifts to the left.

16. Inflation is defined as a period of
    a. rising nominal GDP.
    b. generally rising prices.
    c. falling real GDP.
    d. falling unemployment.

17. Which of the following conditions will result in stagflation?
    a. The aggregate demand curve shifts to the right.
    b. The aggregate demand curve shifts to the left.
    c. The aggregate supply curve shifts to the right.
    d. The aggregate supply curve shifts to the left.

18. Stabilization policy refers to actions by the government to
    a. keep real GDP from rising.
    b. minimize changes in government regulation.
    c. prevent recessions and fight inflation.
    d. equalize the rate of unemployment and inflation.

19. In the period following World War II, the historical record shows
    a. more frequent and more severe recessionary dips in real output than before World War II.
    b. an almost continuous increase in prices.
    c. little if any increase in real GDP.
    d. relatively little inflation.

20. Successful stabilization policy to reduce unemployment would shift
    a. the aggregate supply curve to the left.
    b. the burden of taxes from individuals to corporations.
    c. the aggregate demand curve to the right.
    d. decision making about monetary policy to the Congress.

## Test B

Circle T or F for true or false.

T (F) 1. A study of the economy of Luxembourg would be an example of microeconomics.

(T) F 2. GDP is an example of a macroeconomic aggregate.

(T) F 3. A decrease in nominal GDP necessarily implies a recession.

(T) F 4. Real GDP is a better measure of national output than is nominal GDP.

T (F) 5. Deflation can occur only as a result of shifts in the aggregate supply curve.

T (F) 6. Even during the Great Depression of the 1930s prices did not decline.

T (F) 7. On the eve of World War II, national output, or real GDP, was not much greater than at the end of the Civil War.

T (F) 8. Stagflation refers to the simultaneous occurrence of rising prices and little if any increase in output.

(T) F 9. Stabilization policy refers to attempts by the government to influence both prices and output by shifting the aggregate demand curve.

T (F) 10. Stabilization policy to combat a recession would call for policies that shift the aggregate demand curve to the left.

## STUDY QUESTIONS

1. Why is GDP, a measure of domestic production, not a good measure of national well-being?

2. Why does GDP exclude the sales of existing goods and assets such as used college textbooks and existing homes?

3. Which is the better measure of the change in domestic output, nominal GDP or real GDP? Why?

4. Why does GDP include only final goods and exclude intermediate goods?

5. Should measures of GDP include estimates of non-market economic activity? Why?

6. How can stabilization policy help to reduce unemployment? Inflation?

7. If stabilization policy has the strongest and most immediate impact on aggregate demand, what are the implications for prices when the government wants to reduce unemployment? What are the implications for unemployment when the government wants to reduce prices?

8. What might account for the differences in the American economy's record of economic growth and inflation after 1950 as compared with the period before World War II?

## ECONOMICS IN ACTION

The text describes recessions as a period of decline in GDP. This is also the definition that is used by many media commentators. The beginnings and ends of recessions are actually determined by a group of economists associated with the National Bureau of Economic Research. They look at a broader range of measures of economic activity than just GDP. Much controversy surrounded the dating of the 1990-91 recession. The following is taken from a report by Professor Robert Hall, Stanford University, chairman of the NBER Business Cycle Dating Committee, written after data through October 1991 were available. Using Figure 22-2 can you date the beginning and end of the recession? The Committee's decisions are reported in the answers section of the Study Guide, but make your own determination before looking at their decision.

**FIGURE 22-2**

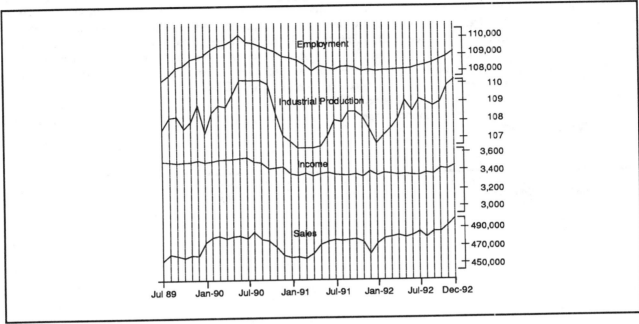

In April 1991, the NBER's Business Cycle Dating Committee determined that a recession had started _____. Figure 1 [22-2] shows the data that most strongly influenced the committee: real personal income less transfers, real sales in manufacturing and trade, nonagricultural employment (because 1990 was a census year, the committee looked at private nonagricultural employment, and nonagricultural employment minus Census workers), and industrial production. The figure shows the basic problem of dating a business cycle: that different cyclical indicators have different turning points.

The U.S. economy in 1990 reflected the combined influence of two different forces. One was a very broad slowdown starting in the spring. The other was a sharp contraction in industries (automobile and others) following the spike in oil prices in August. The result was an unusual combination of leading employment and lagging industrial production. The peak date was a reasonable compromise. It embodied the notion that breadth, or dispersion, is an important characteristic of a recession. When measures that span all sectors of the economy—income and employment—peak earlier, the fact that goods production stayed strong for _____ added months should not control the date of the recession.

Figure 1 [Figure 22-2] also shows some of the challenges that will face the NBER Business Cycle Dating Committee in determining the date of the trough in economic activity. First, the figure makes it completely clear that any such determination in the near future would be quite premature. Should the economy begin to contract again, it is a distinct possibility that the trough would occur in late 1991 or 1992. A trough date cannot be assigned until activity has reached a sufficiently high level that a contraction would be a new recession, not a continuation of the existing one.

Economist James Tobin has argued that the traditional approach to dating business cycles is misguided in that it assumes that any increase in economic activity signals the end of a recession. Tobin argues that in a growing economy, output and employment have to increase simply to keep pace with a growing population. He would prefer growth-oriented dating and definitions of business cycles, recoveries, and recessions. On this view, anytime the growth of output and employment failed to match the growth in the potential output would be candidates to be called recession or growth-recession. According to Tobin's definition, periods of recession begin earlier and last somewhat longer than those defined by the NBER.

1. How would you date the recession? Why?
2. Do you think the definition of recessions should be growth-oriented as advocated by Tobin? Why?

SOURCES: *NBER Reporter*, (National Bureau of Economic Research, Winter 1991/92), pp. 1-3.
James Tobin, "Comments," *Brookings Papers on Economic Activity*, 1993:1, pp. 200-208.

*Chapter* **23**

# Unemployment and Inflation: The Twin Evils of Macroeconomics

## LEARNING OBJECTIVES

After completing this chapter you should be able to:

- describe how the Bureau of Labor Statistics measures the number of unemployed and in what ways this number may be an overestimate or an underestimate of the unemployment level.

- explain the differences between frictional, structural, and cyclical unemployment.

- explain why unemployment insurance only spreads the financial burden of unemployment that individuals would otherwise face, but does not eliminate the economic cost of unemployment.

- summarize the debate over how much unemployment is consistent with full employment.

- distinguish between real and mythical costs of inflation.

- explain how the concept of real wages suggests that inflation has not systematically eroded the purchasing power of wages.

- distinguish between changes in prices that reflect a change in relative prices and changes that reflect general inflation.

- distinguish between real and nominal rates of interest.

- describe how the difference between real and nominal rates of interest is related to expectations about the rate of inflation.

- explain how the taxation of nominal interest income can mean that, during a period of inflation, savers will receive a reduced real return after taxes.

- explain why and how usury ceilings, based on nominal interest rates, can have undesirable impacts during periods of rapid inflation.

- distinguish between creeping and galloping inflation.

- explain why the variability of inflation is important to an understanding of the cost of inflation.

## IMPORTANT TERMS AND CONCEPTS

Unemployment rate
Potential GDP
Labor force
Discouraged workers
Frictional unemployment
Structural unemployment
Cyclical unemployment
Full employment
Unemployment insurance
Purchasing power

Real wage
Relative prices
Redistribution by inflation
Real rate of interest
Nominal rate of interest
Expected rate of inflation
Inflation and the tax system
Usury laws
Creeping inflation
Galloping inflation

## CHAPTER REVIEW

Ever since the Employment Act of 1946 committed the federal government to deliberate macroeconomic policy, policymakers have been facing the choice between the twin evils of macroeconomics. Attempts to lower unemployment have usually meant (more/less) inflation and attempts to fight inflation have

(1) usually meant _____ unemployment. How is one to make the choice? Economics cannot provide a definitive answer to this question, but the material in this chapter will help you understand the issues and enable you to make a more informed choice.

Unemployment has two sorts of costs. The personal costs include not only the lost income for individuals out of work, but also the loss of work experience and the psychic costs of involuntary idleness. The economic costs for the nation as a whole can be measured by the output of goods and services that might have been produced by those who are unemployed.

Unemployment insurance can help ease the burden of unemployment for individual families, but

(2) it (can/cannot) protect society against the lost output that the unemployed might have produced. Employing these people in the future does not bring back the hours of employment that have already been missed. Unemployment compensation provides (complete/partial) protection for (all/some) unemployed workers.

Economists have attempted to measure the economic cost of unemployment by estimating what

(3) output would have been at full employment. These figures are estimates of (potential/actual) GDP. The economic cost of unemployment is the difference between potential GDP and _____.

(4)     Full employment (is/is not) the same as zero unemployment. Some unemployment occurs naturally from the normal workings of labor markets, as people initially look for jobs, improve their own skills, look for better jobs, move to new locations, and so forth. Such unemployment is called _____ unemployment and involves people who are temporarily without a job more or less voluntarily. Full employment would not eliminate this kind of unemployment. Full employment would eliminate unemployment that is due to a decline in the economy's total production; that is, at full employment there would be no _____ unemployment. Unemployment may also occur because people's skills are no longer in demand due to automation or massive changes in production. This type of unemployment is called _____ unemployment.

Unemployment statistics come from a monthly survey by the Bureau of Labor Statistics. People are asked if they have a job. If they answer no, they are asked if they are laid off from a job they expect to return to, are actively looking for work, or are not looking for work. From these answers government statisticians derive estimates of employment, unemployment, and the labor force. These numbers are not above criticism. When unemployment rates are high, some people give up looking for work because they believe that

(5) looking for work is not worth the effort. These people are called _____ workers. An increase in the number of people who have given up looking for work means a(n) (increase/decrease) in the amount of statistical unemployment and is an important reason why some observers feel that the official

unemployment statistics (understate/overstate) the problem of unemployment. Part-time workers are counted as employed. If part-time work is involuntary and these individuals would prefer full-time work, official unemployment statistics will (understate/overstate) the problem of unemployment.

(6)     In the 1970s it was argued that the increased importance of young workers in the labor force increased the percentage of (cyclical/frictional/structural) unemployment and (decreased/increased) the full employment rate of unemployment. Young workers have naturally higher rates of unemployment because they more frequently enter and leave the labor force, and because they change jobs more often. If liberal unemployment compensation induces people to call themselves unemployed even if they have no intention of looking for work then official statistics will (overstate/understate) unemployment.

There are important and valid reasons why people are concerned about continuing inflation. Nevertheless, quite a few popular arguments against inflation turn out to be based on misunderstandings. Many
(7)  people worry that a high rate of inflation reduces their standard of living, or their (real/nominal) income. But the facts show that periods of high inflation are usually accompanied by equally large if not larger increases in wages. For most workers, the real standard of living, or the change in wages adjusted for the change in prices, continues to increase, even during periods of rapid inflation. A worker whose wages double when prices double is able to consume (more/less/the same) goods and services (than/as) before the rise in prices and wages. In this case one would say that real wages (increased/were unchanged/decreased).

(8)        During inflationary periods most prices increase at (the same/different) rates. As a result, goods and services with smaller than average price increases become relatively (more/less) expensive than they were before. Analogously, goods and services with larger than average price increases become relatively _____ expensive. Relative prices change all the time, during both inflationary and noninflationary periods. Changes in relative prices usually reflect shifts in demand and/or supply curves or various forms of government interventions. It is inaccurate to blame inflation for an increase in relative prices.

But inflation does have real effects. One important effect is the redistribution of wealth between borrowers and lenders in inflationary periods. If lenders expect higher prices in the future they will
(9)  demand (higher/lower) interest rates to compensate them for the loss of purchasing power of the future dollars used to repay loans. Economists have thus found it useful to distinguish between nominal and real interest rates. If one looks at interest rates only in terms of the dollars that borrowers must pay lenders, one is looking at _____ interest rates. If one looks at interest rates in terms of the expected purchasing power the borrower will pay the lender, one is looking at _____ interest rates. The difference between these two measures of interest rate is related to expectations of _____. Real rates are often measured as the difference between the nominal rate and the rate of inflation.

If a change in the rate of inflation is accurately foreseen, and if nominal interest rates are correctly
(10)  adjusted to reflect the change in expected inflation, then nominal interest rates (will/will not) change while real interest rates will (also change/be unchanged). More typically, expectations of inflation are incorrect, in which case inflation will result in a redistribution of wealth between borrowers and lenders. Who gains and who loses will depend on whether the adjustment of nominal interest rates is too large or too small. The tax treatment of interest payments can have a substantial impact on the real after-tax rate of return. Problems here reflect the fact that the tax system, originally designed for a world of no inflation, focuses on (nominal/real) interest rates.

(11)        Legal ceilings on interest charges for different types of loans are called _____ ceilings. These ceilings are almost universally written in terms of (nominal/real) interest rates rather than _____ interest rates. During periods of rapid inflation, (nominal/real) interest rates may rise, bumping into usury ceilings, while _____ interest rates may show little if any change. The result will be frustrated borrowers and lenders and reduced levels of economic activity in the affected areas.

Over the long run, small unexpected differences in the rate of inflation can compound to create large differences in profits and losses. Since most business investments depend on long-term contracts, this area of economic activity may suffer during periods of high inflation. The difficulty of making long-term contracts is a real cost of inflation.

(12)    Long-term inflation that proceeds at a fairly moderate and steady pace is referred to as _____ inflation. Inflation that progresses at exceptionally high and, often, accelerating rates, if only for brief periods of time, is called _____ inflation. There is no simple borderline between the two. In different countries or in different periods of time, the dividing line will vary considerably.

# IMPORTANT TERMS AND CONCEPTS QUIZ

Choose the best definition for the following terms.

1. _____ Unemployment rate
2. _____ Potential GDP
3. _____ Labor force
4. _____ Discouraged workers
5. _____ Frictional unemployment
6. _____ Structural unemployment
7. _____ Cyclical unemployment
8. _____ Unemployment insurance
9. _____ Purchasing power
10. _____ Real wage
11. _____ Relative prices
12. _____ Real rate of interest
13. _____ Nominal rate of interest
14. _____ Usury laws
15. _____ Creeping inflation
16. _____ Galloping inflation

a. Government transfer payments to eligible workers if unemployed.
b. Percentage of labor force unemployed.
c. Interest payments, in percentage terms, measured in dollars.
d. Number of people holding or seeking jobs.
e. Prices increasing at exceptionally high rate.
f. Unemployed people who cease looking for work, believing that no jobs are available.
g. Unemployment attributable to decline in economy's total production.
h. Unemployment due to normal workings of the labor market.
i. Legal maximum interest rate.
j. Interest payment, in percentage terms, measured on purchasing power.
k. Volume of goods and services that money wage will buy.
l. Unemployment due to changes in nature of economy.
m. Automatic adjustment of nominal interest rates during periods of inflation.
n. Price of an item in terms of some other item.
o. Prices rising for a long time at a moderate rate.
p. Volume of goods and services that a sum of money will buy.
q. Level of real output attainable if all resources were fully employed.

# BASIC EXERCISES

These exercises are designed to illustrate the difference between real and nominal interest rates.

1. **When Are High Interest Rates Really Low?**

   Let R = nominal interest rate,

   $\pi$ = actual rate of inflation, and

   $\rho$ = real rate of interest.

   It is usual to estimate actual real interest rates as $\rho = R - \pi$. Consider the data in Table 23-1. Column 1 shows data on nominal interest rates on one-year government securities issued in December of each year from 1970 through 1990. Column 2 shows the rate of inflation from December to December as measured by the consumer price index. Note that for 1970 the rate of inflation is from December 1970 to December 1971, the same period for which a holder of the government security earned interest.

## FIGURE 23-1

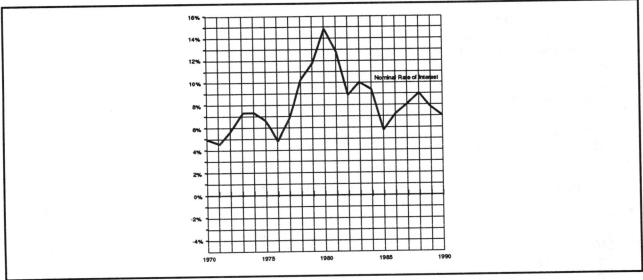

## TABLE 23-1
## NOMINAL INTEREST RATES AND INFLATION

| | Nominal Interest Rate on 1 Year Government Securities (December) | Rate of Inflation (December to December) | Real Interest Rate |
|---|---|---|---|
| 1970 | 5.00% | 5.70% | _____ % |
| 1971 | 4.61% | 4.40% | _____ % |
| 1972 | 5.52% | 3.20% | _____ % |
| 1973 | 7.27% | 6.20% | _____ % |
| 1974 | 7.31% | 11.00% | _____ % |
| 1975 | 6.60% | 9.10% | _____ % |
| 1976 | 4.89% | 5.80% | _____ % |
| 1977 | 6.96% | 6.50% | _____ % |
| 1978 | 10.30% | 7.60% | _____ % |
| 1979 | 11.98% | 11.30% | _____ % |
| 1980 | 14.88% | 13.50% | _____ % |
| 1981 | 12.85% | 10.30% | _____ % |
| 1982 | 8.91% | 6.20% | _____ % |
| 1983 | 10.11% | 3.20% | _____ % |
| 1984 | 9.33% | 4.30% | _____ % |
| 1985 | 7.67% | 3.60% | _____ % |
| 1986 | 5.87% | 1.90% | _____ % |
| 1987 | 7.17% | 3.60% | _____ % |
| 1988 | 8.99% | 4.10% | _____ % |
| 1989 | 7.72% | 4.80% | _____ % |
| 1990 | 7.05% | 5.40% | _____ % |

SOURCES: Federal Reserve, Bureau of Labor Statistics

a. Complete column 3 by computing real interest rates.
b. The nominal interest rates from column 1 are plotted in Figure 23-1.
   Plot the real interest rates you calculated in column 3 in Figure 23-1.
c. How can actual real rates be negative?
d. When were interest rates higher, 1980 or 1987?

This exercise has made use of data on actual inflation to estimate actual real interest rates. Remember that when individuals decide to borrow or lend they typically know the nominal interest rate they will receive or have to pay, but they cannot know what the real interest rate will turn out to be, as that will depend upon future inflation. At the same time, economists argue that decisions to borrow and lend will be strongly influenced by expectations of inflation and the corresponding expectations for real interest rates.

2. **Who Gains and Loses from an Adjustment of Nominal Interest Rates?**

This problem is designed to illustrate how the adjustment of nominal interest rates, when it is an accurate reflection of future inflation, can leave the real costs and returns to borrowers and lenders unchanged. For simplicity the exercise ignores taxes.

   Angela Abbott has a manufacturing firm. After paying other costs she expects a cash flow of $10 million, out of which she must pay the principal and interest on a $5 million loan. If prices are unchanged and if the interest rate is 5 percent, Angela expects a nominal and real profit of $4,750,000. This result is shown in the first column of Table 23-2.

   The next three columns reflect three possible alternatives. The second column shows the consequences of unexpected inflation of 10 percent. In the third column, nominal interest rates have adjusted in expectation of an inflation of 10 percent, which actually occurs. And in the last column, nominal interest rates reflect the consequences of expecting a higher rate of inflation than actually occurs.

a. Fill in the missing figures in the second column. Compare the real returns to both Angela and her lender with those of the noninflationary situation in column 1. Who gains and who loses when there is unexpected inflation?
b. Fill in the missing figures in the third column. This is the case in which nominal interest rates have adjusted appropriately. (The approximation is to add the rate of inflation, 10 percent, to the rate of interest in the noninflationary situation, 5 percent. The extra 0.5 percent comes from a more complex and complete adjustment.) Compare the real returns in rows 7 and 9 with the comparable figures in column 1. Who gains and who loses now?
c. Fill in the missing figures in column 4, where interest rates have adjusted in anticipation of a rate of inflation higher than the rate that actually occurs. Who gains and who loses when inflation turns out to be less than expected?

**TABLE 23-2**

|  | (1) | (2) | (3) | (4) |
|---|---|---|---|---|
| 1. Price level | 1.00 | 1.10 | 1.10 | 1.10 |
| 2. Sales revenue minus labor and materials costs * | 10,000,000 | 11,000,000 | 11,000,000 | 11,000,000 |
| 3. Principal repayment | 5,000,000 | 5,000,000 | 5,000,000 | 5,000,000 |
| 4. Interest rate | 0.05 | 0.05 | 0.155 | 0.20 |
| 5. Interest payment [(4) × (3)] | 250,000 | _____ | _____ | _____ |
| 6. Total nominal payment to lender [(3) + (5)] | 5,250,000 | _____ | _____ | _____ |
| 7. Real payment to lender [(6) ÷ (1)] | 5,250,000 | _____ | _____ | _____ |
| 8. Nominal profits [(2) − (6)] | 4,750,000 | _____ | _____ | _____ |
| 9. Real profits [(8) ÷ (1)] | 4,750,000 | _____ | _____ | _____ |

* Inflation of 10 percent is assumed to increase sales revenue, labor costs, and materials costs by 10 percent each. As a result, the difference between sales revenue and labor plus material costs also increases by 10 percent in column 2, 3, and 4.

# SELF-TESTS FOR UNDERSTANDING

## Test A

Circle the most appropriate answer.

1. Indicate which examples go with which concepts.
   a. An older, unemployed telephone operator replaced by new, computerized switching machines.
   b. An unemployed college senior looking for her first job.
   c. An ex-construction worker who has given up looking for work because of a belief that no one is hiring.
   d. An unemployed retail clerk who is laid off because of declining sales associated with a general business recession.

   frictional unemployment     _____

   structural unemployment     _____

   cyclical unemployment     _____

   discouraged worker     _____

2. Which of the following factors implies that official statistics may understate the magnitude of the problem of unemployment? (There may be more than one correct answer.)
   a. Discouraged workers.
   b. The loss of expected overtime work.
   c. Generous unemployment benefits.
   d. Involuntary part-time work.

3. Which of the following people are eligible for unemployment compensation?
   a. A mechanic for Ford Motor Company laid off because of declining auto sales.
   b. A housewife seeking paid work after six years spent at home with two small children.
   c. A college senior looking for his first job.
   d. An engineer who quits to find a better job.

4. Which one of the following groups experiences the highest rate of unemployment?
   a. Married men.
   b. College graduates.
   c. Teenage workers.
   d. Non-white workers.

5. The measure of output that the economy could produce with the full employment of all people and factories is called
   a. real GDP.
   b. potential GDP.
   c. nominal GDP.
   d. expected GDP.

6. The difference between potential GDP and actual GDP is a reflection of
   a. frictional unemployment.
   b. cyclical unemployment.
   c. galloping inflation.
   d. nominal interest rates.

7. In 1992 unemployment insurance provided benefits to about _____ of the unemployed.
   a. one-quarter
   b. one-third
   c. one-half
   d. all

8. In 1992 unemployment insurance replaced a bit less than _____ of lost income for those who were insured.
    a. one-quarter
    b. one-third
    c. one-half
    d. all

9. Unemployment insurance
    a. eliminates the cost of unemployment to the economy as a whole.
    b. means that no unemployed worker need suffer a decline in his or her standard of living.
    c. helps to protect insured individuals by spreading the cost.
    d. must be paid back by the unemployed once they find a new job.

10. The real rate of interest relevant for a lender about to lend money is measured as the
    a. nominal interest rate divided by the rate of inflation.
    b. nominal interest rate minus the expected rate of inflation.
    c. rate of inflation minus the nominal interest rate.
    d. the increase in nominal GDP divided by the rate of increase in prices.

11. A nominal interest rate of 10 percent and inflationary expectations of 4 percent imply a real interest rate of about _____ percent.
    a. 4
    b. 6
    c. 10
    d. 14

12. Nominal interest rates of 9 percent are consistent with real interest rates of 4 percent if expectations of inflation are equal to
    a. 4 percent.
    b. 5 percent.
    c. 9 percent.
    d. 14 percent.

13. If suddenly everyone expects a higher rate of inflation, economists would expect nominal interest rates to
    a. rise.
    b. fall.
    c. stay unchanged.

14. In a world with no inflation and no taxes, nominal interest rates of 5 percent offer a real return of 5 percent. If suddenly it is expected that prices will rise by 6 percent, what increase in nominal interest rates is necessary if the expected real interest rate is to remain unchanged at 5 percent?
    a. 1 percent.
    b. 5 percent.
    c. 6 percent.
    d. 11 percent.

15. If inflation is unexpected, there is apt to be a redistribution of wealth from
    a. borrowers to lenders.
    b. lenders to borrowers.
    c. rich to poor.
    d. poor to rich.

16. Usury laws are designed to limit
    a. increases in nominal wages.
    b. real interest rates.
    c. the rate of inflation.
    d. nominal interest rates.

17. With overall inflation at 5 percent, if the price of jeans increases by 7 percent and the price of hand calculators declines by 3 percent, we would say that
    a. the relative price of jeans has increased.
    b. calculators are now less expensive in terms of jeans.
    c. both a and b are correct.
    d. only a is correct.

18. The dividing line between creeping and galloping inflation
    a. is 10 percent.
    b. is 50 percent.
    c. is 100 percent.
    d. will depend upon the particular country and historical circumstances.

19. If your wages go up by 10 percent when prices go up by 7 percent, the increase in your real wage is about _____ percent.
    a. 3
    b. 7
    c. 10
    d. 17

20. The historical evidence suggests that in periods with high rates of inflation, nominal wages
    a. increase at about the same rate as before.
    b. increase at much lower rates than inflation.
    c. also increase at high rates.
    d. remain unchanged.

## Test B

Circle T or F for true or false.

T  F   1.  In periods of high unemployment the only people whose incomes are reduced are those who are out of work.

T  F   2.  The official unemployment statistics are adjusted to include those people with part-time jobs who are looking for full-time work.

T  F   3.  All major social groupings, young–old, men–women, blacks–whites, have essentially the same rate of unemployment.

T  F   4.  Unemployment insurance protects society against lost output from unemployment.

T  F   5.  Anyone who is officially counted as unemployed can collect unemployment benefits.

T  F   6.  Potential GDP is an estimate of the maximum possible output our economy could produce under conditions similar to wartime.

T  F   7.  The definition of full-employment is an unemployment rate of zero.

T  F   8.  Inflation does not redistribute wealth between borrowers and lenders because nominal interest rates are automatically adjusted to reflect actual inflation.

T  F   9.  The historical record shows that creeping inflation will always lead to galloping inflation.

T  F  10.  Predictable inflation is likely to impose less cost than unpredictable inflation.

# Appendix:
# How Statisticians Measure Inflation

## LEARNING OBJECTIVES

After completing this appendix you should be able to:

♦ construct a price index from data on prices and the composition of the market basket in the base year.

♦ use a price index to compute real measures of economic activity by deflating the corresponding nominal measures.

♦ use a price index to compute the rate of inflation from one period to the next.

♦ explain how the market baskets differ for the Consumer Price Index and the GDP deflator.

## IMPORTANT TERMS AND CONCEPTS

Index number
Index number problem
Consumer Price Index
Deflating by a price index
GDP deflator

## IMPORTANT TERMS AND CONCEPTS QUIZ

Choose the best definition for the following terms.

1. ___b___ Index number
2. ___d___ Consumer Price Index
3. ___a___ Deflating
4. ___c___ GDP deflator
5. ___f___ Index number problem

a. Dividing a nominal magnitude by a price index to express the magnitude in constant purchasing power.

b. Magnitude of some variable relative to its magnitude in base periods.
c. Price index obtained by dividing nominal GDP by real GDP.
d. Measure of price level based on typical urban household's spending.
e. Average change in consumer prices.
f. Differences between consumption patterns of actual families and the market basket used for a price index.

## BASIC EXERCISE

The following exercise should help you review the material on price indexes presented in the appendix to Chapter 23.

Table 23-3 presents data on expenditures and prices for a hypothetical family that buys only food and clothing. We see that in 1990 this family spent $5,000 on food at $2 per unit of food, and $10,000 on clothing at $25 per unit. Note that between 1990 and 1991, dollar expenditures by this family increased by 15.65 percent, rising from $15,000 to $17,348. Is this family able to consume 15.65 percent more of everything? Clearly not, since prices have risen. How much inflation has there been on average? What is the increase in real income for this family? These are the sorts of questions that a good price index can help you answer.

**TABLE 23-3**
**HYPOTHETICAL PRICES AND EXPENDITURES**

| Year | Food | | Clothing | | Total Expenditures |
| | Price | Expenditures | Price | Expenditures | |
| --- | --- | --- | --- | --- | --- |
| 1990 | $2.00 | $5,000 | $25.00 | $10,000 | $15,000 |
| 1991 | $2.36 | $5,900 | $26.50 | $11,448 | $17,348 |

1. Use the data in Table 23-3 to construct a family price index (FPI) using 1990 as the base year.
   a. Divide expenditures by price to find the quantities of each good purchased in 1990. This is the base-period market basket.

   Quantity of food      _____

   Quantity of clothing      _____

   b. Use 1991 prices to find out how much the base-period market basket would cost at 1991 prices.
   1991 cost of 1990 market basket _____
   c. Divide the 1991 cost of the base-period market basket by the 1990 cost of the same market basket and multiply by 100 to compute the value of the FPI for 1991.
   FPI for 1991 _____
   d. Convince yourself that if you repeat steps b and c using 1990 prices you will get an answer of 100 for the value of the FPI for 1990.
   e. Measure the increase in the cost of living by computing the percentage change in your price index from 1990 to 1991.
   Inflation between 1990 and 1991 _____
   f. Divide total dollar expenditures in 1991 by the 1991 FPI and multiply by 100 to get a measure of real expenditures for 1991.

   Real expenditures in 1991 (1990 prices)      _____

   Percentage change in real expenditures 1990 to 1991      _____

Remember the following points about price indexes:
- Most price indexes, like the Consumer Price Index, are computed by pricing a standard market basket of goods in subsequent periods.
- A price index can be used to measure inflation and to deflate nominal values to adjust for inflation.
- Different price indexes, such as the Consumer Price Index and the GDP deflator, will show slightly different measures of inflation because they use different market baskets.

2. (Optional) Compute a new FPI using 1991 as the base period rather than 1990. Now the value of your price index for 1991 will be 100 and the price index for 1990 will be something less than 100. Does this index give the same measure of inflation as the index with 1990 as the base period? Do not be surprised if it does not. Can you explain why they differ?

TABLE 23-4
INDEX OF CONSUMER PRICES (1982–1984 = 100)

|      | Canada | France | Italy | Japan | United Kingdom | United States | Germany |
|------|--------|--------|-------|-------|----------------|---------------|---------|
| 1970 | 35.1   | 28.7   | 16.8  | 38.5  | 21.8           | 38.8          | 52.9    |
| 1975 | 50.1   | 43.9   | 28.8  | 66.0  | 40.2           | 53.8          | 71.2    |
| 1980 | 76.1   | 72.2   | 63.2  | 91.0  | 78.5           | 82.4          | 86.8    |
| 1985 | 108.9  | 114.3  | 121.1 | 104.1 | 111.1          | 107.6         | 104.8   |
| 1990 | 135.5  | 133.2  | 159.6 | 111.4 | 148.2          | 130.7         | 112.1   |

Source: *1993 Economic Report of the President,* Table B-105.

## SUPPLEMENTARY EXERCISES

1. Table 23-4 contains data on consumer prices for seven countries. Try to answer each of the following questions or explain why the information in Table 23-4 is insufficient to answer the question.
   a. In 1970 which country had the lowest prices?
   b. In 1990 which country had the highest prices?
   c. Over the period 1970 to 1990, which country experienced the most inflation as measured by the percentage change in the consumer price index? Which country experienced the least inflation?

2. Go to the library to document the current unemployment situation of different workers. *Employment and Earnings* is published monthly by the Bureau of Labor Statistics. It contains detailed data on employment and unemployment by age, sex, and race of workers. The *Survey of Current Business* is another good source, although less detailed than *Employment and Earnings*. The *Economic Report of the President*, issued annually, is a good source for historic data.

3. Learn more about the composition of the market basket for the Consumer Price Index. A good place to start is "New basket of goods and services being priced in revised CPI," Charles Mason and Clifford Butler, *Monthly Labor Review*, January 1987, pages 3-22.

## ECONOMICS IN ACTION

There is general agreement that inflation at a constant rate imposes less cost than inflation that fluctuates widely around a similar mean. Some argue that it does not matter what the rate of inflation is as long as it does not vary too much. If inflation could actually be held constant at a given rate, then borrowers and lenders, consumers, and producers would all come to expect this unchanged rate of inflation, and they could devise contracts for borrowing, lending, and wages that incorporated simple inflationary expectations. Using this line of reasoning it does not matter whether inflation averages 0 percent or 10 percent. Inflation that averaged 0 percent but fluctuated between plus 5 percent and minus 5 percent would be as bad as inflation that averaged 10 percent while fluctuating between 5 percent and 15 percent. Based on this view, policy should focus more on the stabilization of the rate of inflation and less on the average rate of inflation.

Others are skeptical that it is possible to stabilize inflation when the average rate is high and wonder whether higher rates of inflation are not necessarily associated with more variable rates. *The Economist*, in its November 7, 1992 issue, examined the question of what rate of inflation countries should aim for. Part of their investigation looked at historical data on the variability of inflation for a number of industrialized countries. Similar data for 22 countries* is shown in Figure 23-2, which plots the average rate of inflation over the period 1961 to 1991 on the horizontal axis and the standard deviation in the rate of inflation over the same period on the vertical axis. (The standard deviation is a statistical measure of variability. Larger numbers are associated with greater variability.)

**FIGURE 23-2**

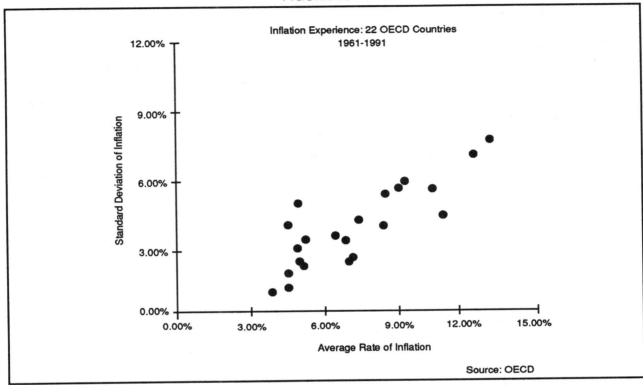

1. What does Figure 23-2 suggest about the link between the average rate of inflation and the variability of inflation?
2. If higher rates of inflation mean greater variability, how low a rate of inflation should countries strive for? Is an average rate of zero possible? Would it be desirable?

You might want to consult the article in *The Economist*, "Zero Inflation: How Low is Low Enough?," November 7, 1992, pp. 23-26.

---

*Australia, Austria, Belgium, Canada, Denmark, Finland, France, Germany, Greece, Ireland, Italy, Japan, Luxembourg, Netherlands, New Zealand, Norway, Portugal, Spain, Sweden, Switzerland, United Kingdom, and United States.

## STUDY QUESTIONS

1. Why doesn't unemployment insurance eliminate the cost of unemployment for the economy as a whole?
2. Consider the following numbers for two hypothetical months:

|  | Month 1 | Month 2 |
| --- | --- | --- |
| Employed | 92 | 91 |
| Unemployed | 8 | 7 |
| Not in the Labor Force | 60 | 62 |
| Rate of Unemployment | 8.0% | 7.1% |

How might the concept of discouraged workers be relevant for explaining why the decline in employment is associated with a decline in the unemployment rate?

---

3. Do you believe the official rate of unemployment overstates or understates the seriousness of unemployment? Why?

4. Which concepts of unemployment—frictional, structural, and cyclical—are relevant when considering the full employment rate of unemployment? Why?

5. When does an increase in the price of textbooks reflect a change in relative prices and when does it reflect inflation?

6. During a period of inflation which is likely to be higher, nominal or real interest rates? Why?

7. Do you agree or disagree with the argument that the taxation of interest and capital gains should be based on real returns rather than nominal returns? Why?

8. Which is likely to have more adverse effects, steady or variable inflation? Why?

*Chapter* **24**

# Income and Spending: The Powerful Consumer

---

## LEARNING OBJECTIVES

After completing this chapter you should be able to:

- distinguish between spending, output, and income.
- describe what spending categories make up aggregate demand.
- distinguish between investment spending as a part of aggregate demand and financial investment.
- explain why, except for some technical complications, national product and national income are necessarily equal.
- explain how disposable income differs from national income.
- derive a consumption function given data on consumption and disposable income and compute the marginal propensity to consume at various levels of income.
- explain why the marginal propensity to consume is equal to the slope of the consumption function.
- distinguish between factors that result in a *movement along* the consumption function and factors that result in a *shift of* the function.
- explain why consumption spending is affected by a change in the level of prices even if real income is unchanged.
- describe why permanent and temporary changes in taxes of the same magnitude would be expected to have different impacts on consumption spending.

---

---

## IMPORTANT TERMS AND CONCEPTS

Aggregate demand
Consumer expenditure (C)
Investment spending (I)
Government purchases (G)
Net exports (X – IM)
C + I + G + X – IM
National income
Disposable income (DI)
Circular flow diagram
Transfer payments
Scatter diagram
Consumption function
Marginal propensity to consume (MPC)
Movements along versus shifts of the consumption function
Money fixed assets
Temporary versus permanent tax changes

---

## CHAPTER REVIEW

This chapter introduces two key concepts that economists use when discussing the determination of an economy's output: *aggregate demand* and the *consumption function*. These basic concepts will be fundamental to the material in later chapters.

(1) The total amount that all consumers, business firms, government agencies, and foreigners are willing to spend on goods and services is called aggregate _____. Economists typically divide this sum into four components: consumption expenditures, investment spending, government purchases, and net exports. Food, clothing, movies, and hamburgers are examples of (consumption/investment/government) expenditures. Factories, office buildings, machinery, and houses would be examples of _____ spending. Red tape, bombers, filing cabinets, and the services of bureaucrats are examples of _____ purchases. American wheat and tractors sold abroad are examples of (exports/imports), and American purchases of French wines, Canadian paper, and Mexican oil are examples of _____. The difference between exports and imports is called _____. Economists use national income accounts to keep track of these components of demand. Appendix B to this chapter provides an introduction to these accounts.

There is a close analogy between the demand for a single product and aggregate demand. As seen in the study of consumer demand in microeconomics, economists argue that demand should be seen as a schedule showing how the quantity demanded depends upon a number of factor, including price. In later chapters we will see that aggregate demand is also a schedule showing how the demand by everyone for newly produced goods and services is affected by a variety of factor, including the overall level of prices or, for short, the price level.

(2) Two other concepts that are closely related to aggregate demand are *national product* and *national income*. National product is simply the output of the economy. National income is the (before/after)-tax income of all the individuals in the economy. Disposable income is the income of individuals after _____ have been paid and any _____ payments from the

---

government have been counted. The circular flow diagram shows that national product and national income are two ways of measuring the same thing: Producing goods and selling them results in income for the owners and employees of firms.

Economists use the concept of a *consumption function* to organize the determinants of consumption expenditures. Specifically, the consumption function is the relation between aggregate real consumption expenditures and aggregate real disposable income, holding all other determinants of con-

(3) sumer spending constant. Higher disposable income leads to (<u>more/less</u>) consumption spending. A change in disposable income leads to a (<u>shift in/movement along</u>) the consumption function. A change in one of the other factors that affect consumer spending, such as wealth, the level of prices, the rate of inflation, or interest rates, leads to a _____ _____ the consumption function. (Two, more technical, aspects of the consumption function, the *marginal propensity to consume* and the *average propensity to consume*, are considered more fully in the Basic Exercise section of this chapter.)

An increase in the price level affects consumption spending and is an important reason why aggregate

(4) demand, _____ + _____ + _____ + _____ − _____ , is a schedule. If prices are higher we expect (<u>more/less</u>) consumption spending. Consumption spending changes because the value of many consumer assets is fixed in money terms, and an increase in the price level will (<u>increase/decrease</u>) the purchasing power of these assets. It is important to remember that higher prices will lead to lower real consumption expenditures even if real disposable income is constant. A doubling of *all* prices will also double wages—the price for an hour of labor services. If wages and prices both double, there is no change in the purchasing power of labor income, but there is a loss to consumers from the decline in the purchasing power of their money fixed assets. It is this latter decline that leads to a shift in the consumption function in response to a change in the price level.

Separately from the level of prices, the rate of inflation may also affect consumption spending. On the one hand, the notion that one should buy now, before prices increase still further, suggests that inflation stimulates consumption spending. On the other hand, the notion that one may have to save more in order to meet higher prices tomorrow, suggests that inflation depresses consumption spending. For rates of inflation experienced in the United States there is no clear evidence as to which tendency is greater. Economists have also found it difficult to detect a large impact on consumption spending from changes in interest rates. While a higher real interest rate provides an increased incentive to consume less and save more, it also means that one can reach a given dollar target with less savings.

A change in income taxes immediately changes disposable income. The consumption function, then, tells us how a change in disposable income will affect consumption spending. For example, a

(5) reduction in income taxes would (<u>increase/decrease</u>) disposable income. After computing the change in disposable income, one could estimate the initial impact on consumption spending by multiplying the change in disposable income by the (<u>marginal/average</u>) propensity to consume. A permanent increase in taxes would be expected to have a (<u>larger/smaller</u>) effect on consumption expenditures than a temporary tax increase of the same magnitude because the permanent increase changes consumers' long-run income prospects by (<u>more/less</u>) than the temporary increase. The same argument works in reverse and implies that temporary tax changes have a (<u>larger/smaller</u>) impact on consumption expenditures than do permanent tax changes.

## IMPORTANT TERMS AND CONCEPTS QUIZ

Choose the best definition for the following terms.

1. _____ Aggregate demand
2. _____ Consumer expenditure (*C*)
3. _____ Investment spending (*I*)
4. _____ Government purchases (*G*)
5. _____ Net exports (*X–IM*)
6. _____ National income
7. _____ Disposable income (*DI*)
8. _____ Transfer payments
9. _____ Consumption function
10. _____ Marginal propensity to consume
11. _____ Movement along the consumption function
12. _____ Shift of the consumption function
13. _____ Money fixed asset

a. Relation between aggregate real consumption expenditures and aggregate real disposable income.

b. Income of individuals after taxes and transfer payments.

c. Purchases of newly produced goods and services by all levels of government.

d. Total amount spent by consumers on newly produced goods and services.

e. Change in consumption due to a change in disposable income.

f. Gross national product divided by price level.

g. Total amount consumers, firms, government agencies and foreigners are willing to spend on final goods.

h. Total spending by firms on new plants and equipment and by consumers on new homes.

i. Change in consumption divided by change in disposable income.

j. Item whose value is fixed in terms of dollars.

k. Exports minus imports.

l. Total earnings of all individuals in economy.

m. Change in consumption due to a change in any factor affecting consumption other than disposable income.

n. Government grants to individuals.

## BASIC EXERCISES

Note that the first three problems are based on income and consumption data for individual families rather than aggregate income and consumption. Along with the fourth problem, they will give you practice using and understanding the MPC.

1. Table 24-1 reports some data on disposable income and consumption.
    a. For each change in income compute the marginal propensity to consume.
    b. The average propensity to consume is defined as the ratio of consumption expenditures to disposable income or APC = *C* + *DI*. For the income of $10,000 the average propensity to consume is .90 = $9,000 + $10,000. Use the data on income and consumption to fill in the column for the APC.
    c. Are the average and marginal propensities equal? Do the differences surprise you? Can you explain them? Perhaps steps d to f will help.
    d. Use the graph of Figure 24-1 to draw the consumption function consistent with the data in Table 24-1. (Locate each income–consumption data pair and then draw a line connecting the points.)
    e. The MPC is represented by what part of your graph?
    f. The APC can be represented by the slope of a ray from the origin to a point on the consumption function. Remember the slope of any straight line, including a ray, is the vertical change over the horizontal change. When measured from the origin, the vertical change of a ray to a point on the consumption function is *C* and the horizontal change is *DI*. Thus the slope of the ray, (*C* + *DI*), is the APC. Draw rays to represent the APC for incomes of $10,000 and $50,000. How does the slope of your rays change as income increases? Is this change consistent with changes in the APC you calculated in step c?

## FIGURE 24-1

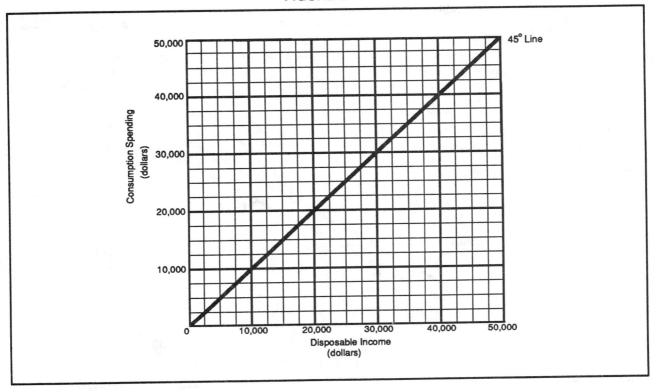

## TABLE 24-1

| Average Propensity to Consume | Disposable Income | Change in Disposable Income to | Marginal Propensity Consume | Change in Consumption Expenditures | Consumption Expenditures |
|---|---|---|---|---|---|
| _____ | $10,000 | | | | $9,000 |
| | | $10,000 | _____ | $7,500 | |
| _____ | $20,000 | | | | $16,500 |
| | | $10,000 | _____ | $7,500 | |
| _____ | $30,000 | | | | $24,000 |
| | | $10,000 | _____ | $7,500 | |
| _____ | $40,000 | | | | $31,500 |
| | | $10,000 | _____ | $7,500 | |
| _____ | $50,000 | | | | $39,000 |

**FIGURE 24-2
CONSUMPTION FUNCTIONS FOR 1992 AND 1993**

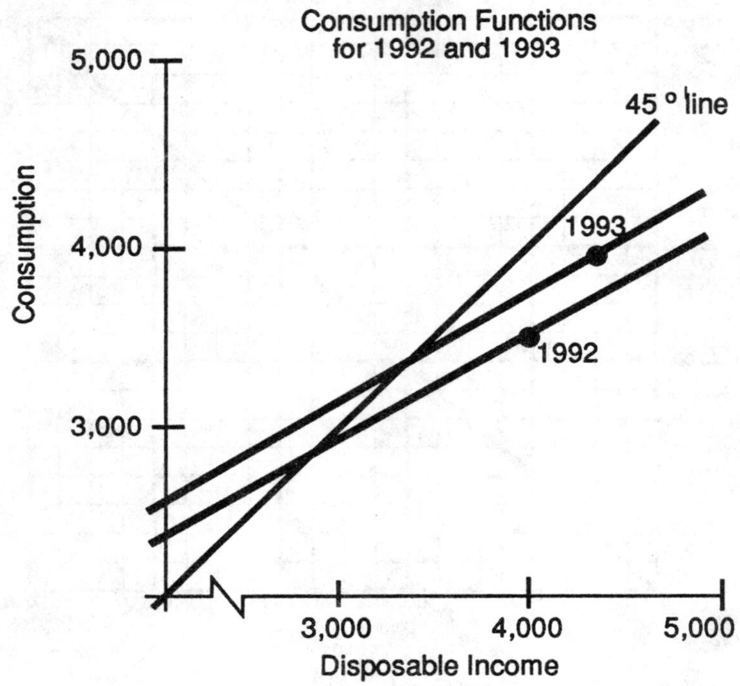

2. Imagine an economy made up of 100 families, each earning $10,000 and 100 families each earning $50,000. Each family consumes according to the consumption function described in Table 24-1.

   a. Fill in the following:

   Consumption of a family earning $10,000 _____

   Consumption of a family earning $50,000 _____

   Aggregate consumption of all 200 families _____

   b. What is the APC of the richer families? _____

   What is the APC of the poorer families? _____

   c. Randy argues that since the lower-income families are spending a greater proportion of their income than the higher-income families, a redistribution of income from high- to low-income families will increase total consumption expenditures. Test Randy's assertion by assuming that the government takes $5,000 from each high-income family and gives it to each low-income family, and that all families adjust their consumption in line with the consumption function described in Table 24-1. Then fill in the following:

   Consumption of a family with $15,000 income _____

   Consumption of a family with $45,000 income _____

   Aggregate consumption of all 200 families _____

   d. Explain why in this example aggregate consumption is unaffected by the redistribution of income.

3. (Optional) Use the data in Table 24-1 to compute an algebraic expression for the consumption function.

Consumption = _____ + 0._____ × (disposable income)

4. The lower line in Figure 24-2 shows the location of the consumption function of Baulmovia in 1992. In 1992 Baulmovian disposable income was $4.0 trillion and consumption spending was $3.6 trillion. In 1993 there was a significant surge in consumer confidence that shifted the consumption function to the higher line in Figure 24-2 in 1993 Baulmovian disposable income was $4.4 trillion and consumption spending was $3.96 trillion.

Consider an estimate of MPC by looking at the change in consumption spending and the change in disposable income from 1992 to 1993.

a. What is this estimate of MPC? _____
b. How does this estimate of MPC compare to the slope of either consumption function? Explain any differences.

## SELF-TESTS FOR UNDERSTANDING

### Test A

Circle the most appropriate answer.

1. Which of the following is not a part of aggregate demand?
   a. Consumption expenditures.
   b. National income.
   c. Net exports.
   d. Investment expenditures.

2. When thinking about aggregate demand, economists use the term investment to refer to all except which one of the following?
   a. The newly built house that Roberta just bought.
   b. The stock in General Electric that Ralph bought with his summer earnings.
   c. The new factory that is being built on the edge of town.
   d. The new machinery that Sherry bought to start her own company.

3. Which of the following would be an example of a government transfer payment?
   a. Wages paid to government bureaucrats.
   b. A tax refund for excess withholding.
   c. The purchase of paperclips by a government agency.
   d. Social security payments.

4. In a circular flow diagram all but which one of the following would be depicted as an injection into the stream of spending?
   a. The Defense Department's purchase of a new airplane.
   b. Joyce and Jim's purchase of an existing house.
   c. Alice's spending to rebuild her restaurant after the fire.
   d. The set of new micro-computers that Elaine's company bought for all its top management.

5. National income refers to
   a. the income of consumers before taxes.
   b. the sum of everyone's before-tax income.
   c. employee wage and salary payments.
   d. the income of federal government employees only.

6. Disposable income is equal to the income of individuals after
   a. subtracting taxes.
   b. adding transfer payments.
   c. adding taxes to transfer payments.
   d. subtracting taxes and adding transfer payments.

7. A graphical representation of how consumption spending varies with changes in disposable income is called the
   a. aggregate demand curve.
   b. income-expenditure schedule.
   c. consumption function.
   d. Phillips curve.

8. A change in which one of the following would be associated with a movement along the consumption function?
   a. Current disposable income.
   b. Wealth.
   c. The price level.
   d. Expected future incomes.

9. A change in all but which one of the following would be associated with a shift in the consumption function?
   a. Wealth.
   b. Interest rates.
   c. Current disposable income.
   d. The price level.

10. A consumption function is an example of a
    a. time series graph.
    b. two-variable diagram.
    c. contour diagram.

11. If an increase in prices is matched by an increase in wages and salaries such that there is no change in real disposable income, then
    a. there should be no effect on consumption spending.
    b. the increase in prices will lead to a movement along the consumption function.
    c. one should expect MPC to decline.
    d. the impact of the change in prices on the purchasing power of money fixed assets should lead to a shift in the consumption function.

12. The impact of a change in real disposable income on consumption spending can be represented as a
    a. movement along a given consumption function.
    b. a shift in the consumption function.
    c. a shift in MPC.
    d. a change in the price level.

13. MPC refers to
    a. Y-axis is intercept of the consumption function.
    b. the slope of the consumption function.
    c. the ratio of consumption spending to income.
    d. the slope of a ray from the origin to a point on the consumption function.

14. If MPC is 0.7, then a $100 billion change in disposable income will be associated with what change in consumption spending?
    a. $20 billion.
    b. $30 billion.
    c. $70 billion.
    d. $100 billion.

15. If a $100 billion increase in disposable income results in a $75 billion increase in consumption spending, then MPC is
    a. 0.25
    b. 0.50
    c. 0.75
    d. 1.0

16. If MPC is 0.80, what decrease in taxes will initially increase consumption spending by $16 billion?
    a. $12.8 billion.
    b. $16 billion.
    c. $20 billion.
    d. $64 billion.

17. If consumption spending declines by $45 billion when disposable income declines by $50 billion, what is MPC?
    a. 0.9
    b. 0.1
    c. –0.1
    d. –0.9

18. If MPC is .8, a $100 billion change in the wealth of consumers will lead to
    a. a $100 billion change in consumption spending.
    b. an $80 billion change in consumption spending.
    c. a movement along the consumption function.
    d. a shift in the entire consumption function.

19. An increase in interest rates
    a. always leads to a decrease in consumption spending as it provides an increased incentive for greater saving.
    b. can be modeled as a movement along the consumption function.
    c. always leads to an increase in consumption spending as the higher interest rate allows savers to reach fixed objectives with smaller savings.
    d. does not appear to have influenced consumption spending very much one way or the other.

20. Which type of tax change would be expected to have the largest impact on consumption spending?
    a. The tax rebate of 1975.
    b. The tax surcharge of 1969.
    c. The permanent reduction in tax rates of 1964.
    d. The reduction in tax withholding announced by President Bush in 1992.

## Test B

Circle T or F for true or false.

T F 1. Aggregate demand is the aggregate of individual household consumption decisions.

T F 2. The consumption function reflects the close relationship between consumption spending and national output.

T F 3. The U.S. government has often used changes in income tax rates as a way of influencing consumer spending.

T F 4. A change in consumption divided by the change in disposable income that produced the change in consumption is called the marginal propensity to consume.

T F 5. An increase in the level of prices is likely to reduce consumption expenditures.

T F 6. The effect of a change in the level of prices on consumption would be viewed graphically as a shift in the consumption function.

T F 7. By increasing household wealth, a big increase in the stock market is likely to lead to a movement along the consumption function.

T  F    8.   The magnitude of the impact of a change in taxes on consumption expenditures is likely to depend on whether consumers view the change in taxes as permanent or temporary.

T  F    9.   A temporary decrease in taxes is likely to have a smaller impact on consumption than will a permanent decrease.

T  F  10.   The initial impact of a change in income taxes on consumption spending can be calculated by multiplying the change in disposable income by MPC.

# Appendix A: The Saving Function and the Marginal Propensity to Save

## LEARNING OBJECTIVES

Working through the exercise below should help you understand the basic message of Appendix A to Chapter 24: *We could just as easily have used the saving function instead of the consumption function.* When you have completed the exercise you should be able to

- compute savings, given data on disposable income and consumption.
- compute the marginal propensity to save.
- show that the MPC and the MPS sum to 1.0.

## IMPORTANT TERMS AND CONCEPTS

Aggregate saving
Saving function
Marginal propensity to save (MPS)

## IMPORTANT TERMS AND CONCEPTS QUIZ

Choose the best definition for the following terms.

1. _____ Aggregate saving
2. _____ Saving function
3. _____ Marginal propensity to save

a. Change in consumer savings divided by change in disposable income.

b. Consumer savings divided by disposable income.
c. Schedule relating consumer saving to disposable income.
d. Disposable income minus consumption.

## BASIC EXERCICES

1. Table 24-2 reproduces the income and consumption data from Table 24-1. Use the data in Table 24-2 to compute the amount of saving at each level of income. Remember that saving is just the difference between disposable income and consumption, that is $S = DI - C$.

2. For each change in income, compute MPS. (You will first need to compute the change in savings.)

## TABLE 24-2

| Average Propensity to save | Savings | Consumption Expenditures | Disposable Income | Change in Disposable Income | Change in Savings | Marginal Propensity to Save |
|---|---|---|---|---|---|---|
| _____ | _____ | $9,000 | $10,000 | | | |
| | | | | $10,000 | _____ | _____ |
| _____ | _____ | $16,500 | $20,000 | | | |
| | | | | $10,000 | _____ | _____ |
| _____ | _____ | $24,000 | $30,000 | | | |
| | | | | $10,000 | _____ | _____ |
| _____ | _____ | $31,500 | $40,000 | | | |
| | | | | $10,000 | _____ | _____ |
| _____ | _____ | $39,000 | $50,000 | | | |

3. Using results from Tables 24-1 and 24-2, show that the sum of MPC and MPC for each change in income is 1.0.

4. Use the data on income and saving to compute the average propensity to save.

5. Again, using results from Tables 24-1 and 24-2, show that the sum of the APC and the APS at each level of income is 1.0.

6. It is because APC plus APS always equals 1.0 and MPC plus MPS always equals 1.0 that we can use the saving or consumption factor interchangeably.

Some simple algebra also gives the same result. Start with the identity:

$$DI = C + S.$$

Now divide both sides of the equation by $DI$ and interpret your results in terms of APC and APS.

We also know that since any change in income must be spent or saved

$$\Delta DI = \Delta C + \Delta S.$$

where $\Delta$ means change. Now divide both sides of the equation by $\Delta DI$ and interpret your results in terms of MPC and MPS.

# Appendix B:
# National Income Accounting

## LEARNING OBJECTIVES

After completing this appendix you should be able to:

♦ describe the three alternative ways of measuring GDP and explain why, except for bookkeeping or statistical errors, they give the same answer.

♦ explain why national income accounting treats government purchases of goods and services differently from government transfer payments.

♦ explain the difference in theory and practice between the following macro measurements: GDP, NDP, national income, personal income, and disposable income.

## IMPORTANT TERMS AND CONCEPTS

National income accounting
Gross National Product (GNP)
Gross Domestic Product (GDP)
Gross private domestic investment
Investment
Government purchases
Transfer payments
Net exports

National Income
Net Domestic Product (NDP)
Net National Product (NNP)
Depreciation
Value added
Personal income
Disposable Income (*DI*)

## APPENDIX REVIEW

Although included in an appendix, this material on national income accounting deserves special treatment. When working through this material, do not lose sight of the forest for the trees. The forest is composed of broad income concepts, such as gross domestic product (GDP), net domestic product (NDP), and national income, what each of these concepts measures and how they relate to one another. This appendix is an introduction to the forest rather than to each individual tree.

The *national income accounts* measure economic activity: the production of goods and services and the incomes that are simultaneously generated. Accurate measurement of production and income is an important prerequisite to attempts to understand and control the economy. National income accounts are centered around measurement of the gross domestic product. Consumption (*C*), investment (*I*), government purchases of goods and services (*G*), and net exports (*X − IM*) are parts of GDP. Other concepts, such as *net domestic product* (NDP) and *national income*, are alternative measures of total economic activity.

(1)     GDP is defined as the sum of the money values of all _____ goods and services that are (produced/sold) during a specified period of time. Economists use money values or market prices to add up the very different types of output that make up GDP. Two of the three exceptions mentioned in Appendix B—government output and inventories—arise because some production is not sold on markets.

The emphasis on *final* goods and services is important, because it avoids double counting of intermediate goods. (The need to avoid double counting is also the key to why the three alternative ways of measuring GDP are conceptually equivalent.) The third part of the definition says that GDP is a statement of production, not sales. It is only production that creates new goods available for consumption or investment. Thus GDP, as a measure of production, is the appropriate measure of how much new consumption or investment our economy can enjoy.

There are three ways to measure GDP. Perhaps the simplest way to measure GDP is to add up the purchases of newly produced final goods and services by private individuals and firms-for consumption and investment—and by the government. For the United States in 1992, this sum of *C + I + G + X − IM* was estimated to be about $5.7 trillion.

(2)     Net exports are (imports/exports) minus _____. We must add exports to *C + I + G* because, even though bought by foreigners, exports are American products and GDP is a measure of total U.S. production. We subtract imports because *C* and *I* and *G* are measures of total spending, including spending on imports, and we want a measure that reflects only those goods and services (purchased/produced) in the United States.

All of a firm's sales receipts eventually end up as income for someone, directly in the case of workers, creditors, and firm owners, and indirectly in the case of payments to suppliers, who in turn use this money to pay their workers, creditors, and so forth. Thus, instead of measuring GDP as purchases of final goods and services, we could equivalently add up all incomes earned in the production of goods and services.

(3) This sum of factor incomes is also called national _____ and is the second way to measure GDP. It is conceptually similar to GDP but differs for U.S. national income accounts because

of three items. Indirect business taxes are included in market prices paid by consumers but (do/do not) result in income for any factor of production as they are immediately collected by the government. National income plus indirect business taxes is equal to NDP or _____ _____ product, which is almost, but not quite, equal to GDP. Adjusting for income that Americans receive for working abroad and for income that foreigners receive while working in the United States gives us net domestic income. The difference between NDP and GDP is _____ and, conceptually, refers to the portion of current total production that is used to replace those parts of the capital stock that have deteriorated as a result of current production. If GDP were all one edible good, we could eat NDP while maintaining our productive capacity. Eating GDP would reduce our productive capacity as we would not be replacing worn-out plants and machines.

To measure GDP as the money value of final goods and services, one would start by collecting sales data for final goods. The second way of measuring GDP, total factor incomes, would start with the collection of income data from firms and individuals. The third way of measuring GDP looks at the difference between a firm's sales receipts and its purchases from other firms. This difference, also called

(4) a firm's _____ _____, is the amount of money a firm has to pay the factors of production that it has employed, including the profits firm owners pay themselves. Thus, the sum of total value added in the economy is the third way to measure GDP.

Two other income concepts should be noted. The first, personal income, is just that, income received by persons. As such, starting from national income, we subtract income that is kept by corporations and payroll taxes, that are never received by persons, e.g. social security. We must add transfer payments, as these payments, while not remuneration for work are clearly income for the persons receiving them.

(5) Our last income concept, disposable personal income, is equal to personal income after _____.

In this discussion of national income accounting, the important lesson is the close link between income and production or output, the upper and lower halves of the circular flow diagram.

## IMPORTANT TERMS AND CONCEPTS QUIZ

Choose the best definition for the following terms.

1. _____ National income accounting
2. _____ Net domestic product
3. _____ Depreciation
4. _____ Value added

a. Bookkeeping and measurement system for national economic data.

b. Value of an economy's capital used up during a year.

c. Revenue from sale of product minus amount paid for goods and services purchased from other firms.

d. Loss on value of business assets from inflation.

e. GDP minus depreciation.

## BASIC EXERCISES

These problems are designed to give you practice in understanding alternative ways of measuring GDP.

1. Consider the following two-firm economy. Firm A is a mining company that does not make purchases from firm B. Firm A sells all its output to firm B, which in turn sells all its output to consumers.

|  | Firm A | Firm B |
|---|---|---|
| Total sales | $500 | $1,700 |
| Wages | 400 | 800 |
| Profits | 100 | 400 |
| Purchases from other firms | 0 | 500 |

a. What are the total sales for the economy? $_____

b. What is the total value of sales for final uses? $_____

c. What is the total of all factor incomes? $_____

d. What is value added for firm A? $_____

e. What is value added for firm B? $_____

f. What is the total value added of both firms? $_____

g. What is GDP? $_____

h. What is national income? $_____

2. Table 24-3 contains information on a three-firm economy. Firm A sells only to other firms. Firm B has both an industrial and a household division. Firm C sells only to final consumers. Note also that production by firm C was greater than sales, thus the entry showing the addition to inventories. Simple addition shows that the sum of factor incomes, in this case wages and profits, is equal to $4,700. Answer the following questions to see if the two other ways of measuring GDP give the same answer. The tricky part of this question is the treatment of production that has not been sold, but added to inventories. You may want to review the discussion of inventories in Appendix B before answering the following questions.

a. Calculate value added for each firm and the sum of value added for all firms.

Value Added, firm A _____

Value Added, firm B _____

Value Added, firm C _____

Sum _____

**TABLE 24-3**

|  | Firm A | Firm B | Firm C |
| --- | --- | --- | --- |
| TOTAL SALES | $1,000 | $2,500 | $3,000 |
| Sales to firm B | $400 |  |  |
| Sales to firm C | $600 | $1,000 |  |
| Sales to consumers |  | $1,500 | $3,000 |
| Change in inventories |  |  | $200 |
| Wages | $750 | $1,800 | $1,200 |
| Profits | $250 | $300 | $400 |

b. GDP is defined as the production of newly produced final goods and services. It is typically calculated by summing sales of newly produced final goods and services. Calculate sales for final use for each firm and the sum for all firms.

Sales for final use, firm A     _____

Sales for final use, firm B     _____

Sales for final use, firm C     _____

Sum     _____

## SELF-TESTS FOR UNDERSTANDING

### Test A

Circle the most appropriate answers.

1. GDP is
   a. the sum of all sales in the economy.
   b. the sum of all purchases in the economy.
   c. the sum of money value of all newly produced final goods and services produced during a year.
   d. equal to $C + I + G + X + IM$.
2. Conceptually, GDP can be measured by all but which one of the following:
   a. Add up all factor payments by firms in the economy.
   b. Add up all purchases of final goods and services, $C + I + G + (X - IM)$.
   c. Add up total sales of all firms in the economy.
   d. Add up value added for all firms in the economy.
3. When measuring GDP, money values are for the most part determined by
   a. the cost of production.
   b. market prices.
   c. estimates prepared by national income accountants who work for the U.S. Commerce Department.
   d. banks and eastern money interests.
4. Which of the following is not valued at market prices when computing GDP?
   a. Imports.
   b. Investment.
   c. Government output.
   d. Exports.
5. Which of the following would add to this year's GDP?
   a. Jim purchases a new copy of the Baumol Blinder textbook for this course.
   b. Jill purchases a used copy of the Baumol Blinder textbook for this course.
   c. Susan purchases 100 shares of GM stock.
   d. Steve sells his three year old car.
6. Which of the following transactions represents the sale of a final good as opposed to sale of an intermediate good?
   a. Farmer Jones sells her peaches to the Good Food Packing and Canning Company.
   b. Good Food sells a load of canned peaches to Smith Brothers Distributors.
   c. Smith Brothers sells the load of canned peaches to Irving's Supermarket.
   d. You buy a can of peaches at Irving's.

7. Which of the following events results in an addition to gross private domestic investment?
   a. Managers of the Good Earth, a newly formed food co-op, buy a used refrigerator case for their store.
   b. Sony's office in Tokyo buys a new IBM computer.
   c. The U.S. Air Force purchases a new plane for the president.
   d. United Airlines purchases 20 new planes so it can expand its service.

8. Gross private domestic investment includes all but which one of the following?
   a. The new home purchased by Kimberly and Jason.
   b. The new Japanese computer purchased by Acme Manufacturing to automate their production line.
   c. The increase in the inventory of newly produced but unsold cars.
   d. The construction of a new plant to manufacture micro computers for IBM.

9. When measuring GDP, government purchases include all but which one of the following:
   a. Salaries paid to members of Congress.
   b. Newly produced red tape purchased by government agencies.
   c. Social security payments to older Americans.
   d. Concrete for new highway construction.

10. If net exports are negative it means that
    a. the national income accountant made a mistake.
    b. exports are greater than imports.
    c. Americans are consuming too many foreign goods.
    d. imports are greater than exports.

11. Which accounts for the largest proportion of national income?
    a. Profits.
    b. Employee compensation.
    c. Rents.
    d. Interest.

12. In the national income accounts, transfer payments are
    a. counted twice, once as part of government purchases and again when spent by consumers.
    b. counted as part of government purchases.
    c. included in personal and disposable income.
    d. not included anywhere.

13. The difference between personal income and disposable personal income is given by
    a. depreciation.
    b. personal income taxes.
    c. social security taxes.
    d. government transfer payments.

14. Which of the following is not part of the difference between GDP and national income?
    a. Depreciation.
    b. Indirect business taxes.
    c. Transfer payments from the government.
    d. Income earned by Americans working abroad.

15. Depreciation explains the difference between
    a. GDP and NDP.
    b. NDP and National Income.
    c. National Income and Personal Income.

16. Value added by a single firm is measured as total sales revenue
    a. minus factor payments.
    b. plus indirect business taxes.
    c. plus depreciation.
    d. minus the purchase of intermediate goods.

17. An increase in government transfer payments to individuals will lead to an initial increase in which one of the following?
    a. GDP.
    b. NDP.
    c. Government purchases of goods and services.
    d. Disposable income.

18. In measuring GDP, government outputs are
    a. appropriately valued at zero.
    b. valued by estimates of their market prices.
    c. valued at the cost of inputs needed to produce them.

19. If net domestic product equals $5 trillion and indirect business taxes are $300 billion, then national income would equal
    a. $5.3 trillion.
    b. $5 trillion.
    c. $4.7 trillion.
    d. Insufficient information to determine national income.

20. NDP is
    a. always greater than GDP.
    b. considered by many economists to be a more meaningful measure of the nation's economic output than is GDP.
    c. conceptually superior to GDP because it excludes the output of environmental "bads."
    d. measured by subtracting indirect business taxes from GDP.

## Test B

Circle T or F for true or false.

T F 1. GDP is designed to be a measure of economic well-being, not a measure of economic production.

T F 2. If you measured GDP by adding up total sales in the economy, you would be double or triple counting many intermediate goods.

T F 3. Production that is not sold but is instead added to inventories is not counted in GDP.

T F 4. If GM started its own steel company rather than continuing to buy steel from independent steel companies, GDP would be lower because intrafirm transfers are not part of GDP but all interfirm sales are.

T F 5. Since the output of government agencies is not sold on markets, it is not included in GDP.

T F 6. Value added is the difference between what a firm sells its output for and the cost of its own purchases from other firms.

T F 7. The difference between GDP and NDP is net exports.

T F 8. Disposable income is usually greater than net NDP.

T F 9. Corporate profits are the largest component of national income.

T F 10. The sum of value added for all firms in the economy is equal to the sum of all factor incomes—wages, interest, rents, and profits.

## SUPPLEMENTARY EXERCISE

1. Consider the following nonlinear, consumption function.

$$C = 100 \sqrt{DI}.$$

Restricting yourself to positive values for disposable income, graph this function. What happens to MPC as income increases? Can you find an explicit expression for MPC as a function of income? (A knowledge of simple calculus will be helpful.) Use this new consumption function to re-answer Basic Exercise question 2 about income redistribution. Does your answer change? If so, why?

What is the savings function that goes with this consumption function? Does MPC + MPS = 1? Does APC + APS = 1?

## STUDY QUESTIONS

1. What are the four major components of GDP? (Why are imports subtracted when everything else is added?)
2. What is the difference between national income and disposable income?
3. How is MPC different from the proportion of disposable income that is spent on consumption?
4. MPC can be represented by what part of the consumption function?
5. Why would a change in the price level or in expected future incomes lead to shift in the consumption function rather than a movement along the function?
6. If planning a reduction in income taxes to increase consumption spending by $200 billion, what difference would it make if MPC were 0.75 or 0.90? Would you expect any differences if the reduction in taxes were to be permanent or temporary? Why?
7. Why is knowledge of the consumption function sufficient for one to be able to describe the savings function for an economy?
8. What are the different ways one can measure GDP?
9. Economists often use national income or GDP interchangeably as a measure of the level of aggregate economic activity. What is the difference between national income and GDP?

## ECONOMICS IN ACTION

### Do Tax Incentives Increase Savings?

During the 1980s a number of specialized programs to increase household savings were introduced. One of the most controversial was the Individual Retirement Account or IRA. Under rules adopted in 1981, all employees could make a tax-deductible $2,000 contribution to an IRA. Previously, IRAs had been limited to individuals without an employer-provided pension plan. Not only did the contribution reduce one's immediate taxable income by $2,000 but interest earnings on IRAs were tax free until the time of withdrawal.[1] In exchange for these advantages, withdrawals before the age of 59-1/2 were subject to substantial tax penalties. Since regular savings can only be done with after-tax, not pre-tax, dollars and the interest earnings of regular savings are taxed on a year by year basis, IRAs offered taxpayers significant advantages and were heavily promoted by banks and other financial institutions. It was hoped that IRAs would lead to a significant increase in household savings.

---

[1]Each wage earner could contribute up to $2,000. There was also a provision for a $250 contribution for a non-working spouse. Taxes on the $2,000 contribution and accumulated interest earnings would be due at the time of withdrawal.

---

Why were IRA accounts controversial? There were several reasons. For one, the advantages of an IRA depended upon one's marginal tax rate. An IRA postponed rather than reduced taxes, but being able to use that money until taxes were due could offer a significant benefit, especially to wealthy taxpayers with high marginal tax rates. For example, a $2,000 IRA contribution in 1982 by the wealthiest taxpayers reduced 1982 income taxes by $1,000, while the same contribution by a low-income family would have reduced 1982 taxes by only $220. A second area of controversy was whether IRAs would actually increase savings or only lead households to change the way they saved. That is, were people being given tax breaks for doing what they would have done anyway or would people save more? A related concern was that the money for opening an IRA could come from an existing, taxable savings account. If so, there might be only a shuffling of financial assets for tax advantages rather than any increase in savings. These concerns plus the continuing decline in personal savings as a proportion of disposable income led Congress to restructure and limit the tax advantages of IRAs in 1986.

What does the evidence show about the effectiveness of IRAs? Work by economists Harvey Galper and Charles Byce showed that wealthier taxpayers were more likely to make an IRA contribution and were more likely to make the largest possible contribution. At the same time, a substantial proportion of moderate-income taxpayers making IRA contributions were making the maximum possible contribution. In a series of papers, economists Steven Venti and David Wise used detailed microeconomic data to examine the savings behavior of individual households. They found a great deal of variability. Some households are thrifty while others appear to be spendthrifts. With regard to IRAs, Venti and Wise found that by 1985 two-thirds of IRAs were held by families with incomes less than $50,000. Venti and Wise also considered whether IRAs increased savings. They found little evidence of asset or saving switching and concluded that the introduction of IRAs resulted in a net increase in saving. Venti and Wise argue that the restrictions on IRAs, and the special feelings many people have about retirement savings made them poor substitutes for other forms of savings.

1. Should the United States use expanded tax incentives to induce households to increase their own savings? If so, how would should such a program be structured? How does your program provide incentives for new savings and not just an advantage for asset adjustments in pursuit of tax advantages?

---

SOURCES: Galper, Harvey, and Charles Byce, "IRAs: Facts and Figures," *Tax Notes*, June 2, 1986.
Venti, Steven F., and David A. Wise, "Government Policy and Personal Retirement Saving," in *Tax Policy and the Economy*, 6, (National Bureau of Economic Research, MIT Press, 1992) pp. 1-41.

*C h a p t e r* **25**

# Demand-Side Equilibrium: Unemployment or Inflation?

## LEARNING OBJECTIVES

After completing this chapter you should be able to:

- describe some of the major determinants of investment spending by firms and explain which of these determinants can be directly affected by government action.
- describe how income and prices, both American and foreign, affect exports and imports.
- draw an expenditure schedule, given information about consumption spending, investment spending, and net exports.
- determine the equilibrium level of income and explain why the level of income tends toward its equilibrium value.
- describe how a change in the price level affects the expenditure schedule and the equilibrium level of income.
- describe how the impact of a change in prices on the expenditure schedule and the equilibrium level of income can be used to derive the aggregate demand curve.
- explain why equilibrium GDP can be above or below the full employment level of GDP.

## IMPORTANT TERMS AND CONCEPTS

Investment tax credit
Equilibrium level of GDP
Expenditure schedule
Induced investment
$Y = C + I + G + (X - IM)$
Income–expenditure (or 45–degree line) diagram
Aggregate demand curve
Full-employment level of GDP (or potential GDP)
Recessionary gap
Inflationary gap
Coordination of saving and investment

# CHAPTER REVIEW

This chapter is the introduction to explicit models of income determination. The model discussed in this chapter is relatively simple and is not meant to be taken literally. Do not be put off by the simplicity of the model or its lack of realism. Careful study now will pay future dividends in terms of easier understanding of later chapters, in which both the mechanics and policy implications of more complicated models are described,

The central focus of this chapter is on the concept of the *equilibrium level of income and output*. (You may want to review the material in Chapter 24 on the equality of national income and national output.) The models discussed in this chapter show us how spending decisions are reconciled with production decisions of firms to determine the equilibrium level of GDP.

When considering the determination of the equilibrium level of GDP, it is important to distinguish between output and income on the one hand and total spending on the other hand. If total spending exceeds current production, firms will find that their inventories are decreasing. They are then likely to

(1) take steps to (<u>decrease/increase</u>) production and output. Analogously, if total spending is less than current output, firms are likely to find their inventories _____, and they are likely to take steps to _____ production.

The concept of equilibrium refers to a situation in which producers and consumers are satisfied with things the way they are and see no reason to change their behavior. Thus the equilibrium level of GDP must be a level of GDP at which firms have no reason to increase or decrease output; that is, at the equilibrium level of GDP, total spending and output will be equal. The determination of the equilibrium level of output thus reduces to

1. describing how total spending changes as output (and income) changes, and
2. finding the one level of output (and income) at which total spending equals output.

In the simplified model discussed in this chapter, there are three components to total spending: consumption, investment, and net exports. Chapter 24 discussed the important role that income plays as a determinant of consumption expenditures. There is no such central factor influencing investment expenditures. Instead, investment expenditures are influenced by a variety of factors, including business people's expectations about the future, the rate of growth of demand as measured against existing capacity, technology and product innovation, interest rates, and tax factors. If any of these factors change, investment spending is likely to change.

(2) Net exports are the difference between exports and imports, specifically _____ minus _____. Exports reflect foreign demand for American production and imports come from American demand for foreign goods and services. It should not be surprising that both are influenced by income and prices. The tricky part is keeping straight whose income influences which demand and how changes in American and foreign prices influence net exports.

The income-expenditure diagram is a useful tool for analyzing the determination of the equilibrium level of output. To find the equilibrium level of output and income we need to know how total spending changes as income and output change, and we need to know where total spending equals income. The relationship between total spending, $C + I + G + (X - IM)$, and income is given by the *expenditure schedule*. The 45-degree line shows all com-binations of spending and income that are equal. The one place where

(3) spending is equal to income is given by the _____ of the expenditure schedule and the 45–degree line. This is the equilibrium level of output because it is the only level of output where total spending is equal to output. At any other level of output, total spending will not be equal to output. (You should be sure that you understand why the economy tends to move to the equilibrium level of output rather than getting stuck at a level of income and output at which total spending is either larger or smaller than output. Consider what happens to business inventories when spending is greater

or less than output. Do not get confused between this automatic tendency to move to the equilibrium level of output and the lack, sometimes, of an automatic mechanism to ensure full employment.)

Any particular expenditure schedule relates total spending to income for a given level of prices. If prices change, total spending will change, even for the same level of real income. In particular, a higher price

(4) level is apt to mean (more/less) consumption spending because of the decline in the purchasing power of the money assets of consumers. This effect of prices on consumption will lead to a (downward/upward) shift in the expenditure schedule and a new equilibrium of income that is (higher/lower) than before. In the opposite case, a lower price level would mean _____ consumption spending and a new, (higher/lower) equilibrium level of income. The relationship between the price level and the equilibrium level of income on the income–expenditure diagram is called the *aggregate demand curve.* As our model of income determination becomes more realistic we will see that a change in the price level affects more than consumption spending. The simplified introductory model of this chapter is sufficient to illustrate the principle behind deriving the aggregate demand curve.

The aggregate demand curve is derived from the income–expenditure diagram and, from the viewpoint of demand, shows how the equilibrium level of income changes when the _____

(5) _____ changes. The qualifier "from the viewpoint of demand" is important. Complete determination of the equilibrium level of income/output and the equilibrium price level comes from the interaction of the aggregate demand and aggregate supply curves.

In Chapter 27 we will see how equilibrium depends upon aggregate demand and aggregate supply. At this point we are considering only the demand side of the economy. Nothing that has been said so far implies that, with regard to demand, the equilibrium level of output must equal the full-employment level of output. It may be larger or it may be smaller. It all depends upon the strength of aggregate demand. Appendix A shows how statements about the strength of aggregate demand relative to the full-employment level of output have an alternative and equivalent interpretation in terms of the amount of savings or leakages that would occur at full-employment relative to the strength of investment demand or injections at full-employment. If the equilibrium level of output exceeds the full-employment level of

(6) output, the difference is called the _____ gap. In a case where the equilibrium level of output is less than the full-employment level of output, the difference is called the _____ gap.

## IMPORTANT TERMS AND CONCEPTS QUIZ

Choose the best definition for the following terms.

1. _____ Investment tax credit
2. _____ Equilibrium level of GDP
3. _____ Expenditure schedule
4. _____ Induced investment
5. _____ Income-expenditure diagram
6. _____ Aggregate demand curve
7. _____ Recessionary gap
8. _____ Inflationary gap
9. _____ Potential GDP

a. Graph of quantity of national product demanded at each possible price level.
b. Line showing relationship between GDP and total spending.
c. Full-employment level of GDP.
d. Reduction in tax liability proportional to business investment spending.
e. Amount by which GDP exceeds full-employment GDP.
f. Level of output where aggregate demand equals total production.
g. Investment spending that changes with changes in GDP.
h. Table or graph showing how saving depends on consumption.
i. Amount by which full-employment GDP exceeds GDP.
j. Two variable graph that allows plotting of total real expenditures against real income.

## BASIC EXERCISES

These exercises are designed to give you practice with manipulations on the income–expenditure diagram. They are based on data for income (output), consumption spending, investment spending, and net exports given in Table 25-1.

1. This exercise shows you how the expenditure schedule is derived and how it helps to determine the equilibrium level of income. For this exercise it is assumed that prices are constant with the price level having a value of 100.
    a. Use the data on consumption spending and income to show how consumption spending varies with income in Figure 25-1.
    b. Add investment spending to the line drawn in Figure 25-1 to show how consumption plus investment spending vary with income.

### FIGURE 25-1

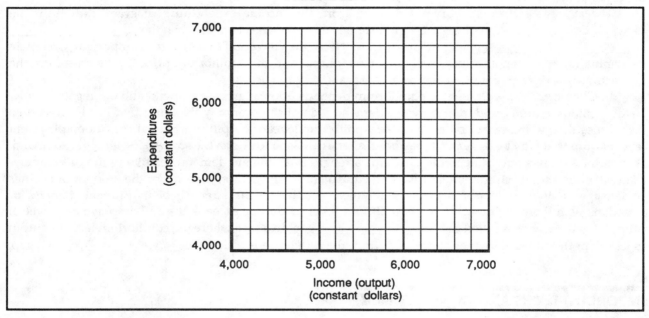

### TABLE 25-1
### (PRICE LEVEL = 100)

| Income (Output) Y | Taxes T | Disposable Income DI | Consumption Spending C | Investment Spending I | Government Purchases G | Exports X | Imports IM | Total Spending |
|---|---|---|---|---|---|---|---|---|
| 5,600 | 700 | 4,900 | 4,300 | 900 | 800 | 500 | 600 | _____ |
| 5,800 | 700 | 5,100 | 4,400 | 900 | 800 | 500 | 600 | _____ |
| 6,000 | 700 | 5,300 | 4,500 | 900 | 800 | 500 | 600 | _____ |
| 6,200 | 700 | 5,500 | 4,600 | 900 | 800 | 500 | 600 | _____ |
| 6,400 | 700 | 5,700 | 4,700 | 900 | 800 | 500 | 600 | _____ |
| 6,600 | 700 | 5,900 | 4,800 | 900 | 800 | 500 | 600 | _____ |

c. Now draw the expenditure schedule, $C + I + G + (X - IM)$ in Figure 25-1.
d. Next, draw a line representing all the points where total spending and income could be equal. (This is the 45–degree line. Do you know why?)
e. The 45–degree line represents all the points that *could be* the equilibrium level of income. Now circle the one point that *is* the equilibrium level of income. What is the equilibrium level of income on your graph?
f. Check your answer by filling in the Total Spending column in Table 25-1 to see where total spending equals income. You should get the same answer from Table 25-1 as you do from the graph.
g. Why isn't the equilibrium level of output $5,800 billion? If for some reason national output and income started out at $5,800 billion, what forces would tend to move the economy toward the equilibrium you determined in Questions e and f?
h. Using the data in Table 25-1 and assuming that the full-employment level of output income is $6,000 billion, is there an inflationary or recessionary gap? How large is the gap? If the full-employment level of income were $6,500 billion, how large would the inflationary or recessionary gap be?
i. Assume now that an increase in business confidence leads to an increased level of investment spending. Specifically, assume that investment spending rises to $1,000 billion at all levels of national income. As a result of this shift, what happens to each of the following?
   • The expenditure schedule.
   • The equilibrium level of income.
   • Consumption spending at the new equilibrium level of income.

2. This exercise explores the implications of changes in the price level. It is designed to show how a change in the price level implies a shift in the expenditure schedule and can be used to derive the aggregate demand curve.
   a. The data in Table 25-1 assumed that prices were constant with the price level at a value of 100. Mark the point in Figure 25-2 that shows the price level of 100 and the equilibrium level of income you found when answering questions e and f of Exercise 1.

## FIGURE 25-2

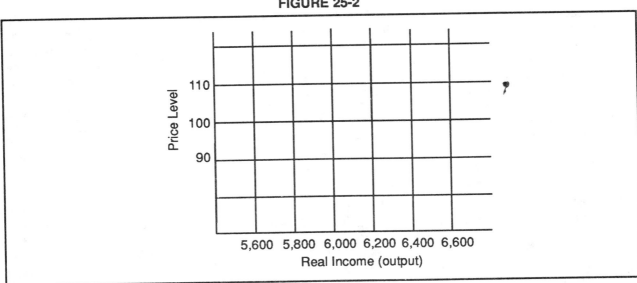

**TABLE 25-2**

| Real<br>Income<br>(Output) | Total<br>Spending<br>(Price Level = 90) | Total<br>Spending<br>(Price Level = 110) |
|---|---|---|
| 5,600 | 6,000 | 5,800 |
| 5,800 | 6,100 | 5,900 |
| 6,000 | 6,200 | 6,000 |
| 6,200 | 6,300 | 6,100 |
| 6,400 | 6,400 | 6,200 |
| 6,600 | 6,500 | 6,300 |

**TABLE 25-3**
**REAL INCOME AND TOTAL SPENDING**
**WHEN INVESTMENT SPENDING = $1,000**

| Real<br>Income<br>(Output) | Total<br>Spending<br>(Price Level = 90) | Total<br>Spending<br>(Price Level = 100) | Total<br>Spending<br>(Price Level = 110) |
|---|---|---|---|
| 5,600 | 6,100 | 6,000 | 5,900 |
| 5,800 | 6,200 | 6,100 | 6,000 |
| 6,000 | 6,300 | 6,200 | 6,100 |
| 6,200 | 6,400 | 6,300 | 6,200 |
| 6,400 | 6,500 | 6,400 | 6,300 |
| 6,600 | 6,600 | 6,500 | 6,400 |

b. Economic research has determined that if prices rose to 110, consumption spending would decline by $100 billion at every level of real income. Table 25-2 shows the relevant information. Each entry in the column for a price level of 110 should be 100 less than the values you calculated for total spending in question 1.f. What is the new equilibrium level of income on the income-expenditure diagram with this higher price level? Mark the point in Figure 25-2 that show the price level of 110 and this new equilibrium level of income.

c. This same research determined that if prices fell to 90, real consumption spending would increase over amounts shown in Table 25-1 by $100 billion at every level of real income. What is the new equilibrium level of income on the income–expenditure diagram for this lower price level? Mark the point in Figure 25-2 that shows the price level of 90 and his new equilibrium level of income.

d. The points you have marked in Figure 25-2 help to trace what curve?

e. Connect these points to verify that your curve has a (negative/positive) slope.

3. Question 1.i. asked you to consider the impact of an increase in investment spending. We saw then that an increase in investment spending shifts the expenditure schedule and leads to a new equilibrium on the income–expenditure diagram. What about the aggregate demand curve? Assume that the increase in business confidence means that investment spending rises to $1,000 regardless of the level of income or the price level. Table 25-3 contains information on total spending that includes the increase in investment spending. Use this information to plot the aggregate demand curve in Figure 25-2 following the increase in investment spending. How does this curve compare to the one you derived in question 2?

## SELF-TESTS FOR UNDERSTANDING

### Test A

Circle the most appropriate answer.

1. Government policies can directly affect all but which one of the following determinants of investment spending?
   a. Interest rates.
   b. The state of business confidence.
   c. Tax incentives.
   d. The overall state of aggregate demand.

2. The demand for imports into the United States is affected by all but which one of the following?
   a. American GDP
   b. American prices
   c. Foreign GDP
   d. Foreign prices

3. The demand for American exports is affected by all but which one of the following?
   a. American GDP
   b. American prices
   c. Foreign GDP
   d. Foreign prices

4. On balance, net exports are likely to _____ when domestic income increases.
   a. decrease
   b. remain unchanged
   c. increase

5. Of production, income and spending, _____ and _____ are always equal while _____ equals the other two only in equilibrium.
   a. spending and income; production
   b. production and spending; income
   c. income and production; spending

6. The expenditure schedule is a relationship between
   a. the equilibrium level of income and prices.
   b. consumption spending and income.
   c. total spending and income.
   d. consumption spending and prices.

7. The expenditure schedule is derived by showing how which of the following vary with income? (There may be more than one correct answer.)
   a. C - consumption
   b. DI - disposable income
   c. G - government purchases
   d. I - investment spending
   e. IM - imports
   f. T - taxes
   g. X - exports
   h. Y - GDP

8. If investment spending increased at all levels of income, the expenditure schedule would _____.
   a. shift down
   b. show no change
   c. shift up

9. An increase in the demand for exports will cause
   a. the expenditure schedule to shift up.
   b. no change in the expenditure schedule.
   c. the expenditure schedule to shift down.

10. A reduction in purchases of goods and services by the government will cause
    a. the expenditure schedule to shift up.
    b. no change in the expenditure schedule.
    c. the expenditure schedule to shift down.

11. In the income–expenditure diagram, the equilibrium level of output is given by the intersection of the expenditure schedule and the
    a. consumption function.
    b. aggregate demand curve.
    c. 45–degree line.
    d. level of full-employment output.

12. When total spending is less than output
    a. inventories are likely to be increasing.
    b. inventories are likely to be decreasing.
    c. there will be a shift in the expenditure schedule.
    d. firms are likely to raise prices.

13. From an initial position of equilibrium, consider an increase in investment spending that shifts the expenditure schedule up. If there were no change in the level of output, what would happen to inventories?
    a. Inventories would increase.
    b. Inventories would decrease.
    c. Inventories would not be affected.

14. When total spending is equal to output,
    a. the resulting level of output is called the full-employment level of output.
    b. the level of income is given by the intersection of the expenditure schedule and the 45–degree line.
    c. there is never an inflationary gap.
    d. the expenditure schedule and the aggregate demand curve coincide.

15. At the equilibrium level of income which one of the following is not necessarily true?
    a. The expenditure schedule will intersect the 45–degree line.
    b. There will be no unexpected changes in business inventories.
    c. There will be no unemployment.
    d. The equilibrium level of output and the price level will together determine one point on the aggregate demand curve.

16. If, at the full-employment level of income, consumers' savings plans are equal to firms' investment plans, then
    a. the equilibrium level of income will be equal to the full-employment level of income.
    b. there will be an inflationary gap.
    c. firms will find their inventories increasing.
    d. the economy will be producing less than potential output.

17. There is a recessionary gap when the equilibrium level of income
    a. is less than potential GDP.
    b. equal to the full-employment level of GDP.
    c. is greater than potential GDP.
    d. imports exceed exports.

18. A lower price level will _____the equilibrium level of income on the income-expenditure diagram.
    a. decrease
    b. not affect
    c. increase

19. The aggregate demand curve is a relationship between the price level and
    a. consumption spending.
    b. the equilibrium level of income on the income-expenditure diagram.
    c. full-employment GDP.
    d. the interest rate.

20. A lower price level will lead to which of the following? (There may be more than one correct answer.)
    a. An increase in exports.
    b. A shift in the consumption function.
    c. A shift in the expenditure schedule.
    d. A shift in the aggregate demand curve.

## Test B

Circle T or F for true or false.

T  F   1.  It is an easy task for government policymakers to influence the state of business confidence.

T  F   2.  The expenditure schedule refers to a relationship between total spending and the level of output (and income).

T  F   3.  The equilibrium level of GDP never equals the full-employment level of GDP.

T  F   4.  If total spending exceeds national output, the resulting decrease in inventories will lead firms to reduce the level of output and production.

T  F   5.  The intersection of the expenditure schedule and the 45–degree line determines one point on the aggregate demand curve.

T  F   6.  The vertical difference between the 45–degree line and the aggregate demand curve is called the inflationary gap.

T  F   7.  The term recessionary gap refers to a situation  in which the equilibrium level of GDP is less than the full-employment level of GDP.

T  F   8.  Because consumers usually invest their savings at financial institutions, there can be no difference between desired savings and desired investment for the economy.

T  F   9.  An increase in the level of prices, through its impact on consumption spending and net exports, will lead to a movement along the expenditure schedule.

T  F  10.  The aggregate demand curve refers to a relationship between the equilibrium level of income and the price level.

# Appendix A: The "Leakages" and "Injections" Approach

## LEARNING OBJECTIVES

The exercise below is intended to illustrate the basic content of Appendix A to Chapter 25: *The condition for the equilibrium level of income can be stated as Y = C + I + G + (X – IM) or it can be stated as S + T + IM = I + G + X.* Both statements lead to the same result.

## IMPORTANT TERMS AND CONCEPTS

$S + T + IM = I + G + X$
Saving schedule
Leakages schedule
Injections schedule
Induced investment

## BASIC EXERCISE

Table 25-4 reproduces some data from Table 25-1.

1. Using the definition of saving, $S = DI - C$, determine the level of consumer saving at each level of national income.

2. At what level of income is the sum of injections, $I + G + X$, equal to the sum of leakages, $S + T + IM$? How does this level of income compare with the equilibrium level of income you computed in question e of the first Basic Exercise to this chapter?

3. Just as tabular results on spending have a graphical representation in the income–expenditure diagram, there is a graphical representation of the leakages and injections formulation. Use the data from Table 25-4 to draw schedules for leakages and injections in Figure 25-3. Using Figure 25-3, equilibrium is determined by_____

_____

What is the equilibrium level of income in Figure 25-3? _____.

4. In this example, only savings varied with income. What would happen if investment, imports or taxes varied with income? There would be no change in the principle that is used to determine the equilibrium level of income. In the income-expenditure diagram, the equilibrium level of income is determined by the intersection of the expenditure schedule and the 45–degree line. In the diagram of leakages and injections, equilibrium is the level of income leakages equal injections. The difference is that the expenditure schedule, the schedule for leakages, or the schedule for injections may be steeper or flatter. Complete Table 25-5 by indicating whether various schedules get steeper, flatter or show no change. Be sure you can explain why in each case. (Government purchases and taxes will be discussed in Chapter 28. Why doesn't it make sense to think of exports varying with income?)

5. We can also show the equivalence of the leakage/injection approach using a little high school algebra. Equilibrium on the income–expenditure diagram is the one level of national income where

$$Y = C + I + G + (X - IM).$$

## TABLE 25-4
### (PRICE LEVEL = 100)

| Income (Output) Y | Savings S | Taxes T | Imports IM | Total Leakages | Investment Spending I | Government Purchases G | Exports X | Total Injections |
|---|---|---|---|---|---|---|---|---|
| 5,600 | _____ | 700 | 600 | _____ | 900 | 800 | 500 | 2,200 |
| 5,800 | _____ | 700 | 600 | _____ | 900 | 800 | 500 | 2,200 |
| 6,000 | _____ | 700 | 600 | _____ | 900 | 800 | 500 | 2,200 |
| 6,200 | _____ | 700 | 600 | _____ | 900 | 800 | 500 | 2,200 |
| 6,400 | _____ | 700 | 600 | _____ | 900 | 800 | 500 | 2,200 |
| 6,600 | _____ | 700 | 600 | _____ | 900 | 800 | 500 | 2,200 |

## FIGURE 25-3

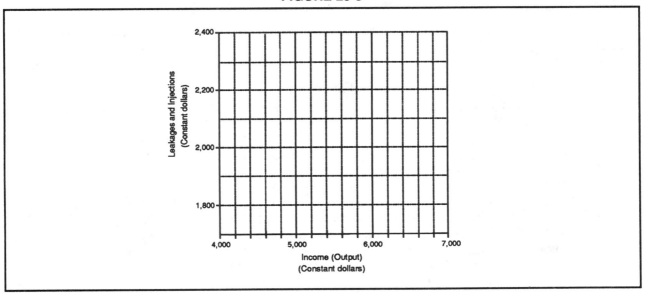

## TABLE 25-5

| | Expenditure Schedule | Leakages Schedule | Injections Schedule |
|---|---|---|---|
| Investment spending increases with income | _____ | _____ | _____ |
| Imports increase with income | _____ | _____ | _____ |

In this economy the only difference between national income ($Y$) and disposable income ($DI$) is taxes. Represented symbolically: $Y = T + DI$. We also know that consumers either spend or save their income, that is $DI = C + S$. Using this last expression for disposable income we can rewrite our expression for $Y$ as $Y = T + C + S$. Substituting this expression for national income into the equation for equilibrium gives

$$T + C + S = C + I + G + (X - IM)$$

Subtracting C from both sides of this expression, putting all the leakages on the left side of the equal sign, and putting all of the injections on the right side, yields our alternative but equivalent formulation of the equilibrium condition, or

_____ + _____ + _____ = _____ + _____ + _____

# Appendix B: The Simple Algebra of Income Determination

## BASIC EXERCISE

This exercise is meant to illustrate the material in Appendix B to Chapter 25. If we are willing to use algebra we can use equations rather than graphs or tables to determine the equilibrium level of output. If we have done all our work accurately, we should get the same answer regardless of whether we use graphs, tables, or algebra.

The following equations are consistent with the numbers in Table 25-1

1) $C = 1850 + .5\ DI$
2) $DI = Y - T$
3) $T = 700$
4) $I = 900$
5) $G = 800$
6) $X = 500$
7) $IM = 600$
8) $Y = C + I + G + (X - IM)$

1. Equation 1 is the consumption function. It shows how consumption spending changes with changes in disposable income. To derive the expenditure schedule we need to figure out how spending changes with changes in national income. Start by substituting equations 2 and 3 for disposable income and taxes into equation 1 to see how C varies with Y.

   9) $C = $ _____ + _____$Y$.

2. Now use equation 9, along with equations, 4, 5, 6 and 7 to show how total spending varies with Y.

   10) $C + I + G + (X - IM) = $ _____ + _____ $Y$.

3. To find the one level of income where spending equals output (and income) substitute the right-hand side of equation 10 for the right-hand side of equation 8 and solve for the equilibrium level of Y.

   $Y = $ _____

Equation 10 is the expenditure schedule. Equation 8 is the 45–degree line. Substituting the right-hand side of equation 10 for the right hand side of equation is the algebraic way of finding the intersection of these two lines.

## ECONOMICS IN ACTIONS

### Military Spending and Aggregate Demand

Some critics on the left argue that America's economic strength is dependent upon large military outlays. These critics point out that the periods of lowest unemployment over the past 50 years were also periods of war—World War II, Korea, and Vietnam. Many also argue that the years of economic expansion under Presidents Reagan and Bush were associated with a substantial increase in defense spending and that unemployment in the early 1990s has been aggravated by defense-related layoffs.

Others are not so sure, arguing that employment will be determined by the level of aggregate demand relative to full employment. Defense spending increases aggregate demand and employment, but so does any other type of spending. While increased military spending has been associated with periods of full employment, this does not mean that only military spending can result in low rates of unemployment. Increases in other types of spending, public or private, also increase employment and lower unemployment. On this view, the historical correlation between defense spending and full employment may really reflect politics not economics. That is, it may be easier to organize the political commitment for high levels of defense spending than for high levels of non-defense spending.

When evaluating these arguments, it is also instructive to look at data. World War II saw the most dramatic increase in defense spending when measured as a proportion of GDP. From about 3 percent in 1940, defense spending climbed to over 40 percent of GDP by 1943. The Korean conflict saw an increase in defense spending from less than 5 percent of GDP to just over 13 percent in two years. The Vietnam increase was substantially smaller, less than 2 percent of GDP. It began after a four year period when both the unemployment rate and defense as a proportion of GDP had been falling. The increase in defense spending under President Reagan actually started in 1979 and was a bit smaller than the Vietnam increase. Furthermore, as in the immediate pre-Vietnam period, the unemployment rate continued to decline even after the growth in defense budgets stopped. From 1987 to 1989, the unemployment rate declined from 6.1 percent to 5.2 percent as real defense spending declined by 4 percent.

To argue that full employment is not dependent upon high levels of defense spending does not imply that changes in defense spending will not affect aggregate demand and employment. In the absence of offsetting changes increases in defense spending would add to aggregate demand while decreases would subtract. The closing of a military base and the termination of defense contracts will typically have an immediate and significant impact on particular communities and states. A number of observers have argued that planned reductions in military spending should be accompanied by special government financed adjustment assistant for the individuals and communities suddenly without jobs. Others would argue that jobs losses from defense cutbacks should be treated no differently than job losses from any other cause. That is, individuals and communities should be eligible for the same assistance they would receive for any job loss but should not receive special treatment.

1. Are concerns about full employment an appropriate argument in support of high levels of defense spending?
2. Reductions in defense spending are sometimes referred to as a "peace dividend." Assuming that planned reductions in defense are realized, what should the federal government do with the peace dividend?
3. Should there be special assistance for individuals and communities who are affected by base closings and the cancellation of military contracts?

You might want to look at the following recent articles about defense conversion:

Jurgen Brauer and John T. Marlin, "Converting Resources from Military to Non-Military Uses," *The Journal of Economic Perspectives*, (Vol. 6, Number 4), Fall 1992, pp. 145-164.

Michelle R. Garfinkel, "The Economic Consequences of Reducing Military Spending," *Review*, Federal Reserve Bank of St. Louis, (Nov./Dec. 1990) pp. 47-58.

## STUDY QUESTIONS

1. Why is investment spending so volatile?

2. If one says that investment is a flighty bird does that mean that policy changes by the government will have no impact on investment?

3. "Exports will change with changes in foreign but not domestic income. They will also change if foreign or domestic prices change." How can it be that exports respond to domestic prices but not domestic income?

4. How do imports respond to changes in domestic income, foreign income, domestic prices and foreign prices?

5. The expenditure schedule shows how total spending changes with domestic income. What categories of spending does the expenditure schedule need to include?

6. What would happen to the expenditure schedule if the marginal propensity to consume were larger or smaller? Why?

7. What would happen to the expenditure schedule if there were a change in any of the following: investment spending, government purchases of goods and services, exports or imports?

8. According to the text, equilibrium occurs at the intersection of the expenditure schedule and the 45–degree line. Why there? What prevents points to the left or right of the intersection from also being points of equilibrium?

9. Why do we say the expenditure schedule is drawn for a given level of prices?

10. What happens to the expenditure schedule if prices increase or if they decrease?

11. Plotting different price levels and the corresponding equilibrium level of income from the income–expenditure diagram results in what curve?

*Chapter* **26**

# Changes on the Demand Side: Multiplier Analysis

---

## LEARNING OBJECTIVES

After completing this chapter you should be able to:

- explain why any autonomous increases in expenditures will have a multiplier effect on GDP.
- calculate the value of the multiplier in specific examples.
- explain how and why the value of the multiplier would change if MPC changed.
- explain why the multiplier expression, $1/(1 - \text{MPC})$, is oversimplified.
- explain the difference between an autonomous and an induced increase in consumption expenditures.
- explain how and why economic booms and recessions tend to be transmitted across national boundaries.
- explain why an increase in savings may be good for an individual but bad for the economy as a whole.
- describe how any change in autonomous spending leads to a shift in the aggregate demand curve.

---

## IMPORTANT TERMS AND CONCEPTS

The multiplier
Induced increase in consumption
Autonomous increase in consumption
Paradox of thrift

---

## CHAPTER REVIEW

The main topic of this chapter is the *multiplier*. It is a fundamental concept in economics, which is why a whole chapter is devoted to explaining how it works. The multiplier has already played an important but unheralded role in Chapter 25, so those of you who paid close attention then should have an easier time grasping the concept of multiplier analysis presented here.

(1)     The idea of the multiplier is that a change in autonomous spending by one sector of the economy will change the equilibrium level of income by (<u>more than/the same as/less than</u>) the change in autonomous spending. We have been studying the determination of the equilibrium level of income in the income–expenditure diagram. Multiplier analysis investigates changes in the equilibrium level of income when the expenditure schedule shifts. In this chapter we will be concerned with parallel shifts in the expenditure schedule which are represented graphically as a change in the vertical axis intercept of the expenditure schedule. A parallel shift in the expenditure schedule shows the same change in spending at all levels of income and is thus a change in (<u>autonomous/induced</u>) spending. Spending that changes when income changes, such as the response of consumption spending to a change in income, is called an _____ change.

    Multiplier analysis shows that the equilibrium level of GDP changes by a multiple of the change in autonomous spending, which is where the term "multiplier" comes from. The basic reason for this multiplier result is relatively simple: Increased spending by one sector of the economy means increased sales receipts for other sectors of the economy. Higher sales receipts will show up in bigger paychecks, or profits, or both; in short, higher income for some people. These higher incomes will then induce more consumer spending, which in turn will result in still higher incomes and more consumption spending by others, and so on and so on.

    You may be wondering at this point whether the multiplier is finite or whether income will increase without limit. Another way of looking at this question is to ask what determines the value of the multiplier. There are several alternative, but equally good, ways of answering this question. In the text the value is determined by summing the increments to spending and income that follow from the original autonomous change in spending. When consumption is the only induced spending, the oversimplified multiplier

(2) expression turns out to be $1/(1 - \underline{\hspace{3cm}})$.

    Here is an alternative derivation of the same result. We know that in equilibrium national output, or income, will equal total spending:

$$Y = C + I + G + (X - IM).$$

Now assume that there is an autonomous increase in investment spending which induces subsequent increases in consumption spending. At the new equilibrium, we know that the change in the equilibrium level of national output must equal the change in total spending. If net exports and government purchases are the same at all levels of income, the change in total spending will have two parts. One is the autonomous change in investment spending and the other is the induced change in consumption spending. We know that

(3)
$$\begin{pmatrix} \text{Change in} \\ \text{equilibrium} \\ \text{level of} \\ \text{income} \end{pmatrix} = \begin{pmatrix} \text{Autonomous} \\ \text{change in} \\ \text{investment} \\ \text{spending} \end{pmatrix} + \begin{pmatrix} \text{Induced change in} \\ \underline{\hspace{2cm}} \\ \underline{\hspace{2cm}} \end{pmatrix}$$

It is possible to represent this symbolically. Let $\Delta Y$ represent the change in the equilibrium level of income and $\Delta I$ represent the autonomous change in investment spending. What about the induced change in consumption spending? The discussion in Chapter 24 told us that consumption spending will change

(4) as disposable _____ changes. Further, with the use of the concept of the marginal propensity to consume, we can represent the change in consumption spending as the product of the change in disposable income multiplied by the _____. When taxes are constant, disposable income changes dollar for dollar whenever GDP or $Y$ changes. We could represent the induced change in consumption spending as $\Delta DI \times MPC$. As $\Delta DI = \Delta Y$, the change in consumption can also be represented as $\Delta Y \times MPC$. If we substitute all these symbols for the words above, we see that

$$\Delta Y = \Delta I + (\Delta Y \times MPC).$$

We can now solve this equation for the change in income by moving all terms in $\Delta Y$ to the left-hand side of the equation:

$$\Delta Y - (\Delta Y \times MPC) = \Delta I.$$

If we factor out the $\Delta Y$ we can rewrite the expression as

$$\Delta Y (1 - MPC) = \Delta I.$$

We can now solve for $\Delta Y$ by dividing both sides of the equation by $(1 - MPC)$.

$$\Delta Y = \left( \frac{1}{1 - MPC} \right) \Delta I.$$

Therefore we find that

$$\begin{pmatrix} \text{Change in} \\ \text{equilibrium} \\ \text{level of} \\ \text{income} \end{pmatrix} = \text{Multiplier} \times \begin{pmatrix} \text{Autonomous} \\ \text{change in} \\ \text{investment} \\ \text{spending} \end{pmatrix}$$

Would our calculation of the multiplier be any different if we considered a change in net exports or an autonomous change in consumption spending? The Basic Exercises to this chapter are designed to help answer this question.

The multiplier expression we just derived, $1/(1 - MPC)$, is the same as the one in Chapter 26 the text and is subject to the same limitations[1]. That is, this expression is oversimplified. There are four important

(5) reasons why real world multipliers will be (smaller/larger) than our formula. These reasons are related to the effects of _____ _____, _____, _____ taxes, and the _____ system.

The simplified multiplier expression we derived above is applicable when analyzing a shift in the expenditure schedule in the 45-degree line diagram. As such, this expression assumes that prices (do/do not) change. In Chapter 25 we saw that the income–expenditure diagram is only a building-block on the way to the aggregate demand curve. (Remember from Chapter 22 that even the aggregate demand curve is only part of the story. For a complete analysis we need to consider both the aggregate demand and the aggregate _____ curves.) To complete our analysis on the demand side, we need to see how our multiplier analysis affects the aggregate demand curve. The multiplier analysis we have done by using the income–expenditure diagram shows us that if prices are constant, the equilibrium level of income will change following any change in (autonomous/induced) spending. This result is true at all price levels and implies that a shift in the expenditure schedule following a change in autonomous spending leads to a (movement along/shift in) demand curve. In fact, it leads to a (horizontal/vertical) shift in the aggregate demand curve. The magnitude of the shift can be computed with the help of the multiplier, as shown in Figure 26-4 of the text and Figure 27-4 of the study guide.

---

[1]A somewhat more general expression for the multiplier is $1/(1 - \text{slope of the expenditure schedule})$. The multiplier is based on summing the rounds of spending induced by an autonomous increase in spending. In the model of this chapter only consumption spending change as income change. As taxes do not vary with changes in income, every dollar change in national income is also a dollar change in disposable income which induces a change in consumption spending determined by the MPC. In this case consumption spending goes up by MPC for every dollar increase in national income and the slope of the expenditure schedule is equal to the MPC.

## IMPORTANT TERMS AND CONCEPTS QUIZ

Choose the best definition for the following terms.

1. _____ Multiplier

2. _____ Induced increase consumption

3. _____ Autonomous increase in consumption

4. _____ Paradox of thrift

a. Increase in consumer spending due to an increase in disposable income.

b. Attempts to increase savings that cause national income to fall with little net impact on savings.

c. Ratio of change in spending to change in equilibrium GDP.

d. Ratio of change in equilibrium GDP to change in autonomous spending that cause GDP to change.

e. Increase in consumer spending not due to increased incomes.

## BASIC EXERCISES

These exercises are designed to illustrate the concepts of the multiplier and the paradox of thrift.

1. **The Multiplier**

   a. Using the data in Table 26-1, fill in the values for total spending and then find the equilibrium level of income.

   b. Table 26-2 has a similar set of data except that investment spending has risen by $100 billion. Find the equilibrium level of income after the rise in investment spending.

   c. What is the change in the equilibrium level of income following the increase in investment spending? _____

   d. What is the value of the multiplier for this increase in autonomous investment spending? _____

      (Remember that the multiplier is defined as the ratio of the change in the _____ of _____ divided by the change in _____ that produced the change in income.)

   e. Now let us verify that the value of the multiplier that you found in question d is the same as the simplified formula 1/(1 – MPC). To do this we will first need to calculate the MPC for the economy in Table 26-1. Write the value of the MPC here: _____ (If you do not remember how to calculate the MPC, review the material in Chapter 24 of the textbook and in this study guide.)

   f. Now calculate the value of the multiplier from the oversimplified formula 1/(1 – MPC). Write your answer here: _____ .

   g. (Optional) The multiplier can also be calculated as

$$\frac{1}{(1 - \text{slope of the expenditure schedule})}$$

   The slope of the expenditure schedule tells us how total spending changes when income changes. Calculate the slope of the expenditure schedule by dividing any of the changes in the last column of Table 26-1 by the corresponding change in income in the first column. What is the slope of the expenditure schedule and how is it related to the multiplier?

2. **International Trade**

   Assume that an increase in income abroad has increased the demand for exports by $100 billion. Table 26-3 shows consumption spending, investment spending, and net exports following this increase in foreign demand.

## TABLE 26-1
## (CONSTANT PRICES)

| Income (Output) Y | Taxes T | Disposable Income DI | Consumption Spending C | Investment Spending I | Government Purchases G | Exports X | Imports IM | Total Spending C + I + G + (X − IM) |
|---|---|---|---|---|---|---|---|---|
| 5,500 | 800 | 4,700 | 4,100 | 800 | 850 | 500 | 650 | _____ |
| 5,750 | 800 | 4,950 | 4,300 | 800 | 850 | 500 | 650 | _____ |
| 6,000 | 800 | 5,200 | 4,500 | 800 | 850 | 500 | 650 | _____ |
| 6,250 | 800 | 5,450 | 4,700 | 800 | 850 | 500 | 650 | _____ |
| 6,500 | 800 | 5,700 | 4,900 | 800 | 850 | 500 | 650 | _____ |
| 6,750 | 800 | 5,950 | 5,100 | 800 | 850 | 500 | 650 | _____ |
| 7,000 | 800 | 6,200 | 5,300 | 800 | 850 | 500 | 650 | _____ |

## TABLE 26-2
## (CONSTANT PRICES)

| Income (Output) Y | Taxes T | Disposable Income DI | Consumption Spending C | Investment Spending I | Government Purchases G | Exports X | Imports IM | Total Spending C + I + G + (X − IM) |
|---|---|---|---|---|---|---|---|---|
| 5,500 | 800 | 4,700 | 4,100 | 900 | 850 | 500 | 650 | _____ |
| 5,750 | 800 | 4,950 | 4,300 | 900 | 850 | 500 | 650 | _____ |
| 6,000 | 800 | 5,200 | 4,500 | 900 | 850 | 500 | 650 | _____ |
| 6,250 | 800 | 5,450 | 4,700 | 900 | 850 | 500 | 650 | _____ |
| 6,500 | 800 | 5,700 | 4,900 | 900 | 850 | 500 | 650 | _____ |
| 6,750 | 800 | 5,950 | 5,100 | 900 | 850 | 500 | 650 | _____ |
| 7,000 | 800 | 6,200 | 5,300 | 900 | 850 | 500 | 650 | _____ |

## TABLE 26-3
## (CONSTANT PRICES)

| Income (Output) Y | Taxes T | Disposable Income DI | Consumption Spending C | Investment Spending I | Government Purchases G | Exports X | Imports IM | Total Spending C + I + G + (X − IM) |
|---|---|---|---|---|---|---|---|---|
| 5,500 | 800 | 4,700 | 4,100 | 900 | 850 | 600 | 650 | _____ |
| 5,750 | 800 | 4,950 | 4,300 | 900 | 850 | 600 | 650 | _____ |
| 6,000 | 800 | 5,200 | 4,500 | 900 | 850 | 600 | 650 | _____ |
| 6,250 | 800 | 5,450 | 4,700 | 900 | 850 | 600 | 650 | _____ |
| 6,500 | 800 | 5,700 | 4,900 | 900 | 850 | 600 | 650 | _____ |
| 6,750 | 800 | 5,950 | 5,100 | 900 | 850 | 600 | 650 | _____ |
| 7,000 | 800 | 6,200 | 5,300 | 900 | 850 | 600 | 650 | _____ |

## TABLE 26-4
## (CONSTANT PRICES)

| Income (Output) Y | Taxes T | Disposable Income DI | Consumption Spending C | Investment Spending I | Government Purchases G | Exports X | Imports IM | Total Spending $C + I + G + (X - IM)$ |
|---|---|---|---|---|---|---|---|---|
| 5,500 | 800 | 4,700 | 4,050 | 900 | 850 | 600 | 650 | _____ |
| 5,750 | 800 | 4,950 | 4,250 | 900 | 850 | 600 | 650 | _____ |
| 6,000 | 800 | 5,200 | 4,450 | 900 | 850 | 600 | 650 | _____ |
| 6,250 | 800 | 5,450 | 4,650 | 900 | 850 | 600 | 650 | _____ |
| 6,500 | 800 | 5,700 | 4,850 | 900 | 850 | 600 | 650 | _____ |
| 6,750 | 800 | 5,950 | 5,050 | 900 | 850 | 600 | 650 | _____ |
| 7,000 | 800 | 6,200 | 5,250 | 900 | 850 | 600 | 650 | _____ |

a. What is the new equilibrium level of domestic income following the increase in net exports?
_____

b. What is the change in the equilibrium level of income from its equilibrium in Table 26-2?
_____

c. What is the multiplier for the change in the equilibrium level of income following the $100 billion increase in net exports, and how does it compare to the multiplier computed above for a change in investment spending?
_____

3. **The Paradox of Thrift**

Assume that in the aggregate all consumers suddenly decided to save $50 billion more than they have been saving at every level of income. If people want to save more it means they must consume
_____ .

This change is an (autonomous/induced) change in savings and consumption. Table 26-4 shows the new values for consumption spending following the increased desire to save. Notice that the numbers for consumption spending in Table 26-4 are all $50 billion less than the numbers in the earlier tables, while investment spending and net exports are unchanged from Table 26-3.
a. Using the data in Table 26-4, find the new equilibrium level of income.
b. What is the change in the equilibrium level of income compared with Table 26-3?
_____

c. At this point we can conclude that if consumer saving shows an autonomous increase while investment spending and net exports are unchanged, then the equilibrium level of income will (rise/fall).
d. The multiplier for this change is _____ .
e. How does this multiplier compare with the multiplier you computed for the increase in investment spending?
f. Why is the specific numerical value you have calculated likely to be an overstatement of the multiplier response of a real economy to a change in investment spending, net exports, or saving?

## SELF-TESTS FOR UNDERSTANDING

### Test A

Circle the most appropriate answer.

1. The multiplier is defined as the ratio of the change in
   a. autonomous spending divided by the change in consumption expenditures.
   b. the equilibrium level of income divided by the increase in consumption spending.
   c. the equilibrium level of income divided by the change in autonomous spending that produced the change in income.
   d. consumption spending divided by the change in autonomous spending.

2. The multiplier shows that
   a. any increase in induced spending will be a multiple of the increase in income.
   b. an autonomous increase in spending will increase income by more than the increase in autonomous spending.
   c. to influence income, any change in autonomous spending must be a multiple of the induced changes in spending.
   d. an induced change in spending will lead to a multiple increase in income.

3. The oversimplified multiplier formula is
   a. 1/MPC.
   b. 1/(MPC–1)
   c. MPC × (1–MPC)
   d. 1/(1–MPC)

4. The secret behind the multiplier is
   a. the government's printing press.
   b. understanding that an autonomous increase in investment spending leads to an autonomous increase in consumption spending.
   c. understanding that an autonomous increase in investment spending induces additional increases in spending as income increases.
   d. the gnomes of Zurich.

5. Actual multipliers will be less than theoretical multipliers because of which of the following? (There may be more than one correct answer.)
   a. Inflation.
   b. Accounting practices.
   c. International trade.
   d. The government deficit.
   e. Income taxes.
   f. Price controls.
   g. The financial system.

6. An autonomous change in spending can be modeled as
   a. a horizontal shift in the expenditure schedule.
   b. a tilt in the slope of the expenditure schedule.
   c. a vertical shift in the expenditure schedule.
   d. an increase in MPC.

7. Which one of the following is not the beginning of a multiplier process?
   a. An autonomous increase in net exports.
   b. An induced increase in consumption spending.
   c. An autonomous increase in investment spending.
   d. An autonomous increase in savings.

8. The multiplier will be largest for which type of change
   a. An increase in investment spending.
   b. An autonomous decrease in consumption spending.
   c. A decrease in exports.
   d. An increase in government purchases.
   e. The multiplier should be similar for all changes.

9. If MPC were 0.6 and prices did not change, the multiplier would be
   a. $\dfrac{1}{0.6} = 1.67$.
   b. 0.6.
   c. $\dfrac{1}{1 - 0.6} = 2.5$.
   d. $\dfrac{1}{1 + 0.6} = 0.63$.

10. If MPC were 0.7 instead of 0.6, the textbook multiplier would be
    a. larger than in question 9.
    b. smaller than in question 9.
    c. the same as in question 9.

11. The textbook multiplier would be largest if MPC were
    a. 0.73.
    b. 0.45.
    c. 0.89.
    d. 0.67.

12. When compared with changes in investment spending, the multiplier associated with autonomous changes in consumption spending will be
    a. larger.
    b. smaller.
    c. about the same.

13. A boom in Japan would likely lead to an increased demand for
    (There may be more than one correct answer.)
    a. Japanese exports.
    b. American exports.
    c. American imports.
    d. Japanese imports

14. If a $100 billion increase in exports led to $300 billion increase in GDP, we could conclude that the multiplier is
    a. 1.
    b. 2.
    c. 3.
    d. 4.

15. An increase in which of the following will not lead to an increase in GDP?
    a. Investment spending.
    b. Government purchases of goods and services.
    c. Exports.
    d. Imports.

16. The multiplier is useful in calculating
    a. the slope of the consumption function.
    b. the horizontal shift in the aggregate demand curve following an increase in autonomous spending.
    c. the vertical shift of the expenditure schedule following a change in autonomous spending.
    d. the shift of the consumption function following an increase in autonomous spending.

17. The multiplier response following an increase in exports would have what impact on the aggregate demand curve?
    a. Horizontal shift to the left.
    b. No impact.
    c. Horizontal shift to the right.

18. The multiplier response following a decrease in investment spending would have what impact on the aggregate demand curve?
    a. Horizontal shift to the left.
    b. No impact.
    c. Horizontal shift to the right.

19. An autonomous increase in savings
    a. is necessarily accompanied by an increase in consumption spending.
    b. will shift the expenditure schedule down.
    c. will not affect the level of income as neither the aggregate demand nor the aggregate supply curve will shift.
    d. shifts the aggregate demand curve to the right.

20. When compared with increases in autonomous spending, multiplier responses to decreases in autonomous spending are likely to be
    a. smaller.
    b. larger.
    c. about the same.
    d. zero.

## Test B

Circle T or F for true or false.

T F 1. The multiplier is defined as the ratio of a change in autonomous spending divided by the resulting change in the equilibrium level of income.

T F 2. Multiplier responses mean that the equilibrium level of national income is likely to change by less than any change in autonomous spending.

T F 3. Multiplier increases illustrated on the income–expenditure diagram are based on the assumption that prices do not change.

T F 4. Actual multiplier responses to changes in autonomous spending are likely to be less than that suggested by the theoretical formula $1/(1 - MPC)$.

T F 5. If income increases because of an autonomous increase in investment spending, the resulting increase in consumption spending is called an induced increase.

T F 6. An autonomous increase in savings by all consumers will immediately lead to a higher level of real GDP, as resources are freed for higher levels of investment.

T F 7. The multiplier for autonomous increases in investment spending is always greater than the multiplier for autonomous increases in consumption spending.

T F 8. An increase in European income that resulted in an increased demand for American exports would have no effect on the equilibrium level of American income.

T  F  9.  The multiplier works for increases in autonomous spending, but because of price and wage rigidities the multiplier is irrelevant when we examine decreases in autonomous spending.

T  F  10.  The impact of a shift in the aggregate demand curve on prices and real output will depend upon the slope of the aggregate supply curve.

# Appendix A
# Basic Exercises: Appendix A

The following exercise is meant to give you practice working with the algebraic representation of the multiplier found in Appendix A.

1. The consumption function can be represented as $C = a + b\,DI$. In this economy $DI = Y - T$. Substitute the expression for disposable income into the consumption function and then substitute the consumption function into the following in order to solve for national income: $Y = C + I + G + (X - IM)$.

   What is the resulting expression for national income? Identify the multiplier in your expression.

2. An autonomous change in spending would be a change in $a$, $I$, $G$, $X$ or $IM$. What does your equation for national income ($Y$) indicate will happen if $a$ or any of the other components of autonomous spending change?

# Appendix B
# Basic Exercises: Appendix B

The following exercise is meant to illustrate the major point of Appendix B: When the demand for imports increases with domestic GDP, the multiplier will be smaller.

1. Table 26-5 is similar to 26-1 except that imports increase with income. Compute total spending to verify that the equilibrium level of income in Table 26-5 is the same as in Table 26-1.

2. Table 26-6 is based on the assumption that investment spending has increased by $125.

   The new equilibrium level of income is _____.

3. We calculate the multiplier as before: the change in the equilibrium level of income divided by the change that changed income. Now the multiplier is _____.

4. Explain any difference between this multiplier and the one you calculated for Table 26-2.

## TABLE 26-5
## (CONSTANT PRICES)

| Income (Output) Y | Taxes T | Disposable Income DI | Consumption Spending C | Investment Spending I | Government Purchases G | Exports X | Imports IM | Total Spending C + I + G + (X − IM) |
|---|---|---|---|---|---|---|---|---|
| 5,500 | 800 | 4,700 | 4,100 | 800 | 850 | 500 | 625 | |
| 5,750 | 800 | 4,950 | 4,300 | 800 | 850 | 500 | 637.5 | |
| 6,000 | 800 | 5,200 | 4,500 | 800 | 850 | 500 | 650 | |
| 6,250 | 800 | 5,450 | 4,700 | 800 | 850 | 500 | 662.5 | |
| 6,500 | 800 | 5,700 | 4,900 | 800 | 850 | 500 | 675 | |
| 6,750 | 800 | 5,950 | 5,100 | 800 | 850 | 500 | 687.5 | |
| 7,000 | 800 | 6,200 | 5,300 | 800 | 850 | 500 | 700 | |

## TABLE 26-6
## (CONSTANT PRICES)

| Income (Output) Y | Taxes T | Disposable Income DI | Consumption Spending C | Investment Spending I | Government Purchases G | Exports X | Imports IM | Total Spending C + I + G + (X − IM) |
|---|---|---|---|---|---|---|---|---|
| 5,500 | 800 | 4,700 | 4,100 | 925 | 850 | 500 | 625 | _____ |
| 5,750 | 800 | 4,950 | 4,300 | 925 | 850 | 500 | 637.5 | _____ |
| 6,000 | 800 | 5,200 | 4,500 | 925 | 850 | 500 | 650 | _____ |
| 6,250 | 800 | 5,450 | 4,700 | 925 | 850 | 500 | 662.5 | _____ |
| 6,500 | 800 | 5,700 | 4,900 | 925 | 850 | 500 | 675 | _____ |
| 6,750 | 800 | 5,950 | 5,100 | 925 | 850 | 500 | 687.5 | _____ |
| 7,000 | 800 | 6,200 | 5,300 | 925 | 850 | 500 | 700 | _____ |

## SUPPLEMENTARY EXERCISES

1. In 1963 the President's Council of Economic Advisers was considering how large a tax cut would be necessary to return the economy to full employment. These economists estimated that actual output was about $30 to $35 billion less than potential, or full-employment, output. That is, they wanted a tax cut that would increase output by $30 to $35 billion, yet they recommended a tax cut of only $13 billion, to be divided between consumers ($10 billion) and businesses ($3 billion). How could these economists expect that total spending could rise by $30 to $35 billion when taxes were only reduced by $13 billion? Even if consumers and businesses spent the whole reduction in taxes, spending would only rise by $13 billion, not nearly enough to return the economy to full employment. What is wrong with this line of reasoning?

2. Use the data in Table 26-1 and a piece of graph paper to draw the income-expenditure diagram.
   a. Show how the expenditure schedule shifts as a result of the increase in investment spending in Basic Exercise 1b. Does your graph give you the same result as Basic Exercise 1c?
   b. Show how the expenditure schedule shifts following the increase in net exports in Basic Exercise 2. How does the new equilibrium level of income, and hence the multiplier, on your graph, compare to your answers in the Basic Exercise?
   c. Show how the expenditure schedule shifts after the increase in savings described in Basic Exercise 3. How does your graph compare with your answer to 3c?

3. If you have access to a micro computer try programming or using a spread sheet to simulate the following model to investigate the dynamics of the multiplier.

   Assume that consumption spending responds to income with a one-period lag as follows

   $$C = 340 + .8DI (-1)$$

   where $C$ is consumption and $DI$ is disposable income. Other important elements of the model are:

   $$DI = Y-T$$
   $$T = 800$$
   $$I = 900$$
   $$G = 850$$
   $$X = 500$$
   $$IM = 650$$

a. If confirm that the equilibrium level of income is 6,000. That is, if income last period was 6,000, then $C + I + G + (X - IM)$ will equal 6,000 this period.

b. Now assume that investment spending increases by 100. Assuming that consumption responds with the one-period lag, simulate your model to investigate how the change in investment spending affects income over time. Does the level of income appear to converge to a new equilibrium value? What is that value? What is the multiplier for the change in investment spending? How does the multiplier from your simulation compare to the oversimplified formula of $1/(1-MPC)$?

c. Investigate the impact of increases and decreases in net exports. Investigate the impact of a change in government purchases. Investigate the impact of autonomous changes in consumption spending, that is a change in the constant term of the consumption function. How would you model an autonomous change in savings?

d. What happens if the MPC changes? You will need first to determine the initial equilibrium level of income for given levels of investment spending, net exports, and autonomous consumption spending. Then simulate your model to see how the change in the MPC affects the multiplier.

## ECONOMICS IN ACTION

### Autonomous and Induced Changes in Consumption Spending

As Chapter 26 discusses, the multiplier shows how an autonomous increase in spending, through its impact on income, induces additional spending. The final result is that the equilibrium level of income increases by more than, or by a multiple of, the original autonomous change. Chapter 24 discussed the close link between disposable income and consumption spending. As seen in Chapter 26, the induced changes in consumption spending are an important part of the multiplier process.

Can changes in consumption spending ever initiate multiplier changes or are they only a part of a process that must be initiated by some other element of spending? To answer this question one must distinguish between factors that shift the consumption function and factors that lead to a movement along the consumption function. As a particular example, consider material from the 1991 Report of the Council of Economic Advisers.

Each January, the President's Council of Economic Advisers issues its annual report. The Council's report is published along with the Economic Report of the President. The volume's statistical appendix reports numerous data series that measure the macroeconomic performance of the economy. The report itself includes commentary on recent developments, a forecast for the upcoming year, and a detailed study of two or three topics of interest. The report is a mixture of politics and economic analysis as it is, in part, a brief for the policies of the President.

The January 1992 report was issued at the beginning of an election year and after the sluggish economic performance of 1991. When discussing factors influencing consumer spending, the report noted the large accumulation of consumer debt, both installment and mortgage debt, that had occurred during the economic expansion of the 1980s.

> By the end of the expansion, many consumers had accumulated relatively high levels of debt. At the same time, the value of their largest asset, their homes—was flat or declining. Householders' expectations of continued increases in the equity of their homes were not being realized. After rising at an average annual rate of 7.5 percent—about twice the rate of inflation—from the end of 1984 through 1989, the value of owner-occupied housing and land fell 1.6 percent in 1990. In addition, the value of other household assets, such as durable goods, stocks, bonds, pensions and other financial assets, grew only slowly in 1990. Total household net worth—the difference between the household sector's assets and liabilities—fell 2 percent in 1990 (page 43).

The report went on to note:

During 1991, real consumer spending rose 0.3 percent. Real disposable personal income, a key determinant of consumer spending rose 0.4 percent during 1991. . . Consumer confidence was on a roller coaster, falling in the second half after a strong post-Operation Desert Storm rebound. In fact, consumer confidence by year-end was very low, which suggests that consumer spending in early 1992 will be sluggish. (page 57)

1. What factors does the report cite to explain the slow growth in consumer spending?
2. Which of these factors reflect a movement along an unchanged consumption function and which reflect a shift in the consumption function? Which would initiate a multiplier process and which would be part of the multiplier response to an autonomous change in spending?

SOURCE: *Economic Report of the President,* Transmitted to Congress, January 1992, (United States Government Printing Office: Washington, D.C.)

## STUDY QUESTIONS

1. Looking just at the expenditure schedule, how can you represent a change in autonomous spending? A change in induced spending?
2. How can it be that a change in autonomous spending results in an even larger change in the equilibrium level of income?
3. What happens to the value of the multiplier if the MPC is larger? Smaller? Why?
4. What are the four shortcomings of the multiplier formula $1/(1-MPC)$?
5. Do these shortcomings mean that the formula overstates or understates the likely value of the multiplier?
6. What is the mechanism by which a recession in Europe may lead to a decline in output in the United States?
7. If an increase in savings is good for an individual, how can it be bad for a nation as a whole? (Explain the reasoning behind the paradox of thrift.)
8. How would results differ if an autonomous increase in savings were matched by an increase in investment spending, as contrasted with the situation where savings increase without any increase in investment spending?
9. What is the relation between the multiplier analysis on the income-expenditure diagram following an autonomous change in spending and the resulting shift of the aggregate demand curve?

*Chapter* **27**

# Supply-Side Equilibrium: Unemployment *and* Inflation?

## LEARNING OBJECTIVES

After completing this chapter you should be able to:

- describe how the aggregate supply curve is derived from an analysis of business costs and why it slopes upward.
- distinguish between factors that will lead to a movement along or a shift in the aggregate supply curve.
- explain why the aggregate supply curve normally gets steeper as output increases.
- use a graph depicting both the aggregate demand curve and the aggregate supply curve to determine the price level and the final equilibrium level of real GDP.
- use the same graph as above to analyze how factors that shift either the aggregate demand curve or the aggregate supply curve will affect the equilibrium level of prices and output.
- use the same graph to explain what kinds of shifts in the aggregate demand curve and the aggregate supply curve can give rise to a period of stagflation.
- explain why an inflationary gap is apt to self-destruct.
- explain why a recessionary gap is not apt to self-destruct.
- use the aggregate demand/aggregate supply diagram to show how increases in prices reduce the value of the multiplier.

## IMPORTANT TERMS AND CONCEPTS

Aggregate supply curve
Productivity
Equilibrium of real GDP and the price level
Inflationary gap
Self-correcting mechanism
Stagflation
Recessionary gap
Inflation and the multiplier

## CHAPTER REVIEW

In Chapter 4 we first learned that for individual commodities equilibrium price and quantity are determined by the intersection of the relevant demand and supply curves. The same logic holds when analyzing the economy as a whole. The level of prices and aggregate output is determined by the intersection of the aggregate demand and aggregate supply curves. In Chapter 25 we saw how the aggregate demand curve could be derived from analyzing how changes in the price level affect the spending decisions that underlie the expenditure schedule. In this chapter we will derive the aggregate supply curve and use both curves to show how the price level and a aggregate output are determined.

The aggregate supply curve is a schedule, showing for each possible price level, the total quantity of goods and services that all businesses are willing to supply during a specified period of time, holding all other factors influencing aggregate supply constant. You should note that the same logic applies here as to discussions of the supply decisions of individual firms. Businesses will adjust supply in pursuit of profits.

If prices rise while production costs per unit of output remain unchanged, we expect firms to
(1) (increase/decrease) output. In fact, if prices stayed higher and production costs did not increase at all, there would be no limit to the increase in profits firms could derive from increases in output. However, even if the prices of inputs do not increase, production costs will eventually rise as firms try to expand output, putting a limit on the profitable increase in output. (Remember that in the short run the supply curve for an individual firm is the upward sloping portion of the firm's marginal cost curve.) The increase in output induced by an increase in the price level is a (movement along/shift in) the aggregate supply curve. Any change in production costs in the face of an otherwise unchanged price level-for example, an increase in energy prices imposed by a foreign supplier or an increase in money wages–will also affect profits and will lead to an adjustment in the quantity of goods and services that businesses are willing to supply. This time, however, the change in supply is a _____ _____ the aggregate supply curve. The aggregate supply curve would also shift following a change in productivity or in the available supplies of labor or capital. For example, as investment increases the stock of capital, the aggregate supply curve will shift to the (left/right).

The increase in production costs associated with higher levels of output, the very increase that put a limit on the profitable increase in supply and helped to define the aggregate supply curve, is likely to be especially severe near full-employment levels of output and is an important reason why the slope of the aggregate supply curve depends upon the level of resource utilization. Near full employment, the
(2) aggregate supply curve is (steeper/flatter).

Now, having derived both the aggregate demand curve and the aggregate supply curve, we are in a position to use both to determine the final equilibrium level of prices and aggregate output, or GDP. See, for example, Figure 27-1, where the equilibrium price level of 100 and the equilibrium level of GDP
(3) of $6000 billion are given by the (intersection/slope) of the aggregate demand and supply curves. A higher price level, say, 110, implies (1) a lower quantity of aggregate demand as consumers respond to the loss of purchasing power of their money assets and net exports (increase/decrease) following the increase in domestic prices, and (2) a larger quantity of aggregate supply as firms respond to higher prices. Clearly, more supply and less demand cannot be a point of equilibrium, since firms would experience continual (increases/decreases) in inventories. The result is likely to be reduced output and price reductions that move the economy toward equilibrium. Similarly, a lower price level, such as 90, would induce analogous, although opposite, reactions.

Nothing in the analysis so far guarantees that the intersection of the aggregate demand and aggregate supply curves will be at the level of output corresponding to full employment. If the final equilibrium level of output is different from the full-employment level of output, the result is either a recessionary gap or
(4) an inflationary gap. Consider Figure 27-2, which shows a(n) _____ gap. The gap (is/is not) likely to self-destruct as continuing increases in the price of inputs lead to shifts in the aggregate supply curve. As unemployment falls below frictional levels and material inputs become scarce, higher input prices will shift the aggregate supply curve (inward/outward) leading to a (movement along/shift in) the aggregate demand curve, (higher/lower) prices, (higher/lower) output, and the elimination of the inflationary

FIGURE 27-1                    FIGURE 27-2

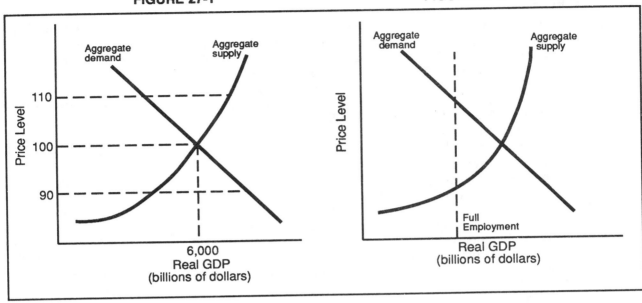

gap. Note that the simultaneous increase in prices and wages does not prove that increasing wages cause inflation. Both are best seen as a symptom of the original inflationary gap.

By contrast, the rigidity of wages and other input prices in the face of unemployment means that

(5) a recessionary gap is (<u>more/less</u>) likely to self-destruct than an inflationary gap.

*Stagflation* refers to the simultaneous occurrence of increasing prices and increasing employment. The previous analysis suggests that stagflation is a natural result of the self-destruction of a(n)

(6) (<u>inflationary/recessionary</u>) gap. Stagflation can also occur as a result of adverse shifts in the aggregate _____ curve.

## IMPORTANT TERMS AND CONCEPTS QUIZ

Choose the best definition for the following terms.

1. _____ Aggregate supply curve
2. _____ Productivity
3. _____ Self-correcting mechanism
4. _____ Stagflation

a. Economy's way of restoring equilibrium through inflation or deflation.
b. Amount of a given input required to produce a unit of output.
c. Graph of total quantity of goods and services produced at each possible price level.
d. Inflation that occurs while the economy is growing slowly or in recession.
e. Amount of output produced per unit of input.

## BASIC EXERCISES

1. This first exercise reviews the derivation of the aggregate demand curve and then uses both the aggregate demand and aggregate supply curves to determine the equilibrium level of income. Figure 27-3 shows an income–expenditure diagram in the top half and a price level–aggregate output diagram in the bottom half. The middle expenditure schedule in the top half duplicates the original situation described in Basic Exercise 1 of Chapter 26 and assumes that the price level with this expenditure schedule is 100. The dashed line extending into the bottom figure shows how this output level, together with its associated price level, can be plotted in the lower diagram. It is one point on the aggregate demand curve.

   a. A decrease in the price level to 90 would increase consumption spending because a reduction in prices (<u>decreases/increases</u>) the purchasing power of consumer money assets and increases net exports. The (<u>movement along/shift in</u>) the consumption function and the change in net exports shifts the expenditure schedule up. The new expenditure schedule, for a price level of 90, is shown in the top half of Figure 27-3. What is the equilibrium level of income in the income-expenditure diagram for a price level of 90?

   b. Plot the combination of prices and output from a in the lower diagram. This is a second point on the aggregate demand curve.

   c. A price level of 110 would depress consumer spending and net exports, shifting both the consumption function and the expenditure schedule. Use the expenditure schedule for a price level of 110 to plot a third point on the aggregate demand curve.

   d. Draw the aggregate demand curve by connecting the three points now plotted in the lower diagram.

   e. Using the aggregate demand curve you have just derived and the aggregate supply curve that is already drawn, what is the equilibrium level of prices and real GDP?

   f. If the level of full-employment output were $6 trillion, would there be an inflationary gap or recessionary gap? How, if at all, might such a gap self-destruct and where would the price level and real GDP end up?

   g. If the level of full-employment output were $6.125 trillion, would there be an inflationary gap or recessionary gap? How, if at all, might such a gap self-destruct and where would the price level and real GDP end up?

   h. If the level of full-employment output were $6.25 trillion, would there be an inflationary or recessionary gap? How, if at all, might such a gap self-destruct and where would the price level and real GDP end up?

2. This exercise reviews the impact of higher prices on the simple multiplier derived in Chapter 26. Consider Figure 27-4. The heavy lines show an initial expenditure schedule and the associated aggregate demand curve. The initial equilibrium is at a level of income $Y^*$, and price level $P^*$. The dashed expenditure schedule comes from an increase in investment spending. Note that the shift in the expenditure schedule leads to a shift in the aggregate demand curve. In fact, the initial new equilibrium on the income-expenditure diagram, $Y$, is equal to the (<u>horizontal/vertical</u>) shift of the aggregate demand curve in the lower half of the diagram.

   a. Is the combination $Y_1$, $P^*$ the final equilibrium?

   b. If $Y_1$, $P^*$ is not the final equilibrium, describe what will happen during the transition to the final equilibrium

## FIGURE 27-3

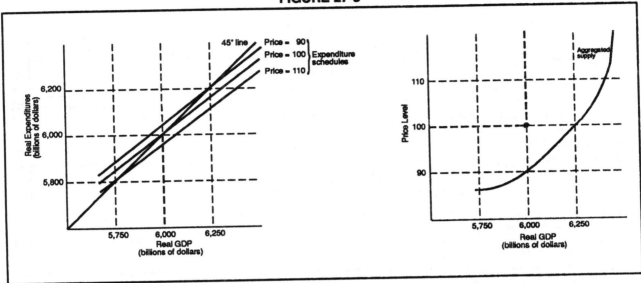

## FIGURE 27-4

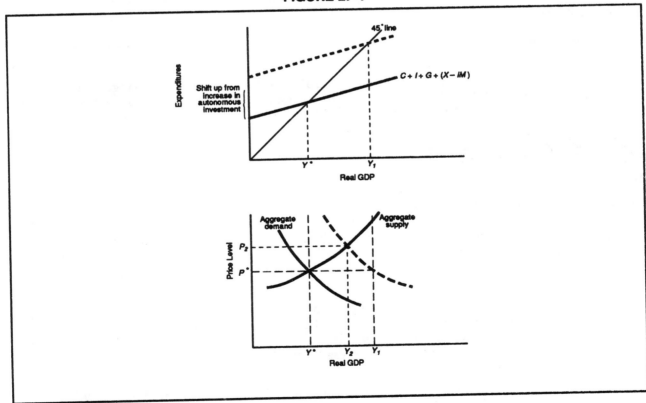

## TABLE 27-1

|  | Aggregate demand curve | Aggregate supply curve | Equilibrium real GDP | Price level |
|---|---|---|---|---|
| A reduction in business investment spending |  |  |  |  |
| An increase in the price of many basic commodities used as inputs in the production of final goods and services |  |  |  |  |
| An increase in the demand for exports caused by an economic boom abroad |  |  |  |  |
| An increase in the labor productivity due to a technological breakthrough |  |  |  |  |
| An upward shift in the consumption function due to a stock market boom |  |  |  |  |
| A large increase in energy prices |  |  |  |  |

3. In Table 27-1, fill in the blanks as indicated to analyze the response to each change. In the first two columns use S or M for "shift in" or "movement along." In the last two columns use + or –.

## SELF-TESTS FOR UNDERSTANDING

### Test A

Circle the most appropriate answer.

1. The aggregate supply curve
   a. slopes down to the right.
   b. has a positive slope.
   c. slopes up to the left.
   d. has a negative slope.

2. The slope of the aggregate supply curve reflects the fact that
   a. inflation reduces the value of the oversimplified multiplier.
   b. the costs of important inputs, such as labor, are relatively fixed in the short run.
   c. the marginal propensity to consume is less than 1.0.
   d. recessionary gaps take a long time to self-destruct.

3. The aggregate supply curve will shift following changes in all but which of the following?
   a. The price level.
   b. Wage rates.
   c. Technology and productivity.
   d. Available supplies of factories and machines.

4. The equilibrium price level and the equilibrium level of real GDP.
   a. are determined by the intersection of the aggregate demand, and aggregate supply curves.
   b. will always occur at full employment.
   c. can be found in the income-expenditure diagram.
   d. do not change unless the aggregate demand curve shifts.

5. A change in the equilibrium price level
   a. will lead to a shift in the aggregate supply curve.
   b. will lead to a shift in the aggregate demand curve.
   c. reflects a shift in the aggregate demand curve and/or aggregate supply curve.
   d. will always lead to stagflation.

6. A higher price level will lead to which of the following? (There may be more than one correct answer.)
   a. A reduction in the purchasing power of consumers' money fixed assets.
   b. A downward shift in the consumption function.
   c. An increase in imports.
   d. A decrease in exports.
   e. A downward shift in the expenditure schedule.

7. Near full employment, the slope of the aggregate supply curve is likely to
   a. become negative.
   b. drop to zero.
   c. decrease, but still remain positive.
   d. increase.

8. An inflationary gap occurs
   a. when the equilibrium level of GDP exceeds potential GDP.
   b. whenever there is an upward shift in the expenditure schedule.
   c. whenever aggregate supply exceeds aggregate demand.
   d. during periods of high unemployment.

9. From an initial position of full employment, which one of the following will not lead to a recessionary gap?
   a. A shift in the aggregate supply curve in response to an increase in energy prices.
   b. A reduction in investment spending due to an increase in business taxes.
   c. A reduction in consumer spending due to an adverse shift in consumer expectations.
   d. An increase in exports the follows a business expansion in Europe.

10. Which of the following is not associated with the elimination of an inflationary gap?
    a. Rising prices.
    b. Falling output.
    c. Increased employment.
    d. Increased unemployment.

11. Which of the following is most likely to lead to an inflationary gap?
    a. An increase in government purchases of goods and services to fight a recession.
    b. An increase in exports that occurs when unemployment rates are high.
    c. A significant increase in energy prices.
    d. Any increase in spending that shifts the aggregate demand curve to the right when GDP is at or beyond potential GDP.

12. The economy's self-correcting mechanisms are likely to work better when
    a. there is an inflationary gap.
    b. there is a recessionary gap.
    c. there is a federal government deficit.
    d. the multiplier is working.

13. Which of the following is most likely to lead to stagflation?
    a. An increase in aggregate demand that comes from an increase in government purchases of goods and services.
    b. An increase in exports that occurs when unemployment rates are high.
    c. A significant increase in energy prices.
    d. Any increase in spending that shifts the aggregate demand curve to the right when GDP is at or beyond potential GDP.

14. Which of the following lead to an increase in net exports? (There may be more than one correct answer.)
    a. Decrease in exports.
    b. Decrease in imports.
    c. Increase in imports.
    d. Increase in exports.

15. From an initial position of equilibrium, exports increase by $100 billion as both Japan and Europe experience business booms. This change will lead to which of the following? (There may be more than one correct answer.)
    a. An upward shift of the expenditure schedule.
    b. A shift to the right in the aggregate supply curve.
    c. A shift to the right in the aggregate demand curve.
    d. An increase in net exports.

16. At the new equilibrium following the increase in exports, American GDP will be _____ and the American price level will be _____.
    a. higher, lower
    b. lower, lower
    c. higher, higher
    d. lower, higher

17. There is likely to be a greater change in prices and a smaller change in output following the increase in exports if
    a. the initial position of equilibrium for the American economy is below potential GDP.
    b. the aggregate supply curve does not shift.
    c. there is an autonomous increase in savings.
    d. initial unemployment rates in the United States are low.

18. Year-to-year changes in GDP and prices are probably best seen as the result of
    a. shifts in the aggregate demand curve that move the economy along an unchanged aggregate supply curve.
    b. shifts in the aggregate supply curve that move the economy along an unchanged aggregate demand curve.
    c. shifts in the both the aggregate demand and aggregate supply curves.

19. Prices rise following an increase in autonomous spending whenever the
    a. aggregate demand curve shifts.
    b. multiplier is greater than 1.0.
    c. aggregate demand curve has a negative slope.
    d. aggregate supply curve is not horizontal.

20. The aggregate demand curve-aggregate supply curve diagram shows that the multiplier will be smaller on the income–expenditure diagram whenever
    a. the aggregate demand curve slopes down and to the right.
    b. the aggregate demand curve slopes up and to the right.
    c. the aggregate supply curve slopes up and to the right.
    d. the MPC is less than 1.0.

**Test B**

Circle T or F for true or false.

T F 1. The aggregate supply curve shows for each possible price the total quantity of goods and services that the nation's businesses are willing to supply.

T F 2. The aggregate supply curve slopes upward because businesses will expand output as long as higher prices make expansion profitable.

T F 3. The aggregate supply curve is likely to be steeper at low levels of unemployment.

T F 4. The impact of unemployment on wages and prices means that recessionary gaps are likely to quickly self-destruct.

T F 5. If the aggregate supply curve shifts inward, the result will be stagflation.

T F 6. The economy's self-correcting mechanisms insure that the aggregate demand and aggregate supply curves will always intersect at potential output.

T F 7. The final equilibrium level of prices and aggregate output is determined by the slope of the aggregate supply curve.

T F 8. A period of excessive aggregate demand is likely to be followed by a period of stagflation as the inflationary gap self-destructs.

T F 9. During the elimination of an inflationary gap, the real cause of inflation is excessive wage demands on the part of labor.

T F 10. Analysis of the aggregate supply curve shows that the multiplier derived from the income–expenditure diagram typically understates the final change in output.

## SUPPLEMENTARY EXERCISE

The following equations are consistent with Basic Exercise 1.

$$T = 800$$
$$DI = Y - T$$
$$C = 740 + .8DI - 3.5P$$
$$I = 800$$
$$G = 850$$
$$X - IM = -50 - 0.5P$$
$$C + I + G + (X - IM) = Y \text{ (45–degree line)}$$

Aggregate supply curve
$$Y = 3750 + 25P$$

$T$ = taxes
$DI$ = disposable income
$C$ = consumption expenditures
$I$ = investment expenditures
$G$ = government purchases
$X$ = exports
$IM$ = imports
$Y$ = GDP
$P$ = price level

1. Use the consumption function along with the level of investment spending, government purchases, and net exports to determine an expression for the expenditure schedule. (Don't forget to substitute for disposable income and note that this expression will involve the variable $P$.)

2. Use the expenditure schedule and the equation for the 45–degree line to determine an expression for the aggregate demand curve.

3. Now use both the aggregate demand curve and the aggregate supply curve to determine the equilibrium level of prices and GDP.

4. Resolve the system on the assumption that investment expenditures decrease to $750.

## ECONOMICS IN ACTION

### How Variable is the Aggregate Supply Curve?

What explains fluctuations in GDP—shifts in the aggregate demand curve or shifts in the aggregate supply curve? Keynesian analysis focuses on shifts in aggregate demand as the major source of fluctuations in output. On this view, the aggregate supply curve shifts out year by year more or less regularly and deviations from potential or full-employment output are the result of shifts in the aggregate demand curve that are greater or less than the shift in the aggregate supply curve. In recent years an alternative view has argued that the growth of potential output and the associated shifts in the aggregate supply curve may be less regular and more variable than had been suspected.

What difference does it make whether potential output grows smoothly or fluctuates from year to year? Estimates of potential output and the difference of actual output from potential are an important determinant of changes in fiscal and monetary policy. For example, when the economy is operating below potential, expansionary policies that increase aggregate demand can increase output and employment. If the aggregate supply curve is relatively flat to the left of full employment, the increase in output may have little impact on prices. The magnitude of changes in fiscal and monetary policy to increase aggregate demand will be influenced by estimates of the shortfall from potential output.

But if GDP is low in part because of an adverse shift in the aggregate supply curve, then expansionary policy that ignores the decrease in potential output could turn out to be too expansionary, push the economy above potential, and create unwanted inflationary pressures. On the other hand, if GDP increased above traditional estimates of potential output because of a favorable shift in the aggregate supply curve, stabilization policy that tried to reduce aggregate demand because of a concern about possible inflationary pressures would unnecessarily increase unemployment.

Why is it so difficult to figure out how the aggregate supply curve is shifting? As economists John Boschen and Leonard Mills point out, potential GDP is not directly observable. Neither is the aggregate demand curve or the aggregate supply curve. The level of output and prices that we observe give us information about where these curves intersect, but by themselves do not identify one curve or the other. In order to identify the aggregate supply curve one needs to use economic theory and make appropriate assumptions about factors that affect aggregate supply, just as we have done with regard to factors that affect aggregate demand. These theories of the aggregate supply curve are then tested by comparing implications of the models with data from the real world. Models of the aggregate supply curve are still in their infancy and estimates of the importance of supply-side factors in explaining fluctuations in output cover a wide range. Boschen and Mills surveyed recent attempts to model shifts in the aggregate supply curve. A number of these estimates suggest that a third of the variation in output might be attributed to variability in the growth of potential GDP while others range as high as 50 to 70 percent.

1. What are the implications for stabilization policy if fluctuations in the aggregate supply curve account for 10 percent or 50 percent of the fluctuations in output?

SOURCE: John Boschen and Leonard Mills, "Monetary Policy with a New View of Potential GNP," *Business Review*, Federal Reserve Bank of Philadelphia, (July/August 1990), pp. 3-10.

## STUDY QUESTIONS

1. Why is the aggregate supply curve drawn sloping upward to the right?
2. Why is the slope of the aggregate supply curve likely to get steeper as output increases?
3. What factors influence the position of the aggregate supply curve?
4. What market forces move the economy to the equilibrium level of output and prices given by the intersection of the aggregate demand curve and aggregate supply curve?

5. Evaluate the following statement: "All periods of inflation are caused by excessive demands for high wages on the part of labor."

6. What is the process by which an inflationary gap self-destructs?

7. Is an adverse supply shock likely to give rise to an inflationary gap or a recessionary gap? Why?

8. What are some of the reasons the economy's self-correcting mechanisms might not work as quickly in the face of a recessionary gap?

9. What is meant by stagflation and when is it likely to occur?

10. How do considerations of aggregate supply reduce the value of the multiplier calculated in Chapter 26?

11. Consider a shift in the expenditure schedule, say due to a $100 billion increase in exports. Which increase in net exports would have the largest multiplier impact on the economy, one that occurs when unemployment rates are high and GDP is less than potential GDP or the same increase in exports that occurs at a time when GDP is close to potential? Why?

*Chapter* **28**

# Managing the Economy with Fiscal Policy

## LEARNING OBJECTIVES

After completing this chapter you should be able to:

- describe the process by which a change in government purchases of goods and services will lead to a shift in the aggregate demand curve.

- describe the process by which a change in taxes will lead to a shift in the aggregate demand curve.

- explain why taxes that depend upon income reduce the value of the multiplier below the over-simplified expression in Chapter 26.

- show on an income-expenditure diagram how a change from fixed to variable taxes affects the slope of the expenditure schedule.

- explain why the multiplier for a change in income taxes will be less than the multiplier for a change in government purchases of goods and services.

- explain why economists treat government transfer payments like taxes, not like govern-ment purchases of goods and services.

- describe the process by which a change in government transfer payments will lead to a shift in the aggregate demand curve.

- explain why active stabilization policy need not imply that government must get bigger and bigger.

- use the aggregate demand and supply diagram to show how supply-side tax cuts hope to reduce the impact on prices associated with the elimination of a recessionary gap.

- describe the kernel of truth in supply-side economics.

- discuss the reservations that most economists have in regard to supply-side economics.

## IMPORTANT TERMS AND CONCEPTS

Fiscal policy
Fixed taxes
Variable taxes
Government transfer payments
Effect of income taxes on the multiplier
Supply-side tax cuts

## CHAPTER REVIEW

The models of income determination in earlier chapters included a rather passive government. This chapter uses a more realistic model of taxes and provides a framework for considering how and when the government should vary spending and taxes. The government's plans for spending and taxes are called
(1) (fiscal/monetary) policy. The only trick is to understand how government spending and taxes affect the curves we have already derived, that is, how government spending and taxes affect the expenditure schedule, the aggregate demand curve, and the aggregate supply curve. After this, the analysis proceeds exactly as before: For a given price level, the equilibrium level of income on the income-expenditure diagram is determined by the intersection of the (consumption/expenditure) schedule and the 45-degree line. A change in prices will affect consumption spending and net exports. The different price levels and the associated equilibrium levels of income on the income-expenditure diagram can be combined to form the aggregate _____ curve. This curve together with the aggregate _____ curve will determine the final equilibrium for income and prices, just as before. A change in the government's fiscal policy will shift one or more of the curves and lead to new equilibrium values for income and prices.

There are three important ways government fiscal policy influences total spending in the economy:

1. The government *purchases goods* and *services*.

2. The government *collects taxes*, reducing the spending power of households and firms. Particular taxes may affect incentives for working, saving, investing or spending.

3. The government gives *transfer payments* to some individuals, thereby increasing their purchasing power.

Government purchases of goods and services are a direct addition to total spending in the economy;
(2) that is, they shift the expenditure schedule (up/down) by the full amount of the purchases. Thus, if government spending increased by $1, the expenditure schedule would shift up by $_____. (An increase in autonomous investment spending or exports of $1 would also shift the expenditure schedule up by $_____.) Thus, changes in government spending shift the expenditure schedule in exactly the same way as other changes in autonomous spending and should have similar multiplier effects.

(3)     Government taxes (are/are not) a direct component of spending on currently produced goods and services. Personal income taxes affect consumption spending through their impact on disposable income. Following a decrease in personal income taxes, consumers' disposable income will be (higher/lower). The initial effect on consumption spending will depend in part on whether consumers view the tax change as permanent or temporary. The largest impact will come from a (permanent/temporary) tax cut. The change in consumption spending will be determined by the marginal _____ to consume which is (less than/equal to/greater than) 1.0. Thus, changes in personal income taxes affect spending, but indirectly through their effect on consumption expenditures. A change in corporate income taxes will change corporate profits after taxes, and is likely to affect _____ expenditures.

The third important function of the government regarding total spending in the economy is the magnitude of government transfer payments. These payments, like taxes, are not a direct element of total spending on goods and services. Also, like personal taxes, they affect total spending because they affect
(4) people's disposable _____ and thus their _____ expenditures. Remember that taxes are earned but not received while transfers are received but not earned. Thus in the models we will be working with, disposable income is equal to GDP (–/+) taxes (–/+) transfers and transfers can be thought of as negative taxes.

An important feature of income taxes (and some transfer payments) is that they vary with GDP.
(5) Typically taxes go (down/up) as GDP goes up. If taxes change whenever income changes they are called _____ taxes. Taxes that do not change when GDP changes are called _____ taxes. Understanding the difference between fixed and variable taxes is important for understanding how to model changes in taxes on the income-expenditure diagram and for understanding how income taxes affect the value of the multiplier.

In Chapter 26 we saw that the multiplier process arises because any autonomous increase in spending means higher income for those who supply the newly demanded goods. These higher incomes will lead to more consumption spending, and so on, and so on. This process continues to take place, but now we see that each round of spending results in an increase in income *before* taxes. Because some of the increase in before-tax income goes to pay higher taxes, after-tax income (or disposable income) will increase by

**(6)** (more/less). Thus, each induced round of consumption spending, responding to the increase in disposable income, will be (smaller/larger) than before.

To summarize, in an economy with income taxes (and transfer payments) that vary with income, each round in the multiplier process will be smaller than before, and thus the multiplier effect on income,

**(7)** from any increase in automatic spending, will be (smaller/larger) than before. The impact of income taxes on the multiplier is another important reason why the formula for the multiplier in Chapter 26 was oversimplified.

We can see these same results graphically on the income-expenditure diagram. In Chapter 26 we assumed that taxes did not vary with income, that is the model of Chapter 26 considered only fixed taxes. A $1 change in GDP meant a $1 increase in disposable income and led to an increase in consumption spending given by the MPC. Since in the model of Chapter 26 consumption spending was the only type of spending that changed when GDP changed, the slope of the expenditure schedule was equal to the

**(8)** _____. Now when we consider the impact of variable taxes, we see that a $1 increase in GDP leads to a(n) (smaller/equal/larger) increase in disposable income and a(n) _____ increase in consumption spending as compared with the case of fixed taxes. The result is that increases in GDP are associated with smaller increases in total spending and a (flatter/steeper) expenditure schedule. As we saw in Chapter 26, the multiplier can be derived from the slope of the expenditure schedule. A flatter expenditure schedule means a smaller multiplier.

Modeling the impact of a change in taxes will depend upon whether the change is in the fixed or variable component of taxes. A reduction in fixed taxes would increase disposable income, and thus consumption, by the same amount at every level of GDP. Thus, it can be modeled as a parallel shift in the expenditure schedule. A change in variable taxes would be a change in the tax rate. A reduction in variable taxes means less of any increase in income goes for taxes and more ends up in disposable income. The larger change in disposable income means that a given change in GDP will be associated with a larger change in consumption spending. The result is that a change in variable taxes leads to a change in the slope of the expenditure schedule. Following a reduction in tax rates the expenditure schedule would

**(9)** become (flatter/steeper).

Let us be more specific about how we can model a change in the fixed component of taxes. (Changes in transfer payments will have similar but opposite effects since transfer payments can be viewed as negative taxes.) We saw earlier that a $1 change in government purchases will shift the expenditure schedule by $1. Consider a permanent $1 reduction in the fixed component of income taxes. What is the magnitude of the initial shift of the expenditure schedule that initiates the multiplier process? At the initial equilibrium level of income, the reduction in income taxes will increase dispos-

**(10)** able income and increase _____ spending. It is this initial impact on spending that determines the magnitude of the shift in the expenditure schedule. Our discussion of the consumption function in Chapter 24 showed that a $1 increase in disposable income will increase consumption spending by less than $1 because the _____ is (less than/equal to/greater than) 1.0. The result is that a $1 change in the fixed component of taxes shifts the expenditure schedule by (less/more) than a $1 change in government purchases. As a result, the multiplier associated with changes in income taxes will be (larger/smaller) than the multiplier associated with changes in government purchases.

We have added government purchases of goods and services, taxes, and transfers to our model of income determination. Taken together, these variables are an important determinant of the equilibrium level of income. Changes in these variables, just like the autonomous changes we considered in earlier chapters, will have multiplier effects on the equilibrium level of GDP. Thus deliberate manipulation of these variables may help the government achieve its desired objectives for GDP and prices. Manipulation of government fiscal policy variables for GDP objectives is an example of stabilization policy. For example,

(11)   if the government wants to increase GDP, it can decide to (<u>increase/decrease</u>) government purchases of goods and services, _____ personal taxes, _____ corporate taxes, or _____ transfer payments to individuals.

   One of the reasons it is so difficult to agree on fiscal policy is that there are so many choices, all of which could have the same impact on national income, but very different impacts on other issues, such as the size of the public versus private sector, the burden of taxes between individuals and corporations, the composition of output between consumption and investment spending, and the amount of income redistribution through transfers to low-income families.

   One might believe that if we could decide upon the amounts of government purchases, taxes, and transfers, effective fiscal policy would be simply a technical matter of choosing the right numbers so that the expenditure schedule would intersect the 45–degree line, and the aggregate demand curve would intersect the aggregate supply curve at full-employment. In actuality, uncertainties about (1) private components of aggregate demand, (2) the precise size of the multiplier, (3) exactly what level of GDP is associated with full employment, and (4) the slope of the aggregate supply curve all mean that fiscal policy will continue to be subject to much political give and take. One hopes that appropriate economic analysis will contribute to a more informed level of debate.

   Changes in government spending or tax rates shift the aggregate demand curve directly, in the case of government purchases, and indirectly through impacts on private spending, in the case of taxes and transfer payments. Any shift in the aggregate demand curve, including government shifts, affects both
(12)   prices and output as we move along the aggregate _____ curve. Thus, expansionary fiscal policy, designed to increase GDP, is also likely to (<u>increase/decrease</u>) prices. Supply-side policies attempt to minimize the impact on prices through changes in fiscal policy that shift the aggregate supply curve at the same time that they shift the aggregate demand curve. Recently there has been much attention given to supply-side tax cuts, including such measures as speeding up depreciation allowances, reducing taxes for increased research and development expenditures, reducing the corporate income tax, reducing taxes on income from savings, reducing taxes on capital gains, and reducing income taxes to encourage more work effort.

   Most economists have a number of reservations about the exaggerated claims of ardent supporters of supply-side tax cuts: Specific effects will depend on exactly which taxes are reduced; increases in aggregate supply are likely to take some time, while effects on aggregate demand will be much quicker. A realistic assessment suggests that by themselves supply-side tax cuts are likely to lead to increased income inequality and to bigger, not smaller, government budget deficits. Do not let these serious objections to exaggerated claims blind you to the kernel of truth in supply-side economics: Marginal tax rates are important for decisions by individuals and firms. Reductions in marginal tax rates can improve economic incentives.

---

## IMPORTANT TERMS AND CONCEPTS QUIZ

Choose the best definition for the following terms.

1. _____ Fiscal policy
2. _____ Fixed taxes
3. _____ Variable taxes
4. _____ Government transfer payments
5. _____ Supply-side tax cuts

a. Tax deductions that businesses may claim when they invest.
b. Money the government gives to individuals in the form of outright grants.
c. Taxes that do not change when GDP changes
d. The government's plan for spending and taxes.
e. Tax policy designed to shift the aggregate supply curve to the right.
f. Taxes that change when GDP changes.

## BASIC EXERCISE

This exercise is designed to show how changes in government purchases and taxes will have multiplier effects on the equilibrium level of income and how these multipliers can be used to help determine appropriate fiscal policy. To simplify the numerical calculations, the exercise focuses on the shift in the expenditure schedule, holding prices constant. That is, we will consider how changes in fiscal policy shift the aggregate demand curve. Table 28-1 has data on GDP, taxes, disposable income, consumption investment, government spending, exports and imports. This table is the same as Table 26-1 except that here taxes vary with income while in Table 26-1 they did not. Alternatively one could say that Table 28-1 considers an economy with variable taxes while Table 26-1 assumed that taxes were fixed taxes.

1. Complete the column for total spending to verify that the initial equilibrium level of income is the same as you found in Table 26-1.

   Equilibrium level of GDP _____

2. Assume now that government purchases decrease by $200 to $650 as shown in Table 28-2. Following the decrease in government purchases, the new equilibrium level of income is _____.

### TABLE 28-1
### (CONSTANT PRICES)

| Income (Output) Y | Taxes T | Disposable Income DI | Consumption Spending C | Investment Spending I | Government Purchases G | Exports X | Imports IM | Total Spending C + I + G + (X − IM) |
|---|---|---|---|---|---|---|---|---|
| 5,500 | 675.0 | 4,825.0 | 4,200 | 800 | 850 | 500 | 650 | _____ |
| 5,750 | 737.5 | 5,012.5 | 4,350 | 800 | 850 | 500 | 650 | _____ |
| 6,000 | 800.0 | 5,200.0 | 4,500 | 800 | 850 | 500 | 650 | _____ |
| 6,250 | 862.5 | 5,387.5 | 4,650 | 800 | 850 | 500 | 650 | _____ |
| 6,500 | 925.0 | 5,575.0 | 4,800 | 800 | 850 | 500 | 650 | _____ |
| 6,750 | 987.5 | 5,762.5 | 4,950 | 800 | 850 | 500 | 650 | _____ |
| 7,000 | 1,050.0 | 5,950.0 | 5,100 | 800 | 850 | 500 | 650 | _____ |

### TABLE 28-2
### (CONSTANT PRICES)

| Income (Output) Y | Taxes T | Disposable Income DI | Consumption Spending C | Investment Spending I | Government Purchases G | Exports X | Imports IM | Total Spending C + I + G + (X − IM) |
|---|---|---|---|---|---|---|---|---|
| 5,500 | 675.0 | 4,825.0 | 4,200 | 800 | 650 | 500 | 650 | _____ |
| 5,750 | 737.5 | 5,012.5 | 4,350 | 800 | 650 | 500 | 650 | _____ |
| 6,000 | 800.0 | 5,200.0 | 4,500 | 800 | 650 | 500 | 650 | _____ |
| 6,250 | 862.5 | 5,387.5 | 4,650 | 800 | 650 | 500 | 650 | _____ |
| 6,500 | 925.0 | 5,575.0 | 4,800 | 800 | 650 | 500 | 650 | _____ |
| 6,750 | 987.5 | 5,762.5 | 4,950 | 800 | 650 | 500 | 650 | _____ |
| 7,000 | 1,050.0 | 5,950.0 | 5,100 | 800 | 650 | 500 | 650 | _____ |

**TABLE 28-3**
**(CONSTANT PRICES)**

| Income (Output) Y | Taxes T | Disposable Income DI | Consumption Spending C | Investment Spending I | Government Purchases G | Exports X | Imports IM | Total Spending C + I + G + (X − IM) |
|---|---|---|---|---|---|---|---|---|
| 5,500 | 425.0 | 5,075.0 | 4,400 | 800 | 650 | 500 | 650 | _____ |
| 5,750 | 487.5 | 5,262.5 | 4,550 | 800 | 650 | 500 | 650 | _____ |
| 6,000 | 550.0 | 5,450.0 | 4,700 | 800 | 650 | 500 | 650 | _____ |
| 6,250 | 612.5 | 5,637.5 | 4,850 | 800 | 650 | 500 | 650 | _____ |
| 6,500 | 675.0 | 5,825.0 | 5,000 | 800 | 650 | 500 | 650 | _____ |
| 6,750 | 737.5 | 6,012.5 | 5,150 | 800 | 650 | 500 | 650 | _____ |
| 7,000 | 800.0 | 6,200.0 | 5,300 | 800 | 650 | 500 | 650 | _____ |

3. The multiplier for this decrease in government purchases is _____ (This multiplier can be computed by dividing the change in the equilibrium level of income by the change in government purchases.)

4. Now consider a subsequent across-the-board reduction in income taxes of $250. Table 28-3 shows the new relevant data for national income, taxes, disposable income, and consumption. The new equilibrium level of income after the reduction in taxes is

   _____.

5. The multiplier for the across-the-board change in taxes is _____.

6. Why did it take a larger reduction in taxes to restore GDP to its initial level following the reduction in government purchases?

7. Question 4 asked you to analyze the impact of a reduction in income taxes. Was this reduction in taxes self-financing? That is, was the increase in GDP stimulated by the reduction in taxes large enough so that on balance there was no decrease in government tax revenues? (Be sure to compare tax receipts at the equilibrium level of income in Table 28-2 with those at the equilibrium in Table 28-3.)

8. Now let us use the multipliers computed in questions 3 and 5 to figure out what changes in government purchases or taxes would be necessary to raise the equilibrium level of income from its initial value given in question 1 to its full-employment level of $6,250. Assuming no change in tax rates, the necessary increase in government purchases is $_____ billion. Assuming no change in government purchases, the necessary reduction in taxes is $_____. (You can answer these questions by figuring out what appropriate change in government purchases or taxes, when multiplied by the relevant multiplier, will equal the desired change in income.) How would you choose between using changes in government purchases of goods and services on the one hand and reductions in taxes on the other?

9. What is the new equilibrium level of income if, from the initial equilibrium given in question 1, investment expenditures rather than government purchases fall by $200? (Now investment spending will be $600 while government purchases stay at $650. Create a new version of Table 28-1 if necessary.) What can one say about multipliers for autonomous changes in public versus private purchases of goods and services?

# SELF-TESTS FOR UNDERSTANDING

## Test A

Circle the most appropriate answer.

1. Fiscal policy involves decisions about all but which one of the following?
   a. Income tax rates.
   b. Eligibility rules for transfer payments.
   c. The money supply.
   d. Government purchases of goods and services.

2. The impact of transfer payments on disposable income suggests that an increase in transfer payments will have the same effect as
   a. an increase in taxes.
   b. an increase in government purchases of goods and services.
   c. a decrease in government purchases of goods and services.
   d. a decrease in taxes.

3. A simultaneous reduction in income taxes and transfer payments of $15 billion will leave aggregate disposable income
   a. lower than before the change.
   b. unchanged.
   c. higher than before the change.

4. Fixed taxes
   a. do not vary with GDP.
   b. increase whenever GDP increases.
   c. are the best way to model income taxes in the American economy.
   d. will be a constant proportion of GDP.

5. Variable taxes mean that the difference between GDP and disposable income will _____ as GDP increases.
   a. decrease
   b. stay the same
   c. increase

6. With fixed taxes, when other categories of aggregate demand—investment spending, net exports, government purchases—do not vary with GDP, the slope of the expenditure schedule will be
   a. less than the MPC.
   b. equal to the MPC.
   c. greater than the MPC.

7. With variable taxes, when other categories of aggregate demand—investment spending, net exports, government purchases—do not vary with GDP, the slope of the expenditure schedule will be
   a. less than the marginal propensity to consume.
   b. equal to the marginal propensity to consume.
   c. greater than the marginal propensity to consume.

8. The initial impact of a change in income taxes is on _____ and
   _____.
   a. imports, exports
   b. disposable income, investment
   c. GDP, consumption
   d. disposable income, consumption

9. A change in fixed taxes can be modeled as
   a. a shift in the consumption function.
   b. a twist of the expenditure schedule.
   c. a parallel shift in the expenditure schedule.
   d. a change in the MPC.

10. Equal reductions in government purchases and taxes are likely to
    a. shift the expenditure schedule down.
    b. leave the expenditure schedule unchanged.
    c. shift the expenditure schedule up.

11. Equal increases in transfer payments and taxes are likely to
    a. reduce aggregate demand at all levels of GDP.
    b. have equal and offsetting impacts on aggregate demand for no net impact.
    c. increase aggregate demand at all levels of GDP.

12. If the basic expenditure multiplier is 2.0 and if the government wishes to decrease the level of GDP by $80 billion, what decrease in government purchases of goods and services would do the job?
    a. $20 billion.
    b. $40 billion.
    c. $80 billion.
    d. $160 billion.

13. Instead of decreasing government expenditures, the same objectives, in terms of reducing GDP, could also be achieved by
    a. reducing government transfer payments.
    b. reducing taxes.
    c. increasing both taxes and government transfer payments by equal amounts.
    d. reducing both taxes and government transfer payments by equal amounts.

14. If the basic expenditure multiplier is 2.0, a reduction in personal income taxes of $25 billion is likely to
    a. increase GDP by $50 billion.
    b. increase GDP by more than $50 billion.
    c. increase GDP by less than $50 billion.

15. A 10 percent reduction in income tax rates would
    a. lower the value of the basic expenditure multiplier.
    b. raise the value of the basic expenditure multiplier.
    c. not affect the value of the basic expenditure multiplier.

16. An increase in tax rates will lead to all but which one of the following?
    a. A decrease in the multiplier.
    b. A movement along the aggregate demand curve.
    c. A reduction in the equilibrium level of GDP.
    d. A shift of the expenditure schedule.

17. Assume that from a position of full employment the government wants to reduce defense spending by $50 billion in response to an easing of international tensions. To avoid a possible recession, the government simultaneously decides to reduce income taxes. The necessary change in taxes to keep the equilibrium level of income unchanged is
    a. less than $50 billion.
    b. $50 billion.
    c. more than $50 billion.

18. Political conservatives could still argue for active stabilization policy as long as the government agreed to _____ during periods of boom and _____ during recessions.
    a. increase taxes; increase government spending
    b. increase government spending; lower taxes
    c. lower government spending; lower taxes
    d. lower taxes; increase government spending

19. Which one of the following is *not* an example of supply-side policies?
    a. Lowering the corporate income tax rate.
    b. Establishing tax-free retirement savings accounts.
    c. Reducing tax rates on capital gains.
    d. Requiring firms to depreciate assets over a longer rather than a shorter period of time.

20. Critics of supply-side tax cuts would agree with all but which one of the following?
    a. Supply-side tax cuts are likely to increase inequality in the distribution of income.
    b. Supply-side tax cuts will substantially reduce the rate of inflation.
    c. Supply-side tax cuts are likely to mean bigger deficits for the federal government.
    d. Supply-side tax cuts will have a larger initial impact on aggregate demand than on aggregate supply.

## Test B

Circle T or F for true or false.

T  F  1.  An increase in income tax rates will increase the multiplier.

T  F  2.  With income taxes, a $1 change in GDP will lead to a smaller change in consumption than would a $1 change in disposable income.

T  F  3.  Income taxation reduces the value of the multiplier for changes in government purchases but does not affect the multiplier for changes in investment.

T  F  4.  Since taxes are not a direct component of aggregate demand, changes in taxes do not have multiplier effects of income.

T  F  5.  Changes in government purchases of goods and services and in government transfer payments to individuals are both changes in government spending and thus have the same multiplier effects on the equilibrium level of income.

T  F  6.  A reduction in taxes matched by an equal reduction in government purchases of goods and services is likely to leave the expenditure schedule unchanged.

T  F  7.  Active stabilization policy implies that the government must get bigger and bigger.

T  F  8.  Since income taxes and transfer payments to individuals have their first impact on the disposable income of consumers, they should have similar multipliers.

T  F  9.  Only the aggregate supply curve will shift following a supply-side tax cut that increases investment spending by firms.

T  F  10.  There is general agreement among economists that supply-side tax cuts will increase output with little impact on prices.

## SUPPLEMENTARY EXERCISES

1. In his analysis of the impact of the 1964 tax cut, which reduced taxes on a permanent basis, Arthur Okun estimated that the MPC was 0.95.[1] At the same time, Okun estimated that the basic expenditure multiplier, applicable for any increase in autonomous spending, was only 2.73, not 20, which comes from the oversimplified formula of Chapter 26. (1/(1 − MPC). How can such a large MPC be consistent with such a small multiplier?

2. The 1964 reduction in personal taxes was about $10 billion. Okun estimated that this tax reduction raised GDP by $25.9 billion. The ratio of the change in GDP to the change in taxes was only 2.59, not 2.73, the value of the basic expenditure multiplier. How can you account for this discrepancy? (*Hint:* In his analysis, Okun assumed prices did not change, so price effects on consumption expenditures are not part of the answer. You should think about whether the basic expenditure multiplier—the multiplier for a shift in the expenditure schedule—is the appropriate multiplier to apply directly to the change in taxes.)

3. What is it like to advise the President of the United States about economic policy? Martin S. Feldstein was Chairman of the Council of Economic Advisers during the Reagan administration. You might enjoy reading his observations on the workings of the Council and the Chair of the Council, "The Council of Economic Advisers and Economic Advising in the United States," *The Economic Journal*, September 1992, pages 1223-1234.

---

[1]Arthur M. Okun, :Measuring the Impact of the 1964 Tax Cut." in W.W. Heller, ed., *Perspectives on Economic Growth* (New York: Vintage Books, 1968), pages 25-49.

# Appendix: Algebraic Treatment of Fiscal Policy and Aggregate Demand

## BASIC EXERCISE

This exercise is meant to illustrate the material in the Appendix to Chapter 28. Just as in the Appendix to Chapter 25, we can use equations rather than graphs or tables to determine the equilibrium level of output and relevant multipliers. If we have done our work accurately, we should get the same answer regardless of whether we use graphs, tables, or algebra.

The following equations underlie the numerical example in the Basic Exercise.

$$
\begin{aligned}
C &= 340 + 0.8DI \\
T &= -700 + 0.25Y \\
DI &= Y - T \\
Y &= C + I + G + (X - IM)
\end{aligned}
$$

1. What is the equilibrium level of income if investment spending is $800 billion, net exports are $150 billion, and government purchases are $650 billion? Be sure that $C + I + G + (X–IM) = Y$

2. Assume that both across-the-board taxes and government purchases decline by $50 billion so that government purchases are $600 billion and the tax equation is

$$T = -750 + 0.25Y$$

Is the equilibrium level of income unchanged following the balanced reduction in the size of the government? Why? What about the government deficit $(G - T)$?

---

3. What is the multiplier for the following:
   - change in investment spending
   - change in net exports
   - change in government purchases
   - change in taxes (that is, change in intercept of tax equation)

## STUDY QUESTIONS

1. How does the multiplier for a change in government spending compare to the multipliers in earlier chapters for changes in investment spending, net exports, and the autonomous component of consumption spending?

2. Consider a change from fixed to variable taxes. Does this change make the multiplier larger or smaller? Why?

3. How does one show the impact on the expenditure schedule of a change from fixed taxes to variable taxes?

4. Consider a change in taxes. How does one show the change in the expenditure schedule when the change in taxes is a change in fixed taxes? When it is a change in the tax rate underlying variable taxes?

5. Why wouldn't an equal increase in government purchases and taxes leave aggregate demand unchanged?

6. If you were charged with recommending changes in government purchases, taxes and transfers to shift the aggregate demand curve to the right, what sorts of changes in each of these elements of fiscal policy would do the job?

7. How would you choose between the alternatives you proposed when answering question 6?

8. Why is designing fiscal policy to achieve full-employment subject to such intense political debate rather than being a technical exercise best left to economists?

9. "Active stabilization policy—the deliberate use of fiscal policy to avoid recessions and inflation—must inevitably lead to bigger and bigger government." Do you agree or disagree? Why?

10. What are some examples of supply-sides tax cuts? Explain how and why each of your examples is expected to affect the aggregate supply curve.

11. If supply-side tax cuts could increase the equilibrium level of output without increasing prices they would be a superior instrument for short-run stabilization policy. Are supply-side tax cuts likely to work in this way? Why or why not? If not, what are supply-side tax cuts good for?

## ECONOMICS IN ACTION

### Tax Rates and Tax Revenue

In the spring and summer of 1993, as Congress considered President Clinton's deficit reduction proposals, a spirited debate took place about the link between tax rates and tax revenues. In the early 1980s supply-siders had argued that a reduction in tax rates would actually increase tax revenues. In 1993 the question was whether an increase in tax rates on the wealthiest taxpayers would increase tax revenues.

Kurt Hauser, an investment counselor in San Francisco, writing in the *Wall Street Journal*, argued that changes in tax rates have made no difference in federal revenues. Mr. Hauser argued that, despite numerous changes in the federal tax code and reductions in the top marginal tax rate for personal income from 92 percent to 28 percent, total federal government revenues—personal, corporate, social security, and other federal taxes—had varied only slightly from the historical average of 19.5 percent of GDP. He found no correlation between changes in tax rates and changes in federal revenue as a proportion of GDP. As for President Clinton's proposals, Mr. Hauser offered the prediction that within a couple of quarters, federal revenues would adjust to the historic 19.5 percent level.

Laura Tyson, Professor of Economics at Berkeley and chair of the President's Council of Economic Advisers, took exception to Mr. Hauser's argument. Focusing on revenues from personal income taxes, Tyson argued that tax revenues were responsive to changes in tax rates. Looking just at personal income tax receipts as a proportion of GDP, Tyson argued that its ups and downs were correlated with changes in tax rates. Specifically she argued that although other factors influence tax revenues, a strong and statistically significant relationship exists between the marginal tax rate for a hypothetical family of four that earns twice the median income and personal income tax revenues as a proportion of GDP.

It should be noted that the changes in taxes finally adopted in the summer of 1993 included increased income tax rates for a limited number of taxpayers: the proportion of social security income subject to tax was increased for social security recipients with significant other income, and the marginal tax rate was increased for the wealthiest taxpayers. A number of economists argued that the Clinton administration had overestimated the likely increase in revenue from these changes. In their opinion, tax-free municipal bonds, stock options instead of salary, deferred compensation along with adjustments in work effort, and tax reducing deductions can all be manipulated to minimize taxes. For most taxpayers the return to such tax avoidance strategies is quite small. When marginal tax rates become high enough and when there is a significant difference between the tax rate on regular income and capital gains, there can be a significant incentive for the wealthiest taxpayers to consider these strategies. Economist Robert Barro saw confirmation of such behavior when he noted that from 1981 to 1990 the proportion of taxes paid by the top one-half of one percent of the income distribution (about $220,000 in 1991) increased as marginal tax rates for the wealthiest taxpayers declined, tax loopholes were closed, and the difference between tax rates on regular income and capital gains was eliminated.

   1. What has happened to total tax revenues and the proportion of taxes paid by the wealthiest taxpayers?

SOURCES: "The Tax and Revenue Equation," W. Kurt Hauser, *Wall Street Journal*, May 7, 1993.
    "Higher Taxes, Lower Revenues," Robert J. Barro, *Wall Street Journal*, July 9, 1993.
    "Higher Taxes Do So Raise Money," Laura Tyson, *Wall Street Journal*, August 3, 1993.

# Money and the Banking System

## LEARNING OBJECTIVES

After completing this chapter you should be able to:

♦ distinguish between various functions of money. Which are unique to money? Which are shared with other assets?

♦ distinguish between commodity money and fiat money.

♦ explain the differences between M1 and M2 as measures of money.

♦ describe the historical origins of fractional reserve banking and explain why the industry is so heavily regulated today.

♦ explain how the banking system as a whole can create deposits, given an initial injection of bank reserves.

♦ use the required reserve fraction to derive the oversimplified deposit creation multiplier.

♦ explain why the deposit creation multiplier, based on the required reserve fraction, is oversimplified.

## IMPORTANT TERMS AND CONCEPTS

Run on a bank
Barter
Unit of account
Money
Medium of exchange
Store of value
Fiat money
Commodity money
Ml versus M2
Near moneys
Liquidity

Fractional reserve banking
Deposit insurance
Federal Deposit Insurance Corporation (FDIC)
Required reserves
Asset
Liability
Balance sheet
Net worth
Deposit creation
Excess reserves

## CHAPTER REVIEW

Whether it is the root of all evil or not, there is no argument that money has an important influence on the way our economy operates. The right amount of money can help to keep employment up and prices stable. Too much money may lead to excessive inflation; too little money may lead to excessive unemployment. This chapter is an introduction to money. What is it? Where did it come from? What role do banks play in the creation of money? Chapter 30 discusses how the government now regulates the amount of money in the economy, and Chapter 31 discusses the influence of money on economic activity.

It is possible that a society could be organized without money. If everyone were self-sufficient there would, by definition, be no trading between individuals and no need for money. Even if people concentrated their productive activities on what they did best and traded with each other to get goods they did not produce themselves, they might still be able to get along without money. Direct trading of goods for

(1) goods, or goods for services, is called _____. For it to be successful there must be a double coincidence of wants. As societies become more complicated and people become ever more specialized, it is clear that barter becomes (<u>less difficult/more difficult</u>).

When a society uses a standard object for exchanging goods and services, a seller will provide goods or services to a buyer and receive the standard object as payment. The efficiency of such a system should be obvious. You no longer have to find someone who not only has what you want but also wants what you have. Anyone who has what you want will now do. Economists would call the standard object

(2) _____. If the object serving as money has intrinsic value, such as gold or jewelry, it is called _____ money. When objects serve as money it is useful that they are divisible, of uniform quality, durable, storable at little or no cost, and compact. Many commodity monies fail on one or more of these criteria. Today money has little intrinsic value and is called _____ money. Such money has value because everyone believes that everyone else will exchange goods and services for it. The bedrock for this foundation of faith is that the government will stand behind the money and limit its production.

When it comes to measuring the quantity of money, exactly where one draws the line is a bit unclear. We have defined money as a standard object used for exchanging goods and services. On this count, the sum of all coins and currency outside of banks plus the wide variety of checking accounts at banks and credit unions surely belongs in any measure of money. The measure that includes only these items is

(3) known as _____. If one also includes savings accounts (because they can easily be transferred into checking accounts), money market deposit accounts, and money market mutual funds, one is measuring _____.

Below are some data for December 1992.

| | |
|---|---:|
| Currency | $292.3 billion |
| Travelers checks | 8.1 billion |
| Checkable deposits | 726.1 billion |
| Savings deposits including money market deposit accounts | 2,056.2 billion |
| Money market mutual funds plus other deposit type securities | 414.3 billion |

SOURCE: H.6 Statistical Release, Board of Governors of the Federal Reserve System, June 3, 1993.

How big is

(4) M1? $_____ billion.

M2? $_____ billion.

Given the importance of bank deposits in all measures of money, it is important to understand *how the banking system can create money*. Banks subject to deposit reserve requirements must hold reserves that are at least as great as some stated percentage of their deposits. Reserves can be either cash in a bank's vaults or money that the bank has on deposit at its local Federal Reserve Bank. We will learn more about the Federal Reserve System in Chapter 30. The stated percentage is the required reserve ratio. Thus, only some of the money used to open or to add to a bank deposit must be kept by the bank to meet reserve requirements. The rest can be used to make loans in the search for more profits. This system is known as fractional reserve banking.

(5)    The multiple creation of deposits is the counterpart to bank (lending/borrowing). Consider an individual bank that is subject to a 10 percent reserve requirement. Following a new deposit of $1,000, the maximum amount of the new deposit that this bank could lend out and still meet the reserve requirement is $_____. As the proceeds of the loan are deposited in other banks, new deposits will be created. For the banking system as a whole, the maximum amount of loans that can be made, and thus the maximum amount of deposits that can be created following an increase in bank reserves, is limited by the _____ _____. The precise sequence of the multiple deposit creation is illustrated in the Basic Exercise for this chapter.

Mathematical formulas have been devised to determine the maximum increase in deposits that can be created by the banking system following an increase in bank reserves:

(6)
$$\begin{pmatrix} \text{Maximum} \\ \text{increase} \\ \text{in} \\ \text{deposits} \end{pmatrix} = \begin{pmatrix} \text{Initial} \\ \text{increase} \\ \text{in bank} \\ \text{reserves} \end{pmatrix} \times \begin{pmatrix} \underline{\qquad} \end{pmatrix}$$

The increase in bank reserves may come from a deposit of cash. In this case, while deposits are up, cash outside banks is down, as some was deposited to start the process of multiple deposit creation. Thus, following a cash deposit, the maximum increase in the money supply will be (more/less) than the maximum increase in deposits.

The deposit creation formula is oversimplified for two reasons:

1. The formula assumes that the proceeds of each loan will eventually be redeposited in the banking system. If some of the proceeds of a loan do not get redeposited, then the deposit creation multiplier will be (larger/smaller).

(7)

2. The formula also assumes that every bank makes as large a loan as possible; that is, each bank is assumed to hold no _____ reserves. If banks do choose to hold such reserves, then the money creation formula would be (larger/smaller).

The discussion of the deposit creation multiplier showed how deposits can be created following an increase in bank reserves. The emphasis was on how a change in reserves leads to a change in deposits. One should not be surprised to learn that *total* deposits in all banks are similarly limited by *total* reserves. The cash deposit discussed in the text results in an increase in total reserves of the banking system. Most increases in reserves at one bank are offset by a decrease in reserves at some other bank, with no increase in total reserves. Consider Derek, who takes money out of his account at Bank A. Derek uses the money to buy a home computer, and the dealer deposits this money in his bank, Bank B. At the same time reserves increase at Bank B, they decrease at Bank A. The process of multiple deposit creation initiated at Bank

(8)  B is offset by a process of multiple deposit _____ starting with Bank A, and the net effect is (some/no) increase in deposits. The important factor for expanding deposits is new reserves available to the banking system. We will learn in Chapter 30 how the Federal Reserve is able to influence the volume of reserves available to the banking system.

## IMPORTANT TERMS AND CONCEPTS QUIZ

Choose the best definition for the following terms.

1. _____C_____ Run on a bank
2. _____j_____ Barter
3. _____g_____ Unit of account
4. _____m_____ Money
5. _____ Medium of exchange *m*
6. _____d_____ Store of value
7. _____t_____ Commodity money
8. _____n_____ Fiat money
9. _____s_____ M1
10. _____k_____ M2 k
11. _____o_____ Near moneys
12. _____e_____ Liquidity
13. _____f_____ Fractional reserve banking
14. _____p_____ Deposit insurance
15. _____v_____ FDIC
16. _____u_____ Required reserves
17. _____b_____ Asset
18. _____r_____ Liability
19. _____l_____ Balance sheet
20. _____h._____ Net worth
21. _____q_____ Deposit creation
22. _____a_____ Excess reserves

a. Reserves in excess of the legal minimum.
b. Item an individual or firm owns.
c. Many depositors concurrently withdrawing cash from their accounts.
d. Item used to hold wealth from one point in time to another.
e. Ease with which an asset can be converted into cash.

f. System where bankers keep reserves equal to only a portion of total deposits.
g. Standard unit for quoting prices.
h. Value of all assets minus the value of all liabilities.
i. Amount of money balances the public will hold at a given price level.
j. System of exchange where people trade one good for another without using money.
k. Sum of coins, paper money, checkable deposits, money market mutual funds, and most savings account balances.
l. Accounting statement listing values of assets on the left-hand side and those of liabilities and net worth on the right-hand side.
m. Standard object used in exchanging goods and services.
n. Object, without value as commodity, which serves as money by government decree.
o. Liquid assets which are close substitutes for money.
p. System which guarantees depositors against loss if bank goes bankrupt.
q. Process by which banking system turns one dollar of reserves into several dollars of deposits.
r. Item an individual or firm owes.
s. Sum of coins, paper money, and checkable deposits.
t. Object used as a medium of exchange that also has substantial nonmonetary uses.
u. Minimum amount of reserves a bank must hold.
v. Government agency that insures depositors' checking and savings accounts.

## BASIC EXERCISE

This exercise is designed to help you understand the multiple creation of bank deposits by working through a specific simplified example.

1. Column 1 of Table 29-1 is partly filled in for you to show the changes in the balance sheet of Bank A immediately following Janet's cash deposit of $10,000. At this point, bank deposits have increased by $_____ and the stock of money in the economy—that is, bank deposits plus currency outside banks—is (higher/lower/unchanged). Assuming the required reserve fraction is 10 percent, fill in the last two rows of column 1, showing the initial changes in required and excess reserves.

## TABLE 29-1
## BALANCE SHEET CHANGES

|  | (1)<br>Bank A | (2)<br>Bank A | (3)<br>Bank B | (4)<br>Bank B | (5)<br>Bank C |
|---|---|---|---|---|---|
| **Assets** | | | | | |
| Reserves | $10,000 | | | | |
| Loans | 0 | | | | |
| **Liabilities** | | | | | |
| Deposits | $10,000 | | | | |
| **Addendum** | | | | | |
| Required reserves | | | | | |
| Excess reserves | | | | | |

Note: Required reserve ratio is 10 percent.

2. Assume that Bank A responds to Janet's deposit by making as large a loan as it can to Earl, given the required reserve ratio. Now fill in column 2 to represent the changes in Bank A's balance sheet after the loan has been made and Earl has taken the proceeds of the loan in cash.

3. Earl uses the money from the loan to buy a car and the car dealer deposits this cash in Bank B. Fill in column 3 to represent the changes in Bank B's balance sheet following this cash deposit. At this point, total bank deposits have increased by $_____ and the stock of money in the economy has increased by $_____.

4. Assume now that Bank B also makes as large a loan as possible. Fill in column 4 to represent changes in Bank B's balance sheet after it makes the loan and this latest borrower takes the proceeds in cash.

5. Assume that the proceeds of this loan eventually get deposited in Bank C. Fill in column 5 to represent the changes in the balance sheet of Bank C following the increase in deposits. At this point total bank deposits have increased by $_____ and the stock of money has increased by $_____.

6. Fill in the following sequence of increased deposits following the initial increase at Bank A, assuming that each bank makes the largest possible loan.

| Increased deposits at Bank A | $10,000 |
|---|---|
| Increased deposits at Bank B | _____ |
| Increased deposits at Bank C | _____ |
| Increased deposits at Bank D | _____ |
| Increased deposits at Bank E | _____ |

If you have not made any mistakes you will notice that each increase in deposit is less than the previous increase and can be expressed as

$(1.0 - 0.1) \times$ (the previous increase in deposits).

Mathematically this is an infinite geometric progression with decreasing increments. If we carried the sum out far enough it would approach a limit given by $10,000 + _____ , or $_____ . (If you have a suitable electronic calculator or microcomputer you might try testing this result by actually calculating the sum for a very large number of terms.) This specific numerical example illustrates the more general principle that the multiplier for the maximum increase in deposits following an increase in bank reserves is 1 + _____ _____ _____ .

## SELF-TESTS FOR UNDERSTANDING

### Test A

Circle the most appropriate answer.

1. Money serves all but which one of the following functions?
   a. Medium of exchange.
   b. Hedge against inflation.
   c. Unit of account.
   d. Store of value.

2. Which of the following is *not* an example of commodity money?
   a. Gold coins.
   b. Wampum.
   c. A $10 bill.
   d. Diamonds.

3. Where was paper money first used?
   a. China.
   b. Egypt.
   c. India.
   d. Italy.

4. Which of the following does not belong in M1?
   a. The coins in your pocket.
   b. Jodi's checking account.
   c. The cash in the vault at the bank downtown.
   d. The traveler's check that Heather has left over from last summer.

5. The difference between M2 and M1 includes which of the following? (There may be more one correct answer.)
   a. Traveler's checks.
   b. Money market mutual fund balances.
   c. Marketable U.S. government debt.
   d. Savings deposits.

6. Liquidity is defined as the
   a. viscosity of financial assets.
   b. ease with which assets can be converted to money.
   c. net worth of a financial institution.
   d. ratio of liabilities to assets.

7. A bank's (or your) net worth is found by
   a. summing up all assets.
   b. adding total assets to total liabilities.
   c. subtracting total liabilities from total assets.
   d. dividing total assets by total liabilities.

8. Which of the following is not an asset for a bank?
   a. Excess reserves.
   b. Holdings of U.S. government securities.
   c. Checking account balances.
   d. Mortgage loans made by the bank.

9. The key item that makes balance sheets balance is a bank's
   a. holdings of excess reserves.
   b. assets.
   c. required reserves.
   d. net worth.

10. If a bank holds more reserves than required, the difference is
    a. the bank's net worth.
    b. liquidity.
    c. solvency.
    d. excess reserves.

11. Banks could increase profits by
    a. holding more commodity money and less fiat money.
    b. reducing their liabilities.
    c. holding fewer excess reserves in order to make more loans.
    d. substituting M2 for M1.

12. If Damien deposits cash that he used to keep under his mattress in his checking account, the initial deposit will result in
    a. an increase M1.
    b. a decrease in M2.
    c. an increase in the net worth of the banking system.
    d. no change in M1.

13. The most important government regulation of banks in terms of limiting the multiple creation of deposits is
    a. bank examinations and audits.
    b. limits on the kinds of assets that banks can buy.
    c. the required reserve ratio.
    d. requirements to disclose the volume of loans to bank officials.

14. If the minimum reserve requirement for all bank deposits is 10 percent, then the maximum multiple creation of deposits by the banking system as a whole following a cash deposit of $2,000 would be
    a. $(0.1) \times (\$2,000) = \$200$.
    b. $(1 + 0.1) \times (\$2,000) = \$2,200$.
    c. $(\$2,000) + (1 - 0.1) = \$2,222$.
    d. $(\$2,000) + (0.1) = \$20,000$.

15. The maximum increase in the money supply would be
    a. smaller than in question 14.
    b. larger than in question 14.
    c. the same as in question 14.
    (In fact, it would be $_____18,000_____.)

16. If the reserve requirement is 15 percent instead of 10 percent, then the maximum multiple creation of deposits would be
    a. smaller than in question 14.
    b. larger than in question 14.
    c. the same as in question 14.

17. If banks hold some of every increase in deposits in the form of excess reserves, then the amount of deposits actually created following a cash deposit would be
    a. less than that indicated in question 14.
    b. the same as that indicated in question 14.
    c. more than that indicated in question 14.

18. If the required reserve ratio is 20 percent and Rachel deposits $100 in cash in the First National Bank, the maximum increase in deposits by the banking system as a whole is
    a. 0.
    b. $20.
    c. $100.
    d. $500.

19. If the required reserve ratio is 20 percent and Rachel deposits $100 in the First National Bank by depositing a check from her mother written on the Second National Bank, the maximum increase in deposits by the banking system as a whole is
    a. 0.
    b. $20.
    c. $100.
    d. $500.

20. If a bank's total reserve holdings are $35 million and it has $12 million of excess reserves, then its required reserves are
    a. $12 million.
    b. $23 million.
    c. $35 million.
    d. $47 million.

## Test B

Circle T or F for true or false.

T F 1. A major advantage of the use of money rather than barter is that money avoids the problems of finding a "double coincidence of wants."

T F 2. Fiat money in the United States may be redeemed for gold from the U.S. Treasury.

T F 3. Many assets serve as a store of value but only money is also a medium of exchange.

T F 4. In periods with high rates of inflation, money is a good store of value.

T F 5. Banks could increase their profitability by holding higher levels of excess reserves.

T F 6. The existence of deposit insurance is an important reason for the dramatic decline in the number of bank failures.

T F 7. The oversimplified deposit creation multiplier of 1 divided by the required reserve ratio is an underestimate of the more appropriate, but more complicated, deposit multiplier.

T F 8. Multiple deposit creation applies to increases in the money supply but reductions in the money supply can come about only through government taxation.

T F 9. Required reserves are part of a bank's liabilities, whereas excess reserves are part of a bank's assets.

T F 10. If a bank's liabilities exceed its assets, the bank is said to have negative net worth.

## SUPPLEMENTARY EXERCISES

1. If the required reserve ratio is 20 percent and banks want to hold 10 percent of any increase in deposits in the form of excess reserves and people want to hold $1 more in currency for every $10 increase in deposits, what is the eventual increase in deposits following a $1,000 cash deposit in the First National Bank? What is the eventual increase in the money supply?

2. If $M$ is the required reserve fraction, $E$ is the ratio of excess reserves to deposits, and $C$ is the ratio of currency to deposits, what is the formula that relates the change in deposits to a change in reserves?

## ECONOMICS IN ACTION

### The Reform of Deposit Insurance

As described in the text, the establishment of federal deposit insurance had a dramatic effect on the number of bank failures. Some critics argue that experience since the late 1970s suggests that we may have had too much of a good thing. Economist Edward J. Kane has been especially critical of the actions of federal government officials, both elected and appointed, concerning deposit insurance. He was one of the first to describe the collapse of the Federal Savings and Loan Insurance Corporation (FSLIC), the deposit insurance agency for S&Ls, as resulting from a combination a moral hazard and a principal-agent problem.[1]

Moral hazard arose because deposit insurance provided an incentive for some S&Ls to engage in risky behavior. The period of high interest rates in the late 1970s and early 1980s had left these institutions with little or negative net worth. Owners of these institutions saw high-risk but potentially high-return loans as their only salvation. Insurance protected their depositors. Negative net worth meant that their own investment in the S&L had already been wiped out. They literally had nothing to lose by engaging in risky behavior.

Kane also charges that Congress and bank regulators (the agents) failed to act in the best interest of U.S. taxpayers (the principals). Kane charges that at critical points, and with the support and encouragement of key members of Congress, the FSLIC allowed bankrupt institutions to continue in business. Succumbing to lobbying pressures to focus on the original book value of assets rather than current market value allowed officials to pretend that bankrupt institutions were still solvent. The result was that problems were deferred as the cost of appropriate action increased. Opposition to increased federal spending and the impact on the deficit that would accompany the official closing of failed institutions further contributed to delay.

What is an appropriate stance for deposit insurance? There have been a large number of proposals. They include the mandatory use of market prices to value assets; mandatory and higher net worth requirements for financial institutions; automatic rules for closing insolvent institutions that remove the element of discretion on the part of regulators; deposit insurance premiums that vary with the riskiness of a bank's portfolio; and public notice of the results of bank examinations.

A number of observers have also argued that the present deposit insurance limit is so high that depositors have little incentive to concern themselves with the riskiness of a bank's portfolio. If a smaller amount, perhaps the first $40,000 or $50,000 of deposits, were insured and it was clear that deposits above this level had no insurance protection, depositors with large balances, including businesses, would have a real incentive to pay attention to the riskiness of their bank's assets. According to this view, a bank that was imprudent would (and should) suffer a run on its deposits with little reason to expect that the run would spill over and harm sound banks.

---

[1]Moral hazard refers to the tendency of insurance to make people less concerned with the risks associated with their behavior, after all its covered by insurance. Principal-agent relationships occur whenever one party, the principal, has to hire others, the agents, to act on their behalf. An example would be stockholders who hire executives to manage corporations. It is often difficult for the principals to monitor the behavior of their agents to insure that the agents act to promote the principal's interests and not their (the agent's) own.

1.  What changes, if any, do you think there should be to the system of deposit insurance? Why? How far should the government go to protect depositors? How does one design a system of deposit insurance that addresses the problem of moral hazard?

You might want to consult the following:

*Reforming Federal Deposit Insurance*, Congressional Budget Office, (GPO: Washington, D.C.) September 1990.

*The S&L Insurance Mess: How Did It Happen*, Edward J. Kane, (The Urban Institute Press: Washington, D.C.) 1991.

*The S&L Debacle*, Lawrence J. White, (Oxford University Press: New York) 1991.

## STUDY QUESTIONS

1.  What functions does money share with other assets and what functions are unique to money?

2.  How does fiat money differ from commodity money? In particular, how do they compare with regard to the list of desirable characteristics discussed in the text?

3.  Where would you draw the line if asked to come up with a measure of money for the American economy?

4.  Rank the following in terms of their liquidity and justify your ranking: a 12 month savings certificate, the balance in your checking account, a corporate bond issued by Microsoft, some left-over traveler's checks from your most recent trip, a share of stock in Dupont, a $20 bill, a piece of lakeside vacation property.

5.  What is full-bodied money? Is money in the United States today full-bodied? If not, where does its value come from?

6.  If the government is going to insure deposits, it seems natural that it be allowed to examine a bank's books and put limits on some types of loans to control its risk. Alternatively, the need for deposit insurance could be eliminated if reserve requirements were set at 100 percent. What do you think would happen to bank service charges if reserve requirements were 100 percent? What other changes might you expect? In particular think about the incentive to create alternatives to bank deposits.

7.  How can you tell when something is an asset or a liability?

8.  As a bank is worth more if its assets exceed its liabilities, in what sense does its balance sheet balance?

9.  As the government controls the printing press, how can banks create money?

10. In what ways is the deposit creation multiplier, 1/m, oversimplified? Does adjusting for these complications make the deposit creation multiplier larger or smaller?

*Chapter* **30**

# Monetary Policy and the National Economy

---

## LEARNING OBJECTIVES

After completing this chapter you should be able to:

- distinguish between the concepts "money" and "income."
- analyze arguments in favor of and opposed to the independence of the Federal Reserve System.
- draw and explain the logic behind both the supply-of-money schedule and the demand-for-money schedule.
- analyze the impact of changes in the three major monetary policy instruments both in words and by using the demand-for- and supply-of-money schedules.
- explain how bond prices and interest rates are related.
- describe the impact of open market operations on bond prices and interest rates.
- explain why the Fed's control of the stock of money is not exact.
- explain how some suggested reforms might change the degree of control that the Fed has over the stock of money.
- describe how changes in monetary policy affect the expenditure schedule and the aggregate demand curve.
- use the expenditure schedule and aggregate demand curve to describe how changes in monetary policy affect the economy's macroeconomic equilibrium, that is, interest rates, investment spending, GDP, and prices.
- explain how the impact of higher prices on the demand for money helps to explain why the aggregate demand curve has a negative slope.

## IMPORTANT TERMS AND CONCEPTS

Central bank
Federal Reserve System
Federal Open Market Committee (FOMC)
Independence of the Fed
Reserve requirements
Open market operations
Bond prices and interest rates
Contraction and expansion of the money supply

Federal Reserve lending to banks
Moral suasion
Supply of money
Demand for money
Opportunity cost
Equilibrium in the money market
Monetary policy
Why the aggregate demand curve slopes down

## CHAPTER REVIEW

In Chapter 29 we learned how deposits are created by the actions of banks. In this chapter we will see how actions taken by the Federal Reserve System can influence the stock of money. Reserve requirements and the total amount of bank reserves are important keys to the Federal Reserve's control of bank deposits and the stock of money. We will also see how the equilibrium in the money market influences the economy's overall macroeconomic equilibrium. The emphasis in this chapter is on building models. In subsequent chapters we will use these models to understand policy issues.

(1)      The Federal Reserve System was established in _____ and is the nation's _____ bank. There are _____ district banks throughout the country, with headquarters in Washington, D.C. The people in charge in Washington are the seven members of the _____ of _____ of the Federal Reserve System. Major decisions about the stock of money are made by the FOMC, or the _____ _____ _____ Committee. Government spending and taxes are the nation's (fiscal/monetary) policy. Policy actions by the Federal Reserve constitute the nation's _____ policy.

We saw in Chapter 29 that the multiple creation of bank deposits is limited by the required reserve ratio and by the volume of bank reserves. Reserve requirements help to determine the deposit creation multiplier. The other two major policy instruments—open market operations and lending to banks—directly affect total bank reserves. We also saw in Chapter 29 that controlling reserve requirements and the volume of bank reserves does not allow for the precise control of the stock of money because of possible

(2) changes in (excess/required) reserve holdings by banks and in currency holdings by the public. These slippages in the deposit creation formula are an important reason why the Federal Reserve's control over the stock of money, while strong and important, is not complete.

A reduction in reserve requirements does not change total bank reserves, but it will initially result

(3) in a(n) (increase/decrease) in noninterest-earning excess reserves. Multiple deposit creation will take place as banks try to put these nonearning excess reserves to work. Thus, a reduction in minimum reserve requirements should be associated with a (larger/smaller) volume of deposits and is an example of a(n) (expansionary/contractionary) change in monetary policy. An increase in reserve requirements will typically force banks to curtail lending in order to meet new, higher holdings of (excess/required) reserves. Such an increase would be an example of a _____ change in monetary policy.

(4)      Open market operations—the purchase and sale of government _____— represent the most important and most commonly used instrument of monetary policy. Open market operations affect bank behavior by adding to or subtracting from the amount of bank reserves. The essence of an open market purchase is that the Fed creates bank reserves when it (buys/sells) a government security. The result is a(n) (increase/decrease) in noninterest-earning excess reserves, and the usual multiple deposit creation process is set in motion. An open market sale has exactly opposite effects. Payment to the Fed for government securities means a(n) (reduction/increase) in bank reserves and initiates a process of multiple deposit (creation/destruction).

Banks can add to their reserve holdings by borrowing directly from the Fed. Such borrowings might facilitate a multiple expansion of deposits or, more frequently, might forestall a multiple destruction of deposits. The Fed influences the volume of borrowing by changing the interest rate it charges banks and
(5) by _____ _____, which is the Fed's way of letting banks know that they are misusing their borrowing privileges. More bank borrowing would mean a (higher/lower) amount of bank reserves than otherwise, and eventually a (higher/lower) volume of bank deposits. When banks borrow reserves from the Fed they must pay interest on these borrowings. In the United States the interest rate for these borrowings is called the _____ _____.

Monetary policy decisions, affecting reserve requirements and the total volume of bank reserves, can be seen as putting an upper limit on the possible creation of bank deposits and hence on the stock of money. How much banks will want to exploit the potential to create deposits will be determined by the profitability of increased bank operations—more loans and more deposits. Higher interest rates on
(6) loans will induce banks to make (more/fewer) loans, hold (more/fewer) nonearning excess reserves, and borrow (more/less) from the Fed (if they can). All of these actions will expand the volume of deposits and hence the stock of money. In brief, considering just banks, higher interest rates should be associated with a (larger/smaller) stock of money.

This behavior by banks is summarized in Figure 30-1, which shows an upward-sloping supply of money schedule. Movements along the schedule are related to the decisions of commercial banks. Shifts in the schedule come from changes in monetary policy. For example, an open market purchase increases
(7) the amount of bank reserves and shifts the money supply schedule to the (left/right). Changes in other monetary policy variables will also shift the money supply schedule. To repeat, monetary policy decisions determine the position of the money supply schedule; they do not, by themselves, determine either the stock of money or the interest rate. The actual stock of money and the interest rate will be determined by the intersection of the supply-of-money schedule and the _____ for-money schedule.

Figure 30-2 shows a demand schedule for money. The schedule has a negative slope because, as the
(8) interest rate rises, the demand for money (increases/decreases). The increase in interest rates means that the opportunity cost of holding money has (increased/decreased). If nominal GDP increases, that is, if real GDP or prices increase, the demand schedule will shift to the (right/left) as more transactions associated with a higher GDP will lead to a(n) (increased/decreased) demand for money at every interest rate. If nominal GDP decreases, the demand schedule will shift to the _____.

Equilibrium values for the stock of money and the rate of interest will be determined by the forces of both supply and demand consistent with the process described in Chapter 4. Graphically, the equi-
(9) librium can be represented by the _____ of the demand and supply curves, as in Figure 30-3. Changes in monetary policy will change the equilibrium values for both the stock of money and the rate of interest. An expansionary change in monetary policy would be represented by a shift of the (demand/supply) schedule to the (left/right), a(n) (increase/decrease) in the stock of money, and a(n) (increase/decrease) in the interest rate. A contractionary change in monetary policy would be represented by a shift of the supply schedule to the _____, a(n) _____ in the stock of money, and a(n) _____ in the interest rate.

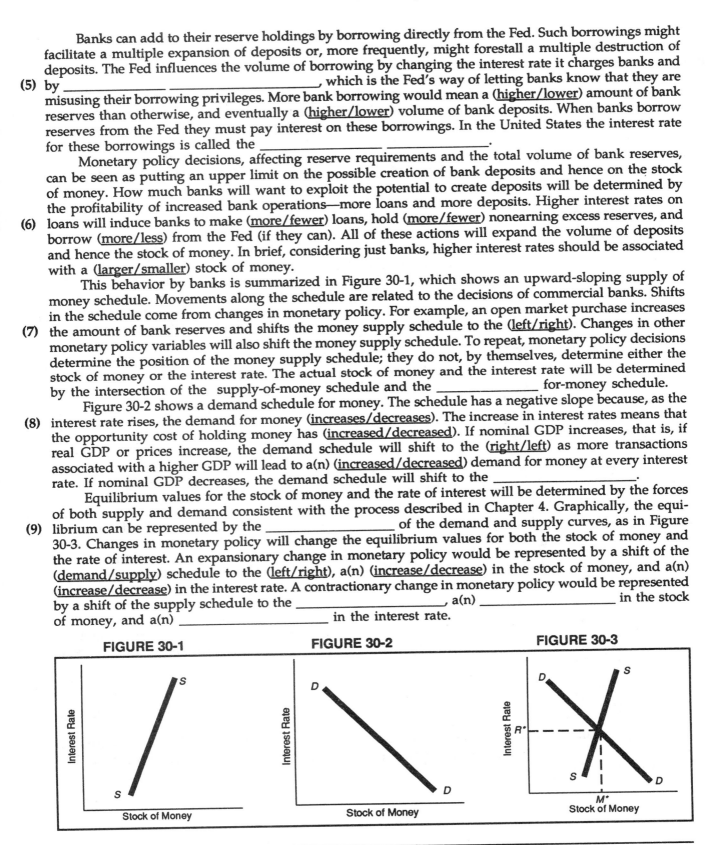

FIGURE 30-1          FIGURE 30-2          FIGURE 30-3

With an understanding of how the demand and supply for money work together to determine interest rates, we are in a position to see how changes in monetary policy affect aggregate demand. Policy
(10) shifts in the (supply/demand) of money schedule will change interest rates as we move along the _____ for money schedule. The change in interest rates will affect interest sensitive categories of demand, especially investment spending. Changes in investment spending lead to a (shift in/movement along) the expenditure schedule. The (shift in/movement along) the expenditure schedule will shift the aggregate (demand/supply) curve through the multiplier process described in Chapter 26. Overall macroeconomic equilibrium is reestablished at the new intersection of the aggregate demand curve and the aggregate supply curve. The division of effects, as between real output and prices, is determined by the slope of the aggregate _____ curve. This sequence of events is diagrammed at the end of Chapter 30 of the text.

The same reasoning helps us to understand two other important points:

*Why the aggregate demand curve has a negative slope*

Higher prices not only reduce the purchasing power of money fixed assets, they also increase the transactions demand for money. With an unchanged supply-of-money schedule, the increase in the demand for money that comes with a higher price level will shift the demand-for-money schedule to the right, leading to an increase in interest rates and lower investment spending. Thus higher prices affect aggregate demand through their impact on investment as well as consumption and net exports.

*Why the multiplier formula 1/(1 – MPC) is oversimplified*

Increases in nominal GDP from the multiplier process increase the transactions demand for money. Interest rates rise as the demand-for-money schedule moves along an unchanged supply-of-money schedule. The reduction in investment spending induced by the rise in interest rates is the third important reason why the multiplier process of Chapter 26 was oversimplified.

## IMPORTANT TERMS AND CONCEPTS QUIZ

Choose the best definition for the following terms.

1. ____b____ Central bank
2. ____h____ Federal Reserve System
3. ____k, a____ Federal Open Market Committee
4. ____e____ Reserve requirement
5. ____j____ Open-market operations
6. ____f____ Moral suasion
7. ____i____ Discount rate
8. ____a____ Opportunity cost
9. ____d____ Equilibrium in the money market
10. ____g____ Monetary policy

a. Foregone value of next best alternative that is not chosen.
b. A bank for banks responsible for the conduct of monetary policy.

c. Branch of Treasury responsible for minting coins.
d. Quantity of money and level of interest rate where money demand equals money supply.
e. Minimum amount of reserves a bank must hold.
f. Fed's informal requests and warnings to persuade banks to limit their borrowings.
g. Actions Fed takes to affect money supply, interest rates, or both.
h. Central bank of the United States.
i. Interest rate Fed charges on loans to banks.
j. Fed's purchase or sale of government securities.
k. Chief policymaking committee of the Federal Reserve System.

## BASIC EXERCISES

1. **Instruments of Monetary Policy**

   This exercise is designed to review the impact of various changes in monetary policy instruments.

   a. Use Figure 30-4 to analyze the impact of an open market sale. The sale of a government security by the Fed results in a(n) (<u>increase/decrease</u>) in total bank reserves. This change in bank reserves can be represented as a shift of the supply-of-money schedule to the _____. (Be sure you can explain in words why the schedule shifts.) Draw a new supply-of-money schedule that represents the result of the open market sale. As a result of this (<u>expansionary/contractionary</u>) change in monetary policy, the equilibrium stock of money will (<u>fall/rise</u>) and interest rates will _____.

   b. Use Figure 30-5 to analyze the impact of a reduction in minimum reserve requirements. The initial result of a reduction in minimum reserve requirements will be a(n) (<u>increase/decrease</u>) in excess reserves. The likely response by banks to this change in excess reserves will result in a process of multiple deposit (<u>creation/destruction</u>). In Figure 30-5 such a development can be represented as a shift of the supply-of-money schedule to the _____. Draw the new supply-of-money schedule. As a result of this _____ change in monetary policy, the equilibrium stock of money will _____ and interest rates will _____.

   c. Use Figure 30-6 to analyze the impact of an increase in the discount rate. An increase in this rate will make banks (<u>more/less</u>) willing to borrow from the Fed. One expects that the volume of member bank borrowing will _____. The change in member bank borrowing is a direct change in bank reserves; so, as a result of the increase in the discount rate, total bank reserves will _____ and the supply-of-money schedule will shift to the _____. Draw the new supply-of-money schedule in Figure 30-6. As a result of this _____ change in monetary policy, the equilibrium stock of money will _____ and interest rates will _____.

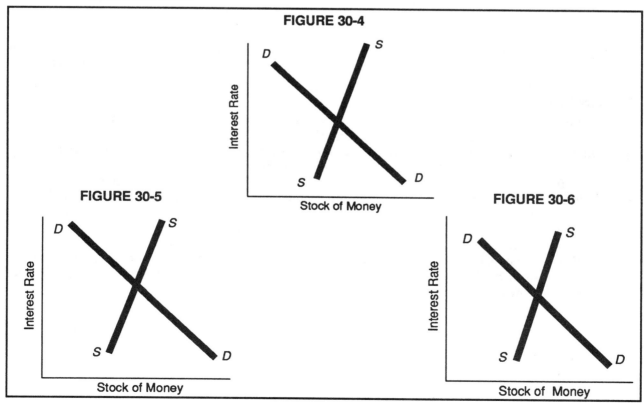

FIGURE 30-4

FIGURE 30-5

FIGURE 30-6

**FIGURE 30-7**

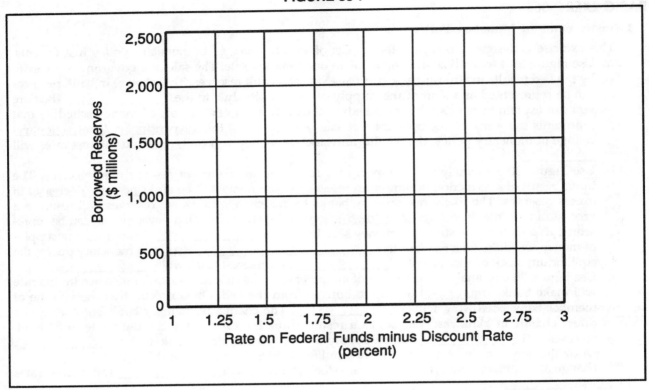

d. You should also be able to analyze the impact of each opposite change in monetary policy; that is, an open market purchase, an increase in minimum reserve requirements, and a decrease in the discount rate.

2. **Borrowing from the Fed**

Consider the data in Table 30-1 on interest rates and borrowings by depository institutions from the Federal Reserve. The federal funds rate is a market interest rate: it is the interest rate on most short term lending and borrowing between depository institutions. Follow the instructions below to explore the influence of market interest rates on bank borrowings from the Fed.

a. The financial incentive to borrow from the Fed can be represented by the difference between the discount rate and market interest rates, represented here by the federal funds rate. Plot the data from the last two columns of Table 30-1, one point for each month, in the two-variable diagram in Figure 30-7. What does this data suggest is likely to happen to bank borrowings from the Fed if market interest rates increase while the discount rate remains unchanged?

b. Whenever the federal funds rate exceeds the discount rate, banks can make money by borrowing cheaply from the Fed and by lending at the higher federal funds rate. Why then wasn't there more borrowing in 1989?

## TABLE 30-1

|  |  | Discount Rate (percent) | Federal Funds Rate (percent) | Fed Funds Rate minus Discount Rate (percent) | Borrowings from the Federal Reserve ($ millions) |
|---|---|---|---|---|---|
| Jan | 1989 | 6.50 | 9.12 | 2.62 | 1,662 |
| Feb | 1989 | 6.59 | 9.36 | 2.77 | 1,487 |
| Mar | 1989 | 7.00 | 9.85 | 2.85 | 1,813 |
| Apr | 1989 | 7.00 | 9.84 | 2.84 | 2,289 |
| May | 1989 | 7.00 | 9.81 | 2.81 | 1,720 |
| Jun | 1989 | 7.00 | 9.53 | 2.53 | 1,490 |
| Jul | 1989 | 7.00 | 9.24 | 2.24 | 694 |
| Aug | 1989 | 7.00 | 8.99 | 1.99 | 675 |
| Sep | 1989 | 7.00 | 9.02 | 2.02 | 693 |
| Oct | 1989 | 7.00 | 8.84 | 1.84 | 555 |
| Nov | 1989 | 7.00 | 8.55 | 1.55 | 349 |
| Dec | 1989 | 7.00 | 8.45 | 1.45 | 265 |

Source: *Economic Report of the President, 1990*, Tables C–69 and C–71.

## SELF-TESTS FOR UNDERSTANDING

### Test A

Circle the most appropriate answer.

1. The Federal Reserve is responsible for the conduct of
   a. domestic economic policy.
   b. fiscal policy.
   c. international economic policy.
   d. monetary policy.

2. The Federal Reserve is a bank for
   a. the Treasury.
   b. households.
   c. businesses.
   d. banks.

3. Which of the following is *not* an instrument of monetary policy?
   a. Open market operations.
   b. Lending to banks.
   c. Antitrust actions to promote competition in banking.
   d. Required reserve ratios.

4. Who has direct responsibility for open market operations?
   a. The Board of Governors.
   b. The Federal Open Market Committee.
   c. The President of the United States.
   d. The Banking Committee of the U.S. Senate.

5. Open market operations involve the Fed buying and selling
   a. stocks in American companies.
   b. U.S. government securities.
   c. gold.
   d. corporate bonds.

6. When making an open market purchase, the Fed gets the money to make the purchase from
   a. the Treasury.
   b. the Bureau of Printing and Engraving.
   c. cash in its vault.
   d. making a computer entry on its own books to credit the reserve account of the bank from which it purchases the security.

7. An open market purchase will lead to all but which one of the following?
   a. Supply-of-money schedule shifts to the right.
   b. Expenditure schedule shifts up.
   c. Multiplier increases.
   d. Aggregate demand curve shifts to the right.

8. An open market sale will result in all but which one of the following?
   a. decrease in the stock of money.
   b. increase in interest rates.
   c. lower investment spending.
   d. higher prices.

9. The immediate impact of a change in reserve requirements will be on the
   a. total volume of bank reserves.
   b. division of reserves (between required reserves and excess reserves).
   c. demand for money.
   d. discount rate.

10. An increase in reserve requirements will lead to all but which one of the following?
    a. An initial increase in required reserves.
    b. A reduction in the stock of money.
    c. An increase in interest rates.
    d. Higher investment spending.

11. A reduction in the discount rate will lead to all but which one of the following?
    a. An increased incentive for banks to borrow from the Fed.
    b. An expansion of bank reserves as banks borrow more.
    c. The money supply schedule shifts to the left.
    d. A reduction in interest rates.

12. Which of the following is *not* an example of expansionary monetary policy?
    a. An open market purchase.
    b. A reduction in reserve requirements.
    c. An increase in the interest rates charged on loans by the Fed to commercial banks.
    d. A reduction in the discount rate.

13. If the Fed wants to reduce the stock of money, which of the following policy actions would be inappropriate?
    a. An increase in minimum reserve requirements.
    b. The sale of a government bond from the Fed's portfolio.
    c. An increase in the discount rate.
    d. An open market purchase.

14. Which of the following help to explain why the Fed does not have precise control of the money supply? (There may be more than one correct answer.)
    a. Banks may vary the amount of excess reserves they desire to hold.
    b. Open market operations can change the volume of bank reserves.
    c. Changes in the amount of currency as opposed to bank deposits that individuals and businesses want to hold.
    d. Changes in reserve requirements will affect the deposit creation multiplier.

15. Important determinants of the demand for money include all but which one of the following?
    a. The discount rate.
    b. The level of real output.
    c. Market interest rates.
    d. The price level.

16. A change in which of the following would lead to a shift in the demand-for-money schedule?
    a. Market interest rates.
    b. Reserve requirements.
    c. GDP.
    d. The discount rate.

17. The positive slope of the supply-of-money schedule indicates that
    a. at higher interest rates people will demand more money.
    b. banks are likely to respond to higher interest rates by holding fewer excess reserves.
    c. minimum reserve requirements increase directly with interest rates.
    d. the Fed is likely to engage in expansionary monetary policy actions as interest rates increase.

18. An increase in interest rates from 8 percent to 9 percent would be associated with _____ in the price of existing bonds.
    a. a decline
    b. no change
    c. an increase

19. Changes in interest rates resulting from changes in monetary policy are likely to affect investment spending and initially lead to a shift in the
    (There may be more than one correct answer.)
    a. Expenditure schedule
    b. Aggregate supply curve
    c. Consumption function
    d. Aggregate demand curve

20. Knowing that an increase in the level of prices will increase the demand for money for transactions purposes helps to explain why
    a. the aggregate supply curve has a positive slope.
    b. the aggregate demand curve has a negative slope.
    c. equilibrium occurs at the intersection of the aggregate demand and aggregate supply curves.
    d. the multiplier response to a change in autonomous spending may be greater than 1.0.

## Test B

Circle T or F for true or false.

T  F  1.  The independence of the Federal Reserve System is now so well established that it is beyond debate.

T  F  2.  Most power in the Federal Reserve System is held by the 12 district Federal Reserve banks.

T  F  3.  Monetary policy decisions by the Federal Reserve are subject to review by the President of the United States before being implemented.

T  F  4.  An open market purchase by the Fed lowers interest rates without changing the stock of money.

T  F  5.  A reduction in minimum reserve requirements is likely to lead to an increase in both the stock of money and the interest rate.

T  F  6.  Changing the discount rate is the most frequently used instrument of monetary policy today.

T  F  7.  Since many forms of money do not earn interest, people's demand for money is unaffected by changes in interest rates.

T  F  8.  Higher interest rates would normally lead banks to reduce their holdings of excess reserves.

T  F  9.  The impact of changes in monetary policy on interest-sensitive categories of demand affects GDP and prices as the economy moves along a given aggregate demand curve.

T  F  10.  The impact of the price level on the demand for money, and hence interest rates, helps to explain why the aggregate demand curve has a negative slope.

## SUPPLEMENTARY EXERCISES

1. Consider an economy where consumption and investment spending are given by

$$C = 650 + .6 \, DI$$

$$I = 1710 - 30r$$

where $r$ is the interest rate. In this economy, taxes are one-sixth of income and net exports are 100.

a. If government purchases are 900 and $r$ is 12 (that is, 12 percent), what is the equilibrium level of income?

b. If the Fed lowers the interest rate to 8, what happens to the equilibrium level of income?

c. The Fed can lower the interest rate by an appropriate increase in bank reserves; that is, an appropriate shift in the money supply schedule. But what is appropriate? Assume the demand for money is

$$M^D = .25Y - 10r$$

and the supply of money is

$$M^S = 5BR + 2.5r$$

where $BR$ is the amount of bank reserves. If $BR = 270$, what is the equilibrium level of income? $r$? and $M$?

d. What increase in $BR$ will reduce the interest rate to 8 and produce the increase in $Y$ you found in question 2? What happens to $M$? (You might start by trying an increase in $BR$ of 10 and figuring out what happens to $Y$ and $r$. Then use these results to figure out how to get $r$ to drop to 8.)

2. **Bond Prices and Interest Rates**

a. Consider a bond that pays $90 a year forever. If interest rates are 9 percent, such a bond should sell for $1,000 as ($90 + $1,000) = .09. Assume now that interest rates fall to 6 percent. With bond payments of $90, what bond price offers investors a return of 6 percent? If interest rates rise to 15 percent, what must be the price of the bond paying $90 to offer investors a return of 15 percent?

b. Bonds that pay only interest and never repay principal are called consols. Most bonds pay interest for a certain number of years and then repay the original borrowing or principal. Bond prices reflect the present value of those interest and principal payments as follows:

$$\text{Price} = \sum_{t=1}^{N} \frac{\text{INT}}{(1+r)^t} + \frac{\text{PRIN}}{(1+r)^N}$$

where INT = interest payments
$r$ = interest rate
PRIN = principal
$N$ = number of years of interest payments (also number of years to principal payment)

It may be easier to answer the following questions if you have access to a microcomputer or sophisticated hand calculator.

Verify that if INT = $90, PRIN = $1,000, $N$ = 10, and $r$ = .09, the price of the bond = $1,000.

Calculate the price of the bond when $r$ = .06 and when $r$ = .15 while INT, PRIN, and $N$ remain unchanged. These calculations show what would happen to the price of an existing bond if interest rates change. Do your results confirm the negative correlation between bond prices and interest rates discussed in the text?

## ECONOMICS IN ACTION

### Independence of the Federal Reserve

In the October 1993, Congressman Henry Gonzales (D-Texas), Chairman of the House Banking Committee, convened a series of committee hearings to consider issues related to the degree of independence of the Federal Reserve. The secrecy surrounding meetings of the Federal Open Market Committee (FOMC) and appointment procedures for presidents of the twelve district Federal Reserve Banks were among the items of special concern to Congressman Gonzales.

With regard to the meetings of the FOMC, Congressman Gonzales proposed that decisions be disclosed within a week and that detailed transcripts and videotapes of each meeting be released within 60 days. He argued that his proposals would promote individual accountability and that "Accurate information does not undermine markets. Partial information and leaked information undermines market efficiency."[1] Alan Greenspan, Chairman of the Board of Governors, and the other Federal representatives who appeared before the Committee argued that videotaping would hinder free debate as individuals concerned that their remarks might be misinterpreted and "cause unnecessary volatility in financial markets," would self-censor what they said. "Unconventional policy prescriptions and ruminations about the longer-term outlook for economic and financial market developments might never be surfaced . . . for fear of igniting a speculative reaction when the discussion was disclosed." Chairman Greenspan went on to argue that premature disclosure "could inhibit or even thwart" the ability of the FOMC to implement decisions. He was especially concerned that immediate disclosure would compromise the ability of the FOMC to implement "contingent plans—that is, if a given economic or financial event occurs, a particular policy action would ensue."[2]

Currently the president of each district bank is appointed by the district bank's Board of Directors, subject to the approval of the Board of Governors in Washington, D.C. District bank presidents serve as voting members of the FOMC on a rotating basis. Critics of the Federal Reserve argue that, in view of their membership on the FOMC and the importance of monetary policy, district bank presidents should be selected or reviewed by elected officials rather than appointed bodies. Options might include appointment by the President and/or confirmation by the Senate. Again Chairman Greenspan spoke against these changes, arguing that the current system represents a deliberate choice by the Congress to isolate decisions about monetary policy from political pressures. He argued that the Federal Reserve is accountable to the Congress and the public through reporting requirements and the daily scrutiny of the business and financial press. However he warned that "if accountability is achieved by putting the conduct of monetary policy under the close influence of politicians subject to short-term election-cycle pressures, the resulting policy would likely prove disappointing over time. . . . The public–private and regional makeup of the Federal Reserve was chosen by Congress, in preference to a unitary public central bank, only after long and careful debate. The system was designed to avoid an excessive concentration of authority in federal hands and to ensure responsiveness to local needs."[3]

---

[1]"Greenspan Warns Against Easing Fed's Secrecy," *The New York Times*, October 20, 1992.

[2]Testimony by Alan Greenspan, Chairman, Board of Governors of the Federal Reserve System, before the Committee on Banking, Finance and Urban Affairs, U.S. House of Representatives, October 13, 1993. A complete transcript of the Committee Hearing should be available by the Spring of 1994.

[3]*Ibid.*

1. When and in how much detail should decisions and minutes of the FOMC be released? Is Greenspan right when he argues that the advance announcement of contingent plans limits their effectiveness?
2. Who should select district bank presidents? Should voting membership on the FOMC be restricted to members of the Board of Governors and exclude district bank presidents?

## STUDY QUESTIONS

1. What is the difference between money and income?
2. How much independence do you think is desirable for the Fed? Why?
3. What are the major instruments of monetary policy? Use a demand and supply diagram to show how changes in each instrument affects the stock of money and interest rates.
4. Open market operations are the most used instrument of monetary policy. Reserve requirements are changed only infrequently and the changes in the discount rate tend to be passive rather than active. What do you think explains the heavy reliance on open market operations rather than other instruments of monetary policy?
5. Why do interest rates and bond prices move inversely to each other?
6. Why can't the Fed control the stock of money to the penny? Would you favor reforms that increase the ability of the Fed to control the stock of money? If so, which reforms and why? If not, why not?
7. Why does the supply-of-money schedule have a positive slope while the demand-for-money schedule has a negative slope?
8. What are the links by which changes in monetary policy affect spending and thus output, employment, and prices? Use an expenditure diagram and an aggregate demand-aggregate supply diagram to illustrate your answer.
9. "Recognizing that an increase in prices increases the demand for money for transactions purposes helps to explain why the aggregate demand curve has a negative slope." What is the logic behind this statement?

*Chapter* **31**
# The Debate over Monetary Policy

## LEARNING OBJECTIVES

After completing this chapter you should be able to:

♦ compute velocity given data on nominal income and the stock of money.

♦ describe the determinants of velocity.

♦ explain the difference between the quantity theory and the equation of exchange.

♦ describe why the equation of exchange is not a theory of income determination and why monetarists' use of the same equation turns it into a theory of income determination.

♦ explain how investment spending and interest rates interact to help determine how monetary policy works in a Keynesian model of income determination.

♦ explain how expansionary fiscal policy and related increases in the demand for money, interest rates, and velocity interact to determine how fiscal policy works in a monetarist model.

♦ distinguish between lags affecting fiscal policy and those affecting monetary policy.

♦ explain why the Fed cannot control $M$ and $r$.

♦ explain how and why the slope of the aggregate supply curve helps to determine the effectiveness of stabilization policy.

♦ explain how long lags might mean that efforts to stabilize the economy could end up destabilizing it.

♦ explain how automatic stabilizers help to reduce fluctuations in GDP.

♦ summarize the views of advocates and opponents of activist stabilization policy by the government.

♦ describe and distinguish between different types of economic forecasting: econometric models, leading indicators, survey data, and judgmental forecasts.

## IMPORTANT TERMS AND CONCEPTS

Quantity theory of money
Velocity
Equation of exchange
Effect of interest rate on velocity
Monetarism
Effect of fiscal policy on interest rates
Lags in stabilization policy

Shape of the aggregate supply curve
Controlling $M$ versus controlling $r$
Automatic stabilizers
Econometric models
Leading indicators
Judgmental forecasts
Rules versus discretionary policy

## CHAPTER REVIEW

This is one of the most important and most difficult of the macroeconomic chapters. While not much new material is introduced, the chapter summarizes and synthesizes many of the concepts presented in preceding chapters concerning the theory of income determination as it discusses a number of issues that confront policymakers.

Earlier chapters presented an essentially Keynesian model of income determination. The monetarist viewpoint is a modern manifestation of an even older tradition known as the quantity theory of money. The concept of *velocity* is perhaps the most important tool associated with this theory. Velocity is the average number of times per year that a dollar changes hands to accomplish transactions associated with

(1) GDP. Velocity is measured as nominal _____ divided by the stock of _____. Alternative measures of money, for example, $M_1$ and $M_2$, give rise to alternative measures of velocity, $V_1$ and $V_2$.

Related to the concept of velocity is something called the equation of exchange, which is simply another way of defining velocity. The equation of exchange says:

(2)        Money supply × velocity = _____  _____.

In symbols, it is: _____ × _____ = _____ × _____. Statisticians and national income accountants measure the stock of money and nominal GDP. Economists then calculate velocity by division. Different values of the stock of money could be consistent with the same level of nominal GDP if _____ changes appropriately.

The quantity theory asserts that there is a close link between changes in nominal GDP and changes

(3) in the stock of _____. This link comes about because the quantity theory assumes that velocity (does/does not) change very much. If velocity is constant, then a change in the money stock translates directly into a change in _____ _____. If velocity is 5 and the money stock increases by $20 billion, then nominal GDP will rise by $_____ billion.

(4)     Historical data, as well as an analysis of the determinants of velocity, suggest that one (should/should not) expect velocity to be constant. Velocity reflects how much money people hold to make transactions, which in turn reflects such institutional factors as the frequency of paychecks and the efficiency of moving money between checking accounts and other assets, such as savings accounts. In Chapter 30 we saw that the amount of money people want to hold, and hence velocity, is also affected by the interest rate as a measure of the _____ _____ of holding money.

*Monetarism*, like the quantity theory, starts with the equation of exchange. But rather than assuming that velocity does not change, monetarists try to predict *how* velocity will change. From a monetarist perspective, determinants of nominal GDP are broken down into implications for the stock of money and

(5) implications for _____. After accounting for appropriate changes, simple multiplication can be used to predict nominal GDP.

At first glance it may appear that a Keynesian approach to income determination cannot analyze changes in monetary policy whereas a monetarist approach ignores fiscal policy. Such a conclusion would be oversimplified and misleading. In formal theory the two viewpoints are closer than is commonly recognized. Keynesian theory implies that monetary policy can have important impacts on aggregate

demand through its impact on interest rates and investment spending. In Chapter 30 we saw that
(6) expansionary monetary policy will lead to a(n) (decline/increase) in interest rates. In Chapter 25 we saw that as a result of lower interest rates investment spending will (increase/decrease). In Chapter 25 we also saw that an increase in investment spending shifts both the expenditure schedule and the aggregate demand curve. Putting all the pieces together we can see that expansionary monetary policy will tend to (increase/decrease) GDP. Restrictive monetary policy would work in exactly the opposite way.

Monetarists are able to analyze the impact of changes in fiscal policy as follows: Expansionary fiscal
(7) policy will be associated with (higher/lower) interest rates. As a result, velocity will (increase/decrease) and a monetarist would forecast a (higher/lower) value for nominal GDP. Neither alone nor together are Keynesian and monetarist theories sufficient to determine output and prices as both are theories of the (demand/supply) side of the economy and ignore the other side.

The impact of changes in fiscal policy on interest rates is not only important to a monetarist analysis of changes in fiscal policy, it is also one of the reasons why the multiplier formula for Chapter 26 is oversimplified; increases in autonomous spending will tend to increase interest rates which in turn induce partially offsetting changes in investment spending.

The choice between monetary and fiscal policy is often influenced by how quickly changes in policy can occur and how long it takes for changes, once made, to affect the behavior of firms and consumers.
(8) In general, lags in formulating policy are shorter for (fiscal/monetary) policy, whereas spending responses of firms and households are typically shorter for _____ policy.

A major controversy in monetary policy is whether, when formulating monetary-policy decisions, the Federal Reserve should pay greater attention to the money supply or to the interest rates. Imagine, for instance, that the Fed is happy with the stock of money and the interest rate given in Figure 31-1. Suddenly the demand-for-money schedule shifts to the right because of an increase in the demand for money from some factor other than interest rates. Draw in the new schedule. If the Fed did nothing, then,
(9) as a result of this shift in the demand for money, the stock of money would be (higher/lower) and the interest rate would _____. To maintain the original money supply, M*, the Fed should shift the supply-of-money schedule to the _____; while to maintain the same rate of interest, the Fed should shift the supply curve to the _____. It should be obvious that the Fed cannot do both at the same time.

Decisions to stick to original monetary targets are likely to mean greater changes in interest rates, while decisions to stabilize interest rates will mean greater changes in the stock of money. The appropriate choice will depend upon the state of the economy and the source of the original unexpected changes in interest rates and the stock of money.

**FIGURE 31-1**

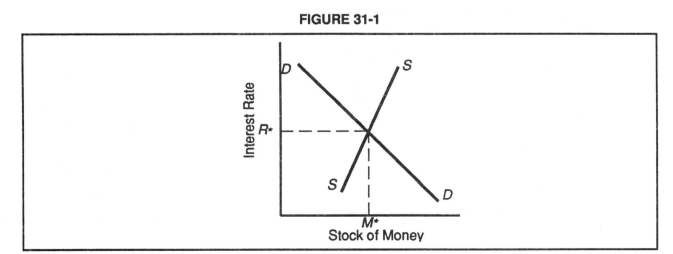

Stabilization policy affects the economy primarily by shifting the aggregate demand curve. The final result, however, in terms of changes in output and prices, also depends upon the slope of the aggregate supply curve. A flat aggregate supply curve means that shifts in the aggregate demand curve will have (10) large effects on (<u>output/prices</u>) with only a small change in _____. On the other hand, shifts of the aggregate demand curve will have big effects on prices without much change in output if the aggregate supply curve is (<u>steep/flat</u>). While some argue that the aggregate supply curve is flat and others that it is steep, an emerging consensus sees the slope of the aggregate supply curve as dependent upon the degree of resource utilization. When the economy is operating close to full-employment, the aggregate supply curve is likely to be (<u>flat/steep</u>), while during periods of significant slack in the economy, the aggregate supply curve is likely to be _____.

Some economists favor an activist-oriented approach to stabilization policy. Others favor less activ- (11) ism and rely on _____ stabilizers to keep the economy on an even keel. Beyond views about the slope of the aggregate supply curve, these differences reflect differing political philosophies and judgments concerning the importance of such factors as the economy's self-correcting mechanisms, the length of various policy lags, the stability of the multiplier and velocity, and the accuracy of economic forecasting.

It takes time before someone notices that the economy is not operating as hoped for and before the appropriate part of the government can decide what policy measures should be adopted. Once a particular policy is decided upon, there may not be much effect on output and prices until the buying habits of households and firms adjust to the new policy. Because of lags, it is not enough to design policies just for today's problems. Economists must also try to predict the future. One way they attempt to do this is through the use of mathematical formulas called econometric models. Another method concentrates on historical timing relationships of some economic variables, called leading indicators.

In addition, the U.S. government and several private organizations periodically ask people and firms about their spending plans for the future. This survey data can also be a useful tool in forecasting. Forecasters who look at the results of all these techniques, as well as such things as sun spots, the length (12) of women's skirts, and so forth, make what are called _____ forecasts. The more accurate the economic forecasts, the more demanding the standards we can set for stabilization policy. At the present time economic forecasts (<u>are/are not</u>) good enough for fine-tuning the economy.

Active use of fiscal policy to correct persistent and sustained deviations from potential output calls for changes in government spending or taxes. The fact that spending, taxes, and monetary policy can be changed (13) means that government spending (<u>must/need not</u>) take an ever larger proportion of the economic pie.

## IMPORTANT TERMS AND CONCEPTS QUIZ

Choose the best definition for the following terms.

1. _____ Quantity theory of money
2. _____ Velocity
3. _____ Equation of exchange
4. _____ Monetarism
5. _____ Automatic stabilizers
6. _____ Econometric models
7. _____ Leading indicators

a. Features of the economy that reduce its sensitivity to shifts in demand.
b. Mode of analysis that uses the equation of exchange to organize and analyze macroeconomic data.

c. Average number of times a dollar is spent in a year.
d. Variables that normally turn down prior to recessions and turn up prior to expansions.
e. Theory of aggregate demand stating that nominal GDP is proportional to the money stock.
f. Sets of mathematical equations that form a model of the economy.
g. Features of the economy that move opposite the business cycle.
h. Formula that states that nominal GDP equals the product of money stock and velocity.

## BASIC EXERCISE

1. This exercise is designed to give you practice computing and using velocity.
   Table 31-1 contains historical data for nominal GDP, $M_1$ and $M_2$
   a. Use this data to compute $V_1$, velocity based on $M_1$; and $V_2$, velocity based on $M_2$.
   b. Assume you are a monetarist working for the Federal Reserve and are asked to predict nominal GDP one year in advance. Even if you knew the money supply, $M$, you would still need an estimate of $V$. One way to estimate velocity is to use data from the previous year. The idea is that, since you can't know velocity for, say, 1982 until you know nominal GDP and $M_1$ or $M_2$ for 1982, you might use velocity for 1981 to predict GDP for 1982. Table 31-2 assumes that the Federal Reserve can control the money supply exactly. Use your numbers for veloci to fill in the blank columns in Table 31-2 to predict income.
   c. Which years show the largest prediction errors? Why?

### TABLE 31-1

|      | Nominal GDP ($billions) | $M_1$ ($billions) | $M_2$ ($billions) | $V_1$ | $V_2$ |
|------|-------------------------|-------------------|-------------------|-------|-------|
| 1980 | 2,708.0 | 395.8 | 1,563.1 | _____ | _____ |
| 1981 | 3,030.6 | 422.7 | 1,711.2 | _____ | _____ |
| 1982 | 3,149.6 | 455.6 | 1,872.4 | _____ | _____ |
| 1983 | 3,405.0 | 497.9 | 2,069.2 | _____ | _____ |
| 1984 | 3,777.2 | 536.8 | 2,281.3 | _____ | _____ |
| 1985 | 4,038.7 | 586.3 | 2,474.2 | _____ | _____ |
| 1986 | 4,268.6 | 672.3 | 2,694.2 | _____ | _____ |
| 1987 | 4,539.9 | 737.3 | 2,866.6 | _____ | _____ |
| 1988 | 4,900.4 | 768.6 | 2,997.8 | _____ | _____ |
| 1989 | 5,250.8 | 790.9 | 3,155.8 | _____ | _____ |
| 1990 | 5,522.2 | 810.9 | 3,289.4 | _____ | _____ |
| 1991 | 5,677.5 | 863.3 | 3,395.7 | _____ | _____ |
| 1992 | 5,950.7 | 963.0 | 3,471.4 | _____ | _____ |

Source: *Economic Report of the President*, 1993, Tables B-1 and B-65;
*Economic Indicators*, May 1993

### TABLE 31-2

|      | Actual $M_1$ (billions) | $V_1$ from Previous Year | Estimated Income ($billions) | Actual Income ($billions) | Estimated Income ($billions) | $V_2$ from Previous Year | Actual $M_2$ (billions) |
|------|-------------------------|--------------------------|------------------------------|---------------------------|------------------------------|--------------------------|-------------------------|
| 1981 | 422.7 | _____ | _____ | 3,030.6 | _____ | _____ | 1,711.2 |
| 1982 | 455.6 | _____ | _____ | 3,149.6 | _____ | _____ | 1,872.4 |
| 1983 | 497.9 | _____ | _____ | 3,405.0 | _____ | _____ | 2,069.2 |
| 1984 | 536.8 | _____ | _____ | 3,777.2 | _____ | _____ | 2,281.3 |
| 1985 | 586.3 | _____ | _____ | 4,038.7 | _____ | _____ | 2,474.2 |
| 1986 | 672.3 | _____ | _____ | 4,268.6 | _____ | _____ | 2,694.2 |
| 1987 | 737.3 | _____ | _____ | 4,539.9 | _____ | _____ | 2,866.6 |
| 1988 | 768.6 | _____ | _____ | 4,900.4 | _____ | _____ | 2,997.8 |
| 1989 | 790.9 | _____ | _____ | 5,250.8 | _____ | _____ | 3,155.8 |
| 1990 | 810.9 | _____ | _____ | 5,522.2 | _____ | _____ | 3,289.4 |
| 1991 | 863.3 | _____ | _____ | 5,677.5 | _____ | _____ | 3,395.7 |
| 1992 | 963.0 | _____ | _____ | 5,950.7 | _____ | _____ | 3,471.4 |

**FIGURE 31-2**

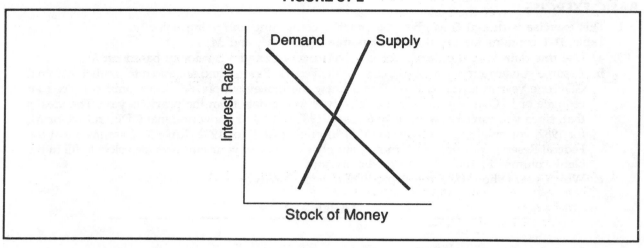

2. For this exercise you are asked to assume the role of adviser to the Federal Reserve's Open Market Committee. Figure 31-2 uses the demand and supply for money to show the actual stock of money and the rate of interest. Assume that initially the economy is at full-employment with price stability. The next meeting of the Open Market Committee begins with a report detailing the increase in the stock of money and interest rates since the last meeting. What to do is not so obvious, however, as suggested by the following arguments offered by two different members of the Committee:

A: This report confirms my fear that aggregate demand is expanding too rapidly. We risk unnecessary inflation and should move to reduce aggregate demand by an appropriate change in monetary policy.

B: This report confirms my concern that there has been an increase in the demand for money that is unrelated to GDP. Businesses and individuals have been harmed buying esoteric and risky financial securities. As a result of these losses there has been a general increase in the demand for money. If we do not take appropriate action the increase in interest rates since our last meeting will reduce aggregate demand and threatens recession.

You are asked to use Figure 31-2 to illustrate what each speaker is arguing and what actions they are suggesting. For each speaker try to determine what curve has shifted and how. Each is arguing for a particular policy to shift the supply-of-money schedule. What is that shift and how is it consistent with the speaker's analysis?

## SELF-TESTS FOR UNDERSTANDING

### Test A

Circle the most appropriate answer.

1. Velocity is measured by
   a. dividing the money stock by nominal GDP.
   b. computing the percentage change in nominal GDP from year to year.
   c. dividing nominal GDP by the stock of money.
   d. subtracting the rate of inflation from nominal interest rates.

2. The equation of exchange says that
   a. for every buyer there is a seller.
   b. $M \times V$ = Nominal GDP.
   c. demand equals supply.
   d. P.T. Barnum was right when he said, "There is a sucker born every minute."

3. According to the equation of exchange an increase in $M$ may lead to
   a. an increase in $Y$ (real GDP).
   b. an increase in $P$.
   c. a reduction in $V$.
   d. an increase in nominal GDP.
   e. any of the above.

4. According to the quantity theory an increase in $M$ will lead to
   (There may be more than one correct answer.)
   a. an increase in $Y$ (real GDP).
   b. an increase in $P$.
   c. a reduction in $V$.
   d. an increase in nominal GDP.
   e. any of the above.

5. Between 1956 and 1957 the money supply ($M_1$) was essentially constant and yet nominal GDP rose by slightly over 5 percent. It must be that
   a. velocity increased.
   b. velocity decreased.
   c. velocity was unchanged.

6. From 1985 to 1986 $M_1$ increased by 14.7 percent. $V_1$ declined from 6.89 to 6.35. It must be that nominal GDP increased by _____ percent.
   a. less than 14.7.
   b. exactly 14.7.
   c. more than 14.7.

7. The historical record shows
   a. that both $V_1$ and $V_2$ have been stable since 1929.
   b. that both $V_1$ and $V_2$ have been quite variable since 1929.
   c. continual increases in $V_1$ since 1929.
   d. that $V_2$ has been more stable than $V_1$ since 1929.

8. Initially the stock of money is $600 billion and velocity is 5. If one can be sure that velocity will not change, what increase in $M$ will be required to increase real GDP by $25 billion?
   a. $5 billion.
   b. $10 billion.
   c. $25 billion.
   d. Insufficient information.

9. Which of the following developments is *not* likely to lead to an increase in velocity?
   a. An increase in the expected rate of inflation.
   b. A reduction in the required reserve ratio for banks.
   c. An increase in interest rates as a result of an expansionary change in fiscal policy.
   d. A widespread trend toward more frequent pay periods.

10. If expansionary fiscal policy increases interest rates, a monetarist would expect that nominal GDP would _____ even if there is no change in the stock of money.
    a. decrease
    b. be unaffected
    c. increase

11. Which of the following is *not* likely to increase nominal GDP according to a monetarist analysis of income determination?
    a. An open market purchase that increases the stock of money.
    b. An increase in government spending.
    c. A technological change in banking practices that increases velocity.
    d. An increase in income taxes.

12. Keynesian analysis argues that the change in interest rates that accompanies an open market purchase is likely to
    a. increase velocity.
    b. have no effect on velocity.
    c. reduce velocity.

13. Which of the following make the value of the multiplier less than $1/(1-MPC)$? (There may be more than one correct answer.)
    a. The increase in interest rates that accompanies an increase in nominal GDP when the supply-of-money curve is constant.
    b. Income taxes.
    c. An increase in imports that normally accompanies an increase in GDP.
    d. Higher prices that reduce the purchasing power of money fixed assets and reduce net exports.

14. Which of the following is an example of a lag in policymaking as opposed to a lag in spending by firms and households?
    a. The construction of a new plant, induced by lower interest rates, cannot start for nine months, because it takes that long to prepare architectural drawings and contractors' bids.
    b. Congress takes five months to consider a presidential tax proposal.
    c. Through multiplier impacts, a $3 billion increase in defense spending eventually raises GDP by $5 billion.
    d. Refrigerator sales rise in the month following a $300 tax rebate.

15. Policy lags are probably shorter for _____ policy. Expenditure lags are probably shorter for _____ policy.
    a. fiscal; monetary
    b. monetary; fiscal
    c. fiscal; fiscal
    d. monetary; monetary

16. Assume that the stock of money and interest rates are both at levels desired by the Federal Reserve. Following a shift in the demand for money, the Fed can control
    (There may be more than one correct answer.)
    a. $M$ but not $r$.
    b. $r$ but not $M$.
    c. both $M$ and $r$.
    d. neither $M$ nor $r$.

17. Stabilization policy will be effective in combating recession if the aggregate supply curve is _____ and effective in combating inflation if the aggregate supply curve is _____.
    a. flat; steep
    b. steep; flat
    c. flat; flat
    d. steep; steep

18. If the aggregate supply curve is relatively flat, then
    a. velocity will be constant.
    b. both monetary and fiscal policy will have relatively large effects on output without much effect on prices.
    c. a change in interest rates will have little impact on investment.
    d. monetary policy will be effective while fiscal policy will not.

19. Which of the following is not an example of an automatic stabilizer?
    a. Unemployment compensation.
    b. The corporate income tax.
    c. Increased highway building enacted during a recession.
    d. Personal income taxes.

20. Forecasting by extrapolating previous timing relationships between changes in the stock of money and GDP is an example of
    a. judgmental forecasts.
    b. econometric models.
    c. leading indicators.
    d. automatic stabilizers.

## Test B

Circle T or F for true or false.

T  F   1.   If the stock of money is $1 trillion and nominal GDP is $6 trillion, then velocity is 6.

T  F   2.   The quantity theory is not really a theory because velocity, by definition, is equal to the ratio of nominal GDP divided by the money stock.

T  F   3.   Monetarist and Keynesian theories are both incomplete in that they concentrate on demand and ignore the supply side of the economy.

T  F   4.   Expansionary monetary policy that increases the stock of money will only increase prices with no impact on real output.

T  F   5.   The lag between a change in fiscal policy and its effects on aggregate demand is probably shorter than the lag between a change in monetary policy and its effects on aggregate demand.

T  F   6.   The lag in adopting an appropriate policy is probably shorter for fiscal policy than for monetary policy.

T  F   7.   By simultaneously using open market operations and making changes in minimum reserve requirements, the Fed would be able to achieve any desired combination of the money stock and the interest rate.

T  F   8.   The shape of the aggregate supply curve is likely to be relatively steep when the economy is operating near full-employment and relatively flat during periods of high unemployment and low rates of capacity utilization.

T  F   9.   Long lags will help make for better stabilization policy because there is more time for a complete analysis of possible actions.

T  F  10.   Automatic stabilizers reduce the sensitivity of the economy to shifts in aggregate demand.

**FIGURE 31-3**

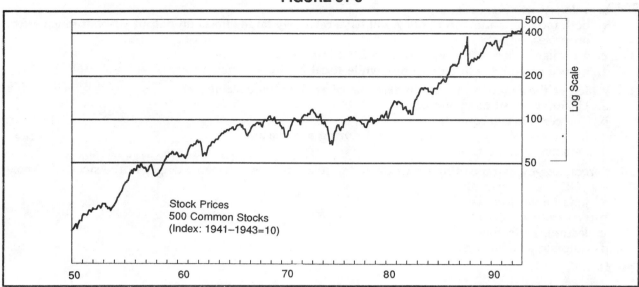

## SUPPLEMENTARY EXERCISE

### Leading Indicator

Is the stock market a good leading indicator of overall economic conditions? Figure 31-3 shows stock prices over the postwar period. Using just Figure 31-3 make an estimate of how many recessions there have been since 1950. Try to date each one approximately. Now go to the library and find a recent copy of the *Survey of Current Business*, a monthly publication of the Commerce Department that publishes data on a large number of economic series and keeps track of recessions as identified by the National Bureau of Economic Research. How many recessions does the NBER identify? How many did you identify? How many false indications of recession were there? What about the forecasting record of other leading indicators? What are the stock market and other leading indicators saying about a possible recession in the next 6 to 12 months?

In addition to the problem of false turning points, there are two other limitations to a purely mechanical use of leading indicators that you should be aware of:

a. Most large declines in a leading indicator are the result of not one large decline, but rather a series of consecutive small declines. At the same time each series has so many ups and downs that most small declines are followed by a small increase. One needs some way of separating those small declines that signal the start of a major slump from those that are quickly reversed.

b. A leading indicator that always changes direction a fixed amount of time before the economy does would be an extremely useful variable. However, the length of time between movements in most leading indicators and the economy may be quite variable.

## STUDY QUESTIONS

1. What is the difference between the equation of exchange, the quantity theory and monetarism?
2. What do you think explains the different historical experience of $V_1$ and $V_2$?
3. How would a monetarist explain the impact of expansionary fiscal policy on GDP and prices?
4. Why can't one use monetarism to determine nominal GDP, Keynesian analysis to determine real GDP, and then compute the price level by dividing the one by the other?
5. What is the difference between policy lags and expenditure lags? Which are likely to be more important for fiscal policy? monetary policy?
6. What's wrong with the following? "Long lags make for better policy as they provide more time for determining the best policy."
7. Why can't the Fed control both $M$ and $r$?
8. Do you think monetary policy should focus on stabilizing interest rates or stabilizing the growth in the stock of money? Why?
9. Why are concerns about excessive levels of government spending not a legitimate reason to oppose active stabilization policy?
10. Do you favor a more or less activist stabilization policy? Why?

## ECONOMICS IN ACTION

### What to Do?

What indicators should the Federal Reserve use when formulating monetary policy? General agreement exists that monetary policy should contribute to broad macroeconomic objectives—price stability, full employment, economic growth—although some would argue that greater weight should be placed on particular objectives, e.g. price stability or full employment. However, the Fed does not control the rate of inflation or the rate of unemployment. For that matter it does not even control interest rates or any measure of money. It has strong influence over these latter variables, which in turn are important for things like GDP, employment, and prices. But strong influence is not control. A related problem is that observations on different macroeconomic variables are available at different times. Estimates of GDP come only every three months. Unemployment and inflation are measured monthly. Data on $M_1$ and $M_2$ are announced every week while interest rates are available at a moment's notice.

At times the Fed has put more emphasis on interest rates and at others on $M_1$, $M_2$, or bank reserves as indicators of monetary policy. The Humphrey–Hawkins Act requires that the Fed announce ranges it expects for the growth of money. When testifying before Congress in July of 1993, and reporting on growth ranges expected for 1994, Alan Greenspan, Chairman of the Board of Governors of the Federal Reserve System, urged caution in interpreting the announced ranges.

The historical relationships between money and income, and between money and the price level have largely broken down, depriving the aggregates of much of their usefulness as guides to policy. At least for the time being, $M_2$ has been downgraded as a reliable indicator of financial conditions in the economy, and no single variable has yet been identified to take its place. . . . In the meantime, the process of probing a variety of data to ascertain underlying economic and financial conditions has become even more essential to formulating sound monetary policy. . . . In these circumstances it is especially prudent to focus on longer-term policy guides. One important guide post is real interest rates, which have a key bearing on longer-run spending decisions and inflation prospects.

Greenspan emphasized what he called the equilibrium real rate of interest:

> . . . specifically the real rate level that, if maintained, would keep the economy at its production potential over time. . . . Real rates, of course, are not directly observable, but must be inferred from nominal interest rates and estimates of inflation expectations. The most important real rates for private spending decisions almost surely are the longer maturities. Moreover, the equilibrium rate structure responds to the ebb and flow of underlying forces affecting spending.

Greenspan concluded:

> While the guides we have for policy may have changed recently, our goals have not. As I have indicated many times to this Committee, the Federal Reserve seeks to foster maximum sustainable economic growth and rising standards of living. And in that endeavor, the most productive function the central bank can perform is to achieve and maintain price stability.

1. What indicators of monetary policy would you favor if you were a member of the Federal Open Market Committee?
2. When is it appropriate to emphasize measures of the stock of money and when it is appropriate to emphasize interest rates?
3. While one can observe nominal interest rates, how does one measure the equilibrium real rate of interest in a way that makes it operational for the conduct of monetary policy?

---

SOURCES: Testimony by Alan Greenspan, Chairman of the Board of Governors of the Federal Reserve System, before the Subcommittee on Economic Growth and Credit Formation of the Committee on Banking, Finance, and Urban Affairs, U.S. House of Representatives, July 20, 1993.

*C h a p t e r* **32**

# Budget Deficits and the National Debt: Fact and Fiction

## LEARNING OBJECTIVES

After completing this chapter you should be able to:

- ◆ explain how measures to balance the budget may unbalance the economy.
- ◆ explain how appropriate fiscal policy depends on the strength of private demand and the conduct of monetary policy.
- ◆ explain the difference between the government's budget deficit and the national debt.
- ◆ discuss some facts about budget deficits and the national debt: When have budget deficits been largest? What has happened to the national debt as a proportion of GDP?
- ◆ describe how the concept of structural deficits or surpluses differs from officially reported deficits or surpluses.
- ◆ describe how traditional accounting procedures will overstate the interest component of government expenditures during a period of inflation.
- ◆ distinguish between real and fallacious arguments about the burden of the national debt.
- ◆ describe the inflationary consequences of a budget deficit and explain why deficits will be more inflationary if they are monetarized.
- ◆ evaluate arguments supporting the crowding-out and crowding-in properties of government deficit spending.
- ◆ explain how increased deficits can be associated with either higher or lower interest rates, higher or lower rates of inflation, and faster or slower growth in real output.
- ◆ explain how changing the mix of monetary and fiscal policy could change the budget deficit while leaving GDP and prices unchanged.
- ◆ explain why most economists measure the true burden of deficits by their impact on the capital stock.

## IMPORTANT TERMS AND CONCEPTS

Budget deficit
National debt
Real versus nominal interest rates
Inflation accounting
Structural deficit or surplus
Monetization of deficits
Crowding-out
Crowding-in
Burden of the national debt
Mix of monetary and fiscal policy

## CHAPTER REVIEW

Ever since 1980 the federal government's budget deficits have been very much like the weather: everyone has been talking about them but no one seems able to do anything about them. By itself this chapter cannot make government deficits larger or smaller, but it can help to increase your understanding of the impacts of both government deficits and the national debt.

(1)  The government runs a deficit when its (spending/revenue)exceeds its _____. There is a surplus when _____ is greater than _____. The national debt measures the government's total indebtedness. The national debt will increase if the government budget shows a (deficit/surplus). The national debt will decrease if the government budget shows a _____.

What is appropriate deficit policy? Earlier chapters discussed the use of fiscal and monetary policy to strike an appropriate balance between aggregate demand and aggregate supply in order to choose between inflation and unemployment. Considerations of balanced budgets, per se, were absent from that discussion. The conclusion that budget policy should adapt to the requirements of the economy is shared by many economists.

Some have advocated a policy of strict budget balance. There is good reason to expect that such a policy would balance the budget at the cost of unbalancing the economy. Consider an economy in an initial equilibrium at full-employment with a balanced budget. An autonomous decline in private spending

(2) would shift the expenditure schedule (down/up), resulting in a shift of the aggregate demand schedule to the (right/left). In the absence of any further policy action the result would be a (decline/increase) in GDP. The change in GDP will also mean a(n) (decline/increase) in tax revenues. The government's budget will move from its initial position of balance to one of (deficit/surplus). At this point, deliberate policy actions to reestablish budget balance would call for either a(n) (decrease/increase) in taxes or a(n) (decrease/increase) in government spending. In either case the result would be an additional shift in the expenditure schedule and aggregate demand curve that would (accentuate/counteract) the original shift that was due to the autonomous decline in private spending.

The fact that tax revenues depend on the state of the economy is important to understanding many complicated issues about the impact of deficits. As seen above, it helps to explain why a policy of budget balancing can unbalance the economy in the face of declines in private spending. It helps to explain why deficits can sometimes be associated with a booming economy and at other times with a sagging economy. It also helps to explain interest in alternative measures of the deficit. The concept of structural deficits, or structural surpluses is an attempt to control for the effects of the economy on the deficit. It does so by looking at spending and revenues at a specified high-employment level of income. Changes in tax

(3) revenues due to changes in income (will/will not) affect the actual deficit but (will/will not) affect the

structural deficit. For this reason, many analysts prefer to use the structural deficit as a measure of the stance of fiscal policy.

Inflation and, especially the impact of inflation on interest rates, raises complicated measurement problems. As we learned in Chapter 23, during periods of inflation, increases in nominal interest rates that reflect expectations of future inflation may not imply any change in real interest rates. To the extent that nominal interest rates include such inflationary premiums, a portion of interest payments is not payment for the use of the purchasing power embodied in the original loan; rather it is a repayment of the purchasing power of the original loan balance itself.

Are deficits inflationary? The short answer is yes and the more complete answer asks for more details. If the alternative to any deficit is more taxation or less spending, then any deficit, whether the result of deliberate policy or of a reduction in autonomous spending, will mean a higher price level, a higher level of output, and less unemployment than the alternative of a balanced budget. This is so because the deficit keeps the aggregate demand curve farther to the right than would be the case with either a decrease in spending or an increase in taxes. The exact inflationary consequences of a budget deficit depend on where along the aggregate supply curve the economy finds itself and what monetary policy is doing. A government deficit during a period of recession may find the economy operating on a relatively flat portion

(4) of the aggregate supply curve. If so, any reduction in the deficit will likely have a (large/<u>small</u>) impact on the price level but could have a relatively large impact on output and employment. In this situation, a deliberate increase in the deficit from expansionary fiscal policy could increase output and employment substantially (<u>with</u>/without) much impact on prices. On the other hand, substantial budget deficits at a time of full-employment will find the economy on a relatively steep portion of the aggregate supply curve. In this case, a reduction in the deficit is likely to have a (<u>large</u>/small) impact on output and a _____ impact on the price level.

A deficit that is associated with a deliberate reduction in taxes will increase output, prices, and interest rates as it shifts the aggregate demand curve to the right. Concerns about the impact of the deficit on interest rates may lead the Federal Reserve to increase the money supply. If the Federal Reserve acts

(5) to increase the stock of money by buying government securities, one says it has _____ the deficit. As we learned in Chapter 30, expansion of the money supply will imply a further expansionary shift in the aggregate demand curve and will mean even higher prices.

Many feelings about the burden of the national debt may be as deeply ingrained and just as irrational as a Victorian's ideas about sex or a football coach's ideas about winning. Many fallacious arguments about the burden of the debt do, however, contain some elements of truth. Arguments about the burden of future interest payments or the cost of repaying the national debt are not relevant when considering debts held

(6) by domestic citizens but are relevant when considering debts held by _____. To the extent that debt is held by domestic citizens, interest payments and debt repayments impose little burden on the nation as a whole; they are only transfers from taxpayers to bondholders, who may even be the same individuals. However, the impact on incentives by using higher taxes to accomplish these transfers should not be ignored.

A real burden of the debt would arise from a deficit in a high-employment economy that crowded

(7) out private (consumption/<u>investment</u>) spending and left a smaller capital stock to future generations. There will continue to be arguments as to whether U.S. deficits have entailed such a burden. The federal government's deficit has shown its largest increases during periods of _____ and _____. Government deficits during periods of slack may actually result in a benefit rather than a burden if, as a result of increased demand, they lead to (<u>crowding in</u>/crowding out) rather than _____. Major concerns about deficits during the late 1980s are that they occurred during a period of (<u>high</u>/low) employment and that they are thus likely to have led to crowding _____.

## IMPORTANT TERMS AND CONCEPTS QUIZ

Choose the best definition for the following terms.

1. _____ Budget deficit
2. _____ National debt
3. _____ Structural deficit
4. _____ Inflation accounting
5. _____ Monetization of deficits
6. _____ Crowding-out
7. _____ Crowding-in

a. Amount by which revenue exceeds spending.
b. Deficit under current fiscal policy if the economy was at full-employment.

c. Amount by which government spending exceeds revenue.
d. Increase in private investment spending induced by increase in government spending.
e. Adjusting standard accounting procedures for changes in purchasing power.
f. Contraction of private investment spending induced by deficit spending.
g. Federal government's total indebtedness.
h. Purchases of government bonds used to finance deficit by central bank.

## BASIC EXERCISE

This exercise is designed to show how a rigid policy of balanced budgets may unbalance the economy. To simplify the calculations, the exercise assumes that prices do not change and thus focuses on the horizontal shift in the aggregate demand curve.

1. Fill in the last column of Table 32-1 to determine the initial equilibrium level of income. The equilibrium level of income is _____.

2. What is the deficit at the initial equilibrium level of income? _____

3. The high employment level of income is $6,750. Is the structural budget in surplus or deficit?

    _____

    What is the magnitude of the structural surplus or deficit? _____

4. Investment spending now declines by $125 billion. Use Table 32-2 to compute the new equilibrium level of income. What is the new equilibrium level of income?

    _____

    How has the deficit changed, if at all? _____

    How has the structural (<u>deficit/surplus</u>) changed, if at all?

    _____

### TABLE 32-1
### (Constant Prices)

| Income (Output) Y | Taxes T | Disposable Income DI | Consumption Spending C | Investment Spending I | Government Purchases G | Exports X | Imports IM | Total Spending $C + I + G + (X - IM)$ |
|---|---|---|---|---|---|---|---|---|
| 6,000 | 800.0 | 5,200.0 | 4,500 | 900 | 950 | 500 | 600 | _____ |
| 6,250 | 862.5 | 5,387.5 | 4,650 | 900 | 950 | 500 | 625 | _____ |
| 6,500 | 925.0 | 5,575.0 | 4,800 | 900 | 950 | 500 | 650 | _____ |
| 6,750 | 987.5 | 5,762.5 | 4,950 | 900 | 950 | 500 | 675 | _____ |
| 7,000 | 1,050.0 | 5,950.0 | 5,100 | 900 | 950 | 500 | 700 | _____ |

## TABLE 32-2
### (Constant Prices)

| Income (Output) Y | Taxes T | Disposable Income DI | Consumption Spending C | Investment Spending I | Government Purchases G | Exports X | Imports IM | Total Spending C + I + G + (X − IM) |
|---|---|---|---|---|---|---|---|---|
| 6,000 | 800.0 | 5,200.0 | 4,500 | 775 | 950 | 500 | 600 | _____ |
| 6,250 | 862.5 | 5,387.5 | 4,650 | 775 | 950 | 500 | 625 | _____ |
| 6,500 | 925.0 | 5,575.0 | 4,800 | 775 | 950 | 500 | 650 | _____ |
| 6,750 | 987.5 | 5,762.5 | 4,950 | 775 | 950 | 500 | 675 | _____ |
| 7,000 | 1,050.0 | 5,950.0 | 5,100 | 775 | 950 | 500 | 700 | _____ |

5. If the government is committed to a balanced budget, would it raise or lower taxes to restore a balanced budget? _____ What would this change in taxes do to the equilibrium level of national income? _____ _____

6. If the government decides to change government purchases to eliminate the deficit, would it raise or lower spending? _____ What would this change do to the equilibrium level of national income? _____ _____

7. (Optional) How large a lump-sum change in taxes, that is, the same change at every level of income, would balance the budget? $ _____ billion. The new equilibrium level of income would be $_____ billion.

8. (Optional) How large a change in government spending would balance the budget?
   $_____ billion. The new equilibrium level of income would be $_____ billion.

## SELF-TESTS FOR UNDERSTANDING

### Test A

Circle the most appropriate answer.

1. The federal government deficit is
   a. the excess of tax revenues over transfer payments.
   b. another term for political gridlock.
   c. total indebtedness of the government.
   d. the difference between government spending and the government's revenue for a given year.

2. The national debt is
   a. equal to the cumulation of past federal government deficits.
   b. another term for the federal government's deficit.
   c. what the United States, government, and private businesses owe foreigners.
   d. the excess of spending over revenue for a given year.

3. The ratio of the national debt to GDP
   a. has declined continuously since World War II.
   b. has increased continuously since World War II.
   c. is about 3 to 1.
   d. has risen over the 1980s from its recent low point in the 1970s.

4. The structural deficit is
   a. equal to the deficit minus interest payments on the national debt.
   b. equal to zero, by definition.
   c. defined as the deficit the government would run if the economy were at full-employment.
   d. the excess of government investment spending over allocations for these projects.

5. At high levels of unemployment, the government's actual deficit will be _____ the structural deficit.
   a. smaller than
   b. the same as
   c. larger than

6. During the 1980s the structural deficit of the federal government
   a. decreased continuously.
   b. fluctuated but showed no trend.
   c. increased substantially.
   d. had been offset by higher tax revenues.

7. Many observers argue that the structural deficit is a better measure of the stance of fiscal policy than the actual deficit because the
   a. actual deficit can be larger or smaller than expected if GDP is smaller or larger than expected.
   b. actual deficit does not include the impact of automatic stabilizers.
   c. structural deficit is based on real rather than nominal interest rates.
   d. structural deficit represents what the President proposes rather than what is enacted by Congress.

8. Until the 1980s, large government deficits were associated with periods of
   (There may be more than one correct answer.)
   a. high inflation.
   b. war.
   c. recession.
   d. low unemployment.

9. A decline in private investment spending will lead to all but which one of the following?
   a. A downward shift in the expenditure schedule.
   b. A decline in the equilibrium level of GDP.
   c. An increase in the government deficit or a reduction in the surplus.
   d. A decline in the structural budget deficit or surplus.

10. Rigid adherence to budget balancing will
    a. help the economy adjust to shifts in private spending.
    b. have little impact on business cycles.
    c. accentuate swings in GDP from autonomous changes in private spending.
    d. help maintain full-employment.

11. If the Federal Reserve monetizes a budget deficit, there will be a(n)
    a. smaller inflationary impact.
    b. unchanged inflationary impact.
    c. larger inflationary impact.

12. The inflationary consequences of a budget deficit are likely to be greatest when
    a. the deficit is the result of a decline in private spending.
    b. the deficit is the result of a deliberate decision to raise taxes and monetize the resulting deficit.
    c. the economy is operating along a relatively flat portion of the aggregate supply curve.
    d. there is an increase in both the actual and structural deficit during a period of low unemployment.

13. Using real interest rates when measuring the deficit during a period of inflation would have what impact?
    a. It would make the deficit smaller.
    b. It would leave the deficit unchanged.
    c. It would make the deficit larger.

14. An increase in the deficit is likely to be correlated with which of the following? (There may be more than one correct answer.)
    a. Faster growth in GDP.
    b. Lower interest rates.
    c. A reduction in the rate of inflation.
    d. Higher interest rates.
    e. Greater inflation.
    f. A slowing of the rate of growth of GDP.

15. The macroeconomic impact of a reduction in government spending to reduce the deficit could be offset by
    a. an increase in taxes.
    b. an open market purchase.
    c. a reduction in taxes.
    d. an open market sale.

16. A deficit that follows a decline in private spending is likely to be associated with which of the following?
    a. Higher inflation.
    b. Lower interest rates.
    c. A reduction in unemployment.
    d. A reduction in the national debt.

17. Which of the following is a valid argument about the burden of the national debt for an economy whose debt is held entirely by its own citizens?
    a. Future generations will find interest payments a heavy burden.
    b. When the debt is due, future generations will be burdened with an enormous repayment.
    c. The debt will bankrupt future generations.
    d. If the deficits causing the debt reduced private investment spending, then future generations would be left with a smaller capital stock.

18. "Crowding-out" refers to
    a. increased population pressures and arguments for zero population growth.
    b. the effects of government deficits on private investment spending.
    c. what happens at the start of the New York City marathon.
    d. the impact of higher prices on the multiplier.

19. Crowding-out is likely to occur if (There may be more than one correct answer.)
    a. the amount of private savings is unchanged.
    b. the economy is operating near full-employment.
    c. the rate of unemployment is high.
    d. inflation is low.

20. Crowding-in is more likely to occur when
    a. the economy is operating near full-employment.
    b. prices are rising.
    c. the government lowers expenditures.
    d. there is substantial slack in the economy.

## Test B

Circle T or F for true or false.

T F 1. A policy calling for continuous balance in the government's budget will help offset shifts in autonomous private demand.

T F 2. A balanced high-employment budget is necessary if the equilibrium level of GDP is to equal the full-employment level of GDP.

T F 3. Inflation accounting would increase the interest portion of government expenditures during periods of inflation.

T F 4. Increases in the government's deficit are always associated with increases in interest rates.

T F 5. The inflationary impact of any budget deficit depends on the conduct of monetary policy.

T F 6. Recent government deficits have meant that the ratio of national debt to GDP has never been higher than it is today.

T F 7. Interest payments on the national debt, whether to domestic citizens or foreigners, are not really a burden on future generations.

T F 8. A major limitation of the simple crowding-out argument is the assumption that the economy's total pool of savings is fixed.

T F 9. Crowding-in is likely to occur when the economy is operating with slack employment, whereas crowding-out is likely to occur at full-employment.

T F 10. Government deficits may impose a real burden on future generations if, as a result of crowding out, there is less private investment and a smaller capital stock in the future.

## SUPPLEMENTARY EXERCISES

### 1. Government Deficits and Interest Rates

Between 1957 and 1958, the federal government's budget shifted from a surplus of $2.3 billion to a deficit of $10.3 billion. At the time this was the largest deficit since World War II and was bigger than any deficit during the Great Depression. At the same time, interest rates declined dramatically. The rate on three-month Treasury bills declined from an average of 3.267 percent in 1957 to 1.839 percent in 1958. The rate on three- to five-year securities fell from 3.62 to 2.90 percent.

Between 1974 and 1975, the federal government's budget deficit increased from $11.6 billion to $69.4 billion. At the same time, interest rates again declined. The rate on three-month Treasury bills declined from 7.886 to 5.838 percent, while the rate on three- to five-year securities declined more modestly from 7.81 to 7.55 percent.

Between 1981 and 1982 the federal government deficit increased dramatically from $58.8 billion to $135.5 billion. At the same time, interest rates declined. The rate on three–month Treasury bills declined from 14.029 percent to 10.686 percent. Interest rates on longer term government securities also declined.

Between 1991 and 1992 the federal government deficit went from $210.4 billion to $298 billion, the largest year-to-year increase to date. At the same time, interest rates on long-term government bonds declined from 7.86 percent to 7.01 percent while rates on short-term government borrowing declined almost two percentage points from 5.42 percent to 3.45 percent.

How do you explain the seemingly contradictory results that larger deficits are associated with lower, not higher, interest rates? Do these observations prove that larger deficits will always be associated with lower interest rates?

## 2. Repudiate the National Debt?

If the national debt is so onerous, we could solve the problem by simply repudiating the debt; that is, we would make no more interest or principal payments on the outstanding debt.

Imagine that in keeping with democratic principles such a proposition were put to American voters. Who do you think would vote pro and who would vote con? Which side would win? Would the outcome of the vote be different if the debt were held entirely by foreigners? By banks and other financial institutions? (The Treasury publishes data on who holds the national debt in the *Treasury Bulletin*. This data is also published in the annual *Economic Report of the President*. You might want to look at these data and consider what would happen to depositors, shareholders, and pensioners, both current and prospective, if the national debt held by banks, corporations, and pension funds was suddenly worthless.)

Repudiating the national debt might well limit future budget flexibility. What would be the likely consequences during periods of future recession? Inflation? War?

## 3. Continual Budget Deficits

What are the long-run consequences of continual budget deficits? If you have access to a programmable hand calculator or to a microcomputer, experiment with the following simulation model to discover how results depend on particular coefficients.

a. Assume that nominal GDP grows at a constant rate, $\lambda$:

$$GDP_t = (1 + \lambda) \, GDP_{t-1}$$

b. Assume that tax receipts are proportional to nominal GDP:

$$T_t = \tau \, GDP_t$$

c. Assume that government purchases of goods and services plus all transfer payments except for interest on the national debt are also some constant percentage of nominal GDP:

$$G_t = g \, GDP_t; \; g > \tau$$

(This specification means that, not counting interest payments, the government deficit is a constant proportion [g – t] of nominal GDP).

d. Assume that the government must pay interest on the national debt at a rate of interest $R$:

$$\text{Interest payments} = IP_t = R \, (\text{Debt}_t)$$

e. The government's total deficit is:

$$\text{Deficit}_t = G_t + IP_t - T_t$$

f. The government debt grows as follows:

$$\text{Debt}_{t+1} = \text{Debt}_t + \text{Deficit}_t$$

g. Use these relationships to simulate your model economy and investigate what happens to the ratio of debt to GDP. To start your simulations you will need values for the four parameters, $\lambda$, $\tau$, $g$, and $R$, and initial values for GDP and the national debt. Try starting with the following:

|  |  |  |  |
|---|---|---|---|
| $\lambda$ | = 0.08 | $R$ | = 0.05 |
| $\tau$ | = 0.20 | GDP | = 6,000 |
| $g$ | = 0.22 | Debt | = 2,500 |

What happens to the ratio of debt to GDP as your model economy evolves?

   h. Try experimenting with some alternative parameters and initial values.
      (i)   Change the initial value of GDP then change the initial value of the national debt. Do these changes affect what happens over time?
     (ii)   Now change $\tau$ and $g$. What happens? Do these changes affect the eventual ratio of debt to GDP? If so, how?
    (iii)   Finally, change $\lambda$ and $R$, individually and then together. Remember that $\lambda$ is the growth rate of nominal GDP and $R$ is nominal interest rates. Higher inflation would be expected to change both $\lambda$ and $R$, whereas a change in real growth or real interest rates would change them individually. Do these changes affect the eventual ratio of debt to GDP? If so, how?

# ECONOMICS IN ACTION
## Huffing and Puffing

Writing in the Summer 1989 issue of *The Brooking Review*, economist Charles Schultze asks whether the federal government deficit is best characterized as a wolf at the door, a domesticated pussycat, or termites in the basement. Schultze attributes the view of the deficit-as-wolf to Wall Street financial circles and some economists. Many who see the deficit as wolf are fearful of a sudden collapse of confidence in the U.S. economy and the dollar. In this view, the resulting sharp drop in the exchange value of the dollar would force the Federal Reserve to defend the dollar by raising interest rates, plunging the economy into a prolonged and serious recession.

Schultze identifies himself with those who hold the termite view. In Schultze's view the result of trying to muddle through, putting up with current deficits, will not be a sudden collapse but rather a steady erosion in the growth prospects of the American economy. When domestic savings decline and the government deficit increases, a country can sustain investment only through increased borrowing from abroad. [Appendix A to Chapter 25 showed that equilibrium on the income-expenditure diagram can be expressed as

$$Y = C + I + G + X - IM, \text{ or as}$$
$$I + G + X = S + T + IM.$$

This latter expression can be rewritten as $I = S - (G - T) + (IM - X)$. When $S$ declines, and $G - T$ increases, then to avoid a drop in $I$, $IM - X$ must increase.] For much of the 1980s increased government deficits were, to a large extent, offset by an increased trade deficit. Schultze notes that continuation of large deficits matched by large foreign borrowing may allow the United States to sustain the level of private investment, but it does so by "increasing the future diversion of national income to overseas interest payments . . . depressing the future path of American living standards." What would happen if foreigners reduce their investments in the United States? In the absence of an increase in domestic savings or a reduction in the deficit, the result must be a decline in private investment and slower growth in American living standards.

Schultze identifies economists on both the political left and right as among those who argue that the deficit is benign, only a pussycat. The pussycat arguments Schultze identifies include: inflation adjustments advocated by Robert Eisner (discussed in Chapter 32); the debt neutrality arguments of Robert Barro (discussed in the text); the lower overall deficit when the budgets of state and local governments are combined with that of the federal government; and the lack of a capital budget on the part of the federal government. Schultze argues that if one reduces the deficit by subtracting the inflation premium in nominal interest rates, there should be a corresponding and offsetting decline in the income and savings of bond holders. While the deficit may be smaller, the final result is no change in net national savings or investment. Like many other economists, Schultze is skeptical of the applicability of arguments about debt neutrality. When discussing the surpluses of state and local governments, Schultze argues that such surpluses are to a large extent accounting artifacts that reflect growing reserves by state and local governments for future pension payments. Even if, as Schultze would prefer, one counts these reserves as private savings, one is still left with a substantial drop in private savings during the 1980s. Finally, Schultze argues that the establishment of a separate capital budget might reduce the deficit in the federal government's operating budget but, again, it would not change the fundamental imbalance between actual domestic savings and the level of private investment necessary to sustain acceptable economic growth.

1. Which view of the deficit do you think is most appropriate and why?

"Of Wolves, Termites, and Pussycats," *The Brookings Review*, Summer 1989, pp. 26 - 33.

## STUDY QUESTIONS

1. What is the difference between the government's deficit and its debt? What is the link between the two?

2. What does the historical record show about when the federal government has run large deficits?

3. Why are policies to stabilize the deficit likely to destabilize the economy?

4. When is a budget deficit appropriate and why? When it is inappropriate?

5. What does the historical record show about the ratio of federal government debt to GDP?

6. What is the difference between the structural deficit and the actual deficit? Which is usually larger and why? Which is a more accurate measure of the stance of fiscal policy?

7. Does an increase in the deficit always indicate a move to expansionary fiscal policy? Why?

8. Does an increase in the deficit always lead to higher interest rates and more inflation? Why?

9. Why do economists argue that foreign-held debt imposes more of a burden than government debt held by Americans?

10. What are the real burdens of the debt?

11. Since deficits are a results of fiscal policy decisions, how does the impact of deficits depend upon monetary policy?

12. What is crowding-out and crowding-in? When is one more likely than the other and why?

*Chapter* **33**

# The Trade-Off Between Inflation and Unemployment

## LEARNING OBJECTIVES

After completing this chapter you should be able to:

- explain how prices can rise following either the rapid growth of aggregate demand or the sluggish growth of aggregate supply.
- explain what the Phillips curve is and what it is not
- explain how the slope of the Phillips curve is related to the slope of the aggregate supply curve.
- explain how the source of fluctuations in economic activity—whether predominantly from shifts of the aggregate demand curve or from shifts of the aggregate supply curve—will affect the Phillips curve.
- explain why the economy's self-correcting mechanism means that the economy's true long-run choices lie along a vertical Phillips curve.
- use the long-run Phillips curve to show how the temporary impact of aggregate demand policy on unemployment can have a permanent impact on the rate of inflation.
- explain how and why one's views on appropriate aggregate demand policy are likely to depend upon one's views on
  - the social costs of inflation vs. unemployment.
  - the slope of the short-run Phillips curve.
  - the efficiency of the economy's self-correcting mechanism.
  - how quickly inflationary expectations adjust.
- explain how the accuracy of expectations about inflation can affect the slope of both the aggregate supply curve and the Phillips curve.
- discuss the implications of and evidence for the hypotheses of rational expectations.
- discuss measures that have been advocated to reduce the natural rate of unemployment.
- calculate how indexing would be applied to wages and interest rates, given the appropriate data on prices.
- discuss the advantages and disadvantages of universal indexing.

## IMPORTANT TERMS AND CONCEPTS

Demand-side inflation
Vertical (long-run) Phillips curve
Rational expectations
Supply-side inflation
Trade-off between inflation and unemployment in
    the short-run and in the long-run
Phillips curve

Stagflation caused by supply shocks
Self-correcting mechanism
Natural rate of unemployment
Inflationary expectations
Wage-price controls
Indexing (escalator clauses)
Real versus nominal interest rates

## CHAPTER REVIEW

This chapter discusses the hard choices that policymakers must make when deciding how to respond to inflation or unemployment. Chapters 28 through 31 discussed how changes in various tools of fiscal and monetary policy can be used to influence aggregate demand. Chapter 33 uses this material to study the policy implications for fighting unemployment and inflation. Here, as in many other areas of life, one cannot have one's cake and eat it too. Actions taken to reduce unemployment will often lead to higher rates of inflation, while actions to reduce inflation will often lead to higher rates of unemployment. Economists can help to define the nature of this trade-off, examine the factors that are responsible for it, and clarify the implications of different choices, but they cannot tell anyone which choice to make. In a democratic society, this decision is left to the political process.

(1)    Any shift in the aggregate demand or aggregate supply curve, whether induced by policy or not, is likely to affect both prices and output. The nature of the association between changes in prices and changes in output will depend upon which curve shifts. If fluctuations in economic activity are predominantly the result of shifts in the aggregate demand curve, higher prices will be associated with (higher/lower) levels of output. The transition to higher prices is a period of inflation. The associated higher level of output will require more employment, leading to a lower level of unemployment. Hence, shifts in the aggregate demand curve imply that inflation and unemployment are (negatively/positively) correlated. That is, if you plotted the rate of unemployment on the horizontal axis and the rate of inflation on the vertical axis, the resulting curve, called the _____ curve, would have a (positive/negative) slope.

(2)    Data for the 1950s and 1960s was consistent with the view sketched above and seemed to imply that policymakers could choose between inflation and unemployment. In particular, it used to be thought that the Phillips curve implied that policymakers could permanently increase output beyond the level of full employment or potential output at the cost of only a small increase in the rate of inflation. Subsequent experience has shown that this view is (correct/incorrect). We saw earlier that output beyond the level of potential output results in a(n) (inflationary/recessionary) gap. The economy's self-correcting mechanism will shift the aggregate supply curve to reestablish long-run equilibrium at the _____ rate of unemployment. Continual shifts of the aggregate demand curve would be necessary to maintain a lower rate of unemployment. These continual shifts of the aggregate demand curve will imply an ever-increasing rate of inflation. The only true long-run choices lie along a _____ Phillips curve.

   In the short run, shifts in the aggregate demand curve will move the economy up or down the short-run Phillips curve; but the economy's self-correcting mechanism implies that this trade-off is only temporary. How long this trade-off lasts depends upon the speed of the economy's self-correcting mechanism. Differing views about the speed of the mechanism are an important part of differences in Keynesian and monetarist policy prescriptions.

   Changes in money wages are an important determinant of shifts in the aggregate supply curve that lead an inflationary gap to self-destruct. It is the original increase in prices above wages that induces firms to expand output. As workers recognize that the purchasing power of their money wages has declined, the subsequent increases in wages to restore real wages will lead to shifts in the aggregate supply curve.

Rather than always being a step behind, workers can try to protect their real wages by anticipating the increase in prices. On this view the expectation of higher prices will lead to higher wages and a shift in the aggregate supply curve in anticipation of inflation. Compared with cases where the aggregate supply curve did not shift, a shift in the aggregate demand curve accompanied by an expectations-induced shift

(3) in the aggregate supply curve will have a (larger/smaller) impact on output and a _____ impact on prices. The result will be a (higher/lower) rate of inflation and the slope of the short-run Phillips curve will be (steeper/flatter).

Economists associated with the hypothesis of rational expectations have focused attention on the formation of expectations. While much remains to be learned, these economists argue that errors in predicting inflation cannot be systematic. An implication of this view is that, except for random elements, the short-run Phillips curve is vertical. Not only is there no long-run trade-off between inflation and unemployment, but, according to this view, there is also no systematic short-run trade-off.

Others are less convinced that expectations are rational in the sense of no systematic errors. These economists believe that people tend to underpredict inflation when it is rising and overpredict it when it is falling. Long-term contracts also make it difficult to adjust to changing expectations of inflation. These economists argue that policy measures to shift the aggregate demand curve can affect output and employment in the short run. But remember that these short-run impacts are constrained by the true long-

(4) run menu of choices which lie along a _____ Phillips curve.

Most economists believe that aggregate demand policy will affect employment and inflation in the short run and will also affect the place where the economy ends up on the long-run Phillips curve. Thus, to fight a recession rather than to wait for the economy's self-correcting mechanism will mean more employment in the short run and is likely to mean more inflation in the long run as compared to a status quo policy that waits on the economy's self-correcting mechanisms. (See Figures 33-14 and 33-15 in the text.) Whether one wants to use aggregate demand policy or wait for natural processes depends on one's assessment of the costs of inflation and unemployment; the efficiency of the economy's self-correcting mechanisms; the current level of output vis-a-vis full employment, especially as it has implications for the slope of the short-run Phillips curve; and the quickness with which inflationary expectations adjust.

A number of policies have been advocated in the hope that they will improve the inflation-unemployment trade-off. These policies run the gamut from presidential exhortations to elaborate wage-price monitoring bureaucracies to proposals for new forms of labor contracts that tie a portion of wages to profits.

*Voluntary wage-price guideposts* call for business and labor to set wages and prices in line with standards determined, in part, by increases in labor productivity. The logic of these guidelines is that labor wage can increases in line with increases in productivity without adding to inflationary pressures from the cost side. Thus, if labor productivity is increasing at 2 percent a year and the government is aiming to hold inflation to 3 percent a year, the guidepost standard for wage increases would be 5 percent.

More drastic forms of income policies include wage-price controls or even a wage-price freeze. Neither policy is a desirable long-run option. If adhered to for a long time, either policy undermines the allocative role of prices and results in inefficient alternatives. Historically, the Nixon wage-price freeze was a tactical device in order to allow time for a program of controls. A wage-price freeze or a set of

(5) controls might work if it resulted in a significant lowering of inflationary _____. However, if there is no change in the underlying forces of aggregate demand and supply, there (is/is not) likely to be much change in expectations.

A number of individuals have argued that rather than trying to reduce the rate of inflation we should simply learn to live with it and rely on automatic adjustments of monetary payments to reflect changes in prices, a process known as indexing. The automatic adjustment of social security benefits, as well as other government transfer programs, and escalator clauses in wage contracts are examples of

(6) _____. A number of observers also advocate this mechanism for interest rates.

Indexing does seem to offer some relief from many of the social costs of inflation discussed in Chapter 23. As workers, firms, and lenders scramble to protect them-selves against anticipated future increases

(7) in prices, current prices and interest rates will (increase/decrease) to reflect the expectation of inflation.

If actual inflation turns out to be greater or less than expected, there will be a redistribution of wealth that many feel is essentially arbitrary. Uncertainty over future prices may make individuals and businesses extremely reluctant to enter into long-term contracts. Indexing offers relief from these problems. Labor contracts and other agreements could be written in real rather than nominal terms, and arbitrary redistributions would be avoided because money payments would reflect actual, not expected, inflation. At the same time, there is concern that learning to live with inflation may make the economy (more/less) inflation prone.

## IMPORTANT TERMS AND CONCEPTS QUIZ

Choose the best definition for the following terms.

1. _____ Vertical Phillips curve
2. _____ Rational expectations
3. _____ Phillips curve
4. _____ Self-correcting mechanism
5. _____ Natural rate of unemployment
6. _____ Inflationary expectations
7. _____ Wage-price controls
8. _____ Indexing

a. Graph depicting unemployment rate on horizontal axis and inflation rate on vertical axis.

b. Legal restrictions on the ability of industry and labor to raise wages and prices.
c. Unemployment rate at full employment.
d. Vertical line at natural rate of inflation.
e. Forecasts which make optimal use of available and relevant data.
f. Adjustments of monetary payments whenever a specified price index changes.
g. The economy's way of curing inflationary and recessionary gaps via changes in the price level.
h. Vertical line at the natural rate of unemployment.
i. Beliefs concerning future price level increases.

## BASIC EXERCISE

This exercise is designed to illustrate the nature of the inflation-unemployment trade-off that policymakers must face when planning aggregate demand policy.

1. Figure 33-1 shows an economy with a recessionary gap. Which of the following monetary and fiscal policies could be used to help eliminate this gap?
   - open market (purchase/sale).
   - (increase/decrease) of minimum reserve requirements.
   - (increase/decrease) in taxes.
   - (increase/decrease) in government transfer payments to individuals.
   - (increase/decrease) in government purchases of goods and services.

2. Assume the full-employment level of income is $6,500 billion. Draw a new aggregate demand curve, representing one or more of the appropriate policies you identified in Question 1, that will restore full employment for this economy. Following a shift in the aggregate demand curve, prices will rise to _____.

3. Consider the following statement:

   "The increase in prices that resulted when we restored full employment was a small price to pay for the increased output. Why not try moving even farther along the aggregate supply curve? If we further stimulate the economy to lower unemployment we can increase output to, say, $6,700 billion and prices will only rise to 109. We can thus have a permanent increase in output of $200 billion every year in return for a one-time increase in prices of just under 6 percent. That's a pretty favorable trade-off." What is wrong with the reasoning of this argument?

**FIGURE 33-1**

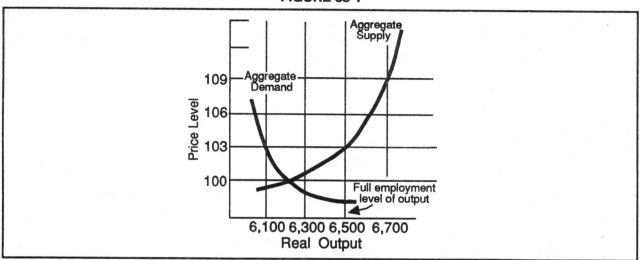

**FIGURE 33-2**                    **FIGURE 33-3**

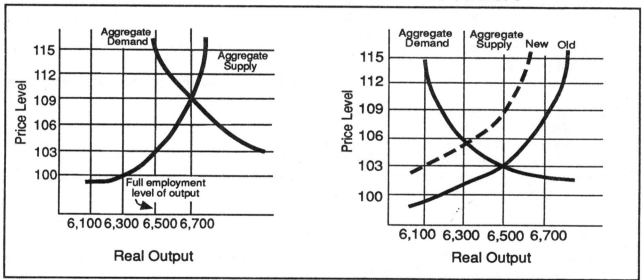

Is the output-price combination of $6,700 billion and 109 a viable long-run equilibrium position? (Figure 33-2 illustrates such a combination. What is apt to happen to the aggregate supply curve? Draw in the new aggregate supply curve that restores full employment.) What would happen if government policymakers tried to keep output at $6,700 billion on a permanent basis? (That is, what would happen if every time the aggregate supply curve shifted, policymakers undertook appropriate expansionary fiscal or monetary policy to shift the aggregate demand curve in an effort to avoid any reduction in output.)

4. Figure 33-3 shows an economy following an adverse shift in the aggregate supply curve. Equilibrium used to be an output of $6,500 and a price level of 103.
   a. What is the new equilibrium immediately following the adverse shift in the supply curve?
      Output _____
      Prices _____

b. If there is to be no decline in employment, the government will need to implement (expansionary/restrictive) policies to shift the aggregate demand curve. The government could maintain employment, but at the cost of an increase in prices to _____.

c. Alternatively, the government could avoid any increase in prices. Such a decision would require (expansionary/restrictive) policies and would result in a new equilibrium level of output of _____.

## SELF-TESTS FOR UNDERSTANDING

Circle the most appropriate answer.

1. If fluctuations in economic activity are caused by shifts in the aggregate demand curve, then
   a. prices and output will be negatively correlated.
   b. the short-run Phillips curve will be vertical.
   c. the long-run Phillips curve will have a negative slope.
   d. the rates of inflation and unemployment will tend to be negatively correlated.

2. If fluctuations in economic activity are the result of shifts in the aggregate supply curve, then
   a. prices and output will be positively correlated.
   b. the short-run Phillips curve will have a negative slope.
   c. the long-run Phillips curve will be horizontal.
   d. the rate of inflation and rate of unemployment will tend to be positively correlated.

3. The Phillips curve
   a. is a statistical relationship that summarizes the historical correlation between unemployment and inflation.
   b. is the set of long-term equilibrium relationships between the rate of unemployment and the rate of inflation.
   c. is the third turn at the Indianapolis 500 Speedway.
   d. shows how nominal interest rate changes when expectations of inflation change.

4. The economy's self-correcting mechanisms mean that in the long run the Phillips curve is likely to
   a. have a negative slope.
   b. have a positive slope.
   c. be horizontal.
   d. be vertical.

5. The difference between the short-run and long-run Phillips curves suggests that activist policy to eliminate a recessionary gap is likely to result in
   a. a temporary period of higher inflation and a permanently lower rate of unemployment.
   b. temporarily higher inflation and lower unemployment.
   c. a temporary period of lower unemployment and a permanently higher rate of inflation.
   d. permanently lower unemployment and inflation.

6. The positively sloped aggregate supply curve is drawn on the assumption that
   a. the cost of productive inputs remains unchanged as output changes.
   b. wages are fully indexed.
   c. the Phillips curve is never vertical.
   d. wage and price controls limit the impact of inflation.

7. An increase in wages, due either to inflation that has occurred in the past or inflation that is expected to occur in the future, can be modeled as
   a. an upward shift in the aggregate supply curve.
   b. an inward shift in the production possibilities frontier
   c. a downward shift in the aggregate demand curve.
   d. a leftward shift in the long-run Phillips curve.

8. An increased emphasis on expectations of future inflation in wage settlements will
   a. lead to a flatter Phillips curve.
   b. have no impact on the Phillips curve.
   c. lead to a steeper Phillips curve.

9. Stabilization policy faces a trade-off between inflation and unemployment in the short run because changes in monetary and fiscal policy have their most immediate impact on the _____.
   a. aggregate supply curve
   b. Phillips curve
   c. production possibilities frontier
   d. aggregate demand curve

10. Which of the following are necessary for expectations to meet the economist's definition of rational expectations? (There may be more than one correct answer.)
    a. They are based on relevant and available information.
    b. They can only be made by economists and statisticians.
    c. There are no systematic errors.
    d. They are always correct.

11. A strong believer in rational expectations would be surprised by which one of the following occurrences?
    a. An announcement by the Fed that it will increase the rate of growth of the money supply leads to expectations of higher inflation.
    b. Plans to lower taxes give rise to expectations of higher prices.
    c. Plans to fight inflation by restrictive policy succeed in reducing the rate of inflation with no increase in unemployment.
    d. An examination of the record shows that people consistently underestimate the rate of inflation during periods when it is increasing.

12. The hypothesis of rational expectations implies that increases in output beyond the level of potential output can be produced
    a. by expected increases in prices.
    b. only by unexpected increases in prices.
    c. by any increase in prices whether expected or not.
    d. by preannounced increases in the money supply or reductions in taxes.

13. Consider a shift to the right of the aggregate demand curve due to expansionary monetary and fiscal policy. Assume that the adoption of expansionary policies leads to expectations of inflation that induce a simultaneous shift in the aggregate supply curve. The resulting change in output will be _____ if there were no shift in the aggregate supply curve.
    a. smaller than
    b. the same as
    c. larger than

14. Under the same conditions as question 13, the resulting change in prices will be _____
    if there were no shift in the aggregate supply curve.
    a. smaller than
    b. the same as
    c. larger than

15. Which of the following is *not* a feasible alternative for aggregate demand policy following an adverse
    shift of the supply curve to the left?
    a. Do nothing and initially experience both higher prices and lower output.
    b. Avoid the reduction in output at the cost of even higher prices.
    c. Avoid the increase in prices at the cost of an even greater decline in output.
    d. Avoid both the reduction in output and increase in prices by using both fiscal and monetary policy
       to shift the aggregate demand curve.

16. Restrictive monetary and fiscal policy adopted to reduce the rate of inflation will work quicker and
    have a smaller impact on unemployment when
    a. changes in inflationary expectations take a long time.
    b. the long-run Phillips curve is vertical.
    c. expectations of inflation adjust quickly to the change in macro policy.
    d. the natural rate of unemployment equals the natural rate of inflation.

17. If job retraining or other measures are successful in reducing the natural rate of unemployment,
    a. the long-run Phillips curve will shift to the left.
    b. the aggregate supply curve will become less steep.
    c. the short-run Phillips curve will become vertical.
    d. the natural rate of inflation will increase.

18. Wage-price controls
    a. may be effective if they succeed in changing expectations of inflation.
    b. were used with great success by President Nixon.
    c. have little long-run impact on economic efficiency.
    d. can be imposed on some parts of the economy without affecting the rest of the economy.

19. A general policy of indexing
    a. is an attempt to shift the aggregate supply curve downward and to the right.
    b. would help to balance the federal government's budget.
    c. is an attempt to ease the social cost of inflation, not an attempt to improve the terms of the
       inflation-unemployment trade-off.
    d. runs little risk of accelerating the rate of inflation.

20. Which of the following is an example of indexing?
    a. Tax penalties on firms that grant excessive wage increases.
    b. The adjustment of nominal interest rates in response to expectations of inflation.
    c. The average change in prices on the New York Stock Exchange.
    d. Increases in social security checks computed on the basis of changes in the consumer price index.

## Test B

Circle T or F for true or false.

T  F  1. Inflation occurs only as a result of shifts in the aggregate demand curve.

T  F  2. In contrast to expansionary monetary or fiscal policy, an autonomous increase in private
          spending will increase output without increasing prices.

T  F  3. It fluctuations in economic activity are predominantly the result of shifts in the aggregate supply
          curve, the rate of unemployment and the rate of inflation will tend to be positively correlated.

T  F  4. The economy's self-correcting mechanism implies that the only long-run policy choices for
          the economy lie along a vertical Phillips curve.

T F 5. The natural rate of unemployment is given by the position of the long-run Phillips curve.

T F 6. A belief that the economy's self-correcting mechanism works quickly is an argument in favor of activist demand-management policy.

T F 7. Expectations of inflation that lead to higher wages will be somewhat self-fulfilling as the increase in wages shifts the aggregate supply curve.

T F 8. One can minimize the inflationary effects of fighting a recession by using fiscal policy rather than monetary policy.

T F 9. Following an adverse shift in the aggregate supply curve, aggregate demand policies can stop the rise in prices with no increase in unemployment.

T F 10. The economy's self-correcting mechanism means that, in the face of a recessionary gap, output and prices will eventually be the same with or without expansionary stabilization policy.

## SUPPLEMENTARY EXERCISE

The following statement on wages, prices, and productivity comes from the 1962 *Annual Report of the Council of Economic Advisers*, page 186.

If all prices remain stable, all hourly labor costs may increase as fast as economy-wide productivity without, for that reason alone, changing the relative share of labor and non-labor incomes in total output. At the same time, each kind of income increases steadily in absolute amount. If hourly labor costs increase at a slower rate than productivity, the share of non-labor incomes will grow or prices will fall, or both. Conversely, if hourly labor costs increase more rapidly than productivity, the share of labor incomes in total product will increase or prices will rise, or both. It is this relationship among long-run economy-wide productivity, wages, and prices which makes the rate of productivity change an important benchmark for noninflationary wage and price behavior.

The principles described in this quotation formed the basis of wage-price guideposts used by the Kennedy and Johnson administrations. The claim of the guideposts was that wage increases equal to the increase in labor productivity plus the target rate of inflation would, in combination with price increases equal to the target rate of inflation, allow equal percentage increases in both wages and profits. Table 33-1 is designed to check this assertion.

**TABLE 33-1**
**ACME MANUFACTURING COMPANY**

| | (1) | (2) | (3) |
|---|---|---|---|
| 1. Employment (people) | 100 | 100 | 100 |
| 2. Labor productivity (gizmos per employee) | 4,000 | 4,400 | 4,400 |
| 3. Total output [(1) × (2)] | 400,000 | _____ | _____ |
| 4. Price per gizmo | $ 5.00 | $ 5.00 | $ 5.25 |
| 5. Total revenue [(4) × (3)] | $2,000,000 | _____ | _____ |
| 6. Hourly wage | $ 8.00 | $ 8.80 | $ 9.24* |
| 7. Total wages [(6) × (2000) × (1)] | $1,600,000 | $ 1,760,000 | $1,848,000 |
| 8. Profits plus overhead [(5) − (7)] | $ 400,000 | _____ | _____ |

* If $x$ is the percentage increase in labor productivity and $y$ is the rate of inflation, the correct adjustment of wages is $(1+x)$ $(1+y) - 1 = x + y + xy$. In our case, this formula works out to 15.5 percent, slightly greater than the 15 percent implied by looking just at $x + y$.

1. Column 1 of Table 33-1 illustrates the initial position of the Acme Manufacturing Company, a company that produces gizmos. According to the guideposts, if wages increased at the same rate as labor productivity, profits would also increase even if prices were held constant. In column 2, productivity and wage are both assumed to increase by 10 percent. Complete column 2 to see if profits increased when price is unchanged, while wages increase at the same rate as productivity.
2. Column 3 is meant to illustrate a situation of general inflation of 5 percent. Complete column 3 to see what happens to profits when increases in wages equal the increase in productivity plus the target rate of inflation of 5 percent.
3. If things work so simply why can't we eliminate inflation overnight by adopting an inflation target of zero?

## ECONOMICS IN ACTION

### How Much Inflation?

How much inflation should an economy tolerate in the long run? The concept of the natural rate of unemployment suggests that we are likely to end up with the same amount of unemployment in the long run, but it leaves open the question of how much inflation we should accept. Some argue that inflation is a necessary part of industrial economies. *The Economist* argues that inflationary experience since World War II is the exception not the rule. Bursts of inflation were typically followed by periods of stable or falling prices. By 1930, prices in Britain were not much different than in 1660 according to *The Economist*.

Those who favor low rates of inflation argue that a stable price level allows markets to function better. It is movements in relative prices that signal the need for resource reallocations. An increase in relative prices attracts resources while reductions are a signal for resources to move to other industries. Those who favor price stability argue that inflation obscures movements in relative prices and reduces the efficiency of market economies. Over time the uncertainty associated with inflation discourages risk taking, reduces long-term investment, and limits economic growth. The strong advocates of this position conclude that "These arguments suggest that the best inflation rate is the one that plays the least role in decision-making. This must be zero; anything higher will generate unnecessary uncertainty and inefficiency."[*]

Others argue that a little inflation need not be a bad thing. The imperfections of price indices is likely to mean that inflation at a rate of 1 or 2 percent a year is really no inflation at all. Some inflation may also facilitate real adjustments, especially in labor markets. In industries with falling demand, where wages need to decline if jobs are to be preserved, workers and unions have typically resisted cuts in nominal pay. A freeze in nominal pay while inflation continues may accomplish the necessary reduction in real pay while avoiding the labor unrest that can follow attempts to reduce nominal pay.

Even if a country were convinced of the virtues of zero inflation, the short-run costs of reducing inflation might outweigh the long-run benefit. *The Economist* argues that a major part of short-run costs reflect the assumption of continuing inflation in many parts of the economy and the subsequent slowness of expectations to adjust. On this view, the credibility of policies and institutions committed to low rates of inflation can work to reduce the short-term costs of adjustment by keeping the lid on expectations. Advocates of this position see an independent central bank that is credibly committed to an inflation target of zero as critical to successful policy.

1. What rate of inflation should the government strive for and why? While fiscal and monetary policy are likely to have a strong impact on prices as they affect aggregate demand, how should the government respond if an adverse shift in the aggregate supply curve suddenly raises prices?

---

[*]"Zero Inflation: How Low is Low Enough," *The Economist*, November 7, 1992, pp. 23-26.

## STUDY QUESTIONS

1. Why does the slope of the Phillips curve depend upon the source of macroeconomic fluctuations?

2. Does the Phillips curve offer macroeconomic policy makers a menu of choices between the rate of unemployment and inflation? Why?

3. What is meant by the statement that the economy's self-correcting mechanisms mean that in the long run the Phillips curve is vertical?

4. What is the natural rate of unemployment?

5. How does the expectation of future inflation and the expectations-related shifts in the aggregate supply curve affect the Phillips curve?

6. How can expectations of inflation be rational if they are not always correct?

7. What sort of policies might reduce the natural rate of unemployment?

8. Should wages and interest rates be fully indexed?

9. Should stabilization policy aim to reduce inflation to zero? Why?

*Chapter* **34**

# Productivity and Growth in the Wealth of Nations

## LEARNING OBJECTIVES

After completing this chapter you should be able to:

♦ explain why growth in labor productivity is the major determinant of the growth in living standards.

♦ explain what factors are important for growth in labor productivity.

♦ discuss arguments and evidence about the international convergence of living standards and productivity levels.

♦ evaluate arguments and evidence about deindustrialization of the American economy.

♦ discuss and evaluate arguments about the cause of the slowdown in the growth of labor productivity since the 1960s.

♦ evaluate the argument that growth in labor productivity will lead only to increased unemployment.

♦ explain why productivity growth less than that of other countries need not imply a loss of export competitiveness, but can lower real wages relative to those in other countries.

## IMPORTANT TERMS AND CONCEPTS

Labor productivity
Standard of living
GNP per capita
Gross Domestic Product (GDP)
GDP per labor hour
GDP per capita
Deindustrialization

## CHAPTER REVIEW

The growth in labor productivity is the major determinant of living standards over long periods of time. Growth in labor productivity explains why, on the average, your parents are wealthier than their parents and their parents' parents. Continued growth in labor productivity will mean that your children and their children will be wealthier than you.

Discussions of productivity usually focus on labor productivity which is defined as the amount of output per unit of labor input. For a firm producing a single output, measuring labor productivity per hour is a simple matter of dividing output by total labor hours. For the American economy, output is usually measured in terms of real GDP and labor input is preferably measured in terms of total labor hours. An increase in labor productivity means that (more/less) output can be produced with the same number of labor hours. If aggregate output were unchanged, an increase in labor productivity would mean

(1) (more/less) unemployment. But remember that total output and the unemployment rate are determined by the intersection of the aggregate _____ and aggregate _____ curves. An increase in productivity means that the production possibilities frontier has shifted (out/in); that is, there has been a(n) (increase/decrease) in potential GDP. It is macroeconomic policy that helps to determine whether we take advantage of new possibilities. What makes labor more or less productive? While there are many factors, certainly the intensity of work, the quality of training, the availability of more and better equipment, and the level of technology are important factors. The nature of labor/ management relations and public policy are cited by some as factors that can help or impede the growth of labor productivity.

(2) Sustained growth in labor productivity (is/is not) a relatively new phenomenon, tracing back about (2,000/200) years. As the following equation shows, growth in labor productivity is the basic determinant of living standards or output per capita:

$$\left( \frac{\text{Total output}}{\text{Total population}} \right) = \left( \frac{\text{Total output}}{\text{Total hours worked}} \right) \times \left( \frac{\text{Total hours worked}}{\text{Number of workers}} \right) \times \left( \frac{\text{Number of workers}}{\text{Total population}} \right).$$

The expression on the left of the equal-sign is output per person or per capita. The first expression on the right side of the equal-sign is labor productivity. The second and third expressions measure the number of hours a typical worker works and the proportion of the population that works. (This last term is sometimes referred to as the employment ratio.) Notice that several of the numerators and denominators on the right-hand side of the equal-sign can be canceled, establishing the equality of the expression. If the number of hours per worker does not change and the proportion of the population that works is constant–that is if the second and third terms on the right-hand side do not change–then the only way that output or GDP per capita can increase is if labor productivity increases. If hours per worker decline, then increases in labor productivity will imply a smaller increase in output per capita. Much of the difference between the growth in labor productivity and the growth in output per capita over the past 100 years can be accounted for by the decline in the number of hours worked each year by a typical worker. Over the past 20 years there has been a sharp increase in the employment ratio, a change that is related to the increased labor force participation of women along with the changing age structure of the population as baby boomers finished school and began working. These latter changes can be important for several decades but are unlikely to be sustained over a century or two. Thus in the long run, changes in GDP per capita will be dominated by changes in labor productivity.

(3) There is much concern about the growth in labor productivity in different countries. Long-term data for a number of industrial countries shows a (convergence/divergence) in levels of labor productivity. The quick dispersion of new technologies enables all industrial countries to share in the benefits of new

innovations. If levels of productivity are converging, then it must be true that those countries that start with lower levels of productivity will show a (faster/slower) growth in labor productivity and those countries that start with higher levels of productivity will show a _____ growth in labor productivity. The concept of convergence indicates how difficult it is for any single country to sustain levels of labor productivity far in advance of other countries. It also suggests that a single

(4) industrialized country is not doomed to fall further behind the rest of the world. However, there is evidence that many developing countries (are/are not) participating in this process of convergence. See Chapter 38 for more discussion on prospects for these countries.

Popular discussions of changes in the growth of labor productivity and changes in the structure of employment are often based on limited data. When measured just from the end of World War II there has been a dramatic decline in the rate of growth of labor productivity in the United States and other industrialized countries in the last 20 years. (Note that a decline in the rate of growth (must/need not) imply a decline in the level of labor productivity.) When viewed over a longer period of time, it is unclear which period is unusual, the 1970s and 1980s when labor productivity growth was 1 to 2 percent per year, or the period from 1950 to 1970 when labor productivity grew by over 3 percent per year.

There has been much recent concern about the declining share of manufacturing employment and the increasing share of service employment in the American economy. At least two pieces of evidence are relevant to a broader consideration of this issue. All major industrialized economies have experienced increases in the size of their service industries. The record of productivity growth for

(5) American manufacturing shows (no/a significant) trend toward a declining rate of growth.

While the slowdown in productivity growth has been worldwide, the growth of labor productivity in the United States has been below that of other countries for some time. To the extent that this relative performance reflects the forces of convergence, there is less need for concern. Should this relative performance continue for a prolonged period of time, it would still be possible to sustain high levels of employment with appropriate macroeconomic policy, but there would be serious implications for American competitiveness in international markets. We could continue to export and reap the gains of international specialization that are explained in Chapter 35, but we would do so at the cost of a decline in our standard of living relative to that of the rest of the world. The experience of the British economy comes most immediately to mind.

## IMPORTANT TERMS AND CONCEPTS

Choose the best definition for the following terms.

1. _____ Labor productivity
2. _____ Standard of living
3. _____ Deindustrialization

a. Total output divided by population.
b. GDP minus net exports.
c. Alleged decline in manufacturing due to a country's lagging growth in productivity.
d. Output per unit of labor input.

## TABLE 34-1

| | GDP per capita 1989 | GDP per capita in 2089 assuming annual growth rate of | | | |
| --- | --- | --- | --- | --- | --- |
| | | 1.00% | 1.50% | 2.00% | 2.50% |
| Canada | $18,544 | $50,158 | $82,188 | $134,345 | $219,074 |
| France | $17,093 | $46,233 | $75,757 | $123,833 | $201,932 |
| Germany | $16,397 | $44,351 | $72,672 | $118,790 | $193,710 |
| Japan | $16,090 | $43,520 | $71,312 | $116,566 | $190,083 |
| United Kingdom | $15,023 | $40,634 | $66,583 | $108,836 | $177,477 |
| United States | $20,630 | $55,800 | $91,433 | $149,457 | $243,717 |

Source: *Statistical Abstract of the United States, 1992,* Table 1375
Note: All figures in U.S. dollars using estimates of purchasing power parities to adjust between national currencies.

## BASIC EXERCISES

1. Productivity growth compounds like interest on a savings account. Over long periods of time, small differences in the growth of productivity compound to quite substantial differences in the level of income. Table 34-1 reports data for GDP per capita for a number of countries for 1989. The columns for the year 2089 compound the actual data for 1989 by assumed growth rates of 1 to 2.5 percent per year for 100 years. Note how small differences in the assumed growth rates, even a difference as small as one-half of one percent, can compound to significant differences over 100 years.

   a. Pick a particular country and calculate how much output per capita increases over 100 years if it grows at 1 percent per year. In 2089 output per capita would be _____ as large as it was in 1989. (Try another country to be sure that your answer does not depend upon which country you choose. It shouldn't.)

   b. Assume now that output per capita grows at 2 percent per year for 100 years. How does the increase in output per capita compare to the situation where it increased 1 percent per year? Is it twice as large or even larger?

   c. If labor productivity in the United States grew at 1 percent per year while it grew at 2 percent per year in the rest of the world, our standard of living would not compare favorably to that of other countries after 100 years. The extrapolation of growth trends is a matter of mathematics, not economics. However, economies can offer insights as to whether mechanical trends can be realized. For example, what are the implications of the concept of convergence for the long-term maintenance of a 1 percent differential in the growth of labor productivity?

   d. (Optional) Assume that output per capita in the United States grows at 1.5 percent per year while in Japan it grows at 2 percent per year. How many years will it take for output per capita in Japan to catch up with that of the United States?

2. This exercise investigates whether a decline in the growth of labor productivity results in a decline in the level of productivity. Assume that annual labor productivity is originally 23,900 of GDP per worker, and that it grows at an annual rate of 2.0 percent for 23 years, and 0.5 percent for the next 19 years.

   a. What is labor productivity at the end of the first 23 years?
      $_____

   b. What is labor productivity at the end of 42 years?
      $_____

   c. Does the decline in the rate of growth of productivity lead to a decline in the level of productivity?

   d. What happens to GDP per capita over the same 42 years if the proportion of the population that is employed increases from 39.5 percent to 46.7 percent.

## SELF-TESTS FOR UNDERSTANDING
### Test A

Circle the most appropriate answer.

1. Labor productivity is defined as
   a. output per capita.
   b. GDP divided by population.
   c. the growth in output per worker.
   d. output per unit of labor input.

2. A country's standard of living is usually measured as
   a. GDP per capita.
   b. output per worker.
   c. the growth in GDP.
   d. output per unit of labor input.

3. If more output can be produced with the same number of labor hours, we would say that labor productivity
   a. has decreased.
   b. is unchanged.
   c. has increased.

4. Declines in the number of hours worked per year by an average worker will mean that compared to the growth in labor productivity, the growth in GDP per capita will be
   a. smaller.
   b. about the same.
   c. larger.

5. If the proportion of a country's population that is employed increases, then the growth in GDP per capita will be _____ than the growth in labor productivity.
   a. smaller
   b. the same
   c. larger

6. Which of the following would not explain differences in labor productivity between countries?
   a. The amount of capital per worker.
   b. The level of technology.
   c. The size of the labor force.
   d. The amount of training received by workers.

7. There is some evidence that by the time of the American Civil War, average living standards were
   a. lower than at the time of the American Revolution.
   b. quite similar to living standards today.
   c. starting a decline that lasted to the end of the 19th century.
   d. about equal to those of Ancient Rome.

8. The text notes that the share of employment in agriculture in the United States has dropped from about 90 percent in 1800 to about 3 percent today. This decline is best explained by
   a. a declining demand for food.
   b. the significant increases in labor productivity in agriculture.
   c. an increasing proportion of food imported from abroad
   d. the significant increase in standards of living in the U.S. from 1800 to 1990.

9. If the growth in labor productivity declines from 3 percent per year to 1.5 percent per year, then
   a. labor will become less productive over time.
   b. standards of living will increase only if there is an expansion in average hours per worker.
   c. labor productivity will continue to increase although at a slower rate than before.
   d. the result will be a declining standard of living.

10. A comparison of labor productivity across countries shows that
    (There may be more than one correct answer)
    a. labor productivity in the United States is now about the average of other industrialized counties.
    b. Japan has now emerged as the world's most productive economy.
    c. labor productivity in the United States still exceeds that of all other countries.
    d. a tendency toward convergence among the world's leading industrialized countries.

11. Lagging productivity growth in a single country is likely to lead to
    a. massive unemployment.
    b. greater exports.
    c. lower exports.
    d. a lower standard of living relative to other countries.

12. From 1967 to 1992 the share of the employment in service employment in the United States has grown
    a. less rapidly than that of other countries.
    b. about the same as in other countries.
    c. more rapidly than that of other countries.

13. The record shows that over the past two to three decades manufacturing employment in the United States (there may be more than one correct answer)
    a. has declined as a share of total employment in the U.S.
    b. has increased as a proportion of total manufacturing employment among the world's 25 leading industrial countries.
    c. has increased as labor productivity in manufacturing continued to decline.
    d. shown little change when measured as a percent of total U.S. employment.

14. Historical evidence shows that since 1800 productivity in the United States has increased at an average annual rate of
    a. less than 1 percent.
    b. slightly more than 1 percent.
    c. slightly less than 2 percent.
    d. 3.9 percent.

15. The record shows that over the past 20 years, labor productivity
    a. has increased in every industrialized country except the United States.
    b. has fallen in all industrialized countries.
    c. has grown more slowly than from 1950 to 1970 in most industrialized countries.
    d. has increased most rapidly in the United States.

16. The record of productivity growth in the United States
    a. has exceeded that of other countries ever since World War II.
    b. has been slower than that of a number of other countries for many decades.
    c. has been higher in service industries than in manufacturing industries.
    d. dooms us to a future of high unemployment and dwindling exports.

17. The convergence hypothesis suggests that the growth of labor productivity in the most advanced country
    a. will exceed that of all other countries.
    b. will be less than that of many countries.
    c. must decline.

18. A major factor leading to the convergence of growth rates across countries is probably
    a. the use of the dollar as the international currency of commerce.
    b. the increased levels of GDP devoted to military spending in many countries.
    c. the quick pace by which new technologies are spread among countries.
    d. the emergence of Japan as a major industrial country.

19. While there is evidence of a convergence of productivity and standards of living among industrialized countries, the record with regard to less-developed countries shows
    a. a similar tendency toward convergence, although at a lower level of GDP per capita.
    b. a mixed picture with some tendency toward greater differences.
    c. that most countries have had growth rates in excess of those of industrialized countries.
    d. increases in standards of living that exceed increases in productivity.

20. In the absence of increases in productivity, American goods can be made competitive in international trade if
    a. there is a reduction in the real wages of American workers relative to workers in other countries.
    b. inflation increases.
    c. the United States increases tariffs on foreign goods.
    d. foreign currency becomes less expensive in terms of dollars.

## Test B

Circle T or F for true or false.

T F 1. Long-term, it makes little difference whether productivity grows at 1 percent per year or at 3 percent per year.

T F 2. Output per worker has been increasing more or less steadily for the last two millennia.

T F 3. Although productivity growth has slowed in the United States, it still remains higher than in most other industrialized countries.

T F 4. Since 1970 the growth in productivity in the United States has been about three times as high as it was right after World War II.

T F 5. There is clear evidence of a long-term decline in the productivity of American manufacturing workers.

T F 6. The historical record shows a convergence of living standards in the major industrial countries.

T F 7. Most developing countries are seeing their living standards converge with living standards in the industrial world.

T F 8. A decline in the rate of growth of American labor productivity means a decline in the productivity of American workers.

T F 9. The experience of Great Britain suggests that growth in labor productivity will only lead to massive unemployment.

T F 10. If productivity growth in the United States is lower than that of our major international competitors, we will lose export markets as foreigners can undersell us in everything.

# ECONOMICS IN ACTION

## Recent Productivity Growth

News of productivity growth for 1991 and 1992 seemed very much a good news/bad news situation. After almost two decades of low growth, a high rate of productivity growth was good news. At the same time, given the sluggish growth in output following the 1990-91 recession, high productivity growth held down the recovery in employment. Economist Robert Gordon argues that high productivity growth is only bad news in the shortest run. If high productivity growth results in slow growth in employment, Gordon argues that the reason must be too little stimulus to output. Over the long run, increased productivity helps to lower inflation and increase real standards of living as potential output grows more rapidly.

A number of observers argued that faster productivity growth signaled the beginning of a new era and an end to the record of subpar growth since 1973. These observers pointed to corporate downsizing and the disproportionate reduction in middle-management, white-collar employment as a sign that American business was becoming lean and mean. Economist Martin Neil Bailey was cautiously optimistic that productivity growth would remain high. He argued that the 1970s and 1980s saw significant disruptions that now appear to be behind us—gyrations in oil prices, corporate restructuring in response to new pressures for international competitiveness, the introduction of new safety and environmental regulation, and major changes in the age/sex composition of the workforce. Some argued that having made significant investments in computers, American business was now in position to reap the productivity benefits of new information technologies.

Others were not so sure. It is expensive to find and train new workers. Severance packages and the risk that good workers will be unavailable when business picks up, make it expensive to let workers go. To avoid the extra expenses associated with firing and then hiring, it can be rational during a recession for businesses to hold on to a larger workforce than necessary if it is believed that any decline in output will be short and temporary. The result of this behavior would be a sharp slowdown in productivity growth as the economy slips into recession and high rates of productivity growth as the economy recovers. The hard question is whether recent experience reflects a new higher trend for the growth of productivity or only a normal cyclical recovery, similar to that of other business cycles. Writing in early 1993 in the *Brookings Papers on Economic Activity* Gordon concluded that available evidence was most consistent with the hypothesis of a normal cyclical recovery and not the dawning of a new era.

If experience in 1991-92 was a normal business cycle recovery, one would expect that productivity growth would then adjust downward, perhaps towards the record of the previous twenty years when productivity grew at less than 1 percent per year. Some who argued that 1992 was the dawning of a new era were predicting that productivity growth would reflect the experience of the past 70 to 80 years and average almost 2 percent per year. If the optimists are right, GDP would be about 10 percent larger after 10 years. The cumulative difference in output would be even larger, amounting to almost $3 trillion more output over 10 years. If the optimists are right a somewhat more expansionary macro policy could deliver faster growth and price stability. If they are wrong, policies for faster growth would only mean more inflation.

1. What is appropriate macro policy when there is uncertainty about the growth of potential output?
2. What has happened to the growth of productivity since 1992?

---

SOURCES: See Robert J. Gordon "The Jobless Recovery: Does it Signal a New Era of Productivity-Led Growth?", *Brookings Papers on Economic Activity*, 1993: 1, pp. 271-306, and "Comments" by Martin Neil Bailey, pp. 307-314.

George A. Kahn, "Sluggish Job Growth: Is Rising Productivity or an Anemic Recovery to Blame?", *Economic Review*, Federal Reserve Bank of Kansas City, (Vol. 78, No. 3), Third quarter 1993, pp. 5-25.

## STUDY QUESTIONS

1. What is the difference between measures of labor productivity and output per capita?
2. Why is the growth of labor productivity so important for the growth in standards of living?
3. What factors are important for growth in labor productivity?
4. Is it possible for the growth in a country's standard of living to exceed the growth in labor productivity? If so, how, and is it likely that such a difference could be sustained over a long period of time?

5. What explains the apparent convergence of labor productivity and standards of living among the world's leading industrial countries?

6. What does the convergence hypothesis suggest about the growth of labor productivity in the United States compared to that of other industrialized countries?

7. Do you agree or disagree with the deindustrialization hypothesis? Why?

8. Why don't increases in labor productivity just lead to increased unemployment?

9. How can a country remain competitive in world markets if its growth in labor productivity lags that of other countries?

*Chapter* **35**

# International Trade and Comparative Advantage

## LEARNING OBJECTIVES

After completing this chapter, you should be able to:

- list the important factors that lead countries to trade with one another.
- explain how voluntary trade, even if it does not increase total production, can be mutually beneficial to the trading partners.
- explain in what ways international and intranational trade are similar and dissimilar.
- distinguish between absolute and comparative advantage.
- explain how absolute advantage and comparative advantage are related to the location and slope of a country's production possibilities frontier.
- explain how trade means that a country's consumption possibilities can exceed its production possibilities.
- explain how world prices are relevant for determining a country's consumption possibilities.
- explain how specialization, consistent with the law of comparative advantage, can increase total world production.
- explain how world prices are determined by the interaction of demand and supply curves for trading partners.
- use a pair of demand and supply diagrams to illustrate the impact of quotas and tariffs.
- contrast the efficiency and distribution effects of tariffs and quotas.
- analyze the arguments used to advocate trade restrictions.
- explain the role of adjustment assistance in a country favoring free trade.
- explain the fallacy in the "cheap foreign labor" argument.

## IMPORTANT TERMS AND CONCEPTS

Imports
Exports
Specialization
Mutual gains from trade
Absolute advantage
Comparative advantage
"Cheap foreign labor" argument
Tariff
Quota
Export subsidy
Trade adjustment assistance
Infant-industry argument
Strategic trade protection
Dumping

## CHAPTER REVIEW

The material in this chapter discusses the basic economic forces that influence the international division of labor in the production of goods and the resulting pattern of international trade. The basic economic

(1) principle underlying an efficient international distribution of production is (absolute/comparative) advantage. It is important to remember that actual production and trade decisions are also affected by important policy interventions such as tariffs, quotas, and export subsidies.

Trade between states is, in principle, no different than trade between nations. Economists and others spend more time studying international trade rather than intranational trade for several reasons: International trade involves more than one government with a resulting host of political concerns; it usually involves more than one currency; and the mobility of labor and capital between nations is more difficult than within nations.

Exchange rates—that is, the number of units of one country's currency that are changeable into another country's currency—are an important determinant of international trade and will be discussed in the next chapter. However, the real terms of trade—how many import goods a country can get indirectly through export production rather than through direct domestic production—are the important measure of the benefits of trade, and they are considered here in some detail.

Individual countries can try to meet the consumption needs of their citizens without trade by producing everything their populations need. Alternatively, they can specialize in the production of fewer commodities and trade for commodities they do not produce. Even if there were no differences between countries, specializing and trading would still make sense if there were important economies of

(2) _____ in production.

An important reason for trade is that differences in oil deposits, fertile soil, and other natural resources, as well as differences in labor inputs and productive capital, will affect the efficiency with which

(3) countries can produce different goods. It is the law of (absolute/comparative) advantage that then indicates where countries should concentrate their production to maximize the potential gains from trade.

Assume country A can produce 2,000 bushels of wheat if it produces one less car, while country B can produce only 1,200 bushels of wheat. For the same world production of cars, world production

(4) of wheat will increase if country (A/B) produced 10 fewer cars and country _____ produced 10 more cars. (World wheat production would increase by _____ bushels.) In this case country A has a comparative advantage in producing _____.

Looking only at its own domestic production, the opportunity cost of one more car in country A

(5) is _____ bushels of wheat. Country B can produce one more car by giving up only _____

bushels of wheat. Thus it should not be surprising if country B concentrates on the production of _____ and trades with country A, which concentrates on the production of _____.[1] It is also important to realize that comparative advantage is not a static concept. The mix of industries that maximizes a country's comparative advantage is not something that can be determined once for all time. Rather, there will need to be continuous adjustments in response to innovations and competition from foreign producers. Countries that try to isolate themselves from foreign competition have usually ended up with stagnating industries and incomes.

    As countries concentrate production on those goods in which they have a comparative advantage, equilibrium world prices and trade flows—that is, exports and imports—will be determined at the point

**(6)** where world _____ equals world _____. This price is not at the intersection of domestic demand and supply curves; instead, it occurs at a point where the excess supply from (<u>importing/exporting</u>) countries (domestic supply minus domestic demand) equals the excess demand by _____ countries (domestic demand minus domestic supply).

    Advanced courses in international trade show how prices derived under conditions of free trade will lead competitive profit-maximizing firms to exploit the comparative advantage of individual countries and help to achieve an efficient allocation of resources. Most countries do not have unrestricted free trade.

**(7)** Rather, imports are often restricted by the use of _____ and _____, and exports are often promoted through the use of export _____. Tariffs reduce the quantity of imports by raising their _____ while quotas raise the price of imports by restricting _____. Either a tariff or a quota could be used to achieve the same reduction in imports, but the choice between the two has other consequences.

**(8)**     Tariff revenues accrue directly to the _____ while the benefits of higher prices under a quota are likely to accrue to private producers, both foreign and domestic. (The government might be able to capture some of these profits by auctioning import licenses, but this is not usually done.)

    Tariffs still require foreign suppliers to compete among themselves. This competition will favor the

**(9)** survival of (<u>high/low</u>)-cost foreign suppliers. What about domestic firms? They (<u>do/do not</u>) have to pay the tariff, so high-cost domestic suppliers (<u>can/cannot</u>) continue in business. Quotas are apt to be distributed on almost any grounds except efficiency and thus have no automatic mechanism that works in favor of low-cost foreign suppliers.

    Why do countries impose tariffs and quotas? Many trade restrictions reflect the successful pleadings of high-cost domestic suppliers. Free trade and the associated reallocation of productive resources in line with the law of comparative advantage would call for the elimination of these firms in their traditional lines of business. It is not surprising that managers and workers resist these changes. If everyone is to benefit from the increased output opportunities offered by free trade, then a program of trade

**(10)** _____ assistance will be necessary to help those most affected by the realignment of productive activities.

**(11)**     Other traditional justifications for trade restriction include the national _____ argument and the _____ -industries argument. In both cases it is extremely difficult to separate firms with legitimate claims from those looking for a public handout. In recent years some have argued that the threat of trade restrictions should be used in a strategic manner to convince others not to impose restrictions.

    Much of the free trade fuss in the United States is concerned about competing with low-cost foreign producers who pay workers lower wages. Concerns about wages need to be joined with measures of productivity. A clear understanding of comparative advantages shows that the standard of living of

**(12)** workers in (<u>the exporting/the importing/both</u>) country(ies) can rise as a result of trade and specialization.

---

[1]Does the law of comparative advantage imply that all countries should specialize in the production of just a few commodities? No, it does not, for several reasons. One important reason is that production possibilities frontiers are likely to be curved rather than straight lines. The implication of the curved frontier is that the opportunity cost of cars in terms of wheat for country B will rise as B produces more cars. Simultaneously, the opportunity cost of cars in terms of wheat for country A will fall as A concentrates on wheat. In equilibrium, the opportunity cost, or slope of the production possibilities frontier, in both countries will be equal. At this point neither country has an incentive for further specialization. Exactly where this point will occur will be determined by world demand and supply for cars and wheat.

The workers with the highest standard of living, i.e., the highest wages, will be those who are most productive. While measures of absolute advantage are important when considering the standard of living workers will enjoy, even countries with high wages can benefit from trade when high wages are associated with high productivity and trade induces adjustments in the structure of worldwide production consistent with the principle of _____ advantage.

## IMPORTANT TERMS AND CONCEPTS QUIZ

Choose the most appropriate definition for the following terms.

1. _____ Imports
2. _____ Exports
3. _____ Specialization
4. _____ Absolute advantage
5. _____ Comparative advantage
6. _____ Tariff
7. _____ Quota
8. _____ Export subsidy
9. _____ Trade adjustment assistance
10. _____ Infant-industry argument
11. _____ Strategic trade policy
12. _____ Dumping

a. Maximum amount of a good that can be imported per unit of time.
b. Threats to implement protectionist policies designed to promote free trade.
c. Selling goods in a foreign market at higher prices than those charged at home.
d. Domestically produced goods sold abroad.
e. Selling goods in a foreign market at lower prices than those charged at home.
f. Tax on imports.
g. Decision by a country to emphasize production of particular commodities.
h. Provision of special aid to those workers and firms harmed by foreign competition.
i. Ability of one country to produce a good less inefficiently (relative to other goods) than another country.
j. Foreign-produced goods purchased domestically.
k. Tariff protection for new industries, giving them time to mature.
l. Payment by the government that enables firms to lower prices to foreign buyers.
m. Ability of one country to produce a good using fewer resources than another country requires.

## BASIC EXERCISES

1. This exercise is designed to review the law of comparative advantage.
    a. Assume that the  hours of labor shown below are the only input necessary to produce hand calculators and backpacks in Canada and Japan.

    |  | Calculators | Backpacks |
    |---|---|---|
    | Canada | 6 | 4 |
    | Japan | 2 | 3 |

    Which country has an absolute advantage in the production of hand calculators? _____. Which country has an absolute advantage in the production of backpacks? _____.
    b. If labor in Canada is reallocated from the production of calculators to the production of backpacks, how many calculators must be given up in order to produce one more backpack? _____. What about Japan? How many calculators must it give up in order to produce one more backpack? _____. Which country has a comparative advantage in the production of backpacks? _____. Which country has a comparative advantage in the production of calculators? _____. According to the law of comparative advantage, _____ should concentrate on the production of backpacks while _____ concentrates on the production of calculators.

c. Assume each country has 12 million hours of labor input that initially is evenly distributed in both countries between the production of backpacks and calculators: 6 million for each. Fill in the following table of outputs.

|  | Output of Calculators | Output of Backpacks |
|---|---|---|
| Canada | _____ | _____ |
| Japan | _____ | _____ |
| Total | _____ | _____ |

d. Assume that Canada now reallocates 1.8 million labor hours away from the production of calculators and into backpacks. The change in Canadian calculator output is −_____. The change in Canadian backpack output is + _____.

e. What reallocation of labor in Japan is necessary to be sure that world output of calculators (Japan plus Canada) remains unchanged? _____ labor hours. What are the changes in Japanese output from this reallocation? The change in Japanese calculator output is + _____. The change in Japanese backpack output is −_____.

f. By assumption, the world output of calculators has not changed, but the net change in the world output of backpacks is a(n) (increase/decrease) of _____ backpacks.

g. Questions c through f showed how specialization according to the law of comparative advantage could increase the output of backpacks without decreasing the output of calculators. Adjustments in line with the law of comparative advantage could alternatively increase the output of both goods. Suppose Japan had reallocated 900,000 labor hours to the production of calculators. Fill in the following table and compare total outputs with your answers to Question c.

| | Calculators Labor Input (millions of hours) | Output |
|---|---|---|
| Canada | 4.2 | _____ |
| Japan | 6.9 | _____ |
| Total | | _____ |

| | Backpacks Labor input (millions of hours) | Output |
|---|---|---|
| Canada | 7.8 | _____ |
| Japan | 5.1 | _____ |
| Total | | _____ |

h. Work through questions d and e again, but assume this time that the initial reallocation of 1.8 million labor hours in Canada is away from backpacks and to the production of calculators. Calculate the reallocation in Japan necessary to maintain world backpack output. What happens to the total output of calculators? Why?

i. Assume that the production of backpacks in Canada requires 9 hours rather than 4 hours. Work through the original output levels in question c and the reallocation of labor in questions d and e to see what now happens to total output of calculators and backpacks. Does your answer to question f differ from your original answer? Why?

**FIGURE 35-1**

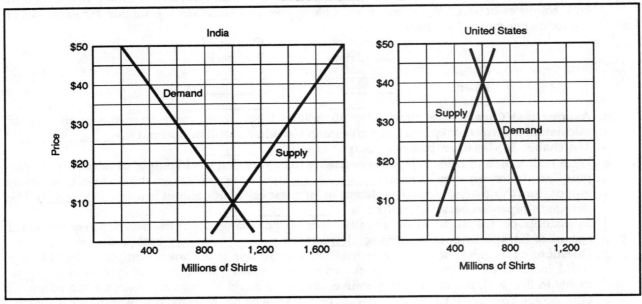

2. This exercise is designed to give practice in analyzing the impact of quotas and tariffs. To simplify the analysis, the question assumes that the world is composed of only two countries, the United States and India.

a. Figure 35-1 shows the demand and supply for shirts in the United States and India. Prices in India are expressed in terms of American dollars. In the absence of international trade, what are the domestic price and quantity of shirts in India and the United States?

|  | Price | Quantity |
|---|---|---|
| India | _____ | _____ |
| United States | _____ | _____ |

b. Assume now that India and the United States are free to trade without restrictions. What is the world price of shirts? _____. What happens to the production of shirts in India? _____. What happens to the production of shirts in the United States? _____. Who exports and who imports how many shirts? _____.

c. Assume that American producers are able to persuade the government to impose a quota limiting shirt imports to 200 million. Following imposition of the quota, what are prices and production in India and the United States?

|  | Price | Quantity |
|---|---|---|
| India | _____ | _____ |
| United States | _____ | _____ |

Compared to the free trade equilibrium described in b, shirt prices have increased in (India/the United States) and decreased in _____. The production of shirts has increased in _____ and decreased in _____. For the world as a whole, shirt production has (increased/decreased).

d. What tariff would have yielded the same results as the quota of 200 million shirts? _____.

e. Discuss the reasons for choosing between a tariff and a quota.

## SELF-TESTS FOR UNDERSTANDING

### Test A

Circle the most appropriate answer.

1. Even if there were no differences in natural resources, climate, labor skills, etc., nations would still find it advantageous to specialize production and trade
   a. because of differences in absolute advantage.
   b. to take advantage of economies of scale.
   c. to take advantage of differences in national currencies.
   d. when inflation rates differ.

2. International trade is different from intranational trade because of
   a. political issues that arise from different governments.
   b. limitations of the ability of labor and capital to move between countries compared to their ability to move within countries.
   c. the use of different currencies.
   d. all of the above.

3. Economists argue that
   a. efficiency in international trade requires countries to produce those goods in which they have an absolute advantage.
   b. efficiency in international trade requires countries to produce those goods in which they have a comparative advantage.
   c. efficiency in international trade requires countries that have an absolute advantage in the production of all goods to become self-sufficient.
   d. countries with export surpluses will have a comparative advantage in the production of all goods.

4. On a per capita production possibilities frontier showing the production of clothes on the vertical axis and cars on the horizontal axis, the absolute advantage in the production of clothes would be determined
   a. by the slope of the per capita production possibilities frontier.
   b. where the per capita production possibilities frontier cuts the horizontal axis.
   c. by the area under the per capita production possibilities frontier.
   d. where the per capita production possibilities frontier cuts the vertical axis.

5. On a per capita production possibilities frontier showing the production of clothes on the vertical axis and cars on the horizontal axis, the comparative advantage in the production of clothes would be determined
   a. by the slope of the per capita production possibilities frontier.
   b. where the per capita production possibilities frontier cuts the horizontal axis.
   c. by the area under the per capita production possibilities frontier.
   d. where the per capita production possibilities frontier cuts the vertical axis.

6. Which of the following is an example of comparative advantage?
   a. Wages of textile workers are lower in India than in America.
   b. The slope of the production possibilities frontier between tomatoes and airplanes differs for Mexico and the United States.
   c. American workers must work an average of only 800 hours to purchase a car, while Russian workers must work 1,600 hours.
   d. In recent years Swedish income per capita has exceeded that of the United States.

7. Specialization and free trade consistent with the law of comparative advantage will enable
   a. increased world production of all traded goods.
   b. increases in the standard of living for workers in both exporting and importing countries.
   c. countries to consume at some point outside their production possibilities frontier.
   d. all of the above.

8. From a worldwide perspective, economic efficiency is enhanced if production and trade is organized according to the law of comparative advantage. Economic efficiency within a single country is enhanced if regional production and trade are organized according to
   a. absolute advantage.
   b. the political power of particular states or regions.
   c. which regions have the highest unemployment.
   d. comparative advantage.

9. If shoes can be produced with two hours of labor input in Italy and three hours of labor input in the United States, then it is correct to say that
   a. Italy has an absolute advantage in the production of shoes.
   b. Italy has a comparative advantage in the production of shoes.
   c. the United States has an absolute advantage in the production of shoes.
   d. the United States has a comparative advantage in the production of shoes.

10. Assuming that shoes are produced as in question 9 and shirts can be produced with four hours of labor in both countries, then it is correct to say that
    a. the United States has a comparative advantage in the production of shirts.
    b. Italy has a comparative advantage in the production of shirts.
    c. Italy has an absolute advantage in the production of shirts.
    d. the United States has an absolute advantage in the production of shirts.

11. Under free trade, world prices for exports and imports would be such that
    a. countries would specialize production along lines of absolute advantage.
    b. all countries would show a slight export surplus.
    c. the quantity supplied by exporters would just equal the quantity demanded by importers.
    d. every country would be self-sufficient in all goods.

12. All but which one of the following have been used to restrict trade?
    a. Export subsidies.
    b. Tariffs.
    c. Quotas.
    d. "Voluntary" export agreements.

13. A tariff affects trade by
    a. imposing a tax on imported goods.
    b. limiting the quantity of goods that can be imported.
    c. offering a subsidy to producers who export for foreign sales.
    d. the voluntary actions of foreign manufacturers to limit their exports.

14. A quota affects trade by
    a. imposing a tax on imported goods.
    b. limiting the quantity of goods that can be imported.
    c. offering a subsidy to producers who export for foreign sales.
    d. the voluntary action of foreign manufacturers to limit their exports.

15. Which of the following is an example of a tariff?
    a. Japanese car manufacturers agree to limit exports to the United States.
    b. U.S. law limits the imports of cotton shirts to 20 million.
    c. Television manufacturers outside Great Britain must pay a 5 percent duty on each set they ship to Great Britain.
    d. Foreign bicycle manufacturers receive a rebate of taxes from their own government for each bicycle they export.

16. One economic advantage of tariffs over quotas is that tariffs
    a. typically give preferential treatment to long-term suppliers.
    b. expose high-cost domestic producers to competition.
    c. force foreign suppliers to compete.
    d. help avoid destructive price wars.

17. The imposition of a tariff on steel will lead to all but which one of the following?
    a. A lower volume of steel imports.
    b. Higher domestic steel prices.
    c. Reduced domestic demand for steel.
    d. Reduced domestic production of steel as higher steel prices reduce demand.

18. The imposition of a quota on steel will lead to all but which one of the following?
    a. A lower volume of steel imports.
    b. Increased domestic production of steel.
    c. Lower domestic steel prices.
    d. Reduced domestic demand for steel.

19. A quota that limits the importation of foreign computer chips is likely to be in the interest of all but which of the following? (There may be more than one correct answer.)
    a. Domestic chip manufacturers.
    b. Domestic computer manufacturers.
    c. Labor employed domestically in the production of computer chips.
    d. Consumers interested in buying computers.

20. Which one of the following is not a justification for trade restrictions?
    a. Some industries would be so vital in times of war that we cannot rely on foreign suppliers.
    b. A temporary period of protection is necessary until an industry matures and is able to compete with foreign suppliers.
    c. Competition from foreign suppliers will help keep prices to consumers low.
    d. The threat of trade restrictions may prevent the adoption of restrictions by others.

## Test B

Circle T or F for true or false.

T F 1. A country with an absolute advantage in producing all goods is better off being self-sufficient than engaging in trade.

T F 2. Countries gain from trade only when it allows them to adjust productive resources to take advantage of economies of scale.

T F 3. A country with an absolute advantage in the production of all goods should only export commodities.

T F 4. The unequal distribution of natural resources among countries is one important reason why countries trade.

T F 5. Which of two countries has a comparative advantage in the production of wine rather than cloth can be determined by comparing the slopes of the production possibility frontiers of both countries.

T  F   6.  It is possible for all countries to simultaneously expand exports and reduce imports.

T  F   7.  A quota on shirts would reduce the volume of imported shirts by specifying the quantity of shirts that could be imported.

T  F   8.  The infant-industry argument is used to justify protection for industries that are vital in times of war.

T  F   9.  Dumping of goods by the United States on Japanese markets would necessarily harm Japanese consumers.

T  F  10.  If foreign labor is paid less, foreign producers will always be able to undersell American producers.

# SUPPLEMENTARY EXERCISES

1. Demand and supply for widgets in Baulmovia and Bilandia are as follows:

    *Baulmovia*

    Demand: $Q = 156 - 7\,P$

    Supply:  $Q = -44 + 18\,P$

    *Bilandia*

    Demand: $Q = 320 - 10\,P$

    Supply:  $Q = -20 + 10\,P$

    a. In the absence of trade, what is the price of widgets in Baulmovia? In Bilandia? What quantity is produced in Baulmovia? In Bilandia?
    b. With free trade what is the one common world price for widgets? Which country exports widgets? Which country imports widgets? What is the volume of exports and imports?
    c. Manufacturers in the importing country have convinced the government to impose a tariff on widget imports of $4.50 a widget. What will happen to trade and the price of widgets in the two countries?
    d. What quota would have the same impact on trade?
    e. What factors might lead one to prefer a tariff over a quota?

2. Ricardia is a small country that produces wine and cloth. The production possibilities frontier for Ricardia is

$$W = \sqrt{324 - C^2}$$

where $W$ = millions of barrels of wine and $C$ = millions of bolts of cloth.
    a. Use a piece of graph paper. Label the vertical axis "wine" and the horizontal axis "cloth." Draw the production possibilities frontier.
    b. Since Ricardia is a small country, it can export or import cloth or wine without affecting world prices. World prices are such that Ricardia can export one million barrels of wine for 750,000 bolts of cloth or it can export 750,000 bolts of cloth for one million barrels of wine. The government's chief economist argues that regardless of consumption preferences, Ricardia should produce 14.4 million bolts of cloth and 10.8 million barrels of wine. Do you agree? Why? (Hint: Consider what a graph of consumption possibilities looks like. For any production combination of wine and cloth,

Ricardia's consumption possibilities are given by a negatively sloped straight line through the production point. The slope of the consumption possibilities line reflects world prices. A movement up the straight line to the left of the production point would imply exporting cloth in order to consume more wine. A movement down the straight line to the right would reflect exporting wine in order to consume more cloth. Exactly what Ricardia chooses to consume is a matter of preferences, but its choice is constrained by its consumption possibilities line, which in turn is determined by Ricardia's production choice and world prices for cloth and wine. Why does the production point 10.8 million barrels of wine and 14.4 million bolts of cloth offer the greatest consumption possibilities?)

## STUDY QUESTIONS

1. Why do countries trade with each other? Why don't they try to be self-sufficient in the production of all goods?

2. What is the difference between absolute advantage and comparative advantage? (Use a per capita production possibilities frontier to illustrate your answer.)

3. Why do economists argue that a country with an absolute advantage in the production of all goods can still gain from trade if it specializes in a manner consistent with the law of comparative advantage? (Consider a two-good, two-country example.)

4. Why isn't it possible for all countries to improve their balance of trade by increasing exports and decreasing imports?

5. Why aren't a country's consumption possibilities limited by its production possibilities?

6. When considering a single commodity that is traded without tariffs or quotas, what are the two conditions that characterize equilibrium and determine world price and the location of production?

7. How are these conditions changed if the importing country imposes a tariff? A quota?

8. Use a demand-supply diagram to show an initial free trade equilibrium and how that equilibrium would be affected by a tariff or quota.

9. It is often asserted that for every tariff there is a corresponding quota in the sense of having the same impact on prices and production. Is this statement correct and if so what difference(s) would one policy make over the other?

10. How do you evaluate the arguments supporting strategic trade policies?

11. What is the role of trade adjustment assistance and why do many think it a necessary element of a policy that favors free trade?

12. What is the infant-industry argument? Do you believe it is ever a compelling argument? Why? Why not?

13. Some industries argue for trade protection on the grounds of national defense. Do you believe this is ever a compelling argument? Why? Why not?

14. "In order to increase the consumption possibilities of Americans, the United States should never prohibit dumping by foreign manufacturers." Do you agree? Why? Why not?

15. Why isn't it obvious to many economists that the United States should enact tariffs to level the playing field and protect American workers from unfair competition from low-wage foreign workers?

# ECONOMICS IN ACTION

## Jobs, Foreign Investment, and Free Trade

On June 14, 1993, *The New York Times* reported on the resolution of an issue that had divided some of President Clinton's top advisers: How far should the government go to encourage foreign-owned companies to build factories in the United States? The issue at the center was whether the expansion of an automobile factory in Tennessee, owned by the Nissan Motor Company, should be declared a foreign trade zone.

Designation as a foreign trade zone would allow Nissan to import auto parts and pay the 2.5 percent tariff for finished cars rather than the 4 to 11 percent tariffs assessed on individual auto parts. It was estimated the reduction in tariffs would save Nissan $20 a car or about $5 million a year.

The *Times* reported that approval of foreign trade zones had been routine in recent years. There are about 200 zones or subzones, including many auto assembly plants or refineries using foreign oil. Domestic auto makers have been among the biggest beneficiaries of such approvals. This time, however, objections were raised by American auto makers and by Mickey Kantor, President Clinton's special trade representative. The auto manufacturers argued that there were already too many car factories in the United States. Expansion of the Nissan plant could cause existing plants to close. Mr. Kantor appeared to argue against routine approval on the grounds its eventual approval could be used as a bargaining chip with Japan on other issues. There was also speculation that Mr. Kantor hoped to use disapproval of the foreign trade zone as a reason for American auto makers to support other elements of the President's economic plan.

On the other side, favoring approval were Laura D'Andrea Tyson, Chairwoman of the Council of Economic Advisers; Vice President Al Gore, former senator from Tennessee; and Ron Brown, Secretary of Commerce. Those supporting the foreign trade zone argued that allowing foreign auto makers to expand production in the United States created more American jobs than importing fully assembled cars. Concern was also voiced that potential foreign investors could be scared off by a reversal of what had been seen as routine.

Nissan also argued that the foreign trade zone would help create U.S. jobs. "We certainly should not have a disincentive to build vehicles here," said Gail O'Sullivan Neuman, vice president and general counsel for the Nissan factory. Others speculated that Nissan was trying to protect itself from possible future trade restrictions and adverse changes in the exchange rate.

1. If you were one of the President's advisers what would you have recommended?

*Chapter* **36**

# The International Monetary System: Order or Disorder?

---

## LEARNING OBJECTIVES

After completing this chapter you should be able to:

- identify the factors that help determine a country's exchange rate under a system of floating exchange rates.

- distinguish between long-, medium-, and short-run factors that help determine the demand and supply of currencies.

- use a demand and supply diagram to show how changes in GDP, inflation, or interest rates can lead to an appreciation or depreciation of the dollar under a system of floating exchange rates.

- show, on a supply-demand graph, how fixed exchange rates can lead to a balance of payments deficit or surplus.

- explain why, under the gold standard, countries lost control of their domestic money stock.

- describe the options, other than changing the exchange rate, that were available under the Breton Woods system to a country wanting to eliminate a balance of payments deficit or surplus.

- explain why, under a system of fixed exchange rates, there was very little risk in speculating against an overvalued currency.

- explain how speculators can reduce the uncertainty exporters and importers face under a system of floating exchange rates.

---

## IMPORTANT TERMS AND CONCEPTS

International monetary system
Exchange rate
Appreciation
Depreciation
Revaluation
Supply of and demand for foreign exchange
Floating exchange rates
Purchasing-power parity theory
Fixed exchange rates
Balance of payments deficit and surplus
Current account
Capital account
Balance of trade
Gold standard
Gold-exchange system (Bretton Woods system)
International Monetary Fund (IMF)
"Dirty" or "managed" floating
The European Exchange Rate Mechanism (ERM)

## CHAPTER REVIEW

Meeting: President Richard M. Nixon and H. R. Haldeman, Oval Office, June 23, 1972 (10:04-11:39 A.M.)

> Haldeman: Burns is concerned about speculation against the lira.
> Nixon: Well, I don't give a (expletive deleted) about the lira...There ain't a vote in it.

(Statement of Information: Appendix III, Hearings before the committee on the Judiciary, House of Representatives, Ninety-third Congress, Second Session, May–June 1974, page 50)

Soon after 1972, even American presidents paid attention to exchange rates. So should you. Even if you are never President, exchange rates are important for all Americans. Consumers are affected by the price of imports, and jobs for workers can be affected by the price of exports and imports. This chapter discusses exchange rates, that is, the price of one currency in terms of another. The discussion in the text covers the economic factors that determine exchange rates, the implications of attempts by governments to fix exchange rates, and a review of recent history focusing on the evolution of the world's current mixed international monetary system.

Discussions of international monetary arrangements involve a whole new vocabulary of fixed and floating exchange rates, current and capital accounts, appreciating and depreciating currencies and devaluations and revaluations. It may help you to keep the vocabulary straight if you remember that most of the analysis of international monetary arrangements is merely an application of the supply-demand analysis originally introduced in Chapter 4.

(1)    Find out how much it would cost, in dollars, to buy one German mark. This figure is the current dollar/mark _____ rate, expressed in dollars. Many newspapers now publish exchange rates on a daily basis. A student in Germany could do the same thing and get a price for dollars in terms of marks. If you both call on the same day you should both get the same price (ignoring sales commissions.)[1] If the dollar price of one mark increases, so that it takes more dollars to buy one mark, we say that the dollar has _____ relative to the mark. Alternatively, we could say that the mark has _____ relative to the dollar.

[1] In the United States you might get a price of 62.5 cents for one mark. The German student would get a price of 1.6 marks for one dollar. If $x$ is the dollar price of one mark, then $1/x$ is the mark price of one dollar.

Under a system of floating exchange rates, exchange rates will be determined by market forces of
(2) _____ and _____. Consider an example using two countries, Germany and the United States. The demand for German marks has three major sources:

(1)   the demand by Americans for German exports, such as cars, cameras, and machine tools;

(2)   the demand by Americans for German financial assets, such as stocks and bonds; and

(3)   the demand by Americans for German physical assets, such as factories and machines.

The supply of German marks also has three sources: the demand by Germans for American (exports/imports), American _____ assets, and American _____ assets. (Note that the demand and supply of marks has an interpretation in terms of the demand and supply of dollars. The demand for marks by Americans is simultaneously a _____ of dollars. Understanding this mirror-image aspect of exchange rates may help keep the vocabulary and analysis straight.)

Under a system of floating rates, the equilibrium exchange rate will be at a level where demand equals supply. A change in any factor that affects demand or supply will change the exchange rate. For example, a sudden demand for German wines on the part of Americans would shift the
(3) (demand/supply) curve for marks. The dollar price of marks will (increase/decrease), a result economists call a(n) (appreciation/depreciation) of the mark in terms of the dollar. Conversely, a sudden demand for California wines on the part of Germans would shift the _____ curve of marks and would mean a(n) (appreciation/depreciation) of the mark in terms of the dollar. A simultaneous boom in the United States and recession in Germany are likely to lead to a(n) _____ of the mark in terms of the dollar.

In the long run, the exchange rate between two currencies should be determined by comparing
(4) prices of traded goods according to the theory of _____ _____ _____. In order that its goods remain competitive on world markets, a country with a very high rate of inflation will see its exchange rate (appreciate/depreciate). In the medium run, a country that experiences an economic boom will find its imports rising and its exchange rate _____. In the short run, exchange rates will be affected by the movement of large pools of investment funds that are sensitive to differences in interest rates. Restrictive monetary policy that increases interest rates will attract funds, (appreciating/depreciating) the exchange rate.

Governments may try to peg the exchange rate. In fact, from the end of World War II until 1973,
(5) the world operated on a system of fixed exchange rates, established at the _____ Woods conference. At the time, it was thought that fixed exchange rates were necessary to stimulate the growth of international trade, so countries could reap the benefits of specialization according to the law of comparative advantage. Pegging an exchange rate is very similar to any other sort of price control and is subject to similar problems.

If, say, the Japanese government pegs the exchange rate at too high a level, the supply of Japanese
(6) yen will exceed the demand for yen, and Japan will experience a balance of payments (deficit/surplus). If the government pegs the rate too low, then (demand/supply) will exceed _____ and the result will be a balance of payments _____.

A government pegging its exchange rate and faced with a deficit will need to use its holdings of
(7) international reserves, that is, gold or foreign currencies, in order to (buy/sell) its own currency. A country faced with a surplus will need to supply its own currency. As a result, it will find its international reserves (increasing/decreasing).

Under fixed exchange rates, most of the pressure for adjustment is placed on countries experiencing a
(8) balance of payments (deficit/surplus). If nothing else, such a country will eventually run out of international reserves. If a country does not want to change its exchange rate, other adjustment options include monetary and fiscal policies that (increase/decrease) interest rates, (increase/decrease) the rate of inflation, or induce a general (contraction/expansion) in the level of economic activity. Many of these adjustments occurred automatically under the gold standard as a balance of payments deficit led to an outflow of gold and a(n) (increase/reduction) in the stock of money.

A major weakness of the Bretton Woods system of fixed exchange rates was that deficit countries (9) (liked/disliked) adjusting their domestic economies for balance of payments reasons rather than for domestic political and economic reasons. Another weakness was the special role accorded the U.S. dollar.

In recent years the world's major industrialized countries have operated under a mixed system of floating rates. Exchange rates are allowed to change on a daily basis in response to market forces. At the same time, many governments intervene by buying or selling currencies, hoping to influence the exchange rate to their advantage. Some have worried that floating exchange rates would be so volatile as to destroy world trade. However, market-determined prices need not be volatile, and importers and exporters can (10) often relieve the business risk of changes in exchange rate by dealing with _____.

## IMPORTANT TERMS AND CONCEPTS QUIZ

Choose the best definition for each of the following terms.

1. _____ International monetary system
2. _____ Exchange rate
3. _____ Appreciation
4. _____ Depreciation
5. _____ Devaluation
6. _____ Revaluation
7. _____ Floating exchange rates
8. _____ Purchasing-power parity theory
9. _____ Fixed exchange rates
10. _____ Balance of payments deficit
11. _____ Balance of payments surplus
12. _____ Current account
13. _____ Capital account
14. _____ Balance of trade
15. _____ Gold standard
16. _____ Gold-exchange system
17. _____ International Monetary Fund
18. _____ Dirty float

a. Value of currencies linked to the dollar whose value was linked to gold.
b. Price of one currency in terms of another.
c. Exchange rates determined in free market by supply and demand.
d. Difference between merchandise exports and imports.

e. Set of institutions that facilitate international movements of currencies.
f. System where exchange rates change in response to market forces, but with intervention by central banks.
g. International agency that extends loans for infrastructure to developing countries.
h. Amount by which quantity supplied of a country's currency exceeds quantity demanded in a given year.
i. Balance of trade involving purchases and sales of assets.
j. International agency that monitors exchange rate policies of member countries.
k. Reduction in official value of a currency.
l. Balance of trade in goods and services plus unilateral transfers.
m. System where currencies are defined in terms of gold.
n. Increase in the amount of foreign currency a unit of a given currency can buy.
o. Exchange rates set by the government.
p. Amount by which quantity demanded of a country's currency exceeds quantity supplied.
q. Idea that exchange rates adjust to reflect differences in the prices of traded goods.
r. Drop in the amount of foreign currency a unit of a given currency can buy.
s. Increase in official value of a currency.

## BASIC EXERCISES

1. This exercise is designed to contrast the impact of similar events under systems of fixed and floating exchange rates.

   Assume that the world is divided into two countries, the United States and France. Table 36-1 lists a number of events. Fill in the missing blank spaces in the table to analyze the impact of these events on (1) the dollar-franc exchange rate under a system of floating rates, and (2) the French balance of payments under a system of fixed exchange rates. Assume that each event takes place from an initial equilibrium that under fixed exchange rates entails neither a deficit nor a surplus. Figure 36-1 illustrates such an equilibrium at an initial exchange rate of 16 cents per franc.

**TABLE 36-1**

| Event | Shift in Demand Curves for Francs (left, right, no shift) | Shift in Supply Curve for Francs (left, right, no shift) | Floating Rates | Fixed Rates |
|---|---|---|---|---|
| | | | Appreciation or Depreciation of Franc | Change in French Balance Payment |
| a. Federal reserve policy raises interest rates in the United States | | | | |
| b. A change in tastes increases American demand for haute couture fashions from Paris. | | | | |
| c. The U.S. economy enters a recession. | | | | |
| d. Major labor strikes in France have resulted in a sudden increase in the (franc) price of French goods. | | | | |
| e. A terrible freeze destroys French wine grapes and increase the demand for American wine. | | | | |

* Appropriate answers would be deficit, surplus, or no charge

**FIGURE 36-1**

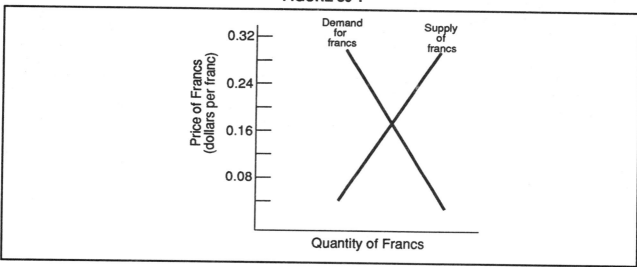

## TABLE 36-2
## AMERICAN INTERNATIONAL TRANSACTIONS
## 1990
## (billions of dollars)

| Line | Item | Demand for dollars (Gain of foreign currency) | Supply of dollars (Loss of foreign currency) |
|------|------|-----------------------------------------------|-----------------------------------------------|
| 1 | Exports | 389.3 | |
| 2 | Imports | | 498.3 |
| 3 | Net military transactions | | 7.8 |
| 4 | Travel and transportation (net) | 9.0 | |
| 5 | Net income from investments and other services | 49.8 | |
| 6 | Private transfers | | 13.5 |
| 7 | U.S. government transfers (nonmilitary) | | 20.4 |
| 8 | Change in U.S. assets abroad | | 44.3 |
| 9 | Change in foreign assets in the U.S. | 71.0 | |
| 10 | Change in the U.S. government assets | 0.1 | |
| 11 | Change in foreign official assets in the U.S. | 34.2 | |

Source: *Survey of Current Business*, June 1993

2. This exercise is designed to illustrate the theory of purchasing power parity.

Assume that the United States and France are the only suppliers of wine on the world market. Consumers of wine are indifferent between French and California wines and buy whichever is cheaper. Initially, the dollar-franc exchange rate is assumed to be 16 cents to the franc and California wine sells for $4.80 a bottle.

Ignoring transportation costs, the initial dollar price of French wines must be $4.80. Accordingly, we know that the initial franc price of French wine is _____ francs.

Assume now that inflation in the United States has raised the price of California wine to $7.20 a bottle, while inflation in France has raised the price of French wine to 40 francs. Based on this data, answer each of the following:
   a. If the exchange rate is fixed at 16 cents to the franc, what is the new dollar price of French wine? $_____ What would happen to the sales of French and California wines? What happens to the American balance of payments?
   b. If the dollar-franc exchange rate is free to adjust, what is the new exchange rate; that is what dollar price of a franc is necessary to equalize the dollar (or franc) price of both wines? _____ This change in the dollar price of a franc is an (appreciation/depreciation) of the franc and a _____ of the dollar.
   c. Assuming that the change in the price of wine is typical of the change in other prices, which country had the higher rate of inflation? _____
   d. From Questions a and c, it is seen that the purchasing-power parity theory implies that under fixed exchange rates a country with more inflation will experience a balance of payments (deficit/surplus).
   e. From Questions b and c, it is seen that the purchasing-power parity theory implies that under floating exchange rates a country with more inflation will have a(n) (appreciating/depreciating) currency.

3. Table 36-2 contains data on American international transactions in 1990. Use the information in this table to compute the following:

Balance of trade       _____

Balance on goods and services   _____

Balance on current account   _____

Balance on capital account   _____

Do these figures show an overall balance of zero? In what sense does the balance of payments balance?

# SELF-TESTS FOR UNDERSTANDING
## Test A

Circle the most appropriate answer.

1. The exchange rate between the American dollar and the French franc tells us
   a. how much gold each currency is worth.
   b. the dollar price of a franc and the franc price of a dollar.
   c. whether the French are running a balance of payments deficit.
   d. how many pounds each currency will purchase.

2. If an American can buy a Finnish mark for 20 cents, how many marks must a Finn spend to buy a dollar?
   a. 0.20 marks
   b. 1 mark
   c. 5 marks
   d. 20 marks

3. If the German mark appreciates relative to the British pound, then a mark will buy
   a. fewer pounds than before.
   b. more pounds than before.
   c. the same number of pounds as before.

4. If under a system of floating exchange rates the Mexican peso used to cost 33 cents and now costs 28 cents, one would say that
   a. the peso has appreciated relative to the dollar.
   b. the peso has depreciated relative to the dollar.
   c. there has been a devaluation of the peso relative to the dollar.
   d. there has been a revaluation of the peso relative to the dollar.

5. If the dollar price of a mark falls from 60 cents to 50 cents, one would say that the (There may be more than one correct answer.)
   a. mark has appreciated against the dollar.
   b. dollar has appreciated against the mark.
   c. dollar has depreciated against the mark.
   d. mark has depreciated against the dollar.

6. If the yen appreciates against the mark, then we know that the
   a. mark has appreciated against the dollar.
   b. dollar has also appreciated against the yen.
   c. mark has depreciated against the yen.
   d. yen has appreciated against the dollar.

7. Under a system of floating exchange rates, an increase in the demand for dollars by foreigners will cause a(n) _____ of the dollar.
   a. devaluation
   b. appreciation
   c. revaluation
   d. depreciation

8. Which of the following would cause an appreciation of the dollar? (There may be more than one correct answer.)
   a. An increase in American GDP.
   b. An increase in foreign GDP.
   c. A decrease in American interest rates.
   d. A decrease in foreign interest rates.
   e. An increase in inflation in the United States.
   f. An increase in inflation in the rest of the world.

9. Which of the following would cause a depreciation of the dollar?
   a. A decrease in American GDP.
   b. An increase in foreign GDP.
   c. An increase in American interest rates.
   d. A decrease in foreign interest rates.
   e. A decrease in inflation in the United States.
   f. A decrease in inflation in the rest of the world.

10. Under a system of floating exchange rates, which one of the following conditions will tend to depreciate the French franc relative to the German mark?
    a. An economic boom in Germany.
    b. A higher level of inflation in France than in Germany.
    c. An increase in interest rates in France.
    d. A sudden increase in German demand for imports from France.

11. Which of the following would lead to an appreciation of the franc relative to the mark?
    a. A recession in Germany.
    b. Less inflation in Germany than in France.
    c. An increase in French interest rates.
    d. A boom in France.

12. An economic boom is likely to mean (There may be more than one correct answer.)
    a. more imports.
    b. a depreciation of a country's currency.
    c. a balance of payments deficit under a system of floating exchange rates.
    d. an appreciation of a country's currency.

13. Purchasing-power parity theory says that
    a. only the volume of exports and imports determines exchange rates; interest rates have nothing to do with exchange rates.
    b. all countries are better off with a system of fixed exchange rates.
    c. adjustment of fixed exchange rates should be symmetrical between deficit and surplus countries.
    d. in the long run, exchange rates adjust to reflect differences in price levels between countries.

14. If inflation in Germany is at an annual rate of 2 percent and inflation in the United States is at 8 percent, then the purchasing-power parity theory suggests that in the long run the dollar price of one mark will
    a. increase at an annual rate of 8 percent.
    b. decrease at an annual rate of 6 percent.
    c. increase at an annual rate of 6 percent.
    d. increase at an annual rate of 2 percent.

15. In Question 14 above, one would say that the higher rate of inflation in the United States results in a(n)
    a. depreciation of the mark relative to the dollar.
    b. appreciation of the mark relative to the dollar.
    c. appreciation of the dollar relative to the mark.
    d. cross-subsidy of the mark by the dollar.

16. Assume that the mark—dollar exchange rate is fixed, that Germany and the United States are the only two countries in the world, and that inflation rates differ as described in Question 14. Which country will have a balance of payments surplus?
    a. The United States.
    b. Germany.

17. From an initial position of equilibrium under a system of fixed exchange rates, which of the following would lead to a balance of payments deficit?
    (There may be more than one correct answer.)
    a. A boom in the domestic economy.
    b. An increase in domestic interest rates.
    c. Domestic inflation in excess of inflation in the rest of the world.
    d. A devaluation by a country's major trading partner.

18. If the country of Zenon tries to fix its exchange rate at a level above that determined by demand and supply, it will likely
    (There may be more than one correct answer.)
    a. run a balance of payments deficit.
    b. run a balance of payments surplus.
    c. find its exports being priced out of world markets.
    d. see reduced interest by foreigners in investing in Zenon.

19. Which one of the following policies would not help to eliminate a deficit under a system of fixed exchange rates?
    a. Monetary and fiscal policies to raise the level of unemployment.
    b. A devaluation of the exchange rate.
    c. Monetary and fiscal policies to increase the rate of inflation.
    d. A change in monetary policy that increases interest rates.

20. If it takes 13 cents to buy one Swedish krona and 52 cents to buy one Dutch guilder, then how many kronor should it take to buy one guilder?
    a. (.13 + .52) = .25.
    b. (.52 + .13) = 4.00.
    c. (1.0 + .13) = 7.69.
    d. (1.0 + .52) = 1.92.

## Test B

Circle T or F for true or false.

T F 1. If one mark used to cost 60 cents and now costs 40 cents, the dollar has appreciated relative to the mark.

T F 2. A pure system of floating exchange rates requires government intervention—purchases and sales of its own currency—in order to work properly.

T F 3. Under a system of floating exchange rates, a sudden increase in the demand for U.S. exports will lead to appreciation of the dollar relative to other currencies.

T F 4. Under a system of fixed exchange rates, a sudden increase in American imports would increase the American balance of payments deficit (or reduce the size of the surplus).

T F 5. Purchasing-power parity is a theory of the short-run determination of exchange rates.

T F 6. Under a system of fixed exchange rates, a country that attempts to peg its exchange rate at an artificially low level will end up with a balance of payments surplus.

T F 7. Today, world international monetary relations are based on the gold standard.

T F 8. A major advantage of the gold standard was that countries could control their own domestic money stock.

T F 9. The Bretton Woods gold-exchange system established a system of fixed exchange rates based on the convertibility of dollars into gold.

T F 10. Under the Bretton Woods system of fixed exchange rates, both surplus and deficit countries felt the same pressure to correct any imbalance in their balance of payments.

## SUPPLEMENTARY EXERCISES

1. **The Risks of Speculation Against Fixed Exchange Rates**

   Assume that in the mid-1960s you are treasurer for a large multinational corporation with 10 million British pounds to invest. The fixed official exchange rate vis-a-vis the U.S. dollar has been $2.80. At this exchange rate Britain has been experiencing large and growing deficits in its balance of payments and has been financing this deficit by buying pounds with foreign currencies. Britain's holdings of foreign currencies are running low, and there is a general feeling that Britain will have to devalue the pound. Exactly how large the devaluation will be and exactly when it will occur are uncertain, but given the history of chronic deficits, there is absolutely no chance that the pound will be revalued.

   Complete Table 36-3 to measure the risks of speculating against the pound. (Changing from pounds to dollars and back again will involve transactions costs. Table 36-3 abstracts from these costs, which are apt to be small.)

   What is the worst outcome?

   As the talk of devaluation heats up, what are you apt to do? How will your actions affect the British deficit and the pressures for devaluation?

2. **World Trade Under Fixed and Flexible Exchange Rates**

   Some observers worried that the introduction of a system of floating exchange rates would have adverse effects on the volume of world trade, as exporters and importers would have trouble coping with short-run fluctuations in exchange rates. Go to the library and look up data on the volume of international trade. (You might try data from one of a variety of international organizations, including the United Nations, the International Monetary Fund, or the World Bank.) What is the percentage change in the annual physical volume of trade since the establishment of current mixed system of floating exchange rates in 1973? How does the growth in trade compare with growth in world output, that is the sum of all countries' GDP?

### TABLE 36-3

|  | (1) | (2) | (3) |
|---|---|---|---|
| Initial holdings of pounds | 10,000,000 | 10,000,000 | 10,000,000 |
| Current exchange rate | $2.80 | $2.80 | $2.80 |
| Number of dollars if you sell pounds for dollars | _____ | _____ | _____ |
| Possible new exchange rate | $2.80* | $2.60 | $2.40 |
| Number of pounds following reconversion to pounds after devaluation | _____ | _____ | _____ |

* This exchange rate assumes Britain takes other steps and does not devalue the pound

## ECONOMICS IN ACTION

### Hedging One's International Investments

The movement of exchange rates complicates the lives of companies and individual investors who by choice or necessity have to deal with international investments. Imagine that interest rates in Britain offer a better return than in the United States. Do you want to convert your dollars into pounds, invest in Britain, and then convert back to dollars? The higher interest return may look tempting, but any advantage of higher interest rates in Britain could be completely offset by an adverse movement in the dollar/pound exchange rate. For example, assume that a pound cost $1.60 when you invest to take advantage of a 10 percent interest rate in Britain compared to a 5 percent interest rate in the United States. What happens if at the end of the year, when you go to convert your pounds back into dollars, the pound has depreciated to $1.45 or appreciated to $1.75? As the example shows, changes in exchange rates can have a major impact on international investors and on the dollar value of international earnings of corporations.[1] Economists would say that these changes add to the variability and risk of international investments. If potential returns are sufficiently attractive, there is an incentive to learn how to manage the associated risk.

It is often argued that one should fully hedge international investments. That is, if you make an investment in Britain you should at the same time take other actions that lock-in the exchange rate you will use to convert your pounds back into dollars. While such actions mean you would not benefit from an appreciation of the pound, you would also avoid the loss that would accompany a depreciation. The use of future markets, that is dealing with speculators in foreign exchange, is one way to lock-in a particular exchange rate.

How important is it to hedge one's international investments? Economist Kenneth Froot argues that whether one should hedge international investments depends upon one's time horizon. Using almost 200 years worth of data on exchange rates between the dollar and the pound along with investment returns in the United States and the United Kingdom, Froot argues that hedging reduced the variance of international investments that were held for short horizons, e.g. one or two years, but that as one's investment horizon lengthened, there was less need to hedge international investments. How can this be?

Consider the following simple example. Assume that over longer time horizons, exchange rates tend toward levels defined by purchasing power parity, real interest rates are the same in the United States and Britain, and nominal investment returns reflect any differences in inflation. If inflation is higher in Britain, then nominal interest rates in Britain should be higher than in the United States. Note that nominal interest rates in Britain are measured in terms of pounds while in the United States they are measured in terms of dollars. If exchange rates are determined by purchasing power parity, the pound will depreciate at a rate that just offsets the difference in nominal interest rates. An U.S. investor would not be disadvantaged by the depreciation in the pound and would receive no benefit from dealing with speculators who would incorporate the difference in rates of inflation into the future exchange rates offered investors. This view suggests that one should evaluate particular investments in the United States or Britain on their merits and that markets may work to minimize the risks associated with changes in the exchange rates if one is investing for the long term.[2]

How do businesses respond to the ups and downs of the dollar? A recent story in *The New York Times* talked about how Eastman Kodak and other companies deal with changes in exchange rates. These changes are of growing importance as American companies increase foreign operations. For example, in 1992 about 46 percent of Kodak's sales came from foreign countries. David Fiedler, director of foreign exchange for Kodak, reported that in the short term he uses financial hedges to protect against changes

---

[1] Changes in exchange rates are not just an issue for a system of flexible exchange rates. The system of fixed rates under the Bretton Woods agreement included long periods of stable exchange rates marked by sudden and often large adjustments of official exchange rates. If one of those large changes occurred when you had made an international investment, you could be much worse or better off, but usually worse.

[2] Froot's findings are new and controversial. Measures of the returns one might have received in the past are no guarantee of what one will receive in the future. Even if over the long term one need not worry about movements in exchange rates, an investment that does poorly in either country will have been a mistake.

---

in exchange rates. Over the longer term he views questions of foreign exchange as a "business problem like any other business problem." That is, exchange rate risk is something that should be given careful consideration from the very beginning, when making decisions about markets, suppliers, and production sites. "Before 1988, Mr. Fiedler . . . often had to respond to currency swings within minutes after a phone call about foreign developments startled him from sleep. 'That's a real motivator to think of another way,' he said."

1. If you were to make a personal financial investment in a foreign stock market, in what market would you invest? How do you evaluate the exchange rate risks of your choice?
2. What strategies might business follow, other than financial hedges, to minimize the risks associated with international operations?

SOURCES: "Companies Learn to Live with Dollar's Volatility," *The New York Times*, August 31, 1992.

Kenneth A. Froot, "Currency Hedging over Long Horizons," Working Paper No. 4355, National Bureau of Economic Research, May 1993.

## STUDY QUESTIONS

1. If you know the dollar price of a German mark, how can you figure out how many marks it takes to buy a dollar?
2. What is the difference between an appreciation and a depreciation of the dollar? Which is better for American tourists? For American exporters?
3. What factors would cause an appreciation of the dollar? What factors would cause a depreciation?
4. Is it possible for the dollar to appreciate against the pound and, at the same time, for the pound to appreciate against the dollar? Why?
5. What is meant by purchasing-power parity? How is it possible for exchange rates to vary from levels determined by purchasing-power parity?
6. How did the gold standard work to maintain fixed exchange rates?
7. What was the difference between the gold standard and the gold-exchange (Bretton Woods) system?
8. What is a balance of payments deficit? Is it possible to have an overall deficit under a system of floating exchange rates? Fixed exchange rates?
9. Under a system of fixed exchange rates, what policies might a country adopt to eliminate a balance of payments deficit? Surplus?
10. Who bore most of the burden for adjustment under the gold-exchange system, deficit or surplus countries? Why wasn't the burden of adjustment equal?
11. Under fixed exchange rates, balance of payment deficits reflect an overvalued exchange rate. The overvalued exchange rate increases the price of a country's exports. A devaluation would help to correct the balance of payments deficit by lowering the price of exports, increasing the demand for exports, and increasing employment in export industries. Yet most countries have resisted devaluation even when facing chronic deficits. What do you think explains this reluctance?
12. What steps might exporters and importers take to minimize the risk of currency fluctuations under a system of floating exchange rates?
13. Why is it said that under fixed exchange rates currency speculation was destabilizing, while under floating exchange rates it is likely to be stabilizing?
14. When would a country prefer a system of fixed exchange rates and when might it prefer a system of floating exchange rates?
15. What is meant by the term "dirty" or "managed" float?

Chapter **37**

# Macroeconomics in a World Economy

## LEARNING OBJECTIVES

After completing this chapter you should be able to:

♦ explain how an appreciation or depreciation in the exchange rate affects net exports.

♦ explain the J-curve and its relevance to an understanding of the impact of a change in exchange rates.

♦ use an aggregate demand—aggregate supply diagram to show how an appreciation or depreciation of the exchange rate affects GDP and the price of domestically produced goods.

♦ explain why the reaction of international capital flows to changes in interest rates works to offset the impact of changes in fiscal policy.

♦ explain why the reaction of international capital flows to changes in interest rates works to enhance the impact of changes in monetary policy.

♦ explain in what way government deficits and trade deficits are linked.

♦ explain how a change in the mix of fiscal and monetary policy affects macroeconomic variables such as GDP, real interest rates, prices, the trade deficit, and the exchange rate.

♦ evaluate the likely impact of proposals to reduce the U.S. trade deficit.

## IMPORTANT TERMS AND CONCEPTS

Exports
Imports
Net exports
Closed economy
Open economy
Exchange rate
Appreciation

Depreciation
Trade deficit
J-curve
International capital flows
Budget deficits and trade deficits
$G - T = (S - I) - (X - IM)$

---

# CHAPTER REVIEW

This chapter integrates the discussion of international trade and exchange rates of the last two chapters with the earlier discussions of income determination and fiscal and monetary policy. An economy that

**(1)** did not trade with any other economy would be called a _____ economy. Today all industrial economies and most developing economies have extensive links with other economies through trade in goods and services and financial assets. Such economies are called _____ economies. These international linkages can affect important macroeconomic outcomes such as GDP and prices. A complete and rigorous examination of these linkages is the stuff of more advanced courses in economics, but with a few minor modifications we can use the model of income determination that we developed in earlier chapters to shed light on a number of important issues.

We start with a review of factors affecting the demand for exports and imports. As we saw in Chapter 25, the demand for exports and imports is influenced by income and prices. An increase in foreign income

**(2)** will (<u>decrease/increase</u>) the demand for American exports and is an important reason why economic fluctuations abroad (<u>are/are not</u>) felt in the United States. Exports and imports are also influenced by changes in the exchange rate, these changes alter the relative price of foreign and domestic goods. An appreciation of the dollar makes foreign goods (<u>less/more</u>) expensive. The result is likely to be a(n) (<u>decrease/increase</u>) in American imports and a(n) _____ in American exports. Putting these two effects together shows that an appreciation of the exchange rate will lead to a(n) (<u>decrease/increase</u>) in net exports, (X – IM). Similar reasoning shows that a depreciation of the dollar will lead to a(n) _____ in exports, a(n) _____ in imports and a(n) _____ in net exports.

A change in net exports that comes from a change in exchange rates is analogous to any other autonomous

**(3)** change in spending. It shifts the expenditure schedule and leads to a (<u>movement along/shift in</u>) the aggregate demand curve. More precisely, following an appreciation of the dollar, net exports (<u>decline/increase</u>), the expenditure schedule shifts (<u>down/up</u>), and the aggregate demand curve shifts to the (<u>left/right</u>). Opposite results follow from a depreciation of the dollar.

A change in exchange rates can also lead to a shift in the aggregate supply curve through its impact on the price of imported intermediate goods. An appreciation of the dollar makes imported

**(4)** inputs (<u>less/more</u>) expensive. This result can be modeled as a(n) (<u>downward/upward</u>) shift in the aggregate supply curve. A depreciation of the dollar makes imported inputs _____ expensive and leads to a(n) _____ shift in the aggregate supply curve.

Once we understand the impact of a change in interest rates on international capital flows and on the exchange rate, we will have all the pieces necessary to examine the impact of changes in fiscal and

**(5)** monetary policy. We saw in Chapter 36 that an increase in interest rates is apt to (<u>decrease/increase</u>) the demand by foreigners for American financial assets. This change in the demand for dollars should lead to a(n) (<u>appreciation/depreciation</u>) of the dollar. Tracing through the impact of this capital-flow-induced change in the exchange rate is the key to understanding how fiscal and monetary policy work in an open economy.

To review, consider a change in fiscal policy. A move to expansionary fiscal policy, say a(n)

**(6)** (<u>decrease/increase</u>) in taxes, would shift the expenditure schedule (<u>up/down</u>) and shift the aggregate demand curve to the (<u>right/left</u>). With no changes in monetary policy (that is, no shift in the supply of money schedule), there will be a(n) (<u>decrease/no change/increase</u>) in interest rates. The impact of this change in interest rates on international capital flows will lead to a(n) (<u>appreciation/depreciation</u>) in the exchange rate. This change in the exchange rate will shift the aggregate demand curve to the (<u>left/right</u>) and shift the aggregate supply curve (<u>down/up</u>). The shift in the aggregate demand curve, induced by

---

the change in the exchange rate, works to (<u>enhance/offset</u>) the original expansionary change in fiscal policy. The shift in the aggregate supply curve works to (<u>lower/raise</u>) prices and to (<u>increase/decrease</u>) output. If the shift in the aggregate supply curve induced by the change in exchange rates were large enough, it could offset the impact on output from the exchange-rate-induced shift in the aggregate demand curve. Evidence suggests that the shift in the aggregate supply curve is small and that, on net, the shifts in the two curves work to (<u>enhance/offset</u>) the impact of expansionary fiscal policy on output.

(7) A move to restrictive monetary policy can be analyzed in the same way. The initial effects will include an increase in interest rates that leads to a(n) (<u>appreciation/depreciation</u>) of the exchange rate. The impact of the change in the exchange rate will (<u>enhance/offset</u>) the original restrictive change in monetary policy.

Our equilibrium condition that $Y = C + I + G + (X - IM)$ can be manipulated to illustrate the important link between government budget deficits and trade deficits. Remembering that GDP equals disposable income plus net taxes and that disposable income equals consumption spending plus savings enables us to rewrite this equilibrium condition[1] as

$$G - T = (S - I) - (X - IM).$$

If the government runs a deficit—that is, if the government wants more output than it can command through taxes—then either private savings must exceed private investment, $(S - I)$, or additional output must be forthcoming from foreigners—that is, imports must exceed exports. It is changes in income, interest rates, exchange rates, and prices that enforce equilibrium and the link between budget deficits and trade deficits.

(8) The impact of a change in exchange rates on imports and exports usually takes some time. Economists refer to the lag in the adjustment of the balance of trade following a change in exchange rates as the _____ curve. Is the American trade deficit a problem? One's answer to this question depends upon whether one views capital inflows over the 1980s as a market response to extravagant spending requiring high interest rates in the United States to attract foreign capital or as the result of an autonomous increase in foreign demand for investment in the United States. Many feel that evidence on interest rates and consumption spending is more consistent with the first rather than the second view.

(9) A number of suggestions have been made to reduce the trade deficit. Many argue that the United States should alter the mix of fiscal and monetary policy. According to this view, (<u>contractionary/expansionary</u>) fiscal policy and _____ monetary policy were responsible for the increase in the trade deficit during the 1980s. Reversing these actions, that is, a move to _____ fiscal policy and _____ monetary policy, could work in reverse and lower the trade deficit. Rapid economic growth abroad would increase American (<u>exports/imports</u>). Protectionism would lower imports, but retaliation by foreign governments could (<u>lower/raise</u>) American exports with little change in net exports. One also needs to consider the impact of protectionism on exchange rates. For any of these measures to work, the equilibrium condition described above, $G - T = (S - I) - (X - IM)$, shows us that a reduction in the trade deficit must be accompanied by a combination of lower budget deficits, higher savings, or lower investment.

---

[1] This condition can also be written as $G + I + X = I + T + IM$. In terms of the circular flow diagram of Figure 7-1 in the text, this formulation says that injections must equal leakages.

## IMPORTANT TERMS AND CONCEPTS QUIZ

Choose the best definition for the following terms.

1. _____ Exports
2. _____ Imports
3. _____ Closed economy
4. _____ Open economy
5. _____ Trade deficit
6. _____ J-curve

a. Domestically produced goods sold abroad.
b. Graph depicting response of inflation to changes in the exchange rate.

c. Economy that trades with other economies.
d. Time series graph depicting response of net exports to changes in the exchange rate.
e. Foreign-produced goods purchased domestically.
f. Economy that does not trade with other economies.
g. Amount by which imports exceed exports.

## BASIC EXERCISE

This exercise is designed to review how the operation of fiscal and monetary policy is affected by interest-sensitive capital flows in an open as compared to a closed economy.

1. Table 37-1 is designed to help you review the impact of changes in the exchange rate on various macroeconomic variables. First, complete the column for an appreciation of the exchange rate. Then complete the column for a depreciation of the exchange rate. In each cell indicate how each variable changes, i.e. increases or decreases, shifts left, right, up or down, as appropriate. Be sure you can explain why each variable shows the change you have indicated. If the change in GDP and the price level seems ambiguous, see if you can resolve the ambiguity by assuming, as in the text, that any shift in the aggregate demand curve is greater than the shift in the aggregate supply curve.

### TABLE 37-1

| Macroeconomic Variable | Exchange Rate Appreciation | Exchange Rate Depreciation |
|---|---|---|
| Exports | | |
| Imports | | |
| Net Exports | | |
| Aggregate Demand Curve | | |
| Aggregate Supply Curve | | |
| Real GDP | | |
| Price Level | | |

2. Table 37-2 shows the impact on GDP and the price level of changes in fiscal and monetary policy. The completed upper portion of the table ignores any impact on exchange rates. Remembering that changes in interest rates are likely to influence the international investment of funds and hence the demand for dollars, complete Table 37-2 to determine whether capital flows offset or enhance these changes in monetary and fiscal policy. You should specify the change in interest rates; determine how the exchange rate is affected; consider the impact of the change in the exchange rate on GDP and prices; and, finally, combine your results from the change in policy and the change in exchange rates to determine the overall impact. Figure 37-1 may be helpful when completing Table 37-2.

3. What general conclusion can you draw about the effectiveness of monetary and fiscal policy in a world of interest-sensitive capital flows and flexible exchange rates?

**TABLE 37-2**

|  | Increase in *G* | Decrease in *G* | Open Market Sale | Open Market Purchase |
|---|---|---|---|---|
| Aggregate Demand Curve<br>Real GDP | Right<br>Up | Left<br>Down<br>Down | Left<br>Down<br>Down | Right<br>Up |
| Interest Rate | _____ | _____ | _____ | _____ |
| Exchange Rate | _____ | _____ | _____ | _____ |
|    Real GDP | _____ | _____ | _____ | _____ |
|    Price Level | _____ | _____ | _____ | _____ |
| Overall Impact | _____ | _____ | _____ | _____ |
|    Real GDP | _____ | _____ | _____ | _____ |
|    Price Level | _____ | _____ | _____ | _____ |

**FIGURE 37-1**

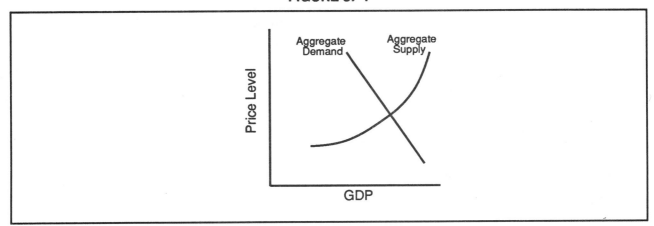

## SELF-TESTS FOR UNDERSTANDING

### Test A

Circle the most appropriate answer.

1. An appreciation of the exchange rate will make
   a. both exports and imports cheaper.
   b. exports more expensive for foreigners but imports cheaper for domestic citizens.
   c. exports cheaper for foreigners but imports more expensive for domestic citizens.
   d. both exports and imports more expensive.

2. A depreciation of the exchange rate will lead to
   a. an increase in exports and imports.
   b. a decrease in exports and an increase in imports.
   c. an increase in exports and a decrease in imports.
   d. a decrease in both exports and imports.

3. A depreciation of the exchange rate will lead to _____ in net exports.
   a. a decrease
   b. no change
   c. an increase

4. An increase in net exports will
   a. shift the aggregate demand curve to the left.
   b. have no impact on the aggregate demand curve.
   c. shift the aggregate demand curve to the right.

5. A depreciation of the exchange rate will
   a. shift the aggregate supply curve up.
   b. have no impact on the aggregate supply curve.
   c. shift the aggregate supply curve down.

6. Evidence suggests that when the exchange rate changes, shifts in the aggregate demand curve will _____ shifts in the aggregate supply curve.
   a. be smaller than
   b. just offset
   c. dominate

7. A depreciation of the exchange rate tends to
   a. raise GDP and the price of domestically produced goods.
   b. raise GDP but lower the price of domestically produced goods.
   c. lower GDP but raise the price of domestically produced goods.
   d. lower GDP and the price of domestically produced goods.

8. An increase in foreign GDP is likely to lead to
   a. a decrease in our exports.
   b. little if any change in our exports.
   c. an increase in our exports.

9. Higher foreign interest rates are likely to be followed by
   (There may be more than one correct answer.)
   a. an inflow of international capital.
   b. an increase in foreign investments by domestic citizens.
   c. an appreciation of the exchange rate.
   d. an increase in net exports.

10. An increase in domestic interest rates should lead to which one of the following?
    a. Capital outflow.
    b. Appreciation of the dollar.
    c. Increase in exports.
    d. Upward shift in the expenditure schedule.

11. An appreciation in the dollar vis-a-vis other currencies should lead to all but which one of the following?
    a. A decrease in exports.
    b. An increase in imports.
    c. A shift of the aggregate demand curve to the right.
    d. A downward shift of the aggregate supply curve.

12. A move to expansionary fiscal policy will lead to all but which one of the following?
    a. An increase in interest rates.
    b. An appreciation of the dollar.
    c. An increase in American exports.
    d. An increase in the American trade deficit.

13. A move to expansionary monetary policy will lead to all but which one of the following?
    a. A decrease in interest rates.
    b. An appreciation of the dollar.
    c. An upward shift in the expenditure schedule.
    d. An increase in inflationary pressures.

14. Taking account of interest-sensitive international capital flows means that in an open economy the impact of fiscal policy is
    a. smaller than in a closed economy.
    b. the same as in a closed economy.
    c. larger than in a closed economy.

15. Taking account of interest-sensitive international capital flows means that in an open economy the impact of monetary policy is
    a. smaller than in a closed economy.
    b. the same as in a closed economy.
    c. larger than in a closed economy.

16. The J-curve refers to
    a. What Julius Erving does with his body when he drives for the bucket.
    b. the delayed impact of higher rates of inflation on interest rates.
    c. the delayed impact of a change in the exchange rate on a country's trade deficit.
    d. the pitch that won the 1983 World Series.

17. In an open economy equilibrium requires that
    a. $G - T = I + S + X - IM$.
    b. $G - T = S - I + (IM - X)$.
    c. $G - T = I + X - S - IM$.
    d. $G - T = S - X - (I + IM)$.

18. If there is no change in the balance of domestic savings and investment, then any increase in the government deficit must be matched by
    (There may be more than one correct answer.)
    a. an increase in the trade deficit.
    b. a reduction in the equilibrium level of output.
    c. a capital inflow.
    d. a reduction in interest rates.

19. Which of the following would help to reduce the U.S. trade deficit?
   a. Higher government deficits.
   b. Increased domestic investment.
   c. Increased domestic savings.
   d. A decrease in exports.

20. An increase in the government deficit need not lead to an increase in the trade deficit if there is (There may be more than one correct answer.)
   a. an increase in private savings.
   b. a decrease in private investment.
   c. an increase in consumption spending.
   d. an increase in imports.

## Test B

Circle T or F for true or false.

T  F  1. International trade means that an economic boom in the United States is likely to lead to recession in the rest of the world.

T  F  2. A change in exports has no multiplier impacts.

T  F  3. A shift in the expenditure schedule coming from an autonomous change in domestic investment spending would be expected to have no impact on a country's trade deficit.

T  F  4. A depreciation in the exchange rate is inflationary.

T  F  5. A depreciation in the exchange rate should help to reduce a country's trade deficit.

T  F  6. Under floating exchange rates, a country with a trade surplus will also experience a capital outflow.

T  F  7. International capital flows make monetary policy less effective.

T  F  8. International capital flows are unaffected by changes in fiscal policy.

T  F  9. Increased protectionism may only lead to an appreciation of the dollar.

T  F  10. The only way to reduce the trade deficit is by reducing the government's budget deficit.

## ECONOMICS IN ACTION

### Fixed or Flexible Exchange Rates for Europe?

As part of plans for a united Europe, the European Economic Community (EEC) countries were to adopt a single currency by 1996 at the earliest and 1999 at the latest. The development of a single currency was seen as an integral part of a united Europe and a natural evolution of the European Monetary System (EMS), established in 1979.

Under the EMS, member countries committed to maintain exchange rates within a fairly narrow band around established parities. While there were periodic adjustments of parities in the early years of the EMS, from 1987 through 1991 there were no parity adjustments. Many saw this record of stable exchange rates as a successful first step toward a single currency. Harmonization of macro policies were also important to the plans for a single currency. To join the single currency bloc, countries were to keep inflation below 3 percent per year and government deficits less than 3 percent of GDP. In addition, there were to be no exchange rate devaluations for at least two years. By the beginning of 1992, adjustments of exchange rate parities had been avoided for five years, but there was wide divergence in meeting the other two targets.

In the summer of 1992, the British pound, Italian lira, and Spanish peseta came under strong speculative attack. In all cases there was significant pressure for depreciation vis-à-vis the German mark. As each exchange rate reached the lower limit of the agreed upon trading band, governments were initially required to use their holdings of foreign exchange to purchase their own currencies but had to ask for help from other EEC countries in defending the established parities. In the end, the earlier parities could not be defended. The lira and pound left the EMS while there were adjustments of exchange rates withing the EMS for the peseta and other weak currencies. In the summer of 1993 there was similar downward pressure on the French franc. This time the result was a significant widening of the allowable trading bands.

The turbulence in exchange rates and financial markets left a number of observers unsure of the desirability of establishing a single currency in Europe. Those who had pressed for a single currency argued that integrated markets would work best if exchange rate uncertainty could be removed. They saw a single European currency as a boon to trade, commerce, and economic growth. However, experience in 1992 and 1993 showed the difficulty of sustaining fixed exchange rates when individual countries pursue divergent macro policies. In Germany there was a significant expansion of aggregate demand connected with the integration of East and West Germany. To minimize the inflationary impact of the increase in public spending, the Bundesbank had increased interest rates in Germany. The resulting flow of capital to Germany worked to appreciate the mark and depreciate other currencies.

A traditional defense to avoid depreciation would be to raise interest rates to increase the demand for your currency, although at the cost of restricting domestic aggregate demand. The risk of increasing unemployment made other countries reluctant to pursue this option. An alternative would be to accept the depreciation and be done with it. While depreciation solves the exchange rate problem and lowers the price of one's exports, it is likely to be seen as inflationary as it increases the cost of imported foreign goods. Depreciation would also admit the difficulty of maintaining fixed parities and thus question the desirability of attempts to move to a single currency. Concerns about the credibility of their commitment to fixed exchange rates led governments to resist exchange rate adjustments until the reality of market forces overwhelmed their ability to defend earlier parities.

As of this writing it is unclear whether the wider trading bands adopted in the summer of 1993 will be sufficient. Persistent differences in the rate of inflation across countries would appear to require continual adjustments in exchange rates. Wider trading bands can help to accommodate temporary fluctuations in demand and supply but are not capable of dealing with a persistent trend in one direction. On the other hand, a commitment to fixed exchange rates requires that the most inflation prone economies take corrective action or their goods will be priced out of the market. It is this discipline on domestic macro policy that many find an appealing part of a commitment to fixed exchange rates.

1. What has happened to exchange rates between European currencies since the summer of 1993? What are the costs and benefits of continued efforts to establish a single currency as compared with a system of more flexible exchange rates? Do you think Europe should move to a single currency? Why?

---

SOURCE: "The European Community: Back to the Drawing Board," *The Economist*, July 3-9, 1993

---

## STUDY QUESTIONS

1. What is the difference between an open and a closed economy?
2. How does an appreciation in the exchange rate affect net exports? What about a depreciation? Why?
3. How does a change in net exports, induced by a change in the exchange rate, affect the aggregate demand curve? The aggregate supply curve? Which effect is likely to be larger?
4. What is meant by the J-curve pattern of adjustment to a change in exchange rates?
5. Does an increase in interest rates lead to an appreciation or depreciation of the exchange rate? Why?

---

6. Consider a move to contractionary fiscal policy that reduces aggregate demand. What is the likely impact on interest rates, international capital flows, the exchange rate and net exports? Do these changes tend to enhance or offset the original change in fiscal policy?

7. Consider a move to expansionary monetary policy that increases aggregate demand. What is the likely impact on interest rates, international capital flows, the exchange rate and net exports? Do these changes enhance or offset the original change in monetary policy?

8. What is the link between government deficits and trade deficits? Under what conditions does an increase in the government deficit lead to an increase in the trade deficit?

9. Some have argued for a change in the mix of fiscal and monetary policy—easier monetary policy and contractionary fiscal policy—as a way to reduce both government deficits and the trade deficit. Would these changes have the desired impact? Why?

10. Why isn't increased protectionism a sure-fire way to reduce the trade deficit?

*Chapter* **38**

# Growth in Developed and Developing Countries

## LEARNING OBJECTIVES

After completing this chapter you should be able to:

- ♦ distinguish between growth in total GDP and GDP per capita.
- ♦ describe what exponential growth is and explain why it usually cannot continue forever.
- ♦ explain why the composition of aggregate demand is an important determinant of the rate of economic growth.
- ♦ describe other factors that are important in determining an economy's rate of growth.
- ♦ describe the arguments for and against continued growth.
- ♦ distinguish between embodied and disembodied growth.
- ♦ discuss some of the important factors that impede the growth of incomes in LDCs.
- ♦ discuss what things LDCs can do for themselves to increase their growth.
- ♦ describe what role developed countries can play in assisting LDCs.
- ♦ explain what the World Bank is and what it does.

## IMPORTANT TERMS AND CONCEPTS

Output per capita
Exponential growth
Social infrastructure
Exchange between present and
    future consumption
Embodied growth
Disembodied growth

Less developed countries (LDCs)
Growth rate in GDP vs. per capita income
Multinational corporations
Disguised unemployment
Entrepreneurship
Brain drain
World Bank

# CHAPTER REVIEW

This chapter discusses some of the general issues concerned with economic growth: Can it continue forever? Is it desirable? What actions can countries take to influence their rates of growth? Economics cannot always offer definitive answers to these questions, but it can help you to think about the issues in a systematic fashion.

(1)     Growth that occurs at a constant percentage rate for a number of years is called _____ growth. This snowballing effect, when projected into the future, seems to suggest doom for the human race. Simple extrapolations of population at current rates of growth lead to ridiculous conclusions. The clear implication is that growth cannot continue at current rates forever and that actual growth experience will be more a matter of economic choices than mechanical extrapolations.

Many factors that are clearly important for growth are not well understood. Examples include

(2) _____, _____, and the _____ _____. Other factors influencing growth rates that countries *can* do something about, include accumulating more capital by higher levels of (consumption/investment) and devoting more resources to _____ and _____. Some new ideas and inventions require new machines before they can help increase output. Growth from these sorts of inventions is called (disembodied/embodied) economic growth. If new ideas permit more output from existing resources, the resulting growth is called _____ growth.

In a full-employment economy, more of anything, including investment spending or research and development, requires less of something else. This reduction, which is necessary to release resources for

(3) an increase in investment or research and development, is the _____ cost of increased investment. In a full-employment economy, resources for more investment would be available if current (consumption/savings) decreased and the amount of _____ increased.

The tools of economics cannot help you determine whether an economy should grow faster or slower; they can, however, identify the sources of growth and the consequences of more or less growth. In particular, a number of economists oppose zero economic growth on the grounds that a move in this direction would require extensive government controls and may seriously hamper efforts to eliminate poverty and to protect the environment. Solutions to these last two problems are likely to require more rather than fewer resources. Many feel that it is easier to reach a political agreement to devote resources to problems of poverty and the environment if total output is expanding rather than if it is not growing.

Concerns about economic growth are an everyday reality for citizens in developing countries. While it is common to develop lists of "the problems" of developing countries, it is important to remember that there is much diversity among these countries and that their problems are not all alike. Density of population shows a wide diversity among LDCs, as do recent gains in per capita incomes.

While income per capita increased in a number of developing countries during the 1970s, more recent developments have been less favorable, illustrating the fragility of recent growth trends. The world recession in the early 1980s had adverse impacts on a number of countries. High levels of external debt are a serious burden for some countries; there is evidence that recent growth has been accompanied by a worsening distribution of income; the rate of population growth remains high in many countries; and many LDCs have seen little if any increase in per capita income in recent years.

As for narrowing the income gap with the developed countries, it should be remembered that growth

(4) in the developed countries (has/has not) stopped. Even if developed countries and LDCs show the same percentage growth in income, the absolute differences in incomes will (increase/decrease) due to the (higher/lower) base of the developed countries.

LDCs face many problems in their quest for higher incomes. A fundamental problem is the lack of physical capital. More capital would help to increase labor productivity. LDCs can accumulate more capital in either of two ways. They can try to get it either from domestic sources or from foreign sources. The

(5) first option, domestic sources, would require (more/less) consumption in order to increase savings and investment.[1] This option will be (easy/difficult) for many countries because of their current extremely low levels of income. The second option, foreign sources, is not without its own risks. Profit-maximizing private businesses will clearly want as good a deal for themselves as possible. Mutual gain is still possible, however, especially if the LDCs insist upon the training of native workers for positions of responsibility and the development of social infrastructures, such as transportation and communication systems.

Population growth continues to be high for many LDCs primarily because of recent dramatic declines
(6) in (birth/death) rates. These declines appear to be the result of relatively (inexpensive/expensive) public health measures rather than the result of advancements in medical technology. High rates of population growth result in tremendous demands on a country to ensure that people do not starve. The experience of advanced economies suggests that birthrates may decrease as income rises. A lack of trained technical workers, extensive unemployment—especially disguised unemployment—a lack of entrepreneurship, and other social impediments to business activity, as well as extensive government interferences in markets, are additional problems facing LDCs.

What can the advanced economies do for the LDCs? They can help them accumulate both technical skills and physical capital. Training individuals from LDCs will add to the pool of technical skills for these countries if those receiving education return to their native countries. The fact that many of these
(7) individuals have not returned is referred to as the _____ _____. Aid in acquiring physical capital can be provided by long-term loans at preferential terms or by direct grants. Aid can be given by individual countries or through international organizations, drawing on the resources of many countries, such as the _____ Bank.

## IMPORTANT TERMS AND CONCEPTS QUIZ

Choose the best definition for the following terms.

1. _____ Exponential growth
2. _____ Social infrastructure
3. _____ Embodied growth
4. _____ Disembodied growth
5. _____ Disguised unemployment
6. _____ Brain drain
7. _____ Multinational corporation
8. _____ Entrepreneurship
9. _____ World Bank

a. Educated individuals from developing countries who emigrate to wealthier countries.
b. Transportation network, telecommunications system, and schools.
c. Growth due to better ideas that can be implemented with existing factors of production.
d. Companies with operations in many countries.
e. The excess of savings over investment.
f. International organization that makes loans to developing countries to finance investments in social infrastructure.
g. Situation where more people are employed than the most efficient number required.
h. Starting new firms, introducing innovations, and taking the necessary risks in seeking business opportunities.
i. Innovations that require new capital before they can affect economic growth.
j. Growth at a constant percentage rate.

[1]We have seen earlier that $Y = C + I + G + X - IM$. If one wants to increase $I$ and $Y$ cannot be expanded, then reductions in $C$, $G$, or ($X - IM$) will do. In an analysis of opportunities for growth, it is often useful to reclassify elements of $G$ and $X$ as either $C$ or $I$. With respect to $G$, highways and dams would be _____, while bureaucrats and paper clips would be _____. With this reclassification, the only way to increase $I$ is to reduce _____ or to get resources from abroad through an increase in _____.

## TABLE 38-1

| Country | GDP (Trillions of dollars) | Income per capita |
|---|---|---|
| United States | $5.61 | $22,204 |
| Brazil | _____ | _____ |
| Britain | _____ | _____ |
| Canada | _____ | _____ |
| China | _____ | _____ |
| France | _____ | _____ |
| Germany | _____ | _____ |
| India | _____ | _____ |
| Indonesia | _____ | _____ |
| Italy | _____ | _____ |
| Japan | _____ | _____ |
| Mexico | _____ | _____ |
| Spain | _____ | _____ |

## BASIC EXERCISE

Complete Table 38-1 with your best estimates of total output and income per capita in 1992 for each of the countries listed below in terms of American dollars. Data for the United States is given as a starting point. Check the accuracy of your estimates in the answers section of the Study Guide.

## SELF-TESTS FOR UNDERSTANDING

### Test A

Circle the most appropriate answer.

1. If the objective of economic growth is an increase in individual material welfare which of the following is an appropriate indicator?
   a. Growth in total output.
   b. Growth in inflation.
   c. Growth in inventiveness.
   d. Growth in output per capita.

2. If something, say GDP, increases by the same percent each year, then the absolute increases in GDP will
   a. become smaller.
   b. stay the same.
   c. become larger.

3. Assume GDP grows at a constant percent each year. One would refer to this growth as an example of
   a. exponential growth.
   b. technical growth.
   c. disembodied growth.
   d. embodied growth.

4. While there are many factors that affect economic growth, economic policy is likely to be most effective in influencing which of the following?
   (There may be more than one correct answer.)
   a. Inventiveness.
   b. The work ethic.
   c. The level of investment spending.
   d. Research and development activities.

5. Which of the following is not an example of investment in social infrastructure?
   a. The construction of the trans-Amazon highway in Brazil.
   b. Substantial investments in public education in the United States.
   c. The development of Indonesian oil fields by American oil companies.
   d. Investments in public health to reduce the incidence of infant mortality.

6. Which of the following is the appropriate measure of the opportunity cost of increased investment undertaken to raise the rate of growth?
   a. The resulting increase in future consumption.
   b. The rate of interest.
   c. The present consumption goods that could have been produced with the resources used to produce the investment goods.
   d. Zero, because economic growth is really without cost.

7. An economy at full-employment can increase investment only if it reduces
   (There may be more than one correct answer.)
   a. consumption spending.
   b. government purchases.
   c. exports.
   d. imports.

8. Innovation
   a. is really the same as invention.
   b. can only be successful when there are large increases in investment spending.
   c. is another name for embodied growth.
   d. refers to putting inventions into practice.

9. Disembodied economic growth
   a. refers to increased output from reallocation of existing resources.
   b. has a zero opportunity cost because it requires only new ideas.
   c. has never been important in the real world.
   d. is likely to mean more resource depletion than embodied growth.

10. Skeptics of attempts to limit economic growth would agree with all but which one of the following?
    a. Economic growth provides resources to fight pollution without having to change current levels of consumption.
    b. Reducing poverty at home and abroad will be easier with greater economic growth.
    c. To reduce or stop growth would require elaborate and repressive government controls.
    d. The irony of economic growth is that it reduces personal satisfaction at the same time it increases the material possessions.

11. The recent record of growth in income per capita in LDCs shows
    a. greater growth during the 1980s than the 1970s.
    b. equal increases in all LDCs.
    c. slower growth during the 1980s as compared with the 1970s and with many industrial countries.
    d. substantial increases for all but a handful of LDCs.

12. Output per capita will increase whenever the growth rate of GDP _____ that of population.
    a. is less than
    b. is equal to
    c. exceeds

13. High rates of population growth in many developing countries are the result of
    a. recent dramatic increases in birthrates.
    b. recent dramatic declines in death rates.
    c. the application of advanced medical technology.
    d. the success of compulsory programs of birth control.

14. Reductions in death rates in many developing countries are for the most part due to
    a. advanced medical treatments for cancer that have been borrowed from industrialized countries.
    b. the adoption of relatively inexpensive public health measures.
    c. the efforts of Peace Corps volunteers.
    d. comprehensive programs of national health insurance in most developing countries.

15. Which of the following is not among the obstacles to high levels of income in the LDCs?
    a. Large rural—urban migration with dramatic increases in urban unemployment.
    b. Domestic savings rates that are so high they depress aggregate demand.
    c. A lack of entrepreneurial talent.
    d. Numerous well-intentioned government interventions that discourage the efficiency of private business.

16. For many LDCs the greatest contribution to economic growth is likely to be made by expanding
    a. general basic education.
    b. the number of college graduates.
    c. technical training.
    d. the use of direct controls to determine the composition of output.

17. Which one of the following is *not* likely to help LDCs achieve higher levels of income?
    a. Any increase in savings and investment that can be squeezed out of existing low levels of income.
    b. Central control of trade and investment.
    c. Agricultural research appropriate to the crops and climates of specific countries.
    d. Removal of impediments to innovation and entrepreneurial talent.

18. If a country tries to maintain an overvalued exchange rate, that is maintain the exchange rate at a level higher than would be sustained by demand and supply, the result will be to make
    a. imports cheaper and exports more expensive.
    b. imports more expensive and exports cheaper.
    c. both imports and exports cheaper.
    d. both imports and exports more expensive.

19. As a percent of GDP, foreign aid from the U.S. to developing countries is _____ that of many other industrialized countries.
    a. less than
    b. equal to
    c. greater than

20. Which one of the following has *not* been an important source of loans and grants for development projects in LDCs?
    a. The World Bank.
    b. The International Monetary Fund.
    c. The United States.
    d. The Soviet Union.

## Test B

Circle T or F for true or false.

T  F   1.  GDP per capita will increase whenever total GDP increases.

T  F   2.  The fact that population growth has recently been exponential is a good reason to believe that it will continue that way forever.

T  F   3.  Zero economic growth would be easy to achieve.

T  F   4.  Zero economic growth would be an unambiguous gain for the environment.

T  F   5.  Increased investment spending leading to more capital accumulation is likely to increase the rate of economic growth.

T  F   6.  Embodied economic growth refers to ideas and inventions that require new machinery.

T  F   7.  Disembodied economic growth means that an economy can have higher rates of growth without having to sacrifice any current consumption.

T  F   8.  For any year that the growth rate of income per capita in the LDCs matches that of the developed countries, the absolute difference in income will decrease.

T  F   9.  Recently all LDCs have shared equally in increases in income per capita.

T  F  10.  Historical evidence refutes the Malthusian law of population growth.

T  F  11.  Research suggests that expenditures on technical training rather than general education are likely to have a greater impact on the rate of economic growth in LDCs.

T  F  12.  Disguised unemployment is only a problem for developed economies and has little relevance for LDCs.

T  F  13.  Unlike the United States, LDCs have not experienced any substantial rural–urban migration.

T  F  14.  The only real constraint to growth in the LDCs is a lack of entrepreneurship.

T  F  15.  In order to avoid the problem of default on loans, the World Bank makes loans only to developed countries, such as Britain and France.

## SUPPLEMENTARY EXERCISES

1. The total volume of U.S. aid to LDCs is much greater than aid from other countries. However, the U.S. economy is much larger than other economies. How does the U.S. commitment to development assistance stack up when measured as a percent of national output? Has the volume of aid from all developed economies, both in total and as a percent of national output, been increasing or decreasing? What about OPEC countries and the former Soviet bloc countries? A good place to start to answer these questions is the library. *World Development Report* typically contains data on official development assistance from major industrialized countries and OPEC countries. *The United States Statistical Yearbook* is another source of data.

   Some observers argue that looking only at foreign aid is incomplete as a measure of a country's concern for others. These people suggest that in view of many multilateral defense agreements, that have been an important part of American foreign policy one must also consider military expenditures.

What do you think of the argument? What is its quantitative significance? What does it imply at a time when superpower military tensions apperar to be diminishing dramatically? The *Statistical Abstract of the United States* is another place to start looking for data.

2. In 1950, the world's population was estimated to be 2.5 billion. From 1950 to 1990 it grew at an average annual rate of 1.9 percent to 5.3 billion. Assume that population has always grown at an annual rate of 1.9 percent. If we started with a population of two, how many years would it take for the world population to reach 5.3 billion? How long will it take for the world's population to double if it continues to grow at 1.9 percent per year?

3. Assume that growth policies were successful in raising the growth rate of income per capita in Mexico above that of the United States. Because of the initial higher level of incomes in the United States, $22,204 vs. $7,170, it would take a number of years for Mexican incomes to reach parity with those in the United States. Initially the absolute difference would increase even though the Mexican growth rate exceeds that of the United States.

Assume that the growth rate of income per capita in Mexico is 4 percent per year while it is only 1.5 percent per year in the United States.

   a. How many years will it take until income per capita in Mexico equals that of the United States? What would income be at that time?

   b. While the ratio of income per capita in Mexico to that in the United States will decline continuously, the absolute difference will initially increase. In what year would the difference in income per capita be greatest? What is the differential?

# ECONOMICS IN ACTION

## Understanding Economic Growth

What do we know about the growth experiences of different countries? In recent years much effort has gone into developing consisten measures of the economic performance of most countries in the world, many of which did not exist as separate nations until after World War II. A recent study by economists Stephen Parente and Edward Prescott used some of this data to look at the growth experience of 102 countries that had populations of at least one million in 1969 and for which data exists for the years 1960 through 1985. Looking at output per capita, Parente and Prescott find little variation in the range of disparity between the richest and poorest countries over time. The ratio of incomes in the five richest countries to that in the five poorest countries was about 29 to 1 in both 1960 and 1985. While this finding suggests that the distribution of income pre capita across countries has changed little, Parente and Prescott find that there were significant changes in the position of individual countries within the distribution. Some saw a substantial improvement in income per capita in both absolute and relative terms, while others experienced significant declines in income per capita.[1]

Is there a small set of factors that distinguish those countries with high rates of growth from those with low rates? In a number of cases, analysts have found important correlations to explain the growth experience of particular countries but many of these findings are fragile. That is, conclusions as to what factors are important for economic growth are likely to change as the number of countries, the number of variables, or the time period of the study changes. One needs to be careful about premature generalizations from one or a limited number of studies. Over time, as the number of studies has grown larger and larger, some variables appear to be consistently correlated with high rates of economic growth. The ratio of investment to output is one such variable. Countries with a higher share of output devoted to investment tend to have higher rates of economic growth. Political and military instability appears to be correlated with lower rates of growth. There is some evidence of convergence in the levels of income across countries, although there is still wide disagreement about the exact form of convergence and the applicability of

---

[1]The ten countries that had the largest declines in income per capita were Zambia, Mozambique, Madagascar, Angola, Chad, Liberia, Ghana, Zaire, Nicaragua, and Afghanistan, most of which experienced major military conflicts at some point between 1960 and 1985.

convergence among industrialized countries for less developed countries. Some economists argue that convergence depends upon education. A country with low incomes but an educated workforce would be expected to grow rapidly and catch up with similar countries. The immediate post-World War II experience in Europe and Japan would be examples of such experience.

Can we ever hope to find a small set of factors that will explain the growth experience of different countries? When thinking about this questions, it may be useful to remember the mathematical distinction between necessary and sufficient conditions. For example, increased investment in physical capital and increased spending on education may be necessary for higher rates of economic growth, but by themselves may not be sufficient if social and economic institutions are not supportive. Institutional factors that economists have argued can help to shape the impact of increased investment include the role of markets as opposed to central planning; incentives for entrepreneurs to create new businesses and adopt new technologies; the structure of government regulation; and so forth. Most of these institutional factors are difficult to measure but can have a significant impact on statistical correlations. The lesson that many economists draw from all this is not that economic analysis cannot explain growth rates, but rather that the way economic variables are likely to interact in a particular country will depend upon the institutions of that country. A country looking to change needs to think about both changes in important economic variables and the structure of social and economic institutions.

1. Pick a region of the world and go to the library to see what you can learn about the actual growth experience of the countries in that region. Try to find out such things as the proportion of output devoted to investment, the structure of educational opportunity and achievement, and the importance of international trade. Also find out what you can about social and economic institutions for these countries. Can you explain the growth experience of these countries compared with other countries? One place to start your investigation is *World Development Report*, an annual publication of the World Bank. Each volume contains detailed data on social and economic variables for a large number of countries.

SOURCES: Robert J. Barro and Jong-Wha Lee, "Losers and Winners in Economic Growth," Working Paper No. 4341, National Bureau of Economic Research, April 1993.

Stephen L. Parente and Edward C. Prescott, "Changes in the Wealth of Nations," *Quarterly Review*, Federal Reserve Bank of Minneapolis, (Spring 1993), pp. 3-16.

## STUDY QUESTIONS

1. Why can we be reasonably sure that exponential population growth will not continue forever?

2. Can a country influence its prospects for economic growth by changing the composition of aggregate demand? If so, how? (What can a capitalistic society that relies on markets to allocate resources do to affect the composition of demand and output?)

3. How might the government influence important but intangible growth factors such as the work ethic, entrepreneurship and innovation?

4. Do you think that the United States should pursue policies that work to increase the rate of American economic growth? Why or why not?

5. What is the difference between embodied and disembodied growth? Can you think of examples of each?

6. Why do many observers argue that high rates of population growth have had a negative impact on the ability of LDCs to enhance economic well-being even if they add to the growth of GDP?

7. What are appropriate strategies for developed countries to adopt in order to enhance the growth prospects of developing countries?

8. What are appropriate strategies for developing countries to adopt in order to enhance their own growth prospects?

*C h a p t e r* **39**

# Comparative Economic Systems: What Are the Choices?

## LEARNING OBJECTIVES

After completing this chapter, you should be able to:

- describe how in theory and practice the decisions about economic coordination and ownership—markets or planning; capitalism or socialism—are distinct choices.

- evaluate the record of market and planned economies regarding:
  - the choice of goods to produce
  - the efficiency of production
  - the distribution of income
  - economic growth
  - fluctuations in economic activity.

- describe the role of the "profit motive" in capitalism and the implications of its absence under socialism.

- explain how the Soviet Union was able to achieve high rates of economic growth in the face of substantial inefficiencies of production and why it was unable to sustain high rates of growth.

- describe how the Soviet planning process worked: who made the decisions, the role of Five-Year and One-Year Plans, and the meaning of material balance.

- explain the practical problems in moving from planning to markets and from social to private ownership.

- contrast Chinese and Soviet styles of planning.

- contrast the Japanese corporatist and American individualistic styles of doing business.

# IMPORTANT TERMS AND CONCEPTS

Welfare state
Collectivization
Central Planning
Capitalism
Socialism
Planning
Free markets
Consumer sovereignty
Privatization
Workers' management
Soviet Five-Year and One-Year Plans
Material balance
Material incentives
Sequencing
Great Leap Forward
Great Proletarian Cultural Revolution
Export-led growth
Industrial policy
Transition
Perestroika
Glasnost

# CHAPTER REVIEW

Countries must make choices about how to organize their economies. The discussion in this chapter looks at two crucial decisions: How should economic activity be coordinated? And who should own the means of production? The alternatives are compared using indicators of both equity and efficiency, and the experiences of three countries—the Soviet Union, China, and Japan—are considered in terms of the above issues.

(1) When considering how to coordinate economic activity, economies can choose to emphasize _____ or _____. These options are not simple all-or-nothing alternatives. For most countries the choice is a matter of emphasis and degree. That is, market economies allow for government intervention in many areas, and most planned economies rely on market forces in several areas.

(2) When considering ownership of the means of production, economies can choose to emphasize private ownership, that is, _____; or public ownership, that is, _____. Again, most countries do not choose one to the exclusion of the other.

Are socialism/planning and capitalism/markets the only feasible combinations? Both theory and real-world examples suggest that this pairing (is/is not) inevitable. For example, Yugoslavia was a (socialist/capitalist) country that relied heavily on (markets/planning) for the coordination of economic
(3) activity and France is a _____ country that uses mild forms of _____.

What difference does it make whether a country emphasizes markets or planning? We can keep score on the following five issues:
(4)    1. *What goods to produce.* Market economies respond to the preferences of _____ and planned economies to the preferences of _____. Which option one values depends, in part, on how much one values individual _____. A major shortcoming of planned economics is the lack of a feedback mechanism to correct any imbalance between the preferences of consumers and planners. In a market economy an imbalance of

production and demand will result in shortages or surpluses that in turn lead to changes in prices as markets adjust to equate demand and supply. It is the change in _____ that corrects imbalances and provides the incentive for firms and consumers to adjust their behavior.

2. *Production efficiency.* Here _____ economies have a clear advantage over _____ economies. The _____ motive is a powerful device for promoting efficiency. Planned economies have not yet found an alternative incentive that works as well.

3. *The distribution of income.* Governments help to influence the distribution of income in all economies, although the degree to which they do so varies. If planning is associated with socialism, there is apt to be more equality in the distribution of income.

4. *Growth.* One can find examples of planned economies that have grown faster than market economies and vice versa. Countries will probably continue to make choices based on political systems, value judgments, traditions, and aspirations.

5. *Business fluctuations.* Here _____ economies clearly have the better track record.

How one strikes the final balance on these five issues is a matter of trade-offs, the basic stuff of economics. Remember that one does not have to make all-or-nothing choices. While planning infringes on individual freedom, complete freedom does not exist anywhere. The experience of many countries indicates a variety of choices between markets and planning, socialism and capitalism, and the degree of individual freedom.

(5)     The Soviet Union was a (capitalist/socialist) economy with comprehensive, centralized planning. An understanding of how Soviet planning worked is important to an understanding of current pressures facing the economics that have emerged from the Soviet bloc. The broad objectives of Soviet policy were set forth in the (Five/One)-Year Plans while more detail for implementation was provided in _____-Year Plans. Soviet planning relied extensively on targets and quotas. Because of the complexity of the Soviet economy it was a problem to ensure that all the quantity targets were mutually consistent. The Soviets referred to consistency as achieving _____ balance. Input-output analysis could be used here, but the enormity of the information requirements made it unfeasible for detailed planning.

A central planner needed to know the detailed production requirements of all goods as well as the capabilities of individual enterprises. She then needed to figure out how all these requirements interacted to be sure that planned increases in production were mutually consistent. It is a virtue of a market economy that all this information need not be centralized in a single individual or agency. Production is efficiently coordinated as individual enterprises respond to changes in the prices of their inputs and their outputs.

The Soviet style of central planning, under which orders flowed down from the top while information flowed up from the bottom, placed a tremendous burden on the transmission of information. The result, almost of necessity, was a considerable amount of inefficiency. Because rewards were based on achieving one's quota,

(6) plant managers had an incentive to (be conservative/take risks). There was (little/strong) incentive for innovation. Compared with American experience, inventories of strategic materials were often excessively high and many consumer goods were of low quality.

Immediately before and after World War II the Soviet economy reported high economic growth. Much came from the initial adjustment of output to favor investment over consumption and the reallocation of labor from agriculture to industry. Over time, growth can be sustained only if there are continual

(7) increases in productivity. Under the Soviet system of central planning there were (few/many) incentives for plant managers to take the risks associated with invention and innovation necessary to increase productivity. Declining economic growth and the growing inefficiencies of Soviet planning helped set the stage for Gorbachev's attempts at (glasnost/perestroika)—an increased emphasis on markets instead of planning—and _____, the introduction of democratic ideas into political and economic spheres.

The transition of the former Soviet bloc economies is still unfolding. Most have found the move from planned economies to market economies difficult. Privatization has been slower than many hoped due to difficulties associated with the identification of ownership rights, the valuation of assets, the scarcity of managerial talent, and the unattractiveness of unprofitable enterprises. The freeing of prices, a necessary step to an increased reliance on markets, made overt the inflation previously repressed. Concerns about large-scale unemployment in state–owned enterprises along with the inadequacies of tax revenues introduced pressures for large increases in the stock of money. High rates of domestic inflation made it difficult to establish convertible currencies and hindered the development of international trade with the West. There have been continuing arguments about whether the transition should proceed more quickly—the so-called big bang—or more slowly. The economic and political transformation of these economies is still in progress.

(8)      China is a (market/planned) economy with extensive (private/state) ownership. Chinese planning and economic growth have moved in fits and starts related to domestic ideological struggles. Chinese planning was patterned after Soviet planning, but the Chinese version was (less/more) centralized and placed less emphasis on (agricultural/industrial) development. During the 1980s the Chinese moved to increase the role of markets significantly.

The success of the Japanese economy has attracted a great deal of attention. Japanese experience has been characterized by export-led growth, under which business firms pay special attention to opportunities

(9) in (domestic/foreign) markets, and deliberate industrial policy that calls for close cooperation between industry, banks, and the government. This cooperation represents a policy of _____

_____. The industrial structure of Japan is (less/more) concentrated than in the United States and labor-management relations have been (less/more) adversarial. A number of observers believe the most important lessons we can learn from the Japanese relate to their ability to organize and motivate people.

## IMPORTANT TERMS AND CONCEPTS QUIZ

Choose the most appropriate definition for the following terms.

1. _____ Capitalism
2. _____ Socialism
3. _____ Consumer sovereignty
4. _____ Workers' management
5. _____ Export-led growth
6. _____ Material balance
7. _____ Industrial policy
8. _____ Privatization
9. _____ Perestroika
10. _____ Glasnost
11. _____ Sequencing
12. _____ Five-Year Plans
13. _____ One-Year Plans

a. Employees make most of the decisions concerning how an enterprise is run.
b. Cooperative planning for economic growth between government agencies and private firms.
c. Private individuals own the means of production.

d. Decisions about what goods are produced reflect consumer preferences.
e. Strategy of emphasizing production of goods for export.
f. The state owns the means of production.
g. Mutually consistent planning targets for all inputs.
h. Government regulation of firms that produce consumer goods.
i. An increased emphasis on markets instead of planning.
j. Multi-year plans that set general goals.
k. The introduction of democratic ideas in political and economic spheres.
l. Detailed plans that set targets for the production and distribution of particular commodities.
m. The question of when to abolish price controls as free markets are being established.
n. The sale of publicly owned businesses to individuals.

## SELF-TESTS FOR UNDERSTANDING

### Test A

Circle the most appropriate answer.

1. The question of how economic activity is coordinated is a choice between
   a. socialism and capitalism.
   b. glasnost and perestroika.
   c. markets and planning.
   d. inflation and unemployment.

2. The form of economic organization in which the state owns the means of production is called
   a. socialism.
   b. consumer sovereignty.
   c. capitalism.
   d. laissez faire.

3. Capitalism is a form of economic organization in which
   a. economic planning is done in the nation's capital.
   b. business and government work closely on industrial planning.
   c. individuals own the means of production.
   d. all the benefits of increased productivity are appropriated by the owners of capital.

4. Market economies have a clear edge over planned economies on which of the following? (There may be more than one.)
   a. What to produce.
   b. How to produce.
   c. Income distribution.
   d. Economic growth.
   e. Business cycles.
   f. Individual freedom.

5. Market economies clearly do much worse than planned economies in which one of the following areas?
   a. Avoiding business fluctuations.
   b. Fostering a high rate of growth.
   c. Achieving efficiency in the production of goods and services.
   d. Achieving equality in the distribution of labor income.

6. Experience suggests that
   a. planning can only work in socialist economies.
   b. personal freedom tends to be greatest in economies that rely on markets and capitalism.
   c. it is easy for socialist economies to provide appropriate incentives for managerial efficiency and innovation.
   d. the distribution of labor income is typically much more equal in socialist than in capitalist economies.

7. Experience suggests that
   a. planning need not be synonymous with socialism.
   b. it is easy for socialist economies to provide appropriate incentives for managerial efficiency.
   c. market economies have avoided the business cycle fluctuations of planned economies.
   d. technological innovations are more easily introduced in planned economies than in ones that rely on markets.

8. Match each of the following with the appropriate country.

    _____ Material balance        a. China

    _____ Workers' management      b. Japan

    _____ Export-led growth        c. Soviet Union

    _____ Great Leap Forward       d. Yugoslavia

9. Which of the following are associated with Stalin's economic policies? (There may be more than one.)
    a. Central planning.
    b. Perestroika.
    c. Collectivization.
    d. Glasnost.

10. Soviet planning as implemented under Stalin gave priority to
    a. agriculture.
    b. consumer goods.
    c. private ownership.
    d. heavy industry.

11. The Soviet planning system
    a. made extensive use of input-output analysis to ensure that each One-Year Plan had internal consistency.
    b. saved on information requirements by having plant managers maximize profits.
    c. was one of consumer sovereignty, since Soviet citizens were free to buy consumer goods of their own choosing.
    d. created incentives for plant managers to play it safe by establishing easy quotas and stockpiling strategic materials.

12. Under Soviet–style planning, orders flowed _____ and information flowed _____.
    a. up; up
    b. up; down
    c. down; up
    d. down; down

13. The term "material balance" refers to
    a. inventories at the end of each planning period.
    b. consistency in plans so that the quantity demanded and the quantity supplied of each commodity are equal.
    c. the former wealth of Kremlin leaders.
    d. the choices planners must make as they balance competing claims for consumption and investment goods.

14. Which of the following are associated with Gorbachev's attempts at reform? (There may be more than one.)
    a. Keiretsu.
    b. Perestroika.
    c. Kaizen.
    d. Glasnost.

15. Which of the following helps to explain why privatization of publicly owned enterprises has been a slow process?
    a. An abundance of managerial talent.
    b. Excessive profits of state–owned enterprises
    c. The ease of valuing enterprise assets.
    d. The identification of ownership rights.

16. Compared to Soviet-style planning, planning in China
    a. has been less influenced by concerns about ideological purity.
    b. has been less centralized.
    c. placed an even greater emphasis on industrialization.
    d. placed an even greater emphasis on material incentives to motivate workers.

17. In China, the record of the economy shows
    a. a consistent and unwavering commitment to highly centralized planning.
    b. extensive use of material incentives to motivate workers.
    c. a greater emphasis on agricultural development compared with the Soviet Union.
    d. a consistent emphasis on economic efficiency that protected the economy from domestic ideological struggles.

18. Compared with the United States, Japan shows
    a. a less concentrated industrial structure.
    b. a greater emphasis on internal as opposed to foreign markets.
    c. more adversarial labor-management relations.
    d. closer cooperation between government and industry.

19. Export-oriented growth means that business must pay close attention to
    a. domestic consumer demand.
    b. world markets.
    c. government decrees.
    d. the preferences of central planners.

20. Compared with the United States, which one of the following is not true of Japanese labor markets?
    a. Lifetime employment guarantees.
    b. Greater loyalty to employers.
    c. Less worker resistance to the introduction of production techniques.
    d. Large pay differentials between workers and managers.

## Test B

Circle T or F for true or false.

T  F  1. Socialism must be accompanied by central planning.

T  F  2. *Consumer sovereignty* is the term used for the form of economic organization in which individuals own the means of production.

T  F  3. Planned economies have done a better job of avoiding business cycles than have market economies.

T  F  4. Market economies are clearly superior to planned economies in production efficiency.

T  F  5. A major problem with planned economies is devising an incentive mechanism for managers that promotes efficiency.

T  F  6. Under Soviet planning One-Year Plans set broad objectives while Five-Year Plans contained the details of implementation.

T  F  7. Many observers now conclude that the transition from planning to markets will involve an inevitable, but hopefully temporary, decline in living standards.

T  F  8. The Chinese system of planning is a direct copy of Soviet planning.

T  F  9. Average living standards in Japan now exceed those in the United States.

T  F  10. Japan's emphasis on export-led growth is based on an abundance of natural resources.

## STUDY QUESTIONS

1. How can there be markets without private ownership and planning without socialism?

2. Which scores better—markets or planning—in deciding what to produce? Why?

3. Which scores better—markets or planning—in deciding how to produce things? Why?

4. How do capitalism and socialism compare with regard to the distribution of income?

5. How do you evaluate the importance of personal freedom when it comes to choosing between markets and planning?

6. Why couldn't Soviet planners use input-output analysis described in Chapter 10 to achieve material balance and implement Five- and One-Year Plans?

7. Why was the Soviet economy unable to sustain its earlier economic growth?

8. What is the difference between perestroika and glasnost?

9. If you were in charge in Moscow or Warsaw and interested in introducing free markets and private ownership, would you advocate as many changes as fast as possible or slower, step-by-step changes? Why?

10. Would the United States be better off if it adopted Japanese-style industrial planning?

## ECONOMICS IN ACTION

### Manage the Transition?

In early 1993 *The Economist* examined the Polish experience with the transition from a planned to market economy. On the positive side was a new abundance of consumer goods. There were signs of strong economic growth, although absolute levels of income and industrial production were still substantially below peaks in 1989 when the old regime collapsed. Inflation, which had reached almost 600 percent in 1990, was down to 45 percent in 1992 and was expected to fall to 30 percent in 1993. *The Economist* concluded that the Polish economy appeared to have turned the corner. "Poland provides an excellent example of how reform works when politicians are weak. Much of what happened did not go according to plan; muddle and spontaneity have shaped the progress of reform just as much as has careful planning."[1]

*The Economist* noted the strong growth in the uncontrolled capitalist sector as contrasted with the slow progress in privatization of large state-owned enterprises. Small, private manufacturing businesses along with export and import firms seemed best able to adapt. The weakness of government regulation and taxes enabled the most nimble to become their own bosses and exploit profitable opportunities. By contrast, state enterprises found it hard to deal with the new realities. When subsidies were cut off in early 1990 they responded by raising prices instead of cutting costs. The resulting reduction in demand along with the loss of easy sales to what had been eastern bloc economies added to their problems. The resulting demands on the government by managers and workers in these industries for higher subsidies delayed the moves to privatization and added to political instability. While many Poles seemed willing to accept an initial decline in living standards as part of the price of political freedom, others grew resentful of the sudden changes.

The complexity of trying to sell entire enterprises led to interest in alternative approaches to privatization. One idea called for large holding companies run by western managers. Polish citizens would receive vouchers they could use to buy shares in the holding companies. The holding companies would use the vouchers to buy state enterprises. For the most part privatization has occurred in other ways. Some have been accomplished by local governments working to implement worker/management buy-outs and joint ventures. Others have taken place inadvertently as enterprises sold assets to private companies in order to avoid bankruptcy.

---

[1]"Poland's Economic Reforms," *The Economist*, January 23–29, 1993.

---

*The Economist* argued that the Polish experience offered several lessons: Change should not be managed from the center. Decision making should be left to local governments. Private ingenuity can be a valuable alternative to the difficulties of government. Cracking down on what appear to be illegal business practices may be counterproductive. Rather than trying to sell state enterprises outright, it might be best to let them wither away by selling off assets piecemeal.

1. With the passage of time from early 1993, how do you read the lessons of managing the transition from a planned to market economy?

# Answer Key

## CHAPTER 1
### Chapter Review

(1) information; value

### Important Terms and Concepts Quiz
| | | |
|---|---|---|
| 1. f | 5. l | 9. d |
| 2. b | 6. a | 10. k |
| 3. e | 7. c | 11. j |
| 4. g | 8. i | |

### Self-Tests For Understanding
#### Test A
1. c   p. 3
2. a   pp. 3-4
3. c   p. 4
4. b   pp. 4-5
5. a   p. 5
6. d   pp. 5-6
7. b   p. 6
8. a   pp. 6-7
9. c   p. 7
10. c   p. 8
11. d   pp. 8-9
12. b   p. 9

#### Test B
1. F   p. 11
2. F   pp. 15-17
3. T   p. 7
4. T   pp. 15-16
5. F   p. 14
6. F   p. 14
7. F   p. 12
8. F   p. 14
9. F   p. 8
10. F   p. 9

### Appendix Review
(1) horizontal; vertical; origin
(2) vertical; horizontal; constant; positive; up; negative; no
(3) ray; 45–degree
(4) tangent
(5) contour

### Important Terms and Concepts Quiz: Appendix
| | | |
|---|---|---|
| 1. f | 6. o | 11. c |
| 2. g | 7. k | 12. j |
| 3. d | 8. p | 13. e |
| 4. m | 9. l | 14. i |
| 5. h | 10. b | 15. n |

### Basic Exercises: Appendix
1. a. 300
   b. increase; 500
   c. decrease; 200
   d. –50
   e. Slope equals vertical change divided by horizontal change or the change in salary divided by the change in the quantity demanded. Information about the change in the number of new Ph.D. economists demanded as salary changes is given the reciprocal of the slope. For example, the demand curve implies that a $1,000 change in salary will reduce the quantity demand by 20.
2. a. 9
   b. 10
   c. above
   d. non-economics

3.  a. straight
    b. $5; the slope shows the change in total cost as output changes. In Chapter 5 you will learn that the slope of the total cost curve is called marginal cost.
    c. 1000; A business firm may have certain costs that it must meet regardless of the level of output. In Chapter 6 you will learn that this Y axis intercept is called fixed costs.
    d. The slope of the curve line declines as output increases to 10,000. After 10,000 the slope increases. This is a case where marginal cost decreases initially and then increases.

**Self-Tests For Understanding: Appendix**

**Test A**

1.  b  p. 19
2.  b  p. 19
3.  c  p. 19
4.  d  p. 20
5.  a  p. 20
6.  a  p. 20
7.  3; 1; 2; 4   pp. 20-21
8.  A&E; C; B&D; none   p. 22
9.  d  slope = vertical change/horizontal change = (16-10)/(8-5) = $-^6/_3$ = –2
10. c  p. 21
11. b  p. 22
12. b  p. 22
13. b  p. 22
14. d  p. 22
15. c  p. 22
16. a  p. 24
17. d  p. 22
18. a  slope = $^2/_5$ = 0.4
19. b  p. 20
20. b  p. 24

**Test B**

1.  F  p. 19      6.  T  p. 22
2.  F  p. 20      7.  F  p. 23
3.  T  p. 20      8.  T  p. 22
4.  T  p. 20      9.  T  p. 24
5.  F  p. 21      10. F  p. 24

# CHAPTER 2

**Chapter Review**

(1) domestic; product; GDP
(2) inputs; outputs, free; private
(3) open; closed; closed
(4) inflation; real; per capita
(5) recessions
(6) production
(7) labor; 10¢; service
(8) proprietorship; partnership; corporations; mixed
(9) horizontal; vertical

**Important Terms and Concepts Quiz**

1.  d      6.  k      11. b
2.  i      7.  e      12. n
3.  m      8.  c      13. o
4.  a      9.  h      14. l
5.  g      10. j

**Basic Exercises**

1.  a. No, increases in aggregate income due to inflation or population do not increase individual purchasing power.
    b. 8.1 times; column 3: 1,995; 3,521; 8,576; 16,177
    c. 2.1 times; column 5: 7,256; 7,588; 10,600; 15,304
2.  15.98; 28.47; 22.78; 22.08; 26.62; 28.90; 23.43; 26.28; 27.37; 33.10; 32.50
3.  The graph in Figure 2-1a exaggerates the increase as it omits the origin. While there was a substantial increase in gold prices during the first half of 1993, the value of gold as an investment is by no means a sure thing. For example $10,000 invested in gold in 1980 was worth only $5,624 at the end of 1992. A similar investment in U.S. government securities would have been worth $27,599 by the end of 1992 while the value of a balanced portfolio of stocks would have grown to $54,520.
4.  The trend line from 1968 to 1983 seems to tell a similar story; but, just as in the 1960s, the trend line does not mean that appropriate macroeconomic policy cannot lower the rate of unemployment.

## Self-Tests For Understanding

### Test A

1. a and d    p. 28
2. c    pp. 28-29
3. d    p. 30
4. a    p. 33
5. d    p. 33
6. b    As it uses dollars of constant purchasing power, real GDP changes only if the volume of output changes.
7. c    p. 33
8. d    p. 34
9. c    p. 38
10. d    bread is the output
11. d    p. 36
12. c    p. 40
13. a    p. 40
14. b    p. 41
15. d    Imports are goods produced abroad and bought in America.
16. a    Exports are goods produced in America and sold in foreign countries.
17. d    p. 39
18. a    p. 44
19. c    p. 47
20. a    p. 45

### Test B

1. T    p. 28
2. F    p. 34
3. F    p. 31
4. T    p. 29
5. T    p. 35
6. F    p. 35
7. F    p. 36
8. F    p. 36
9. T    p. 38
10. T    p. 40

## Supplementary Exercise

1987 dollars:

Public: 1,030; 1,131; 2,043

Private: 4,267; 5,284; 10,765

Proportion of per capita real income:

Public: 13.6%; 10.7%; 13.3%

Private: 56.2%; 49.8%; 70.3%

## CHAPTER 3

### Chapter Review

**(1)** scarce
**(2)** opportunity cost
**(3)** scarce; specialized; fewer; more; more; consumption
**(4)** slope
**(5)** increase; increasing; specialized
**(6)** inside; inefficient;
**(7)** will

### Important Terms and Concepts Quiz

| | | | | | |
|---|---|---|---|---|---|
| 1. g | | 8. s | | 15. h | |
| 2. i | | 9. f | | 16. d | |
| 3. n | | 10. q | | 17. o | |
| 4. r | | 11. p | | 18. k | |
| 5. m | | 12. b | | 19. t | |
| 6. j | | 13. e | | | |
| 7. a | | 14. l | | | |

### Basic Exercise

1. a. 560,000; 40,000; rises; 120,000; continue to rise; specialized
   b. Point A is not attainable; point B is attainable; point C is attainable; on and inside
   c. Point B is inefficient. You should be able to shade a small triangular area above and to the right of point B out to and including a small segment of the PPF.
2. a. Catskill, the economy that produces the greater amount of capital goods will have the greater shift. That is, next year the PPF for Catskill should lies outside that of Adirondack.
   b. An economist would measure the cost of economic growth by the differences in the output of consumption goods or 120,000 loaves of bread, 400,000–280,000.

### Self-Tests For Understanding

### Test A

1. c    p. 57
2. c    p. 62
3. d    p. 60
4. d    p. 67
5. a    p. 60
6. b    p. 61

7.  c   p. 60
8.  b   p. 67
9.  d   p. 61
10. d   p. 62
11. b   p. 65
12. b   On the PPF, output of computers must decline by 500.
13. b   Borrowing money would enable firm to pay for additional resources.
14. a   p. 61
15. b   Reflects economic growth.
16. c   More money helps a single firm buy resources. An economy's resources are given by its natural resources, population and capital.
17. c   p. 57
18. a   p. 70
19. b   p. 67
20. d   p. 68

**Test B**
1.  F   p. 57
2.  F   p. 58
3.  T   pp. 61-62
4.  T   pp. 65-66
5.  F   p. 56
6.  F   pp. 60-61
7.  T   p. 67
8.  T   p. 67
9.  F   Any economic unit with limited resources will need to make choices.
10. F   Dollar bills are not a factor of production.

**Supplementary Exercises**
3.  a. 300,000 cars; 1,000 tanks
    c. yes, it bows out.
    d. $\frac{1}{2}C^*$, $\frac{1}{2}T^*$ should be on straight line connecting $C^*$ and $T^*$. Combination is attainable, lies inside frontier; inefficient, not on frontier as frontier bows out.
    e. 6 cars; 30 cars; 120 cars
    f. opportunity cost = (0.6)T cars; yes, opportunity cost increases as the production of tanks increases.
    g. new frontier lies everywhere outside the old frontier.
4.  a. When $I$ = 1,600 the sustainable level of $C$ = 10,292.

b.  $C$ drops by 400 to 9,892 and then rises to its new sustainable level of 10,574.
c.  The increase in consumption, 10,574 to 10,761, is less than in question b. Additional machines add to output but at a decreasing rate. This increase at a decreasing rate is an example of declining marginal productivity, a concept that is discussed in Chapter 6.
d.  There can be too much of a good thing. Additional machines allow for an increase in total output, but additional machines also increase the amount of output that must be allocated to investment in order to maintain the larger number of machines. With a large enough increase in the number of machines, the increase in investment needed to maintain machines swamps the increase in output available for consumption. Past this point, additional investment will actually lower the sustainable level of consumption. What is this critical point? In this problem, it depends upon the exponents on $L$ and $M$ in equation (1) and the rate of depreciation, assumed to be 8 percent. Ask your instructor for more details.

# CHAPTER 4

**Chapter Review**
(1) price; negative; more; movement along; shift in
(2) price; positive; more; shift in
(3) demand
(4) $300; 4000; less; 6000; 2000; surplus; reduction; shortage; demanded; supplied; increase
(5) intersection; equilibrium
(6) demand; supply; movement along; supply; demand; demand
(7) maximum; minimum
(8) hard; auxiliary restrictions
(9) shortages; decrease
(10) high

## Important Terms and Concepts Quiz

| | | |
|---|---|---|
| 1. k | 7. o | 13. d |
| 2. e | 8. p | 14. j |
| 3. g | 9. n | 15. b |
| 4. c | 10. h | 16. a |
| 5. i | 11. f | |
| 6. q | 12. m | |

## Basic Exercises

1. b. 40; 1100
   c. increased; 50; increased; 1200
   d. increase; decrease; 55; 1100
2. a. demand; right; rise; rise
   b. supply; right; fall; rise
   c. supply; left; rise; fall
   d. demand; left; fall; fall
3. a. 100; 100; neither, as ceiling exceeds equilibrium price
   b. 110; 80; shortage
      Price ceilings lead to shortages when they are less than the free market equilibrium price.
   c. 90; 120; surplus
   d. 100; 100; neither, as floor is less than equilibrium price
      Price floors lead to surpluses when they are greater than the free market equilibrium price.

## Self-Tests For Understanding

### Test A

1. c. p. 78
2. a p. 78
3. c p. 79
4. d pp. 84 and 88
5. c p. 79
6. b p. 88
7. a p. 88
8. a p. 89
9. d p. 81
10. b p. 84
11. c p. 85
12. a p. 84
13. a pp. 89-90
14. b, d p. 90, cotton cloth is an input; skirts, pants and blouses may be related inputs
15. b p. 90
16. b pp. 86-87
17. c p. 83
18. a p. 96
19. d pp. 91-92
20. b p. 81

### Test B

1. F The law of supply and demand is an empirical regularity, not a Congressional statute.
2. T p. 78
3. T p. 79
4. F p. 84
5. F p. 78
6. T p. 83
7. T p. 81
8. F p. 84
9. F p. 90
10. T pp. 91-92
11. F p. 96
12. T p. 91
13. F p. 93
14. F The increase in price and quantity comes from the movement along the supply curve following the shift in the demand curve.

## CHAPTER 5

### Chapter Review

(1) average; marginal
(2) marginal; marginal; profits; revenue; cost
(3) total
(4) marginal; marginal; positive; zero; equals

### Important Terms and Concepts Quiz

| | |
|---|---|
| 1. i | 7. b |
| 2. g | 8. j |
| 3. e | 9. l |
| 4. a | 10. f |
| 5. k | 11. c |
| 6. d | |

### Basic Exercises

1. a. Total Profits: 1,500; 3,600; 5,200; 6,300; 6,600; 6,100; 5,000; 3,400; 1,300; –1,300; 5 widgets
   b. Marginal Revenue: 3,100; 2,700; 2,300; 1,900; 1,500; 1,100; 700; 300; –100
      Marginal Cost: 1,000; 1,100; 1,200; 1,600; 2,000; 2,200; 2,300; 2,400; 2,500, 5 widgets. The 5th widget adds 300 to profit. Increasing output to 6 widgets would lower profit by 500.
   c. profit; does not; does not
2. is not; horizontal; vertical; horizontal

## Self-Tests For Understanding
### Test A
1. b  p. 106
2. c  p. 108
3. c  p. 108
4. d  p. 116
5. b  if marginal cost were zero or negative, total cost would be constant or decline. See p. 111.
6. a  p. 111
7. b  p. 111
8. d  p. 109
9. d  p. 110
10. a  Review Basic Exercise 2.
11. c  p. 117
12. c  p. 116
13. c  p. 117
14. b  p. 118
15. c  pp. 114-115
16. a  p. 120
17. b  p. 117
18. b  p. 108
19. a  p. 108, zero accounting profits leave nothing to cover the opportunity cost of owner supplied inputs.
20. d  pp. 122-123

### Test B
1. F  p. 106
2. F  pp. 107-108
3. F  p. 109
4. F  p. 111
5. F  Review Basic Exercise 2
6. T  p. 116
7. T  p. 117
8. T  p. 108
9. F  A firm is making profits if AR>AC but should increase output only if MR>MC.
10. F  pp. 122-123

### Appendix
1. Data on Kristen's batting is consistent with Rule 3 and Rule 4. Note that from game 3 to 4 Kristen's daily batting average actually increased, from .250 to .333 and yet her season batting average declined from .417 to .400. Even though her performance for the 4th game was better than for the 3rd, it was still below her overall average. As a result, and consistent with Rule 4, her season batting average declined.

2. b. The marginal profit curve should equal zero where total profits are maximized.
   c. The marginal cost curve should go through the minimum of the average cost curve.

### Supplementary Exercises: Appendix
1. a. $16,000
   b. Average cost $= 16,000/Q + 120 - .4Q + .002Q^2$
      Marginal cost $= 120 - .8Q + .006Q^2$
   c. It should.
   d. Marginal revenue $= 300 - .5Q$
   f. $Q = 200$
   g. Find the positive value of $Q$ such that marginal cost = marginal revenue
      $120 - .8Q + .006Q^2 = 300 - .5Q$
      $Q = 200$
   h. Price = $250; total revenue = $50,000; total cost = $40,000; total profits = $10,000
   j. Average cost $= 20,000/Q + 120 - .4Q + .0002Q^2$
      No change in profit maximizing level of output; total profits = $6,000

## CHAPTER 6
### Chapter Review
(1) increase; physical; revenue
(2) revenue; price
(3) more; less; reduce; increase
(4) reduce; less; more
(5) production; increasing; decreasing; constant
(6) short
(7) output; total
(8) long run; lower
(9) is unchanged; less; fall; more; rises
(10) indivisible

### Important Terms and Concepts Quiz
1. g       6. c       11. j
2. h       7. o       12. d
3. k       8. i       13. p
4. f       9. n       14. a
5. b      10. e       15. l

### Basic Exercise
1. 100 acres; increasing returns: 0 to 2 workers; decreasing returns: 2 to 4 workers; negative returns: 4 to 6 workers

2. 200 acres; increasing returns: 0 to 2 workers; decreasing returns: 2 to 5 workers; negative returns: 5 to 6 workers. 300 acres; increasing returns: 0 to 2 workers; decreasing returns: 2 to 6 workers. The output-labor curve shifts up as land increases.

3. 100: 1; 3; 2; 1; –1; –2
   200: 2; 4; 3.5; 2.5; 1; –1
   300; 3; 4.5; 3.5; 3; 2; 1

4. Marginal returns to land generally decline.

5. increasing; increasing; constant; increasing; decreasing

6. $10,000; $20,000; $17,500; $12,500; $5,000; –$5,000
   Hire 4 workers; $28,000 = (12,000 × $5) – ($8,000 × 4)

## Self-Tests For Understanding

### Test A
1. d p. 133
2. c p. 133
3. d p. 136
4. d p. 135
5. b p. 135
6. b p. 133
7. a p. 137
8. c p. 137
9. d p. 141
10. a p. 145
11. b p. 141
12. a p. 145
13. a b, c, & d influence costs and hence the supply curve. Price is determined by the intersection of supply and demand curves.
14. d p. 154
15. c p. 154
16. c p. 145
17. b pp. 148-150
18. d p. 156
19. a p. 136
20. d p. 150
21. a p. 150

### Test B
1. F p. 156
2. T p. 133
3. F p. 136
4. F p. 156
5. T p. 155
6. F p. 145
7. F p. 145

8. F p. 147
9. T p. 146
10. F pp. 156-158

## APPENDIX
### Appendix Review
(1) production indifference; more
(2) negative; will; diminishing; marginal; do not
(3) straight; horizontal
(4) lowest
(5) expansion

### Important Terms and Concepts Quiz: Appendix
1. c        2. d        3. a

### Basic Exercise: Appendix
1. 200; 2; 100; 3. Total costs are constant along a single budget line. Total costs are greater along higher budget lines.
2. $80

### Self-Tests For Understanding: Appendix
### Test A
1. d p. 161
2. b pp. 161-162. The least costly input combination is where the slope of the isoquant = the ratio of input prices.
3. c p. 162
4. c p. 162
5. c p. 164
6. d Total cost will increase, but the least costly input combination does not change as the slope of the budget line is unchanged.
7. d Production indifference curves are determined by the production function, not input prices.

### Test B
1. F p. 161. Output is constant along a production indifference curve.
2. T p. 162
3. T pp. 162-163
4. F an increase in the price of the input measured on the vertical axis makes the budget line flatter.
5. F a change in the price of one input typically changes the optimal use of all inputs. pp. 164-165.

6. F a change in output prices may induce a movement along the expansion path but it does not shift the production indifference curves or the slope of the budget line. Thus it does not change the cost minimizing input combination for a given level of output.

7. T p. 164

## Supplementary Exercise: Appendix

2. For labor: $MPP_L \cdot P_W = P_L$ or $(M/L)^{1/2} \, 50 = 12$. For machines: $MPP_M \cdot P_W = P_M$ or $(L/M)^{1/2} \, 50 = 48$.

Solving the two expressions for $L$ in terms of $M$ shows that when the price of labor hours is 12 and the price of machine hours is 48, then $L = 4M$.

From the production function
$W = L^{1/2} \, M^{1/2}$
Knowing that for the least-cost combination of inputs $L = 4M$, the equation can be rewritten as
$500,000 = M^{1/2} \, (4M)^{1/2}$
$500,000 = (4M^2)^{1/2} = 2M$
$M = 250,000$ machine hours
$L = 1,000,000$ labor hours

3. a. Total output = $500 \sqrt{L}$
   b. MPP of labor = $250/\sqrt{L}$; the MPP of labor is the slope of the total product curve.
   c. For this production function, MPP of labor declines continuously, but is never negative.
   d. 1,085,069.45 labor hours; (Find the quantity of labor such that the MRP of labor is equal to the price of labor. $(250/\sqrt{L}) \times 50 = 12$.) Output = 520,833.33 widgets.

4. For this production function, the expansion path is a straight line.

5. Constant: $(2M)^{1/2} \, (2L)^{1/2} = 2M^{1/2}L^{1/2} = 2W$ A doubling of inputs doubles output.

6. a. Set marginal cost = marginal revenue. Marginal cost: when $P^L = 12$ and $P^M = 48$, the least cost combination of inputs uses four hours of labor input for each hour of machine time. (See the answer to question 2 above.) To produce one widget, a firm would use two hours of labor with a half-hour of machine time for a total cost of $48. As the production function exhibits constant

returns to scale, average and marginal cost are equal at $48 per widget.

Marginal revenue = $100 - .00008W$

To find the profit maximizing level of output set marginal cost = marginal revenue.

$$48 = 100 - .00008W$$
$$W = 650,000$$
$$L = 1,300,000$$
$$M = 325,000$$
$$P_W = \$74$$

b.     Output: $W = (200,000)^{1/2}L^{1/2}$
Labor Input: $L = W^2/200,000$
Total (labor) cost = $12W^2/200,000$
Marginal (labor) cost = $24W/200,000$
$= .00012W$

Marginal revenue = $100 - .00008W$

Set marginal cost = marginal revenue
$$.00012W = 100 - .0008W$$
$$.0002W = 100$$
$$W = 500,000$$
$$L = 1,250,000$$
$$P_W = \$80.$$

# CHAPTER 7
## Chapter Review
**(1)** elasticity; demand
**(2)** zero; infinite; changes
**(3)** elastic; inelastic; unit elastic
**(4)** will not; 1.0
**(5)** greater; increase; decrease; will not; increase; decrease
**(6)** cross
**(7)** complements; negative; increase; right
**(8)** substitutes; positive; decrease; left
**(9)** shift in

## Important Terms and Concepts Quiz
| | |
|---|---|
| 1. f | 5. d |
| 2. e | 6. h |
| 3. b | 7. a |
| 4. g | 8. i |

## Basic Exercises
1. straight
   a. %Δ price: 18.2%; 22.2%; 28.6%; 40%
   %Δ quantity: 28.6%; 22.2%; 18.2%; 15.4%
   elasticity: 1.57; 1.00; 0.64; 0.38; decreases

b. Total Revenue: $576,000; $640,000; $640,000; $576,000; $448,000.
Total revenue increases (decreases) as price declines if the elasticity of demand is greater (less) than 1.0. Total revenue increases (decreases) as price increases if the elasticity of demand is less (greater) than 1.0.

2. b. 1.0
   c. 1.0
   d. 1.0
   Do not be fooled by appearances.

**Self-Tests For Understanding**

**Test A**

1. b  Slope is the reciprocal of the change in the quantity demanded divided by the change in price.
2. a  p. 78, Chapter 4
3. c  p. 170
4. a  p. 170
5. c  pp. 171-172
6. b  p. 170
7. d  p. 170
8. b  p. 177
9. a  p. 177
10. b  p. 177
11. a  p. 170
12. b  p. 177
13. b  p. 177
14. a  p. 180
15. c  pp. 180-181
16. c  p. 180
17. c  pp. 180-181
18. a  pp. 180-181
19. a  p. 183
20. d  p. 181
21. b  p. 180

**Test B**

1. F  p. 170
2. F  p. 175
3. T  p. 174
4. F  True for any demand curve with a negative slope, whether elastic or inelastic.
5. F  Inelastic means only that the absolute value of the percentage change in the quantity demanded is less than the percentage change in price.
6. T  p. 177
7. F  p. 181

8. T  p. 181
9. F  They are substitutes.
10. T  p. 179
11. T  p. 183
12. F  p. 183
13. F  p. 180
14. F  p. 183

**APPENDIX**

**Basic Exercises: Appendix**

1. Not much; plotting historical data is an inappropriate way to estimate a demand curve.
2. a.  1990: P = 22; Q = 380
       1991: P = 23; Q = 395
       1992: P = 24; Q = 410

When only the demand curve shifts, the historical data on price and quantity trace out the supply curve. If you connect the three pairs of points, you should have a graph of the supply curve. Each point comes from the intersection of the demand curve for the specific year with the unchanging supply curve. In this case, the points of market equilbrium provide no information about the demand curve.

With shifts in both demand and supply curves, the points of market equilibrium trace out neither curve. Try drawing the demand and supply curves for each year on the same diagram. As both curves shift, a line connecting the successive points of market equilibrium gives no information about either curve.

**Economics In Action**

1. elasticity of demand = (3570/1997) + (5.50/3.75) = 1.22
While the elasticity of demand is an indicator of the change in total revenue, a profit maximizing firm is interested in profits not revenues. Increased output may entail increased costs. In Mr. Grant's case, changing from first to second run movies dramatically cut the proportion of the ticket price claimed by movie distributors. The cut was so dramatic that net revenue before paying employees, utilities, etc., but after paying the admission tax and after paying the distributors, was unchanged at 61¢ a ticket.

2. a. If total revenue is to remain unchanged the price elasticity of demand would have to equal 1.0.

  b. Data on historical quantities is not a good way to measure demand. The relevant question is what would have been the demand for air travel in the summer of 1992 if fares had not been reduced. It is also relevant to note that some air travelers, those buying their tickets at the last minute, paid full fare and were not eligible for the discounted fares. At the same time it does appear that the fare war was a bonanza for travelers and not so good for airlines. A significant reduction in ticket prices appears to have induced only a modest increase in air travel.

# CHAPTER 8

## Chapter Review

(1) marginal; will; decrease
(2) consumer's; consumer's surplus; price; greater; increase
(3) greater; marginal; more; up; negative
(4) shift in; utility; normal; inferior
(5) substitution; income; fewer; substitution; income; negative; substitution; income
(6) horizontal; negative

## Important Terms and Concepts Quiz

1. d          4. i          7. a
2. h          5. b          8. c
3. e          6. g

## Basic Exercises

1. a. 110; 100; 80; 70; 50; 30; 20
   b. 2; 4; 5
   c. Col. 3: 20; 30; 20; 0; –40; –100; –170; 2
      Col. 5: 50; 90; 110; 120; 110; 80; 40; 4
      Col. 7: 70; 130; 170; 200; 210; 200; 180; 5
   d. Consumer's; quantities are the same
2. a. 1
   b. 1
   c. 4
   d. 5
   e. 1
   f. 2

## Self-Tests For Understanding

### Test A

1.  b   p. 192
2.  d   p. 193
3.  a   marginal utility = change in total utility = 300 – 200 = 100.
4.  c   p. 195
5.  d   if MU > P then the difference between total utility and total spending will increase.
6.  c   p. 194
7.  c   p. 195
8.  a   p. 196
9.  c   p. 200
10. b   p. 200
11. b   p. 201
12. d   p. 201
13. d   p. 202
14. c   p. 202
15. c   p. 201
16. a   p. 202
17. c   p. 203
18. b   p. 202
19. a   p. 202
20. d   p. 203

### Test B

1.  F   p. 192
2.  F   p. 201
3.  T   p. 202
4.  T   p. 202
5.  T   p. 194
6.  F   p. 202
7.  T   p. 201
8.  F   the label of inferior goods implies nothing about rationality. It refers to the impact of a change in income on the quantity demanded.
9.  F   p. 199
10. F   p. 204

## APPENDIX

### Appendix Review

(1) straight; negative; intercept; slope
(2) indifference; indifferent; are; never; negative
(3) in; more; substitution; decreases
(4) budget; indifference; highest; budget line
(5) budget line

## Important Terms and Concepts Quiz: Appendix

1. c    2. d      3. a      4. e

## Basic Exercise: Appendix

1. b.   20; 10
   c.   3; 2
   e.   equals the slope of the budget line
2. a.   Z
   Neither is an inferior good as point Z shows an increase in the quantity demanded for both following the increase in income.
   b.   Y

## Self-Tests For Understanding: Appendix

### Test A

1. c   p. 208
2. c   p. 210
3. d   p. 210
4. d   p. 209
5. b   p. 211
6. d   p. 212
7. c   p. 212
8. a   p. 210
9. b   pp. 211-212
10. b   p. 212

### Test B

1. F   p. 208
2. T   p. 210
3. F   p. 209
4. F   p. 212
5. F   p. 212
6. T   p. 212
7. F   p. 215
8. F   Budget line shows commodity bundles consumer can buy. A single indifference curve shows bundles about which she is indifferent.
9. T   pp. 215-217
10. T   a doubling of money income and prices leaves the budget line unaffected.

## Supplementary Exercise: Appendix

2. $F = (Y + 20P_C - 12P_F)/2P_F$
   $C = (Y - 20P_C + 12P_F)/2P_C$
   where $P_F$ = price of food, $P_C$ = price of clothing and $Y$ = income. The demand curves come from solving the following two equations for $F$ and $C$:

Optimal purchases require that the marginal rate of substitution equals the ratio of market prices, or

$$(F + 12)/(C = 20) = P_C/P_F$$

The budget constraint requires that:

$$F \bullet P_F + C \bullet P_C = Y$$

3. $F = 114; C = 43$
4. $F = 84; C = 44$
5. $F = 124; C = 48$; no

# CHAPTER 9

## Chapter Review

(1) Many; Identical; Easy; Perfect; do not; zero
(2) horizontal; marginal
(3) marginal; losses; variable; sunk; marginal cost; variable
(4) horizontal; demand; supply
(5) loss; two; better; opportunity; economic; accounting
(6) profits; (shaded rectangle should go from the y axis to a quantity of 1450 and from 20 to 15.30, the difference between the market price and the firm's average cost when producing 1450 units of output); enter; right; fall; $15.00 (minimum average cost; see the Basic Exercise); long-run average

## Important Terms and Concepts Quiz

| | | |
|---|---|---|
| 1. g | 6. k | 11. i |
| 2. m | 7. o | 12. l |
| 3. c | 8. f | 13. h |
| 4. n | 9. j | 14. d |
| 5. a | 10. b | |

## Basic Exercise

1. 1400; $5,544 = (P − AC)Q$; $5,310; $5,330
2. 1200; −$4,380 = (P − AC)Q$; −$4,550; −$4,532; −$10,140 (fixed costs)
3. 0; price does not cover average variable cost.
4. Firm's short-run supply curve is the portion of its marginal cost curve above average variable cost.

5. While under perfect competition marginal revenue equals price, one also needs to consider how a change in output affects costs. That is, the relevant comparison is with marginal cost, not average cost.
6. $15.00; 1300 widgets

## Self-Tests For Understanding

### Test A

1. b   p. 222
2. c   p. 222
3. a   p. 224
4. d   a horizontal demand curve is perfectly elastic.
5. c   p. 225 Average revenue = price.
6. c   pp. 225-226
7. b   p. 230
8. c   p. 230
9. b   p. 231
10. b   p. 238
11. c   p. 238
12. d   p. 238
13. d   p. 235
14. b   p. 235
15. c   pp. 227 and 235
16. c   pp. 232 and 236
17. a   p. 242
18. a   pp. 241-242
19. c   firms will expand output until MC = P. (p. 227)
20. d   p. 238

### Test B

1. F   p. 222
2. F   If $P >$ AC, a firm can increase profits by expanding output as long as $P >$ MC.
3. F   p. 238
4. F   pp. 227-229
5. F   p. 224
6. F   If $P >$ AC, a firm can increase profits by expanding output only if MC $< P$.
7. F   p. 230
8. T   p. 238
9. F   p. 228
10. F   p. 223

## Supplementary Exercise

1.  a. Average Cost =
       $10,140/Q + .00001Q^2 - .02Q + 16.3$
    b. Average variable cost =
       $.00001Q^2 - .02Q + 16.3$

    c. Marginal cost =
       $.00003Q^2 - .04Q + 16.3$
3.  To find the minimum of either average cost curve sets its derivative equal to zero.
    For AC, $Q = 1300$; AC = 15.00; at $Q = 1300$, MC = 15.00
    For AVC, $Q = 1000$; AVC = 6.30; at $Q = 1000$, MC = 6.30
4.  Supply = 0 if $P < 6.30$
    Supply =

$$\frac{.04 + \sqrt{-.0002 + .00012P}}{.00006} \quad \text{if } P > 6.30$$

## CHAPTER 10

### Chapter Review

(1) are not
(2) selection; planning; distribution
(3) was not; efficient
(4) efficient; decreasing
(5) utility; cost
(6) increase; cost; greater; is not; equals
(7) price; marginal cost; price; price
(8) utility; cost; equals
(9) input-output

### Important Terms and Concepts Quiz

1. c       3. a       5. g
2. f       4. e       6. b

### Basic Exercise

1. $22; $12
2. $10; more
3. decrease; $3; fewer
4. $18

### Self-Tests For Understanding

### Test A

1. d   conditions for efficiency say nothing about necessities and luxuries. Prices will depend upon consumer preferences and production costs as explained on page 252-253.
2. b   p. 254
3. d   p. 252
4. c   p. 254
5. d   slope of the PPF is technologically determined.
6. c   p. 246

7. b   p. 246
8. c   p. 258
9. b   p. 259
10. b   p. 257
11. c   pp. 252-253
12. a   p. 258
13. b   increased production typically increased marginal cost, while increased consumption typically lowers marginal utility.
14. c   p. 246
15. b   imposing Leon's preferences would be equivalent to imposing those of a central planner.
16. c   p. 246
17. a   p. 259
18. b   p. 259

**Test B**
1. T   p. 252
2. F   p. 246
3. F   p. 257
4. T   p. 257
5. F   p. 257
6. F   p. 256
7. T   pp. 260-261
8. T   pp. 261-262
9. F   p. 254
10. T   pp. 259-260

## APPENDIX

### Basic Exercises: Appendix
1. every consumer must have the same marginal utility for every commodity.
   a. No
   b. increase; 1; increase; 2; inefficient
   c. All consumers respond to the same set of prices and consume so that marginal utility equals price.
2. Ratio of marginal physical product for two inputs is the same in all alternative uses.
   a. 120; 1200; 160; 800; +40; +400. Note that this reallocation of inputs should work to move the ratio of marginal physical products in the production of corn and tomatoes toward equality.
   c. In competitive markets, profit maximizing firms adjust the use of inputs until the ratio of marginal physical products is equal to the ratio of input prices. By adjusting to common prices, the ratio of marginal physical products is equated across alternative uses.

## CHAPTER 11

### Chapter Review
(1) one; no
(2) natural; barriers; entry
(3) negative; lower
(4) marginal; marginal revenue; price; is not
(5) average; less; below; above
(6) demand; greater; less; less; will not; higher; lower
(7) price; price; marginal revenue; less; greater; greater
(8) down
(9) will not; does not; maker

### Important Terms and Concepts Quiz
1. e      3. d      5. f
2. a      4. b

### Basic Exercise
1. a. Total revenue: $114,000; $120,900; $127,400; $133,500; $139,200
      Total cost: $84,816; $90,441; $96,516; $103,041; $110,016
      14
   b. Marginal revenue: $6,900; $6,500; $6,100; $5,700
      Marginal cost: $5,625; $6,075; $6,525; $6,975
      revenue; cost; 14
   c. 9,100
   d. 30,884
2. Total revenue: $114,000; $120,900; $127,400; $133,500; $139,200
   Marginal revenue: $6,900; $6,500; $6,100; $5,700
   Total cost: $96,816; $103,441; $110,516; $118,041; $126,016
   Marginal cost: $6,625; $7,075; $7,525; $7,975
   a. 13 widgets; $9,300; $13,000; $200
   b. $17,459
3. No change in output = 14 widgets; no change in price = $9,100; profits down $13,000 to $17,884. No change in pollution as output is unchanged. The differences between questions 2 and 3 reflect the differences between the effects of a change in marginal and fixed costs. Note that in Question 2 marginal cost changed as the tax was imposed on each widget produced. In Question 3 marginal cost is unchanged as the pollution charge is independent of the number of widgets produced.

## Self-Tests for Understanding
### Test A
1. d   p. 269
2. c   p. 270
3. b   p. 271
4. d   pp. 270-271
5. c   p. 270
6. c   p. 273
7. c   p. 273
8. a   Rule 4 in the Appendix to Chapter 5, p. 128
9. a   p. 273
10. d   p. 275
11. c   p. 276
12. c   p. 277
13. c   p. 272
14. b   p. 278
15. b   pp. 281-282
16. b   An increase in fixed costs would leave marginal cost curve unchanged.
17. c   p. 282
18. c   p. 280
19. b   profit maximizing level of output is determined where marginal cost equals marginal revenue. A change in fixed cost will not change marginal revenue or marginal cost and will not change the profit maximizing level of output.
20. a   see question 2 in the Supplementary Exercises.

### Test B
1. F   p. 269
2. T   p. 271
3. F   p. 277
4. F   monopolist would face downward sloping market demand curve.
5. T   p. 273
6. F   as compared to the competitive situation, price is up and quantity is down. See discussion on page 277.
7. T   p. 279
8. F   even if price exceeds average cost, profits will decline if marginal revenue is less than marginal cost.
9. F   p. 281-282
10. F   p. 282

## Supplementary Exercises
1. a. Total revenue = $11,900Q - 200Q^2$
      Marginal revenue = $11,900 - 400Q$
      Average cost = $225Q + 52,416/Q$
      Marginal cost = $450Q$

   c. $11,900 - 400Q = 450Q$; $850Q = 11,900$; $Q = 14$
   d. Per-unit charge:
      TC = $52,416 + 225Q^2 + 1,000Q$
      AC = $225Q + 52,416/Q + 1,000$
      MC = $450Q + 1,000$
      Fixed charge:
      TC = $65,416 + 225Q^2$
      AC = $225Q + 65,416/Q$
      MC = $450Q$
      Note that the addition of a fixed cost element does not change marginal cost.
2. If a monopolist is originally producing where demand is inelastic, then an increase in market price will increase profits. The increase in price reduces costs as quantity declines and increases revenue as the percentage decline in the quantity sold is more than offset by the percentage increase in price. Thus the initial point could not have been a point of profit maximization. Similar reasoning rules out b, the case of unit elastic demand, as a point of profit maximization. Again profits increase as the reduction in quantity from an increase in price reduces costs while revenue is unchanged from the assumption of unit elasticity of demand.

# CHAPTER 12
## Chapter Review
(1) monopolistic; negative; marginal revenue; marginal cost; zero; entry; average
(2) oligopoly; cartel; price leadership
(3) zero; lower; larger
(4) payoff; strategy
(5) will; will not; marginal; cost
(6) entry; exit; opportunity cost; capital

## Important Terms and Concepts Quiz
1. g    5. i    9. k
2. c    6. j    10. d
3. f    7. e
4. a    8. h

## Basic Exercises
1. a. Profit-maximizing level of output = 1,000 meals
   b. Marginal revenue: $2,200; $1,400; $600; -$200

Marginal cost: $998; $1,000; $996; $1,000
Profit-maximizing level of output
= 1,000 meals
MC is less than MR at less than 1,000 meals
MC exceeds MR at more than 1,000 meals
See also the Supplementary Exercise to this chapter.

2. a. 1,000; $200; Marginal revenue exceeds marginal cost up to 1,000 sets and is less than marginal cost beyond 1,000 sets.
   b. No change in price or quantity. It is the kink in the demand curve that gives rise to the discontinuity in marginal revenue. Fluctuations of marginal cost within this discontinuity have no impact on the profit maximizing level of output or price.
   c. Marginal cost would have to rise above $150 a set.
   d. Marginal cost would have to fall below $50 a set.

## Self-Tests For Understanding

### Test A

| | | | | | |
|---|---|---|---|---|---|
| 1. | b | p. 287 | 11. | d | p. 292 |
| 2. | c | p. 286 | 12. | c | p. 294 |
| 3. | a | p. 287 | 13. | c | p. 296 |
| 4. | b | p. 289 | 14. | b | p. 297 |
| 5. | a | p. 290 | 15. | c | pp. 297-298 |
| 6. | b | p. 286 | 16. | c | p. 298 |
| 7. | c | p. 288 | 17. | d | pp. 301-302 |
| 8. | b | p. 290 | 18. | c | p. 302 |
| 9. | d | p. 289 | 19. | b | p. 303 |
| 10. | b | p. 292 | 20. | a | p. 306 |

### Test B

| | | | | | |
|---|---|---|---|---|---|
| 1. | T | p. 292 | 6. | T | p. 292 |
| 2. | T | p. 287 | 7. | T | p. 295 |
| 3. | F | pp. 288-289 | 8. | F | p. 297 |
| 4. | F | p. 289 | 9. | T | p. 302 |
| 5. | F | p. 291 | 10. | F | pp. 304-305 |

## Supplementary Exercise

Total Revenue = $25Q - Q^2/100$
Marginal Revenue = $25 - Q/50$
Average Cost = $10,000/Q + 5$
Marginal Cost = 5
Profit-maximizing level of output:
$25 - Q/50 = 5$; $Q = 1000$

## CHAPTER 13

### Chapter Review

(1) opportunity
(2) marginal cost; marginal utility; on
(3) little
(4) externalities; detrimental; beneficial externalities
(5) higher; higher
(6) private; inefficient; much; less
(7) depletability; excludability; public
(8) difficult; rider
(9) zero; zero
(10) does not; less
(11) irreversible
(12) limited

### Important Terms and Concepts Quiz

| | | | | | |
|---|---|---|---|---|---|
| 1. | q | 7. | l | 13. | o |
| 2. | h | 8. | p | 14. | g |
| 3. | e | 9. | f | 15. | m |
| 4. | b | 10. | k | 16. | c |
| 5. | n | 11. | i | | |
| 6. | j | 12. | d | | |

### Basic Exercise

1. Col. 1: $2,640,000; $11; 100; $2,112,000; $10.56
2. Col. 2: $2,640,000; $11; 100; $2,200,000; $11; cost of producing widgets unchanged; cost per hour of police service up 4.17 percent.
3. Col. 3: 80; $2,640,000; $11; 100; $3,300,000; $16.50; cost of producing widgets unchanged; cost per hour of police service up 50 percent over 10 years.

### Self-Tests For Understanding

### Test A

1. c p. 312
2. c Chapter 3 showed that production inside the PPF is inefficient.
3. d p. 313
4. c p. 314
5. d (and possibly b) p. 313
6. d p. 313
7. a p. 314
8. a p. 314
9. a p. 314
10. c p. 318
11. d p. 319
12. c p. 319

13. b When busy with a patient, a doctor is unavailable to others; nonpaying patients can be excluded.
14. b p. 319
15. a p. 324
16. c p. 324
17. b p. 323
18. d p. 328
19. b It is easier to introduce labor saving innovations into the production of TVs than in the other examples where labor requirements may be more or less fixed.
20. b The adjustment of nominal interest rates during periods of inflation is not an argument that private markets make inappropriate decisions about savings and investment.

**Test B**

| | | | | |
|---|---|---|---|---|
| 1. | F | p. 310 | 6. F | p. 318 |
| 2. | F | pp. 313-314 | 7. T | p. 319 |
| 3. | T | p. 313 | 8. T | p. 319 |
| 4. | F | p. 315 | 9. T | p. 320 |
| 5. | F | p. 318 | 10. F | p. 321 |

**Supplementary Exercises**

1. b. Widgets:
   $MP(L) = 22.61$
   $AP(L) = 45.23$
   Recitals:
   $MP(L) = 50$
   $AP(L) = 50$
   c. Widgets:
   $MP(L) = 25.63$
   $AP(L) = 51.26$
   Recitals:
   $MP(L) = 50$
   $AP(L) = 50$
   Productivity of widget workers is up 13.3 percent. No increase in the productivity of musicians.
   d. Opportunity cost of recitals has risen 13.3 percent from .45 widgets to .51 widgets.
   PPF: $M = 50[40,000 - W^2/(3600K)]$
   e. The new production possibilities frontier is never inside the original frontier.

## CHAPTER 14

### Chapter Review

(1) proprietorship; partnership; corporation; limited
(2) stock; bonds; plowback (or retained earnings)
(3) are not; more; bonds; meet bond payments
(4) falls; loss; increase
(5) diversification; program; takeover
(6) are not; riskiness
(7) higher; lower; insurance
(8) random walk; today

### Important Terms and Concepts Quiz

| | | | | | |
|---|---|---|---|---|---|
| 1. | e | 6. | n | 11. | h |
| 2. | i | 7. | l | 12. | c |
| 3. | k | 8. | j | 13. | a |
| 4. | m | 9. | d | 14. | o |
| 5. | b | 10. | g | | |

### Basic Exercises

1. a. 16%; 10%; 6.25%; 4%
   b. $40; no; the price of the stock adjusts so that the dividend yield offers a return that is competitive with other options.
   c. Stock price will fall to $25; stock price will rise to $64.
   d. At the previous price of $40; a dividend of $8 offers a 20 percent return, twice that available on corporate bonds. The increased demand for XYZ stock will increase its price now.
   e. $80; $80 stock price and $8 dividend imply a 10 percent return.
2. The return on the diversified portfolio will be an average of the returns on individual stocks. The diversified portfolio misses the big gainers but minimizes the impact of the worst performers.

### Self-Tests For Understanding

**Test A**

1. b p. 335
2. a p. 335
3. b p. 336
4. b pp. 337-338
5. a p. 338
6. c pp. 338-339
7. d pp. 340-341

8.  c   p. 341
9.  b   p. 339
10. d   p. 342
11. a   p. 343
12. a   p. 343
13. b   p. 349 Changes in the price of outstanding shares mean gains or losses for current stockholders.
14. c   p. 345
15. c   p. 346
16. d   p. 345
17. a   p. 350
18. b   p. 353 Speculators succeed when they buy low (excess supply) and sell high (excess demand).
19. d   p. 352
20. c   p. 354

**Test B**
1. T   p. 335        6.  F   p. 349
2. T   p. 335        7.  F   p. 349
3. F   pp. 339-340   8.  F   p. 350
4. F   p. 343        9.  F   pp. 354-356
5. F   p. 348        10. F   p. 353

### Supplementary Exercises
1. The prices of bonds for all companies are likely to move together in response to changes in economy-wide interest rates. Stock prices are more heavily influenced by the fortunes and misfortunes of individual companies. As a result, changes in share prices are more likely to differ across companies.

# CHAPTER 15
## Chapter Review
(1) productivity; revenue
(2) negative; more; positive; higher; below; intersection
(3) discounting; fewer; lower; negatively
(4) is not
(5) all; no
(6) most; part; is
(7) higher; equal; low
(8) increase; increase; more
(9) greater; greater; innovation; greater

### Important Terms and Concepts Quiz
1. g    6.  o    11. i
2. c    7.  e    12. a
3. j    8.  n    13. f
4. m    9.  h    14. l
5. d    10. k

### Basic Exercise
1. Economic profit = Net revenue - opportunity cost of labor - cost of other inputs; Economic profit = $400 - ($8 × 40) - $30 = $400 - $350 = $50.
2. $30; The rent for the sunny plot should reflect the difference in the cost of production as compared to the marginal plot.
3. If the owner of the sunny plot tried charging a rent that exceeded the $30 difference in production costs, Darlene would make a greater profit by growing her flowers on the marginal plot. With a rent of $30 for the sunny plot she would be indifferent about using either plot.

### Self-Tests For Understanding
**Test A**
1.  d   p. 363
2.  a   p. 362
3.  c   p. 363
4.  b   p. 364
5.  b   p. 367
6.  c   p. 367
7.  a   p. 361
8.  c   pp. 365-366
9.  d   p. 365
10. d   p. 373
11. a   p. 373
12. b   p. 373
13. c   p. 375
14. a   p. 379
15. c   p. 377
16. b   pp. 378-379
17. b   p. 376
18. b   p. 380
19. c   p. 381
20. a   p. 383

**Test B**
1. F   p. 363        6.  T   p. 379
2. T   p. 365        7.  F   p. 373
3. T   p. 367        8.  F   p. 374
4. F   p. 365        9.  T   p. 379
5. F   p. 375        10. F   pp. 380-82

## APPENDIX

### Important Terms and Concepts Quiz: Appendix

1. a

### Basic Exercises: Appendix

1.  a. $4,000; $1,818.18; $2,066.12; 3,884.30; -$115.70
    b. cost; no
    c. $4,000; $1,904.76; $2,267.57; $4,172.33; $172.33
    d. present value of returns; yes
    e. 5 percent: $200; $4,200; $2,200; $110; $2,310
       10 percent: $400; $4,400; $2,400; $240; $2,640
    f. 5 percent: $1,800; $90; $4,390; $190
       10 percent: $1,600; $160; $4,260; -$140

2.  The contest sponsors can meet their payments to Mr. Calhoun by investing a smaller sum in 1993 and using both the initial investment along with the interest earnings to make the necessary future payments. Present value calculations show how much must be invested today to fund the future payments. Assuming the first payment was made right away, the sponsors need to invest a sum sufficient to fund 19 future payments of $50,000, or

    Necessary sum =
    present value =

    $$\sum_{t=1}^{19} \frac{50,000}{(1+i)^t}$$

    If the interest rate is 6.5% the present value of the future payments is only $557,906. Including the first payment to Mr. Calhoun brings the total cost of $1,000,000 to $607,906. A higher interest rate would mean a lower present value, while a lower interest rate would mean a higher present value.

## CHAPTER 16

### Chapter Review

(1) leisure; more; decrease; income
(2) more; substitution; increases; offset; slope; position; income
(3) demand; higher
(4) does; do not
(5) minimum; higher; decrease; supply
(6) unskilled; unions; National Labor Relations; Taft-Hartley
(7) monopolist; demand; right
(8) monopsonist; wages; lower; higher; two; bilateral
(9) collective bargaining; mediation; arbitration; mediator; arbitrator

### Important Terms and Concepts Quiz

| | | |
|---|---|---|
| 1. c | 7. k | 13. e |
| 2. h | 8. f | 14. n |
| 3. l | 9. m | 15. o |
| 4. b | 10. a | 16. i |
| 5. d | 11. r | |
| 6. q | 12. j | |

### Basic Exercise

1. 60; 55; 50; 45; 40; 35; 30; 25; 20; 15
2. $2400; $2200; $2000; $1800; $1600; $1400; $1200; $1000; $800; $600
3. 7
4. Total profits with 7 workers: $4,900
   (315 × $40) − (7 × $1100)
   Total profits with 6 workers: $4,800
   (285 × $40) − (6 × $1100)
   Total profits with 8 workers: $4,800
   (340 × $40) − (8 × $1100)
5. $1000; 800; 8; $5600; if 7 workers, profits = $5600 as MRP = wage for eighth worker.
6.  a. $1800
    b. 900 workers
    c. $1400 and 600 workers, or $1200 and 700 workers

### Self-Tests For Understanding

**Test A**

1. d  p. 391
2. a  p. 395
3. b  p. 391
4. c  p. 391
5. b  p. 393
6. b  p. 395
7. a  p. 394
8. b  p. 392
9. a  p. 391
10. c  p. 391

11. d   p. 396
12. b   the marginal physical product of labor ($MPP_L$) derives from the production function for schmoos. An increase in employment that comes from an increase in the demand for schmoos will lead to a movement along the $MPP_L$ schedule, not a shift in the schedule.
13. c   pp. 396-397
14. a   p. 397
15. d.  p. 402
16. c   p. 403
17. a   p. 405
18. d   p. 405
19. b   p. 407
20. d; a; e; f; b; c; f    pp. 405; 408; 411-412

**Test B**
1. T   p. 393
2. T   p. 407
3. F   p. 391
4. F   a change in wages leads to a movement along the supply curve.
5. F   p. 401
6. F   p. 405, a union is a monopolist, the sole supplier of labor. A monopsonist is the sole buyer of something.
7. F   p. 410
8. F   p. 407
9. F   p. 409
10. T   p. 411

## APPENDIX

### Important Terms and Concepts Quiz: Appendix
1. b

### Basic Exercise: Appendix
1. $1000; 8; no; Tony is a monopsonist. The marginal cost of labor is greater than average wages for a monopsonist when the supply of labor curve has a positive shape.
2. greater
   Total labor cost:  $300; $800; $1,500; $2,400; $3,500; $4,800; $6,300; $8,000; $9,900; $12,000
   Marginal labor cost:  $300; $500; $700; $900; $1,100; $1,300; $1,500; $1,700; $1,900; $2,100
4. 6 workers
5. $800

6. $6,600 = $40 × 285 - 6 × $800. The competitive solution, hiring 8 workers at $1,000, would have produced profits of only $5,600 ($40 × 340 - 8 × $1,000).
7. Both wages and employment would increase. Tony would hire 7 workers at $1100 a month. The "high" minimum wage increases employment because Tony is a monopsonist. The minimum wage changes Tony's marginal cost of labor schedule.
8. No. If the union had more than 7 workers, it might want a lower wage to increase employment. If the union had 7 or fewer workers, it might be able to extract a higher wage by bargaining for some of Tony's profits.

## CHAPTER 17

### Chapter Review
**(1)** 14; 350; absolute; relative
**(2)** Lorenz; zero; 45-degree; positive; below; very little
**(3)** 44.2; 4.5
**(4)** efficiency
**(5)** marginal; decrease
**(6)** decrease; break-even; negative; small
**(7)** different; are not; overstate; employers

### Important Terms and Concepts Quiz
1. a       4. g       7. e
2. c       5. b       8. j
3. i       6. f       9. h

### Basic Exercise
1. 12,000; 12,365; 13,740; 13,988; 12,487; 13,419; 13,587; 15,399; 18,119; 18,847
3. Col. 4: 365; 1,375; 248; -1,500; 932; 168; 1,811; 2,720; 728
   Col. 5: 235; 4,525; 1,051; 1,501; 1,268; 82; 1,139; 3,430; 1,122
   Col. 6: 39.2; 76.7; 80.9; 150,132.6; 57.6; 32.6; 38.6; 55.8; 60.6
   The marginal tax rates in column 6 should be equivalent to the slopes of the line segments you graphed in Figure 17-1. In 1992 as income increased above $21,200, income plus social security taxes would have taken 22.65 percent of increases in income.

## Self-Tests For Understanding
### Test A

1. d p. 428
2. c p. 425
3. b p. 425
4. a p. 425
5. b p. 428
6. c p. 428
7. d p. 430, even in the absence of economic discrimination, incomes will differ.
8. a p. 430
9. d p. 428
10. b p. 428
11. b p. 427
12. d p. 441
13. c p. 441, with a 50 percent tax rate, earnings of $8,000 reduce negative tax payments by $4,000 to $2,000, for a total income of $10,000.
14. c p. 441
15. a reducing the tax rates raises costs which can only be offset by a reduction in the minimum guarantee.
16. a, d p. 441
17. a p. 431
18. a differences in schooling might reflect discrimination in access to schooling.
19. d pp. 431-432
20. b pp. 433-435

### Test B

1. T in principle, growth can push all incomes past an absolute standard. Relative standards will increase with economic growth.
2. F p. 425
3. F p. 428
4. T p. 428
5. T p. 429
6. F p. 432
7. T p. 433
8. F p. 426
9. T pp. 430-431
10. F p. 443

## CHAPTER 18
### Chapter Review

(1) regulate; nationalize
(2) scale; scope; is not; below; above; fixed; marginal
(3) high
(4) fully distributed; marginal; lower
(5) less; demand; marginal; stand alone
(6) less; performance
(7) reduces; inefficiency; efficiency

### Important Terms and Concepts Quiz

| | | |
|---|---|---|
| 1. c | 6. e | 11. d |
| 2. g | 7. l | 12. h |
| 3. n | 8. f | 13. j |
| 4. k | 9. a | 14. m |
| 5. o | 10. b | |

### Basic Exercise

1. Output:

| | | | |
|---|---|---|---|
| 60 | 90 | 120 | 150 |

   Average Cost:

| | | | |
|---|---|---|---|
| 26.25¢ | 22.5¢ | 20.625¢ | 19.5¢ |

   Marginal Cost:

| | | | |
|---|---|---|---|
| 15.0¢ | 15.0¢ | 15.0¢ | 5.0¢ |

2. $6.75 million loss at all levels of output.
3. No; fixed costs are never covered.

### Self-Tests For Understanding
### Test A

1. ICC = d p. 453
   FCC = c p. 453
   FERC = g p. 453
   Fed. Res. = a p. 453
   SEC = f p. 453
2. c p. 457, proponents argue that regulation is often necessary to protect consumers.
3. b p. 454
4. d p. 454
5. c p. 454
6. b p. 455
7. a p. 455
8. c p. 459
9. c p. 459
10. d p. 460
11. d p. 462
12. d p. 462
13. c when there are shared or overhead costs, marginal cost pricing will allow lower prices than any of the alternatives.
14. b p. 465
15. b p. 467
16. a p. 467
17. a pp. 464-465
18. d pp. 466-467
19. d pp. 467-468
20. a p. 451

**Test B**

| | | | | | | |
|---|---|---|---|---|---|---|
| 1. | F | p. 452 | 6. | T | p. 456 | |
| 2. | F | p. 454 | 7. | T | pp. 462-463 | |
| 3. | F | pp. 464-465 | 8. | F | p. 459 | |
| 4. | F | p. 465 | 9. | T | p. 471 | |
| 5. | T | p. 455 | 10. | F | p. 471 | |

# CHAPTER 19

## Chapter Review

(1) Sherman; was not
(2) Clayton; price discrimination; tying; interlocking directorates
(3) reason; is not; conduct; was
(4) merger; vertical; horizontal; conglomerate
(5) less; innovation
(6) increasing; reduction; increase
(7) concentration; little

## Important Terms and Concepts Quiz

| | | | | | |
|---|---|---|---|---|---|
| 1. | d | 4. | i | 7. | a |
| 2. | f | 5. | g | 8. | c |
| 3. | b | 6. | h | | |

## Basic Exercise

1. Total Revenue: $2,400,000; $3,093,750; $3,675,000; $4,143,750; $4,500,000; $4,743,750; $4,875,000; $4,893,750
Marginal Revenue: $37; $31; $25; $19; $13; $7; $1
Price $33; Output 143,750; Profits $806,250
2. Centerville; Total Revenue: $480,000; $1,125,000; $1,680,000; $2,145,000; $2,520,000; $2,805,000; $3,000,000; $3,105,000
Marginal Revenue: $43; $37; $31; $25; $19; $13; $7
Price $30; Quantity 100,000
Middletown: Total Revenue: $1,920,000; $1,968,750; $1,995,000; $1,998,750; $1,980,000; $1,938,750; $1,875,000; $1,788,750
Marginal Revenue: $13, $7; $1; -$5; -$11; -$17; -$23
Price $45; Quantity 43,750
Profits: $1,031,250
3. Middletown; Centerville; yes

## Self-Tests For Understanding

**Test A**

1. c p. 479
2. a p. 479
3. a p. 480
4. c p. 481
5. d p. 479
6. c p. 480
7. b p. 480
8. c p. 480
9. d p. 480 Apple and IBM are competitors.
10. c p. 481
11. c p. 482
12. a p. 482, merger with supplier.
13. d p. 482, merger of competing firms.
14. b p. 482, merger of unrelated firms.
15. c p. 482
16. c p. 485, each firm produces 10 percent of industry output. Four firms produce 40 percent.
17. b p. 486
18. c p. 490
19. d p. 487
20. b p. 491, Chapter 13 defined rent seeking as activity in search of profits that does not contribute to production.

**Test B**

| | | | | | | |
|---|---|---|---|---|---|---|
| 1. | T | p. 476 | 6. | F | p. 490 | |
| 2. | T | p. 479 | 7. | F | p. 486 | |
| 3. | F | p. 479 | 8. | F | p. 484 | |
| 4. | F | p. 482 | 9. | F | p. 488 | |
| 5. | T | p. 485 | 10. | F | pp. 490-491 | |

# CHAPTER 20

## Chapter Review

(1) direct; indirect; personal income; payroll; corporate
(2) average; marginal; progressive; proportional; regressive
(3) payroll; regressive; do not; zero
(4) sales; property; assessed; market; is not; federalism
(5) equity; horizontal equity; vertical equity; vertical; benefits; benefits
(6) burden; greater; excess burden; does not; smallest
(7) higher; lower; smaller
(8) incidence; flypaper; shifting
(9) demand; supply; inelastic; workers; firms

## Important Terms and Concepts Quiz

1. b
2. p
3. i
4. n
5. r
6. g
7. s
8. k
9. a
10. m
11. h
12. t
13. o
14. c
15. d
16. q
17. e
18. f
19. l

## Basic Exercise

2. $42; 50 million
3. $46; 44 million
4. $4; it is less than increase in tax.
5. All are likely to decline.
7. The first demand curve.
8. $50; 48 million; Figure 20-3; Figure 20-3; consumers

## Self-Tests For Understanding

### Test A

1. b   p. 496
2. c   p. 496
3. d   p. 497
4. c   p. 497
5. d   p. 497
6. c   p. 504
7. c   p. 496
8. d   as long as the marginal tax rate exceeds the average rate it can rise or fall and the average rate will continue to increase. Consider Table 20-1 in the text and Rule 4 in the Appendix to Chapter 5.
9. c   Rule 4 in the Appendix to Chapter 5.
10. c   p. 496
11. b   p. 504
12. b   p. 504
13. c   p. 505
14. c   p. 506
15. c   p. 506
16. b   p. 506
17. a   zero price elasticity of demand means a vertical demand curve. Any increase in price from the sales tax induces no change in behavior.
18. d   p. 507
19. a   p. 513
20. a   p. 513

### Test B

1. F   p. 496
2. F   p. 499
3. T   p. 497
4. T   p. 497
5. T   p. 504
6. F   p. 504
7. F   p. 506
8. T   p. 507
9. F   pp. 510-511
10. F   pp. 511-512

## Supplementary Exercise

2. Revenue = $T \times Q$
   Harris:
   Revenue = 25.608 T = 2.95 T²
       T = $4.34 maximizes revenue;
           revenue = $55.57 billion
   Grossman:
   Revenue = 27.5184T - 10.91 T²
       T = $1.26 maximizes revenue;
           revenue = $17.35 billion

3. Harris: $\Delta Q = 1.475$; elasticity = .275
   Grossman: $\Delta Q = 5.455$; elasticity = 1.107
       When demand is more elastic, every increase in the tax leads to a larger reduction in the quantity demanded. As a result the revenue maximizing tax is lower.
       Harris did not solve for the revenue maximizing tax. Rather he analyzed the impact of $2 increase in cigarette taxes and estimated a net increase in revenue of $28 billion. The approximation to the Harris demand curve for this exercise shows a gross increase in revenue with a $2.24 tax of $37.56 billion.

4. When the supply curve is infinitely elastic (horizontal), consumers pay all of any increase in taxes. If the supply curve were perfectly inelastic (vertical), then producers would pay all of any increase in taxes and there would be no change in the quantity demanded regardless of the elasticity of demand. If the supply curve has a positive slope, that is if the elasticity of supply is not infinite or zero, then the incidence of any increase in taxes will be divided as between consumers and producers depending upon the elasticities of demand and supply.

# CHAPTER 21

## Chapter Review

(1) externality; decrease; taxes
(2) controls

(3) inefficient; efficient; marginal
(4) can never; price
(5) interest; increasing
(6) interest
(7) discourage; incentive; encourage; incentive; encouraging

## Important Terms and Concepts Quiz
1. d        4 e        6. a
2. f        5. h        7. g
3. b

## Basic Exercises
1. a.  15 cents; 10 million
   b.  falls; rises; no change in short run, declines in long run; shifts up by 5 cents; short run—declines; long run—no change or falls to zero, i.e., some firms leave industry; declines as industry output declines in short- and long-run.
   c.  Since the tax is per bag, not per unit of pollution, the pollution control equipment will not reduce a firm's pollution tax.
   d.  No. Since the equipment is only 75 percent effective, the total cost of using the equipment (4 cents plus the 1.25-cent emission tax per bag) is greater than the tax of 5 cents per bag.
   e.  less than 3.75 cents; more than 5.33 cents
   f.  Price rises and industry output declines as at least some high-cost firms leave the industry.
2. Energy:  23.1; 23; 22.9; 22.7; 22.3; 21.9; 22; 21.6; 21.1; 20.8; 20.1; 19.3; 18.8; 18.0; 17.9; 17.3; 16.8; 16.9; 17.0; 16.8; 16.7; 16.8; 16.6
   Energy use rose during the late 1960s as the relative price of energy fell. The rise in energy prices following 1973 led to a significant decline in energy consumption. Energy consumption per thousand dollars of GNP has continued to decline throughout the 1980s even as relative energy prices have fallen. Patterns of energy consumption per thousand dollars of GNP up to 1981 could be interpreted as a movement along a demand curve in response to changes in price, although the introduction of energy conservation practices, e.g., home insulation, energy-

efficient machines and cars, are perhaps best seen as a shift in the demand curve to the left. These shifts mean that as energy prices decline, one would not expect energy consumption to return to earlier levels. The decline in energy consumption during the 1980s at the same time that relative energy prices were declining reflects the continued introduction of energy-saving practices.

## Self-Tests For Understanding
### Test A
1. b   p. 521
2. e   pp. 517-519
3. b   p. 523
4. d   p. 522
5. b   p. 523
6. a   p. 525
7. b   pp. 527-528
8. b   p. 525
9. b   p. 528
10. a   p. 528
11. d   firms have an incentive to reduce pollution as long as it is cheaper to continue to reduce pollution than to pay the tax.
12. c   p. 533
13. b   p. 536
14. d   p. 538
15. a   others are either supply responses or reflect a shift in the demand curve.
16. c   p. 535
17. a   pp. 538-539
18. c   p. 531
19. c   see Basic Exercise 2
20. d   pp. 536-537

### Test B
1. F   p. 517
2. F   pp. 517-519
3. F   pp. 527-528
4. F   as the example of the excise tax in Chapter 20 showed, an increase in price will reduce demand and hence the quantity of output and pollution.
5. F   p. 522
6. F   p. 538
7. F   p. 535
8. F   p. 533
9. T   p. 536
10. T   p. 538

## Supplementary Exercise

1. a. MC = 15.
    MR = 65 - .05Q (P = 65 - .025Q;
    TR = 65Q - .025Q²).
    Set MC = MR to solve for profit
    maximizing output: 15 = 65 - .05Q; Q =
    1000; P = 40¢; Profit = 25¢ on each of
    1000 million bags or $250 million.
   b. If price rises by 5¢, quantity demanded
    will decline to 800 million bags. At price
    of 45¢, profit is 25¢ a bag or $200 million.
    Set MC = MR to determine profit
    maximizing level of output: 20 = 65 -
    .05Q; Q = 900; P = 42.5¢; profits = 22.5¢
    a bag or $202.5 million.
   c. Long run equilibrium price equals
    minimum average cost = 15¢.
    Market quantity = 2000 million bags; 200
    firms producing 10 million bags each.
   d. Short run: For representative firm AC
    = .4(Q - 10)² + 20.
    TC = .4Q³ - 8Q² + 60Q.
    MC = 1.2Q² - 16Q + 60.
    As each firm supplies 1/200 of the
    market, we can find the short-run profit
    maximizing position of each firm by
    setting MC equal to price.
    MC = 65 - .025(Q x 200), or
    1.2Q² - 16Q + 60 = 65 - 5Q.
        The mathematics of solving this
    equation for Q are a bit cumbersome.
    Rounding off, firm output = 9.6 million
    bags; industry output = 1920 million
    bags; and price = 17¢. Note that price is
    now less than average cost.
        Long run: Some firms leave in
    response to short-run losses. Long-run
    equilibrium occurs where remaining
    firms produce at minimum average cost.
    Price = 20¢; market demand = 1800; each
    of 180 firms produce 10 million bags.
    The conditions in this problem—marginal cost
    for the monopolist equal to the minimum
    average cost of competitive firms and the same
    demand curve under either market structure—
    imply the following: 1) by restricting output,
    the monopolist creates less pollution than the
    perfectly competitive industry; 2) the
    monopolist is unable to pass on the full extent
    of the pollution tax; and 3) in long-run
    equilibrium under perfect competition,
    consumers pay all of the pollution tax.

## Economics in Action

1. Simon won the bet and received a check for
   $567.07 from Ehrlich. You can read about
   the bet in John Tierney's article "Betting the
   Planet," *New York Times Magazine,*
   December 2, 1990.

# CHAPTER 22

## Chapter Review

(1) microeconomics; macroeconomics
(2) price; quantity; domestic product
(3) inflation; deflation; recessions; higher;
    higher; left; decrease; stagflation
(4) money; final; nominal; real; real; nominal;
    real; is not
(5) up; depends; risen
(6) inflation; stabilization; recessions; inflation

## Important Terms and Concepts Quiz

| | | |
|---|---|---|
| 1. p | 7. q | 13. g |
| 2. h | 8. l | 14. k |
| 3. e | 9. b | 15. c |
| 4. i | 10. n | 16. f |
| 5. m | 11. d | |
| 6. o | 12. j | |

## Basic Exercises

1. a. c; d
   b. b; yes, 1929-1933
   c. a
   d. c
2. a. shift aggregate demand curve to left
   b. shift aggregate demand curve to right
   c. Real GDP will fall as aggregate demand
    curve is shifted to the left; prices will
    rise as aggregate
    demand curve is shifted to the right.
3. a. col (3): $600; $300; $225; $1,125
    col (6): $868; $416; $297; $1,581
   b. 40.5 percent
   c. $620; $320; $247.50; $1,187.50
   d. 5.56 percent
   e. The increase in real GDP is less than
    the increase in nominal GDP as the
    increase in nominal GDP includes both
    the increase in production and the
    increase in prices. The increase in real

GDP is the better measure of the change in output. It is a weighted average of the increases in the output of hamburgers, shakes, and fries. The weights sum to one and reflect the relative importance of output in GDP for the base year, 1992 in this example.

## Self-Tests For Understanding

### Test A

1. b p. 545
2. d p. 545
3. a p. 545
4. c p. 548
5. a p. 548
6. b p. 549
7. a p. 550
8. a p. 549
9. c p. 549
10. d p. 550
11. d p. 550
12. b pp. 549-550
13. a pp. 551-552
14. d p. 549
15. d p. 548
16. b p. 548
17. d p. 558
18. c p. 559
19. b p. 554
20. c pp. 559-560

### Test B

1. F p. 545
2. T p. 545
3. F Not if the decrease comes from a decrease in prices.
4. T p. 549
5. F If aggregate demand curve shifts to the left, prices will fall.
6. F p. 554
7. F pp. 553-554
8. T p. 558
9. T p. 559
10. F pp. 559-560

## Economics in Action

1. The NBER committee dated the business cycle peak in July 1990 and the trough in March 1991.

## CHAPTER 23

### Chapter Review

(1) more; more
(2) cannot; partial; some
(3) potential; actual GDP
(4) is not; frictional; cyclical; structural
(5) discouraged; decrease; understate; understate
(6) frictional; increased; overstate
(7) real; the same; as; were unchanged
(8) different; less; more
(9) higher; nominal; real; inflation
(10) will; be unchanged; nominal
(11) usury; nominal; real; nominal; real
(12) creeping; galloping

### Important Terms and Concepts Quiz

1. b
2. q
3. d
4. f
5. h
6. l
7. g
8. a
9. p
10. k
11. n
12. j
13. c
14. i
15. o
16. e

### Basic Exercises

1. a. –0.7%; 0.21%; 2.32%; 1.07%; –3.69%; –2.50%; 0.91%; 0.46%; 2.7%; 0.68%; 1.38%; 2.55%; 2.71%; 6.91%; 5.03%; 4.07%; 3.97%; 3.57%; 4.89%; 2.92%; 1.65%.
   c. When actual inflation turns out to be much greater than expected, the difference between nominal interest rates and the actual rate of inflation may be negative.
   d. While the nominal rates were higher in December 1980, the actual real rate from December 1980 to December 1981 was lower than the real rate from December 1987 to December 1988.
2. a. $250,000; $5,250,000; $4,772,727; $5,750,000; $5,227,273. Borrowers gain at expense of lenders.
   b. $775,000; $5,775,000; $5,250,000; $5,225,000; $4,750,000. Both are treated equally.
   c. $1,000,000; $6,000,000; $5,454,545; $5,000,000; $4,545,455. Lenders gain at expense of borrowers.

## Self-Tests For Understanding
### Test A
1. b, a, d, c    pp. 568-570
2. a, b, d    p. 568
3. a    p. 570
4. c    pp. 565-566
5. b    p. 566
6. b    p. 569
7. b    p. 570
8. c    p. 570
9. c    p. 571
10. b    p. 577
11. b    p. 577
12. b    p. 577
13. a    p. 577
14. c    p. 577
15. b    pp. 575-576
16. d    p. 579
17. c    p. 574
18. d    p. 583
19. a    pp. 572-573
20. c    p. 572

### Test B
1. F    Reduced hours, loss of overtime, and involuntary part-time reduce income for individuals counted as employed.
2. F    p. 568
3. F    p. 565
4. F    p. 571
5. F    p. 570
6. F    p. 566
7. F    pp. 569-570
8. F    pp. 576-577
9. F    p. 583
10. T    p. 581

## CHAPTER APPENDIX
### Important Terms and Concepts Quiz: Appendix
1. b    3. a    5. f
2. d    4. c

### Basic Exercises: Appendix
1. a. 2,500; 400
   b. $16,500 = 2,500 \times \$2.36 + 400 \times \$26.50$
   c. 110
   e. 10 percent
   f. $15,771 ($1,990); 5.1 percent

2. 1990 index, using 1991 base, 91.1. 1991 base implies inflation of 9.8 percent. The slightly lower rate of inflation reflects a larger weight on more slowly rising clothing prices when using the 1991 expenditure pattern.

### Supplementary Exercise: Appendix
1. a and b.    Insufficient information; for example, the price index for Canada for 1990 shows how 1990 Canadian prices compare to Canadian prices in 1982-1984, not how Canadian prices compare to those in other countries.
   c. Italy; West Germany

## CHAPTER 24
### Chapter Review
(1) demand; consumption; investment; government; exports; imports; net exports
(2) before; taxes; transfer
(3) more; movement along; shift in
(4) $C$; $I$; $G$; $X$; $IM$; less; decrease
(5) increase; marginal; larger; more; smaller

### Important Terms and Concepts Quiz
1. g    6. l    11. e
2. d    7. b    12. m
3. h    8. n    13. j
4. c    9. a
5. k    10. i

### Basic Exercises
1. a. .75; .75; .75; .75
   b. .9; .825; .8; .7875; .78
   e. slope of consumption function
   f. rays become less steep, that is their slope decreases. For straight line consumption function with a positive Y intercept, the APC will be greater than the MPC although the difference will be getting smaller as income increases.
2. a. $9,000; $39,000; $4,800,000
   b. .78; .9
   c. $12,750; $35,250; $4,800,000
   d. In this example, MPC is the same for the rich and poor. The rich reduce their

consumption by the same amount that the poor increase their consumption.

3. C = 1,500 + .75DI

4. a. Estimated MPC = 3.6/4.0 = .9

   b. The estimate in a is greater than the slope of the consumption function. It overestimates the MPC because it includes the effect of the shift of the consumption function.

## Self-Tests For Understanding

### Test A

1. b pp. 591-592
2. b p. 591
3. d p. 594
4. b Circular flow diagram shows spending on newly produced goods and services.
5. b p. 592
6. d p. 592
7. c p. 600
8. a p. 602
9. c p. 602
10. b p. 596 and Appendix, Chapter 1
11. d pp. 603-604
12. a p. 600
13. b p. 600
14. c $\Delta C = MPC \times \Delta DI$
15. c $MPC = \Delta C/\Delta DI$
16. c $\Delta$ taxes $= -\Delta DI = \Delta C/MPC$
17. a $MPC = \Delta C/\Delta DI$. For 14, 15, 16, and 17, remember:
    $MPC = \Delta C/\Delta DI$. Each question gives you two numbers; you must solve equation for the third.
18. d p. 602
19. d p. 604
20. c changes in withholding affect the timing of when taxes are paid but do not change what a taxpayer owes. pp. 605-606

### Test B

1. F p. 591
2. F p. 600
3. T pp. 595-596
4. T p. 600
5. T p. 603
6. T p. 604
7. F p. 602
8. T pp. 605-606
9. T p. 606
10. T p. 600

## APPENDIX A

### Important Terms and Concepts Quiz: Appendix A

1. d      2. c      3. a

### Basic Exercises: Appendix A

1. $1,600; $3,200; $4,800; $6,400; $8,000
2. change in savings; $1,600; $1,600; $1,600; $1,600; MPS: .4; .4; .4; .4
4. APS: .13; .20; .24; .27; .29
6. $DI/DI = C/DI + S/DI$ or $1 = APC + APS$
   $\Delta DI/\Delta DI = \Delta C/\Delta DI + \Delta S/\Delta DI$ or $1 = MPC + MPS$

## APPENDIX B

### Appendix Review

(1) final; produced
(2) exports; imports; produced
(3) income, do not; net national; depreciation
(4) value added
(5) taxes

### Important Terms and Concepts Quiz: Appendix B

1. a      2. e      3. b      4. c

### Basic Exercises: Appendix B

1. a. $2,200
   b. $1,700
   c. $1,700; wages = $1,200; profits = $500
   d. $500
   e. $1,200
   f. $1,700
   g. $1,700
   h. $1,700
2. a. $1,000; $2,100; $1,600; $4,700
   b. 0; $1,500; $3,200; $4,700

### Self-Tests for Understanding: Appendix B

### Test A

1. c p. 612
2. c p. 616
3. b p. 612
4. c p. 612
5. a This year's GDP only includes goods produced this year. p. 612
6. d pp. 616-617

7.  d  Computers shipped to Japan are exports. p. 613
8.  b  Computers from Japan are imports.
9.  c  Social security payments are transfers. p. 613
10. d  p. 614
11. b  p. 615
12. c  p. 618
13. b  p. 618
14. c  pp. 617-618
15. a  p. 618
16. d  p. 616
17. d  p. 618
18. c  p. 612
19. c  p. 618
20. b  p. 615

## Test B

1.  F  p. 612
2.  T  p. 616
3.  F  p. 612
4.  F  No effect on GDP. Value added by GM up. Value added by suppliers down.
5.  F  p. 612
6.  T  p. 616
7.  F  p. 614
8.  F  p. 618
9.  F  p. 615
10. T  These are alternative ways to measure national income.

## Supplementary Exercise: Appendix B

1.  MPC = $50/\sqrt{DI}$; MPC declines as income rises. Thus consumption spending rises following redistribution from rich to poor as increase in consumption by poor is greater than decline in consumption by rich.
    S = $DI - 100\sqrt{DI}$
    MPC + MPS = 1 and APC + APS = 1

# CHAPTER 25

## Chapter Review

(1) increase; increasing; decrease
(2) exports; imports
(3) intersection
(4) less; downward; lower; more; higher
(5) price level
(6) inflationary; recessionary

## Important Terms and Concepts Quiz

1.  d      4.  g      7.  i
2.  f      5.  j      8.  e
3.  b      6.  a      9.  c

## Basic Exercises

1.  e.  $6,200
    f.  5,900; 6,000; 6,100; 6,200; 6,300
    g.  Spending would be greater than output, inventories would decline, firms would increase output.
    h.  inflationary gap, $200; recessionary gap, $300
    i.  Expenditure schedule shifts up; $6,400; $4,700
2.  b.  $6,000
    c.  $6,400
    d.  aggregate demand curve
    e.  negative
3.  New aggregate demand curve should lie to the right of the aggregate demand curve in question 2.

## Self-Tests For Understanding

## Test A

1.  b  pp. 622-623
2.  c  pp. 624-625
3.  a  pp. 624-625
4.  a  Net exports = $X - IM$.
5.  c  p. 625
6.  c  p. 628
7.  a, c, d, e, g    p. 628
8.  c  p. 628
9.  a  p. 628
10. c  p. 628
11. c  p. 631
12. a  p. 630
13. b  p. 630
14. b  p. 631
15. c  p. 634
16. a  p. 637
17. a  p. 634
18. c  p. 632
19. b  pp. 632-633
20. a, b, c    The increase in the purchasing power of money-fixed assets shifts the consumption function and the expenditure schedule leading to a movement along the aggregate demand curve

## Test B
1. F  p. 622
2. T  p. 628
3. F  p. 637
4. F  p. 630
5. T  pp. 632-633
6. F  p. 635
7. T  p. 634
8. F  pp. 636-638
9. F  pp. 632-633
10. T  pp. 632-633

## APPENDIX A
### Basic Exercises: Appendix A
1. 600; 700; 800; 900; 1,000; 1,100
2. Leakages: 1,900; 2,000; 2,100; 2,200; 2,300; 2,400
   Equilibrium income = 2,200
3. The intersection of the leakages schedule and the injections schedule; 2,200
4. Investment: steeper; no change; steeper
   Imports: flatter; steeper; no change
   Exports: affected by foreign, not domestic income
5. $S + T + IM = I + G + X$

## APPENDIX B
### Basic Exercises: Appendix B
1. $C = 1,850 + .5 (Y - T)$
   $= 1,500 + .5Y$
2. $C + I + G + (X - IM) = 3,100 + .5Y$
3. $Y = 3,100 + .5Y$
   $= 6,200$

## CHAPTER 26
### Chapter Review
(1) more than; autonomous; induced
(2) MPC
(3) consumption spending
(4) income; MPC
(5) smaller; international trade; inflation; income; financial
(6) do not; supply; autonomous; shifting; horizontal

### Important Terms and Concepts Quiz
1. d    2. a    3. e    4. b

## Basic Exercises
1. a. 5,600; 5,800; 6,000; 6,200; 6,400; 6,600; 6,800; equilibrium: 6,000
   b. 6,500
   c. 500
   d. 5; equilibrium level; income; autonomous spending
   e. .8
   f. $1/(1 - 0.8) = 1(0.2) = 5$
   g. slope expenditure schedule
      $= 200/250 = 0.8$
2. a. Total spending = 5,800; 6,000; 6,200; 6,400; 6,600; 6,800; 7,000; equilibrium = 7,000
   b. 500
   c. 5; it is the same as the investment spending multiplier.
3. less; autonomous
   a. 6,750
   b. −250
   c. fall
   d. 5
   e. the same
   f. It ignores effects of inflation, taxes, the financial system, and international trade.

### Self-Tests For Understanding
#### Test A
1. c  p. 648
2. b  p. 648
3. d  p. 653
4. c  p. 650
5. a; c; e; g  p. 653
6. c  See Figure 26-1 or 26-3.
7. b  p. 654
8. e  p. 660
9. c  p. 653
10. a  p. 653
11. c  p. 653
12. c  p. 660
13. b; d  Japanese imports from the United States are America exports to Japan.
14. c  p. 648
15. d  An autonomous increase in imports shifts expenditure schedule down.
16. b  p. 658
17. c  p. 658
18. a  p. 659
19. b  p. 658
20. c  pp. 657-658

## Test B

1. F   p. 648
2. F   p. 648
3. T   p. 658
4. T   p. 653
5. T   p. 654
6. F   p. 658
7. F   p. 654
8. F   p. 655
9. F   pp. 657-658
10. T   p. 660

## APPENDIX A

### Basic Exercises: Appendix A

1. $Y = a + b(Y - T) + I + G + X - IM$

   $= \dfrac{1}{1-b}(a - bT + I + G + X - IM)$

   Multiplier $= \dfrac{1}{1-b}$

2. $\Delta Y = \dfrac{1}{1-b}\,\Delta a$

   $\Delta Y = \dfrac{1}{1-b}\,\Delta I$

   $\Delta Y = \dfrac{1}{1-b}\,\Delta G$

   $\Delta Y = \dfrac{1}{1-b}\,\Delta X$

   $\Delta Y = \dfrac{1}{1-b}\,\Delta IM$

## APPENDIX B

### Basic Exercises: Appendix B

2. 6,500
3. multiplier = 500/125 = 4
4. The multiplier is smaller because imports increase with income. The slope of the expenditure schedule = 187.5/250 = 0.75. Multiplier = 1/(1 − 0.75) = 1/0.25 = 4. Alternatively, the marginal propensity to import = 0.05. Multiplier = 1/(1 − 0.8 + 0.05) = 1/(1 − 0.75) = 4.

### Supplementary Exercises: Appendix B

1. It ignores the multiplier.
3. b. Model should show change in income of 400 for multiplier of 4 = 1/(1 − MPC).
   c. Autonomous change in saving is necessarily a change in intercept of consumption function. Review Appendix A to Chapter 7 if necessary.

d. Larger MPC will mean larger multiplier; smaller MPC means smaller multiplier.

## CHAPTER 27

### Chapter Review

(1) increase; movement along; shift in; right
(2) steeper
(3) intersection; decrease; increases
(4) inflationary; is; inward; movement along; higher; lower
(5) less
(6) inflationary; supply

### Important Terms and Concepts Quiz

1. c      2. e      3. a      4. d

### Basic Exercises

1. a. increases; shift in; $6,200
   e. 95; $6,125
   f. Inflationary gap; increasing production costs would shift aggregate supply curve; 100 and $6,000
   g. no gaps
   h. recessionary gap; elimination of gap likely to be very slow; 90; $6,250
2. horizontal
   a. no
   b. At $P^*$ aggregate demand would exceed aggregate supply. Prices would rise. The increase in prices would mean a movement along the dashed aggregate demand curve to the equilibrium, ($Y_2$, $P_2$), given by the intersection of the dashed aggregate demand curve and the solid aggregate supply curve.

   The increase in investment spending, which shifted the expenditure schedule and gave rise to the dashed aggregate demand curve, will lead to an increase in prices as part of the broader multiplier process, reducing net exports and the purchasing power of money-fixed assets. The result of the reduction in net exports and the shift in the consumption function is a downward shift in the expenditure schedule (not drawn) that partially offsets the expansionary impact of the original increase in investment spending and reconciles equilibrium in the income-expenditure diagram with that of the aggregate demand–aggregate supply diagram. That is, to complete the analysis one would need to draw a third expenditure schedule between the solid and dashed ones already shown in Figure 27-4. We know from the equilibrium determined in the aggregate demand–aggregate supply diagram that this final expenditure schedule will intersect the 45-degree line at a real GDP level of $Y_2$.

3. s, m, –, –; m, s, –, +; s, m, +, +; m, s, +, –; s, m, +, +; m, s, –, +

**Self-Tests For Understanding**

**Test A**
1. b  p. 669
2. b  pp. 668-669
3. a  change in the price level leads to a movement along the aggregate supply curve
4. a  p. 673
5. c  p. 673
6. a, b, c, d, e  p. 677
7. d  pp. 672-673
8. a  p. 675
9. d  p. 672
10. c  p. 678
11. d  An increase in $G$ when there is a recessionary gap need not result in an inflationary gap. p. 675
12. a  p. 681
13. c  p. 683
14. b, d  Net exports = exports – imports
15. a, c, d  The increase in net exports leads to shifts on the demand side.
16. c  Shift in aggregate demand curve leads to movement along aggregate supply curve.
17. d  pp. 672-673
18. c  A growing population shifts both curves every year.
19. d  p. 686
20. c  p. 686

**Test B**
1. T  p. 668
2. T  p. 668
3. T  pp. 672-673
4. F  pp. 679-680
5. T  p. 683
6. F  While there is a tendency to move toward full employment or potential output, there is nothing that requires the aggregate demand and supply to always intersect there.
7. F  Equilibrium is determined by intersection of both curves.
8. T  p. 678
9. F  p. 678
10. F  p. 684

**Supplementary Exercises**
1. $C + I + G + (X - IM) = 1{,}700 + .8Y - 5P$
2. $P = 340 - .04Y$ or $Y = 8{,}500 - 25P$
3. $P = 95; Y = 6{,}125$
4. $P = 90; Y = 6{,}000$
   New expenditure schedule:
   $C + I + G + (X - IM) = 1{,}650 + .8Y - 5P$
   New aggregate demand curve:
   $P = 330 - .04Y$

# CHAPTER 28

**Chapter Review**
(1) fiscal; expenditure; demand; supply
(2) up; 1; 1
(3) are not; higher; permanent; propensity; less than; investment
(4) income; consumption; –; +
(5) up; variable; fixed
(6) less; smaller
(7) smaller
(8) MPC; smaller; smaller; flatter
(9) more; steeper
(10) consumption; MPC; less than; less; smaller
(11) increase; decrease; decrease; increase
(12) supply; increase

**Important Terms and Concepts Quiz**
1. d    3. f    5. e
2. c    4. b

## Basic Exercises

1. $6,000
2. $5,500
3. 2.5
4. $6,000
5. 2.0
6. The multiplier for a change in taxes is less than the multiplier for a change in government purchases.
7. No. The increase in GDP from the multiplier process increased tax revenues by $125, an amount less than the reduction in taxes that initiated the multiplier process.
8. $100; $125
9. $5,500; the multipliers are the same.

## Self-Tests for Understanding

### Test A

1. c Money supply is monetary policy decision. p. 691
2. d p. 698
3. b p. 698
4. a p. 691
5. c p. 692
6. b With fixed taxes $\Delta DI = \Delta GDP$ and in this case only $C$ changes as GDP changes.
7. a With variable taxes $\Delta DI < \Delta GDP$ leading to a smaller change in $C$ when GDP changes then in question 6.
8. d p. 691
9. c p. 692
10. a p. 698
11. b These changes leave disposable income unchanged.
12. b $\Delta Y = \Delta G \times$ multiplier, p. 699
13. a A reduction in transfer payments reduces disposable income and aggregate demand.
14. c pp. 697-698
15. b A reduction in income taxes makes the expenditure schedule steeper. pp. 694-695
16. b A change in any variable affecting demand except price will lead to a shift in the aggregate demand curve.
17. c As the multiplier for a change in taxes is smaller than the multiplier for a change in government purchases, it takes a larger change in taxes to offset the change in purchases. p. 697

18. c p. 700-701
19. d p. 703
20. b p. 705

### Test B

1. F See comment to question 15, Test A.
2. T pp. 694-695
3. F Multiplier applies to any change in autonomous spending, i.e. vertical shift in expenditure schedule.
4. F p. 694
5. F p. 698
6. F p. 698
7. F pp. 700-701
8. T p. 698
9. F pp. 705-706
10. F p. 705

## Supplementary Exercises

1. Income taxes are an important reason why Okun's multiplier is less than the oversimplified formula.
2. The tax multiplier is less than the multiplier for changes in autonomous spending.
3. The 1975 income tax rebate was a temporary tax change. The 1964 change was permanent.

## APPENDIX

### Basic Exercise: Appendix

1. $Y = 6,000$
2. No; $Y$ declines by 25 to $5,975; tax and spending multipliers differ. Deficit increases from 50 to 56.25
3. Multipliers:
$\Delta I = 2.5$; $\Delta Y/\Delta I = 1/(1-b(1-t))$
$\Delta G = 2.5$; $\Delta Y/\Delta \Gamma = 1/(1-b(1-t))$
$\Delta(X - IM) = 2.5$; $\Delta Y/\Delta(X - IM) = 1/(1-b(1-t))$
$\Delta T = -2.0$ (change in intercept)
$\Delta Y/\Delta T_0 = -\Delta Y/\Delta I = -b/(1-b(1-t))$

## CHAPTER 29

### Chapter Review

(1) barter; more difficult
(2) money; commodity; fiat
(3) M1; M2
(4) 1026.5; 3497.0
(5) lending; 900; reserve requirement

(6) 1/(reserve requirement); less

(7) smaller; excess; smaller

(8) contraction; no

## Important Terms and Concepts Quiz

| | | |
|---|---|---|
| 1. c | 9. s | 17. b |
| 2. j | 10. k | 18. r |
| 3. g | 11. o | 19. l |
| 4. m | 12. e | 20. h |
| 5. m | 13. f | 21. q |
| 6. d | 14. p | 22. a |
| 7. t | 15. v | |
| 8. n | 16. u | |

## Basic Exercises

1. $10,000; unchanged; col. 1: $1,000; $9,000
2. col. 2: $1,000; $9,000; $10,000; $1,000; 0
3. col. 3: $9,000; 0; $9,000; $900; $8,100; $19,000; $9,000
4. col. 4: $900; $8,100; $9,000; $900; 0
5. col. 5: $8,100; 0; $8,100; $810; $7,290; $27,100; $17,100
6. B: $9,000; C: $8,100; D: $7,290; E: $6,561; 0.1; $100,000; required reserve ratio.

## Self-Tests For Understanding

### Test A

1. b   p. 717
2. c   p. 718
3. a   p. 718
4. c   M1 includes cash in circulation. Vault cash is included in a bank's reserves. p. 720
5. b, d   p. 720 .
6. b   p. 721
7. c   p. 726
8. c   p. 726
9. d   p. 726
10. d   p. 727
11. c   p. 723
12. d   The increase in deposits offsets the reduction in cash in circulation.
13. c   p. 724
14. d   p. 732
15. a   9,000; net increase in money supply = deposit expansion – cash deposit.
16. a   p. 732
17. a   p. 734
18. d   $100 \div (0.2) = 500$, p. 732

19. a   Interbank claims lead to offsetting chains of deposit creation and destruction.
20. b   total reserves = required + excess = nonborrowed + borrowed.

### Test B

| | | | | | |
|---|---|---|---|---|---|
| 1. | T | p. 715 | 6. | T | p. 724 |
| 2. | F | p. 718 | 7. | F | p. 734 |
| 3. | T | p. 717 | 8. | F | pp. 732-733 |
| 4. | F | p. 717 | 9. | F | pp. 726-727 |
| 5. | F | p. 723 | 10. | T | p. 726 |

## Supplementary Exercises

1. 2,500; 1,500
2. Change in deposits = $[1/(M + E + C)]$ × (change in reserves)

---

# CHAPTER 30

## Chapter Review

(1) 1914; central; 12; Board; Governors; Federal Open Market; fiscal; monetary

(2) excess

(3) increase; larger; expansionary; required; contractionary

(4) securities; buys; increase; reduction; destruction

(5) moral suasion; higher; higher; discount rate

(6) more; fewer; more; larger

(7) right; demand

(8) decreases; increased; right; increased; left

(9) intersection; supply; right; increase; decrease; left; decrease; increase

(10) supply; demand; shift in; shift in; demand; supply

## Important Terms and Concepts Quiz

| | |
|---|---|
| 1. b | 6. f |
| 2. h | 7. i |
| 3. k | 8. a |
| 4. e | 9. d |
| 5. j | 10. g |

## Basic Exercises

1. a.   decrease; left; contractionary; fall; rise
   b.   increase; creation; right; expansionary; rise; fall
   c.   less; decline; decline; left; contractionary; fall; rise

2. a. The scatter of points has a positive slope suggesting that an increase in the difference between the federal funds rate and the discount rate is associated with a larger volume of bank borrowing from the Fed.

   b. Remember that borrowing is a privilege not a right. The Fed is likely to use moral suasion to limit bank borrowing when the economic incentive from interest rate differentials gets large.

3. Note that when the interest rate differential increases, the ratio of GDP to money gets larger. That is, individuals economize on the use of money as the opportunity cost of holding M2 balances increases.

## Self-Tests For Understanding

### Test A

1. d pp. 740-741
2. d p. 738
3. c p. 759
4. b pp. 741-742
5. b p. 742
6. d pp. 742-743
7. c Simple multiplier is determined by slope of expenditure schedule, e.g., MPC, tax rates, and slope of aggregate supply curve.
8. d Shift of aggregate demand curve should reduce inflation, that is make prices lower than they otherwise would be.
9. b p. 745
10. d p. 753
11. c Money supply schedule shifts to the right.
12. c p. 746
13. d p. 743
14. a, c Both lead to variability in the deposit creation multiplier.
15. a p. 750
16. c p. 751
17. b p. 748
18. a p. 744
19. a, d It takes time for an increase in investment to affect the aggregate supply curve. pp. 753-754
20. b p. 758

### Test B

1. F pp. 741-742
2. F p. 740
3. F pp. 740-741
4. F pp. 742-743
5. F Reduction in reserve requirement shifts money supply schedule to the right, increasing $M$ and decreasing $R$.
6. F p. 746
7. F p. 750
8. T p. 748
9. F Changes in monetary policy lead to shifts in the aggregate demand curve.
10. T p. 758

## Supplementary Exercises

1. a. 6,000; $C$ = 3,650; $I$ = 1,350; $G$ = 900; $X - IM$ = 100

   b. increases to 6,240

   c. In this model, equilibrium in the income–expenditure diagram depends on the rate of interest. The expenditure schedule is as follows:

   $C + I + G + (X - IM) = 650 + .6(5/6) Y + 1,710 - 30r + 900 + 100 = 3,360 - 30r + .5Y$

   The 45-degree line is $C + I + G + (X - IM) = Y$. Solving these two equations for one expression in $Y$ and $r$ yields

   $$Y = 6,720 - 60r$$

   Setting the demand for money equal to supply of money yields a second expression in $Y$ and $r$.

   $$Y = 20BR + 50r.$$

   When BR = 270 then $Y$ = 2,400, $r$ = 12, and $M$ = 1,380. The value of $M$ can be found from either the demand for money equation or the supply of money equation.

   d. Changing bank reserve shifts the second equation for $Y$ and $r$. A little experimentation should show that bank reserves of 292 will yield an interest rate of 8 and a money stock of 1,480.

2. a. $1,500; $600

   b. $1,220.80; $698.87

# CHAPTER 31

## Chapter Review

(1) GDP; money
(2) nominal GDP; $M$; $V$; $P$; $Y$; velocity
(3) money; does not; nominal GDP; 100
(4) should not; opportunity cost
(5) velocity
(6) decline; increase; increase
(7) higher; increase; higher; demand
(8) monetary; fiscal
(9) higher; higher; left; right
(10) output; prices; steep; steep; flat
(11) automatic
(12) judgmental; are not
(13) need not

## Important Terms and Concepts Quiz

1. e      4. b      6. f
2. c      5. a      7. d
3. h

## Basic Exercises

1.  a.  $V_1$: 6.84; 7.17; 6.91; 6.84; 7.04; 6.89; 6.35; 6.16; 6.38; 6.64; 6.81; 6.58; 6.18
        $V_2$: 1.73; 1.77; 1.68; 1.65; 1.66; 1.63; 1.58; 1.58; 1.63; 1.66; 1.68; 1.67; 1.71
    b.  Col. 3: 2,892.1; 3,266.5; 3,442.4; 3,671.0; 4,125.2; 4,631.5; 4,681.0; 4,732.6; 5,042.6; 5,383.9; 5,878.7; 6,333.2
        Col. 5: 2,964.6; 3,316.1; 3,480.6; 3,753.9; 4,096.7; 4,397.8; 4,539.9; 4,747.6; 5,158.8; 5,473.1; 5,700.6; 5,804.2
    c.  Errors are highest when velocity changes. The greater variation in $V_1$ leads to larger errors for predictions based on $M_1$.

2.  Each speaker is arguing that the demand for money has shifted to the right. In both cases the shift is consistent with the increase in $M$ and $r$.

    Speaker A is arguing that the shift in the demand for money derives from an autonomous shift in the aggregate demand curve to the right. A shift of the money supply curve to the left, an open market sale, would increase interest rates even further, inducing an offsetting shift of the aggregate demand curve to the left. With a bit of luck, the policy induced shift of the aggregate demand curve to the left would offset the autonomous shift in the aggregate demand curve to the right, and there would be no inflation.

    Speaker B is arguing that there has been an autonomous increase in the demand for money. If there is no offsetting increase in supply, interest rates will rise, inducing a shift of the aggregate demand curve to the left. In this case the appropriate action would be to shift the money supply curve to the right and hold interest rates constant to avoid inducing a shift in the aggregate demand curve.

    The appropriate policy response, whether to focus on $M$ or $r$, depends upon the origins of the shift in the demand for money.

## Self-Tests For Understanding

### Test A

| | | |
|---|---|---|
| 1. | c | p. 762 |
| 2. | b | p. 763 |
| 3. | e | p. 763 |
| 4. | a, b, d | p. 763 |
| 5. | a | p. 762 |
| 6. | a | The reduction in $V$ means that the percentage increase in $P$ times $Y$ must be less than the percentage increase in $M$ |
| 7. | d | p. 764 |
| 8. | d | Quantity theory predicts that increases in $M$ will increase nominal GDP, $P$ times $Y$. It does not predict $P$ and $Y$ separately. |
| 9. | b | This change should lower interest rates and reduce velocity. |
| 10. | c | p. 768 |
| 11. | d | Increase in taxes would lower nominal GDP. |
| 12. | c | pp. 765-766 |
| 13. | a, b, c, d | p. 769 |
| 14. | b | p. 770 |
| 15. | b | pp. 770-771 |
| 16. | a, b | p. 773 |
| 17. | a | p. 775 |
| 18. | b | p. 775 |
| 19. | c | p. 781 |
| 20. | c | p. 785 |

## Test B

| | | | | | |
|---|---|---|---|---|---|
| 1. | T | p. 762 | 6. | F | p. 771 |
| 2. | F | p. 763 | 7. | F | pp. 771-773 |
| 3. | T | p. 767 | 8. | T | pp. 776-777 |
| 4. | F | p. 767 | 9. | F | p. 781 |
| 5. | T | p. 770 | 10. | T | p. 781 |

## CHAPTER 32

### Chapter Review

(1) spending; revenue; revenue; spending; deficit; surplus

(2) down; left; decline; decline; deficit; increase; decrease; accentuate

(3) will; will not

(4) small; without; small; large

(5) monetized

(6) foreigners

(7) investment; recession; war; crowding in; crowding out; high; out

### Important Terms and Concepts Quiz

| | | | |
|---|---|---|---|
| 1. | c | 5. | h |
| 2. | g | 6. | f |
| 3. | b | 7. | d |
| 4. | e | | |

### Basic Exercises

1. 6,250; 6,375; 6,500; 6,625; 6,750; equilibrium = 6,500

2. –25

3. surplus; 37.5

4. 6,125; 6,250; 6,375; 6,500; 6,625; equilibrium = 6,250; actual deficit increases to 87.5; no change in structural deficit

5. raise; lower equilibrium level of income.

6. lower; lower equilibrium level of income.

7. 146; 6,016.7

8. –175; 5,900

**Note:** Figuring out the correct answers to 7 and 8 is a bit tricky. With regard to 7, increasing the fixed component of taxes by 87.5 would eliminate the deficit if $Y$ did not change. However, the increase in fixed taxes will reduce $Y$ and result in a smaller net increase in taxes. Letting $FT$ stand for the fixed component of taxes, one can find the necessary increase in fixed taxes by solving the following two equations:

$$\Delta\text{Deficit} = -\Delta FT - 0.25\,\Delta Y$$
$$\Delta Y = -\Delta FT\,[MPC/(0.5)].$$

The first equation shows how the deficit changes when the fixed component of taxes and $Y$ change. The second shows how $Y$ changes when the fixed component of taxes changes. The number 0.25 measures the responsiveness of taxes to income, and the expression $[MPC/(0.5)]$ is the multiplier for a change in fixed taxes in this model. Setting the change in the deficit equal to –87.5, one can solve for the necessary change in fixed taxes and the associated change in $Y$. A similar approach provides the answer to question 8, but note that there are some small but important differences in the two equations:

$$\Delta\text{Deficit} = \Delta G - 0.25\,\Delta Y$$
$$\Delta Y = \Delta G\,[1/(0.5)].$$

### Self-Tests For Understanding

#### Test A

1. d p. 796
2. a p. 796
3. d p. 799
4. c p. 800
5. c p. 801
6. c p. 801
7. a pp. 799-800
8. b, c p. 797
9. d p. 801
10. c pp. 794-795
11. c Monetizations means a further rightward shift of the aggregate demand curve along a steep portion of the aggregate supply curve. p. 809
12. d
13. a pp. 802-804
14. a, b, c, d, e, f pp. 815-816
15. b A reduction in taxes would not reduce the deficit.
16. b p. 816
17. d p. 811
18. b p. 811
19. a,b pp. 811-813
20. d p. 811

#### Test B

1. F p. 795
2. F Depending upon the strength of private demand, a deficit or surplus may be required to insure that aggregate demand and supply curves intersect at full employment.

3. F  p. 804
4. F  p. 816
5. T  pp. 808-810
6. F  p. 799
7. F  pp. 805-806
8. T  p. 813
9. T  p. 813
10. T  p. 811

## Supplementary Exercises

1. It is important to distinguish between deficits during periods of recession and deficits from deliberate increases in $G$ or reductions in $T$. All of the examples come from periods when the economy was falling into recession.

g. The ratio of debt to GDP should approach 0.72.

h. As long as $g$ is greater than $\tau$ and $\lambda$ is greater than $R$, the ratio of debt to GDP tends toward $(1 + \lambda)(g - \tau)/(\lambda - R)$. If $g$ is less than $\tau$, the government runs surpluses that eventually pay off the debt. If $R$ is greater than $\lambda$, then interest payments on the debt are sufficient to make the national debt grow faster than GDP, and the ratio of debt to GDP grows without limit. If $R = \lambda$, the formula above will not work. Interest payments alone keep the ratio of debt to GDP constant. If in addition $G > \tau$, then the ratio of debt to income grows without limit.

Is recent experience a case of adjusting to a lower value for $\tau$ and hence a larger, but stable, ratio of debt to GDP or is it a case of interest rates exceeding the growth of nominal GDP, $(R > \lambda)$, in which case there may be no limit to the ratio of debt to GDP? Would spending and tax policies remain unchanged if the ratio of national debt to GDP appeared to be increasing without limit?

## CHAPTER 33

### Chapter Review

(1) higher; negatively; Phillips; negative
(2) incorrect; inflationary; natural (or full-employment); vertical
(3) smaller; larger; higher; steeper
(4) vertical
(5) expectations; is not
(6) indexing
(7) increase; more

### Important Terms and Concepts Quiz

1. h    5. c
2. e    6. i
3. a    7. b
4. g    8. f

### Basic Exercise

1. purchase; decrease; decrease; increase; increase
2. 103
3. No; aggregate supply curve will shift up as long as output exceeds full-employment level of output; aggregate supply curve will continue to shift up and prices will tend to rise faster and faster.
4. a. 6,300; 106
   b. expansionary; 109
   c. restrictive; 6,100

### Self-Tests For Understanding

### Test A

1. d  p. 826
2. d  p. 831
3. a  p. 828
4. d  p. 834
5. c  pp. 835-837
6. a  p. 838
7. a  The aggregate supply curve shifts up whenever the cost of inputs increases.
8. c  p. 839
9. d  p. 844
10. a, c p. 841
11. d  p. 841
12. b  p. 842
13. a  pp. 838-839
14. c  pp. 838-839

15. d  As any policy induced shift in the aggregate demand curve will mean a movement along the new aggregate supply curve, it is not possible to return to the original equilibrium.
16. c  pp. 839-840
17. a  pp. 844-845
18. a  pp. 846-847
19. c  p. 847
20. d  p. 847

**Test B**
1. F  p. 823
2. F  Any shift in the aggregate demand curve, from whatever source, will affect prices.
3. T  p. 831
4. T  p. 834
5. T  p. 835
6. F  p. 838
7. T  pp. 838-839
8. F  Both monetary and fiscal policy would shift the aggregate demand curve along the aggregate supply curve with similar effects on prices.
9. F  See comments to question 15, Test A.
10. F  pp. 834-837

**Supplementary Exercise**
1. 440,000; $2,200,000; $440,000; profits up 10 percent
2. 440,000; $2,310,000; $462,000; profits up 15.5 percent
3. What happens if inflation differs from the announced target rate?

# CHAPTER 34

## Chapter Review
(1) more; more; demand; supply; out; increase
(2) is; 200
(3) convergence; faster; slower; are not
(4) need not
(5) no

## Important Terms and Concepts Quiz
1. d     2. a     3. c

## Basic Exercises
1. a. 2.7
   b. 7.2, more than twice as great.
   c. The concept of convergence suggests that major differences in the growth of labor productivity cannot be sustained for 100 years.
   d. 50 years, 7 months
2. a. 37,688
   b. 41,434
   c. No, labor productivity still increases but at a slower rate.
   d. GDP per capita increases at an average annual rate of 1.72 percent from $9,441 (23,900 × 0.395) to $19,350 (41,434 × 0.467). The average rate of growth of labor productivity over the same period is 1.32 percent per year. Numbers for this exercise were chosen to illustrate American experience over the period 1950 to 1992. See 1993 *Economic Report of the President,* Tables B-2, B-29, and B-30. Labor productivity was measured as GDP per employee in the civilian labor force and the armed forces. Alternatively, and more appropriately, one could measure labor productivity per hour of labor input. If average hours of work reported in Table B-42 for private nonagricultural industries is representative of average hours for all workers, labor productivity per hour of work increased at an average annual rate of 1.66 percent from $11.55 in 1950 to $23.09 in 1992. The rate of increase in labor productivity per hour of work is greater than the rate of increase in labor productivity per worker because average hours declined from 39.8 hours per week in 1950 to 34.4 in 1992.

## Self-Tests For Understanding
## Test A
1. d  p. 856
2. a  p. 856
3. c  p. 856
4. a  p. 858
5. c  see Chapter Review

6. a, b, c and d  help to determine the productivity of each member of the labor force. p. 856
7. d  pp. 856-857
8. b  pp. 852-853
9. c  p. 862
10. c, d  pp. 860-861
11. d  p. 869
12. a  p. 866
13. a, b  pp. 866-867
14. c  p. 859
15. c  p. 863
16. b  pp. 864-865
17. b  p. 865
18. c  pp. 860-861
19. b  pp. 861-862
20. a  p. 869

**Test B**
1. F  p. 859
2. F  p. 857
3. F  p. 860
4. F  p. 862
5. F  pp. 866-867
6. T  p. 860
7. F  p. 862
8. F  p. 862
9. F  p. 868
10. F  p. 869

# CHAPTER 35

## Chapter Review
(1) comparative
(2) scale
(3) comparative
(4) A; B; 8000; wheat
(5) 2000; 1200; cars; wheat
(6) demand; supply; exporting; importing
(7) tariffs; quotas; subsidies; price; quantity
(8) government
(9) low; do not; can
(10) adjustment
(11) defense; infant
(12) both the exporting and importing; comparative

## Important Terms and Concepts Quiz
1. j   5. i   9. h
2. d   6. f   10. k
3. g   7. a   11. b
4. m   8. l   12. e

## Basic Exercises
1. a. Japan; Japan
   b. $2/_3$; $1 1/_2$; Canada; Japan; Canada; Japan
   c. Calculators; 1,000,000; 3,000,000; 4,000,000
      Backpacks: 1,500,000; 2,000,000; 3,500,000
   d. 300,000; 450,000
   e. 600,000 hours; 300,000 calculators; 200,000 backpacks
   f. increase; 250,000
   g. Calculators: 700,000; 3,450,000; 4,150,000
      Backpacks: 1,950,000; 1,700,000; 3,650,000
      The output of both calculators and backpacks has increased as compared to Question c.
   h. Canadian backpack output would fall to 1,050,000. Japan would need to reallocate 1,350,000 labor hours. Total calculator output would fall to 3,625,000. This reallocation is not in line with the principle of comparative advantage. The opportunity cost of backpacks in terms of calculators is greater in Japan than in Canada.
   i. There will be no change in total world output. Neither country has a comparative advantage. The opportunity cost of increased calculator or backpack production is the same in both countries.
2. a. India: $10; 1,000
      United States: $40; 600
   b. $20; production in India increases to 1200; production in United States decreases to 400; India exports, United States imports 400 shirts.
   c. United States: price = $30, production = 500; imports = 200
      India: price = $15; production = 1100; exports = 200
      United States; India; United States; India; decreased
   d. Tariff of $15

## Self-Tests For Understanding
### Test A
1. b  p. 874
2. d  pp. 875-876
3. b  p. 877
4. d  p. 880
5. a  p. 881
6. b  p. 881
7. d  pp. 882-883
8. d  p. 875
9. a  p. 876
10. a  pp. 878-879
11. c  p. 883
12. a  Export subsidies increase the volume of trade.
13. a  p. 885
14. b  p. 885
15. c  p. 885
16. c  p. 889
17. d  Although domestic demand declines, a tariff induces a greater decline in foreign imports, allowing for an increase in domestic production.
18. c  p. 898
19. b and d  Higher prices hurt the users of computer chips—computer manufacturers and consumers.
20. c  pp. 892-894

### Test B
1. F  p. 877
2. F  pp. 874-875
3. F  Trade should reflect comparative not absolute advantage.
4. T  pp. 873-874
5. T  p. 881
6. F  As world exports must equal world imports, it is not possible for all countries to increase exports without increasing imports.
7. T  p. 885
8. F  pp. 892-893
9. F  pp. 894-895
10. F  pp. 895-896

## Supplementary Exercise
1. a.  Baulmovia: 8,100; Bilandia: 17,150
   b.  12; Baulmovia; Bilandia; 100
   c.  Baulmovia: price = 10;
       Bilandia: price = 14.5;
       Trade = 50.
   d.  50

e.  Tariff revenues accrue to the government. Tariffs do not protect high-cost foreign producers.
2. Production of 14.4 million bolts of cloth and 10.8 million barrels of wine allows Ricardia to choose from the outermost consumption possibilities line. Note that to be on the outermost consumption possibilities line Ricardia must choose to produce at the point where the slope of the production possibilities frontier equals the ratio of world prices.

## Economics in Action
1. Tyson, Gore, and Brown prevailed.

## CHAPTER 36
### Chapter Review
(1) exchange; depreciated; appreciated
(2) demand; supply; exports; financial; physical; supply
(3) demand; increase; appreciation; supply; depreciation; appreciation
(4) purchasing power parity; depreciate; depreciating; appreciating
(5) Bretton
(6) deficit; demand; supply; surplus
(7) buy; increasing
(8) deficit; increase; decrease; contraction; reduction
(9) disliked
(10) speculators

### Important Terms and Concepts Quiz
| | | |
|---|---|---|
| 1. e | 7. c | 13. i |
| 2. b | 8. q | 14. d |
| 3. n | 9. o | 15. m |
| 4. r | 10. h | 16. a |
| 5. k | 11. p | 17. j |
| 6. s | 12. l | 18. f |

### Basic Exercises
1. a.  The demand curve may shift to the left if some Americans now find French investments less attractive. The supply curve shifts to the right as French investors are attracted by higher U.S. interest rates. With floating rates, the franc depreciates. With fixed rates, a deficit results.

b. The demand curve shifts to the right. There is no shift in the supply curve. With floating rates, the france appreciates. With fixed rates, a surplus results.

c. The demand curve shifts to the left as Americans import less. The supply curve might shift to the right if a recession leads to lower dollar prices of U.S. exports. With floating rates, the franc depreciates. With fixed rates, a deficit results.

d. The demand curve shifts to the left. The supply curve might shift to the right if French citizens import more. With floating rates, the franc depreciates. With fixed rates, a deficit results.

e. The demand curve shifts to the left and the supply curve shifts to the left as the increase in the price of French wine leads Americans and French to increase their demand for California wines. With floating rates the franc depreciates. With fixed rates, a deficit results.

2. 30
   a. $6.40. Sales of French wine would increase. Sales of California wines would decrease. The U.S. balance of payments would show a deficit.
   b. 18 cents; appreciation; depreciation
   c. United States (50 percent vs. 33 percent)
   d. deficit
   e. depreciating

3. Balance of trade = –109.0
   (drawn after line 2)
   Balance on goods and services = –58.0
   (drawn after line 5)
   Balance on current account = –91.8
   (drawn after line 7)
   Balance on capital account = 61.0
   (lines 9, 10, 11, and 12)

   If balance of payments accounts were accurate and complete, the balance on current account and the balance on capital account should sum to zero. For 1990 they sum to –30.9 billion. See text page 914 for a discussion of the statistical discrepancy in measuring international transactions.

**Self-Tests For Understanding**

**Test A**
1.  b  p. 901
2.  c  p. 901
3.  b  p. 902
4.  b  p. 902
5. b, d  p. 902
6.  c  p. 902
7.  b  p. 904
8. b, d, f   These factors should increase the demand for American goods or financial assets and, hence, the demand for American dollars.
9.  f  b, c, d, and e should increase the demand for dollars. a should reduce the supply of dollars. f should increase the supply of dollars.
10.  b  p. 906
11.  c  p. 908
12. a, b  p. 907
13.  d  p. 905
14.  c  A 6 percent depreciation of the dollar is necessary to equalize the purchasing power of dollars and marks.
15.  b  p. 906
16.  b  Higher inflation in the U.S. increases supply of dollars as Americans demand less expensive German goods resulting in U.S. deficit and German surplus.
17. a, c, d   All should shift the supply of domestic currency to the right.
18. a, c, d   At the overvalued exchange rate, demand for Zenon currency would be less than under a system of floating exchange rates.
19.  c  p. 917
20.  b  Exchange rates should adjust so that, except for transactions costs, direct conversion between kronor and guilders costs neither more nor less than first converting into dollars and then into kronor or guilders.

**Test B**
1.  T  A depreciating currency buys fewer units of foreign currency; an appreciating currency buys more units of foreign currency.
2.  F  A pure system of floating exchange rates involves no government intervention by definition.
3.  T  p. 907

4.  T   An increase in imports would mean an increase in the supply of dollars by Americans. The shift in the supply schedule for dollars would increase a deficit or reduce any surplus.
5.  F   p. 905
6.  T   p. 911
7.  F   pp. 919-920
8.  F   p. 915
9.  T   p. 915
10.  F   p. 916

## Supplementary Exercises

1.  Col. 1: $28,000,000; £10,000,000
2.  Col. 2: $28,000,000; £10,769,231
3.  Col. 3: $28,000,000; £11,666,667
    If there is no devaluation, you are out only the transactions costs. If the pound is devalued, you stand to make a handsome profit. As the prospect of devaluation increases, there is a greater incentive to sell your pounds before their price falls. Your efforts to sell pounds, along with similar actions by others, will increase the pressure for devaluation.

# CHAPTER 37
## Chapter Review

(1)  closed; open
(2)  increase; are; less; increase; decrease; decrease; increase; decrease; increase
(3)  shift in; decline; down; left
(4)  less; downward; more; upward
(5)  increase; appreciation
(6)  decrease; up; right; increase; appreciation; left; down; offset; lower; increase; offset
(7)  appreciation; enhance
(8)  J
(9)  expansionary; contractionary; contractionary; expansionary; exports; lower

## Important Terms and Concepts Quiz

1.  a       3.  f       5.  g
2.  e       4.  c       6.  d

## Basic Exercises

1.  Appreciation: Exports decrease; Imports increase; Net exports decrease; Aggregate Demand Curve shifts to the left; Aggregate Supply Curve shifts down; Real GDP decreases; Price level decreases.

    Depreciation: Exports increase; Imports decrease; Net exports increase; Aggregate Demand Curve shifts to the right; Aggregate Supply Curve shifts up; Real GDP increases; Price level increases.
2.  Increase in $G$: Interest rate increases; Exchange rate appreciates; GDP and price level down, which work to offset the initial impact of the increase in $G$.

    Decrease in $G$: Interest rate decreases; Exchange rate depreciates; GDP and price level up, which work to offset the initial impact of the decrease in $G$.

    Open Market Sale: Interest rate increases; Exchange rate appreciates; GDP and price level down, which work to enhance the initial impact of the open market sale.

    Open Market Purchase: Interest rate decreases; Exchange rate depreciates; GDP and price level increase, which work to enhance the initial impact of the open market purchase.
3.  The impact of monetary policy is enhanced. The impact of fiscal policy is diminished.

## Self-Tests For Understanding
## Test A

1.  b     p. 929
2.  c     p. 929
3.  c     p. 929
4.  c     p. 929
5.  a     p. 932
6.  c     p. 934
7.  a     p. 933
8.  c     pp. 927-928
9.  b, d   p. 935
10.  b     p. 935
11.  c     The decrease in exports following an appreciation of the dollar shifts the aggregate demand curve to the left.
12.  c     p. 935

13. b  The reduction in interest rates from the move to expansionary monetary policy leads to a capital outflow and a depreciation of the dollar.
14. a  pp. 935-937
15. c  pp. 937-938
16. c  p. 930
17. b  p. 941
18. a, c  p. 941
19. c  p. 503
20. a, b  p. 501

## Test B
1. F  pp. 927-928
2. F  A change in exports, whether from a change in foreign GDP or a change in the exchange rate, is modeled as an autonomous change in spending with multiplier effects similar to those of any other autonomous change.
3. F  Autonomous shifts in investment spending affect interest rates, exchange rates, net exports, and the trade deficit in a manner analogous to changes in fiscal policy.
4. T  p. 933
5. T  p. 929
6. T  p. 936
7. F  p. 938
8. F  pp. 935-936
9. T  p. 945
10. F  p. 943

## CHAPTER 38
### Chapter Review
(1) exponential
(2) inventiveness; entrepreneurship; work ethic; investment; research; development; embodied; disembodied
(3) opportunity; consumption; saving
(4) has not; increase; higher
(5) less (footnote: I; C; C; IM) difficult
(6) death; inexpensive
(7) brain drain; World

### Important Terms and Concepts Quiz
| | | |
|---|---|---|
| 1. j | 4. c | 7. d |
| 2. b | 5. g | 8. h |
| 3. i | 6. a | 9. f |

### Basic Exercise
1. On May 20, 1993, *The New York Times* reported new international income comparisons from the International Monetary Fund using estimates of purchasing power parity to convert various national currencies into American dollars and avoid the transition fluctuations of exchange rates.

| | | |
|---|---|---|
| Brazil: | 0.79 | 5,240 |
| Britian: | 0.90 | 15,720 |
| Canada: | 0.52 | 19,178 |
| China: | 1.66 | 1,450 |
| France: | 1.04 | 18,227 |
| Germany: | 1,25 | 19,500 |
| India: | 1.00 | 1,150 |
| Indonesia | 0.50 | 2,730 |
| Italy | 0.98 | 16,896 |
| Japan | 2.37 | 19,107 |
| Mexico | 0.60 | 7,170 |
| Spain | 0.50 | 12,719 |

Note the different rankings by total output and income per capita. For example, in terms of total output China ranks third, but in terms of income per capita it ranks twelfth. Canada ranks eleventh in terms of total output and third in terms of income per capita.

### Self-Tests For Understanding
### Test A
1. d  p. 950
2. c  p. 952
3. a  p. 952
4. c, d  p. 955
5. c  p. 955
6. c  p. 956
7. a, b, c  p. 956
8. d  p. 957
9. a  p. 958
10. d  pp. 959-960
11. c  pp. 963-965
12. c  p. 965
13. b  p. 968
14. b  p. 968
15. b  p. 969
16. c  p. 969
17. b  pp. 966-971
18. a  p. 971
19. a  p. 973

20. b  As explained in Chapter 36, the IMF helps developed and developing countries with exchange rate and balance of payments issues.

### Test B

1. F  GDP per capita will decrease whenever the growth rate of population exceeds the growth rate of total GDP.
2. F  pp. 952-954
3. F  p. 960
4. F  p. 960
5. T  p. 955
6. T  p. 958
7. F  p. 958
8. F  p. 964
9. F  pp. 963-964
10. T  p. 951
11. T  p. 969
12. F  p. 970
13. F  p. 970
14. F  pp. 965-971
15. F  p. 972

### Supplementary Exercises

2. 1,152 years; 294 days; 36 years; 302 days
3. The absolute difference in incomes would grow from its initial value of $15,034 to $17,303 in the 30th year. After that the absolute difference in incomes would decline until parity is achieved shortly after the start of the 78th year at an income per capita of $69,928.

## CHAPTER 39

### Chapter Review

(1) markets; planning
(2) capitalism; socialism
(3) is not; socialist; markets; capitalist; planning
(4) consumers; planners; freedom; prices; market; planned; profit; planned
(5) socialist; Five; One; material
(6) be conservative; little
(7) few; perestroika; glasnost
(8) planned; state; less; industrial
(9) foreign; industrial planning; more; less

### Important Terms and Concepts Quiz

1. c      6. g      11. m
2. f      7. b      12. j
3. d      8. n      13. l
4. a      9. i
5. e      10. k

### Self-Tests For Understanding

### Test A

1. c        p. 978
2. a        p. 978
3. c        p. 978
4. a, b, f    pp. 982 and 984
5. a        p. 982
6. b        p. 984
7. a        p. 980
8. c; d; b; a  p. 988; p. 980; p. 994; p. 991
9. a, c      p. 985
10. d        p. 985
11. d        p. 988
12. c        p. 987
13. b        p. 988
14. b, d      p. 988
15. d        p. 989
16. b        p. 991
17. c        p. 991
18. d        pp. 994-996
19. b        p. 994
20. d        p. 995

### Test B

1. F  p. 980          6. F  pp. 986-987
2. F  p. 980          7. T  p. 990
3. T  p. 982          8. F  pp. 990-991
4. T  p. 982          9. F  p. 993
5. T  pp. 981-982     10. F  p. 993